CHAPTER SIX **Evaluation** Evaluate a subject by applying standards held in common with your readers and by justifying your judgments.	•Choose an appropriate subje[...] •Present a subject to readers. •Assert a clear, authoritative [...] necessary. •Give reasons for a judgment, based on recognized standards. •Support reasons with evidence from a subject and by comparing or contrasting a subject to similar subjects. •Organize an essay through logically related reasons. •Signal explicitly the stages of an evaluative argument.
CHAPTER SEVEN **Speculation about Causes or Effects** Attempt to convince readers that certain causes or effects offer a plausible explanation for an event, trend, or phenomenon.	•Choose an event, trend, or phenomenon that remains open to speculation about its possible causes or effects. •Present a subject to be speculated about. •Propose likely causes or effects. •Support proposed causes or effects with facts, examples, statistics, cases, quotes from authorities, or anecdotes. •Anticipate readers' questions and preferred causes or effects, counterarguing as needed. •Organize an essay through a logical sequence of causes or effects. •Signal explicitly the stages of cause or effect reasoning.
CHAPTER EIGHT **Proposal to Solve a Problem** Attempt to convince readers to support a proposed course of action.	•Choose a problem that needs solving and come up with a feasible solution. •Describe a problem and solution. •Give reasons why readers should support a solution. •Support each reason with examples, facts, analogies, cases, scenarios, statistics, quotes from authorities, or anecdotes. •Anticipate readers' questions and preferred solutions, counterarguing as needed. •Organize an essay through logically ordered reasons. •Signal explicitly the stages in an argument to support a solution.
CHAPTER NINE **Position Paper** Attempt to convince readers to take seriously a position on a current issue.	•Choose an arguable issue and define it carefully. •Assert a position on an issue. •Give reasons why readers should take a position seriously. •Support each reason with examples, facts, analogies, statistics, anecdotes, or quotes from authorities. •Anticipate readers' questions and their positions on an issue, counterarguing as needed. •Organize an essay through logically ordered reasons. •Signal explicitly the stages in an argument taking a position.

Reading Critically, Writing Well

A Reader and Guide

FIFTH · EDITION

Rise B. Axelrod
California State University, San Bernardino

Charles R. Cooper
University of California, San Diego

Bedford/St. Martin's
Boston/New York

For Bedford/St. Martin's

Executive Editor: Carla Samodulski
Developmental Editors: Michael Gillespie and Jori Finkel
Senior Production Editor: Shuli Traub
Production Supervisor: Dennis J. Conroy
Marketing Manager: Karen Melton
Art Director/Cover Design: Lucy Krikorian
Text Design: Robin Hessel Hoffmann
Copy Editor: Wendy Polhemus-Annibell
Cover Art: © Michael Sheehey/SIS
Composition: Pine Tree Composition
Printing and Binding: R. R. Donnelley & Sons Company

President: Charles H. Christensen
Editorial Director: Joan E. Feinberg
Editor in Chief: Nancy Perry
Director of Editing, Design, and Production: Marcia Cohen
Managing Editor: Erica T. Appel

Library of Congress Catalog Card Number: 98-84407

Manufactured in the United States of America.

4 3 2 1 0 9
f e d c b

For information, write: Bedford/St. Martin's, 75 Arlington Street, Boston, MA 02116 (617-426-7440)

ISBN: 0-312-25029-0

Acknowledgments

Preface

Read, read, read. . . . Just like a carpenter who works
as an apprentice and studies the master. Read!

—William Faulkner

I went back to the good nature books that I had read. And I analyzed them. I
wrote outlines of whole books—outlines of chapters—so that I could see their
structure. And I copied down their transitional sentences or their main sen-
tences or their closing sentences or their lead sentences. I especially paid at-
tention to how these writers made transitions between paragraphs and scenes.

—Annie Dillard

In these quotes, the novelist William Faulkner and essayist Annie Dillard tell us
what many authors know intuitively—that reading critically helps writers learn to
write well. By reading critically, of course, we mean more than just reading for enjoyment or reading to get the gist. Reading critically, as Faulkner and Dillard suggest, requires readers to pay close attention to how texts work.

Our goal throughout the fifth edition of *Reading Critically, Writing Well* continues to be to teach students practical strategies for critical reading. We believe
that as college students become better critical readers, they will also become
more effective writers. To help students improve in both areas, we provide extensive instruction in reading as well as comprehensive guidance in writing.

FEATURES

The special features of this edition of *Reading Critically, Writing Well* include:

Eight Different Types of Real-World Writing

Each assignment chapter (Chapters Two through Nine) focuses on a specific
genre or type of writing that students will encounter during college and on the

job. There are four personal and explanatory genres (autobiography, observation, reflection, and explanation of concepts) and four argumentative genres (evaluation, speculation about causes or effects, proposal to solve a problem, and taking a position on an issue). Some of the reading and writing assignments give students opportunities to think deeply about their own experiences and perceptions, while other assignments require them to think about points of view other than their own.

Combining Methods of Development for Various Purposes

Although some of the assignment chapters emphasize particular writing strategies or methods of development (such as narration in autobiography, description in observation, and argument in position papers), all of the essays included in this book as well as the essays students will write reflect reality by showing how writers use a combination of writing strategies to achieve their purposes.

Engaging Readings That Provoke Response and Reward Analysis

The readings have been carefully selected to show students how other writers—published authors as well as students—have approached each type of writing presented in *Reading Critically, Writing Well*. Varying in length and difficulty, the readings encompass interesting topics that are likely to stimulate lively class discussion and student writing, such as whether teenagers should work while attending school, why some people like horror films, how divorce affects children's relationships with parents, how gender expectations impact individuals, and whether talk shows promote democracy.

- *New Readings.* A third of the readings in the book are new to this edition.

- *New Voices.* Many talented writers, including Chang-Rae Lee, Amanda Coyne, and Natalie Angier, are introduced in this edition.

- *Trusted Favorites.* Audre Lorde, Annie Dillard, Russell Baker, Shelby Steele, John McPhee, Deborah Tannen, Charles Krauthammer, Michael Kinsley, Barbara Ehrenreich, and Brent Staples are among the many distinguished writers whose work appears in this edition.

- *Essays by Student Writers.* To show students strong writing by their peers, every chapter includes one essay written by a student in a composition course. Two of the student essays are new to this edition.

Guided Activities That Teach Critical Reading

This text brings critical reading and writing together by teaching students two fundamental ways of reading: **Reading for Meaning** and **Reading Like a Writer**. While Reading for Meaning gives students insight into how readers will construct meanings from their writing, Reading Like a Writer teaches them how to construct their own texts rhetorically to influence their readers' understanding and response. The two strategies are introduced in Chapter One, developed further in the Guide to Reading at the beginning of each chapter, and applied to every reading selection throughout the text. Mastering these two critical reading strategies, students gain confidence in their ability to write essays of their own in the same genres this book explores.

READING FOR MEANING ACTIVITIES

As writing instructors, we recognize that many students need help reading for meaning. Some students read superficially, barely skimming the surface, while others do not go beyond the meanings that resonate with their own experience. We developed the Reading for Meaning activities to help students get the gist of a reading, but also to suggest how they can reread for further meanings. We want students to gain confidence that they can construct meanings from any text, and we want them to persist at constructing meanings beyond initial impressions and personal connections.

Although the Reading for Meaning activities that follow each reading are organized identically, each one is designed specifically to help students explore and develop the particular meanings of the reading it accompanies. As students complete these activities they learn to perform an active role in constructing meaning. Reading for Meaning activities ask students to write to explore and develop a reading's meanings. This kind of exploratory writing stimulates thinking, especially when it is sustained for at least a page.

We prompt exploratory writing in two ways:

Start Making Meaning. Students are first asked to write about a particular aspect of a reading, such as the significance of an autobiographical event or the main reasons for taking a position on an issue. We designed this part of the activity to ensure that students get the gist of the reading. Students are then asked to continue writing about anything else, either in the reading itself or in their own experience, that contributes to their understanding of the reading. This part of the activity gives students a point of departure to explore additional meanings.

If You Are Stuck. If students are unable to extend their meaning-making for a page, they may skim a variety of suggestions offered in If You Are Stuck. We designed this part of the activity to draw attention to different aspects of a reading, such as problematic assertions, intriguing examples, and provocative word choices. This activity also encourages students to explore ways in which their own points of view differ from or correspond to the points of view in the reading. Furthermore, it invites students to relate the reading to their own experience in a way that deepens their understanding of the reading.

The Reading for Meaning activities—in addition to teaching students to read closely and critically—also give students useful insights about writing. Students nearly always recognize, for example, that writers seek to influence readers' thinking and feeling in particular ways and that writers choose their words and writing strategies carefully to achieve these purposes. Students usually notice that writers attempt to direct readers' attention to key ideas and that the more precisely these ideas are named, defined, and supported, the more likely readers are to understand them. These and other insights, absorbed through much reading for meaning, complement the more recognizably rhetorical principles students learn from our Reading Like a Writer activities.

READING LIKE A WRITER ACTIVITIES

These activities shift student focus from exploring the meanings of a reading selection to analyzing and evaluating how the writer presents those ideas. By completing these activities, students learn how to read rhetorically, examining and assessing the effectiveness of the writer's choices in light of the purpose and audience.

The Guide to Reading at the beginning of each chapter presents several Reading Like a Writer activities that introduce the rhetorical strategies typical of the genre. Each subsequent essay in a chapter is followed by one Reading Like a Writer activity, inviting students to learn more about a particular strategy introduced in the Guide to Reading. Altogether, each chapter invites students to complete nine or ten focused rhetorical analyses of a genre.

Every Reading Like a Writer activity directs students to a specific part of a reading—a few sentences or paragraphs—so that students lose no time wondering where to begin their analysis. Many activities show students the first step to take. At least one activity in every chapter invites students to compare two or more readings in the chapter. Because they are focused and accessible, these activities make it possible for even the most inexperienced readers to complete them and engage in a serious program of rhetorical learning. Each Reading Like a Writer activity has two parts:

Analyze. Students note and annotate a rhetorical feature of the reading. For example, they may be asked to underline the active verbs in several paragraphs to see how a writer dramatizes an autobiographical event or to outline a causal argument to see how the writer sequences causes in order of importance or plausibility. Students may also be asked to consider the strategy's possible effect on the intended readers—for example, judging the persuasiveness of a counterargument in a position paper or deciding whether a comparison/contrast helps explain a concept. This part of the activity teaches students how to identify and think about writers' use of rhetorical strategies.

Write. Students write to present what they have learned by analyzing one particular feature of a reading. They explain or describe what they have noticed and evaluate its effectiveness by citing examples from the reading. Thus they learn to illustrate and support their generalizations with specific details from the text.

Guides to Writing That Support Students' Composing Processes

As writing instructors, we know that students need help writing essays. To provide support for students, each *Reading Critically, Writing Well* chapter concludes with a comprehensive Guide to Writing that escorts students through every stage of the composing process from choosing a topic and gathering information and ideas, to offering constructive criticism of a classmate's draft, to revising and then editing and proofreading an essay. In our experience, all students—

from the most anxious, inexperienced writers to the most confident, expert writers—benefit in some way from the Guides to Writing.

STUDENTS LEARN TO WRITE WELL
BY DEVELOPING A SYSTEMATIC PROCESS

Grounded in research on composing and in learning theory, each Guide to Writing is effective because it:

- scaffolds the writing process, providing temporary support so that students can focus on one part of the process at a time.

- provides prompts so that students can learn the kinds of questions they need to ask themselves.

- applies the rhetorical knowledge gleaned from reading to writing an essay in a genre.

- helps students engage in constructive critical readings of their classmates' writing.

- systematizes the writing process so that students can learn to organize their work and follow through to the end.

GUIDES TO WRITING REDESIGNED FOR THIS EDITION

Following are some of the ways the Guides to Writing have been improved:

- *Easy-to-Follow Sequence of Invention Activities.* Activities for every phase of the invention process have been divided into smaller, more manageable tasks.

- *A New Section on Thesis Statements.* The new section helps students write a strong thesis. Example thesis statements from the chapter's readings illustrate possibilities.

- *New Section on Planning and Organizing.* This section helps students consider how to organize an essay and suggests possible plans for developing their ideas.

- *More Specific Guidelines for Peer Review.* The section called Reading a Draft Critically helps students read each other's drafts, encouraging constructive, practical group work.

- *More Specific Advice for Revising.* Keyed to peer review from the Reading a Draft Critically section, this advice helps students carry out a comprehensive revision of their drafts.

- *Added Advice on Editing and Proofreading.* This section alerts students to common errors in each essay genre. Each Editing and Proofreading section is based on our research into errors college students typically make writing the types of essays in this book.

- *Enhanced Visibility and Ease of Use.* A user-friendly system of headings and bullets helps to orient students throughout the guide. Italics clearly signal actions students are asked to take.

Activities That Ask Students to Reflect on Their Learning

Research has shown that when students reflect on their learning, they clarify their understanding and remember what they have learned longer. Reflecting also enables students to think critically about what they have learned and how they have learned it. *Reading Critically, Writing Well* provides two opportunities for students to reflect on their learning and also to discuss what they have learned with others. These activities are placed at important transitions in each chapter:

- *Reviewing What Makes [this kind of essay] Effective* appears after the readings and before the Guide to Writing. It invites students to look back at one essay they admire and to think about how it achieves its purpose.

- *Reflecting on What You Have Learned* appears at the end of the chapter and invites students to think about the essay they wrote and what influenced their writing.

Complete Catalog of Proven Critical Reading Strategies

In addition to the two critical reading strategies—Reading for Meaning and Reading Like a Writer—highlighted in every chapter, *Reading Critically, Writing Well* offers students an array of additional reading strategies. These strategies include annotating, outlining, summarizing, paraphrasing, contextualizing, and evaluating the logic of an argument. They are presented in Appendix One, A Catalog of Critical Reading Strategies, where they are briefly illustrated. Following a reading in each assignment chapter, one of these various strategies is introduced, encouraging students to use this additional strategy to extend meaning or to deepen their rhetorical analyses.

Expanded Guidelines for Finding and Evaluating Internet Sources

Appendix Two has been redesigned and updated to include guidelines for finding and evaluating Internet sources as well as the most current MLA and APA guidelines for documenting them. It also includes complete coverage of library and field research.

New Index to Methods of Development

The readings in *Reading Critically, Writing Well* are categorized by genre—by social function or writer's purpose. Writers usually employ a combination of rhetorical strategies to achieve their purposes but may emphasize a specific method of development in a particular genre, such as narration in autobiographical event essays (Chapter Two) and argument in position papers (Chapter Nine). The new Index to Methods of Development categorizes entire readings as well as specific passages within readings that employ particular methods of development that instructors may want to emphasize.

Comprehensive Instructor's Manual

The Instructor's Manual has been revised substantially for this edition. In addition to offering a variety of course plans for teaching with *Reading Critically, Writing Well*, the manual includes practical suggestions for using the Reading Like a Writer activities together with the Guide to Writing to help students develop their analysis of the readings and apply what they have learned to the essays they are writing. There is also a discussion of general teaching strategies, such as using reading journals, small groups, portfolios, and computers, as well as an annotated bibliography of research and theory that has influenced *Reading Critically, Writing Well*.

ACKNOWLEDGMENTS

We first want to thank our students at the University of California, San Diego, University of Nevada, Reno, and California State University, San Bernardino, who have been generous and frank with their advice. Some of them contributed essays to this text. We also owe a debt of gratitude to the many reviewers and questionnaire respondents who made suggestions for the revision. They include: Angela Anthony, Raritan Valley Community College; Patricia T. Bates, Louisiana State University–Shreveport; Jurene Brooks, Golden West College; Phil Brown, Kirkwood Community College; Solveig Brownfeld, Northern Virginia Community College–Annandale Campus; Debra Bruno, The George Washington University; H. Jean Bryan, DePaul University; David J. Carlson, Indiana University; Leeann Chen, Yavapai College; George Christian, Des Moines Area Community College; Tony Collins, Alverno College; Ionna M. Colonna, Lakeland Community College; Matilda Cox, Old Dominion University; Priscilla Finley, Elmira College; David Finnell, Northern Virginia Community College–Annandale Campus; Tami Haaland, Montana State University–Billings; Lisa L. Hardaway, Wayne State University; Wanda Hennings, State Center Community College District; Mary Linn Hoffman, Saginaw Valley State University; David E. Isaacs, Crafton Hills College; Larry W. Johnson, Iowa Central Community College; Michael J. Kelly, Slippery Rock University; Marilyn Kurtz, Ph.D., Nassau Community College; Jocelyn Ladner, St. Louis Community College; Susan Toth Lord, Kent State University; Andrew J. Manno, Ph.D., Raritan Valley Community College; Mary McCay, Loyola University–New Orleans; Dr. Marshall Myers, Eastern Kentucky University; Troy D. Nordman, Butler County Community College; Claire O'Donoghue, St. John's University; Ruth E. Oleson, Illinois Central College; Lindee H. Owens, University of Central Florida; Debora A. Person, University of Wyoming; Meredith J. Pool, Virginia Western Community College; Nancy Richard, Delgado Community College; Susan Robb Smith, Lakeland Community College; Katherine Scheil, St. Joseph College; Scott Vander Ploeg, Ph.D., Madisonville Community College; Rocco Versaci, Indiana University; Randal Woodland, University of Michigan–Dearborn.

To the editorial, production, and sales crew at Bedford/St. Martin's, we wish to convey our deepest appreciation. We want to thank our developmental editor, Michael Gillespie, for his many contributions and good humor as well as Nancy Perry and Carla Samodulski for their advice and support. Sincere thanks go especially to Jori Finkel for her insightful editing and to Shuli Traub for her smooth coordination of the production process. Thanks also to Sandy Schechter for her work on the permissions and to Karen Melton for her enthusiasm in marketing the book.

Finally, Charles dedicates this book to his daughter Laura, an artist with recent shows in Los Angeles, New York, and Bruges. She is also an art teacher, a gardener and specialist in gardening history, a lively conversationalist, and an instigator of a writing course for senior art majors at Pasadena College of Art and Design. In addition to thanking her husband Steven for his love and support, Rise wishes to dedicate this book to her nephews Gregory Borenstein, who has just started college, and Max Borenstein, who will be starting college soon. Remember Annie Dillard's provocative advice to writers: "You know when you think about writing a book, you think it is overwhelming. But, actually, you break it down into tiny little tasks any moron could do."

Rise B. Axelrod
Charles R. Cooper

Contents

CHAPTER FOUR   Reflection   117

CHAPTER EIGHT   Proposal to Solve a Problem   335

Introduction

R *eading Critically, Writing Well* is designed to help prepare you for the special demands of learning in college, where all your reading should be critical reading—not only understanding what you read but also analyzing and evaluating it.

When you read a text critically, you alternate between seeking to understand the text on its own terms and questioning the text's ideas and authority. Putting your questions aside even temporarily allows you to be open to new ideas and different points of view. But reading critically requires that eventually you examine every idea—your own as well as those of others—skeptically.

Learning to read critically also helps you to write well. It leads you to a fuller understanding of the subject you plan to write about. Not only do you search out complexities in others' points of view, but also you try to question your own point of view. You seek to go beyond the obvious, to avoid superficiality and oversimplification.

Reading critically helps you to write well in yet another important way: by helping you anticipate what readers will expect and the questions they will pose. Knowing your readers' expectations for the kind of essay you are writing helps you plan your essay with readers in mind. If you are explaining an unfamiliar concept, you can assume your readers will expect concrete examples and comparisons to help them grasp the new and abstract idea. If you are arguing a position on a current issue, you know that readers will expect you not merely to assert your position but also to support it with facts, statistics, expert testimony, or other relevant evidence. Similarly, knowing your readers' expectations will help you anticipate their questions. If you expect readers to accept certain of your ideas but to be skeptical about others, you can bolster with specific details, examples, or quotations those parts of your essay that present your most controversial ideas. Being able to anticipate how readers will respond does not mean, however, that as a writer you always seek to please readers. In fact, good writing often challenges readers. But to challenge readers' assumptions, you need to know what they expect.

You will learn from the activities in this book that reading critically and writing well are intellectually demanding tasks that require your time and effort. Speed reading may be the best strategy when you need to get the gist of an article or sort through a pile of possible sources. But when you need to understand new ideas or to evaluate complex arguments, when you are reading to prepare for class discussion or to write an essay, then you need to read more slowly and thoughtfully. Rereading is also essential.

The same principles apply to writing. Some kinds of writing can be dashed off in a single draft. The more practiced you are in a given kind of writing, the more efficient your writing process will be. If you write a lab report every week for a term, you should be able to write one rather quickly. If you know how to study for essay exams and have written them often, you should become quite adept. But when you need to do a kind of writing you have not mastered or to write about new and difficult material, then you will need more time to develop and organize your ideas.

Slowing down your reading and writing processes probably sounds like a bad idea to you right now, especially as you begin a new term and have just been told how much course work you will have to do. This book offers practical and efficient ways to meet this challenge by introducing basic strategies for reading critically and writing well.

READING CRITICALLY

After you read each selection in *Reading Critically, Writing Well* you will practice two basic strategies for reading critically: *reading for meaning* and *reading like a writer*. These strategies offer different but complementary ways of looking at a text.

When you read for meaning, you look at a text in terms of its ideas and information to understand and respond critically to what is being said. When you read like a writer, your focus shifts from meaning to rhetoric, from *what* is being communicated to *why* and *how* it is communicated. Although experienced readers may combine these two ways of reading— simultaneously reading for meaning and reading like a writer—we separate them here to give you an opportunity to refine your critical reading skills.

In Chapters Two through Nine, you will be asked to apply these two ways of reading critically to a variety of essays. Additional strategies such as summarizing, outlining, and evaluating the logic of an argument will be introduced to extend and deepen your repertoire of critical reading skills. Appendix One presents a complete catalog of these strategies.

READING FOR MEANING

When you read, your primary effort is to make the black marks on the page or computer screen meaningful. But as you know from your experience as a reader, a text may be more or less meaningful depending on your familiarity with the words that are used, as well as your knowledge of the subject and the kind of text or genre you are reading. If you have some knowledge about an issue currently being debated, for example, then an essay arguing for a position on that issue is likely to be relatively easy to read and full of meaning for you. If, however, you know nothing about the issue or the ways people have been stating and supporting their positions on the issue, then the essay will probably be more difficult to read and less obviously meaningful.

As a critical reader, you need to learn that reading for meaning requires you to use your knowledge and experience to create meaning. You must bring to the text your knowledge about the subject and genre, your beliefs and values, your personal experience as well as the historical and cultural contexts you share with others. Reading with this rich context helps you to see many possibilities for meaning in a text. Therefore, you will not be surprised that what you find meaningful in a given reading may overlap to some extent with what others find meaningful in the same reading, but also retain your own unique stamp.

You are not a passive receptacle into which meaning is poured as your eyes move across a text. Instead you actively construct meaning from a text, contributing your own relevant knowledge and point of view while also seeking to assimilate the text's new ideas and information. This highly significant and culturally important activity is what we mean by reading for meaning.

Annotating as you read is a powerful method for making sure you have something relevant to say about a given text. It helps concentrate your attention on the text's language and leaves you with a record of the insights, reactions, and questions that occurred to you in the process of reading for meaning. It simply involves marking the page as you read. You note what you think is important in a reading, what you think it means, and what ideas and questions it raises for you. Annotating is easy to do. All it takes is a text you can write on and something to write with. Here are just a few ways to annotate a text:

- Highlight or underline key words and sentences.
- Bracket important passages.
- Connect related ideas with lines.
- Circle words to be defined.
- Outline the main ideas in the margin.
- Write brief comments and questions in the margin.

Some readers mark up the text extensively, while others mark only the parts they consider significant or problematic. What is important is not how you annotate or even how much you annotate, but *that* you annotate. The simple act of marking the page as you read makes it more likely that you will read closely and attentively. There is no right or wrong way to annotate. (For an example of annotating, see Appendix One, pp. 451–456.)

After annotating, *exploratory writing* is a powerful way of developing your ideas about an essay. You will find that the very act of composing sentences leads you to clarify and extend your ideas, discovering new insights and raising new questions. The key to productive exploratory writing is to refrain from censoring yourself. Simply write without stopping until you have written at least a page. Do not concern yourself with grammar, word choice, spelling, and punctuation. The goal at this stage is to allow ideas to flow freely.

We recommend, then, a two-step procedure: annotating as you read, followed by exploratory writing that develops meanings for a text. You can extend your understanding by adding a third step—conversing with others who have also read the essay. Your instructor will likely give you opportunities, whether in class or online, to discuss the reading with other students.

Previewing the Reading for Meaning Activities

A Reading for Meaning activity follows each selection in the book. Turn to one of these activities now. As you can see, each Reading for Meaning activity consists of two sections: (1) *Start Making Meaning* and (2) *If You Are Stuck.*

START MAKING MEANING

This section asks you to begin constructing meaning by writing about an important aspect of the type of essay you are studying, such as the event's significance in an autobiographical essay or the reasons in a position paper. Then, you are encouraged to write about any meanings you see in the essay. Think of this writing as exploratory—following your thoughts to see where they lead, without being overly concerned about word choice, grammar, spelling. Your aim is simple: Write until you have written at least a page. If you cannot think of anything else to write, try to expand on your annotations, reread and respond to an intriguing passage, or write about one of the suggestions offered in If You Are Stuck.

IF YOU ARE STUCK

To help you write at least a page about the essay's possible meanings, the If You Are Stuck section offers several suggestions focusing on different aspects of the essay. You could respond to one or more of these suggestions or use them as a springboard for your own insights about the essay. You might have no need for these suggestions; they are simply designed to stimulate your thinking about the reading.

READING LIKE A WRITER

Reading like a writer, the second type of critical reading following each essay, shifts your focus from constructing meanings for the essay to analyzing and evaluating how its meanings are presented. Reading like a writer, you look closely at rhetoric—the ways writers make their ideas understandable and seek to influence readers.

To read rhetorically, you need to think about writing in terms of its purpose and audience. Writers make many choices when they write, choices that frequently depend on the writer's purpose and the particular readers being addressed. When you read like a writer, you examine the writer's choices and assess their effectiveness in light of the purpose and audience. This kind of reading helps you make rhetorically effective choices in your own writing.

When you read like a writer, you follow the same simple procedure as you do for reading for meaning: annotating, followed by writing.

Previewing the Reading Like a Writer Activities

A Reading Like a Writer activity follows each selection in the book. Turn to one of these activities now. As you can see, each Reading Like a Writer activity consists of one or two introductory paragraphs followed by two sections: *Analyze* and *Write*.

ANALYZE

The instructions in this section typically ask you to reread specific paragraphs in the essay and underline or bracket certain words or sentences. These annotations you make as you read like a writer focus on the characteristic textual features and rhetorical strategies of the type of essay you are studying. Your aim is to use annotating as a way to begin analyzing the features and strategies typical of the genre and to begin evaluating how well they work in the particular essay you are reading.

WRITE

Here you are asked to write several sentences about what you discovered in analyzing and evaluating the essay's features and strategies in terms of how well they achieve the writer's purpose. Writing even a few sentences can help you develop your analysis and evaluation of an essay writer's strategies.

WRITING WELL

The following section introduces you to the essay-length writing you will do when you undertake the major assignments in Chapters Two through Nine of *Reading Critically, Writing Well.* As you might guess, the briefer writing activities following every reading selection (Reading for Meaning and Reading Like a Writer) prepare you to write your own full-length essay.

Before previewing the essay assignments, pause to think about your own writing experience in high school, college, or on the job.

Thinking about Your Past Writing Experience

1. *Recall* the last time you wrote something fairly difficult, long, or complicated. Do not choose something written in class or under strict time limits.

2. *Write* several sentences describing how you went about planning and writing. Begin by briefly explaining your purpose for writing and identifying your audience. *Note* any assumptions you made about your readers' knowledge of the subject or their expectations of your writing.

You can use one or more of the following questions if you need help remembering how you went about completing the writing. But do not restrict yourself to these questions. Write down whatever comes to mind as you think about your past writing experience.

- How long did it take before you started putting your ideas on paper?

- What kind of plan did you have? How did your plan evolve as you worked?

- What did you change as you were writing? What changes, if any, did you make after completing your first draft?

- What role did other people play in helping you develop your ideas and plans?

THE WRITING ASSIGNMENTS

As you work through the assignments in Chapters Two through Nine of *Reading Critically, Writing Well,* you will learn how to write the following kinds or genres of essays:

Autobiography: telling readers about important events and people in your life

Observation: presenting to readers your firsthand reports about intriguing new places, people, and activities

Reflection: exploring for readers the larger social implications of your experience or observation

Explaining concepts: defining for readers the meaning and importance of key terms in academic disciplines or other areas of expertise

Evaluation: arguing to convince readers that your judgment of a movie, book, performance, essay, noteworthy person, or other subject is justifiable

Speculation about causes or effects: arguing to convince readers that certain causes or effects plausibly explain some event, trend, or phenomenon

Proposal to solve a problem: arguing to convince readers to accept or seriously consider your proposed solution to a problem

Position paper: arguing to convince readers to accept or seriously consider your position on a controversial issue

Each of these writing assignments identifies a genre of writing done every day by countless writers. More than mere school writing exercises, they are real-world writing situations like those you will encounter in college and at work. Pause now to learn a bit more about these assignments.

Previewing the Writing Assignments

Look at the different writing genres that are represented in this book. On the second or third page of each assignment chapter (Chapters Two through Nine) is a brief set of Writing Situations. Read this section in all of the chapters to get a quick sense of the different kinds of writing. Then write several sentences responding to the following questions:

1. Which of these genres have you already written?

2. With which of these genres have you had the most experience? Where and when did you write this kind of essay? What was most challenging about writing it?

3. What other genres would you like to learn to write? Why do they interest you?

THE GUIDES TO WRITING

At the end of Chapters Two through Nine in *Reading Critically, Writing Well,* a Guide to Writing helps you complete the writing assignment. These guides reflect the fact that writing is a process of discovery. As writers, we rarely if ever begin with a complete understanding of the subject. We put together some information and ideas, start writing, and let the writing lead us to understanding. While writing helps us achieve greater understanding, it also raises questions and unexpected complexities, which, in turn, can inspire more writing and, nearly always, generate further ideas and insights.

Experienced writers have learned to trust this fascinating discovery process because they know that writing is an unsurpassed thinking tool. Writing helps you discover, explore, develop, and refine your ideas in a way that cannot compare with sitting around and thinking about a subject. Because writing leaves a record of your thinking, it reduces the burden of remembering and allows you to direct all your energy toward solving the immediate problem. By rereading what you have written, you can figure out where you became derailed or recall points that you forgot were important or see new possibilities you did not notice before.

The Guide to Writing for each assignment leads you through the complex, creative process of discovery: Invention, Drafting, Reading a Draft Critically, Revising, and Editing and Proofreading. Because it helps to approach the first draft of an essay with some notes and other brief writings in hand, the first writing activity in each guide is called *invention,* a term used since classical Greek times to describe speakers' and writers' attempts to discover what they know and might say about a subject. Because *drafting* is most efficient and productive when you clarify your purpose and plan in advance, the Guide to Writing helps you set goals and organize your draft. Also, because nearly any draft can benefit from the advice of thoughtful readers, guidelines are included to help you and your classmates *read each other's drafts critically.* And because *revising* gives you the opportunity to develop your ideas and to make your writing communicate more clearly and effectively, each Guide to Writing includes suggestions for improving your draft. Finally, because you want your finished essay to conform to the conventions of grammar, mechanics, punctuation, and spelling, each Guide concludes with advice on *editing and proofreading* your writing.

Before reading about the resources offered to support your invention, drafting, critical reading, revising, and editing and proofreading, take time to preview a Guide to Writing.

Previewing a Guide to Writing

Turn to one of the Guides to Writing toward the end of any chapter. Skim the guide, reading the headings and the first paragraph in each section to get an idea of what it offers.

INVENTION

Invention begins with finding a subject to write about. The Considering Ideas for Your Own Writing sections following each reading, together with the suggestions in the Guide to Writing, will help you list several possible subjects. This act of listing possibilities is itself inventive because one item often suggests the next, and as the list grows you come to understand your options better and can therefore more confidently choose a subject. In each chapter, you will find suggestions that will help you make a good choice and understand the implications of developing the subject you choose.

Because each writing situation makes unique demands on writers, the invention activities in each chapter differ. To see how the invention activities differ from one kind of writing to the next, compare the activities under Invention in two or three chapters—for example, in Chapter Two on autobiography, Chapter Five on explaining concepts, and Chapter Nine on arguing positions.

The immediate advantage of this genre-specific invention is that it stimulates your thinking, getting you writing days before you begin drafting your essay. Although you will need no more than two hours to complete these invention activities, it is best to spread them over several days. As soon as you start writing the first few sentences about a subject, your mind goes to work on it, perhaps even offering ideas and insights when you are going about your daily activities, not consciously thinking about the subject. More invention writing will inspire more ideas. Your understanding of the subject will deepen and the possibilities will become more wide-ranging and subtle. An assignment that may have seemed daunting will become intellectually invigorating, and you will have pages of invention notes with which to launch your draft.

DRAFTING

After working on invention, you may be eager to begin drafting your essay. If, however, you are having difficulty making the transition from jotting down invention notes to writing a first draft, the Guide to Writing in each chapter will show you how to set achievable goals and devise a workable plan that will ease the process of drafting. The Guide's drafting section offers two activities: Setting Goals and Organizing Your Draft. To set goals, you need to ask yourself questions about your purpose and audience, such as how to interest readers in your subject, describe a person vividly, or counterargue effectively. As you establish your goals, you will also be reminded of the strategies other writers in the chapter use to accomplish similar goals in their essays. Organizing Your Draft points out how other writers in the chapter organize their essays and suggests that you make a scratch outline to develop a plan for your own essay.

READING A DRAFT CRITICALLY

Reading a draft with a critical eye enables you to give a classmate's draft an informed reading. Your critical reading can be supportive and helpful because as a writer yourself you can give the kind of advice writers most need when they have written a draft but are unsure what is working and what needs improvement. In the case of revising a position paper, for example, writers may need advice on how to clarify the position, strengthen the argument, anticipate objections, tighten the logic, and so on. These are the essentials for arguing convincingly for a position on a controversial issue.

Reading a Draft Critically invites you to make practical use of all you have learned about reading a genre. It invites you to try out your newly acquired expertise, and even to show off a bit—while doing a classmate a big favor. Part of the favor you provide is the written record of your critical reading that you hand over to your classmate, a record the classmate can refer to the next day or next week when revising the essay. You do yourself a favor as well. Like your classmate, you too will revise an essay in the same genre. As you read your classmate's essay critically, you will reflect intensely on your own just-completed draft. The more thoughtful and comprehensive your critical reading, the more likely you will be to discover ways to strengthen your own draft.

REVISING

Revising offers the great opportunity of rethinking what you have written, given your purpose and your readers' needs and expectations. Assume you will want to make changes and add new material at this stage. Be prepared to cut sentences, move sentences, reorder paragraphs. You provide the brainpower, and the computer provides the technology to make dramatic changes easy. This section on revising offers a range of suggestions for you to consider, along with the advice you received from your classmates and instructor.

EDITING AND PROOFREADING

Editing and proofreading are like taking a last look at yourself in the mirror before going out. You have given some thought to what you would wear and how you would look; now you check to make sure everything is the way you want it. The same principle applies to your essay. You have spent a lot of time and energy planning and writing; now you want to check to make sure that there are no glaring mistakes in grammar, punctuation, or spelling. If you are unsure whether you have made a mistake or how to fix it, consult a writer's guidebook or handbook.

Thinking about Your Learning

We know from research that if learning is not reviewed, reflected on, and consolidated, it soon fades and might not be available when new occasions arise for using or applying it. Therefore, in each assignment chapter, we provide two occasions for you to pause and reflect on what you have learned.

REVIEWING WHAT MAKES ESSAYS EFFECTIVE

The first occasion for thinking about your learning comes after the Readings section in each chapter. For example, in Chapter Nine, Position Paper, this section is titled Reviewing What Makes Position Papers Effective. You are asked to choose one reading that seemed to you a particularly good example of its genre, to reread it critically in light of all you have learned about the genre, and then to write a page or more justifying your choice. This activity enables you to review the characteristic features and rhetorical strategies of the genre you are about to write. Coming where it does before the Guide to Writing, this activity helps you complete the transition from thinking like a reader to thinking like a writer.

REFLECTING ON WHAT YOU HAVE LEARNED

This final occasion for thinking about your learning comes at the end of each chapter, where you are invited to describe what you are most pleased with in your revised essay and to explain what contributed to this achievement. It reminds you that there is much you have learned and much to learn about writing—from reading others' work, from writing your own essays, and from collaborating with other writers.

Autobiography

A utobiography involves telling stories about key events and describing people who played important roles in your life. Whether writing about an exhilarating childhood game or a difficult relationship, you should evoke for readers a vivid impression to help them see what you saw and hear what you heard. To write autobiography, therefore, you need to revisit the past, immersing yourself in the sights and sounds of memory. You also need to think deeply about the meaning of your experience—why it was and still is significant to you. Thinking deeply about the significance of important events and people in your life can help you discover something about the forces within yourself and within society that have helped to shape who you are and what is important to you.

While writing about your own life can be both enjoyable and instructive, so too can reading about other people's lives. As readers, we often take pleasure in seeing reflections of our own experience in other people's autobiographical writing. We enjoy recognizing similarities between the people and the events we have known and those that we read about. But sometimes the differences can be far more thought-provoking. For example, we may see how certain conditions—such as whether we grew up in the suburbs or the city; whether we are male or female; whether we are of African American, European, Asian, or mixed descent—can profoundly affect our lives and perspectives. Autobiography sometimes affirms our preconceptions, but it is most effective when it leads us to question our certainties, challenging us to see ourselves and others in a new light.

Whether you are reading or writing autobiography, it is important to remember that autobiography is public, not private. While it involves self-presentation and contributes to self-knowledge, it does not require writers to make unwanted self-disclosures. Autobiographers compose themselves for readers; they fashion a self in words, much as a novelist creates a character. As readers, we come to "know" the people we read about by the way they act, look, talk, think, and feel. When you write autobiography, then, you decide how to portray yourself. This decision depends on who you expect to read your essay (your audience) and what you want to communicate to readers (your purpose).

As you work through this chapter, you will learn more about autobiography by reading several different examples of it. You will see that some autobiographical essays center on a single event that occurred over a brief period of hours or days, while other essays focus on a person who played a significant role in the writer's life. Whether you decide to tell a story about a remembered event or to write about another person, you will practice two of the most basic writing strategies—narration and description. As you will see in later chapters of this book, narration and description can play a role not only in autobiography but also in providing explanations and developing arguments.

Whether you choose to write about an event or a person, your study of the reading selections in this chapter will give you ideas for writing effective autobiography. As you read and write about the selections, keep in mind the following assignment, which sets out the goals for writing an autobiographical essay. To support your writing of this assignment, the chapter concludes with a Guide to Writing Autobiography.

THE WRITING ASSIGNMENT

Autobiography

Write an autobiographical essay about a significant event or person in your life. Choose the event or person with your readers in mind: It should be one that you feel comfortable presenting to others and that will lead readers to reflect on their own lives or on the differences between their personal experiences and your own.

Present your experience dramatically and vividly so that readers can imagine what it was like for you. Through a careful choice of words and details, convey the meaning and importance—the autobiographical significance—of this event or person in your life.

AUTOBIOGRAPHICAL WRITING SITUATIONS

You may think only scientists, novelists, politicians, movie stars, and other famous people write their autobiographies. But autobiographical writing is much more widespread, as the following examples indicate:

- As part of her college application, a high-school senior includes a brief autobiographical essay that conveys her reasons for wanting to study science and become a researcher. In the essay, she recalls what happened when she did her first scientific experiment on the nutritional effects of different breakfast cereals on mice.

- Asked to recall a significant early childhood memory for an assignment in a psychology class, a college student writes about a fishing trip he took as a nine-year-old. He reflects on the significance of the trip—it was the first trip he took alone with his father and it began a new stage in their relationship.

- As part of a workshop on management skills, a business executive writes about a person who influenced his ideas about leadership. As he explores his memory and feelings, he realizes that he mistook fear for admiration. He recognizes that he has been emulating the wrong model, an autocratic leader who gets people to perform by using intimidation.

A GUIDE TO READING AUTOBIOGRAPHY

This section focuses on a brief but powerful piece of autobiography by poet-activist Audre Lorde. You will read Lorde's story twice. First, you will read it for meaning, seeking to grasp the significance of the event for Lorde—what it meant at the time and years later when she wrote about it—as well as the meaning it holds for you. Then, you will reread the story like a writer of autobiography, analyzing the parts to see how Lorde crafts her story and to learn the strategies she uses to make her autobiographical writing effective.

AUDRE LORDE

That Summer I Left Childhood Was White

Audre Lorde (1934–1992) is probably best known for her poetry and for her autobiography, Zami: A New Spelling of My Name *(1982).*

In this excerpt from that book, Lorde recalls an incident from 1947, when she was thirteen. Before reading, consider what you know about the history of racism in the United States during and directly after World War II. Did you know, for example, that a million African American men and women served in the military during the war, but that the military was not integrated until 1948? Did you know that it did not become illegal to refuse service in a restaurant on the basis of race until the Civil Rights Act of 1964?

As you read the selection, annotate anything that strikes you as meaningful or especially effective in conveying the drama and significance of the event. Annotating involves writing on the text as you read—noting parts you think are important, identifying words or references you do not know, writing comments and questions in the margin. (To learn more about annotating, see Appendix One, A Catalog of Critical Reading Strategies, pp. 450–456.)

The first time I went to Washington, D.C., was on the edge   1
of the summer when I was supposed to stop being a child. At least that's what they said to us all at graduation from the eighth grade. My sister Phyllis graduated at the same time from high school. I don't know what she was supposed to stop being. But as graduation presents for us both, the whole family took a Fourth of July trip to Washington, D.C., the fabled and famous capital of our country.

It was the first time I'd ever been on a railroad train dur-   2
ing the day. When I was little, and we used to go to the Connecticut shore, we always went at night on the milk train, because it was cheaper.

Preparations were in the air around our house before   3
school was even over. We packed for a week. There were two very large suitcases that my father carried, and a box filled with food. In fact, my first trip to Washington was a mobile feast; I started eating as soon as we were comfortably ensconced in our seats, and did not stop until somewhere after Philadelphia. I remember it was Philadelphia because I was disappointed not to have passed by the Liberty Bell.

My mother had roasted two chickens and cut them up   4
into dainty bite-size pieces. She packed slices of brown bread and butter and green pepper and carrot sticks. There were little violently yellow iced cakes with scalloped edges called "marigolds," that came from Cushman's Bakery. There was a spice bun and rock-cakes from Newton's, the West Indian bakery across Lenox Avenue from St. Mark's School, and iced tea in a wrapped mayonnaise jar. There were sweet pickles for us and dill pickles for my father, and peaches with the fuzz still on them, individually wrapped to keep them from bruising. And, for neatness, there were piles of napkins and a little tin box with a washcloth dampened with rosewater and glycerine for wiping sticky mouths.

I wanted to eat in the dining car because I had read all   5
about them, but my mother reminded me for the umpteenth time that dining car food always cost too much money and

besides, you never could tell whose hands had been playing all over that food, nor where those same hands had been just before. My mother never mentioned that Black people were not allowed into railroad dining cars headed south in 1947. As usual, whatever my mother did not like and could not change, she ignored. Perhaps it would go away, deprived of her attention.

I learned later that Phyllis's high school senior class trip   6
had been to Washington, but the nuns had given her back her deposit in private, explaining to her that the class, all of whom were white, except Phyllis, would be staying in a hotel where Phyllis "would not be happy," meaning, Daddy explained to her, also in private, that they did not rent rooms to Negroes. "We will take you to Washington, ourselves," my father had avowed, "and not just for an overnight in some measly fleabag hotel."

American racism was a new and crushing reality that my   7
parents had to deal with every day of their lives once they came to this country. They handled it as a private woe. My mother and father believed that they could best protect their children from the realities of race in america and the fact of american racism by never giving them name, much less discussing their nature. We were told we must never trust white people, but why was never explained, nor the nature of their ill will. Like so many other vital pieces of information in my childhood, I was supposed to know without being told. It always seemed like a very strange injunction coming from my mother, who looked so much like one of those people we were never supposed to trust. But something always warned me not to ask my mother why she wasn't white, and why Auntie Lillah and Auntie Etta weren't, even though they were all that same problematic color so different from my father and me, even from my sisters, who were somewhere in-between.

In Washington, D.C., we had one large room with two   8
double beds and an extra cot for me. It was a back-street hotel that belonged to a friend of my father's who was in real estate, and I spent the whole next day after Mass squinting up at the Lincoln Memorial where Marian Anderson had sung after the D.A.R.[1] refused to allow her to sing in their auditorium because she was Black. Or because she was "Colored," my father said as he told us the story. Except that

[1]*D.A.R.:* Daughters of the American Revolution. An organization of women descended from Americans who aided in the achievement of American Independence. *(Ed.)*

what he probably said was "Negro," because for his times, my father was quite progressive.

I was squinting because I was in that silent agony that 9 characterized all of my childhood summers, from the time school let out in June to the end of July, brought about by my dilated and vulnerable eyes exposed to the summer brightness.

I viewed Julys through an agonizing corolla of dazzling 10 whiteness and I always hated the Fourth of July, even before I came to realize the travesty such a celebration was for Black people in this country.

My parents did not approve of sunglasses, nor of their 11 expense.

I spent the afternoon squinting up at monuments to free- 12 dom and past presidencies and democracy, and wondering why the light and heat were both so much stronger in Washington, D.C., than back home in New York City. Even the pavement on the streets was a shade lighter in color than back home.

Late that Washington afternoon my family and I walked 13 back down Pennsylvania Avenue. We were a proper caravan, mother bright and father brown, the three of us girls step-standards in-between. Moved by our historical surroundings and the heat of the early evening, my father decreed yet another treat. He had a great sense of history, a flair for the quietly dramatic and the sense of specialness of an occasion and a trip.

"Shall we stop and have a little something to cool off, Lin?" 14

Two blocks away from our hotel, the family stopped for a 15 dish of vanilla ice cream at a Breyer's ice cream and soda fountain. Indoors, the soda fountain was dim and fan-cooled, deliciously relieving to my scorched eyes.

Corded and crisp and pinafored, the five of us seated our- 16 selves one by one at the counter. There was I between my mother and father, and my two sisters on the other side of my mother. We settled ourselves along the white mottled marble counter, and when the waitress spoke at first no one understood what she was saying, and so the five of us just sat there.

The waitress moved along the line of us closer to my fa- 17 ther and spoke again. "I said I kin give you to take out, but you can't eat here. Sorry." Then she dropped her eyes looking very embarrassed, and suddenly we heard what it was she was saying all at the same time, loud and clear.

Straight-backed and indignant, one by one, my family and 18 I got down from the counter stools and turned around and marched out of the store, quiet and outraged, as if we had never been Black before. No one would answer my emphatic questions with anything other than a guilty silence. "But we hadn't done anything!" This wasn't right or fair! Hadn't I written poems about Bataan and freedom and democracy for all?

My parents wouldn't speak of this injustice, not because they had contributed to it, but because they felt they should have anticipated it and avoided it. This made me even angrier. My fury was not going to be acknowledged by a like fury. Even my two sisters copied my parents' pretense that nothing unusual and anti-american had occurred. I was left to write my angry letter to the president of the united states all by myself, although my father did promise I could type it out on the office typewriter next week, after I showed it to him in my copybook diary.

The waitress was white, and the counter was white, and the ice cream I never ate in Washington, D.C., that summer I left childhood was white, and the white heat and the white pavement and the white stone monuments of my first Washington summer made me sick to my stomach for the whole rest of that trip and it wasn't much of a graduation present after all.

19

20

READING FOR MEANING

Write to create meanings for Lorde's autobiographical story.

START MAKING MEANING

Begin by explaining what you think the significance of this event is for Lorde and her possible purpose or purposes for choosing to write about it in the way that she does. Continue by writing about anything else in the selection or in your experience that contributes to your understanding of Lorde's story.

IF YOU ARE STUCK

If you cannot write at least a page, consider writing about

- what surprised you as you read the story and what you could have predicted—and why.

- the young Lorde's reaction to being denied service at the ice-cream counter compared to her parents' reactions.

- this essay as a coming-of-age story, enabling the young Lorde to see herself and others differently or to act differently.

- what the story says about the time in which the event occurred (two years after the end of World War II), the time in which the story was first published (the early 1980s), or the time in which you are now reading it.

READING LIKE A WRITER

This section leads you through an analysis of Lorde's autobiographical writing strategies: *narrating the story, describing places, describing people,* and *conveying the autobiographical significance.* For each strategy you will be asked to reread and annotate part of Lorde's essay to see how she uses the strategy to accomplish her particular purpose.

When you study the selections later in this chapter, you will see how different autobiographers use these same strategies for different purposes. The Guide to Writing Autobiography at the end of the chapter suggests ways you can use these strategies in your own writing.

Narrating the Story

Whether focusing on a single event or a person, writers nearly always tell a story or several brief stories called *anecdotes.* Stories are so pervasive in our culture, indeed in most cultures, that we are all familiar with what makes a story effective. A well-told story draws readers in by arousing their curiosity and keeps them reading by building suspense or tension, making them want to know what will happen.

Storytellers use a variety of techniques to pace the story and intensify dramatic scenes. One way is to speed up the action (as you will see in the next selection, "A Chase," by Annie Dillard). Another way, paradoxically, is to slow down the action, focusing attention on specific details in a kind of cinematic close-up or slow-motion shot. Here is an example from Lorde's essay: "*Straight-backed and indignant, one by one,* my family and I got down from the counter stools. . . ." (paragraph 18). The italicized phrases focus in on the characters' body language as they prepare to leave the restaurant. What we pay attention to as we read is not the main action—their getting down from the counter stools—but the manner in which they do so. The few words Lorde uses to describe the scene speak volumes about her family and how they choose to react to the injustice of being denied service.

ANALYZE

1. *Reread and annotate* the scene in the ice-cream store very closely. Begin with paragraph 13 just before the father proposes a stop for ice cream, and read to the end of the story. *Find and mark* the turning point, the moment when the emotion of the scene reaches a climax.

2. Next, *reread* the paragraphs leading up to the turning point you identified, examining how Lorde paces the narrative in terms of tension and drama. For example, *note* whether the pace stays constant or whether it changes, speeding up or slowing down. *Notice* also what Lorde focuses readers' attention on. *Underline* any word choices that enable you to picture the mood of the narrator and her family before the turning point.

3. Finally, *focus* on the turning point and what follows. Again, *notice* the pacing to see how Lorde signals to readers the intense emotions and drama of the scene we are witnessing. *Underline* any word choices that convey the intensity and significance of Lorde's feelings about what happened.

WRITE

Write several sentences explaining what you have learned about the way Lorde narrates the ice-cream store scene. How does she use pacing to make the scene dramatic? How do her word choices enable you to picture what happened and also to appreciate the significance of this event?

Describing Places

Whether an autobiography centers on an event or a person, it nearly always includes some description of places. This physical description not only enables readers to picture what happened in a particular place, but it also creates for readers an overall or dominant impression of the place that helps convey the story's significance. Vivid language that describes sensory impressions—what the place looked, smelled, and sounded like—is particularly evocative of feeling and mood.

Another important aspect of describing a place is the narrator's point of view, or the vantage point from which the scene is described. Is the scene viewed from a fixed position or as the narrator moves through it? Is the place observed close up or from a panoramic distance, or some combination of perspectives? While point of view indicates the narrator's physical location in relation to the place, it also can imply the autobiographer's emotional attitude to what happened there. For example, when Lorde describes herself as "squinting up at the Lincoln Memorial" (paragraph 8), her physical distance from Lincoln's image underscores and symbolizes how out of reach the freedom and equality he promised still seem to her. Point of view, in this way, can give readers insight into the writer's feelings and the story's significance.

ANALYZE

Lorde describes four different places: the train (paragraphs 3–5), the hotel room (briefly, in paragraph 8), the streets and monuments of

Washington, D.C. (paragraphs 8–14 and 20), and the ice-cream parlor (paragraphs 15–18 and 20). *Choose one* of these locations and *reread* the description. *Note* in the margin which senses—sight, sound, smell, touch, and taste—are evoked and *underline* any sensory details that help you imagine what the place was like for Lorde.

WRITE

Based on your analysis, *write* several sentences about Lorde's description of the one location you chose. *List* the key sensory details that stick in your mind and try to *describe* the feelings they evoke. *Indicate* how Lorde's description of this particular scene conveys its significance for the writer.

Describing People

Autobiographers depict people by describing their physical appearance, revealing aspects of their character or personality, and suggesting the nature of their relationships. Often, a few brief details about the way a person looks, dresses, or acts will be sufficient. Even essays portraying a person who played an important role in the writer's life tend to have less physical description than one might expect. A single gesture or expression can be more revealing than a catalog of visual details. In addition to providing descriptive detail, writers may comment directly on the person's personality traits and relationships with others. Characterizations like these can be especially effective when accompanied by an illustrative story or anecdote that creates a vivid, lasting impression of the person for readers.

ANALYZE

Reread closely and *annotate* paragraphs 7–8, 11, 13, 18–20, putting brackets ([ ]) around the specific physical details that describe Lorde and her family—the way they look and dress, their movements and gestures. Also mark anything they say or Lorde says about them that gives you a sense of their beliefs and attitudes as well as Lorde's relationship with them.

WRITE

Based on your annotations, *write* several sentences explaining how Lorde characterizes her family—particularly her parents—in the story. What do you learn about them and their relationship with Lorde from the way she portrays them? *Cite* one or two specific examples that give you insight into her parents and her relationship with them.

Conveying the Autobiographical Significance

Autobiographers convey the significance of the event or person in two ways: by *showing* that it was important and by *telling* what it meant. Most writers do both. Through your analysis of how Lorde tells the story and describes the place and people, you have seen how she shows the event's significance. Now turn your focus to what she tells her readers.

Autobiographers may tell us what they thought and felt *at the time* of the event, or what they think and feel now *as they look back* at the event. Often, writers do both. As a close reader, you should look for any differences in how the writer understood the experience at the time it occurred and how the writer understands it now in retrospect.

ANALYZE

1. *Reread* paragraphs 5–7, putting a *C* in the margin to mark the places where you think Lorde expresses what she thought and felt as a child at the time of the event. (For example, you would put a *C* next to the first sentence in paragraph 5.)

2. *Write* an *A* in the margin next to parts of paragraphs 5–7 where you think Lorde expresses her adult perspective as she looks back at her past experience and writes about it. (For example, you would put an *A* next to the second sentence in paragraph 5 and the third sentence in paragraph 7 where Lorde chose not to capitalize the word *America*.)

3. *Examine* carefully how Lorde signals to readers which thoughts and feelings she had as a child and which ones she has an adult.

WRITE

Write a few sentences exploring what your analysis reveals about the event's significance to Lorde. Also *indicate* how you think the writer's understanding of its significance changed from when she was a child to when she was an adult.

ANNIE DILLARD

A Chase

Annie Dillard (b. 1945), a poet, essayist, and literary theorist, gained recognition as one of America's finest non-fiction writers with her Pulitzer Prize–winning book Pilgrim at Tinker Creek *(1974). Since then she has published a book of poems,* Tickets for the Prayer Wheel *(1982); a book of literary theory,* Living by Fiction *(1982); an autobiography,* An American Childhood *(1987); and an account of her working life as a writer,* The Writing Life *(1989). In 1992, Dillard published her first novel,* The Living.*

The following selection, from Dillard's autobiography, focuses on an event from the writer's childhood. It occurred one snowy morning, when she and a friend were chased relentlessly by an adult stranger at whom they had been throwing snowballs. Dillard admits that she was terrified, and yet she asserts that she has "seldom been happier since." As you read, think about how this paradox helps you appreciate the significance of the experience for Dillard.

Some boys taught me to play football. This was fine sport. 1
You thought up a new strategy for every play and whispered it to the others. You went out for a pass, fooling everyone. Best, you got to throw yourself mightily at someone's running legs. Either you brought him down or you hit the ground flat out on your chin, with your arms empty before you. It was all or nothing. If you hesitated in fear, you would miss and get hurt: you would take a hard fall while the kid got away, or you would get kicked in the face while the kid got away. But if you flung yourself wholeheartedly at the back of his knees—if you gathered and joined body and soul and pointed them diving fearlessly—then you likely wouldn't get hurt, and you'd stop the ball. Your fate, and your team's score, depended on your concentration and courage. Nothing girls did could compare with it.

Boys welcomed me at baseball, too, for I had, through en- 2
thusiastic practice, what was weirdly known as a boy's arm. In winter, in the snow, there was neither baseball nor football, so the boys and I threw snowballs at passing cars. I got in trouble throwing snowballs, and have seldom been happier since.

On one weekday morning after Christmas, six inches of 3
new snow had just fallen. We were standing up to our boot

tops in snow on a front yard on trafficked Reynolds Street, waiting for cars. The cars traveled Reynolds Street slowly and evenly; they were targets all but wrapped in red ribbons, cream puffs. We couldn't miss.

I was seven; the boys were eight, nine, and ten. The oldest two Fahey boys were there—Mikey and Peter—polite blond boys who lived near me on Lloyd Street, and who already had four brothers and sisters. My parents approved Mikey and Peter Fahey. Chickie McBride was there, a tough kid, and Billy Paul and Mackie Kean too, from across Reynolds, where the boys grew up dark and furious, grew up skinny, knowing, and skilled. We had all drifted from our houses that morning looking for action, and had found it here on Reynolds Street.   4

It was cloudy but cold. The cars' tires laid behind them on the snowy street a complex trail of beige chunks like crenellated castle walls. I had stepped on some earlier; they squeaked. We could not have wished for more traffic. When a car came, we all popped it one. In the intervals between cars we reverted to the natural solitude of children.   5

I started making an iceball—a perfect iceball, from perfectly white snow, perfectly spherical, and squeezed perfectly translucent so no snow remained all the way through. (The Fahey boys and I considered it unfair actually to throw an iceball at somebody, but it had been known to happen.)   6

I had just embarked on the iceball project when we heard tire chains come clanking from afar. A black Buick was moving toward us down the street. We all spread out, banged together some regular snowballs, took aim, and, when the Buick drew nigh, fired.   7

A soft snowball hit the driver's windshield right before the driver's face. It made a smashed star with a hump in the middle.   8

Often, of course, we hit our target, but this time, the only time in all of life, the car pulled over and stopped. Its wide black door opened; a man got out of it, running. He didn't even close the car door.   9

He ran after us, and we ran away from him, up the snowy Reynolds sidewalk. At the corner, I looked back; incredibly, he was still after us. He was in city clothes: a suit and tie, street shoes. Any normal adult would have quit, having sprung us into flight and made his point. This man was gaining on us. He was a thin man, all action. All of a sudden, we were running for our lives.   10

Wordless, we split up. We were on our turf; we could lose ourselves in the neighborhood backyards, everyone for him-   11 self. I paused and considered. Everyone had vanished except Mikey Fahey, who was just rounding the corner of a yellow brick house. Poor Mikey, I trailed him. The driver of the Buick sensibly picked the two of us to follow. The man apparently had all day.

He chased Mikey and me around the yellow house and up   12
a backyard path we knew by heart: under a low tree, up a bank, through a hedge, down some snowy steps, and across the grocery store's delivery driveway. We smashed through a gap in another hedge, entered a scruffy backyard and ran around its back porch and tight between houses to Edgerton Avenue; we ran across Edgerton to an alley and up our own sliding woodpile to the Halls' front yard; he kept coming. We ran up Lloyd Street and wound through mazy backyards toward the steep hilltop at Willard and Lang.

He chased us silently, block after block. He chased us   13
silently over picket fences, through thorny hedges, between houses, around garbage cans, and across streets. Every time I glanced back, choking for breath, I expected he would have quit. He must have been as breathless as we were. His jacket strained over his body. It was an immense discovery, pounding into my hot head with every sliding, joyous step, that this ordinary adult evidently knew what I thought only children who trained at football knew: that you have to fling yourself at what you're doing, you have to point yourself, forget yourself, aim, dive.

Mikey and I had nowhere to go, in our own neighborhood   14
or out of it, but away from this man who was chasing us. He impelled us forward; we compelled him to follow our route. The air was cold; every breath tore my throat. We kept running, block after block; we kept improvising, backyard after backyard, running a frantic course and choosing it simultaneously, failing always to find small places or hard places to slow him down, and discovering always, exhilarated, dismayed, that only bare speed could save us—for he would never give up, this man—and we were losing speed.

He chased us through the backyard labyrinths of ten   15
blocks before he caught us by our jackets. He caught us and we all stopped.

We three stood staggering, half blinded, coughing, in an   16
obscure hilltop backyard: a man in his twenties, a boy, a girl. He had released our jackets, our pursuer, our captor, our hero: he knew we weren't going anywhere. We all played by the rules. Mikey and I unzipped our jackets. I pulled off my sopping mittens. Our tracks multiplied in the backyard's new snow. We had been breaking new snow all morning. We

didn't look at each other. I was cherishing my excitement. The man's lower pants legs were wet; his cuffs were full of snow, and there was a prow of snow beneath them on his shoes and socks. Some trees bordered the little flat backyard, some messy winter trees. There was no one around: a clearing in a grove, and we the only players.

It was a long time before he could speak. I had some difficulty at first recalling why we were there. My lips felt swollen; I couldn't see out of the sides of my eyes; I kept coughing.   17

"You stupid kids," he began perfunctorily.   18

We listened perfunctorily indeed, if we listened at all, for the chewing out was redundant, a mere formality, and beside the point. The point was that he had chased us passionately without giving up, and so he had caught us. Now he came down to earth. I wanted the glory to last forever.   19

But how could the glory have lasted forever? We could have run through every backyard in North America until we got to Panama. But when he trapped us at the lip of the Panama Canal, what precisely could he have done to prolong the drama of the chase and cap its glory? I brooded about this for the next few years. He could only have fried Mikey Fahey and me in boiling oil, say, or dismembered us piecemeal, or staked us to anthills. None of which I really wanted, and none of which any adult was likely to do, even in the spirit of fun. He could only chew us out there in the Panamanian jungle, after months or years of exalting pursuit. He could only begin, "You stupid kids," and continue in his ordinary Pittsburgh accent with his normal righteous anger and the usual common sense.   20

If in that snowy backyard the driver of the black Buick had cut off our heads, Mikey's and mine, I would have died happy, for nothing has required so much of me since as being chased all over Pittsburgh in the middle of winter— running terrified, exhausted—by this sainted, skinny, furious redheaded man who wished to have a word with us. I don't know how he found his way back to his car.   21

READING FOR MEANING

Write to create meanings for Dillard's autobiographical story.

START MAKING MEANING

Begin by explaining what you think the significance of this event is for Dillard and her possible purpose or purposes for choosing to write about it in the way that she does. Continue by writing about anything else in the selection or in your experience that contributes to your understanding of Dillard's story.

IF YOU ARE STUCK

If you cannot write at least a page, consider writing about

- your impression of childhood and gender roles in the United States at the time of Dillard's story (the 1950s), perhaps in comparison with your own experience or Audre Lorde's experience (the 1940s) in the preceding selection.

- why Dillard states proudly, "We all played by the rules" (paragraph 16), perhaps speculating about how we come to know what "rules" to play by.

- why Dillard uses such words as "hero" (paragraph 16) and "sainted" (paragraph 21) to describe the man who chased her, even though she dismisses what he said when he finally caught her as "redundant, a mere formality, and beside the point" (paragraph 19).

- how the description of one key scene—such as the iceballing scene (paragraphs 5–8) or the confrontation scene (paragraphs 15–21)—contributes to your understanding of the event's significance for Dillard.

READING LIKE A WRITER
NARRATING A STORY DRAMATICALLY

The stories writers tell may build up to a single dramatic moment, as in Audre Lorde's "That Summer I Left Childhood Was White." Or they may be full of action and drama, as in Annie Dillard's "A Chase." This activity will help you see how Dillard uses verbs to show dramatic action in her story.

ANALYZE

1. *Underline* each verb in paragraphs 12–16, including the *-ing* forms. To get you started, paragraph 12 begins with the verbs "chased" and "smashed," and in paragraph 14, "chasing" is the first *-ing* form.

2. *Put a second line* under the verbs that name an action. For example, the verb "tore" in the following sentence names an action (double underline), whereas the verb "was" does not name an action (single underline): "The air was cold; every breath tore my throat" (paragraph 14).

3. *Find* two or three sentences in which you think the action verbs help you experience the drama of the chase.

WRITE

Write several sentences explaining what you have learned about Dillard's use of verbs to represent action and to make her narrative dramatic. *Quote* several verbs and sentences as examples.

CONSIDERING IDEAS FOR YOUR OWN WRITING

List several occasions when you were amused, frightened, or surprised by the way another person behaved toward you or toward another person in your presence. Choose one particularly significant event, and recall who was present and what happened. As a writer describing this event, what would you emphasize to make the story dramatic? What significance would you want the story to convey to readers?

RUSSELL BAKER

Smooth and Easy

Russell Baker (b. 1924) began his career as a journalist with the Baltimore Sun *and for many years covered the White House, Congress, and national politics for the* New York Times. *Since 1962, he has written his nationally syndicated "Observer" column. He was awarded the Pulitzer Prize for Distinguished Commentary in 1979, and won a second Pulitzer in 1983 for his autobiography* Growing Up. *His other books include* The Good Times *(1989),* There's a Country in My Cellar *(1990), and* Russell Baker's Book of American Humor *(1993). Recently, he has become a familiar face as host of the PBS program* Masterpiece Theater.

In this selection from Growing Up, *Baker recounts a turning point in his life, an event that occurred toward the end of World War II. The narrative focuses on the test he had to pass to qualify as a Navy pilot. As you read, notice how Baker uses humor to present himself in this difficult situation.*

For the longest time . . . I flew and flew without ever being in control of any airplane. It was a constant struggle for power between the plane and me, and the plane usually won. I approached every flight like a tenderfoot sent to tame a wild horse. By the time I arrived at the Naval Air Station at Memphis, where Navy pilots took over the instruction, it was obvious my flying career would be soon ended. We flew open-cockpit biplanes—"Yellow Perils," the Navy called them—which forgave almost any mistake. Instructors sat in the front cockpit, students behind. But here the instructors did not ride the controls. These were courageous men. Many were back from the Pacific, and they put their destinies in my hands high over the Mississippi River and came back shaking their heads in sorrow.   1

"It's just like driving a car, Baker," a young ensign told me the day I nearly killed him trying to sideslip into a farm field where he wanted to land and take a smoke. "You know how it is when you let in the clutch? Real smooth and easy."   2

I knew nothing about letting in the clutch, but didn't dare say so. "Right," I said. "Smooth and easy."   3

I got as far as the acrobatic stage. Rolls, loops, Immelman turns. Clouds spinning zanily beneath me, earth and river whirling above. An earnest young Marine pilot took me aside after a typical day of disaster in the sky. "Baker," he said, "it's just like handling a girl's breast. You've got to be gentle."   4

I didn't dare tell him I'd never handled a girl's breast, either.   5

The inevitable catastrophe came on my check flight at the   6
end of the acrobatic stage. It was supposed to last an hour,
but after twenty minutes in the sky the check pilot said, "All
right, let's go in," and gave me a "down," which meant "unfit
to fly." I was doomed. I knew it, my buddies knew it. The
Navy would forgive a "down" only if you could fly two successful check flights back-to-back with different check pilots.
If you couldn't you were out.

I hadn't a prayer of surviving. On Saturday, looking at   7
Monday's flight schedule, I saw that I was posted to fly the
fatal reexamination with a grizzled pilot named T. L. Smith. It
was like reading my own obituary. T. L. Smith was a celebrated perfectionist famous for washing out cadets for the
slightest error in the air. His initials, T. L., were said to stand
for "Total Loss," which was all anyone who had to fly for him
could expect. Friends stopped by my bunk at the barracks to
commiserate and tell me it wasn't so bad being kicked out of
flying. I'd probably get soft desk duty in some nice Navy
town where you could shack up a lot and sleep all day. Two
of my best friends, wanting to cheer me up, took me to go
into Memphis for a farewell weekend together. Well, it beat
sitting on the base all weekend thinking about my Monday
rendezvous with Total Loss. Why not a last binge for the
condemned?

We took a room at the Peabody Hotel and bought three   8
bottles of bourbon. I'd tasted whiskey only two or three
times before and didn't much like it; but now in my gloom it
brought a comfort I'd never known. I wanted more of that
comfort. My dream was dying. I would plumb the depths of
vice in these final hours. The weekend quickly turned into
an incoherent jumble of dreamlike episodes. Afterwards I
vaguely remembered threatening to punch a fat man in a
restaurant, but couldn't remember why. At some point I was
among a gang of sailors in a hotel corridor, and I was telling
them to stop spraying the hallway with a fire hose. At another I was sitting fully dressed on what seemed to be a
piano bench in a hotel room—not at the Peabody—and a
strange woman was smiling at me and taking off her
brassiere.

This was startling, because no woman had ever taken her   9
brassiere off in front of me before. But where had she come
from? What were we doing in this alien room? "I'll bet I know
what you want," she said.

"What?"   10

"This," she said, and stepped out of her panties and   11
stretched out flat on her back on the bed. She beckoned. I
stood up, then thought better of it and settled to the floor
like a collapsing column of sand. I awoke hours later on the
floor. She'd gone.

With the hangover I took back to the base Sunday night, I   12
would have welcomed instant execution at the hands of
Total Loss Smith, but when I awoke Monday morning the
physical agony was over. In its place had come an unnatural,
disembodied sensation of great calm. The world was moving
much more slowly than its normal pace. In this eerie state of
relaxation nothing seemed to matter much, not the terrible
Total Loss Smith, not even the end of my flying days.

When we met at the flight line, Total Loss looked just as   13
grim as everybody said he would. It was bitterly cold. We
both wore heavy leather flight suits lined with wool, and his
face looked tougher than the leather. He seemed old enough
to be my father. Wrinkles creased around eyes that had
never smiled. Lips as thin as a movie killer's. I introduced
myself. His greeting was what I'd expected. "Let's get this
over with," he said.

We walked down the flight line, parachutes bouncing   14
against our rumps, not a word said. In the plane—Total Loss
in the front seat, me in the back—I connected the speaking
tube which enabled him to talk to me but didn't allow me to
speak back. Still not a word while I taxied out to the mat, ran
through the cockpit checks, and finished by testing the mag-
netos. If he was trying to petrify me before we got started he
was wasting his efforts. In this new state of peace I didn't
give a damn whether he talked to me or not.

"Take me up to 5,000 feet and show me some rolls," he   15
growled as I started the takeoff.

The wheels were hardly off the mat before I experienced   16
another eerie sensation. It was a feeling of power. For the
first time since first stepping into an airplane I felt in complete mastery of the thing. I'd noticed it on takeoff. It had
been an excellent takeoff. Without thinking about it, I'd automatically corrected a slight swerve just before becoming air-
borne. Now as we climbed I was flooded with a sense of confidence. The hangover's residue of relaxation had freed me
of the tensions that had always defeated me before. Before,
the plane had had a will of its own; now the plane seemed to
be part of me, an extension of my hands and feet, obedient
to my slightest whim. I leveled it at exactly 5,000 feet and
started a slow roll. First a shallow dive to gain velocity, then
push the stick slowly, firmly, all the way over against the

thigh, simultaneously putting in hard rudder, and there we are, hanging upside down over the earth and now—keeping it rolling, don't let the nose drop—reverse the controls and feel it roll all the way through until—coming back to straight-and-level now—catch it, wings level with the horizon, and touch the throttle to maintain altitude precisely at 5,000 feet.

"Perfect," said Total Loss. "Do me another one."   17

It hadn't been a fluke. Somewhere between the weekend's   18
bourbon and my arrival at the flight line that morning, I had become a flyer. The second slow roll was as good as the first.

"Show me your snap rolls," Total Loss said.   19

I showed him snap rolls as fine as any instructor had ever   20
shown me.

"All right, give me a loop and then a split-S and recover   21
your altitude and show me an Immelman."

I looped him through a big graceful arc, leveled out and   22
rolled into the split-S, came out of it climbing, hit the altitude dead on at 5,000 feet, and showed him an Immelman that Eddie Rickenbacker would have envied.

"What the hell did you do wrong on your check last   23
week?" he asked. Since I couldn't answer, I shrugged so he could see me in his rearview mirror.

"Let me see you try a falling leaf," he said.   24

Even some instructors had trouble doing a falling leaf.   25
The plane had to be brought precisely to its stalling point, then dropped in a series of sickening sideways skids, first to one side, then to the other, like a leaf falling in a breeze, by delicate simultaneous manipulations of stick, rudder pedals, and throttle. I seemed to have done falling leaves all my life.

"All right, this is a waste of my time," Total Loss growled.   26
"Let's go in."

Back at the flight line, when I'd cut the ignition, he   27
climbed out and tramped back toward the ready room while I waited to sign the plane in. When I got there he was standing at a distance talking to my regular instructor. His talk was being illustrated with hand movements, as pilots' conversations always were, hands executing little loops and rolls in the air. After he did the falling-leaf motion with his hands, he pointed a finger at my instructor's chest, said something I couldn't hear, and trudged off. My instructor, who had flown only with the pre-hangover Baker, was slack-jawed when he approached me.

"Smith just said you gave him the best check flight he's   28
ever had in his life," he said. "What the hell did you do to him up there?"

"I guess I just suddenly learned to fly," I said. I didn't men-   29
tion the hangover. I didn't want him to know that bourbon
was a better teacher than he was. After that I saw T. L. Smith
coming and going frequently through the ready room and
thought him the finest, most manly looking fellow in the entire corps of instructors, as well as the wisest.

READING FOR MEANING

Write to create meanings for Baker's autobiographical story.

START MAKING MEANING

Begin by explaining what you think the significance of this event is for
Baker and his possible purpose or purposes for choosing to write about it
in the way that he does. Continue by writing about anything else in the selection or in your experience that contributes to your understanding of
Baker's story.

IF YOU ARE STUCK

If you cannot write at least a page, consider writing about

- this selection as a coming-of-age story, one that enables the young
  Baker to see himself and others differently or to act differently from
  the way he would have been able to act before the experience—perhaps comparing his story with Audre Lorde's or Annie Dillard's story.

- the ways Baker makes fun of himself in this story, perhaps speculating about why an autobiographer would use self-deprecating humor.

- how being a man or a woman influences your reading of Baker's story.

- what the story suggests about learning a difficult new skill such as flying an airplane—in light of your experiences as a learner.

A SPECIAL READING STRATEGY

Contextualizing

Contextualizing is a special strategy described in Appendix
One, A Catalog of Reading Strategies. When you use contextualizing to read for meaning, you look for differences between the values and attitudes you bring to your reading and those represented in an essay like Baker's that was written in an earlier
era—in this case, the 1940s. To contextualize, you need to think
about questions like these:

Continued

- What images and ideas come to mind when you think about the World War II period of the 1940s?

- How does Baker's essay reinforce or contradict those images and ideas?

- How do the sensibilities of your own time and culture lead you to react to the attitudes and stereotypes Baker's essay presents?

See Appendix One for additional help in using this strategy.

READING LIKE A WRITER
DESCRIBING PEOPLE

To describe a person who plays an important role in a story, autobiographers usually focus on a few memorable physical details, typical mannerisms, ways of talking, and personality or character traits. This activity will help you see how Baker uses details to describe the check pilot T. L. Smith, also know as Total Loss Smith.

ANALYZE

1. *Reread* paragraph 7, where Baker tells us about the check pilot's reputation, and *underline* any details that convey Baker's attitude toward him at this point in the story.

2. Then closely *examine* paragraphs 13–29, where Baker presents his encounter with Total Loss Smith, and *underline* any descriptive details that let you see what the check pilot is actually like in this encounter with Baker.

WRITE

Write several sentences explaining what you have learned about Baker's way of describing Total Loss Smith. *Cite* a few descriptive details that helped you imagine what Total Loss was like for Baker.

CONSIDERING IDEAS FOR YOUR OWN WRITING

List several occasions when you had a hard time trying to learn something or when you helped someone else learn something challenging. Choose one particularly significant event, and recall who was present and what happened. As a writer describing this event, what would you emphasize to make the story dramatic? What significance would you want the story to convey to readers?

LAURIE ABRAHAM

Divorced Father

Laurie Abraham (b. 1965), a public health reporter, wrote this portrait of her father for a collection of autobiographical essays titled Reinventing Home: Six Working Women Look at Their Home Lives *(1991). She also edited a second essay collection,* Reinventing Love: Six Women Talk About Love, Lust, Sex, and Romance *(1998). As the title of this reading suggests, Abraham's essay is about her father after her parents were divorced. As you read and annotate the essay, note Abraham's feelings about how the divorce changed her father and affected her relationship with him.*

I have seen tears in my father's eyes twice: during the premiere of the Waltons' Christmas special and on the drive to his new apartment. If I had asked about the tears in his eyes the morning he left home, he probably would have blamed them on the sun. It was a too-bright day in June when my father left home, exactly eighteen years after my parents were married. He took his clothes, the old black-and-white TV, the popcorn popper, a pot and skillet, and a few other things. It took only two trips in the brown Pinto station wagon to move half of my father's life. Not that he couldn't have claimed his share of the tables, chairs, and pictures—but he chose to leave the fallout of two decades of acquiring with my mother.

From a house full of things, he went to an apartment of four empty rooms carpeted in gold-and-white shag. Soon, though, a queen-sized bed jutted from the middle of his bedroom wall, a butcher-block table with four matching chairs sat in the dining room, and an L-shaped brown velvet sofa dwarfed the 19-inch TV. He never bought a picture, a coffeetable, a knickknack or anything that said, "Harold Abraham lives here." A few things that my dad had claimed from the divorce, however, definitely bore his mark: cocktail glasses printed with the Dow Jones Industrial Average; four plastic beer mugs (one with the Bud Man, another with "Michelob" tastefully printed in gold); a stoneware coffee mug with sailboats. But these weren't the possessions of a father of two with a master's degree and a CPA degree. These were pieces of "Abe," that hard-drinking wild boy who wore garlic around his neck for a week to gain admission to a fraternity that stole a cow for a pet, a fraternity that was banned from the campus the year after my father left.

Money certainly didn't prevent my father from decorating   3
his apartment. He usually had enough of it, and when he didn't, he spent it anyway. Surprisingly, the explanation for the starkness of his home came to me from people who have less in common with my father than my mother did: low-income teenagers who picked up trash and trimmed grass in a government jobs program.

"Where do you stay?" several of them asked me during   4
the summer that I worked as their supervisor. At first I wondered about their word choice: I always asked new acquaintances where they lived, not where they stayed. But after listening to them all summer I understood why "stay" was the most appropriate word to describe their experiences. They were always moving, from their mother's apartment, to their grandmother's, to an aunt's. None of these places was necessarily bad, just temporary. These kids didn't live at East Seventy-fifth and Superior, they stayed there for a time. My father was doing that, too—staying. He had no intention of living in his apartment, or calling it home. It was a way station between his first wife and the one to come—except on Sundays. When his girls came to visit, my dad rushed to throw together a home.

I know little about my father's childhood, but I won't for-   5
get the few memories that he's let slip over the years. He slept in a dresser drawer because his family could not afford a crib. His dad never said to him, "Harold, how was school today?" He went without many of the furnishings that make up a home, never mind the nurturing. Making a home for his children was important so that he could give us what he never got. He did his best—for us and for the boy whose parents never quite made it to his high school football games.

But since he had been deprived of the emotional suste-   6
nance that makes a home a home, my father was never quite sure what to do with my sister and me once he had us. He relied on food—the most straightforward kind of nurturing—to turn his bachelor's apartment into a home. Breakfast was pancakes. In the beginning, when all three of us were trying to fight off sadness and before my sister and I grew to resent the Sunday morning call, "Your father's here," he flipped them. By high school, the pancakes didn't fly and I slumped in my chair, suffering from the six-pack I had downed the night before. By dinner I'd usually recovered enough to enjoy either spaghetti with Ragú sauce or Kentucky Fried Chicken—always carryout; the restaurant wasn't

home. These dishes were hearty but deliciously junky, the kind of food men with few cooking skills and one chance a week to win their children's approval are apt to serve. Between meals, we'd eat some more: popcorn or pizza rolls while watching football on TV, or ice cream after an awkward, time-filling walk in the woods.

My father's homemaking hit full stride at Christmas, when shortcomings we never could ignore became that much more obvious and sad. First, we'd pick the right tree with my mother. Then, another tree with Dad, if we could arrange a time that was "mutually convenient." To the scratchy strains of "Christmas in Killarney," a Ray Conniff album my parents bought when they were first married, we pushed the lights onto the prickly branches of a spruce or Scotch pine. (We never used garden gloves with my father, although my mother used them; he probably didn't own a pair anyway.) My father's half of the ornaments included a few of the "good" ones—the papier-mâché Santa, the Ohio State football helmet trimmed with holly—but he also had his share of the back-of-the-tree duds such as clear plastic teardrops, one for each of the twelve days of Christmas. Most years, decorating the tree with Dad was fun, but to my sister and me, it wasn't our real tree in our real home. It was what we put up with Dad so he wouldn't be lonely at Christmas.

Long after I began to consider the two times I saw my father almost cry, I realized that there might be a connection between the tears of moving day and those provoked by the Waltons' Christmas show. Its plot was this: Pa Walton was lost during a snowstorm on Christmas Eve. A man was cut off from his family. I doubt back then, watching that show, that Dad imagined one day he would be driving away from his wife and girls, but somehow he identified. And what my father missed the most when he left home was something the Waltons had plenty of—people. That's what my father was forced to give up: lots of people around, people he might not necessarily be close to (like my mom), but who were present. He didn't want to struggle to build a new family from scratch; he needed to be plopped down in the middle of one. And so he was, finally. His second wife comes from a large and raucous family, and my dad has three new stepchildren. Large Christmas Eve parties at his new wife's home have become something of a tradition for us.

For me, the parties are events. I wear red, or something that stands out in a crowd of relatives I see once a year. Yet although I always have a good time, I still feel that my real Christmas is the next day at treeside, in those more intense,

7

8

9

heartfelt moments with my mother. Spending the day with my mother is what I want, but I do not think I could enjoy myself if my father were alone on Christmas. He would never ask my sister or me to spend part of the day with him; he is too proud. Instead, he would call us around eleven in the morning to wish us "Merry Christmas" in a loud voice. His conversation would be punctuated by laughs that seemed to end before they started. I knew from experience that when he wasn't talking, he was gritting his teeth slightly, tightening the line of his jaw. "Love you big bunches," he would say rapidly, before hanging up. Then the phone would ring again right away. He had forgotten to tell me that I left my sweatshirt at his apartment. "Oh, thanks, Dad; I'll get it next time we come over," I would say.

"Okay, then. Merry Christmas."   10

"Merry Christmas, Dad."   11

I am grateful to my new stepfamily for sheltering my father and me from this coldest cold. Without them, my father would get lost in the snow.   12

READING FOR MEANING

Write to create meanings for Abraham's portrait of her father.

START MAKING MEANING

Begin by explaining what you have learned about the significance of Abraham's relationship with her father during the period about which she is writing. Continue by writing about anything else in the reading or in your experience that contributes to your understanding of Abraham's essay.

IF YOU ARE STUCK

If you cannot write at least a page, consider writing about

- the picture you get of Abraham's father from the list of things he took to his new apartment (paragraphs 1 and 2).

- the contrast between the two different Christmas memories (paragraphs 7 and 8).

- the distinction between where you *stay* and where you *live* (paragraph 4).

- your impression of what Abraham's childhood was like after her parents divorced or after her father remarried, perhaps comparing her experience with your own or a friend's.

READING LIKE A WRITER
DESCRIBING A PERSON THROUGH ANECDOTES AND RECURRING ACTIVITIES

Writers usually can recall many experiences that might be used to describe a person who played a significant role in their lives. Some of these experiences are one-time occurrences that, like a snapshot, catch the person at a particular place and time. The stories writers tell about one-time occurrences are called *anecdotes,* such as a humorous incident of someone falling down at a birthday party. Other experiences occur more than once, often on a regular basis with only a little variation over a period of time. We call this *recurring activities* because they show what usually happened rather than what once happened, such as several stories of a particular person tripping or falling down, suggesting a clumsy manner. As you analyze Abraham's use of anecdotes and recurring activities, you will see how they differ and what each contributes to the portrait of her father.

ANALYZE

1. *Reread* paragraph 1, where Abraham tells a brief anecdote about her father, and paragraph 6, where she presents a recurring activity central to life with him after the divorce.

2. Try to figure out what makes paragraph 1 an anecdote and paragraph 6 a recurring activity. *Underline* any language that lets you know one is an anecdote, the other a recurring activity.

WRITE

Write several sentences describing how the anecdote and recurring activity differ, pointing to specific details in each paragraph to illustrate the differences. Then *speculate about* what each contributes to Abraham's portrait of her father.

CONSIDERING IDEAS FOR YOUR OWN WRITING

Autobiographers often write about people with whom they have close and somewhat complicated relationships. Like Abraham, you could write about a relationship with a close relative or friend that changed in some significant way.

CHANG-RAE LEE

Uncle Chul Gets Rich

As a young child, Chang-Rae Lee (b. 1963) immigrated from South Korea to the United States with his parents and siblings. In this autobiographical story, Lee presents a portrait of his Uncle Chul, who at the time the story begins had only recently immigrated and was trying to establish himself in business so that he could bring his wife and baby to America.

Chang-Rae Lee did his undergraduate work at Yale and graduate studies at the University of Oregon. He has written a novel, Native Speaker *(1996), and occasionally writes autobiographical pieces for the* New York Times Magazine, *where this selection originally appeared in 1996.*

My father's youngest brother, Uncle Chul, shared the 1 Lees' famously bad reaction to liquor, which was to turn beet-red in the face, grow dizzy and finally get sick. In spite of this, he was always happy to stay up late at family gatherings. After a few Scotches he would really loosen up, and, with the notable exception of my mother, we all appreciated his rough language and racy stories. Only when Mother came in from the kitchen would his talk soften, for he knew he had always fallen short in her eyes. If they were ever alone together, say in the kitchen, after dinner, he would use the most decorous voice in asking for a glass or a fresh bucket of ice, and even offer to help load the dishwasher or run an errand to the store.

On one of those nights we sped off, both happy for a break 2 in the long evening. He asked me about school, what sports I was playing, but the conversation inevitably turned toward my parents, and particularly my mother—how much she had invested in me, that I was her great hope. I thought it was odd that he was speaking this way, like my other relatives, and I answered with some criticism of her—that she was too anxious and overbearing. He stared at me and, with a hard solemnity I had not heard from him before, said that my mother was one of the finest people one could ever know. He kept a grip on the wheel and in the ensuing quiet of the drive I could sense how he must have both admired and despised her. In many respects, my mother was an unrelenting woman. She tended to measure people by the mark of a few principles of conduct: ask no help from anyone, always plan for the long run and practice (her own variation of) the golden rule, which was to treat others much better than oneself.

In her mind, Uncle Chul sorely lacked on all these ac-   3
counts. In the weeks following our drive, my father would be
deciding whether to lend him $10,000 to start a business. As
always after dinner, my parents sat in the kitchen (the scent
of sesame oil and pickled vegetables still in the air) and
spoke in Korean, under the light of a fluorescent ring. My
mother, in many ways the director of the family, questioned
my uncle's character and will. Hadn't he performed poorly
in school, failed to finish college? Hadn't he spent most of
his youth perfecting his skills as a black belt in taekwondo
and his billiards game? Wasn't he a gambler in spirit?

My father could defend him only weakly. Uncle Chul had a   4
history of working hard only when reward was well within
sight, like cash piled high on the end of a pool table. His
older brothers were all respected professionals and aca-
demics. My father was a doctor, a psychiatrist who had
taught himself English in order to practice in America. Uncle
Chul had left Korea after a series of failed ventures and odd
jobs, and found himself broke with a wife and new baby.
How valuable were his taekwondo trophies now? What
could he possibly do in this country?

My parents argued fiercely and my father left the kitchen.   5
But as was my mother's way, she kept on pushing her side of
the issue, thinking aloud. My father was throwing away his
hard-earned money on the naïve wish that his little brother
had magically changed. Uncle Chul was a poor risk and even
now was complaining about his present job, hauling and clean-
ing produce for a greengrocer in Flushing. He would get to the
store at 4 A.M. to prepare vegetables for the day's selling. While
he shared a sofa bed with his nephew in his older brother's
tiny apartment, his wife and infant daughter were still in Seoul,
waiting for him to make enough money to send for them.

But his wages were only $250 a week for 70 hours of work   6
and he loathed the job, the brutal effort that went into clearing a few cents a carrot, a quarter a soda, the niggling, daily
accrual. The owners themselves would toil like slaves to see
a till full of tattered ones and fives at day's end.

I knew Uncle Chul craved the big score, the quick hit, a rain   7
of cash. For the very reasons my mother had so little faith in
him—his brashness, his flagrant ambitions—I admired him.
Over Scotch and rice crackers, he would tell my father about
the millions he was going to make by moving merchandise
wholesale, in bigger-ticket items with decent margins. He
would never touch another orange again. I remember my father absently nodding his head at each vague and grandiose
idea, probably hearing my mother's harangues.

The other men in my father's family were thick-lensed   8
scribblers who worked through their days from A to Z, as-
siduously removing uncertainty by paying close attention to
the thousand details of each passing hour. My father worked
long days at the hospital, and spent weekends poring over
volumes of Freud and Rank and Erikson in his second language, to "catch up" with the American doctors. When my father decided to lend Uncle Chul the $10,000, making it clear
that no further discussion was needed, my mother transferred her worrying energy squarely onto me. It seemed no
accident that her latest criticism was that I was "always
looking for the easy way." I had, in fact, been feeling moody
and rebellious, weary of being a good student and good boy.
I was in the eighth grade, and my friends were beginning to
drink beer and smoke pot. I secretly resolved to join them.

I was also taking solo train trips from Pleasantville, N.Y.,   9
down to the city to visit my older cousins on the weekends,
prompting questions from my mother about what kind of fun
we were having. I didn't tell her that what thrilled me most
was riding the elevated trains between Flushing and Grand
Central, shuttling back and forth with the multitude. My
newcomer's heart was fearful and enthralled, and I naïvely
thought Uncle Chul felt the same way. He had quit working
for the greengrocer after getting the money, and brought
over his wife and child. He was busy scouting out stores for
his first business in America.

But Uncle Chul found that the leases for even the smallest   10
stores were $4,000 a month, and he seemed tense and even a
little scared. I felt a strange pang of guilt because of the extra
pressure on him—the $10,000 and the tenuous faith behind
it. The only thing worse than losing the money was what my
mother would never have to mention again: that he started
working a little too late.

But he did find a store, in the Bronx, and we drove down   11
one Sunday to see it in all its new glory. It seemed as if half
the tenement buildings on the block were burned out or deserted, and the sidewalks were littered with garbage, broken
glass and the rubble of bricks and mortar. My father pulled
up behind Uncle Chul's car and we peered out to see if we
had the right address. The shop couldn't have been more
than eight feet wide. A single foot-wide corridor running its
length was lined with accessories, odd-lot handbags and tie
clips and lighters; the stuff hung on plastic grids on the walls
and overhead. In the back, there was a hot plate on the floor,
two stools and a carton of instant ramen noodles.

Uncle Chul proudly showed us the merchandise and, from a glass display box, gave me a watch; my sister got a faux-pearl necklace. A customer peered in but waved her hand and scurried away. My mother said that we were disturbing the business, and after a rush of bows and goodbyes we were in the car, heading back to Westchester. 12

Uncle Chul had no choice but to be in that neighborhood, in that quarter-size store, with the risk of crime and no insurance. The trade-off was the low rent, and it soon became clear that he had made an excellent choice. With little competition on the block, the money started coming in, and soon he moved to a larger store nearby, and then moved again. His volume and cash flow surged, and after selling each successive business, he staked his profit on the next store. 13

We didn't see him much during this time, but when we did he made sure to show off his success to my parents. My aunt wore designer clothes, and Uncle Chul sported a fat gold Rolex. If we were out somewhere, he would casually pull out a rolled wad of $100's when a check arrived, proclaiming affably to his brothers that it was his turn to pay. 14

But I noticed, too, that he and my aunt looked haggard and pressed. They spoke hurriedly and ate as quickly as they could. My mother would say something like, "You've developed such expensive tastes," and tell him that he was still frittering away his money on useless luxuries. 15

When Uncle Chul amassed the war chest he needed to open the wholesale business he had hoped for, he moved away from New York. He had heard of opportunities in Texas, where goods could be imported across the border and sold at big profits. Within a few years he had more than 50 people working for him, selling, by containers and truckloads, the same purses and belts he started with years before. 16

He bought a sprawling ranch house, brand-new and fitted with jet-action bathtubs and wide-screen televisions. He hired a team of Mexican maids to keep the place running. He traded in his Cadillacs for BMW's and sent his daughters to private school. One summer he paid my sister outrageous wages to sit in his air-conditioned office and practice her Spanish with the retailers. The business was on automatic pilot—effortless. Uncle Chul was now a millionaire several times over, richer than all his brothers combined. 17

I spent time with him again years later, when my mother became terminally ill. He visited regularly, always bearing gifts for the family. To me, he simply gave money. He knew I 18 had quit my first job to become a writer, which meant little to him, except that I would be poor forever. Maybe, someday, my name would be famous, and he invested in that possibility, slipping me a couple of $100's when my mother wasn't looking. He did this naturally, with an ease and power in his grip full of cash. His money was like a weight outside his body, which he could press upon others, like me. But in my mother's presence, his swagger vanished, and he was just Uncle Chul again, prodigal and bereft.

He was especially solemn on the day of her funeral. Of the   19
many people who made their way to the cemetery and later to the house, I suspect Uncle Chul knew he was among those she would be most closely watching. My mother's friends had brought food and electric rice cookers and the men were in the living room, drinking companionably, speaking in low voices. My mother had been dying for nearly two years, and now that it was over waves of exhaustion and relief were washing over everyone in the house.

I remember Uncle Chul padding softly about the house,   20
wary of disturbing even the layer of dust on her furniture. He was speaking in a soft register, his voice faltering, like a nervous young minister on his first encounter with the bereaved. He was nodding and bowing, even helping the ladies gather cups and plates, exercising until the last visitor left a younger brother's respect and obedience to the family and the dead.

In the Korean tradition, mourners brought offerings of   21
money, all token amounts, except for Uncle Chul's fat envelope, which held thousands of dollars. He would have given more, he said, but his wholesale business wasn't doing so well anymore. I knew that wasn't the real reason. He must have known what my mother would have said, perhaps was telling him now—that he couldn't help but be the flashy one again.

READING FOR MEANING

Write to create meanings for Lee's autobiographical story.

START MAKING MEANING

Begin by explaining what you think the significance of Uncle Chul is for Lee as well as Lee's possible purpose or purposes for choosing to write about his uncle in the way that he does. Continue by writing about anything else in the selection or in your experience that contributes to your understanding of Lee's story.

IF YOU ARE STUCK

If you cannot write at least a page, consider writing about

- what Lee admired about his uncle, perhaps thinking of Uncle Chul as Lee's double or alter-ego.

- the male role models in Lee's family, such as his father and his father's brother, possibly comparing them with the men in your family.

- what the story says about work, ambition, and success, perhaps relating Lee's ideas to the American Dream, especially for recent immigrants.

- the attitudes toward the drinking of alcohol expressed in this story, perhaps in comparison with Baker's story, your own attitudes, or attitudes prevalent today.

READING LIKE A WRITER
DESCRIBING A PERSON THROUGH DIALOGUE

Writers use dialogue to represent what people say as well as how they say it. Dialogue may be presented in *direct quotation,* which uses quotation marks to signal to readers what people actually said, or *indirect quotation,* which paraphrases (rewords) or summarizes (gives the gist of) what was said. This activity focuses first on Lee's use of indirect quotation to present his relationship with Uncle Chul. Then, it invites you to compare Lee's strategy of indirect quotation with another writer's use of direct quotation.

ANALYZE

1. *Reread* the second paragraph, sentences 2–4, where Lee reports a conversation he had with Uncle Chul. *Notice* that some of the language in these sentences presents Lee's own thoughts and descriptions, and some of the language represents what he and his uncle said to one another.

2. *Identify* the indirect quotations in these sentences by underlining what each person said.

WRITE

Rewrite one of these sentences in quoted dialogue form. Then *write* several sentences, explaining what you have learned about Lee's use of indirect quotation to present his conversation with Uncle Chul. *Cite* examples from Lee's paragraph to illustrate your explanation.

COMPARE

Reread paragraphs 28–29 in the selection by Russell Baker (pp. 32–33) or look ahead to paragraphs 24–26 in the essay by Brad Benioff (pp. 49–50), where each writer uses direct quotation. *Underline* what each person said. Then try making the direct quotation indirect by paraphrasing or summarizing the language you underlined. What effect does changing the dialogue seem to have? *Write* a few sentences considering how you would decide when to use direct quotation and when to use indirect quotation in your own writing.

CONSIDERING IDEAS FOR YOUR OWN WRITING

Like Lee in "Uncle Chul Gets Rich," you could choose to write about a person who passed in and out of your life several times over a span of years. Whereas Lee writes about an uncle he saw only occasionally, you might write about a distant relative, neighbor, schoolmate, or teacher with whom you have had a relationship over time.

BRAD BENIOFF
Rick

Brad Benioff was a first-year college student when he wrote the following essay for an assignment in his composition class.

Like Laurie Abraham and Chang-Rae Lee in the preceding selections, Benioff focuses his story on a memorable person: his high-school water polo coach, Rick Rezinas. As you read, notice how Benioff uses dialogue to dramatize his relationship with Rick.

I walked through the dawn chill, shivering as much from   1
nervousness as from the cold. Steam curled up from the water in the pool and disappeared in the ocher morning light. Athletes spread themselves about on the deck, lazily stretching and whispering to each other as if the stillness were sacred. It was to be my first practice with the high school water polo team. I knew nothing about the game, but a friend had pushed me to play, arguing, "It's the most fun of any sport. Trust me." He had awakened me that morning long before daylight, forced me into a bathing suit, and driven me to the pool.

"Relax," he said. "Rick is the greatest of coaches. You'll   2
like him. You'll have fun."

The mythical Rick. I had heard of him many times before.   3
All the older players knew him by his first name and always spoke of him as a friend rather than a coach. He was a math teacher at our school, and his classes were very popular. Whenever class schedules came out, everyone hoped to be placed in Mr. Rezinas's class. He had been known to throw parties for the team or take them on weekend excursions skiing or backpacking. To be Rick's friend was to be part of an exclusive club, and I was being invited to join. And so I looked forward with nervous anticipation to meeting this man.

My friend walked me out to the pool deck and steered me   4
toward a man standing beside the pool.

"Rick," announced my friend, "I'd like you to meet your   5
newest player."

Rick was not a friendly looking man. He wore only swim   6
trunks, and his short, powerful legs rose up to meet a bulging torso. His big belly was solid. His shoulders, as if to offset his front-heaviness, were thrown back, creating a deep crease of excess muscle from his sides around the small of

his back, a crease like a huge frown. His arms were crossed, two medieval maces placed carefully on their racks, ready to be swung at any moment. His round cheeks and chin were darkened by traces of black whiskers. His hair was sparse. Huge, black, mirrored sunglasses replaced his eyes. Below his prominent nose was a thin, sinister mustache. I couldn't believe this menacing-looking man was the legendary jovial Rick.

He said nothing at first. In those moments of silence, I felt   7
more inadequate than ever before in my life. My reflection in his glasses stared back at me, accusing me of being too skinny, too young, too stupid, too weak to be on his team. Where did I get the nerve to approach him with such a ridiculous body and ask to play water polo, a man's game? Finally, he broke the silence, having finished appraising my meager body. "We'll fatten him up," he growled.

Thus began a week of torture. For four hours a day, the   8
coach stood beside the pool scowling down at me. I could do nothing right.

"No! No! No!" He shook his head in disgust. "Throw the   9
damn ball with your whole arm! Get your goddamn elbow out of the water!"

Any failure on my part brought down his full wrath. He   10
bellowed at my incompetence and punished me with pushups and wind sprints. Even when I was close to utter exhaustion, I found no sympathy. "What the hell are you doing on the wall?" he would bellow. "Coach ... my side, it's cramped."

"Swim on it! If you can't take a little pain, then you don't   11
play!" With this, he would push me off the wall.

He seemed to enjoy playing me against the older, stronger   12
players. "Goddamn it, Brad! If someone elbows or hits you, don't look out at me and cry, 'It's not fair.' Push back! Don't be so weak!" I got elbowed around until it seemed that none of my internal organs was unscathed. He worked me until my muscles wouldn't respond, and then he demanded more.

"You're not trying! Push it!"   13

"Would you move? You're too slow! Swim!"   14

"Damn it! Get out and give me twenty!"   15

It took little time for me to hate both the game and the   16
man who ruled it.

I reacted by working as hard as I could. I decided to deprive   17
him of the pleasure of finding fault with me. I learned quickly and started playing as flawlessly as possible. I dispensed with looking tired, showing pain, or complaining of cramps. I pushed, hit, and elbowed back at the biggest of players. No

matter how flawless or aggressive my performance, though, he would find fault and let me know it. He was never critical of other players. He would laugh and joke with the other players; but whenever he saw me, he frowned.

I decided to quit.   18

After a particularly demanding practice, I walked up to   19
this tyrant. I tried to hold his gaze, but the black glasses forced me to look down.

"Coach Rezinas," I blurted, "I've decided that I don't want   20
to play water polo." His scowl deepened. Then after a moment he said, "You can't quit. Not until after the first game." And he walked away. The dictator had issued his command.

There was no rule to keep me from quitting. Anger flushed   21
through me. Somehow I would get revenge on this awful man. After the first game? Okay. I would play. I would show him what a valuable player I was. He would miss my talents when I quit. I worked myself up before the first game by imagining the hated face: the black glasses, the thin mustache, the open, snarling mouth. I was not surprised that he placed me in the starting lineup because I was certain he would take me out soon. I played furiously. The ball, the goal, the opposition, even the water seemed to be extensions of Rick, his face glaring from every angle, his words echoing loudly in my ears. Time and time again I would get the ball and, thinking of his tortures, fire it toward the goal with a strength to kill. I forgot that he might take me out. No defender could stand up to me. I would swim by them or over them. Anger and the need for vengeance gave me energy. I didn't notice the time slipping by, the quarters ending.

Then, the game ended. My teammates rushed out to me,   22
congratulating and cheering me. I had scored five goals, a school record for one game, and shut out the other team with several key defensive plays. Now I could get revenge. Now I could quit. I stepped out of the pool prepared with the words I would spit into his face: "I QUIT!"

As I approached him, I stopped dead. He was smiling at   23
me, his glasses off. He reached out with his right hand and shook mine with exuberance.

"I knew you had it in you! I knew it!" he laughed.   24

Through his laughter, I gained a new understanding of the   25
man. He had pushed me to my fullest potential, tapping into the talent I may never have found in myself. He was responsible for the way I played that day. My glory was his. He never hated me. On the contrary, I was his apprentice, his favored pupil. He had brought out my best. Could I really hate

someone who had done that much for me? He had done what he had promised: he had fattened me up mentally as well as physically. All this hit me in a second and left me completely confused. I tried to speak, but only managed to croak, "Coach ... uh ... I, uh. ..." He cut me off with another burst of laughter. He still shook my hand.

"Call me Rick," he said.   26

READING FOR MEANING

Write to create meanings for Benioff's autobiographical story.

START MAKING MEANING

Begin by explaining what you think the significance of Rick is for Benioff as well as Benioff's possible purpose or purposes for choosing to write about his coach in the way that he does. Continue by writing about anything else in the selection or in your experience that contributes to your understanding of Benioff's story.

IF YOU ARE STUCK

If you cannot write at least a page, consider writing about

- Rick's coaching style, perhaps comparing it with other styles of coaching or teaching.

- the notion that how you see yourself reflected in another person's eyes affects what you value or devalue in yourself.

- how being male or female may affect your reading of and response to this story.

- this essay as a coming-of-age story, one that enables Benioff to see the role Rick played in his life—perhaps comparing it to the role Total Loss played for Russell Baker.

READING LIKE A WRITER
DESCRIBING A PERSON THROUGH VISUAL DETAILS AND IMAGES

Visual description enables readers to see the person and to get a sense of how that person appears to others. For example, providing vivid details of someone's facial features could show whether a person looks others directly in the eye, or looks down on others. This activity will help you see how Benioff uses visual description to give readers a picture of Rick as well as an understanding of his significance to the writer.

ANALYZE

1. *Reread* paragraph 6, where Benioff describes Rick. Notice that the writer makes only two general statements characterizing Rick, in the first and last sentences of the paragraph. The remaining sentences in this paragraph offer visual details and images describing Rick's appearance. Because Rick is wearing only swim trunks and sunglasses, Benioff concentrates on the appearance of Rick's body.

2. *Underline* the parts of Rick's body Benioff singles out, beginning with "legs" and "torso" in the second sentence.

3. Then *put a wavy line* under the visual details Benioff uses to describe the parts of Rick's body, beginning with "short, powerful" and "bulging" in sentence 2.

4. *Put a star* by the two comparisons: a simile in sentence 2 (a simile makes an explicit comparison by using the word *like* or *as*), and a metaphor in sentence 3 (a metaphor implicitly compares two items by describing one in terms of the other).

WRITE

Write several sentences explaining the impression you get of Rick as seen through Benioff's eyes. *Quote* the visual details and comparisons that contribute most to this impression.

COMPARE

Reread paragraph 13 in Russell Baker's story (p. 31) to see how he uses visual details and comparisons to describe the check pilot Total Loss Smith. *Underline* the details and comparisons that let you see Total Loss and that give you an understanding of what Baker thought and felt about him at the time. Then, in a few sentences, *compare* Baker's use of visual description with Benioff's.

CONSIDERING IDEAS FOR YOUR OWN WRITING

Think about the coaches, teachers, employers, and other mentors who have influenced your life. Choose one of these people, and consider how you can describe what that person taught you and how he or she went about it. As a writer aiming to describe this individual's significance in your life, how would you reveal what you learned about the person and about yourself? Or as an alternative, you might consider someone with whom you have had continuing disagreements or conflicts, and then speculate on how you can describe your relationship with that person.

Reviewing What Makes Autobiography Effective

In this chapter you have been learning how to read autobiography for meaning and how to read it like a writer. Before going on to write a piece of autobiography, pause here to review and contemplate what you have learned about the elements of effective autobiography.

Analyze

Choose one reading from this chapter that is for you an especially effective example of autobiography. Before rereading the selection, *note* one or two things that led you to remember it as an example of good autobiographical writing.

Then *reread* the selection, adding further annotations about what makes it a particularly successful example of autobiography. To begin, *consider* the writer's purpose, judging how and how well the essay achieves that purpose for its readers. Then *focus* on how well the selection

- tells the story.

- describes the place.

- describes people.

- conveys the autobiographical significance.

You can complete this activity on your own, or your instructor may ask you to work with a small group of students who have chosen the same reading. If you work with others, allow enough time initially for all group members to reread the selection and add their annotations. Then discuss as a group what makes the selection effective. Take notes on your discussion. One student in your group should then report to the class what the group has learned about this reading. If you are working individually, write up what you have learned from your analysis.

Write

Write at least a page, explaining and justifying your choice of this reading as an example of effective autobiographical writing. Assume that your readers—your instructor and classmates—have read the selection but will not remember many details about it. They also may not remember it as an especially successful piece of autobiography. Therefore, you will need to *refer* to details and specific parts of the reading as you explain how it works as autobiography and *justify* your evaluation of its effectiveness. You need not argue that it is the best reading in the chapter or that it is flawless, only that it is, in your view, a strong example of the genre.

A GUIDE TO WRITING AUTOBIOGRAPHY

From the autobiographical selections you have read and analyzed in this chapter, you have seen that some autobiographies tell dramatic stories, while others present vivid portraits of people who played a significant role in the writer's life. Whether the focus is on events or people, you have discovered that the overall purpose for writers of autobiography is to convey the significance—both the meaning and importance—of their past experience. In so doing, autobiographers often present themselves as individuals affected by social and cultural influences.

As a reader of autobiography, you have examined how autobiographers convey through their writing drama and vividness as well as significance. But you may have also found that different readers interpret the significance of an autobiographical selection differently. In other words, you have seen how the meanings readers make are affected by their personal experience as well as their social and cultural contexts.

Having learned how autobiographers invest their writing with drama, vividness, and significance and how readers interpret and respond to autobiographical writing, you can now approach autobiography more confidently as a writer. You can more readily imagine the problems you must solve as a writer of autobiography, the materials and possibilities you have to work with, the choices and decisions you must make. This section offers detailed suggestions for writing autobiographical essays and resources to help you solve the special challenges this kind of writing presents.

INVENTION

The following invention activities will help you choose a memorable *event* or an important *person* to write about, recall details about your subject, and explore its significance in your life. Completing these activities will produce a record of remembered details and thoughts that will be invaluable as you draft your essay.

Choosing a Subject

Rather than limiting yourself to the first subject that comes to mind, take a few minutes to consider your options. List the most promising subjects you can think of, beginning with any you listed for the Considering Ideas for Your Own Writing activities following the readings in this chapter. Here are some other ideas to consider:

Events

- A difficult situation, such as when you had to make a tough choice, when someone you admired let you down (or you let someone else down), or when you struggled to learn or understand something

- An incident charged with strong emotion, such as pride, fear, anger, love, guilt, frustration, or some combination of strong emotions

- An occasion when something did not turn out as you thought it would, such as when you expected to be criticized but were praised or ignored instead, or when you were convinced you would succeed but failed

- An incident in which a single encounter with another person changed the way you view yourself, changed your ideas about how you fit into a particular group or community, or led you to consider seriously someone else's point of view

People

- Someone who inspired a strong emotion in you, such as admiration, envy, disapproval, or fascination

- Someone who surprised or disappointed you

- Someone in a position of power over you, or someone over whom you had power

- Someone with whom you have worked closely, such as another student, a colleague, or a parent

By listing as many subjects as you can, you will have a variety of possible topics to choose from for your autobiographical essay. The subject you ultimately decide on should be one that will give you the pleasure of recalling a past experience and exploring what it means to you. Your subject should also be one that is likely to engage your readers so they will enjoy learning something about your life.

Developing Your Subject

The following activities will help you develop your subject by recalling actions that happened during the event or by telling anecdotes that reveal something about the person. You can recall significant details of the place and people. You can also explore your feelings and thoughts at the time and now as you look back on the event or person. Each activity takes only a few minutes but will help you produce a fuller, more focused draft.

RECALLING THE EVENT OR PERSON.   *If you have chosen to write about an* **event,** *begin by writing for five minutes, telling what happened.* Do not worry about telling the story dramatically or even coherently. Just try to make a rough sketch of the actions that occurred during the event as you remember them now. Later, you may want to fill in more details.

If you have chosen to write about a **person,** *begin by listing anecdotes you could tell about the person.* Then choose one anecdote that reveals something important about the person or your relationship, and write for two or three minutes telling what happened.

DESCRIBING IMPORTANT PEOPLE.   *If you have chosen to write about a **person,** list aspects of the person's appearance and dress, way of walking and gesturing, tone of voice and mannerisms—anything that would help readers see the person as you remember her or him.*

*If you have chosen to write about an **event,** recall other people who were involved, and write a brief description of each person.*

DESCRIBING IMPORTANT PLACES.   *Identify the place where the event happened or a place you associate with the person, and detail what you see in the scene as you visualize it.* Try to recall specific sensory details: size, shape, color, condition, and texture of the scene or memorable objects in it. Imagine the place from head-on and from the side, from a distance and from close-up. Describe what you see with vivid, expressive language.

RECALLING YOUR FEELINGS AND THOUGHTS.   *Write for a few minutes, trying to recall your thoughts and feelings when the event was occurring or when you knew the person.* What did you feel—in control or powerless, proud or embarrassed, vulnerable, detached, judgmental? How did you show or express your feelings? What did you want others to think of you at the time? What did you think of yourself? What were the immediate consequences for you personally?

EXPLORING YOUR PRESENT PERSPECTIVE.   *Write for a few minutes, trying to express your present thoughts and feelings as you look back on the event or person.* How have your feelings changed? What insights do you now have? What does your present perspective reveal about what you were like at the time? Try looking at the event or person in broader, cultural or social terms. For example, consider whether you or anyone else upset gender expectations or felt out of place in some way.

RECONSTRUCTING DIALOGUE.   *Write a few lines of dialogue that you could use to convey something important about the event or to give readers an impression of the person you have chosen to write about.* You may use direct quotation, enclosing the words you remember being spoken in quotation marks, or you may use indirect quotation, paraphrasing and summarizing what was said. Try to re-create the give-and-take quality of normal conversation in the dialogue. Here is a format you can follow:

[Your name]: [What you said]

[Other person's name]: [What the other person said]

[Continue alternating contributions down the page.]

EXPLORING THE SIGNIFICANCE.   *Write several sentences to discover the event's or person's significance.* To help you develop the significance, consider some of these questions:

- What do you not understand fully about the event or relationship? What puzzles you or seems contradictory about it?

- What about your subject do you expect will sound familiar to your readers? What do you think will surprise your readers, perhaps getting them to think in new ways or to question some of their assumptions about themselves or others?

- What will writing about this event or person enable you to suggest about yourself as an individual? What will it let you suggest about the social and cultural forces that helped shape you—for example, how people exercise power over one another, how family and community values and attitudes have an impact on individuals, or how economic and social conditions influence our sense of self?

The exploratory sentences you write to uncover the significance of your subject will help you focus your draft, providing a thesis for your writing. The thesis for an autobiographical essay need not be stated explicitly, however. It may instead be implied, conveyed primarily through carefully selected words and details that reinforce the impression you want readers to get of the person or event.

Exploring the significance before drafting—whether you make your thesis explicit or implicit—will also help you decide which words and details will or will not create the impression you want readers to have of the event or person. But as you draft, you should also expect that your understanding will change or deepen, and that you will have to revise your draft to accommodate these changes in your thinking.

DRAFTING

The following guidelines will help you set goals for your draft, plan its organization, choose relevant details, and decide how to begin.

Setting Goals

Establishing goals for your draft before you begin writing will enable you to make decisions and work more confidently. The following questions will help you set goals for drafting as well as help you recall how the writers you have read in this chapter tried to achieve similar goals.

- *How can I present my subject vividly and memorably to readers?* Should I rely on direct or indirect dialogue to present people and relationships, as Baker, Lee, and Benioff do? Or should I concentrate on presenting action rather than dialogue, like Dillard? Can I use visual or other sensory details as Lorde and Abraham do, to give readers a vivid impression of the person and place while also establishing the significance of my subject?

- *How can I help readers understand the meaning and importance of the event or person?* Can I use the symbolism of the place, as Lorde does with Washington, D.C., to underscore the significance of the event? Can I build the suspense, as Dillard does, in a way that lets readers vicariously share the excitement I felt at the time? Can I use the person as a kind of double, as Lee does, to reflect one side of myself?

- *How can I avoid superficial or one-dimensional presentations of my experience and my relations with others?* Knowing that my readers will not expect easy answers about what makes the event or person significant, how can I satisfy their expectations for writing that has some depth and complexity? How might I employ one or more of the strategies illustrated by the writers I have read in this chapter—the paradox in Dillard's feeling both terror and pleasure as she is chased by the man in the black Buick; the irony implicit in Baker's suggestion that, after the flight, he sees T. L. Smith as the "most manly looking fellow in the entire corps of instructors"; the contradictions Lorde sets up in relating her parents' behavior and their beliefs; Lee's surprise that his uncle admires Lee's mother despite her criticism of him; Benioff's love-hate relationship with the coach? What contradictions, paradoxes, or ironies exist in my own story?

Organizing Your Draft

With goals in mind, plan your draft by making a tentative outline. Although your plan may change as you write and revise your draft, outlining before you begin drafting can help you get organized. If you are uncertain about how to organize your material, review the events or portraits from the readings you admire in this chapter.

For an *event,* outline the sequence of main actions, from the beginning to the end of the event.

For a *person,* outline the order of the character traits, physical details, dialogue, recurring activities, or anecdotes you will use to present the person.

Choosing Relevant Details

The invention activities helped you generate many details, probably more than you can use. To decide which details to include in your draft and which to leave out, consider how well each detail contributes to the overall impression you want to create. But before you discard any details that seem irrelevant, think again about what they might suggest about the significance of your subject. Sometimes, seemingly irrelevant details or ones that do not fit neatly can lead you to new insights.

Writing the Beginning

In order to engage your readers' interest from the start, consider beginning with an arresting bit of dialogue or a compelling graphic description (as Benioff does when he describes the swimming pool in the early morning light), with a startling action or a vivid memory (as Abraham does when she recalls the two times she saw her father cry), or with some background information (as Baker does when he explains his dilemma of flying without feeling in control). You might have to try two or three different beginnings before finding a promising way to start, but do not agonize for too long over the first sentence. Try out any possible beginning and see where it takes you.

READING A DRAFT CRITICALLY

Getting a critical reading of your draft will help you see how to improve it. Your instructor may schedule class time for reading drafts, or you may want to ask a classmate or a tutor in the writing center to read your draft. Ask your reader to use the following guidelines and to write out a response for you to consult during your revision.

Read for a First Impression

1. Read quickly through the draft, without stopping to annotate or comment, and then write two or three sentences giving your general impression.

2. Identify one aspect of the draft that seems especially effective.

Read Again to Suggest Improvements

1. Recommend ways to make the narrative more dramatic and telling.

   For a story presenting an event:

   - Point to any scenes where the action seems to drag or become confusing.

   - Suggest places where the drama might be intensified—by adding a close-up, using more active verbs, or shifting the placement of background information or descriptive detail, for example.

   - Indicate where direct dialogue could add drama to a confrontation scene.

For a story using anecdotes or recurring activities to present a person:

- Note which anecdotes and recurring activities seem especially effective in illustrating something important about the person or the relationship.

- Point to one weak anecdote or recurring activity and suggest how it could be made more effective, such as by adding graphic details and dialogue or by telling how it relates to the person's significance.

- Indicate any passages where the direct quotation of dialogue could be more effectively presented indirectly, through paraphrase or summary, or by combining a striking quote with summary.

2. Indicate any areas where dull or weak description could more vividly or effectively convey the dominant impression of the essay.

- Describe the impression you get from the writer's description of the person or place.

- Identify one or two passages where you think the description is especially vivid; for example, where the visual details and images help you picture the person or place.

- Point to any passages where the description could be made more vivid or where it seems to contradict the impression you got from other parts of the essay.

3. Suggest how the autobiographical significance could be developed.

- Briefly explain your understanding of the significance, indicating anything that puzzles or surprises you about the event or person.

- Note any word choice, contradiction, or irony—in the way people and places are described or in the way the story is told—that alerts you to possible deeper meaning that the writer could develop.

- Point to any passages where the writer needs to clarify the historical, social, or cultural dimensions of the experience or relationship.

4. Suggest how the organizational plan could be improved. Consider the overall plan of the essay, perhaps by making a scratch outline (see Appendix One).

- For an *event*, indicate any passages where narrative transitions or verb tense markers are needed to make the story unfold more logically and clearly.

- For a *person*, suggest where topic sentences or transitions could be added or where the writer could more clearly indicate what the anecdotes or recurring activities contribute to your impression of the person.

REVISING

This section provides suggestions for revising your draft, suggestions that will remind you of the possibilities for developing an engaging, coherent autobiography. Revising means reenvisioning your draft, trying to see it in a new way, given your purpose and readers, in order to develop your autobiography.

The biggest mistake you can make in revising is to focus initially on words or sentences. Instead, first try to see your draft as a whole in order to assess its likely impact on your readers. Think imaginatively and boldly about cutting unconvincing material, adding new material, and moving material around. Your computer makes even drastic revisions easy, but you still need to make the effort and decisions that will improve your draft.

To Make the Narrative More Dramatic and Telling

- If the story seems to meander and have no point, focus the action so that it builds up more directly toward the climax.

- Where the narrative drags or the tension slackens, try using more active verbs, more dialogue, or shorter sentences.

- Where background information or descriptive detail interrupts the drama or slows the pace, consider cutting or moving it.

- If the purpose of an anecdote or a recurring activity is not clear, make explicit what it illustrates.

- If the exact words in a conversation are not striking or important, use indirect instead of direct dialogue or combine the two, paraphrasing or summarizing most of what was said but including a memorable phrase or notable word.

To Describe Places Vividly

- If any details about an important place do not fit together well and do not contribute to the dominant impression or reinforce the significance, omit them from the essay.

- Where readers cannot visualize the place, add more sensory detail.

- Where the description distracts from the action, cut or move the description.

- Where the point of view is confusing, consider simplifying it.

To Describe People Vividly

- Where more graphic description is needed, give visual details showing what the person looks like or how the person gestures.

- If any detail seems inconsistent or contradictory, cut it or use it to develop the significance.

- If the description does not convey the impression you want it to convey, consider cutting some descriptive details and adding others, or rethinking the impression you want your writing to convey and the significance it suggests.

To Develop the Significance

- If readers may not understand the significance, look for passages where you could convey it more directly.

- If the significance seems too pat or simplistic, consider whether you could develop contradictions or allow for ambivalence.

- If readers may not understand the importance of the social, cultural, or historical context, consider giving background information to reveal its influence.

To Make the Organizational Plan More Effective

- If readers may be confused about what happened when, add transitions or verb tense markers.

- If readers may not see clearly how the anecdotes or recurring activities contribute to the portrait of the person, add forecasting or topic sentences to clarify what those elements demonstrate.

EDITING AND PROOFREADING

After you have revised the essay, be sure to spend some time checking for errors in usage, punctuation, and mechanics, and to consider matters of style. If you keep a list of errors you typically make, begin by looking for them. In addition, our research on student writing has shown that essays dealing with autobiographical subjects have a high percentage of errors in verb tense and punctuation. You should proofread your narration for verb tense errors and your description for punctuation errors—such as comma splices and missing commas after introductory elements. Refer to a writer's handbook for help with these problems.

Reflecting on What You Have Learned

In this chapter, you have read critically several pieces of autobiography and have written one of your own. To remember what you have learned, pause now to reflect on the reading and writing activities you completed in this chapter.

Continued

1. *Write* a page or so reflecting on your learning. Begin by describing what you are most pleased with in your autobiographical essay and what you think contributed to your achievement. Be specific about this contribution:

   - If it was something you learned from the readings, *indicate* which readings and specifically what you learned from them.

   - If it came from your invention writing, *point out* the section or sections that helped you most.

   - If you got good advice from a critical reader, *explain* exactly how the person helped you—perhaps by helping you to understand a particular problem in your draft or by adding a new dimension to your writing.

2. Now *reflect* more generally on how you tend to interpret autobiographical writing, your own as well as other writers'. *Consider* some of the following questions: In reading for meaning, do you tend to find yourself interpreting the significance of the event or person in terms of the writer's personal feelings, sense of self-esteem, or psychological well-being? Or do you more often think of significance in terms of larger social or economic influences—for example, whether the writer is male or female, rich or poor, suburban or urban, African American or Anglo? Where do you think you learned to interpret the significance of people's stories about themselves and their relationships—from your family, friends, television, school?

Observation

C ertain kinds of writing are based on fresh observation or direct investigation. Travel writers, for example, may profile a place they have visited; naturalists may describe phenomena they have observed. Investigative reporters or clinical psychologists may write up interviews with individuals, while cultural anthropologists may write ethnographies of groups they have studied in depth. Much of what we know about people and the world we learn from this kind of writing.

Writing about your own observations can offer special challenges and rewards. It requires you to pay more attention than you normally do. You need to look with all your senses and give your curiosity free reign. Taking a questioning or inquiring stance will enable you to make discoveries in even the most mundane settings. In addition, it helps to take voluminous notes because you might not know what is significant until you begin to sort through the observations and quotations you have collected. That way, after the work of observing and interviewing is done, another kind of equally challenging and rewarding work can begin—making meaning of the bits and pieces you have gathered. Analyzing and synthesizing your notes, you interpret your subject, deciding what you want to tell your readers about it. These activities of close observation and careful notetaking, combined with thoughtful analysis and imaginative synthesis, form the basic strategies of researching and learning in many areas of college study.

When writing about your observations, you will have an immediate advantage if you choose a place, an activity, or a person that is new to readers. But even if the subject is familiar, you can still intrigue and inform readers by presenting it in a new light or by focusing on a specific aspect of the subject. By focusing on certain details, you not only help readers imagine what the place looks, sounds, and smells like or picture how the people dress, gesture, and talk, but you also create an impression that conveys your idea or interpretation of the subject.

As you read, discuss, and write about the selections that follow in this chapter, you will learn a lot about observational writing. From the readings and from the suggestions for writing after each reading, you will get many ideas for your own observational essay. As you analyze the readings and think about writing an observation of your own, keep in mind the following assignment. The Guide to Writing Observational Essays, at the end of the chapter, will help you choose a subject as well as plan, draft, and revise your essay.

THE WRITING ASSIGNMENT

Observation

Write an observational essay about an intriguing person, place, or activity in your community. Your essay may be a brief profile of an individual based on one or two interviews; a description of a place or an activity observed once or twice; or a longer, more fully developed profile of a person, place, or activity based on multiple observational visits and interviews conducted over several weeks. Observe your subject closely, and then present what you have learned in a way that both informs and engages readers.

OBSERVATIONAL WRITING SITUATIONS

As we indicated earlier, lots of people—including travel writers, investigative reporters, clinical psychologists, and cultural anthropologists—write essays based on observation and interview. In your other college courses, you may have an opportunity to write an observational essay like one of the following:

- For art history, a student writes about a local artist recently commissioned to paint outdoor murals for the city. The student visits the artist's studio and talks with him about the process of painting murals. The artist invites the student to spend the following day as a part of a team of local art students and neighborhood volunteers working on the mural under the artist's direction. This firsthand experience helps the student describe the process of collaboration involved in mural painting.

- For a journalism course, a student profiles a typical day in the life of an award-winning scientist. He spends a day observing the scientist at home and at work, and interviews colleagues, students, and family, as well as the scientist herself. Her daily life, he learns, is very much like that of other working mothers—a constant effort to balance the demands of her career against the needs of her family. He conveys this idea in his essay by alternating between details about the scientist's work and those about her family life.

• For a sociology class, a student writes about a controversial urban renewal project. To learn about the history of the project, she reads newspaper reports and interviews people who helped plan the project as well as some neighborhood activists who oppose it. She also tours the site with the project manager to see what is actually being done. In addition to presenting different points of view about the project, her essay describes the renovation in detail, including pictures of the neighborhood before and drawings projecting what it will be like afterwards.

A GUIDE TO READING OBSERVATIONAL ESSAYS

This guide introduces you to the observational essay, beginning with "Soup," an intriguing profile of Mr. Yeganeh and his unique restaurant, Soup Kitchen International. First, you will read for meaning, looking closely at the essay for ideas and significance. Then, you will read like a writer, analyzing the strategies that make this particular profile and observational writing in general vivid and informative.

THE NEW YORKER

Soup

"Soup" was initially published anonymously in a 1989 issue of the New Yorker, *a magazine read by many people across the country who enjoy witty cartoons, short stories, reviews of cultural events, and profiles of interesting people and places. The subject of this essay is Albert Yeganeh, the creative and rather demanding owner/chef of a small take-out restaurant that serves only soup. In 1995, Yeganeh's restaurant inspired an episode of the popular television program* Seinfeld.

As you read, you can readily imagine the reporter interviewing the owner, writing down soup names and ingredients, observing people in line, and even standing in line as well for a bowl of soup. Annotate anything that helps you picture Yeganeh and his Soup Kitchen International. Notice

*that the writer relies extensively on dialogue quoted from
the interview to keep the focus on Yeganeh's personality
and ideas.*

When Albert Yeganeh says "Soup is my lifeblood," he 1
means it. And when he says "I am extremely hard to please,"
he means that, too. Working like a demon alchemist in a
tiny storefront kitchen at 259-A West Fifty-fifth Street, Mr.
Yeganeh creates anywhere from eight to seventeen soups
every weekday. His concoctions are so popular that a wait of
half an hour at the lunchtime peak is not uncommon, although there are strict rules for conduct in line. But more on
that later.

"I am psychologically kind of a health freak," Mr. Yeganeh 2
said the other day, in a lisping staccato of Armenian origin.
"And I know that soup is the greatest meal in the world. It's
very good for your digestive system. And I use only the best,
the freshest ingredients. I am a perfectionist. When I make a
clam soup, I use three different kinds of clams. Every other
place uses canned clams. I'm called crazy. I am not crazy.
People don't realize why I get so upset. It's because if the
soup is not perfect and I'm still selling it, it's a torture. It's
my soup, and that's why I'm so upset. First you clean and
then you cook. I don't believe that ninety-nine per cent of
the restaurants in New York know how to clean a tomato. I
tell my crew to wash the parsley *eight* times. If they wash it
five or six times, I scare them. I tell them they'll go to jail if
there is sand in the parsley. One time, I found a mushroom
on the floor, and I fired that guy who left it there." He spread
his arms, and added, "This place is the only one like it in . . .
in . . . the whole earth! One day, I hope to learn something
from the other places, but so far I haven't. For example, the
other day I went to a very fancy restaurant and had borscht.
I had to send it back. It was *junk,* I could see all the chemicals in it. I never use chemicals. Last weekend, I had lobster
bisque in Brooklyn, a very well-known place. It was *junk.*
When I make a lobster bisque, I use a whole lobster. You
know, I never advertise. I don't have to. All the big-shot
chefs and the kings of the hotels come here to see what *I'm*
doing."

As you approach Mr. Yeganeh's Soup Kitchen Interna- 3
tional from a distance, the first thing you notice about it is
the awning, which proclaims "Homemade Hot, Cold, Diet
Soups." The second thing you notice is an aroma so delicious that it makes you want to take a bite out of the air. The

third thing you notice, in front of the kitchen, is an electric signboard that flashes, saying, "Today's Soups . . . Chicken Vegetable . . . Mexican Beef Chili . . . Cream of Watercress . . . Italian Sausage . . . Clam Bisque . . . Beef Barley . . . Due to Cold Weather . . . For Most Efficient and Fastest Service the Line Must . . . Be Kept Moving . . . Please . . . Have Your Money . . . Ready . . . Pick the Soup of Your Choice . . . Move to Your Extreme . . . Left After Ordering."

"I am not prejudiced against color or religion," Mr.   4
Yeganeh told us, and he jabbed an index finger at the flashing sign. "Whoever follows that I treat very well. My regular customers don't say anything. They are very intelligent and well educated. They know I'm just trying to move the line. The New York cop is very smart—he sees everything but says nothing. But the young girl who wants to stop and tell you how nice you look and hold everyone up—*yah!*" He made a guillotining motion with his hand. "I tell you, I hate to work with the public. They treat me like a slave. My philosophy is: The customer is always wrong and I'm always right. I raised my prices to try to get rid of some of these people, but it didn't work."

The other day, Mr. Yeganeh was dressed in chef's whites   5
with orange smears across his chest, which may have been some of the carrot soup cooking in a huge pot on a little stove in one corner. A three-foot-long handheld mixer from France sat on the sink, looking like an overgrown gardening tool. Mr. Yeganeh spoke to two young helpers in a twisted Armenian-Spanish barrage, then said to us, "I have no overhead, no trained waitresses, and I have the cashier here." He pointed to himself theatrically. Beside the doorway, a glass case with fresh green celery, red and yellow peppers, and purple eggplant was topped by five big gray soup urns. According to a piece of cardboard taped to the door, you can buy Mr. Yeganeh's soups in three sizes, costing from four to fifteen dollars. The order of any well-behaved customer is accompanied by little waxpaper packets of bread, fresh vegetables (such as scallions and radishes), fresh fruit (such as cherries or an orange), a chocolate mint, and a plastic spoon. No coffee, tea, or other drinks are served.

"I get my recipes from books and theories and my own   6
taste," Mr. Yeganeh said. "At home, I have several hundreds of books. When I do research, I find that I don't know anything. Like cabbage is a cancer fighter, and some fish is good for your heart but some is bad. Every day, I should have one sweet, one spicy, one cream, one vegetable soup—and they

must change, they should always taste a little different." He added that he wasn't sure how extensive his repertoire was, but that it probably includes at least eighty soups, among them African peanut butter, Greek moussaka, hamburger, Reuben, B.L.T., asparagus and caviar, Japanese shrimp miso, chicken chili, Irish corned beef and cabbage, Swiss chocolate, French calf's brain, Korean beef ball, Italian shrimp and eggplant Parmesan, buffalo, ham and egg, short rib, Russian beef Stroganoff, turkey cacciatore, and Indian mulligatawny. "The chicken and the seafood are an addiction, and when I have French garlic soup I let people have only one small container each," he said. "The doctors and nurses love that one."

A lunch line of thirty people stretched down the block   7
from Mr. Yeganeh's doorway. Behind a construction worker was a man in expensive leather, who was in front of a woman in a fur hat. Few people spoke. Most had their money out and their orders ready.

At the front of the line, a woman in a brown coat couldn't   8
decide which soup to get and started to complain about the prices.

"You talk too much, dear," Mr. Yeganeh said, and mo-   9
tioned her to move to the left. "Next!"

"Just don't talk. Do what he says," a man huddled in a   10
blue parka warned.

"He's downright rude," said a blond woman in a blue coat.   11
"Even abusive. But you can't deny it, his soup is the best."

READING FOR MEANING

Write to create meanings for this observational essay on Yeganeh and his Soup Kitchen International.

START MAKING MEANING

Begin by listing Albert Yeganeh's most memorable or surprising qualities. Continue by noting anything else in the essay about Mr. Yeganeh or his restaurant that seems significant.

IF YOU ARE STUCK

If you cannot write at least a page, consider writing about

- what Yeganeh thinks of the work he does and its importance, giving examples of his views.

- Yeganeh's inversion of the often-stated business principle, "The customer is always right," perhaps comparing it with your own experience as a customer or worker in fast-food restaurants (paragraph 4).

- Yeganeh's apparent obsession with quality, possibly connecting it with your own or someone else's perfectionism.

- the work ethic and entrepreneurship that Yeganeh stands for, compared to your own work experience or your observations.

READING LIKE A WRITER

This section guides you through an analysis of the observational writing strategies illustrated in "Soup": *describing places and people, organizing the observations, engaging and informing readers,* and *conveying an impression of the subject.* In each part, we describe one strategy briefly and then pose a critical reading and writing task that will show you how that particular strategy works in "Soup."

Consider this section a writer's introduction to observational essay writing. You will learn still more about how writers use observational writing strategies from the activities following the other selections later in this chapter. The Guide to Writing Observational Essays at the end of the chapter will suggest how you can use these strategies in your own essay.

Describing Places and People

Observational writing, like autobiography (Chapter 2), succeeds by presenting the subject vividly and concretely. Writers of observation usually describe both places and people, although they may emphasize one over the other. Visual details usually predominate in an observational essay, but some writers accentuate the visual description with especially evocative sounds, smells, and tastes.

Observational writers present people through specific visual details—how they look, how they dress, how they move, what they do. They also show how people talk and interact with one another, often creating dialogues or paraphrasing what people have said. To gain a sense of an individual's personality, readers usually need only a few descriptive details indicating the person's tone of voice, facial expression, or body language.

ANALYZE

1. *Reread* the descriptions of Yeganeh and his establishment in paragraphs 3 and 5–6, and *bracket* the words and phrases used to describe him and his place of business. In paragraph 3, for example, you might bracket the words on the awning "Homemade Hot, Cold, Diet Soups" in the first sentence, and the words "aroma" and "delicious" in the sec-

ond. You could also bracket the vivid image that specifies just how delicious the aroma is: "it makes you want to take a bite out of the air."

2. *Review* the descriptions you have bracketed and *note* in the margin, wherever you can, which of the senses—sight, hearing, touch, smell, or taste—is being evoked.

WRITE

Write several sentences explaining what you have discovered about the essay's use of sensory description to present Yeganeh and his restaurant. Which senses seem to predominate? From your annotations, *give examples* of the descriptive language you find to be especially vivid or memorable.

Organizing the Observations

Observational writers typically present their subjects narratively, as a more or less chronological story of their observations, or topically, as groups of related information the writer wants readers to know about the subject. "Soup" is a good example of topical organization. Other observational essays in this chapter are arranged narratively, as you will discover when you analyze John McPhee's profile of an outdoor vegetable market that also serves as a "Pickpocket Academy." While a narrative plan offers certain advantages—engaging readers and providing the drama of a good novel or movie—a topical plan keeps the focus firmly on the information.

ANALYZE

1. *Make a scratch outline* of "Soup," identifying the topics in the order in which they appear. *Notice* that some paragraphs have more than one topic, such as paragraph 2, which raises the topics of the health benefits of soup, Yeganeh's perfectionism, his emphasis on cleanliness, and how his restaurant compares to others. (For an illustration of scratch outlining, see p. 461.)

2. *Note* in your outline where the information appears to come from: interviews, the writer's firsthand observation, or other sources.

WRITE

Write several sentences commenting on the type of information presented, where it comes from, and how effectively it is put together. Do you think *New Yorker* readers would be surprised by the number of topics covered in this brief essay? Were you? Is the information arranged in a way that is easy to follow and makes sense? If not, how would you rearrange it?

Engaging and Informing Readers

Along with presenting their subjects vividly, observational writers strive to engage their readers and inform them about the subject. Readers expect to learn something new from observational writing, and they anticipate savoring this learning experience. To accomplish these intertwined goals of engaging and informing readers, writers must pace the flow of information and place it within an engaging framework. Strategies for engaging readers include beginning with an arresting image or statement, using active verbs, telling exciting or funny anecdotes, and giving dialogue punch and personality.

Much of the information in observational writing tends to come from interviews and be presented through dialogue, as in "Soup." Information can also come from the writer's background reading or other interviews, and be quoted or summarized. Strategies for presenting information include identifying and defining new terms, listing, dividing into parts, classifying or grouping, and comparing or contrasting. A writer of observation needs to consider carefully what readers are likely to know about the subject as well as what will interest and amuse them.

ANALYZE

1. *Skim* the essay and *insert a question mark* in the margin next to any words that you think *New Yorker* readers, including yourself, might find new, unusual, and informative (such as the names of unfamiliar soups and vegetables).

2. As you skim also *insert an exclamation point* in the margin next to anything you think *New Yorker* readers, again including yourself, might find engaging or amusing (such as the opening quote: "Soup is my lifeblood").

WRITE

Write several sentences describing how the author of "Soup" presents information while also entertaining readers. *Cite* a few examples from your annotations.

Conveying an Impression of the Subject

Readers expect observational essays to convey a particular impression or interpretation of the subject. They want to know the writer's insight into the subject after having spent time observing the place and talking to people. Indeed, observation is like autobiography in that the impression created by the essay gives readers a sense of the significance of the subject. It is what separates profiles from mere exercises in description and narration.

To convey a dominant impression, writers carefully select details of the place and people and put these details together in a particular way.

They may also express an attitude toward the subject as well as an interpretation or evaluation of it. The angle or point of view the writer takes toward the subject invests the description and narration with significance. It also may be stated explicitly: announced at the beginning, woven into the ongoing observations, or presented as a conclusion. More often, however, writers convey an impression by implication. The author of "Soup," for example, does not state an interpretation or evaluation directly but implies it through the quotes, descriptive details, and the little drama presented at the end.

ANALYZE

1. *Underline* any words or phrases that suggest the author's attitudes toward or feelings about Yeganeh as a human being, cook, and businessman.

2. *Note* in the margin any interpretation or evaluation of Yeganeh and his way of doing business stated directly or implied by what he says and does.

WRITE

Write several sentences identifying the overall impression you have of Yeganeh and his Soup Kitchen International. *Quote* from the essay one or two passages that convey this impression most strongly and briefly identify the attitude, interpretation, or evaluation you see in each passage.

JOHN McPHEE

The New York Pickpocket Academy

*John McPhee (b. 1931) lives in Princeton, New Jersey,
where he occasionally teaches a writing workshop in the
"Literature of Fact" at Princeton University. He is highly regarded as a writer of profiles—in-depth reporting about
people, places, and activities—and is a shrewd observer
and masterful interviewer. In his profiles, McPhee inge-
niously integrates information from observations, interviews, and research into engaging, readable prose. Readers
marvel at the way he explains such complex subjects as ex-
perimental aircraft or modern physics and discovers the
complexities of such ordinary subjects as bears or oranges.
Among his books are* Oranges *(1967),* The Control of Nature *(1989),* Assembling California *(1993), and* The Ran-
som of Russian Art *(1994).*

The following selection, from the collection of essays
Giving Good Weight *(1979), is part of a longer profile of
New Jersey farmers who sell produce at open-air farmers'
markets in New York City. The narrator of the story is
McPhee himself, weighing and sacking produce, all the
while looking beyond the zucchini and tomatoes for material that might interest readers. As you read, notice the many
details McPhee provides about the people and the place: the
vegetables and trucks and hats and colors and sounds of the
market. Notice, too, the great variety of examples he presents of crime and honesty, some happening before his eyes
and some told to him by people at the market.*

Brooklyn, and the pickpocket in the burgundy jacket appears just before noon. Melissa Mousseau recognizes him
much as if he were an old customer and points him out to
Bob Lewis, who follows him from truck to truck. Aware of
Lewis, he leaves the market. By two, he will have made another run. A woman with deep-auburn hair and pale, nervous hands clumsily attracts the attention of a customer
whose large white purse she is rifling. Until a moment ago,
the customer was occupied with the choosing of apples and
peppers, but now she shouts out, "Hey, what are you doing?
Your hand is in my purse. What are you doing?" The auburn-
haired woman not only has her hand in the purse but most
of her arm as well. She withdraws it, and with intense ab-

1

sorption begins to finger the peppers. "How much are the peppers? Mister, give me some of these!" she says, looking up at me with a gypsy's dark, starburst eyes. "Three pounds for a dollar," I tell her, with a swift glance around for Lewis or a cop. When I look back, the pickpocket is gone. Other faces have filled in—people unconcernedly examining the fruit. The woman with the white purse has returned her attention to the apples. She merely seems annoyed. Lewis once sent word around from truck to truck that we should regularly announce in loud voices that pickpockets were present in the market, but none of the farmers complied. Hodgson shrugged and said, "Why distract the customers?" Possibly Fifty-ninth Street is the New York Pickpocket Academy. Half a dozen scores have been made there in a day. I once looked up and saw a well-dressed gentleman under a gray fedora being kicked and kicked again by a man in a green polo shirt. He kicked him in the calves. He kicked him in the thighs. He kicked him in the gluteal bulge. He kicked him from the middle of the market out to the edge, and he kicked him into the street. "Get your ass out of here!" shouted the booter, redundantly. Turning back toward the market, he addressed the curious. "Pickpocket," he explained. The dip did not press charges.

People switch shopping carts from time to time. They make   2
off with a loaded one and leave an empty cart behind. Crime on such levels is a part of the background here, something in the urban air, so many parts per million. The condition is accepted with a resignation that approaches nonchalance.

Most thievery is petty and is on the other side of the   3
tables. As Rich describes it, "Brooklyn, Fifty-ninth Street, people rip off stuff everywhere. You just expect it. An old man comes along and puts a dozen eggs in a bag. Women choosing peaches steal one for every one they buy—a peach for me, a peach for you. What can you do? You stand there and watch. When they take too many, you complain. I watched a guy one day taking nectarines. He would put one in a plastic bag, then one in a pocket, then one in a pile on the ground. After he did that half a dozen times, he had me weigh the bag."

"This isn't England," Barry Benepe informed us once, "and   4
a lot of people are pretty dishonest."

Now, in Brooklyn, a heavyset woman well past the middle   5
of life is sobbing pitifully, flailing her arms in despair. She is sitting on a bench in the middle of the market. She is wear-

ing a print dress, a wide-brimmed straw hat. Between sobs, she presents in a heavy Russian accent the reason for her distress. She was buying green beans from Don Keller, and when she was about to pay him she discovered that someone had opened her handbag—even while it was on her arm, she said—and had removed several books of food stamps, a telephone bill, and eighty dollars in cash. Lewis, in his daypack, stands over her and tells her he is sorry. He said, "This sort of thing will happen wherever there's a crowd."

Another customer breaks in to scold Lewis, saying, "This   6
is the biggest rip-off place in Brooklyn. Two of my friends were pickpocketed here last week and I had to give them carfare home."

Lewis puts a hand on his forehead and, after a pensive   7
moment, says, "That was very kind of you."

The Russian woman is shrieking now. Lewis attends her   8
like a working dentist. "It's all right. It will be O.K. It may not be as bad as you think." He remarks that he would call the police if he thought there was something they could do.

Jeffrey Mack, eight years old, has been listening to all this,   9
and he now says, "I see a cop."

Jeffrey has an eye for cops that no one else seems to   10
share. (A squad car came here for him one morning and took him off to face a truant officer. Seeing his fright, a Pacific Street prostitute got into the car and rode with him.)

"Where, Jeffrey?"   11

"There," Jeffrey lifts an arm and points.   12

"Where?"   13

"There." He points again—at trucks, farmers, a falafel man.   14

"I don't see a policeman," Lewis says to him. "If you see   15
one, Jeffrey, go and get him."

Jeffrey goes, and comes back with an off-duty 78th Precinct   16
cop who is wearing a white apron and has been selling fruits and vegetables in the market. The officer speaks sternly to the crying woman. "Your name?"

"Catherine Barta."   17

"Address?"   18

"Eighty-five Eastern Parkway."   19

Every Wednesday, she walks a mile or so to the Green-   20
market. She has lived in Brooklyn close to half her life, the rest of it in the Ukraine. Heading back to his vegetables, the officer observes that there is nothing he can do.

Out from behind her tables comes Joan Benack, the   21
baker, of Rocky Acres Farm, Milan, New York—a small woman with a high, thin voice. Leaving her tropical carrot

bread, her zucchini bread, her anadama bread, her beer bread, she goes around with a borrowed hat collecting money from the farmers for Catherine Barta. Bills stuff that hat, size 7—the money of Alvina Frey and John Labanowski and Cleather Slade and Rich Hodgson and Bob Engle, who has seen it come and go. He was a broker for Merrill Lynch before the stock market imploded, and now he is a blond-bearded farmer in a basketball shirt selling apples that he grows in Clintondale, New York. Don Keller offers a dozen eggs, and one by one the farmers come out from their trucks to fill Mrs. Barta's shopping cart with beans and zucchini, apples, eggplants, tomatoes, peppers, and corn. As a result, her wails and sobs grow louder.

A man who gave Rich Hodgson a ten-dollar bill for a   22
ninety-five-cent box of brown eggs asks Rich to give the ten back after Rich has handed him nine dollars and five cents, explaining that he has smaller bills that he wants to exchange for a twenty. Rich hands him the ten. Into Rich's palm he counts out five ones, a five, and the ten for a twenty and goes away satisfied, as he has every reason to be, having conned Rich out of nine dollars, five cents, and a box of brown eggs. Rich smiles at his foolishness, shrugs, and sells some cheese. If cash were equanimity, he would never lose a cent. One day, a gang of kids began taking Don Keller's vegetables and throwing them at the Hodgson truck. Anders Thueson threw an apple at the kids, who then picked up rocks. Thueson reached into the back of the truck and came up with a machete. While Hodgson told him to put it away, pant legs went up, switchblades came into view. Part of the gang bombarded the truck with debris from a nearby roof. Any indication of panic might have been disastrous. Hodgson packed deliberately, and drove away.

Todd Jameson, who comes in with his brother Dan from   23
Farmingdale, New Jersey, weighed some squash one day, and put it in a brown bag. He set the package down while he weighed something else. Then, reaching for the squash, he picked up an identical bag that happened to contain fifty dollars in rolled coins. He handed it to the customer who had asked for the squash. Too late, Todd discovered the mistake. A couple of hours later, though, the customer—"I'll never forget him as long as I live, the white hair, the glasses, the ruddy face"—came back. He said, "Hey, this isn't squash. I didn't ask for money, I asked for squash." Whenever that man comes to market, the Jamesons give him a bag full of food. "You see, where I come from, that would never, never happen," Todd explains. "If I made a mistake like that in

Farmingdale, no one—no one—would come back with fifty dollars' worth of change."

Dusk comes down without further crime in Brooklyn, and   24
the farmers are packing to go. John Labanowski—short, compact, with a beer in his hand—is expounding on his day. "The white people are educating the colored on the use of beet greens," he reports. "A colored woman was telling me today, 'Cut the tops off,' and a white woman spoke up and said, 'Hold it,' and told the colored woman, 'You're throwing the best part away.' They go on talking, and pretty soon the colored woman is saying, 'I'm seventy-three on Monday,' and the white says, 'I don't believe a word you say.' You want to know why I come in here? I come in here for fun. For profit, of course, but for relaxation, too. I like being here with these people. They say the city is a rat race, but they've got it backwards. The farm is what gets to be a rat race. You should come out and see what I—" He is interrupted by the reappearance in the market of Catherine Barta, who went home long ago and has now returned, her eyes hidden by her wide-brimmed hat, her shopping cart full beside her. On the kitchen table, at 85 Eastern Parkway, she found her telephone bill, her stamps, and her cash. She has come back to the farmers with their food and money.

READING FOR MEANING

Write to create meaning for McPhee's observations of the vegetable market.

START MAKING MEANING

Begin by listing the types of crime McPhee observes at the farmers' market (described in paragraphs 1–5 and 22). Continue by writing about anything else in the essay or in your experience that contributes to your understanding of McPhee's observations.

IF YOU ARE STUCK

If you cannot write at least a page, consider writing about

- the attitudes of the people who work at the market toward the crimes committed there, perhaps related to your own attitude toward "petty thievery."

- the notion that crime is part of the everyday experience of urban living, but is not part of life in suburbia or small-town America.

- the Todd Jameson anecdote in paragraph 23.

- what happens to Catherine Barta and how people at the market treat her, possibly related to your own experience or observation of how people treat others in distress.

READING LIKE A WRITER

ORGANIZING THE OBSERVATIONS

McPhee uses a narrative organization to present his observations chronologically, as they occur along a time line. His story begins "just before noon" (first sentence of paragraph 1) and ends as "dusk comes down" (first sentence of paragraph 24). To keep readers from getting confused about what is happening as the narrative moves along, McPhee uses narrative time markers. These markers include words and phrases that note the time of day (such as "noon" and "by two" in sentences 1 and 4 of paragraph 1) or indicate when something happened relative to when something else happened (such as "until a moment ago" and "but now" in sentence 6). This easy-to-follow chronological structure pushes readers along, keeping them on track as they are catapulted into the noisy, crowded world of the farmers' market.

For most of the essay, the narrative moves forward in time. But McPhee's narrative is not simple. He interweaves into his narrative of what happened that afternoon references to events that occurred at various points in the past. In the middle of paragraph 1, for example, the phrases "Lewis once sent word" and "I once looked up and saw" refer to events that occurred sometime before this particular afternoon. These references to earlier events give McPhee's narrative a thick fabric, enabling readers to imagine not only the swirl of activities occurring that afternoon but also what the market has been like on other occasions.

ANALYZE

1. *Reread* the selection and *underline* the time markers, beginning with "just before noon" in the opening sentence of the essay.

2. *Note* in the margin which time markers refer to events that occurred at other points in the past.

WRITE

Write several sentences describing how McPhee uses time markers to help readers understand which events occurred that afternoon and which occurred at other times. How effectively do the time markers keep you oriented? Indicate any passages in the essay where you are confused about when something happened.

COMPARE

To understand the difference between narrative and topical organization in observational writing, *compare* McPhee's narrative plan with the topical organization used in "Soup" (pp. 65–68). Given the subject and the writer's purpose in each essay, what advantages and disadvantages do you see in the type of organization chosen?

Write several sentences speculating about why each writer chose the particular organizational plan. Instead of working chronologically, could McPhee have organized the essay topically by the various types of crime he observes at the market, using anecdotes as examples of each type? Could the *New Yorker* writer have told the story of a typical day at the soup kitchen, weaving the various topics he discusses into the narrative of a day? *Consider* these alternatives and *speculate* why the writers might have chosen the plans they did.

CONSIDERING IDEAS FOR YOUR OWN WRITING

Public scenes filled with people and action offer good material for observational essays. Crowds also present problems, mainly because of their huge size and scope: So many people are present and so much is happening at once, the observer may not be able to decide where to focus. Notice how McPhee solves this problem by remaining in one location, the stall where he is selling vegetables. The action takes place in one small area of a huge market, focusing on only a few people and events.

You could likewise find such a focus for an observational essay in some large public scene. Here are a few examples to start you thinking: the souvenir sellers or grounds keepers at a baseball game; a lifeguard station at a beach; an unusual store or restaurant at a shopping mall; one stall at a flea market; a small group of riders from the same club at a Harley-Davidson motorcycle reunion; one section of your college library; an ice-skating rink at a city park; a musician, vendor, or guard in a subway station. You need not seek to find some unexpected activity, like the pickpocketing at the Brooklyn farmers' market, but you could probably interest readers in the people and activities in one limited area of a large, amorphous public place.

JOE GLICKMAN

So Wet and Wild:
Paddling for Thrills

Joe Glickman (b. 1959) writes about rivers. He regularly contributes to "The Weekend Warrior" column in the New York Times, *from which our selection comes. His articles have appeared in such diverse publications as* The Village Voice, Outside, *and* The Wall Street Journal. *In addition to his book* Our Wisconsin River *(1997), he co-wrote (with Allen Barra)* That's Not The Way It Was, *about myths in sports.*

In this essay, Glickman recounts some of his experiences during a two-day course in white-water kayaking. His purpose in writing, however, is not so much autobiographical—to convey to readers the personal significance of the experience—as it is informational—to let readers know about white-water kayaking in general and the Zoar Outdoor course in particular. Like Glickman, writers of observation sometimes get involved in the activity or with the people they are observing. This kind of observational research is called participant observation. *Whether you are a participant observer or an outside observer, you need to recognize that your very presence may affect the people and places you are observing. As you read "So Wet and Wild," think about how the essay would have been different had Glickman not participated in the kayaking course. What would his essay have gained or lost?*

I knew I had flipped my boat when I felt frigid water fill   1
my nostrils. Squinting into a blurry montage of percolating
water and submerged rocks, I frantically tried to execute
an Eskimo roll, a nifty move I'd been taught earlier in the
day that was supposed to right the kayak. When that failed—
and it failed miserably—I segued to the next phase of
self-rescue: squirming out of the kayak and swimming to
shore.

Tim Cahill, author of "Pecked to Death by Ducks," an ad-   2
venture travel book, calls river kayaks "maddening, tippy"
vessels "built to capsize for the fun of it." For precisely that
reason, Bruce Lessels, a three-time member of the United
States White-Water Team and head of Zoar Outdoor, a kayak
school in Charlemont, Mass., had us practice two techniques for regaining balance, j-leans and bracingstrokes, at
the start of the two-day white-water course on the Deerfield
River on the Vermont-Massachusetts line.

Ours was the first clinic of the season. We had the river to   3
ourselves, and the water level was high. But in early April,
the air temperature was 45 degrees and the water nearly as
cold. Our group consisted of five students and two instructors: the 6-foot-5-inch, 195-pound Mr. Lessels, who managed to look tall even in a kayak, and Heather Young, a
sturdy 29-year-old who, when she isn't teaching kayaking,
sharpens skis at the slope overlooking the bright red 18th-
century farmhouse that serves as headquarters for Zoar
Outdoor. While my class, advanced beginners/intermediate,
required three to five days of white-water paddling experience, beginners need only be fit and eager.

On Saturday morning, we worked on the basics on   4
the calm Sherman Reservoir, which spans the Vermont-Massachusetts border, one of a string of reservoirs along the 70-
mile Deerfield River. The Eskimo roll, which we learned last, is
intended to right you when you capsize. When it is done correctly, the submerged kayaker bursts out of the water, shakes
his head like a shaggy dog emerging from a bath, and paddles
on. So valuable is the technique that an *Outside* magazine
columnist, David Quammen, wrote that kayakers tend to think
of it on par with the invention of the wheel.

Unable to effect this triumph of Arctic agility in actual   5
conditions, I performed an aptly named "wet exit." Yanking
wildly at the whiffle ball at the head of the neoprene spray
skirt (a watertight apron worn above the waist that
stretches to fit tightly over the oblong cockpit), I wiggled
into the freezing water and then up into the world of light
and oxygen. I had a pulsating sensation in my head that
kayakers call an "ice cream headache."

"Don't worry," Mr. Lessels said, smiling as usual. "Reading   6
the water is a 'feel' thing. You'll get it tomorrow."

That evening, I drove to Northampton, Mass., to meet a   7
friend for dinner. His first question was why I was taking the
course in the first place, since I was an experienced kayaker.
My friend is not a river man; in fact, in his kitchen was a
photo of him in a life jacket floating in an inner tube and
clutching the sides.

"You paddled the entire Missouri River," he said. "What   8
could they teach you?"

My answer? "Everything!"   9

White water forms when a river bed narrows or drops off   10
rapidly, and paddling on it has its risks. In addition to avoiding waterfalls and large rocks, the most obvious dangers,
you need to steer clear of "sweepers" (downed trees) and
"keepers" (holes that form where the river drops over a rock
and reverses itself).

To the uninitiated, a kayak is a kayak, but white-water and   11
touring models are as different as, say, downhill and cross-
country skis. Sea kayaks, which range from 17 to 19 feet
long, are so stable that anyone who can walk a straight line
can paddle a kayak in calm water. River kayaks are shorter,
more maneuverable and, as previously noted, quicker to
capsize. I've spent countless hours paddling tippy flat-water
racing kayaks, but I'd never been in a white-water kayak,
knew little about the hydraulics of white water, and nothing
about the art of running rapids. That's why I called Zoar.

On Sunday morning, we headed to a section of the Deer-   12
field River called Dryway No. 4, a more dynamic stretch than
the Class I and II water we had run the day before. White
water in the East is divided into six categories. Class I is simply moving water with ripples, fine for a paddle in a summer-
camp canoe. Class II is "broken" or white water. Class III is
white water with obstacles like holes and rocks. The difference between Class IV and V, both of which should be
scouted and run only by experts, is subjective and dependent on water levels. Class VI is for lunatics. In his guidebook on the Deerfield River, Mr. Lessels wrote, "Fatal consequences may follow an unsuccessful run."

As we walked to the dam above the dryway, shouldering   13
our stubby 35-pound lime-and-purple boats, I tried to visualize myself doing a solid Eskimo roll, while praying to the
river gods that I wouldn't need one. In a helmet similar to
those worn by hockey players, with neoprene booties, a wet
suit with padded knees, synthetic long underwear, a paddling vest, spray skirt, life jacket and mitts, I looked like a
lacrosse player headed for the beach.

We stood high on the bank adjacent to the dam, shouting to   14
be heard above the roar of the water pouring over the spill-
way. At the bottom of the 15-foot falls, a green bottle bounced
in place, as if trapped in a vicious washing machine. "That's a
killer hole," Ms. Young said of the boiling water that could pin
a boat under for longer than any of us cared to consider. It was
just above the rocks where we would put in. Mr. Lessels, who
won a bronze medal at the 1987 World White-Water Champi-
onships, stared at the churning mess like a hungry man eyeing
a smorgasbord. After considerable discussion about what we
could expect below, we hit the water.

We ran the first stretch of white water and "eddied out."   15
Usually found behind boulders or on the inside of a bend, an
eddy is a pocket of water rushing back upstream. It offers a
kayaker a place to pause in turbulent water with little or no
paddling. In the relative calm of the eddies, Mr. Lessels and
Ms. Young shouted instructions to refine our techniques.

Leapfrogging from eddy to eddy, it took us four hours to   16
travel one mile. And Mr. Lessels was right. My "feel" for the
river improved. I learned when to lean downstream in turbulent water (resisting the very strong impulse to lean upstream), and how to make sharp turns. I was able to ferry
across the rushing river like a hummingbird by pointing my
bow into the current and using a powerful forward sweep
stroke. I learned to surf, balancing at the apex of a recirculat-
ing wave with minimal effort. Most important, I began to
relax.

But that afternoon, we drove to the Zoar Gap: a narrow   17
Class III-plus gauntlet with boulders the size of U.P.S. trucks.
The surrounding hills dropped into the choked river at a
45-degree angle. My damp wet suit quickly chilled in the fun-
neled wind.

"Meaty," said Jim Stirling, an Englishman who lives in Con-   18
necticut and once survived a three-day storm on a solo
trans-Atlantic sailing trip. Two members of our group opted
out. Ms. Young stood on the bank with a throw rope should
any of us go for an unplanned swim in the raging current.

Mr. Lessels led, bounding around the submerged boul-   19
ders like a deer through the forest. I was next. Boiling water
filled my eyes and ears, but I remained upright for the entire
200-yard 30-second ride, one of the biggest thrills of my
kayaking life.

Sitting triumphantly in an eddy, I watched the last two in   20
our group fight through. Mr. Stirling, a short, muscular type,
flipped and rolled upright three times. Nick Nagel, who plays
kayak polo every Sunday and paddles in the Atlantic all year,
tried a tricky turn, spun backward and negotiated the rapids
in reverse.

Water dripping from our helmets, the four of us congre-   21
gated in the rolling eddy, staring back up at a force too powerful to describe. Appropriately enough, it took a hard-core
British sailor, Mr. Stirling, to find the right words. "Wasn't
that giggly," he said.

READING FOR MEANING

Write to create meanings for Glickman's observations of the river
kayaking course.

START MAKING MEANING

Begin by speculating about why Glickman chose to open the essay as
he does, instead of beginning with the material in the second paragraph.

What effect do you think his opening is likely to have on his *New York Times* readers, including yourself? Continue by writing about anything else in the essay or in your experience that contributes to your understanding of Glickman's observations.

IF YOU ARE STUCK

If you cannot write at least a page, consider writing about

- Glickman's conversation with his friend in Northampton (paragraphs 7–9).

- the delight people like Glickman take in death-defying feats, perhaps related to your own inclinations.

- the idea (in paragraph 11) that the sport of kayaking is both a science and an art, possibly comparing kayaking with another sport or activity with which you are familiar.

- an activity you enjoy that makes you feel "giggly," comparing your experience with Glickman's.

READING LIKE A WRITER
ENGAGING AND INFORMING READERS

As they aim to engage readers' interest by vividly describing places and people, writers of observation also try to inform readers about the subject. In "Soup" (pp. 65–68) for example, the writer tells us about different types of soup, their ingredients and proper preparation, and, most importantly, about Albert Yeganeh and his unique restaurant. Similarly, in "So Wet and Wild," Glickman tells us about kayaks and kayaking, equipment and techniques, as well as the hydraulics of white water.

ANALYZE

1. *Reread* paragraphs 1–2, 4–5, 10–11, and 13. *Underline* the information that Glickman presents in these paragraphs.

2. *Note* in the margin the topic being discussed in each of these paragraphs. For example, paragraph 1 mentions the "Eskimo roll" but describes another less elegant self-rescue technique, which is the real topic under discussion.

WRITE

Write several sentences describing the topics Glickman presents in his essay, illustrating each topic with one or two examples from your annotations.

CONSIDERING IDEAS FOR YOUR OWN WRITING

You might choose to profile a leisure or educational activity that brings people together briefly for special training. This kind of mini-course usually meets only a few times (one to five times is typical) on evenings or weekends. The offerings reflect people's diverse interests and differ somewhat from community to community: dog training, motorcycle riding, dancing, cooking, decorating for a holiday, stress reduction, conflict resolution, training for new computer software, public speaking, introduction to political candidates, speed reading. You can find these classes advertised in newspapers and in your college's extension-course catalog. Ask for the instructor's permission to observe the class, and arrange to interview him or her for a few minutes before or after class. Be bold in approaching two or three students to discover why they enrolled in the class and what they have to say about it. Take careful notes on your observations of at least one class meeting.

AMANDA COYNE

The Long Good-Bye: Mother's Day in Federal Prison

Amanda Coyne wrote "The Long Good-Bye" for the May 1997 issue of Harper's, *a monthly magazine that publishes profiles of interesting people and places, autobiographical and reflective essays, as well as informative reports on current social and political issues. As she explains in the essay, Coyne based her observations on a one-day visit to a minimum security women's prison where her sister is incarcerated. Coyne writes about her sister and other women in a similar situation to inform readers and to awaken their concern about the justice system. As you read, you will see that Coyne states her views explicitly (particularly in paragraphs 15 and 16), but notice how she also invests her description of the place and people with feeling.*

You can spot the convict-moms here in the visiting room   1
by the way they hold and touch their children and by the single flower that is perched in front of them—a rose, a tulip, a daffodil. Many of these mothers have untied the bow that attaches the flower to its silver-and-red cellophane wrapper and are using one of the many empty soda cans at hand as a vase. They sit proudly before their flower-in-a-Coke-can, amid Hershey bar wrappers, half-eaten Ding Dongs, and empty paper coffee cups. Occasionally, a mother will pick up her present and bring it to her nose when one of the bearers of the single flower—her child—asks if she likes it. And the mother will respond the way that mothers always have and always will respond when presented with a gift on this day. "Oh, I just love it. It's perfect. I'll put it in the middle of my Bible." Or, "I'll put it on my desk, right next to your school picture." And always: "It's the best one here."

But most of what is being smelled today is the children   2
themselves. While the other adults are plunking coins into the vending machines, the mothers take deep whiffs from the backs of their children's necks, or kiss and smell the backs of their knees, or take off their shoes and tickle their feet and then pull them close to their noses. They hold them tight and take in their own second scent—the scent assuring them that these are still their children and that they still belong to them.

The visitors are allowed to bring in pockets full of coins,   3
and today that Mother's Day flower, and I know from previ-

ous visits to my older sister here at the Federal Prison Camp for women in Pekin, Illinois, that there is always an aberrant urge to gather immediately around the vending machines. The sandwiches are stale, the coffee weak, the candy bars the ones we always pass up in a convenience store. But after we hand the children over to their mothers, we gravitate toward those machines. Like milling in the kitchen at a party. We all do it, and nobody knows why. Polite conversation ensues around the microwave while the popcorn is popping and the processed-chicken sandwiches are being heated. We ask one another where we are from, how long a drive we had. An occasional whistle through the teeth, a shake of the head. "My, my, long way from home, huh?" "Staying at the Super 8 right up the road. Not a bad place." "Stayed at the Econo Lodge last time. Wasn't a good place at all." Never asking the questions we really want to ask: "What's she in for?" "How much time's she got left?" You never ask in the waiting room of a doctor's office either. Eventually, all of us—fathers, mothers, sisters, brothers, a few boyfriends, and very few husbands—return to the queen of the day, sitting at a fold-out table loaded with snacks, prepared for five or so hours of attempted normal conversation.

Most of the inmates are elaborately dressed, many in prison-crafted dresses and sweaters in bright blues and pinks. They wear meticulously applied makeup in corresponding hues, and their hair is replete with loops and curls—hair that only women with the time have the time for. Some of the better seamstresses have crocheted vests and purses to match their outfits. Although the world outside would never accuse these women of making haute-couture fashion statements, the fathers and the sons and the boyfriends and the very few husbands think they look beautiful, and they tell them so repeatedly. And I can imagine the hours spent preparing for this visit—hours of needles and hooks clicking over brightly colored yards of yarn. The hours of discussing, dissecting, and bragging about these visitors—especially the men. Hours spent in the other world behind the door where we're not allowed, sharing lipsticks and mascaras, and unraveling the occasional hair-tangled hot roller, and the brushing out and lifting and teasing . . . and the giggles that abruptly change into tears without warning—things that define any female-only world. Even, or especially, if that world is a female federal prison camp.

While my sister Jennifer is with her son in the playroom, an inmate's mother comes over to introduce herself to my younger sister, Charity, my brother, John, and me. She tells us about visiting her daughter in a higher-security prison before she was transferred here. The woman looks old and tired, and her shoulders sag under the weight of her recently acquired bitterness.

"Pit of fire," she says, shaking her head. "Like a pit of fire straight from hell. Never seen anything like it. Like something out of an old movie about prisons." Her voice is getting louder and she looks at each of us with pleading eyes. "My *daughter* was there. Don't even get me started on that place. Women die there." 6

John and Charity and I silently exchange glances. 7

"My daughter would come to the visiting room with a black eye and I'd think, 'All she did was sit in the car while her boyfriend ran into the house.' She didn't even touch the stuff. Never even handled it." 8

She continues to stare at us, each in turn. "Ten years. That boyfriend talked and he got three years. She didn't know anything. Had nothing to tell them. They gave her ten years. They called it conspiracy. Conspiracy? Aren't there real criminals out there?" She asks this with hands outstretched, waiting for an answer that none of us can give her. 9

The woman's daughter, the conspirator, is chasing her son through the maze of chairs and tables and through the other children. She's a twenty-four-year-old blonde, whom I'll call Stephanie, with Dorothy Hamill hair and matching dimples. She looks like any girl you might see in any shopping mall in middle America. She catches her chocolate-brown son and tickles him, and they laugh and trip and fall together onto the floor and laugh harder. 10

Had it not been for that wait in the car, this scene would be taking place at home, in a duplex Stephanie would rent while trying to finish her two-year degree in dental hygiene or respiratory therapy at the local community college. The duplex would be spotless, with a blown-up picture of her and her son over the couch and ceramic unicorns and horses occupying the shelves of the entertainment center. She would make sure that her son went to school every day with stylishly floppy pants, scrubbed teeth, and a good breakfast in his belly. Because of their difference in skin color, there would be occasional tension—caused by the strange looks from strangers, teachers, other mothers, and the bullies on the playground, who would chant after they knocked him down, "Your Momma's white, your Momma's white." But if she were home, their weekends and evenings would be spent together transcending those looks and heal- 11 ing those bruises. Now, however, their time is spent eating visiting-room junk food and his school days are spent fighting the boys in the playground who chant, "Your Momma's in prison, your Momma's in prison."

He will be ten when his mother is released, the same age 12 my nephew will be when his mother is let out. But Jennifer, my sister, was able to spend the first five years of Toby's life with him. Stephanie had Ellie after she was incarcerated. They let her hold him for eighteen hours, then sent her back to prison. She has done the "tour," and her son is a well-traveled six-year-old. He has spent weekends visiting his mother in prisons in Kentucky, Texas, Connecticut (the Pit of Fire), and now at last here, the camp—minimum security, Pekin, Illinois.

Ellie looks older than his age. But his shoulders do not 13 droop like his grandmother's. On the contrary, his bitterness lifts them and his chin higher than a child's should be, and the childlike, wide-eyed curiosity has been replaced by defiance. You can see his emerging hostility as he and his mother play together. She tells him to pick up the toy that he threw, say, or to put the deck of cards away. His face turns sullen, but she persists. She takes him by the shoulders and looks him in the eye, and he uses one of his hands to swat at her. She grabs the hand and he swats with the other. Eventually, she pulls him toward her and smells the top of his head, and she picks up the cards or the toy herself. After all, it is Mother's Day and she sees him so rarely. But her acquiescence makes him angrier, and he stalks out of the playroom with his shoulders thrown back.

Toby, my brother and sister and I assure one another, will 14 not have these resentments. He is better taken care of than most. He is living with relatives in Wisconsin. Good, solid, middle-class, churchgoing relatives. And when he visits us, his aunts and his uncle, we take him out for adventures where we walk down the alley of a city and pretend that we are being chased by the "bad guys." We buy him fast food, and his uncle, John, keeps him up well past his bedtime enthralling him with stories of the monkeys he met in India. A perfect mix, we try to convince one another. Until we take him to see his mother and on the drive back he asks the question that most confuses him, and no doubt all the other children who spend much of their lives in prison visiting rooms: "Is my Mommy a bad guy?" It is the question that most seriously disorders his five-year-old need to clearly separate right from wrong. And because our own need is perhaps just as great, it is the question that haunts us as well.

Now, however, the answer is relatively simple. In a few   15
years, it won't be. In a few years we will have to explain manda-
tory minimums, and the war on drugs, and the murky conspiracy laws, and the enormous amount of money and time
that federal agents pump into imprisoning low-level drug deal-
ers and those who happen to be their friends and their lovers.
In a few years he might have the reasoning skills to ask why so
many armed robbers and rapists and child-molesters and, indeed, murderers are punished less severely than his mother.
When he is older, we will somehow have to explain to him the
difference between federal crimes, which don't allow for parole, and state crimes, which do. We will have to explain that
his mother was taken from him for five years not because she
was a drug dealer but because she made four phone calls for
someone she loved.

But we also know it is vitally important that we explain all   16
this without betraying our bitterness. We understand the
danger of abstract anger, of being disillusioned with your
country, and, most of all, we do not want him to inherit that
legacy. We would still like him to be raised as we were, with
the idea that we live in the best country in the world with
the best legal system in the world—a legal system carefully
designed to be immune to political mood swings and public
hysteria; a system that promises to fit the punishment to the
crime. We want him to be a good citizen. We want him to
have absolute faith that he lives in a fair country, a country
that watches over and protects its most vulnerable citizens:
its women and children.

So for now we simply say, "Toby, your mother isn't bad,   17
she just did a bad thing. Like when you put rocks in the lawn
mower's gas tank. You weren't bad then, you just did a bad
thing."

Once, after being given this weak explanation, he said,   18
"I wish I could have done something really bad, like my
Mommy. So I could go to prison too and be with her."

It's now 3:00. Visiting ends at 3:30. The kids are getting   19
cranky, and the adults are both exhausted and wired from
too many hours of conversation, too much coffee and
candy. The fathers, mothers, sisters, brothers, and the few
boyfriends, and the very few husbands are beginning to
show signs of gathering the trash. The mothers of the infants
are giving their heads one last whiff before tucking them and
their paraphernalia into their respective carrying cases. The
visitors meander toward the door, leaving the older children
with their mothers for one last word. But the mothers never

say what they want to say to their children. They say things like, "Do well in school," "Be nice to your sister," "Be good for Aunt Berry, or Grandma." They don't say, "I'm sorry I'm sorry I'm sorry. I love you more than anything else in the world and I think about you every minute and I worry about you with a pain that shoots straight to my heart, a pain so great I think I will just burst when I think of you alone, without me. I'm sorry."

We are standing in front of the double glass doors that   20
lead to the outside world. My older sister holds her son, rocking him gently. They are both crying. We give her a look and she puts him down. Charity and I grasp each of his small hands, and the four of us walk through the doors. As we're walking out, my brother sings one of his banana songs to Toby.

"Take me out to the—" and Toby yells out, "Banana   21
store!"

"Buy me some—"   22

"Bananas!!"   23

"I don't care if I ever come back. For it's root, root, root   24
for the—"

"Monkey team!"   25

I turn back and see a line of women standing behind the   26
glass wall. Some of them are crying, but many simply stare with dazed eyes. Stephanie is holding both of her son's hands in hers and speaking urgently to him. He is struggling, and his head is twisting violently back and forth. He frees one of his hands from her grasp, balls up his fist, and punches her in the face. Then he walks with purpose through the glass doors and out the exit. I look back at her. She is still in a crouched position. She stares, unblinking, through those doors. Her hands have left her face and are hanging on either side of her. I look away, but before I do, I see drops of blood drip from her nose, down her chin, and onto the shiny marble floor.

READING FOR MEANING

Write to create meanings for Coyne's observations of children visiting their mothers in federal prison.

START MAKING MEANING

Begin by describing your impressions of the inmates Jennifer and Stephanie. Continue by writing about anything else in the essay or in your experience that contributes to your understanding of Coyne's observations.

IF YOU ARE STUCK

If you cannot write at least a page, consider writing about

- the homey details used to describe the visiting room and the impression they create (paragraphs 1–4).

- the idea that a person may be good, but his or her behavior may be bad (paragraph 18).

- Jennifer's relationship with her son, Toby, compared to Stephanie's relationship with her son, Ellie.

- Coyne's critique of the criminal justice system (paragraphs 15 and 16).

A SPECIAL READING STRATEGY

Scratch Outlining

Outlining, especially scratch outlining, is an easy and surprisingly helpful strategy for reading critically. To outline a long and complicated essay like "The Long Good-Bye: Mother's Day in Federal Prison," you must distinguish between the essay's main ideas and its many supporting details and examples.

Turn to the critical reading strategy, Outlining, in Appendix One (p. 459), and follow the guidelines there for scratch outlining.

READING LIKE A WRITER
DESCRIBING PEOPLE

Writers often focus their observations on people, alone or interacting with others. To present people, writers can choose from a repertoire of strategies. Visual description helps readers see the people in their minds' eye: "You can spot the convict-moms here in the visiting room by the way they hold and touch their children and by the single flower that is perched in front of them—a rose, a tulip, a daffodil" (paragraph 1). Other sensory details—touch, sound, smell, even taste—can add depth to a portrait. Dialogue lets readers hear what people say as well as how they say it, their tone of voice and attitude: "An occasional whistle through the teeth, a shake of the head. 'My, my, long way from home, huh?' " (paragraph 3). Dialogue also reveals how people interact with others. These strategies of description and dialogue, many of which you may have used while writing your autobiographical essay in Chapter 2, enable writers to present a concrete and vivid portrait.

ANALYZE

1. *Reread* paragraphs 5–13 and 26, and *underline* the descriptive details that enable you to picture Stephanie and her son, Ellie.

2. *Note* in the margin, next to the language you have underlined, which descriptive strategy (such as sensory description or dialogue) is being used. *Put a checkmark* next to the parts that you think are especially effective.

WRITE

Write several sentences explaining how Coyne describes Stephanie and Ellie, giving examples from your annotations to show the different strategies she uses. *Add* a few more sentences to identify what you think is the most effective part of the description, explaining why you think it works so well.

CONSIDERING IDEAS FOR YOUR OWN WRITING

You might write about a public place where you can observe parents and children interacting, such as a neighborhood playground, beach, restaurant, or toy store. Another possibility is to visit a place where people live in a communal setting, such as a hospital, home for the elderly, or halfway house. Alternatively, you might consider places where people see each other routinely but do not know each other very well; for example, a gym, a night course at the local community college, or a little league baseball game.

TAMAR LEWIN

Struggling for Personal Attention in Day Care

Tamar Lewin (b. 1949) was a lawyer before becoming a journalist and now is a national correspondent for the New York Times, *where the following essay was published in April 1998. Lewin observed three day-care centers in Houston, Texas, before writing her article. Writers of observation usually focus on one site that they can visit several times to observe the activity and interview the people. Lewin's decision to observe multiple sites of the same type, however, enables her to investigate not only specific day-care practices but also some of the larger concerns people have about the quality of child care in this country. As you read, notice that Lewin's essay includes research (such as quotes from experts on child care) as well as direct observation.*

It is snack time in the toddler room at the Educare Learning Center, and Patricia Jackson and a co-worker are handing out crackers to nine little ones seated around the curved table and to Joseph, who eats in a high chair while making the transition from the infant room next door. 1

"Your hands go in your lap," Ms. Jackson says cheerfully. "Remember, don't eat yet. We've got to say grace." 2

The children, ages 1 to 2, are quiet, starting their crackers and juice only after Ms. Jackson finishes saying: "Lord is great. Lord is good. Let us thank him for our food." Each child eats calmly, then goes to the rug where Ms. Jackson has put out a bin of Duplo blocks. Ty'Shierra builds a tower, Stefan says "Aaayyy" and starts to clap, and Joseph just bangs two blocks together. But everyone plays with the blocks and no one leaves the rug. Ms. Jackson, now alone with the children, intervenes only with an occasional "Don't grab" or "Be nice." And when she announces clean-up time, all the toddlers help put the blocks back into the bin. 3

Such day care routines are the fabric of life for an increasing number of American preschoolers. Most children under 5 are cared for by people other than their parents and, according to the Census Bureau, a rising percentage, nearly a third, are in formal day care centers. Day care regulations vary by state, with some, like New York, imposing stringent standards, including one adult for every seven 3-year-olds. Other states, like Texas, allow more than twice as many children per adult. 4

Recent visits to three Houston centers—Educare, the   5
Magnolia Branch Y.W.C.A. and Center 532 of Kindercare, the
largest national for-profit child-care chain—offer a glimpse
of how such care often forces the workers to change their
emphasis from individual attention to group management.

Nationwide, more children are starting day care as young   6
as 6 weeks and spending 10 or more hours a day in centers.
So questions about what makes good day care have become
a prime concern both to parents and to politicians; the Clinton Administration has proposed a $21 billion program to
improve the quality and availability of child care. And with
welfare reform pushing more mothers of young children into
the work force, the needs for low-cost, high-quality child
care are more urgent than ever.

But there is still passionate debate about how child care   7
affects children. While the largest, longest-running study, by
the National Institutes of Health, has offered reassurance
that high-quality child care does not interfere with mother-
child attachment and fosters intellectual development, other
studies have found that most care is mediocre—and more
than 1 in 10 children are in care that is unsafe and harmful to
their development.

"The key issues are how many infants or children one per-   8
son can care for, how the caregiver is trained and whether
the pay is enough to attract and keep good people," said
Marcy Whitebook, co-director of the Center for the Child
Care Workforce, a nonprofit research and advocacy group in
Washington.

For many years, children's advocates have argued for na-   9
tional standards for training, child-to-adult ratios and group
size. But many conservatives say that the Government
should not favor working parents by investing in child care
and that standards should be left to the states.

Texas, and Educare, are at the far end of the spectrum, al-   10
lowing more children per adult than recommended by professional groups, like the National Association for the Education of Young Children. For accreditation by the association,
a center must have at least 1 adult for every 4 babies under
2, every 6 2-year-olds and every 7 3-year-olds. Texas's licens-
ing requirements allow each adult to look after 9 toddlers
ages 18–23 months, 11 2-year-olds or 15 3-year-olds.

While the most expensive Texas day care centers often   11
have more workers than the state requires, the more affordable ones tend to use the state standards.

Each of the Houston centers visited had a different atmos-   12
phere and culture: The Y program is part of a community

center; Educare has strong Christian underpinnings, with quotations from Scripture posted in the rooms, and Kindercare Learning Centers is a large corporation, offering state-of-the-art toys. Reflecting their neighborhoods, the Y's teachers and children were mostly Hispanic, Educare's were mostly African-American and Kindercare's were mostly white.

Even in the largest groups, there was neither neglect nor   13
bedlam. The rooms were orderly and pleasant, with care providers who—at least while observed by a reporter—were unfailingly warm, loving and instantly responsive to any sign of distress.

"I think it's an ivory-tower issue at those groups who say   14
one teacher can only take care of four children," said Leon J. Wynn, the founder of Educare. "I know that in the real world our ratios work fine. Children learn the majority of what they know from other children, and if you are clear on what they are expected to do, they will do it."

The children at the three Houston centers were well be-   15
haved. However, an as-yet-unpublished analysis of the research by the National Institutes of Health found that over all, there are more behavior problems in day care centers where each adult cares for more children.

And with so many children per adult, there is a limit to   16
how much personal attention each child receives. Most of the workers' pronouncements are either admonitions or what child-care experts refer to as to-whom-it-may-concern statements, like, "It's line-up time."

None of the care providers kept up anything like the   17
stream of language that researchers have found to hum through the best day care centers.

Talk like "Caitlin, is that a pie? Mmmm, delicious. Is it   18
blueberry? Is that your favorite?" is a form of stimulation and responsiveness that researchers say helps children's intellectual development.

At the three Houston centers, workers seemed to see   19
their role more as managing children than interacting with them. If a child was not having a problem, not in need of feeding or diapering or nose-wiping, no one was likely to engage that child.

In one room at Educare recently, Shirley Arceneaux was   20
responsible for 15 children, most of them recently turned 3: 8 were in the kitchen corner, shaking and baking and pouring imaginary food, 3 were building with plastic blocks, 2 were at a table with foam shapes and animals, and 2 were pushing wooden beads up and down a winding wire track.

Although it was noisy and some children wandered around somewhat aimlessly, there was no fighting and no crying.

Ms. Arceneaux monitored the group, reminding children 21
who knocked things over to pick them up, and making sure they shared. But she never joined the play, or discussed what the children were doing. And most of the children quickly sought attention from a visitor in the room, coming over to offer a pretend cup of tea, show off their new shoes, tell about their birthdays or have the drawstrings of their pants tied.

At all three centers, what child-care experts call "teach- 22
able moments" were often overlooked. At the Kindercare in-fant room, there was more than an hour and a half on a recent Thursday morning when no one said a word to 13-month-old LaRhonda, who navigated the room with the staggering gait of a new walker. Once, a teacher picked her up to smell her diaper, decided it was fine, and put her back down, without addressing her. And three times in the pe-riod, LaRhonda got stuck trying to get in or out of a blue plastic tugboat; each time, she whimpered slightly, and was immediately picked up and moved out of the boat. But no one showed LaRhonda how to manage it herself.

The center's rules sometimes run up against children's 23
routines. For example, Kindercare does not allow teachers to give children bottles in their cribs. Most child-care ex-perts would approve, given the chance to make feeding a more personal interaction and the risk of dental problems and choking. But some of the babies accustomed to sucking a bottle as they fell asleep at home cannot drowse off with-out a bottle. So they get a bottle in a highchair, where they gradually droop into a contorted sleep and then are moved to a crib.

During a reporter's visit, there were 10 children in Kinder- 24
care's youngest room, from Audrey, a 6-week-old trying out the center for the day, to Justin, a 15-month-old getting ready to move to the toddler room.

The youngest—Audrey, and Shelbie and Kelby, 10-week- 25
olds—spent most of the day in their cribs and were taken out only when they cried or needed diapering or feeding. And while they seemed content, gazing at the brightly col-ored Easter art hanging nearby and at the older children, no one stopped to talk to them as they sat in bouncy chairs in their cribs, or, if fussy, in the wind-up swing.

There were two care providers in the room. But with the 26
center director, the area manager and a corporate commu-nications officer, there were sometimes six adults in the room—and all had babies playing with their shoes, climbing

into their laps and staying with them as long as they remained available. Jill Eiland, the Kindercare communications officer, took this as an indicator of how friendly and open to strangers the children were; others might see it as an indicator that they craved more adult interaction.

At the Y, where Maria Villegas cares for a group of nine,   27
from 18 months to nearly 3, it was easy to pick out a recent addition: Rosita, who popped up irrepressibly from the line and said "My turn," or "No, me" whenever one child was to be selected to wash hands, get dessert or pour milk. Even with two of the nine absent, Ms. Villegas had her hands full. When the children were in the gym, Gersoon, the youngest, was determined to pick up tiny shreds of paper from the floor and stick them into his mouth. Ms. Villegas tried to be vigilant, crooning "No, mi amor. That's garbage. Basura." But then she had to retrieve Rosita, who had wandered off to the men's locker room.

At all three centers, the quality of the teacher-child rela-   28
tionship would change, noticeably, when there were fewer children—before 8 A.M., when many children had not yet arrived, late in the day, when many had been picked up, and at nap time, when most had gone to sleep.

In Ms. Jackson's room, at 5 P.M., all but four children were   29
gone, and sitting on the rug with the late ones she began to sing a song with a verse for each child. "Where is Donna, where is Donna?" she sang. "Please stand up, do a little jumping and a little clapping, please sit down."

And Donna, who had been placidly content but showed   30
no visible emotion all afternoon, got to her feet and jumped up and down, a slow smile spreading across her face, making her face shine in delight in a whole new way.

READING FOR MEANING

Write to create meanings for Lewin's observations of day care centers.

START MAKING MEANING

Begin by listing the topics in paragraphs 15–23. Continue by writing about anything else in the essay or in your experience that contributes to your understanding of Lewin's observations.

IF YOU ARE STUCK

If you cannot write at least a page, consider writing about

• the similarities among the three Houston child-care centers that Lewin observed.

- the qualities of a good day-care center, possibly comparing your own and Lewin's views.

- the statement that "children learn the majority of what they know from other children" (paragraph 14).

- the debate about whether business should help provide alternatives to child care for working parents (such as telecommuting and flexible work schedules).

READING LIKE A WRITER
CONVEYING AN IMPRESSION THROUGH DIRECT STATEMENT

Some writers of observation adopt the role of the neutral or objective reporter, conveying their impression of the subject through implication, as you have seen in "Soup" (pp. 65–68) and will see in the following selection by Craig Elsten. Other writers, like Tamar Lewin in this essay, state their views openly. They regard observational writing as an opportunity to provide what anthropologist Clifford Geertz calls "thick description," a description of the place, people, and activity that includes the observer's commentary. The commentary can include interpretive as well as evaluative statements and raise important social issues. This activity invites you to analyze Lewin's strategy of commenting directly on the subject.

ANALYZE

1. *Reread* paragraphs 13–30, and *underline* the author's explicit evaluative or interpretive comments.

2. *Note* where Lewin's comments are accompanied by supporting details or examples.

WRITE

Write several sentences briefly explaining Lewin's strategy of direct commentary. *Give examples* of the kinds of comments she makes and indicate whether she supports her comments with specific details.

CONSIDERING IDEAS FOR YOUR OWN WRITING

Like Lewin, you could use observational writing to explore a current controversial issue or problem on campus or in the community. For example, you could observe a rape crisis center, drug intervention program, or birth-control clinic. You could interview a parole officer, former or current gang member, someone enrolled in a Workfare program or who administers such a program. You could observe a class in teaching English as a second language or interview experts in bilingual education. You could observe a school for new drivers or for people who have received driving tickets.

You might also consider observing two or three comparable places as Lewin does. Do not consider this option, however, unless you have a lot of time for advance planning and observing as well as for organizing and writing your essay. If you do wish to observe multiple sites, think about choosing a subject related to your major or the kind of work you hope to do. For example, if you are majoring in an applied science, you could visit different labs on campus to see how they operate. If you want to be an attorney, you could observe criminal and civil trials to see how they compare. If you are a business major, you could observe offices, stores, or restaurants to see how they are managed. If you are a nursing major, you could observe different hospitals or clinics. If you plan to teach, you could visit different schools or several classes in the same school.

CRAIG ELSTEN

Dead Air: Is Anyone Listening?

*Craig Elsten wrote this insightful essay about a campus
radio station when he was a first-year college student. Elsten
uses a variety of observed details, as well as interviews with
station personnel, to portray the offbeat, student-operated alternative music station. While his primary audience is other
students at his college, notice how Elsten provides enough
background to make his profile understandable and appealing to a general readership.*

"Thirty seconds!" 1

Studio A, the nerve center of radio station KSDT, is abuzz 2
with action. Student-DJ Shane Nesbitt frantically flips through
a pile of records, looking for a song to put on the air. His part-
ner, Nathan Wilson, frets at the control board, listening to the
current song, "Chew Me, Chew Me," by a band called Intense
Mutilation. The song is almost over, and Nesbitt and Wilson
have nothing ready to go on afterwards.

A cry of triumph rings out as Nesbitt finds his record of 3
choice, the Pogues' "If I Should Fall from Grace with God."
Quickly, the DJs scramble to cue up a song. Then, Wilson
skillfully starts the Pogues' song at low volume, bringing it
up as Intense Mutilation fades into the distance. The segue is
complete; the crisis is over. Leaning back on his stool, Wilson smoothes his hair and laughs.

"Whew!" he explains, "Business as usual. I just hope some- 4
one is listening."

While student volunteers strive to bring alternative radio 5
to UCSD, most of the campus is unable to tune in. KSDT operates without an FCC license, so it is unable to broadcast
over standard airwaves. The station instead sends its signal
over "cable radio," which works similarly to cable television.
The problem is, almost nobody has cable radio. On campus,
the Revelle and Muir dormitories are able to pick up KSDT
on carrier current at 540 AM, but even then reception is er-
ratic at best.

The obvious question then is, why broadcast at all? 6

"For the fun of it," responds Nesbitt. "On cable radio, we 7
can be less careful and do more crazy things. We can play a
crude rap song and then follow it with a jazz number, or, if
we want, we can just talk for twenty minutes. On regular
radio, we couldn't do that."

"Here there is no pressure," Wilson agrees. "If we screw   8
up and knock the needle off the record, or if we play a lousy
song or say something rude, no one is going to call and complain." Then he adds, "It's kind of a bummer to think that
throughout your whole show, there might not be anyone out
there at all."

The lobby of KSDT is decorated in a fashion that befits al-   9
ternative radio. Posters and stickers, many of bands that
have long since faded out of memory, decorate the walls.
One message stands out from the lobby door, a bumper
sticker reading, "Still Crazy After All These Beers." Nearby, a
sticker for the band Elvis Christ is pasted on a file cabinet.
There, the King does his pelvis thrusts on a crucifix.

There is an old couch in the lobby, one that looks like it   10
has rested many a posterior. Indeed, the sofa looks like it
was purchased from a garage sale—in 1978. The woman at
the lobby desk, when asked, said that she had no idea when
the couch was last cleaned. She did, however, suggest not
rolling on the cushions. "The cockroaches will wake up," she
smiled.

A striking feature of KSDT is its vast collection of records.   11
Over fifteen thousand vinyls, at last count, were stored in
the station library. With modern musical technology being
the way it is, it seems surprising that vinyl records are in use
at all. According to DJ Scott Garrison, however, a lot of stuff
they play is released by minor-label recording companies,
which can't afford to produce CDs.

From a newcomer's standpoint, it seems curious that so   12
few steps have been taken to bring the station to the listeners. After all, KSDT has been in operation for over fifteen
years.

One of the "key people" that keeps the station alive is gen-   13
eral manager Steve Branin. Branin remarks that one of
KSDT's main problems is in its power structure. "The management has been so weak for so many years now that the
DJs have taken over," Branin says. "Now, it seems that we
can't get the DJs to follow any rules at all. We ask them to
play promos [promotions of upcoming events], and they
don't. We ask them to pay quarterly dues [five dollars], and
most DJs don't. Our hands are tied."

With KSDT being primarily a volunteer effort (only the   14
general manager, assistant manager, and secretary are
paid), enforcement of rules becomes difficult. "I've tried sus-
pending a DJ's air privileges," Branin says, "but then the person will just quit. We have a hard enough time getting air
time filled as it is. We need all the DJs we can get."

Branin has attempted this year to start the procedure to   15
obtain an FCC license, but he admits that the station is "at
least five years away from going public."

Assistant manager Brad Darlow feels that the wait will be   16
much longer. "There is no way that KSDT will have an FCC license in the next five years," he says, "because people here
are unwilling to give up any of their freedoms. If we got on
public radio, DJs wouldn't be able to play whatever they
wanted, or to skip their shows. The disorganization here is
incredible, and it's not going to change."

Darlow recalls a weekend afternoon when he walked into   17
the station and found no one around. "Whoever the last DJ
was had left, and the CD that he had going over the air was
skipping, making this horrendous sound. It sounded sort of
like a car engine trying to turn over, but louder. I turned it
off, but who knows how long the station was putting that
sound over the airwaves."

News director Dan Schuck, however, feels that too much   18
is being made of the station's problems. "Sure, a lot of stuff
that could get done around here doesn't," Schuck says, "but
remember, one of the main reasons this place is here is so
people can learn something about radio."

This attitude is shared by several people at KSDT. While   19
some station members are concerned with increasing the
profile of the station on campus, many are pleased just to be
around KSDT's progressive atmosphere or to admire the station's impressive, if eclectic, record library.

"Did you know that we have nine Culture Club albums?"   20
Wilson says. "There are so many obscure albums here, I
could spend years just trying to listen."

Along with the over eleven thousand records in the sta-   21
tion's main library, KSDT has a second room filled with over
four thousand old, unpopular, or little-known albums. This
collection is known affectionately as "Dinosaur Rock."

"This place is a music lover's dream come true," Nesbitt   22
says. "One of the reasons I became a DJ was just so I could
keep on top of what's happening in the current music
scene."

Indeed, one of the best-organized departments at the sta-   23
tion is the music department. Music director Vicky Kim receives albums from across the country every day, sometimes before commercial stations do. "It's funny to see a
band go big on 91X [a San Diego commercial station] that we
have been playing here for a long time," Kim remarked. "The
DJs there will say, 'Here's a brand new band,' and I just have
to laugh."

The situation at KSDT will soon come to a head. Earlier   24
this year, UCSD Associated Students president John Edson
mentioned that if KSDT could not become an FCC licensed
station, it could be shut down to avoid its high cost of operation. Other people in the campus administration have questioned the intelligence of spending the $21,000 per year for a
station that, for all intents and purposes, is nothing but a
training lab.

General manager Branin remains optimistic, however. "I   25
think that once everything gets settled, KSDT could be a real
asset to the campus, as well as to all of San Diego. It would
bring a higher profile to UCSD and would give the students
something to identify with."

Schuck adds, "It would be great if UCSD students driving   26
in to the campus could tune into the station for campus
news instead of having to rely on the *Guardian.* That's my
dream: the day will come when the *Guardian* has to use *us* as
a news source."

Finally, Shane Nesbitt adds, "I don't really care what hap-   27
pens in a couple of years. I'm having fun doing a show right
now."

The Pogues are done playing. Nathan Wilson talks about   28
his romantic problems, while Nesbitt goes off in search of an
industrial band called Sandy Duncan's Eye. The music continues, and the station continues, into the dead of the night.

READING FOR MEANING

Write to create meanings for Elsten's profile of a college radio station.

START MAKING MEANING

Begin by summarizing what you learned about the operations of
KSDT. (See pp. 462–463 for help with summarizing.) Continue by writing
about anything else in the reading or in your experience that contributes
to your understanding of the essay.

IF YOU ARE STUCK

If you cannot write at least a page, consider writing about

- the frustration of not knowing whether anyone is paying attention to
you (like that experienced by the DJs or your own experience as a
speaker or writer).

- the conflict between the desire to do your own thing and the responsibility that comes with access to a medium like radio.

- the idea that because DJs are volunteers, "enforcement of rules becomes difficult" (paragraphs 13–14).

- the definition of *alternative radio* based on Elsten's account and your own observations.

READING LIKE A WRITER
CONVEYING AN INTERPRETATION THROUGH IMPLICATION

In this chapter, you have seen various ways observational writers interpret and evaluate their subjects. Tamar Lewin in her observation of Houston day-care centers states her interpretation explicitly. It is easy to find several sentences where she offers her own commentary on the scene and the action, telling us unmistakably what the point is. By contrast, Craig Elsten, like the author of "Soup," conveys his interpretation of the college radio station primarily through implication. This activity will help you analyze the way Elsten implies his interpretation through descriptive detail, dialogue, and the narrative of what happens and does not happen at the radio station. It also invites you to compare Elsten's implicitness to Lewin's explicitness.

ANALYZE

1. *Reread* the essay and *mark* any words or sentences in which the writer comments directly on the issues that KSDT faces.

2. *Note* any places where the writer's evaluation of the radio station and the people who work there is conveyed indirectly—for example, through narrated events, dialogue, descriptive detail, the title and subtitle.

WRITE

Write several sentences describing your impression of KSDT and the author's attitude toward it. *Give examples* to show what kinds of things Elsten says directly and what he says indirectly about the station and the people working there.

COMPARE

If you have done the Reading Like a Writer activity following Tamar Lewin's essay observing day-care centers (pp. 94–98), *compare* Craig Elsten's strategy of conveying an interpretation through implication to Lewin's strategy of commenting directly on the subject. *Write* a few more sentences explaining what you have learned from comparing the strategies in these two essays.

CONSIDERING IDEAS FOR YOUR OWN WRITING

If you were to write about a student-run organization on your campus, which one might you choose? With the help of other students or using a published list of student organizations, make a list of campus organizations. Choose two or three to consider carefully as possible subjects for an observational essay. What would you expect to learn about these organizations? What might interest your readers about each one? What would you want to learn in a preliminary visit to each organization to decide about which one to write? You might profile the local office for a national organization, such as Big Brothers of America, Amnesty International, Habitat for Humanity, or Meals on Wheels. You can find listings of community service organizations in the phone book, on the Internet, or through a librarian.

Alternatively, you might consider observing individuals who volunteer their time and energy to help others in the community. For example, you could choose someone who coaches a sports team, tutors children, visits senior citizens, or helps out in the hospital.

Reviewing What Makes Observational Essays Effective

In this chapter, you have been learning how to read observational essays for meaning and how to read them like a writer. Before going on to write an observational essay, pause here to review and contemplate what you have learned about the elements of effective observational writing.

Analyze
Choose one reading in this chapter that seems to you especially effective. Before rereading the selection, *jot* down one or two qualities you expect of a good observational essay.

Reread the essay, adding further annotations about what makes this particular essay so effective. Begin by considering the essay's purpose and how well it achieves that purpose for its intended readers. Then focus on how well the essay

- details places and people.

- organizes the observations.

- engages and informs readers.

- conveys an impression of its subject.

Your instructor may ask you to complete this activity on your own or to work with a small group of students who have chosen the same essay. If you work with others, allow enough time initially for all group members to read the selection thoughtfully and to add their annotations. Then discuss as a group what makes the essay effective. Take notes on your discussion. One student in your group should then report to the class what the group has learned about the effectiveness of observational writing. If you are working individually, write up what you have learned from your analysis.

Write

Write at least one page, justifying your choice of this essay as an example of effective observational writing. Assume that your readers—your instructor and classmates—have read the selection but will not remember many details about it. They also might not remember it as especially successful. Therefore, you will need to *refer* to details and specific passages in the essay as you explain how it works and *justify* your evaluation of its effectiveness. You need not argue that it is the best essay in the chapter or that it is flawless, only that it is, in your view, a strong example of the genre.

A GUIDE TO WRITING OBSERVATIONAL ESSAYS

The readings in this chapter have shown you how writers of observational essays present unfamiliar places and people. You have seen that writers collect large amounts of information and ideas from visits and interviews, which must be sorted, organized, and integrated into a readable draft. This Guide to Writing is designed to help you through the stages of invention, drafting, revising, and editing, as you gather the material you will need and solve any problems you encounter as you write.

INVENTION

The following invention activities will help you choose a subject, plan and make observations, and decide on an impression you want your essay to convey to your readers.

Choosing a Subject

List the subjects you are interested in observing. To make the best possible choice and have alternatives in case the subject you choose requires too much time or is inaccessible, you should have a list of several possible subjects. You might already have a subject in mind, possibly one you listed for the Considering Ideas for Your Own Writing activities following the readings in this chapter. The suggestions that follow will help you think of other possible topics:

People

- Anyone doing work that you might want to do—city council member, police officer, lab technician, computer programmer, attorney, salesperson

- Anyone with an unusual job or hobby—dog trainer, private detective, ham radio operator, race car driver, novelist

- A campus personality—coach, distinguished teacher, newspaper editor, oldest or youngest student

- Someone recently recognized for community service or achievement

Places

- Small-claims court, consumer fraud office, city planner's office

- Body-building gym, weight-reduction clinic, martial arts school

- Hospital emergency room, campus health center, hospice, psychiatric unit

- Internet chat room, game parlor, or bulletin board

- Recycling center, airport control tower, theater, museum, sports arena

Activities

- Tutoring, registering voters, rehearsing for a play, repairing a car

- Unconventional sports event—marathon, dog's frisbee tournament, college bowl

- Special courses—rock climbing, folk dancing, dog training, truck driving

Select a topic about which you are genuinely curious. Be sure to check on accessibility, requesting permission to visit one or more times to make detailed observations and to interview your subject. Above all, choose a subject that interests you—and that you think will appeal to your readers.

Researching Your Subject

The writing and research activities that follow will enable you to gather information and ideas about your subject.

MAKING A SCHEDULE. *Set up a tentative schedule for your observational and interview visits.* Figure out first the amount of time you have to complete your essay. Then determine the scope of your project—one-time observation, interview plus follow-up, or multiple observations and interviews. Decide what visits you will need to make, whom you will need to interview, and what library or Internet work you might want to do. Estimate the time necessary for each, knowing you might need to schedule more time than anticipated.

Make phone calls to schedule visits. When you write down your appointments, be sure to include names, addresses, phone numbers, dates and times, and any special arrangements you have made for a visit. Consult Appendix Two, Strategies for Research and Documentation, for helpful guidelines on observing, interviewing, and taking notes.

EXPLORING READERS' AND YOUR OWN PRECONCEPTIONS. *Write for ten minutes about your readers' as well as your own assumptions and expectations.* For example, ask questions about your readers: Who are they? What are they likely to think about the subject? What would they want to know about it? Also reflect: Why do you want to research this subject? What more familiar subject does it resemble? How does it differ? What aspects of it do you expect to be interesting or entertaining?

VISITING A PLACE. *During your visit, take notes on what you observe.* Do not try to impose order on your notes at this stage, simply record whatever you notice. Pay special attention to sensory details that you can draw on later to describe the place and people. Appendix 2 provides useful guidelines for observing a place, taking notes on the spot, supplementing your notes later, and reflecting on what you have seen.

INTERVIEWING A PERSON. *Prepare for the interview by writing out some preliminary questions.* But do not be afraid of abandoning your script during the interview. Listen carefully to what is said and ask follow-up questions. Take notes, and if you like and your subject agrees, you may also tape-record the interview. See Appendix Two for guidelines to help you plan and conduct an interview.

GATHERING INFORMATION. *If you do background reading, take careful notes and keep accurate bibliographic records of your sources.* Try to pick up relevant fliers, brochures, or reports at the place you observe. In addition, you might want to do some research on the Internet or in your college library. (See Appendix Two for help with Internet and library research.)

CONSIDERING YOUR PURPOSE. *Write for ten minutes about the impression of the subject you want to convey to your readers.* After you have researched your subject, you may arrive at a tentative idea about its significance. What makes it worth observing? Your answer to this question might change as you write, but a preliminary answer will give your writing a direction to follow, or what journalists commonly call an *angle* on the subject. This angle will help you choose what to include as well as what to emphasize in your draft. Use the following questions to help clarify the impression you want your essay to convey.

- What visual images or other sensory impressions of the subject stand out in your memory? Think about the feelings these images evoke in you. If they evoke contradictory feelings, consider how you could use them to convey to readers the complexity of your feelings about the place, people, or activities you observed.

- What is most surprising about your observations? Compare the preconceptions you listed earlier with what you actually saw or heard.

- What interests you most about the people you interviewed? Compare the direct observations you made about them with the indirect or secondhand information you gathered about them.

- From your observations, what can you now infer about the society to which your subject belongs? Think of the subject as an anthropologist or archaeologist might, as if the subject were from a different culture or time period.

DRAFTING

The following guidelines will help you set goals for your draft and plan its organization.

Setting Goals

Establishing goals before you draft your essay can make your writing more focused and confident. Ask yourself the following questions now, and keep them in mind as you draft. They will help you maintain your focus while drafting as well as recall how the writers you have read in this chapter tried to achieve similar goals.

- *How can I help my readers picture the subject?* In addition to describing visual details, should I evoke other senses? Can I evoke the senses of taste, as the author of "Soup" does, touch and sound, as in Glickman's essay, or smell, as Coyne does? Should I characterize people by their clothes, facial expressions, and dialogue, as McPhee and Coyne do? Should I use surprising metaphors or similes, as the author of "Soup" does in describing Yeganeh's "working like a demon alchemist"?

- *How can I engage as well as inform my readers?* Should I focus on dramatic interactions among people, as McPhee does? Should I begin with a dramatic moment, like Lewin and Elsten do, a poignant image, like Coyne does, a surprising statement, like in "Soup"? Should I present information through dialogue, as in "Soup," or in my own voice, as in the Lewin and Coyne essays?

- *How should I organize my observations?* Should I organize the observations topically in groups of related information, as the author of "Soup," Lewin, and Elsten do? Or should I arrange them in a chronological narrative order, as McPhee, Glickman, and Coyne do?

- *How can I convey the impression I want to leave with my readers?* Should I make my interpretation of the subject explicit by saying what I think and feel, as Lewin and Coyne do? Or should I try to convey an impression indirectly—by my choice of words, descriptive details, and the story, like the author of "Soup," McPhee, Glickman, and Elsten do?

Organizing Your Draft

With your goals in mind, reread the notes you took about the place and people, and decide how to organize them—grouped into topics or put in chronological order? If you think a topical organization would work best, try grouping your observations and naming the topic of each group. If you think narrating what happened would help you organize your observations, make a time line and note where the information would go. You might want to try different kinds of outlines before settling on a plan and drafting your essay.

Writers who use a narrative structure usually follow a simple, straightforward chronology. Coyne and Glickman, for example, present activities observed over a limited period—a few hours or a few days—in the order in which they occurred. Writers may also punctuate their main narrative with additional events that occurred on other occasions: McPhee, for example, recounts what happened over a few hours at the Brooklyn farmers' market while also weaving in other stories about the market that took place at different times. Glickman inserts details about river kayaking into his narrative, and Coyne provides a lot of background information about the two families she juxtaposes.

Writers who organize their observations topically must limit the number of topics they cover. Lewin, for example, focuses the child-care debate on the kind and quality of interaction between caregivers and children. The author of "Soup" focuses on Yeganeh's ideas about soup and his attitudes toward customers.

READING A DRAFT CRITICALLY

Getting a critical reading of your draft will help you see how to improve it. Your instructor may schedule class time for reading drafts, or you may want to ask a classmate or a tutor in the writing center to read your draft. Ask your reader to use the following guidelines and write out a response for you to consult during your revision.

Read for a First Impression

1. Read the draft without stopping to annotate or comment, and then write two or three sentences giving your general impression.

2. Identify one aspect of the draft that seems to you particularly effective.

Read Again to Suggest Improvements

1. Suggest ways of making descriptions of places and people more vivid.

   - Find a description of a place, and suggest what details could be added to objects in the scene (location, size, color, and shape) or what sensory information (look, sound, smell, taste, and touch) could be included to help you picture the place.

- Find a description of a person, and indicate what else you would like to know about the person's dress, facial expression, tone of voice, and gestures.

- Find direct dialogue, and note if any of the quotes could be paraphrased or summarized without losing impact.

- Find passages where additional quotations could enhance the drama or help bring a person to life.

2. Recommend ways of making the organization clearer or more effective.

   - If the essay is organized chronologically, look for passages where the narrative seems to wander pointlessly or leaves out important information. Also suggest cues that could be added to indicate time sequence (*initially, then, afterwards*).

   - If the essay is organized topically, mark topics that get too much or too little attention, transitions between topics that need to be added or clarified, and topics that should be placed elsewhere.

   - If the essay alternates narration with topical information, suggest where transitions could be made smoother or sequencing could be improved.

3. Suggest how the essay could be made more engaging and informative.

   - If the essay seems boring or you feel overwhelmed by too much information, suggest how the information could alternate with vivid description or lively narration. Also consider whether any of the information could be cut or simplified.

   - List any pressing questions you still have about the subject.

   - If the essay seems abstract, suggest where definitions, examples, or specific descriptive details could be added.

4. Suggest ways to make the overall impression clearer and the essay more coherent.

   - Let the writer know your overall impression of the subject and what you find especially interesting about the subject.

   - Point out any contradictions between what the writer explicitly says or implicitly suggests and your overall impression of the subject.

   - Think of the subject as an anthropologist or archaeologist might, as if it were from a different culture or time period, and tell the writer what you infer about the society.

REVISING

This section offers suggestions for revising your draft, suggestions that will remind you of the possibilities for developing a vivid, informative observational essay. Revising means reenvisioning your draft, trying to see it in a new way, given your purpose and readers.

The biggest mistake you can make in revising is to focus initially on words or sentences. Instead, first try to see your draft as a whole in order to assess its likely impact on your readers. Think imaginatively and boldly about cutting unconvincing material, adding new material, and moving material around. Your computer makes even drastic revisions easy, but you still need to make the effort and decisions that will improve your draft.

Keeping in mind any advice you have received from a critical reader, analyze your draft. Reread carefully, noting which parts need revising and what specific changes you could make. The following suggestions will help you solve problems and strengthen your essay.

To Make Your Description of Places and People More Vivid

- Cull your notes for additional details you could supply about people and objects in the scene.

- If your notes are sparse, consider revisiting the place to add to your observations, or try imagining yourself back at the place and write about what you see.

- Consider where you could add description based on senses other than sight.

- Identify where a simile or metaphor would enrich your description.

- Review dialogue to make sure you directly quote only that language which conveys personality; paraphrase or summarize other dialogue.

To Make the Organization Clearer and More Effective

- If the essay is organized chronologically, keep the narrative focused and well-paced, adding time markers to clarify the sequence of events.

- If the essay is organized topically, make sure it moves smoothly from topic to topic, adding transitions where necessary.

- If the essay alternates narration with topical information, make sure the sequence is clear and easy to follow.

To Make the Essay More Engaging and Informative

- If the essay bores or overwhelms readers, cut information that is obvious or extraneous, and consider alternating information with descriptive or narrative passages.

- If readers have questions about the subject, try to answer them.

- If the essay seems abstract, provide specific definitions, examples, and details.

To Strengthen the Impression Your Essay Conveys

- Examine any contradictions between what you say and how you present the subject to deepen and clarify your interpretation.

- If readers get an impression of the subject you did not expect, consider what in your essay may have given them that impression, and either cut it or use it to enrich your interpretation.

EDITING AND PROOFREADING

After you have revised your essay, be sure to spend some time checking for errors in usage, punctuation, and mechanics. If you have been keeping a list of errors you frequently make, begin by checking your draft against this list. Ask someone else to proofread your essay before you print out a copy for your instructor.

From our research on student writing, we know that observational essays tend to have errors in the punctuation of quotations. Check a writer's guidebook or handbook for guidance on when to enclose a comma, period, question mark, or other punctuation inside or outside of quotation marks. Also make a list of verbs you can include in signal phrases ("he *remarked*," "she *said*") to avoid repetition and add specificity to your dialogue.

Reflecting on What You Have Learned

In this chapter, you have read critically several observational essays and have written one of your own. To better remember what you have learned, pause now to reflect on the reading and writing activities you completed in this chapter.

1. *Write* a page or so assessing your learning. Begin by describing what you are most pleased with in your essay. Then explain what you think contributed to your achievement. Be specific about this contribution.

Continued

- If it was something you learned from the readings, *indicate* which readings and specifically what you learned from them.

- If it came from your invention writing, interviews, or observations, *point out* what helped you most.

- If you got good advice from a critical reader, *explain* exactly how the person helped you—perhaps by helping you understand a particular problem in your draft or by adding a new dimension to your writing.

2. Now *reflect* more generally on the genre of observational writing. *Consider* some of the following questions: As a reader of observational essays, how aware are you of the writer's perspective on the subject? Which writers, of the essays you read in this chapter, would you call objective observers? Which writers make their points of view on the subject most explicit? How can you characterize the point of view in your own observational essay?

Reflection

Reflective writing, like autobiography and observation, comes out of experience. In autobiography and observation, the central aim is to show specific incidents, people, and places—not to tell readers what to think or to draw larger generalizations. Autobiographers and observational writers often suggest larger meanings in what they show, but they seldom explore such meanings directly and in detail. In reflection, however, the focus shifts from showing to telling. Writers present something they did, saw, overheard, or read in order to tell us what they think it suggests about people and society.

The range of topics for reflection is wide. One writer in this chapter reflects on her reluctance to tell people that she is deaf. Another reflects on the difficulties of raising a son, and yet another on young women's obsession with weight and body shape. Many reflective essays explore social customs and problems (such as dating and child rearing), virtues and vices (such as pride, jealousy, and compassion), or hopes and fears (such as the desire for intimacy and the fear of it).

These subjects may seem far-reaching, but writers of reflection have relatively modest goals. They do not attempt to exhaust their subjects, nor do they set themselves up as experts. They simply try out their ideas. One early meaning of the word *essay* was "to try out." From the very first reflective essays by French author Michel de Montaigne in 1580, the essay has been regarded as an exercise in the art of trying out ideas from a personal perspective. Reflective essays have always been short, informal, tentative, exploratory, inconclusive.

Reflective writing is enjoyable to write and to read because it is inventive. Successful reflective writing enables us, as readers and writers, to see even the most familiar things in new ways. Avoiding the obvious, resisting the impulse to moralize, revealing a contradiction, finding fresh language to revitalize old truths, taking a critical view of what we typically accept as true—these are some of the characteristics of the best reflective essays.

The writer of the reflective essay typically addresses readers directly and openly. The writer seems to be sitting across from the reader, talking about what happened and what it might mean. A conversational tone characterizes the reflective essay, and it can be quite seductive.

As you read, discuss, and write about the essays in this chapter, you will learn a good deal about reflective writing. You should also get ideas for a reflective essay of your own, based perhaps on the suggestions for writing that follow each reading. As you work through the selections in this chapter, keep in mind the following assignment, which sets out the goals for writing a reflective essay.

THE WRITING ASSIGNMENT

Reflection

Write a reflective essay based on something you experienced or observed. Describe this occasion vividly so that readers can understand what happened and will care about what you have to say. In reflecting on the particular occasion, explore both your own values and society's dominant attitudes. Reflective writing is like a conversation—you are writing not just for yourself but to share your thoughts with others, to stimulate their thinking as well as your own.

REFLECTIVE WRITING SITUATIONS

Reflective essays are written on all kinds of subjects and in many different contexts. The following examples suggest this variety of topics and situations:

- A former football player writes a reflective essay based on his experience playing professional sports. He recalls a specific occasion when he sustained a serious injury but continued to play because he knew that playing with pain was regarded as a badge of honor, a sign of manliness and dedication. He recalls that he had played many times before with minor injuries, but that this time he feared he might be doing irreparable damage to himself. As he reflects on what happened, he considers whose interests were really being served.

- Writing for a political science course, a student reflects on her first experience voting in a presidential election. She begins by describing a recent conversation with friends about how people decide to vote for one presidential candidate over another. They agreed that most people they know seem to base their decisions on trivial, even bizarre, reasons, rather than on a candidate's experience, voting record in previous offices, character, or even campaign promises. For example, one friend knew someone who voted for a presidential candidate who reminded her of her grandfather, while another friend knew someone who voted against a candidate because he did not like the way the candidate dressed. The writer then reflects on the humorous as well as the serious implications of voting decisions like these.

- A first-year college student in a composition course reflects on a performance of his high-school chorus that far surpassed their expectations. He describes their trip to the statewide competition and their anxious rehearsals before the performance. Their teacher-conductor seemed tense; they complained that their teacher had chosen unnecessarily difficult music. Then the performance began: The student describes their unexpected feelings of confidence, their precision and control, and the exuberance of the performance. He contrasts this memorable occasion with examples of another chorus performance and other personal experiences that turned out worse than expected, trying to discover the secret of the unexpected success. He tries out the possibility that luck, fear of embarrassment, affection for their teacher, or the excitement of a trip to the state capital led to their success. Then he acknowledges the possibility that they did so well simply because they had rehearsed especially attentively for weeks because the music was so challenging. Finally, he gives up trying to establish a reason for their success and instead makes a few general statements about the special pleasures of success in groups like choruses, orchestras, soccer teams, and drama groups, where cooperation and precise timing are essential.

A GUIDE TO READING REFLECTIVE ESSAYS

This guide introduces you to the reflective essay, beginning with a selection by a woman writer reflecting on her deafness and on a hearing aid that changed her life at age thirty. First, you will read the essay for meaning, seeking to understand the writer's experience, to follow her reflections, and to discover your own ideas about deafness and other disabilities. Then, you will read the essay like a writer, analyzing the strategies that make this selection and reflective writing in general vivid and engaging.

NICOLLETTE TOUSSAINT

Hearing the Sweetest Songs

> *This reflective essay by Nicollette Toussaint was pub-*
> *lished in 1994 in* Newsweek, *a weekly news magazine that*
> *occasionally publishes unsolicited personal essays such as*
> *this one.* Newsweek's *broad national readership includes*
> *college students.*
>
> *In this essay, Toussaint writes about her deafness, rela-*
> *tions with family and friends, and thoughts about disabili-*
> *ties. As you read, annotate anything that strikes you as inter-*
> *esting or effective in Toussaint's reflections.*

Every year when I was a child, a man brought a big, black, 1
squeaking machine to school. When he discovered I couldn't
hear all his peeps and squeaks, he would get very excited.
The nurse would draw a chart with a deep canyon in it. Then
I would listen to the squeaks two or three times, while the
adults—who were all acting very, very nice—would watch
me raise my hand. Sometimes I couldn't tell whether I heard
the squeaks or just imagined them, but I liked being the center of attention.

My parents said I lost my hearing to pneumonia as a baby; 2
but I knew I hadn't *lost* anything. None of my parts had
dropped off. Nothing had changed: if I wanted to listen to
Beethoven, I could put my head between the speakers and
turn the dial up to 7. I could hear jets at the airport a block
away. I could hear my mom when she was in the same
room—if I wanted to. I could even hear my cat purr if I put
my good ear right on top of him.

I wasn't aware of *not* hearing until I began to wear a hear- 3
ing aid at the age of 30. It shattered my peace: shoes creak-
ing, papers crackling, pencils tapping, phones ringing, refrig-
erators humming, people cracking knuckles, clearing throats
and blowing noses! Cars, bikes, dogs, cats, kids all seemed to
appear from nowhere and fly right at me.

I was constantly startled, unnerved, agitated—exhausted. 4
I felt as though inquisitorial Nazis in an old World War II film
were burning the side of my head with a merciless white
spotlight. Under that onslaught, I had to break down and
confess: I couldn't hear. Suddenly, I began to discover many
things I couldn't do.

I couldn't identify sounds. One afternoon, while lying on 5
my side watching a football game on TV, I kept hearing a
noise that sounded like my cat playing with a flexible-spring

doorstop. I checked, but the cat was asleep. Finally, I happened to lift my head as the noise occurred. Heard through my good ear, the metallic buzz turned out to be the referee's whistle.

I couldn't tell where sounds came from. I couldn't find my phone under the blizzard of papers on my desk. The more it rang, the deeper I dug. I shoveled mounds of paper onto the floor and finally had to track it down by following the cord from the wall. . . .

For the first time, I felt unequal, disadvantaged and disabled. Now that I had something to compare, I knew that I *had* lost something: not just my hearing, but my independence and my sense of wholeness. I had always hated to be seen as inferior, so I never mentioned my lack of hearing. Unlike a wheelchair or a white cane, my disability doesn't announce itself. For most of my life, I chose to pass as abled, and I thought I did it quite well.

But after I got the hearing aid, a business friend said, "You know, Nicollette, you think you get away with not hearing, but you don't. Sometimes in meetings you answer the wrong question. People don't know you can't hear, so they think you're daydreaming, eccentric, stupid—or just plain rude. It would be better to just tell them."

I wondered about that then, and I still do. If I tell, I risk being seen as *un*able rather than *dis*abled. Sometimes, when I say I can't hear, the waiter will turn to my companion and say, "What does she want?" as though I have lost my power of speech.

If I tell, people may see *only* my disability. Once someone is labeled "deaf," "crippled," "mute" or "aged," that's too often all they are. I'm a writer, a painter, a slapdash housekeeper, a gardener who grows wondrous roses; my hearing is just part of the whole. It's a tender part, and you should handle it with care. But like most people with a disability, I don't mind if you ask about it.

In fact, you should ask, because it's an important part of me, something my friends see as part of my character. My friend Anne always rests a hand on my elbow in parking lots, since several times, drivers who assume that I hear them have nearly run me over. When I hold my head at a certain angle, my husband, Mason, will say, "It's a plane" or "It's a siren." And my mother loves to laugh about the things I *thought* I heard: last week I was told that "the Minotaurs in the garden are getting out of hand." I imagined capering bull-men and I was disappointed to learn that all we had in the garden were overgrown "baby tears."

Not hearing can be funny, or frustrating. And once in a   12
while, it can be the cause of something truly transcendent.
One morning at the shore I was listening to the ocean when
Mason said, "Hear the bird?" What bird? I listened hard until
I heard a faint, unbirdlike, croaking sound. If he hadn't mentioned it, I would never have noticed it. As I listened, slowly I
began to hear—or perhaps imagine—a distant song. Did I
really hear it? Or just hear in my heart what he shared with
me? I don't care. Songs imagined are as sweet as songs
heard, and songs shared are sweeter still.

That sharing is what I want for all of us. We're all just   13
temporarily abled, and every one of us, if we live long
enough, will become disabled in some way. Those of us
who have gotten there first can tell you how to cope with
phones and alarm clocks. About ways of holding a book,
opening a door and leaning on a crutch all at the same time.
And what it's like to give up in despair on Thursday, then
begin all over again on Friday, because there's no other
choice—and because the roses are beginning to bud in the
garden.

These are conversations we all should have, and it's not   14
that hard to begin. Just let me see your lips when you speak.
Stay in the same room. Don't shout. And ask what you want
to know.

READING FOR MEANING

Write to create meanings for Toussaint's reflections on deafness and
disability.

START MAKING MEANING

Begin by considering Toussaint's three reflections (in paragraphs 7,
9–10, and 12–14) and identifying the one reflection that seems to you the
most interesting and insightful. Write a few sentences explaining your
choice. Continue by writing about anything else in the essay or in your experience that contributes to your understanding of the writer's reflections.

IF YOU ARE STUCK

If you cannot write at least a page, consider writing about

- what you find humorous, frustrating, or "transcendent" (as Toussaint
  puts it in paragraph 12) about the writer's experience of deafness.

- Toussaint's feelings about her disability (paragraphs 7, 9, and 10).

- Toussaint's idea that the disabled and "temporarily abled" should share and converse (paragraphs 13 and 14).

- your personal experience with a disability or the experience of someone close to you, comparing it with Toussaint's.

READING LIKE A WRITER

This section leads you through an analysis of Toussaint's reflective writing strategies: *presenting the particular occasion, developing the reflections, maintaining topical coherence,* and *engaging readers.* Each strategy is described briefly and followed by a critical reading and writing task to help you see how Toussaint uses that particular strategy in her essay.

Consider this section a writer's introduction to reflective essay writing. You will learn still more about how writers use reflective writing strategies from the activities following the other selections later in this chapter. The Guide to Writing Reflective Essays at the end of the chapter will suggest how you can use these strategies in your own essay.

Presenting the Particular Occasion

The particular occasion is the main experience that started the writer thinking. Writers may describe this occasion at length, or they may just give a quick sketch to help readers grasp the point. The key in both cases is to present the occasion in a vivid and suggestive way, encouraging readers to want to know more about the writer's thoughts on the experience. To succeed at this, writers rely on the same strategies you practiced in Chapter Two (Autobiography) and Chapter Three (Observation): describing the scene and people through visual details, movement and gesture, and dialogue, as well as building a well-shaped and carefully paced narrative.

Toussaint's essay opens with two specific occasions, separated by many years: The first is an early recollection of school hearing tests (paragraph 1); the second focuses on what happened when Toussaint began wearing a hearing aid at age thirty (paragraphs 3–6). These two occasions for reflection stand out, offering vivid visual and aural details. Here, we focus on the aural (sound) details in Toussaint's reflections on the two occasions. Keep in mind that one of Toussaint's purposes is likely to contrast the experience of being tested as a child with the shock of wearing a hearing aid as an adult.

ANALYZE

1. *Reread* the two occasions for Toussaint's reflections (paragraphs 1 and 3–6) and *underline* the words and phrases that name or suggest sounds.

2. *Analyze* the sounds you have underlined. *Notice* the variety and types of sounds Toussaint identifies.

WRITE

Write several sentences describing how Toussaint uses sounds to present the occasions for her reflections and evaluating how successful her strategy is. What effect do these sounds have on you at the beginning of the essay? How do they prepare you for the reflections that follow?

Developing the Reflections

An occasion introduces a subject, and reflections explore the subject. Reflections include both ideas about self and society and development or exploration of these ideas. What does it mean to explore or develop ideas? It means simply to examine the ideas inventively in any way that illuminates them; for example, by giving examples, posing questions, or comparing and contrasting. In addition, the writer of a reflective essay might examine an idea by placing it in a surprising context—saying what it is not, associating it with other ideas, speculating about where it came from, trying to apply it, taking it seriously or taking it lightly. For example, in paragraph 10, Toussaint asserts this idea: "Once someone is labeled 'deaf,' 'crippled,' 'mute' or 'aged,' that's too often all they are." Then she develops the idea: "I'm a writer, a painter, a slapdash housekeeper, a gardener who grows wondrous roses; my hearing is just part of the whole. It's a tender part and you should handle it with care."

ANALYZE

1. *Look* again at paragraphs 12 and 13, each of which opens with a two-sentence idea about deafness or its implications. *Underline* these ideas. Then *evaluate* the two ideas within the context of the whole essay. How insightful or obvious do these ideas seem to you as one of Toussaint's intended readers? To what extent were you prepared for them through the occasions and the reflections that precede these ideas?

2. *Notice* that the ideas that open paragraphs 12 and 13 are followed by examples. *Reread* these examples. *Consider* whether they seem appropriate, interesting, and detailed enough to develop the ideas.

WRITE

Write several sentences explaining what you have learned about how Toussaint develops her reflections. *Comment* on both the ideas and examples the writer uses to illustrate the reflections.

Maintaining Topical Coherence

Because reflective essays explore ideas on a topic by turning them this way and that, examining them first from one perspective and then from another, and sometimes piling up examples to illustrate the ideas, such essays may seem rambling, with one idea or example added to another in a casual way. It is not always clear where the essay is going, and the essay may not seem to end conclusively. This apparently casual plan or organization is deceptive, however, because in fact the writer has arranged the parts carefully to give the appearance of a mind playfully at work on an idea. This special kind of coherence in reflective essays is called *topical coherence,* where *topical* refers to the topic or subject of the essay and *coherence* to a reader's sense that all the parts of an essay seem relevant to the topic. While each new idea or example may turn the essay in an unexpected new direction, it should somehow seem connected to what has gone before and seem to lead without a break to the next idea or example.

ANALYZE

1. *Reread* paragraphs 7–14, where the reflections are concentrated. As you read, *underline* the cues at the beginning of each paragraph that connect it to the previous paragraph. For example, at the start of paragraph 8, the phrase "But after I got the hearing aid" presents several cues: "the hearing aid" connects to the hearing aid mentioned in paragraph 3 and to the subject of paragraphs 3–7, and "but" and "after" refer back to paragraph 7 by setting up a contrast with it and establishing the time relationship between what happens in paragraphs 7 and 8.

2. *Select* one of the longer paragraphs (7, 11, 12, and 13) and *underline* the cues that connect each sentence to the preceding sentence.

WRITE

Write several sentences explaining how Toussaint tries to maintain topical coherence through cues at paragraph boundaries and between sentences. *Cite* examples from the reading.

Engaging Readers

Readers of reflective essays, like readers of autobiography and observational writing, expect to feel personally engaged. They expect more than mere entertainment; they want the essay to lead them to reflect on their own experiences. They want to question what they know and how they know it. They expect to have their beliefs and values challenged or their minds stretched.

Reflective writers can engage their readers in several ways. They may attempt to present the occasion in a way that makes it seem immediately relevant, even though the occasion may be foreign to readers' experience. Or they may strive to present unexpected ideas about a familiar topic. In either case, they make an effort to discover surprisingly apt examples or comparisons and contrasts. They also take risks they might not otherwise take in their writing because they know they are simply trying out some ideas on the topic without coming to any particular conclusion. Using *I,* they claim the ideas as their own, saying to the reader without coyness, self-effacement, or apology, "Here's my mind at work on a topic that should be of interest to you."

ANALYZE

1. *Review* Toussaint's essay, thinking about what had personal significance to you or struck you as having a larger social significance when you first read the essay. *Mark* those places in the margin.

2. Then, considering again the reflective paragraphs 7–14, *underline* two or three ideas that seem to you surprising and insightful, now that you have had time to analyze the essay. Do you believe the ideas emerge from a deeply felt personal experience? How does Toussaint challenge the usual talk-show banter about disabilities?

3. Finally, *underline* a few examples of language—words, phrases, sentences—that seem to you particularly original and effective. You may find that you can identify few, if any, examples of effective language, or you may find that you can readily identify several.

WRITE

Write several sentences about your personal engagement with Toussaint's essay. *Point out* engaging ideas, examples, or language.

BRENT STAPLES

Black Men and Public Space

Brent Staples (b. 1951) earned his Ph.D. in psychology from the University of Chicago and went on to become a journalist, writing for several magazines and newspapers, including the Chicago Sun-Times. *In 1985, he first became assistant metropolitan editor of the* New York Times *and is now a member of the editorial board. His book,* Parallel Times: Growing Up in Black and White, *was published in 1994.*

The following essay was originally published in Ms. *magazine in 1986, under the title "Just Walk on By." Staples revised it slightly for publication in* Harper's *a year later under the present title. The particular occasion for Staples's reflections is an incident that occurred for the first time in the mid-1970s, when he discovered that his mere presence on the street late at night was enough to frighten a young white woman. Recalling this incident leads him to reflect on issues of race, gender, and class in the United States. As you read, think about why Staples chose the new title, "Black Men and Public Space."*

My first victim was a woman—white, well dressed, probably in her late twenties. I came upon her late one evening on a deserted street in Hyde Park, a relatively affluent neighborhood in an otherwise mean, impoverished section of Chicago. As I swung onto the avenue behind her, there seemed to be a discreet, uninflammatory distance between us. Not so. She cast back a worried glance. To her, the youngish black man—a broad six feet two inches with a beard and billowing hair, both hands shoved into the pockets of a bulky military jacket—seemed menacingly close. After a few more quick glimpses, she picked up her pace and was soon running in earnest. Within seconds she disappeared into a cross street.

That was more than a decade ago. I was twenty-two years old, a graduate student newly arrived at the University of Chicago. It was in the echo of that terrified woman's footfalls that I first began to know the unwieldy inheritance I'd come into—the ability to alter public space in ugly ways. It was clear that she thought herself the quarry of a mugger, a rapist, or worse. Suffering a bout of insomnia, however, I was stalking sleep, not defenseless wayfarers. As a softy who is scarcely able to take a knife to a raw chicken—let alone hold one to a person's throat—I was surprised, embarrassed, and dismayed all at once. Her flight made me feel like an accomplice in tyranny. It also made it clear that I was indistinguishable from the muggers who occasionally seeped into the area from the surrounding ghetto. That first encounter, and those that followed, signified that a vast, unnerving gulf lay between nighttime pedestrians—particularly women—and me.' And I soon gathered that being perceived as dangerous is a hazard in itself. I only needed to turn a corner into a dicey situation, or crowd some frightened, armed person in a foyer somewhere, or make an errant move after being pulled over by a policeman. Where fear and weapons meet—and they often do in urban America—there is always the possibility of death.

In that first year, my first away from my hometown, I was   3
to become thoroughly familiar with the language of fear. At dark, shadowy intersections, I could cross in front of a car stopped at a traffic light and elicit the *thunk, thunk, thunk, thunk* of the driver—black, white, male, or female—hammering down the door locks. On less traveled streets after dark, I grew accustomed to but never comfortable with people crossing to the other side of the street rather than pass me. Then there were the standard unpleasantries with policemen, doormen, bouncers, cabdrivers, and others whose business it is to screen out troublesome individuals *before* there is any nastiness.

I moved to New York nearly two years ago and I have re-   4
mained an avid night walker. In central Manhattan, the near-constant crowd cover minimizes tense one-on-one street encounters. Elsewhere—in SoHo, for example, where sidewalks are narrow and tightly spaced buildings shut out the sky—things can get very taut indeed.

After dark, on the warrenlike streets of Brooklyn where I   5
live, I often see women who fear the worst from me. They seem to have set their faces on neutral, and with their purse straps strung across their chests bandolier-style, they forge ahead as though bracing themselves against being tackled. I understand, of course, that the danger they perceive is not a hallucination. Women are particularly vulnerable to street violence, and young black males are drastically overrepresented among the perpetrators of that violence. Yet these truths are no solace against the kind of alienation that comes of being ever the suspect, a fearsome entity with whom pedestrians avoid making eye contact.

Over the years, I learned to smother the rage I felt at so   6
often being taken for a criminal. Not to do so would surely

have led to madness. I now take precautions to make myself less threatening. I move about with care, particularly late in the evening. I give a wide berth to nervous people on subway platforms during the wee hours, particularly when I have exchanged business clothes for jeans. If I happen to be entering a building behind some people who appear skittish, I may walk by, letting them clear the lobby before I return, so as not to seem to be following them. I have been calm and extremely congenial on those rare occasions when I've been pulled over by the police.

And on late-evening constitutionals I employ what has   7
proved to be an excellent tension-reducing measure: I whistle melodies from Beethoven and Vivaldi and the more popular classical composers. Even steely New Yorkers hunching toward nighttime destinations seem to relax, and occasionally they even join in the tune. Virtually everybody seems to sense that a mugger wouldn't be warbling bright, sunny selections from Vivaldi's *Four Seasons.* It is my equivalent of the cowbell that hikers wear when they know they are in bear country.

READING FOR MEANING

Write to create meanings for Staples's reflections about how people react to him in public spaces.

START MAKING MEANING

Begin by listing some of the ways Staples tries to alleviate people's fear of him and commenting on his feelings about these encounters. Continue by writing about anything else in the essay or in your experience that contributes to your understanding of Staples's reflections.

IF YOU ARE STUCK

If you cannot write at least a page, consider writing about

- whether Staples accurately assesses the woman's feelings in the first encounter he describes, perhaps speculating about how you would feel in this woman's position.

- the extent to which in your view Staples's problem results from social tensions related to race, class (income level), or gender.

- an experience you have had of encountering someone different from you in a public space, comparing your experience to that of Staples or one of the people he encountered.

- whether in your experience the fear of strangers operates the same way in suburban or small-town public spaces as it did for Staples in an urban setting.

READING LIKE A WRITER
PRESENTING THE PARTICULAR OCCASION

Reflective writing generally grows out of a particular occasion—a specific incident or experience that sets the writer's thoughts in motion.

ANALYZE

1. *Reread* paragraph 1, where Staples describes the particular occasion that sets the stage for his reflections. Carefully *examine* how Staples presents the incident. *Annotate* details such as the following:

   - The words Staples uses to describe the woman versus those he uses to describe himself as the woman saw him (for example, his choice of the word *shoved* to describe his hands in his pockets)

   - His description of the scene—time, place, social setting

   - The specific verbs he uses; the quick shifts from what he did to what the woman did in reaction

2. *Consider* how Staples's descriptive and narrative strategies highlight a sense of drama and danger. How might he have decided what was and was not relevant to present this occasion?

WRITE

Write several sentences explaining what you have learned about how Staples creates a vivid narrative of his reflections. *Illustrate* your points with details from the incident he describes.

CONSIDERING IDEAS FOR YOUR OWN WRITING

Staples's essay focuses on what happens in "public space." List any incidents you can recall in which you or others reacted peculiarly or surprisingly in public. Consider different kinds of public space—on the highway, in the classroom, at a concert, at a mall. Also list incidents from your own experience that suggest how people interact privately under different situations—for example, during a first date or at a family gathering.

BARBARA EHRENREICH
Are Families Dangerous?

Barbara Ehrenreich (b. 1941) is the author of seven books, including a critique of the 1980s, The Worst Years of Our Lives: Irreverent Notes from a Decade of Greed *(1990), and a study of the middle class,* Fear of Falling *(1989). Her essays have appeared in such journals and magazines as the* American Scholar, *the* Atlantic Monthly, *and the* New Republic. *She writes a weekly column for* Time *and* The Guardian.*

The following essay was published in Time *magazine in 1994. The occasion for Ehrenreich's reflections is three well-publicized cases of family violence: Brothers Erik and Lyle Menendez, accused of murdering their parents, claimed their parents abused them; Lorena Bobbitt cut off her husband's penis because he abused her; and O. J. Simpson abused his wife, Nicole, but was found not guilty of murdering her. As you read, notice how Ehrenreich weaves these cases in and out of her reflections about how dangerous, even deadly, some families can be. You will find yourself drawn into intense reflection about your own family and into evaluation of Ehrenreich's ideas.*

A disturbing subtext runs through our recent media fixations. Parents abuse sons—allegedly at least, in the Menendez case—who in turn rise up and kill them. A husband torments a wife, who retaliates with a kitchen knife. Love turns into obsession, between the Simpsons anyway, and then perhaps into murderous rage: the family, in other words, becomes personal hell.

This accounts for at least part of our fascination with the Bobbitts and the Simpsons and the rest of them. We live in a culture that fetishes the family as the ideal unit of human community, the perfect container for our lusts and loves. Politicians of both parties are aggressively "pro-family," even abortion-rights bumper stickers proudly link "pro-family" and "pro-choice." Only with the occasional celebrity crime do we allow ourselves to think the nearly unthinkable: that the family may not be the ideal and perfect living arrangement after all—that it can be a nest of pathology and a cradle of gruesome violence.

It's a scary thought, because the family is at the same time our "haven in a heartless world." Theoretically, and sometimes actually, the family nurtures warm, loving feelings, uncontaminated by greed or power hunger. Within the family, and often only within the family, individuals are loved "for themselves," whether or not they are infirm, incontinent, infantile or eccentric. The strong (adults and especially males) lie down peaceably with the small and weak.

But consider the matter of wife battery. We managed to   4
dodge it in the Bobbitt case and downplay it as a force in Tonya Harding's life. Thanks to O. J., though, we're caught up now in a mass consciousness-raising session, grimly absorbing the fact that in some areas domestic violence sends as many women to emergency rooms as any other form of illness, injury or assault.

Still, we shrink from the obvious inference: for a woman,   5
home is, statistically speaking, the most dangerous place to be. Her worst enemies and potential killers are not strangers but lovers, husbands and those who claimed to love her once. Similarly, for every child like Polly Klaas who is killed by a deranged criminal on parole, dozens are abused and murdered by their own relatives. Home is all too often where the small and weak fear to lie down and shut their eyes.

At some deep, queasy, Freudian level, we all know this.   6
Even in the ostensibly "functional," nonviolent family, where no one is killed or maimed, feelings are routinely bruised and often twisted out of shape. There is the slap or put-down that violates a child's shaky sense of self, the cold, distracted stare that drives a spouse to tears, the little digs and rivalries. At best, the family teaches the finest things human beings can learn from one another—generosity and love. But it is also, all too often, where we learn nasty things like hate and rage and shame.

Americans act out their ambivalence about the family   7
without ever owning up to it. Millions adhere to creeds that are militantly "pro-family." But at the same time millions flock to therapy groups that offer to heal the "inner child" from damage inflicted by family life. Legions of women band together to revive the self-esteem they lost in supposedly loving relationships and to learn to love a little less. We are all, it is often said, "in recovery." And from what? Our families, in most cases.

There is a long and honorable tradition of "anti-family"   8
thought. The French philosopher Charles Fourier taught that the family was a barrier to human progress; early feminists saw a degrading parallel between marriage and prostitution. More recently, the renowned British anthropologist Edmund Leach stated that "far from being the basis of the good society, the family, with its narrow privacy and tawdry secrets, is the source of all discontents."

Communes proved harder to sustain than plain old   9
couples, and the conservatism of the '80s crushed the last
vestiges of life-style experimentation. Today even gays and
lesbians are eager to get married and take up family life.
Feminists have learned to couch their concerns as "family issues," and public figures would sooner advocate free co-
caine on demand than criticize the family. Hence our un-
seemly interest in O. J. and Erik, Lyle and Lorena: they allow
us, however gingerly, to break the silence on the hellish side
of family life.

But the discussion needs to become a lot more open and   10
forthright. We may be stuck with the family—at least until
someone invents a sustainable alternative—but the family,
with its deep, impacted tensions and longings, can hardly be
expected to be the moral foundation of everything else. In
fact, many families could use a lot more outside interference
in the form of counseling and policing, and some are so dangerously dysfunctional that they ought to be encouraged
to disband right away. Even healthy families need outside
sources of moral guidance to keep the internal tensions from
imploding—and this means, at the very least, a public philosophy of gender equality and concern for child welfare.
When, instead, the larger culture aggrandizes wife beaters,
degrades women or nods approvingly at child slappers, the
family gets a little more dangerous for everyone, and so, inevitably, does the larger world.

READING FOR MEANING

Write to create meanings for Ehrenreich's reflections on the dangers
in families.

START MAKING MEANING

Begin by listing the dangers in families that Ehrenreich implies or
states in paragraphs 1–6. Continue by writing about anything else in the
essay or in your experience that contributes to your understanding of
Ehrenreich's reflections.

IF YOU ARE STUCK

If you cannot write at least a page, consider writing about

- the advice Ehrenreich gives in her conclusion (paragraph 10), where
  she restates her main points about the dangers in families and comments on how to minimize them.

- the ideas of the "anti-family" thinkers (paragraph 8), restating their arguments, giving your reaction, and supporting your views with comments and examples.

- the reaction you think Ehrenreich expects to get from her readers, supporting your hunches with details or quotations from the reading.

- the extent to which your experience with a family (your own or one you know) supports or does not support Ehrenreich's ideas.

A SPECIAL READING STRATEGY

Reflecting on Challenges to Your Beliefs and Values

Some of the reading you do in college will challenge your beliefs and values. For example, nearly every reader feels challenged by one or more ideas in Ehrenreich's essay. If you reread "Are Families Dangerous?" in order to identify just where it tests your beliefs and values, you can begin to learn more about your beliefs and values themselves. Turn to the critical reading strategy, Reflecting on Challenges to Your Beliefs and Values, in Appendix One (p. 468), and follow the guidelines there.

READING LIKE A WRITER
MAINTAINING TOPICAL COHERENCE

Because writers of reflective essays aim to try out ideas on their readers while not necessarily attempting to reach any definitive conclusions, their essays may appear organized by a "first-I-had-this-idea-and-then-I-had-another-idea" principle. The essay may seem rambling and loosely organized, and yet readers find it coherent; they can read it straight through without encountering any gaps or breaks or confusion. As we saw earlier in the chapter, this kind of coherence in reflective writing is called topical coherence. The writer stays on topic and provides minimal cues about the movement from one idea or example to the next.

Consider how Ehrenreich maintains topical coherence in her reflective essay. For example, she begins paragraph 9 with the phrase "Communes proved harder to sustain than plain old couples." The phrase does not offer any explicit cues, such as repeated words, that connect the paragraph to the previous one, and it introduces what looks like a new topic with the word "communes." But the attentive reader will recognize that a commune is a substitute family where members live together, married or not, sharing resources and work. The word "harder" alerts the reader to the contrast being established: "communes" versus "plain-old couples" or, viewed in other terms, the alternative family (introduced in paragraph 9) versus the conventional family (already discussed in paragraph 8). These minimal cues create coherence while also allowing the writer to give the impression of a mind at work—coming up with one idea and then another without straining to make explicit, conventional connections.

ANALYZE

1. *Reread* Ehrenreich's essay and *underline* the cues in the first sentence of each paragraph that link it to the previous paragraph.

2. Then *choose* one paragraph that seems especially coherent to you and *underline* the cues in each sentence that keep you on track. The cues may be, for example, repeated key words or phrases, pronoun references, or parallel sentence patterns.

WRITE

Write several sentences reporting what you have learned about topical coherence in Ehrenreich's essay. *Cite* examples of several cues from the reading.

CONSIDERING IDEAS FOR YOUR OWN WRITING

Ehrenreich reflects on a topic—violence in families—that she claims most people prefer to ignore. Think of other topics that people are reluctant to discuss openly. They need not be dangerous or negative topics, just topics that tend to remain underground. Some examples include taking credit for one's successes, fear of success, sexually transmitted diseases, sexual dysfunction, male body image, death, lack of money, the difference between opportunities offered to you and to others, pornography, anxieties about speaking in public or about writing. You will think of others.

JERRY ROCKWOOD

Life Intrudes

Jerry Rockwood (b. 1927) is the author of The Crafts-
men of Dionysus: An Approach to Acting *(1966), which
has been used as a text in colleges and theatre schools
throughout the country. He has taught acting at the Stella
Adler Studio, the American Academy of Dramatic Art, the
Cleveland Playhouse, New York University, and Montclair
State College. He has given over one hundred Master
Classes in colleges across the country in conjunction with his
performance of his one-man show,* Edgar Allan Poe, *for
which he won the Barter Theatre Award for acting and the
Buffalo Theatre Critics Award. He has directed extensively
and his production of* Marat/Sade *won the American College Theatre Award and was performed at the Kennedy Center in Washington, D.C. The following essay was originally
published in 1988, in the* New York Times Magazine *as part
of a continuing series of essays "About Men." In this piece,
Rockwood writes about his son's encounter with a bully and
his own feelings and thoughts about aggression.*

I never spoke back. I was quiet and obedient. And so I   1
grew up without aggression, at least the kind of aggression
that can be seen on the surface.

It has cost me dearly. I think one reason I became an actor   2
was to be able to vent my squelched aggression and hostility
through the characters I played on the stage. But one needs
loads of personal aggression to make it in the theater, and,
as a result, I never had the success I wanted. Eventually, I
turned to teaching acting in college.

Now I have been watching my son, Matthew, a year out of   3
college, display a similar lack of aggression. He reminds me
of myself—the way I used to find myself shrinking back or
turning away from unpleasantness. Matthew uses "I choose
not to" as an excuse for avoiding things he ought to face. It
troubles me. It makes me wonder about the values we impose in raising our children.

Education, to a Cherokee father, meant teaching his son   4
to hunt with a bow and arrow, to tread noiselessly through
the woods. To an Eskimo father, it meant showing his boy
how to tap ice for strength and thickness, how to gauge the
depth of the water. Education for these boys meant learning
to deal with the environment.

Was it so with Matthew when he was a boy? I think not.   5
His was a good school. Private. Expensive. With all the right

and beautiful philosophies intended to help kids grow up to be interested and sincere and sensitive and cooperative and creative and aware—to shun violence and war and vice and double-dealings. Disputes in Matthew's school were mediated by sympathetic and understanding teachers. Feelings were aired, points of view pointed out, alternatives proposed. The right stuff.

But I cannot forget an episode that occurred when 6 Matthew was 9 years old. A boy named Kevin, the leader of a small gang of bullies, had it in for him. I remember saying something like, "Look, Math, if Kevin calls you filthy names and teases you, then he's not a very nice kid, and the best thing to do is to ignore him. Laugh it off and walk away."

"But he follows me. And then he starts shoving me. And 7 today he knocked over a bike on me. I don't know what to do!"

Well, what do you do? Tell me, educators and psycholo- 8 gists, what should I have told my son to do? He had discovered that the world inside his fabulously equipped, psychologist-staffed and superior-teacher-laden school was not like the real world outside.

What I did do is this: when I learned that Matthew was de- 9 termined to fight with Kevin, I first tried to talk him out of it. I asked him if he could beat Kevin. He said yes. I saw that he was determined, and so I agreed and even accompanied him. "My father is coming," Matthew had explained to the other boys, "just to make sure that two of you guys don't jump me at once."

We all walked along the beach looking for a secluded 10 place. "Whatever happens, Dad," Matthew said on the way, "don't break it up." I said I wouldn't break it up.

I stood against a telephone pole, gripping with one hand 11 the lowest of the metal spikes used for climbing it. A dozen or more kids stood nearby. Matthew was sturdier than the wiry Kevin; they were the same height. Each waited for the other to move first. Kevin sprang and, in an instant, had Matthew down and in a headlock. His fist smashed again and again into Matthew's face. There was no contest. Kevin was an accomplished street fighter; Matthew simply didn't know how to fight. At last, "Do you give up?" "Yes."

Matthew rose to his feet, his nose bleeding, his lips bloody 12 and swollen. He tried to hold back the tears, but the anger and humiliation were too much. He made a lunge, and Kevin reached all the way back with his right fist and threw all his weight into a solid punch in the neck. There was an audible intake of breath from the spectators at the sound of the punch.

Matthew was stunned and gave a strangulated cry. "Do you give up?" A nod of the head. I put my arm around my son's shoulder and took him home to bathe his wounds.

Later, I tucked him in bed and kissed him goodnight. I knew that his bruises would heal, but I wasn't sure about the humiliation. Even now, all I'm sure of is that Matthew remembers the incident as vividly as I.

13

I am puzzled. I reluctantly allowed my son to have his confrontation, and he did not shrink from it. But was that enough? Should I have taught Matthew to be a street fighter, as well? Should he have been trained to co-exist in this other world? The idea is monstrous to me. But so is the idea of his being beaten up by any punk who comes along. Are we wrong in presenting only half the picture? Do you train a sailor by showing him the ropes and neglect to tell him about wind direction and tides?

14

"Life intrudes," was one of the pet expressions of Stella Adler, a wonderful acting teacher with whom I worked for years. Life intrudes. No matter how solidly we build our dream cabin, we can't ever completely seal up all the cracks. Life will sneak in, force itself upon us. It is there no matter how often we mutter our, yeses and noes and ifs and buts and maybes. It is there, and it may be unwise to pretend it is not.

15

I don't have an answer, just the uncertainty of how to wish the best for Matthew and all of us. If we can't train the street fighters to be gentlemen, must we train the gentlemen to be street fighters? Should we all be Boy Scouts? Be Prepared? Or is that akin to the craziness of putting a hair trigger on the gun?

16

READING FOR MEANING

Write to create meaning for Rockwood's reflections on what a son needs to learn from a father.

START MAKING MEANING

Begin by restating what Rockwood seems to be "puzzled" about, focusing on what he says in paragraphs 14–16. Continue by writing about anything else in the essay or in your experience that contributes to your understanding of Rockwood's reflections.

IF YOU ARE STUCK

If you cannot write at least a page, consider writing about

• what Rockwood decided to do and the results of his decision.

- "the environment" Rockwood mentions in paragraph 4, describing in your own words the larger social and cultural environment in which boys in the United States grow up.

- how you would answer one of the questions Rockwood poses in paragraphs 14 and 16.

- any question you have on the subject of confrontation or real-world education that is not raised by Rockwood, offering your own answer to the question and connecting it in some way with Rockwood's reflections.

- an occasion when "life intruded" on you, describing and reflecting on what happened and connecting your reflections with one or more of Rockwood's reflections.

READING LIKE A WRITER
DEVELOPING THE REFLECTIONS THROUGH QUESTIONS

Writers rely on a number of essential strategies to develop their reflections. One of these strategies is to ask questions. Not every reflective essay includes questions, but enough do to make it a notable feature of this type of writing. Because reflective essays need not offer conclusions about their subjects or answers to the personal and social issues they raise, they sometimes use questions to remain tentative, exploratory, probing. Rockwood's essay is typical in this regard: The writer admits "I am puzzled" (paragraph 14) and "I don't have an answer" (paragraph 16).

ANALYZE

1. *Locate* and *underline* the questions Rockwood asks in paragraphs 5, 8, 14, and 16.

2. *Consider* the purpose of each of these four instances of questioning. Within the context of the entire essay—the occasions, ideas, and reflections—what does each instance of questioning contribute? Does Rockwood answer any of the questions? Do the questions refer to what has gone before in the essay or anticipate what is to come? Are some questions merely rhetorical; that is, easily answered by readers? How many are substantive? How does each instance of questioning develop, extend, or deepen Rockwood's reflections? *Note* your ideas in the margins of the essay.

3. *Select* two questions that seem to you the most surprising, significant, or insightful.

WRITE

Write several sentences explaining what you have learned about how Rockwood uses questions to develop his reflections.

CONSIDERING IDEAS FOR YOUR OWN WRITING

Rockwood makes a difficult decision with deep and mixed feelings—like many decisions you have made. The outcome of his decision, agreeing to let Matthew fight Kevin, is the occasion that sets the stage for his reflections on raising boys. Think about a time when you decided to do something you felt ambivalent about. Maybe you did something dangerous or reckless, generous or helpful. Maybe you ended a relationship. Maybe you said something you should or should not have said after thinking about it for a long time. Try to choose an occasion that involved a difficult decision and that now reveals something important about you, someone you know, or the world. Like Rockwood, you could set up a context for the occasion, but do not wait too long to discuss the occasion itself. Tell it using concrete language, and then reflect on its meaning.

WENDY LEE
Peeling Bananas

> *Wendy Lee wrote the following essay when she was a high school student, and it was published in 1993 in* Chinese American Forum, *a quarterly journal of news and opinion. Lee reflects on growing up in America as the child of parents born in China. While she focuses mainly on going to school, her interest is larger: to discover how she can become American without losing the knowledge and experience of her Chinese heritage. As you read, reflect on how you might hold on to the special qualities of your family or ethnic group while at the same time becoming part of a larger regional or national community.*

When my friend told me that her father had once compared her to a banana, I stared at her blankly. Then I realized that her father must have meant that outside she had the yellow skin of a Chinese, but inside she was white like an American. In other words, her appearance was Chinese, but her thoughts and values were American. Looking at my friend in her American clothes with her perfectly straight black hair and facial features so much like my own, I laughed. Her skin was no more yellow than mine.

In kindergarten, we colored paper dolls: red was for Indians, black for Afro-Americans, yellow was for Chinese. The dolls that we didn't color at all—the white ones—were left to be Americans. But the class wanted to know where were the green, blue or purple people? With the paper dolls, our well-meaning teacher intended to emphasize that everyone is basically the same, despite skin color. Secretly I wondered why the color of my skin wasn't the shade of my yellow Crayola. After we colored the dolls, we stamped each one with the same vacant, smiley face. The world, according to our teacher, is populated by happy, epidermically diverse people.

What does it mean to be a Chinese in an American school? One thing is to share a last name with a dozen other students, so that you invariably squirm when roll-call is taken. It means never believing that the fairy-tales the teacher read during story time could ever happen to you, because you don't have skin as white as snow or long golden hair. "You're Chinese?" I remember one classmate saying. "Oh, I *really* like Chinese food." In the depths of her over-friendly eyes I saw fried egg-rolls and chow mein. Once, for show-and-tell, a girl proudly told the class that one of her ancestors was in the picture of George Washington crossing the Delaware. I promptly countered that by thinking to myself, "Well, my grandfather was Sun Yat-Sen's* physician, so THERE."

In my home, there is always a rather haphazard combination of the past and present. Next to the scrolls of black ink calligraphy on the dining room wall is a calendar depicting scenes from the midwest; underneath the stacked Chinese newspapers, the *L.A. Times.* In the refrigerator, next to the milk and butter, are tofu and bok choy from the weekly trips to the local Chinese supermarket. Spoons are used for soup, forks for salad, but chopsticks are reserved for the main course. I never noticed the disparity between my lifestyle and that of white Americans—until I began school. There, I became acquainted with children of strictly Caucasian heritage and was invited to their home. Mentally I always compared the interiors of their home to my own and to those of my mother's Chinese friends. What struck me was that their home seemed to have no trace of their heritages at all. But nearly all Chinese-American homes retain aspects of the Chinese culture; aspects that reflect the yearning for returning home Chinese immigrants always have.

Chinese immigrants like my parents have an unwavering faith in China's potential to truly become the "middle kingdom," the literal translation of the Chinese words for China. They don't want their first-generation children to forget the way their ancestors lived. They don't want their children to forget that China has a heritage spanning thousands of years, while America has only a paltry two hundred. My mother used to tape Chinese characters over the words in our picture books. Ungratefully my sister and I tore them off because we were more interested in seeing how the story turned out. When she showed us her satin Chinese dresses, we were more interested in playing dress-up than in the stories behind the dresses; when she taught us how to use chopsticks, we were more concentrated on eating the Chinese delicacies she had prepared. (Incidentally, I still have to remind myself how to hold my chopsticks properly, though this may merely be a personal fault; I can't hold a pencil properly either.)

After those endless sessions with taped-over books and flashcards, my mother packed us off to Chinese School.

Sun Yat-Sen (paragraph 3): (1866–1925) Revolutionary leader of China and first president of the Chinese Republic (1911–1912)

There, we were to benefit from interaction with other Chinese-American children in the same predicament—unable to speak, read, or write Chinese nicely. There, we were supposed to make the same progress we made in our American schools. But in its own way, Chinese School is as much of a banana as are Chinese-Americans. A Chinese School day starts and ends with a bow to the teacher to show proper reverence. In the intervening three hours, the students keep one eye on the mysterious symbols of Chinese characters on the blackboard and the other on the clock. Their voices may be obediently reciting a lesson, but silently they are urging the minute hand to go faster. Chinese is taught through the American way, with workbooks and homework and tests. Without distinctive methods to make the experience memorable and worthwhile for its students, Chinese School, too, is in danger of becoming completely Americanized. Chinese-American kids, especially those in their teens, have become bewitched by the American ideal of obtaining a career that makes lots and lots of money. Their Chinese heritage probably doesn't play a big part in their futures. Many Chinese-Americans are even willing to shed their skins in favor of becoming completely American. Certainly it is easier to go forward and become completely American than to regress and become completely Chinese in America.

Sometimes I imagine what it would be like to go back to Taiwan or mainland China. Through eyes misty with romantic sentiment, I can look down a crooked, stone-paved street where a sea of black-haired and slanted-eyed people are bicycling in tandem. I see factories where people are hunchbacked over tables to manufacture plastic toys and American flags. I see fog-enshrouded mountains of Guilin, the yellow mud of Yangtze River, and the Great Wall of China snaking across the landscape as it does in the pages of a *National Geographic* magazine. When I look up at the moon, I don't see the pale, impersonal sphere that I see here in America. Instead, I see the plaintive face of Chang-Oh, the moon goddess. When I look up at the moon, I may miss my homeland like the famous poet Li Bai did in the poem that every Chinese School student can recite. But will that homeland be America or China?

When the crooked street is empty with no bicycles, I see a girl standing across from me on the other side of the street. I see mirrored in her the same perfectly straight black hair and facial features that my Chinese-American friend has, or the same that I have. We cannot communicate, for I only know pidgin Mandarin whereas she speaks fluent Cantonese, a dialect of southern China. Not only is the difference of language a barrier, but the differences in the way we were brought up and the way we live. Though we look the same, we actually are of different cultures, and I may cross the street into her world but only as a visitor. However, I also realize that as a hybrid of two cultures, I am unique, and perhaps that uniqueness should be preserved.

READING FOR MEANING

Write to create meanings for Lee's reflections on the difficulties of embracing two different cultures.

START MAKING MEANING

Begin by restating briefly the occasion for Lee's reflections and listing two or three experiences by which Lee remains aware of her Chinese ethnicity. Continue by writing about anything else in the essay or in your experience that contributes to your understanding of Lee's reflections.

IF YOU ARE STUCK

If you cannot write at least a page, consider writing about

- the traces of Lee's Chinese heritage that she encounters at home, perhaps comparing them to the signs of your ethnic heritage (African, Mexican, Italian, Cambodian, German, or some other) in your home.

- the insights that occur to Lee as she imagines a trip to Taiwan or China (paragraphs 7 and 8).

- Lee's assumption that there is a white American ethnicity or culture that stands in contrast to Chinese ethnicity.

- your personal experience of feeling different ethnically or otherwise, comparing it to Lee's experience.

READING LIKE A WRITER
DEVELOPING THE REFLECTIONS THROUGH COMPARISON
AND CONTRAST

In reflective writing, insights and ideas are central; yet writers cannot merely list ideas, regardless of how fresh and daring their ideas might be. Instead, writers must work imaginatively to develop their ideas, to explain and elaborate them, to view them from one angle and then another. One well-established way to develop ideas is through comparison and contrast.

ANALYZE

1. *Review* the comparisons and contrasts in paragraphs 4, 6, and 8 of Lee's reflections.

2. *Choose* one of these paragraphs to analyze more closely. What exactly is being compared or contrasted? *Underline* details that highlight the comparisons and contrasts.

WRITE

Write several sentences describing how Lee uses comparisons or contrasts to develop her ideas. From the one paragraph you chose to analyze, *identify* the terms of the comparison/contrast (the items being compared) and the ideas they represent.

CONSIDERING IDEAS FOR YOUR OWN WRITING

Consider reflecting on your own ethnicity, beginning, like Lee, with a concrete occasion. If you are among the "white Caucasians" Lee mentions, you may doubt that you have an ethnicity in the sense that Lee has one. Consider, however, that Asians do not comprise a single ethnicity. Among Asian Americans, there are several distinctly different ethnicities, as defined by their countries or regions of origin: Chinese, Japanese, Korean, Cambodian, Vietnamese, Philippino, and others. White Caucasians also represent many national origins: German (still the single largest American immigrant group), Swedish, Russian, Polish, Irish, Italian, British, Greek, French, to mention only a few. In all of these Asian and European—and Latin American and other—immigrant groups, intermarriage and acculturation to whatever is uniquely American have blurred and blended many of the original ethnic distinctions. Nevertheless, Lee's reflections remind us of the likelihood that in nearly every family there are remnants of one or more national or regional ethnicities. This idea for writing invites you to reflect on whatever meanings remain for you personally in your ethnic identities.

KATHERINE HAINES
Whose Body Is This?

Katherine Haines wrote the following essay for an assignment in her first-year composition course.

As the essay's title suggests, the writer reflects on her dismay and anger about our society's obsession with the perfect body—especially the perfect female body. As you read, note the many kinds of details Haines uses to develop her reflections.

"Hey Rox, what's up? Do you wanna go down to the pool with me? It's a gorgeous day." 1

"No thanks, you go ahead without me." 2

"What? Why don't you want to go? You've got the day off work, and what else are you going to do?" 3

"Well, I've got a bunch of stuff to do around the house . . . pay the bills, clean the bathroom, you know. Besides, I don't want to have to see myself in a bathing suit—I'm so fat." 4

Why do so many women seem obsessed with their weight and body shape? Are they really that unhappy and dissatisfied with themselves? Or are these women continually hearing from other people that their bodies are not acceptable? 5

In today's society, the expectations for women and their bodies are all too evident. Fashion, magazines, talk shows, "lite" and fat-free food in stores and restaurants, and diet centers are all daily reminders of these expectations. For instance, the latest fashions for women reveal more and more skin: shorts have become shorter, to the point of being scarcely larger than a pair of underpants, and the bustier, which covers only a little more skin than a bra, is making a comeback. These styles are only flattering on the slimmest of bodies, and many women who were previously happy with their bodies may emerge from the dressing room after a run-in with these styles and decide that it must be diet time again. Instead of coming to the realization that these clothes are unflattering for most women, how many women will simply look for different and more flattering styles, and how many women will end up heading for the gym to burn off some more calories or to the bookstore to buy the latest diet book? 6

When I was in junior high, about two-thirds of the girls I knew were on diets. Everyone was obsessed with fitting into 7 the smallest size miniskirt possible. One of my friends would eat a carrot stick, a celery stick, and two rice cakes for lunch. Junior high (and the onset of adolescence) seemed to be the beginning of the pressure for most women. It is at this age that appearance suddenly becomes important. Especially for those girls who want to be "popular" and those who are cheerleaders or on the drill team. The pressure is intense; some girls believe no one will like them or accept them if they are "overweight," even by a pound or two. The measures these girls will take to attain the body that they think will make them acceptable are often debilitating and life threatening.

My sister was on the drill team in junior high. My sister wanted to fit in with the right crowd—and my sister drove herself to the edge of becoming anorexic. I watched as she came home from school, having eaten nothing for breakfast and at lunch only a bag of pretzels and an apple (and she didn't always finish that), and began pacing the oriental carpet that was in our living room. Around and around and around, without a break, from four o'clock until dinnertime, which was usually at six or seven o'clock. And then at dinner, she would take minute portions and only pick at her food. After several months of this, she became much paler and thinner, but not in any sort of attractive sense. Finally, after catching a cold and having to stay in bed for three days because she was so weak, she was forced to go to the doctor. The doctor said she was suffering from malnourishment and was to stay in bed until she regained some of her strength. He advised her to eat lots of fruits and vegetables until the bruises all over her body had healed (these were a result of vitamin deficiency). Although my sister did not develop anorexia, it was frightening to see what she had done to herself. She had little strength, and the bruises she had made her look like an abused child.

This mania to lose weight and have the "ideal" body is not easily avoided in our society. It is created by television and magazines as they flaunt their models and latest diet crazes in front of our faces. And then there are the Nutri-System and Jenny Craig commercials, which show hideous "before" pictures and glamorous "after" pictures and have smiling, happy people dancing around and talking about how their lives have been transformed simply because they have lost weight. This propaganda that happiness is in a large part based on having the "perfect" body shape is a message that the media constantly sends to the public. No one seems to be able to escape it.

My mother and father were even sucked in by this idea.   10
One evening, when I was in the fifth grade, I heard Mom and
Dad calling me into the kitchen. Oh no, what had I done
now? It was never good news when you got summoned into
the kitchen alone. As I walked into the kitchen, Mom looked
up at me with an anxious expression; Dad was sitting at the
head of the table with a pen in hand and a yellow legal pad in
front of him. They informed me that I was going on a diet. A
diet!? I wanted to scream at them, "I'm only ten years old,
why do I have to be on a diet?" I was so embarrassed, and I
felt so guilty. Was I really fat? I guess so, I thought, otherwise
why would my parents do this to me?

It seems that this obsession with the perfect body and a   11
woman's appearance has grown to monumental heights. It is
ironic, however, that now many people feel that this problem is disappearing. People have begun to assume that
women want to be thin because they just want to be
"healthy." But what has happened is that the sickness slips
in under the guise of wanting a "healthy" body. The demand
for thin bodies is anything but "healthy." How many anorex-
ics or bulimics have you seen that are healthy?

It is strange that women do not come out and object to   12
society's pressure to become thin. Or maybe women feel
that they really do want to be thin, and so go on dieting end-
lessly (they call it "eating sensibly"), thinking this is what
they really want. I think if these women carefully examined
their reasons for wanting to lose weight—and were not allowed to include reasons that relate to society's demands,
such as a weight chart, a questionnaire in a magazine, a certain size in a pair of shorts, or even a scale—they would find
that they are being ruled by what society wants, not what
they want. So why do women not break free from these standards? Why do they not demand an end to being judged in
such a demeaning and senseless way?

Self-esteem plays a large part in determining whether   13
women succumb to the will of society or whether they are
independent and self-assured enough to make their own decisions. Lack of self-esteem is one of the things the women's
movement has had to fight the hardest against. If women
didn't think they were worthy, then how could they even
begin to fight for their own rights? The same is true with
the issue of body size. If women do not feel their body is
worthy, then how can they believe that it is okay to just
let it stay that way? Without self-esteem, women will be
swayed by society and will continue to make themselves unhappy by trying to maintain whatever weight or body shape

society is dictating for them. It is ironic that many of the popular women's magazines—*Cosmopolitan, Mademoiselle, Glamour*—often feature articles on self-esteem and how essential it is and how to improve it, and then in the same issue give the latest diet tips. This mixed message will never give women the power they deserve over their bodies and will never enable them to make their own decisions about what type of body they want.

> *"Rox, why do you think you're fat? You work out all*   14
> *the time, and you just bought that new suit. Why don't*
> *you just come down to the pool for a little while?"*
> *"No, I really don't want to. I feel so self-conscious with*   15
> *all those people around. It makes me want to run and put*
> *on a big, baggy dress so no one can tell what size I am!"*
> *"Ah, Rox, that's really sad. You have to learn to be-*   16
> *lieve in yourself and your own judgment, not other*
> *people's."*

READING FOR MEANING

Write to create meanings for Haines's reflections on women's obsession with thinness.

START MAKING MEANING

Begin by restating briefly the two ideas Haines offers for why women worry excessively about their weight—television and magazines (paragraph 9) and societal influences (paragraph 12)—and explaining why you agree or disagree with her ideas. Continue by writing about anything else in the essay or in your experience that contributes to your understanding of Haines's reflections.

IF YOU ARE STUCK

If you cannot write at least a page, consider writing about

- Haines's belief that an obsession with weight often masks itself as an obsession with health (paragraph 11), describing briefly what she has to say and then commenting on the issue from your point of view.

- the emphasis given to weak self-esteem (paragraph 13) as an explanation for women's obsession with thinness.

- the suggestion that women's preoccupation with body image often begins in early adolescence (paragraph 7), indicating why you agree or disagree and connecting your speculations with Haines's argument.

- whether you think men also strive for some ideal body image, describing that image and speculating about where it comes from, and connecting your speculations with Haines's ideas.

READING LIKE A WRITER
DEVELOPING THE REFLECTIONS THROUGH EXAMPLES

Examples play an important role in reflective writing. Haines makes use of examples throughout her essay, several times anchoring her ideas and general statements in concrete experience. A special kind of fictional example called a *scenario* frames her essay, opening and closing it with relevant dialogue between two characters. Three other examples based on personal experience also stand out, in paragraphs 7, 8, and 10.

ANALYZE

1. *Reread* the example Haines describes in paragraph 8, and *underline* the details that make the example vivid for you.

2. *Look* through the entire essay and *find* the one idea that is most closely related to the example given in paragraph 8. *Underline* this idea. Then *consider* how the idea and example are related.

WRITE

Briefly *summarize* the idea you have chosen. Now, *write* several sentences describing how the example is developed—the extent of the narration and the kinds of details offered, evaluating how well the example supports its idea.

COMPARE

Compare the ways Haines, Staples, Lee, and Ehrenreich begin their reflective essays with examples used as occasions, rather than general statements. *Consider* how the examples are alike and different. *Write* a few sentences about what you have learned about how Haines and the other authors make use of examples to launch their reflections.

CONSIDERING IDEAS FOR YOUR OWN WRITING

Haines is frustrated by the ways in which society influences how we think about and judge ourselves. Haines focuses on how we perceive our own bodies. You could explore this question of cultural ideals of masculine and feminine beauty from another angle. For example, you might think about beauty in terms of different ethnic and racial groups. Or you might think about it historically in terms of the painting and sculpture that have influenced our sense of the beautiful.

You could instead explore our cultural ideas about success. The Horatio Alger rags-to-riches story is the prototypical expression of the American Dream. But we all know that success does not have to be measured in terms of money. In what other ways do we measure success?

Think of a particular occasion that could launch your reflections, something you observed or read or experienced personally to ground your ideas. Also think of a few supporting examples from your experience that could help you develop your ideas.

Reviewing What Makes Reflective Essays Effective

In this chapter, you have been learning how to read reflective writing for meaning and how to read it like a writer. Before going on to write a reflective essay, pause here to review and contemplate what you have learned about the elements of effective reflective essays.

Analyze

Choose one reading from this chapter that seems to you especially effective. Before reading the selection again, *write* down one or two reasons you remember it as an example of good reflective writing.

Reread your chosen selection, adding further annotations about what makes it particularly successful as a reflective essay. *Consider* the selection's purpose and how well it achieves that purpose for its intended readers. (You can make an informed guess about the intended readers and their expectations by noting the publication source of the essay.) Then focus on how well the essay

- presents the particular occasion or occasions for the reflections.

- develops the reflections, paying particular attention to the variety of development strategies the writer uses.

- maintains topical coherence.

- engages readers.

You can review all of these basic features in the Guide to Reading Reflective Essays (p. 119).

Your instructor may ask you to complete this activity on your own or to work with a small group of other students who have

Continued

chosen the same essay. If you work with others, allow enough time initially for all group members to reread the selection thoughtfully and to add their annotations. Then discuss as a group what makes the essay effective. Take notes on your discussion. One student in your group should then report to the class what the group has learned about the effectiveness of reflective writing. If you are working individually, write up what you have learned from your analysis.

Write

Write at least one page, supporting your choice of this reading as an example of effective reflective writing. Assume that your readers—your instructor and classmates—have read the selection but will not remember many details about it. They also might not remember it as especially successful. Therefore, you will need to *refer* to details and specific parts of the essay as you explain how it works and *justify* your evaluation of its effectiveness. You need not argue that it is the best essay in the chapter or that it is flawless, only that it is, in your view, a strong example of the genre.

A GUIDE TO WRITING REFLECTIVE ESSAYS

The readings in this chapter have helped you learn a great deal about reflective writing. At its best, the reflective essay is interesting, lively, insightful, engaging—much like good conversation—and it avoids sounding pretentious or preachy in its focus on basic human and social issues that concern us all. Writers of reflection are not reluctant to say what they think or to express their most personal observations. As you develop your reflective essay, you can review the readings to see how other writers use various strategies to solve problems you might also encounter. This Guide to Writing is designed to help you through the various decisions you will need to make as you plan, draft, and revise a reflective essay.

INVENTION

The following invention activities will spur your thinking by helping you find a particular occasion and general subject, test your subject, develop the particular occasion, and develop your reflections on the subject. Taking some time now to consider a wide range of possibilities will pay off later when you draft your essay, giving you confidence in your choice of subject and in your ability to develop it effectively.

Finding a Particular Occasion and General Subject

As the selections in this chapter illustrate, writers of reflection usually center their essays on one (or more than one) event or occasion. They connect this occasion to a subject they want to reflect upon. In the process of invention, however, the choice of particular occasion does not always come before the choice of general subject. Sometimes writers set out to reflect on a general subject, such as envy or friendship, and must search for the right occasion—an image or anecdote—with which to particularize it.

To help you find an occasion and subject for your essay, make a two-column chart like the one that follows by matching particular occasions to general subjects. In the left-hand column, list several particular occasions—a conversation you have had or overheard, a scene you have observed, something memorable you have read or seen in movies or on television, an incident in your own or someone else's life—that might lead you to reflect more generally. In the right-hand column, list the general subjects—human qualities such as compassion, vanity, jealousy, faithfulness; social customs and mores for dating, eating, working; abstract notions such as fate, free will, the imagination—suggested by the particular occasions in the left-hand column.

Move from left to right *and* from right to left, making your list as long as you can. You will find that a single occasion might suggest several subjects and that a subject might be particularized by a variety of occasions. Each entry will surely suggest other possibilities for you to consider. Do not be concerned if your chart of occasions and subjects starts to look quite messy, as that is a good sign of a mind at work. A full and rich exploration of topics will give you confidence in the subject you finally choose and in your ability to write about it. If you have trouble getting started, review the Considering Ideas for Your Own Writing sections following the readings in this chapter.

As further occasions and subjects occur to you over the next two or three days, add them to your chart.

Particular Occasions	*General Subjects*
Saw junior high girls wearing makeup as thick as a clown's	Makeup; makeover, mask the real self; ideas of beauty
Punk styles of the '90s	New fashions: conformity or rebellion?
Rumor about Diane and Tom spread by a friend of theirs	Malicious like gossip? How do they start? Stop?
Saw film called *Betrayal*	Friendship & betrayal
Television story about a 15-year-old who killed a woman to get her car	Violence in our society. Why are teenage men so violent? Danger in cities.
Buying clothes, I couldn't decide and let the salesperson pressure me	Decisions & indecisiveness; bowing to outside pressure; low self-esteem; can't or won't think of self—conformity again!
Take friends to help me make a decision	

Testing Your Subject

Review your chart, and select an occasion and subject you now think looks promising. To test whether this selection will work, write for fifteen minutes, exploring your thoughts on it. Do not make any special demands on yourself to be profound or even to be coherent. Just put your ideas on paper as they come, letting one idea suggest another. Your aim is to determine whether you have anything to say and whether the topic holds your interest. If you discover that you do not have very much to say or that you quickly lose interest in the subject, choose another one and try again. It might take you a few preliminary explorations to find the right subject.

Developing the Particular Occasion

The following activities will help you recall details about the occasion for your reflection. Depending on the occasion you have identified, choose Narrating an Event or Restating Particulars of Something Read or Viewed.

NARRATING AN EVENT.   *Write for five minutes, narrating what happened during the event.* Write about the people involved, their appearance and behavior (including snippets of dialogue, if appropriate), and the setting.

RESTATING PARTICULARS OF SOMETHING READ OR VIEWED.   *Write for five minutes, restating the particulars of that subject.* Include as many details as you can recall that may be pertinent to your reflections.

Developing Your Reflections on the Subject

To explore your ideas about the subject, try an invention activity called *cubing.* Based on the six sides of a cube, this activity leads you to turn over your subject as you would a cube, looking at it in six different ways. Complete the following activities in any order, writing for five minutes on each. Your goal is to invent new ways of considering your subject.

GENERALIZE ABOUT IT.   *Consider what you have learned from the experience that will be the occasion for your reflections/ideas.* What does it suggest to you? What does it suggest about people in general or about the society in which you live?

GIVE EXAMPLES OF IT.   *Illustrate your subject with specific examples.* Think of what would help your classmates understand the ideas you have about it.

COMPARE AND CONTRAST IT.   *Think of a subject that compares with yours.* Explore the similarities and the differences.

EXTEND IT.   *Take your subject to its logical limits.* Speculate about its implications. Where does it lead?

ANALYZE IT.   *Take apart your subject.* What is it made of? How are the parts related to one another? Are they all of equal importance?

APPLY IT.   *Think about your subject in practical terms.* How can you use it or act on it? What difference would it make to you and to others?

DRAFTING

The following activities will help you set goals for your draft and plan its organization.

Setting Goals

Setting goals and keeping them in mind as you draft your essay can make your writing more focused and confident. Use the following questions to help you establish meaningful goals for your writing.

- *How can I present the occasion vividly and so that it anticipates my reflections?* Should I narrate an event like Staples, refer to shocking events in the news like Ehrenreich, or create an imaginary dialogue like Haines?

- *How can I best develop and extend my reflections?* Should I use questions like Rockwood, make use of comparisons and contrasts like Lee, give examples like Staples and Haines and Lee, refer to authorities and history like Ehrenreich, mention other cultures like Rockwood, or create an imaginary scenario like Lee (paragraphs 7 and 8)?

- *How will I be able to ensure coherence among my ideas and examples?* Like all the writers in this chapter, how can I make clear the connections between my ideas or insights and the examples that develop them? How can I keep my readers on track as they follow the course of my reflections?

- *How can I engage and hold my readers' interests?* Should I reveal the human interest and social significance of my subject by opening my essay with a dramatic scene like Staples, a reminder of bizarre and troubling events in the news like Ehrenreich, a personal disclosure like Rockwood, a familiar dialogue like Haines, or an ironic ethnic stereotype like Lee? Like all the writers in this chapter, should I reveal my personal commitment to the subject, and should I attempt to inspire my readers to think deeply about their own lives?

Organizing Your Draft

You might find it paradoxical to plan a type of essay that tries not to reach conclusions or that seeks to give readers the impression that it is finding its way as it goes. And yet you have seen that reflective essays are orderly and easy to follow. It may be the case that the order—what we call topical coherence in this chapter—is discovered in the writing rather than in the planning beforehand. Certainly, readers may have that impression. Nevertheless, there are some ways that planning can help. For example, you probably want to begin by presenting the occasion for your reflections, often a narrative that is relatively easy to construct. Then you begin offering a series of ideas or insights suggested by the occasion. One approach to planning is to attempt a tentative brief list of these ideas. Another is to list tentatively the key examples you want to weave into your reflections. Or perhaps you could attempt to pair ideas and examples and then decide tentatively on a sequence for the pairs. Search your completed invention exercises for promising material.

Another approach is to draft your opening occasion and then, without a plan for the rest, start drafting, feeling your way along to see what turns up. Often after a page or two, a tentative overall plan will suggest itself. However you go about planning or discovering a plan—and remember that a plan is a meaningful and coherent *sequence* of your reflections—your final draft must be easy to follow, with each part following meaningfully from all of the previous parts. In any event, you may find that you must drastically reorder your first draft, an outcome that is predictable with reflective writing.

READING A DRAFT CRITICALLY

Getting a critical reading of your draft will help you see how to improve it. Your instructor may schedule class time for reading drafts, or you may want to ask a classmate or a tutor in the writing center to read your draft. Ask your reader to use the following guidelines and write out a response for you to consult during your revision.

Read for a First Impression

1. Read the draft without stopping to annotate or comment, and then write two or three sentences giving your general impression.

2. Identify one aspect of the draft that seems to you particularly effective.

Read Again to Suggest Improvements

1. Suggest ways of presenting the occasion more effectively.

   - Read the paragraphs that present the occasion for the reflections, and tell the writer whether the occasion dominates the essay, taking up an unjustified amount of space, or whether it needs more development.

   - Note whether this occasion suggests the significance or importance of the subject, and consider how well it prepares readers for the reflections by providing a context for them.

   - Tell the writer what works well and what needs improvement.

2. Help the writer develop the reflections.

   - Look for two or three ideas that strike you as especially interesting, insightful, or surprising and tell the writer what interests you about them. Then, most important, suggest ways these ideas might be developed further through examples, contrasts, social implications, connections to other ideas, and so on.

   - Identify any ideas you find uninteresting, explaining briefly why you find them so.

- Look for ideas that are merely mentioned and any places that could be developed further. Choose one or two ideas and suggest ways they might be expanded.

3. Recommend ways to strengthen topical coherence.

- Skim the essay, looking for gaps between sentences and paragraphs, those places where the meaning does not carry forward smoothly. Mark these gaps with a double slash (//). Choose two or three gaps and recommend a way to close each one.

- Skim the essay again, looking for irrelevant or unnecessary material that can disrupt coherence and divert the reader's attention. Bracket ([ ]) this material and explain to the writer why it seems to you irrelevant or unnecessary.

- Consider the essay as a sequence of sections. Ask yourself whether some of the sections could be moved, making the essay easier to follow. Circle any section that seems out of place and draw an arrow to where it might be better located.

4. Suggest ways to further engage readers.

- Point to two or three aspects of the essay that draw you in, hold your interest, inspire you to think, challenge your attitudes or values, or keep you wanting to read to the end.

- Try to suggest ways the writer might engage readers more fully. Consider the essay in light of what is most engaging for you in the selections you have read in this chapter.

REVISING

This section provides suggestions for revising your draft, suggestions that will remind you of the possibilities for developing an engaging, coherent, reflective essay. Revising means reenvisioning your draft, trying to see it in a new way, given your purpose and readers, in order to develop your reflections.

The biggest mistake you can make in revising is to focus initially on words or sentences. Instead, first try to see your draft as a whole in order to assess its likely impact on your readers. Think imaginatively and boldly about cutting unconvincing material, adding new material, and moving material around. Your computer makes even drastic revisions easy, but you still need to make the effort and decisions that will improve your draft.

You may have received help with this challenge from classmates who have given your draft a critical reading. If so, use this feedback in deciding which parts of your draft need revising and what specific changes you could make.

To Present the Particular Occasion More Effectively

- If the occasion for your reflections seems flat and inadequately detailed, expand it with relevant details.

- If the occasion fails to illustrate the significance of your subject, revise it to do so.

- If the occasion seems not to anticipate the reflections that follow, revise it or come up with a new, more relevant occasion.

To Develop the Reflections More Fully

- If promising ideas are not yet fully developed, provide further examples, anecdotes, contrasts, and so on.

- If certain ideas now seem too predictable, drop them and try to come up with more insightful ideas.

- If your reflections do not move beyond personal associations, extend them into the social realm by commenting on their larger implications—what they mean for people in general.

To Strengthen Topical Coherence

- If there are distracting gaps between sentences or paragraphs, try to close them by revising sentences.

- If one section seems not to follow from the previous one, consider reordering the sequence of sections.

To Better Engage Readers

- If your beginning—typically the presentation of the occasion—seems unlikely to draw readers in, make its event more dramatic, its comments less predictable, or its significance more pointed. If you cannot see how to make it more interesting, consider another beginning.

- If your reflections seem unlikely to lead readers to reflect on their own lives and their interactions with other people, try to carry your ideas further and to develop them in more varied ways.

EDITING AND PROOFREADING

After you have revised your essay, be sure to spend some time checking for errors in usage, punctuation, and mechanics. If you have been keeping a list of errors you frequently make, begin by checking your draft against this list. Ask someone else to proofread your essay before you print out a copy for your instructor.

From our research on student writing, we know that essays reflecting on a particular occasion have a relatively high frequency of shifts in verb tense and mood. Consult a writer's handbook for information on verb shifts and then edit your writing to correct any shifts in verb tense and mood.

Reflecting on What You Have Learned

In this chapter, you have read critically several reflective essays and have written one of your own. To better remember what you have learned, pause now to reflect on the reading and writing activities you completed in this chapter.

1. *Write* a page or so reflecting on what you learned. Begin by describing what you are most pleased with in your essay. Then explain what contributed to your achievement. Be specific about this contribution.

    • If it was something you learned from the readings, *indicate* which readings and specifically what you learned from them.

    • If it came from your invention writing, *point out* the section or sections that helped you most.

    • If you got good advice from a critical reader, *explain* exactly how the person helped you—perhaps by helping you understand a particular problem in your draft or by adding a new dimension to your writing.

    Try to write about your achievement in terms of what you have learned about the genre of reflection.

2. Now *reflect* more generally on reflective essays, a genre of writing that has been important for centuries and is still practiced in our society today. *Consider* some of the following questions: How comfortable did you feel relying on your own experience or observations as a basis for developing ideas about larger subjects? For developing ideas about the way people are and the ways they interact? How comfortable did you feel merely trying out your own personal ideas on a subject rather than researching it or interviewing people to collect their ideas? How comfortable was it to adopt a conversational rather than a formal tone? How would you explain your level of comfort? How might your gender or social class or ethnic group have influenced the ideas you came up with? What contribution might reflective essays make to our society that other genres cannot make?

Explaining Concepts

E
ssays explaining concepts feature a kind of explanatory writing that is especially important for college students to understand. Each of the essays you will analyze in this chapter explains a single concept, such as *parthenogenesis* in biology, *markedness* in linguistics, and *dating* in sociology. For your own explanatory essay, you will choose a concept from your current studies or special interests.

Our focus here on explaining concepts has several advantages for you as a college student. It gives you strategies for critically reading the textbooks and other concept-centered material in your college courses. It helps give you confidence to write a common type of essay examination and paper assignment. And it acquaints you with the basic strategies or modes of development common to all types of explanatory writing: definition, classification or division, comparison and contrast, process narration, illustration, and causal explanation.

A *concept* is a major idea or principle. Every field of study has its concepts: physics has quantum theory, subatomic particles, the Heisenberg principle; psychiatry has neurosis, schizophrenia, narcissism; composition has invention, heuristics, recursiveness; business management has corporate culture, micromanagement, and direct marketing; and music has harmony and counterpoint. Concepts include abstract ideas, phenomena, and processes. Concepts are central to the understanding of virtually every subject—we create concepts, name them, communicate them, and think with them.

As you work through this chapter, keep in mind that we learn a new concept by connecting it to what we have previously learned. Good explanatory writing, therefore, must be incremental, adding bit by bit to the reader's knowledge. Explanatory writing goes wrong when the flow of new information is either too fast or too slow for the intended readers, when the information is too difficult or too simple, or when the writing is digressive or just plain dull.

The readings in this chapter will help you see what makes explanatory writing interesting and informative. You will also get ideas for writing your own essay about a concept, perhaps from the ideas for writing that follow each reading selection. As you analyze the readings, keep in mind the following assignment and the Writing Situations for Explaining Concepts.

THE WRITING ASSIGNMENT

Explaining Concepts

Choose a concept that interests you enough to study further. Write an essay, explaining the concept. Consider carefully what your readers already know about the concept and how your essay can add to their knowledge of it.

WRITING SITUATIONS FOR EXPLAINING CONCEPTS

Writing that explains concepts is familiar in college and professional life, as the following examples show.

- For a presentation at the annual convention of the American Medical Association, an anesthesiologist writes a report on the concept of *awareness during surgery*. He presents evidence that patients under anesthesia, as in hypnosis, can hear; and he reviews research demonstrating that they can perceive and carry out instructions that speed their recovery. He describes briefly how he applies the concept in his own work: how he prepares patients before surgery, what he tells them while they are under anesthesia, and what happens as they recover.

- A business reporter for a newspaper writes an article about *virtual reality*. She describes the lifelike, three-dimensional experience created by wearing gloves and video goggles wired to a computer. To help readers understand this new concept, she contrasts it with television. For investors, she describes which corporations have shown an interest in the commercial possibilities of virtual reality.

- As part of a group assignment, a college student at a summer biology camp in the Sierra Nevada mountains reads about the condition of mammals at birth. She discovers the distinction between infant mammals that are *altricial* (born nude and helpless within a protective nest) and those that are *precocial* (born well-formed with eyes open and ears erect). In her part of a group report, she develops this contrast point by point, giving many examples of specific mammals but focusing in detail on altricial mice and precocial porcupines. Domestic cats, she points out, are an intermediate example—born with some fur but with eyes and ears closed.

A GUIDE TO READING ESSAYS EXPLAINING CONCEPTS

This guide is designed to introduce you to concept explanation. We ask you to read, annotate, and write about the following essay by David Quammen. First, you will read it for meaning, looking closely at the information the writer gives about the concept. Then, you will reread the essay like a writer to analyze the range of strategies it employs in explaining the concept.

DAVID QUAMMEN

Is Sex Necessary? Virgin Birth and Opportunism in the Garden

> *David Quammen (b. 1948) is a novelist, nature writer, and a columnist for the magazine* Outside. *The readers of* Outside *have special interests in nature, outdoor recreation, and the environment, but few have advanced training in ecology or biology. Quammen has also published articles in* Smithsonian Magazine, Audubon, Esquire, Rolling Stone, *and* Harper's. *His books include the novel* The Soul of Viktor Tronko *(1987) and several essay collections, including* The Song of the Dodo *(1996),* Wild Thoughts from Wild Places *(1998), and* Natural Acts: A Sidelong View of Science and Nature *(1985), from which the following selection is taken.*
>
> *In this essay, Quammen gives us a nonscientist's introduction to parthenogenesis—not only to the facts of it but also to its significance in nature. As you read, annotate anything that helps you understand the concept of parthenogenesis. Notice also Quammen's attempts to amuse as well as inform, and think about how his playfulness might help or get in the way of readers' understanding of the concept.*

Birds do it, bees do it, goes the tune. But the songsters, as usual, would mislead us with drastic oversimplifications.   1

The full truth happens to be more eccentrically nonlibidinous: Sometimes they *don't* do it, those very creatures, and get the same results anyway. Bees of all species, for instance, are notable to geneticists precisely for their ability to produce offspring while doing *without.* Likewise at least one variety of bird—the Beltsville Small White turkey, a domestic dinnertable model out of Beltsville, Maryland—has achieved scientific renown for a similar feat. What we are talking about here is celibate motherhood, procreation without copulation, a phenomenon that goes by the technical name *parthenogenesis.* Translated from the Greek roots: virgin birth.

And you don't have to be Catholic to believe in this one.   2

Miraculous as it may seem, parthenogenesis is actually   3 rather common throughout nature, practiced regularly or intermittently by at least some species within almost every group of animals except (for reasons still unknown) dragonflies and mammals. Reproduction by virgin females has been discovered among reptiles, birds, fishes, amphibians, crustaceans, mollusks, ticks, the jellyfish clan, flatworms, roundworms, segmented worms; and among insects (notwithstanding those unrelentingly sexy dragonflies) it is especially favored. The order *Hymenoptera,* including all bees and wasps, is uniformly parthenogenetic in the manner by which males are produced: Every male honeybee is born without any genetic contribution from a father. Among the beetles, there are thirty-five different forms of parthenogenetic weevil. The African weaver ant employs parthenogenesis, as do twenty-three species of fruit fly and at least one kind of roach. The gall midge *Miastor* is notorious for the exceptionally bizarre and grisly scenario that allows its fatherless young to see daylight: *Miastor* daughters cannibalize the mother from inside, with ruthless impatience, until her hollowed-out skin splits open like the door of an overcrowded nursery. But the foremost practitioners of virgin birth—their elaborate and versatile proficiency unmatched in the animal kingdom—are undoubtedly the aphids.

Now no sensible reader of even this can be expected, I real-   4 ize, to care faintly about aphid biology *qua* aphid biology. That's just asking too much. But there's a larger rationale for dragging you aphidward. The life cycle of these little nebbishy sap-sucking insects, the very same that infest rose bushes and house plants, not only exemplifies *how* parthenogenetic reproduction is done; it also very clearly shows *why.*

First the biographical facts. A typical aphid, which feeds   5 entirely on plant juices tapped off from the vascular system of young leaves, spends winter dormant and protected, as an egg. The egg is attached near a bud site on the new growth of a poplar tree. In March, when the tree sap has begun to rise and the buds have begun to burgeon, an aphid hatchling appears, plugging its sharp snout (like a mosquito's) into the tree's tenderest plumbing. This solitary individual aphid will be, necessarily, a wingless female. If she is lucky, she will become sole founder of a vast aphid population. Having sucked enough poplar sap to reach maturity, she produces—by *live birth* now, and without benefit of a mate—daughters identical to herself. These wingless daughters also plug into the tree's flow of sap, and they also produce further wingless daughters, until sometime in late May, when that particular branch of that particular tree can support no more thirsty aphids. Suddenly there is a change: The next generation of daughters are born with wings. They fly off in search of a better situation.

One such aviatrix lands on an herbaceous plant—say a young climbing bean in some human's garden—and the pattern repeats. She plugs into the sap ducts on the underside of a new leaf, commences feasting destructively, and delivers by parthenogenesis a great brood of wingless daughters. The daughters beget more daughters, those daughters beget still more, and so on, until the poor bean plant is encrusted with a solid mob of these fat little elbowing greedy sisters. Then again, neatly triggered by the crowded conditions, a generation of daughters are born with wings. Away they fly, looking for prospects, and one of them lights on, say, a sugar beet. (The switch from bean to beet is fine, because our species of typical aphid is not inordinately choosy.) The sugar beet before long is covered, sucked upon mercilessly, victimized by a horde of mothers and nieces and granddaughters. Still not a single male aphid has appeared anywhere in the chain.

The lurching from one plant to another continues; the alternation between wingless and winged daughters continues. But in September, with fresh tender plant growth increasingly hard to find, there is another change.

Flying daughters are born who have a different destiny: They wing back to the poplar tree, where they give birth to a crop of wingless females that are unlike any so far. These latest girls know the meaning of sex! Meanwhile, at long last, the starving survivors back on that final bedraggled sugar beet have brought forth a generation of males. The males have wings. They take to the air in quest of poplar trees and first love. *Et voilà.* The mated females lay eggs that will wait out the winter near bud sites on that poplar tree, and the circle is thus completed. One single aphid hatching—call her the *fundatrix*—in this way can give rise in the course of a year, from her own ovaries exclusively, to roughly a zillion aphids.

Well and good, you say. A zillion aphids. But what is the point of it? 9

The point, for aphids as for most other parthenogenetic animals, is (1) exceptionally fast reproduction that allows (2) maximal exploitation of temporary resource abundance and unstable environmental conditions, while (3) facilitating the successful colonization of unfamiliar habitats. In other words the aphid, like the gall midge and the weaver ant and the rest of their fellow parthenogens, is by its evolved character a galloping opportunist. 10

This is a term of science, not of abuse. Population ecologists make an illuminating distinction between what they label *equilibrium* and *opportunistic* species. According to William Birky and John Gilbert, from a paper in the journal *American Zoologist:* "Equilibrium species, exemplified by many vertebrates, maintain relatively constant population sizes, in part by being adapted to reproduce, at least slowly, in most of the environmental conditions which they meet. Opportunistic species, on the other hand, show extreme population fluctuations; they are adapted to reproduce only in a relatively narrow range of conditions, but make up for this by reproducing extremely rapidly in favorable circumstances. At least in some cases, opportunistic organisms can also be categorized as colonizing organisms." Birky and Gilbert also emphasize that "The potential for rapid reproduction is the essential evolutionary ticket for entry into the opportunistic lifestyle." 11

And parthenogenesis, in turn, is the greatest time-saving gimmick in the history of animal reproduction. No hours or days are wasted while a female looks for a mate; no minutes lost to the act of mating itself. The female aphid attains sexual maturity and, bang, she becomes automatically pregnant. No waiting, no courtship, no fooling around. She delivers her brood of daughters, they grow to puberty and, zap, another generation immediately. If humans worked as fast, Jane Fonda today would be a great-grandmother. The time saved to parthenogenetic species may seem trivial, but it is not. It adds up dizzyingly: In the same time taken by a sexually reproducing insect to complete three generations for a total of 1,200 offspring, an aphid (assuming the *same* time re- 12 quired for each female to mature, and the *same* number of progeny in each litter), squandering no time on courtship or sex, will progress through six generations for an extended family of 318,000,000.

Even this isn't speedy enough for some restless opportunists. That matricidal gall midge *Miastor,* whose larvae feed on fleeting eruptions of fungus under the bark of trees, has developed a startling way to cut further time from the cycle of procreation. Far from waiting for a mate, *Miastor* does not even wait for maturity. When food is abundant, it is the *larva,* not the adult female fly, who is eaten alive from inside by her own daughters. And as those voracious daughters burst free of the husk that was their mother, each of them already contains further larval daughters taking shape ominously within its own ovaries. While the food lasts, while opportunity endures, no *Miastor* female can live to adulthood without dying of motherhood.

The implicit principle behind all this nonsexual reproduction, all this hurry, is simple: Don't argue with success. Don't tamper with a genetic blueprint that works. Unmated female aphids, and gall midges, pass on their own gene patterns virtually unaltered (except for the occasional mutation) to their daughters. Sexual reproduction on the other hand, constitutes, by its essence, genetic tampering. The whole purpose of joining sperm with egg is to shuffle the genes of both parents and come up with a new combination that might perhaps be more advantageous. Give the kid something neither Mom nor Pop ever had. Parthenogenetic species, during their hurried phases at least, dispense with this genetic shuffle. They stick stubbornly to the gene pattern that seems to be working. They produce (with certain complicated exceptions) natural clones of themselves.

But what they gain thereby in reproductive rate, in great explosions of population, they give up in flexibility. They minimize their genetic options. They lessen their chances of adapting to unforeseen changes of circumstance.

Which is why more than one biologist has drawn the same conclusion as M. J. D. White: "Parthenogenetic forms seem to be frequently successful in the particular ecological niche which they occupy, but sooner or later the inherent disadvantages of their genetic system must be expected to lead to a lack of adaptability, followed by eventual extinction, or perhaps in some cases by a return to sexuality."

So it *is* necessary, at least intermittently (once a year, for   17
the aphids, whether they need it or not), this thing called
sex. As of course you and I knew it must be. Otherwise
surely, by now, we mammals and dragonflies would have
come up with something more dignified.

READING FOR MEANING

Write to create meanings for Quammen's explanation of parthenogenesis.

START MAKING MEANING

Begin by writing a few sentences briefly explaining parthenogenesis.
Continue by writing about anything else in the essay or in your experience that contributes to your understanding of parthenogenesis. As you
write, you may need to reread parts of the essay, adding to your annotations any further thoughts you have as you read.

IF YOU ARE STUCK

If you cannot write at least a page, consider writing about

- the process of parthenogenesis in aphids (paragraphs 5–8).

- the advantages of nonsexual compared to sexual reproduction (paragraphs 10–14).

- the distinction between equilibrium and opportunistic species (paragraph 11).

- how the theory of evolution helps explain parthenogenesis.

READING LIKE A WRITER

This section guides you through an analysis of Quammen's explanatory writing strategies: *devising a readable plan, using appropriate explanatory strategies, integrating sources smoothly,* and *engaging readers' interest.* Each strategy is described briefly and followed by a critical reading
and writing activity to help you see how Quammen uses the strategy to
explain the concept of parthenogenesis.

Consider this section a writer's introduction to the explanation of
concepts. You will learn more about how different writers use these
strategies later, from the Reading Like a Writer activities following the
other selections in this chapter. Finally, at the end of the chapter, A Guide
to Writing Essays Explaining Concepts suggests how you can use these
same strategies in your own essay.

Devising a Readable Plan

Experienced writers of explanation know that readers often have a hard time making their way through new and difficult material and sometimes give up in frustration. Writers who want to avoid this scenario construct a reader-friendly plan by dividing the information into clearly distinguishable topics. They also give readers road signs—forecasting statements, transitions, and topic sentences—to guide them through the explanation. Writers often provide a forecasting statement early in the essay to let readers know where they are heading.

They also may provide cues like topic sentences to announce each subject of discussion as it comes up, transitions (such as *in contrast* and *another*) to relate what is coming to what came before, and summaries to remind readers what has been explained already.

ANALYZE

1. *Underline* the forecasting sentence, in paragraph 4, that states the two major topics of the essay.

2. *Find* where the first of these topics begins and *underline* the topic sentence that announces it.

3. *Find* where the second topic begins and *underline* the topic sentence that announces it. *Notice* that topic sentences sometimes include transitions and summaries.

WRITE

Write a few sentences, explaining and evaluating how Quammen's use of forecasting and topic sentences makes his explanation easy to follow.

Using Appropriate Explanatory Strategies

When writers organize and present information, they rely on strategies we call the building blocks of explanatory essays: defining, classifying or dividing, comparing and contrasting, narrating a process, illustrating, and reporting causes or effects. The strategies a writer chooses are determined by the topics covered, the kinds of information available, and the writer's assessment of readers' knowledge about the concept. Following are brief descriptions of the writing strategies that are particularly useful in explaining concepts:

Defining: Briefly stating the meaning of the concept or any other word likely to be unfamiliar to readers

Classifying or dividing: Grouping related information about a concept into two or more discrete groups and labeling each group, or dividing a concept into its constituent parts to consider each part separately

Comparing and contrasting: Pointing out how the concept is similar to and different from a related concept

Narrating a process: Presenting procedures or a sequence of steps as they unfold over time to show the concept in practice

Illustrating: Giving examples, relating anecdotes, listing facts and details, and quoting sources to help readers understand a concept

Reporting causes or effects: Identifying the known causes or effects related to a concept

ANALYZE

Quammen makes good use of all these fundamentally important explanatory strategies: defining in paragraphs 1, 8, and 11; classifying in paragraphs 10 and 11; comparing and contrasting in paragraphs 11–14 (as well as establishing the analogy between insects and humans that runs through the essay); narrating a process in paragraphs 5–8; illustrating in paragraph 3; and reporting known effects in paragraphs 12–14. *Review* Quammen's use of each strategy, and *select* one to analyze more closely.

WRITE

Write several sentences, describing how the strategy you have analyzed works in this essay to help readers understand the concept.

Integrating Sources Smoothly

In addition to drawing on experience and observation, writers often do additional research about the concepts they are trying to explain. How writers treat sources depends on the writing situation. Certain formal situations, such as college assignments or scholarly publications, have prescribed rules for citing and documenting sources. As a student, you are expected to cite your sources formally because your writing will be judged in part by what you have read and how you have used your reading. For more informal writing occasions—newspaper and magazine articles, for example—readers do not expect writers to include page references or publication information, only to identify their sources.

Writers may quote, summarize, or paraphrase their sources: quoting when they want to capture the exact wording of the original source; summarizing to convey only the gist or main points; and paraphrasing when they have details to add to the original. Whether they quote, summarize, or paraphrase, writers try to integrate source material smoothly into their writing. For example, they deliberately vary the way they introduce borrowed material, avoiding repetition of the same signal phrase (*X* said, as *Y* put it).

ANALYZE

1. *Look* closely at paragraphs 11 and 16, where Quammen quotes sources directly.

2. *Put brackets* ([ ]) around the signal phrase he uses to introduce each quotation, noticing how he integrates the quotation into his sentence.

WRITE

Write a few sentences, describing how Quammen introduces and integrates quotations into his writing. *Give examples* from paragraphs 11 and 16.

Engaging Readers' Interest

Most people read explanations of concepts because they are helpful for work or school. They do not generally expect the writing to entertain, but simply to inform. Nevertheless, explanations that keep readers awake with lively and relevant writing are usually appreciated. Writers explaining concepts may engage readers' interest in a variety of ways. For example, they may remind readers of what they already know about the concept. They may show readers a new way of using a familiar concept or dramatize that the concept has greater importance than realized. They can connect the concept, sometimes through metaphor or analogy, to common human experiences. They may present the concept in a humorous way to convince readers that learning about a concept can be painless, or even pleasurable.

Quammen relies on many of these strategies to engage his readers' interest. Keep in mind that his original readers could either read or skip his column. Those who enjoyed and learned from previous Quammen columns would be more likely to try out the first few paragraphs of this one, but Quammen could not count on their having any special interest in parthenogenesis. He has to try to generate that interest—and rather quickly in the first few sentences.

ANALYZE

Reread paragraphs 1–4, noting in the margin the various ways Quammen reaches out to interest readers in his subject.

WRITE

Write several sentences, explaining how Quammen attempts to engage his readers' interest in parthenogenesis. What parts seem most effective to you? Least effective?

DEBORAH TANNEN

Marked Women

Deborah Tannen (b. 1945) holds the prestigious title of University Professor in Linguistics at Georgetown University in Washington, D.C. She has written more than a dozen books and scores of articles. Although she does write technical articles in linguistics, she also writes for a more general audience on the ways that language reflects the society in which it develops, particularly the society's attitudes about gender. Both her 1986 book, That's Not What I Meant!: How Conversational Style Makes or Breaks Your Relations with Others, *and her 1990 book,* You Just Don't Understand: Women and Men in Conversation, *were best-sellers.* The Argument Culture: Moving from Debate to Dialogue *was published in 1998. The following selection comes from an article that was originally published in the* New York Times Magazine *in 1993.*

In this essay, Tannen explains the concept of markedness, a "staple of linguistic theory." In this century, linguistics—the study of language as a system for making meaning—has given birth to a new discipline called semiology, *the study of any system for making meaning. Tannen's essay embodies this shift, as it starts with a verbal principle (the marking of words) and applies it to the visual world (the marking of hair style and clothing). As you read the opening paragraphs, notice how Tannen unpacks the meaning of what various conference participants are wearing.*

Some years ago I was at a small working conference of four women and eight men. Instead of concentrating on the discussion I found myself looking at the three other women at the table, thinking how each had a different style and how each style was coherent. 1

One woman had dark brown hair in a classic style, a cross between Cleopatra and Plain Jane. The severity of her straight hair was softened by wavy bangs and ends that turned under. Because she was beautiful, the effect was more Cleopatra than plain. 2

The second woman was older, full of dignity and composure. Her hair was cut in a fashionable style that left her with only one eye, thanks to a side part that let a curtain of hair fall across half her face. As she looked down to read her prepared paper, the hair robbed her of bifocal vision and created a barrier between her and the listeners. 3

The third woman's hair was wild, a frosted blond ava-   4
lanche falling over and beyond her shoulders. When she
spoke she frequently tossed her head, calling attention to
her hair and away from her lecture.

Then there was makeup. The first woman wore facial   5
cover that made her skin smooth and pale, a black line
under each eye and mascara that darkened already dark
lashes. The second wore only a light gloss on her lips and a
hint of shadow on her eyes. The third had blue bands under
her eyes, dark blue shadow, mascara, bright red lipstick and
rouge; her fingernails flashed red.

I considered the clothes each woman had worn during the   6
three days of the conference: In the first case, man-tailored
suits in primary colors with solid-color blouses. In the second, casual but stylish black T-shirts, a floppy collarless
jacket and baggy slacks or a skirt in neutral colors. The third
wore a sexy jump suit; tight sleeveless jersey and tight yellow slacks; a dress with gaping armholes and an indulged
tendency to fall off one shoulder.

Shoes? No. 1 wore string sandals with medium heels; No.   7
2, sensible, comfortable walking shoes; No. 3, pumps with
spike heels. You can fill in the jewelry, scarves, shawls,
sweaters—or lack of them.

As I amused myself finding coherence in these styles, I   8
suddenly wondered why I was scrutinizing only the women.
I scanned the eight men at the table. And then I knew why I
wasn't studying them. The men's styles were unmarked.

The term "marked" is a staple of linguistic theory. It refers   9
to the way language alters the base meaning of a word by
adding a linguistic particle that has no meaning on its own.
The unmarked form of a word carries the meaning that goes
without saying—what you think of when you're not thinking
anything special.

The unmarked tense of verbs in English is the present—   10
for example, *visit.* To indicate past, you mark the verb by
adding *ed* to yield *visited.* For future, you add a word: *will
visit.* Nouns are presumed to be singular until marked for
plural, typically by adding *s* or *es,* so *visit* becomes *visits* and
dish becomes *dishes.*

The unmarked forms of most English words also convey   11
"male." Being male is the unmarked case. Endings like *ess*
and *ette* mark words as "female." Unfortunately, they also
tend to mark them for frivolousness. Would you feel safe en-
trusting your life to a doctorette? Alfre Woodard, who was
an Oscar nominee for best supporting actress, says she iden-

tifies herself as an actor because "actresses worry about eyelashes and cellulite, and women who are actors worry about the characters we are playing." Gender markers pick up extra meanings that reflect common association with the female gender: not quite serious, often sexual.

Each of the women at the conference had to make decisions about hair, clothing, makeup and accessories, and each decision carried meaning. Every style available to us was marked. The men in our group had made decisions, too, but the range from which they chose was incomparably narrower. Men can choose styles that are marked, but they don't have to, and in this group none did. Unlike the women, they had the option of being unmarked.   12

Take the men's hair styles. There was no marine crew cut or oily longish hair falling into eyes, no asymmetrical, two-tiered construction to swirl over a bald top. One man was unabashedly bald; the others had hair of standard length, parted on one side, in natural shades of brown or gray or graying. Their hair obstructed no views, left little to toss or push back or run fingers through and, consequently, needed and attracted no attention. A few men had beards. In a business setting, beards might be marked. In this academic gathering, they weren't.   13

There could have been a cowboy shirt with string tie or a three-piece suit or a necklaced hippie in jeans. But there wasn't. All eight men wore brown or blue slacks and nondescript shirts of light colors. No man wore sandals or boots; their shoes were dark, closed, comfortable, and flat. In short, unmarked.   14

Although no man wore makeup, you couldn't say the men didn't wear makeup in the sense that you could say a woman didn't wear makeup. For men, no makeup is unmarked.   15

I asked myself what style we women could have adopted that would have been unmarked, like the men's. The answer was none. There is no unmarked woman.   16

There is no woman's hair style that can be called standard, that says nothing about her. The range of women's hair styles is staggering, but a woman whose hair has no particular style is perceived as not caring about how she looks, which can disqualify her from many positions, and will subtly diminish her as a person in the eyes of some.   17

Women must choose between attractive shoes and comfortable shoes. When our group made an unexpected trek, the woman who wore flat, laced shoes arrived first. Last to arrive was the woman in spike heels, shoes in hand and a handful of men around her.   18

If a woman's clothing is tight or revealing (in other words,   19
sexy), it sends a message—an intended one of wanting to be
attractive, but also a possibly unintended one of availability.
If her clothes are not sexy, that too sends a message, lent
meaning by the knowledge that they could have been. There
are thousands of cosmetic products from which women can
choose and myriad ways of applying them. Yet no makeup at
all is anything but unmarked. Some men see it as a hostile re-
fusal to please them.

Women can't even fill out a form without telling stories   20
about themselves. Most forms give four titles to choose
from. "Mr." carries no meaning other than that the respon-
dent is male. But a woman who checks "Mrs." or "Miss" com-
municates not only whether she has been married but also
whether she has conservative tastes in forms of address—
and probably other conservative values as well. Checking
"Ms." declines to let on about marriage (checking "Mr." declines nothing since nothing was asked), but it also marks
her as either liberated or rebellious, depending on the observer's attitudes and assumptions.

I sometimes try to duck these variously marked choices   21
by giving my title as "Dr."—and in so doing risk marking myself as either uppity (hence sarcastic responses like "Excuse
me!") or an overachiever (hence reactions of congratulatory
surprise like "Good for you!").

All married women's surnames are marked. If a woman   22
takes her husband's name, she announces to the world that
she is married and has traditional values. To some it will indicate that she is less herself, more identified by her husband's identity. If she does not take her husband's name,
this too is marked, seen as worthy of comment: She has
done something; she has "kept her own name." A man is
never said to have "kept his own name" because it never occurs to anyone that he might have given it up. For him using
his own name is unmarked.

A married woman who wants to have her cake and eat it   23
too may use her surname plus his, with or without a hyphen.
But this too announces her marital status and often results in a tongue-tying string. In a list (Harvey O'Donovan,
Jonathan Feldman, Stephanie Woodbury McGillicutty), the
woman's multiple name stands out. It is marked.

I have never been inclined toward biological explanations   24
of gender differences in language, but I was intrigued to see
Ralph Fasold bring biological phenomena to bear on the
question of linguistic marking in his book *The Sociolinguis-*

tics of Language. Fasold stresses that language and culture are particularly unfair in treating women as the marked case because biologically it is the male that is marked. While two X chromosomes make a female, two Y chromosomes make nothing. Like the linguistic markers *s, es,* or *ess,* the Y chromosome doesn't "mean" anything unless it is attached to a root form—an X chromosome.

Developing this idea elsewhere Fasold points out that girls are born with full female bodies, while boys are born with modified female bodies. He invites men who doubt this to lift up their shirts and contemplate why they have nipples.   25

In his book, Fasold notes "a wide range of facts which demonstrates that female is the unmarked sex." For example, he observes that there are a few species that produce only females, like the whiptail lizard. Thanks to parthenogenesis, they have no trouble having as many daughters as they like. There are no species, however, that produce only males. This is no surprise, since any such species would become extinct in its first generation.   26

Fasold is also intrigued by species that produce individuals not involved in reproduction, like honeybees and leafcutter ants. Reproduction is handled by the queen and a relatively few males; the workers are sterile females. "Since they do not reproduce," Fasold said, "there is no reason for them to be one sex or the other, so they default, so to speak, to female."   27

Fasold ends his discussion of these matters by pointing out that if language reflected biology, grammar books would direct us to use "she" to include males and females and "he" only for specifically male referents. But they don't. They tell us that "he" means "he or she," and that "she" is used only if the referent is specifically female. This use of "he" as the sex-indefinite pronoun is an innovation introduced into English by grammarians in the eighteenth and nineteenth centuries, according to Peter Mühlhäusler and Rom Harré in *Pronouns and People.* From at least about 1500, the correct sex-indefinite pronoun was "they," as it still is in casual spoken English. In other words, the female was declared by grammarians to be the marked case.   28

Writing this article may mark me not as a writer, not as a linguist, not as an analyst of human behavior, but as a feminist—which will have positive or negative, but in any case powerful, connotations for readers. Yet I doubt that anyone reading Ralph Fasold's book would put that label on him.   29

I discovered the markedness inherent in the very topic of gender after writing a book on differences in conversational   30 style based on geographical region, ethnicity, class, age, and gender. When I was interviewed, the vast majority of journalists wanted to talk about the differences between women and men. While I thought I was simply describing what I observed—something I had learned to do as a researcher—merely mentioning women and men marked me as a feminist for some.

31   When I wrote a book devoted to gender differences in ways of speaking, I sent the manuscript to five male colleagues, asking them to alert me to any interpretation, phrasing, or wording that might seem unfairly negative toward men. Even so, when the book came out, I encountered responses like that of the television talk show host who, after interviewing me, turned to the audience and asked if they thought I was male-bashing.

32   Leaping upon a poor fellow who affably nodded in agreement, she made him stand and asked, "Did what she said accurately describe you?" "Oh, yes," he answered. "That's me exactly." "And what she said about women—does that sound like your wife?" "Oh, yes," he responded. "That's her exactly." "Then why do you think she's male-bashing?" He answered, with disarming honesty, "Because she's a woman and she's saying things about men."

33   To say anything about women and men without marking oneself as either feminist or anti-feminist, male-basher or apologist for men seems as impossible for a woman as trying to get dressed in the morning without inviting interpretations of her character.

34   Sitting at the conference table musing on these matters, I felt sad to think that we women didn't have the freedom to be unmarked that the men sitting next to us had. Some days you just want to get dressed and go about your business. But if you're a woman, you can't, because there is no unmarked woman.

READING FOR MEANING

Write to create meanings for Tannen's essay on the concept of markedness.

START MAKING MEANING

Begin by listing two or three effective examples of markedness in Tannen's essay, explaining briefly how these examples help you understand the concept. Continue by writing about anything else in the essay or in your experience that contributes to your understanding of markedness.

IF YOU ARE STUCK

If you cannot write at least a page, consider writing about

- what one marked style in hair and clothes might look like for men.

- other examples of markedness, associated not with gender but with age, ethnicity, social class, income level, or anything else you can think of.

- Tannen's assumption that this essay may mark her for certain readers "as a feminist—which will have positive or negative, but in any case powerful, connotations for readers" (paragraph 29).

- how your earlier reading of David Quammen's essay on parthenogenesis (pp. 163–68) helps you understand Ralph Fasold's ideas about biology and the marking of women.

READING LIKE A WRITER
EXPLAINING THROUGH ILLUSTRATION

Because concepts are abstractions, mental not physical realities, they tend to be hard to grasp. One way to explain a concept is through illustration. Examples, anecdotes, descriptive detail, and specific facts and figures provide concrete images that help readers grasp or visualize concepts. Writers explaining concepts usually give several brief examples and sometimes also present an extended example. In his essay explaining parthenogenesis (pp. 163–68), David Quammen cites several examples of parthenogenetic species (paragraphs 2 and 3) and develops the example of the aphid over several paragraphs (4–8) so that readers can understand fully what is involved in the process of parthenogenesis. The following activity invites you to examine Tannen's use of a variety of brief examples to explain the concept of markedness.

ANALYZE

1. *Reread* paragraphs 1–8, noting Tannen's examples in the margin.

2. *Examine* the first two sentences in paragraph 19 to see how she connects the examples in paragraphs 1–8 to the concept of markedness.

WRITE

Write several sentences, discussing how Tannen uses examples to explain the abstract concept of markedness. *Cite* examples from paragraphs 1–8 to illustrate your answer.

CONSIDERING IDEAS FOR YOUR OWN WRITING

If you are taking a course concerned with language and society, you might want to learn about and then explain another linguistic concept such as semantics, language acquisition, connotation, or discourse community, or a semiotic concept such as signification, code, iconography, or popular culture. Related fields with interesting concepts to learn and write about are gender studies and sociology. Gender studies is concerned with such concepts as femininity, masculinity, the objectification of individuals, and the construction of desire. Sociology uses concepts such as socialization, the family, role model, community, and status to study group dynamics and social patterns.

PHILIP ELMER-DEWITT

Welcome to Cyberspace

> *Philip Elmer-DeWitt (b. 1949) is a* Time *magazine senior editor specializing in technology, including everything from video games to new operating systems. The following selection is excerpted from an article introducing a special Spring 1995 issue of* Time *on the future uses of cyberspace and its potential impact on the economy and politics. Given the context in which this essay was originally published plus the essay's title, Elmer-DeWitt evidently assumes that his readers know relatively little about the subject. As you read and annotate the essay, think about the way he systematically builds his explanation bit by bit.*

It started, as the big ideas in technology often do, with a   1
science-fiction writer. William Gibson, a young expatriate
American living in Canada, was wandering past the video ar-
cades on Vancouver's Granville Street in the early 1980s
when something about the way the players were hunched
over their glowing screens struck him as odd. "I could see in
the physical intensity of their postures how *rapt* the kids
were," he says. "It was like a feedback loop, with photons
coming off the screens into the kids' eyes, neurons moving
through their bodies and electrons moving through the
video game. These kids clearly *believed* in the space the
games projected."

That image haunted Gibson. He didn't know much about   2
video games or computers—he wrote his breakthrough
novel *Neuromancer* (1984) on an ancient manual typewriter—
but he knew people who did. And as near as he could tell,
everybody who worked much with the machines eventually
came to accept, almost as an article of faith, the reality of
that imaginary realm. "They develop a belief that there's
some kind of *actual space* behind the screen," he says.
"Some place that you can't see but you know is there."

Gibson called that place "cyberspace," and used it as the   3
setting for his early novels and short stories. In his fiction,
cyberspace is a computer-generated landscape that characters enter by "jacking in"—sometimes by plugging elec-
trodes directly into sockets implanted in the brain. What
they see when they get there is a three-dimensional representation of all the information stored in "every computer in
the human system"—great warehouses and skyscrapers of
data. He describes it in a key passage in *Neuromancer* as a

place of "unthinkable complexity," with "lines of light ranged in the nonspace of the mind, clusters and constellations of data. Like city lights, receding. . . ."

In the years since, there have been other names given to that shadowy space where our computer data reside: the Net, the Web, the Cloud, the Matrix, the Metaverse, the Datasphere, the Electronic Frontier, the information superhighway. But Gibson's coinage may prove the most enduring. By 1989 it had been borrowed by the online community to describe not some science-fiction fantasy but today's increasingly interconnected computer systems—especially the millions of computers jacked into the Internet.

Now hardly a day goes by without some newspaper article, some political speech, some corporate press release invoking Gibson's imaginary world. Suddenly, it seems, everybody has an E-mail address, from Hollywood moguls to the Holy See. Billy Graham has preached on America Online; Vice President Al Gore has held forth on CompuServe; thousands chose to celebrate New Year's this year with an online get-together called first Night in Cyberspace. . . .

Corporations, smelling a land rush of another sort, are scrambling to stake out their own claims in cyberspace. Every computer company, nearly every publisher, most communications firms, banks, insurance companies and hundreds of mail-order and retail firms are registering their Internet domains and setting up sites on the World Wide Web. They sense that cyberspace will be one of the driving forces—if not the primary one—for economic growth in the 21st century.

All this is being breathlessly reported in the press, which has seized on cyberspace as an all-purpose buzz word that can add sparkle to the most humdrum development or assignment. For working reporters, many of whom have just discovered the pleasures of going online, cyber has become the prefix of the day, and they are spawning neologisms as fast as they type: cyberphilia, cyberphobia, cyberwonk, cybersex, cyberslut. A Nexis search of newspapers, magazines, and television transcripts turned up 1,205 mentions of cyber in the month of January, up from 464 the previous January and 167 in January 1993.

One result of this drum roll is a growing public appetite for a place most people haven't been to and are often hard-pressed to define. In a *Time*/CNN poll of 800 Americans conducted in January by Yankelovich Partners, 57% didn't know what cyberspace meant, yet 85% were certain that information technology had made their life better. They may not know where it is, but they want desperately to get there. The rush to get online, to avoid being "left behind" in the information revolution, is intense. Those who find fulfillment in cyberspace often have the religious fervor of the recently converted.

These sentiments have been captured brilliantly in an   9
IBM ad on TV showing a phalanx of Czech nuns discussing— of all things—the latest operating system from Microsoft. As they walk briskly through a convent, a young novice mentions IBM's competing system, called Warp. "I just read about it in *Wired,*" she gushes. "You get true multitasking . . . easy access to the Internet." An older sister glances up with obvious interest; the camera cuts to the mother superior, who wistfully confesses, "I'm dying to surf the Net." Fade as the pager tucked under her habit starts to beep.

Cybernuns.   10

What is cyberspace? According to John Perry Barlow, a   11
rock-'n'-roll lyricist turned computer activist, it can be defined most succinctly as "that place you are in when you are talking on the telephone." That's as good a place to start as any. The telephone system, after all, is really a vast, global computer network with a distinctive, audible presence (crackling static against an almost inaudible background hum). By Barlow's definition, just about everybody has already been to cyberspace. It's marked by the feeling that the person you're talking to is "in the same room." Most people take the spatial dimension of a phone conversation for granted—until they get a really bad connection or a glitchy overseas call. Then they start raising their voice, as if by sheer volume they could propel it to the outer reaches of cyberspace.

Cyberspace, of course, is bigger than a telephone call. It   12
encompasses the millions of personal computers connected by modems—via the telephone system—to commercial online services, as well as the millions more with high-speed links to local area networks, office E-mail systems and the Internet. It includes the rapidly expanding wireless services: microwave towers that carry great quantities of cellular phone and data traffic; communications satellites strung like beads in geosynchronous orbit; low-flying satellites that will soon crisscross the globe like angry bees, connecting folks too far-flung or too much on the go to be tethered by wires. Someday even our television sets may be part of cyberspace, transformed into interactive "teleputers" by so-called full-service networks like the ones several cable-TV companies (including Time Warner) are building along the old cable lines, using fiber optics and high-speed switches.

But these wires and cables and microwaves are not really   13
cyberspace. They are the means of conveyance, not the des-
tination: the information superhighway, not the bright city
lights at the end of the road. Cyberspace, in the sense of
being "in the same room," is an experience, not a wiring system. It is about people using the new technology to do what
they are genetically programmed to do: communicate with
one another. It can be found in electronic mail exchanged by
lovers who have never met. It emerges from the endless debates on mailing lists and message boards. It's that bond
that knits together regulars in electronic chat rooms and
newsgroups. It is, like Plato's plane of ideal forms, a metaphorical space, a virtual reality.

But it is no less real for being so. We live in the age of   14
information, as Nicholas Negroponte, director of M.I.T.'s
Media Lab, is fond of pointing out, in which the fundamental
particle is not the atom but the bit—the binary digit, a unit
of data usually represented as a 0 or 1. Information may still
be delivered in magazines and newspapers (atoms), but the
real value is in the contents (bits). We pay for our goods and
services with cash (atoms), but the ebb and flow of capital
around the world is carried out—to the tune of several tril-
lion dollars a day—in electronic funds transfers (bits).

Bits are different from atoms and obey different laws. They   15
are weightless. They are easily (and flawlessly) reproduced.
There is an infinite supply. And they can be shipped at nearly
the speed of light. When you are in the business of moving bits
around, barriers of time and space disappear. For information
providers—publishers, for example—cyberspace offers a
medium in which distribution costs shrink to zero. Buyers
and sellers can find each other in cyberspace without the benefit (or the expense) of a marketing campaign. No wonder so
many businessmen are convinced it will become a powerful
engine of economic growth.

At this point, however, cyberspace is less about com-   16
merce than about community. The technology has un-
leashed a great rush of direct, person-to-person communications, organized not in the top-down, one-to-many structure
of traditional media but in a many-to-many model that
may—just may—be a vehicle for revolutionary change. In a
world already too divided against itself—rich against poor,
producer against consumer—cyberspace offers the nearest
thing to a level playing field.

Take, for example, the Internet. Until something better   17
comes along to replace it, the Internet *is* cyberspace. It may
not reach every computer in the human system, as Gibson

imagined, but it comes very close. And as anyone who has spent much time there can attest, it is in many ways even stranger than fiction.

Begun more than 20 years ago as a Defense Department   18
experiment, the Internet escaped from the Pentagon in 1984 and spread like kudzu during the personal-computer boom, nearly doubling every year from the mid-1980s on. Today 30 million to 40 million people in more than 160 countries have at least E-mail access to the Internet; in Japan, New Zealand and parts of Europe the number of Net users has grown more than 1,000% during the past three years.

One factor fueling the Internet's remarkable growth is its   19
resolutely grass-roots structure. Most conventional computer systems are hierarchical and proprietary; they run on copyright software in a pyramid structure that gives dictatorial powers to the system operators who sit on top. The Internet, by contrast, is open (nonproprietary) and rabidly democratic. No one owns it. No single organization controls it. It is run like a commune with 4.8 million fiercely independent members (called hosts). It crosses national boundaries and answers to no sovereign. It is literally lawless.

Although graphics, photos, and even videos have started   20
to show up, cyberspace, as it exists on the Internet, is still primarily a text medium. People communicate by and large through words, typed and displayed on a screen. Yet cyberspace assumes an astonishing array of forms, from the utilitarian mailing list (a sort of junk E-mail list to which anyone can contribute) to the rococo MUDs, or Multi-User Dungeons (elaborate fictional gathering places that users create one "room" at a time). All these "spaces" have one thing in common: they are egalitarian to a fault. Anybody can play (provided he or she has the requisite equipment and access), and everybody is afforded the same level of respect (which is to say, little or none). Stripped of the external trappings of wealth, power, beauty and social status, people tend to be judged in the cyberspace of the Internet only by their ideas and their ability to get them across in terse, vigorous prose. On the Internet, as the famous *New Yorker* cartoon put it, nobody knows you're a dog.

READING FOR MEANING

Write to create meanings for Elmer-DeWitt's explanation of cyberspace.

START MAKING MEANING

Begin by identifying the part of this essay you think would be most helpful to readers unfamiliar with cyberspace, briefly explaining why you think it would help them understand the concept. Continue by writing about anything else in the essay or in your experience that contributes to your understanding of cyberspace.

IF YOU ARE STUCK

If you cannot write at least a page, consider writing about

- William Gibson's use of such words as *faith* and *belief* to suggest that video-game playing or Internet surfing is comparable in some way to a religious experience (paragraph 2).

- the idea that people are "genetically programmed" to communicate with one another (paragraph 13).

- what you think Elmer-DeWitt means when he writes that cyberspace "may—just may—be a vehicle for revolutionary change" (paragraph 16).

- the idea that cyberspace is democratic (paragraphs 19–20).

READING LIKE A WRITER
DEVISING A READABLE PLAN

To help readers understand a new or difficult concept, writers decide what information readers should know about the concept and divide the information into topics. These topics are then put into some kind of order that the writer hopes will make sense to readers. Writers can also help their readers by providing road signs. These road signs might be topic sentences that announce the significance of an individual paragraph. They might be transitional words or phrases—narrative time markers (such as *in the years since* and *now*) or logical markers (such as *but* and *although* to signal a contrast).

This activity invites you to construct an outline of Elmer-DeWitt's essay, and to discover how he uses topic sentences and transitions to help make his essay easy to follow.

ANALYZE

1. *Make* a scratch outline by noting in the margin the topic of each paragraph or group of paragraphs. (For help with making a scratch outline, see Appendix One, p. 461.)

2. *Underline* in the essay any topic sentences or transitions that helped you identify and track the topics as you made your scratch outline.

WRITE

Write several sentences, discussing how Elmer-DeWitt's topic sentences and transitions help make his essay readable, citing a few examples of good topic sentences and transitions.

CONSIDERING IDEAS FOR YOUR OWN WRITING

If you know something about computers and cyberspace, you might consider writing about one of the concepts Elmer-DeWitt mentions but does not explain in detail, such as Internet searches, local area networks, or virtual reality. Or you could explain a more general theme such as interactivity or virtual community. An alternative to these computer terms might be a concept from business, engineering, or another field. Within the field of automotive design, for example, you might consider ergonomics, torque, aerodynamics, or fuel injection. You could begin your research by consulting newspapers, books, and magazines in the field.

JANICE CASTRO

Contingent Workers

Janice Castro (b. 1949) is an associate editor at Time *magazine, where she writes about politics and business. Some of her major reports have addressed the high cost of medical care, drugs in the workplace, quality in American manufacturing, and the state of the U.S. work force. In addition to her articles, Castro has written a book,* The American Way of Health: How Medicine Is Changing and What It Means to You *(1994).*

The following essay, a Time *article originally published in 1993, discusses changes in the way American companies do business, changes that rely on part-time or freelance workers. Castro uses the term* contingent workers *to name both the phenomenon and the people it affects. If you have worked part-time in a fast-food restaurant or a campus computer lab, you may already be familiar with this concept, although you may use a different name for it. As you read, think about how your own experience as a contingent worker relates to what Castro says about it.*

The corporation that is now the largest private employer in America does not have any smokestacks or conveyor belts or trucks. There is no clanging of metal on metal, no rivets or plastic or steel. In one sense, it does not make anything. But then again, it is in the business of making almost everything.

Manpower Inc., with 560,000 workers, is the world's largest temporary employment agency. Every morning, its people scatter into the offices and factories of America, seeking a day's work for a day's pay. As General Motors (367,000 workers), IBM (330,500) and other industrial giants struggle to survive by shrinking their payrolls, Manpower, based in Milwaukee, Wisconsin, is booming along with other purveyors of temporary workers, providing the hands and the brainpower that other companies are no longer willing to call their own.

Even as its economy continues to recover, the U.S. is increasingly becoming a nation of part-timers and free-lancers, of temps and independent contractors. This "disposable" work force is the most important trend in business today, and it is fundamentally changing the relationship between Americans and their jobs. For companies large and small, the phenomenon provides a way to remain globally competitive while avoiding the vagaries of market cycles and the

growing burdens imposed by employment rules, antidis-
crimination laws, health-care costs, and pension plans. But
for workers, it can mean an end to the security and sense of
significance that came from being a loyal employee. One by
one, the tangible and intangible bonds that once defined
work in America are giving way.

Every day, 1.5 million temps are dispatched from agencies   4
like Kelly Services and Manpower—nearly three times as
many as 10 years ago. But they are only the most visible part
of America's enormous new temporary work force. An additional 34 million people start their day as other types of
"contingent" workers. Some are part-timers with some benefits. Others work by the hour, the day or the duration of a
project, receiving only a paycheck without benefits of any
kind. The rules of their employment vary widely and so do
the attempts to label them. They are called short-timers,
per-diem workers, leased employees, extra workers, supple-
mentals, contractors—or in IBM's ironic computer-generated parlance, "the peripherals." They are what you might
expect: secretaries, security guards, salesclerks, assembly-
line workers, analysts and CAD/CAM designers. But these
days they are also what you'd never expect: doctors, high
school principals, lawyers, bank officers, X-ray technicians,
biochemists, engineers, managers—even chief executives.

Already, one in every three U.S. workers has joined these   5
shadow brigades carrying out America's business. Their
ranks are growing so quickly that they are expected to out-
number permanent full-time workers by the end of this
decade. Companies keep chipping away at costs, stripping
away benefits or substituting contingent employees for full-
time workers. This year alone, U.S. employers are expected
to use such tactics to cut the nation's $2.6 billion payroll
costs as much as $800 million. And there is no evidence to
suggest that such corporate behavior will change with improvement in the economy.

No institution is immune to the contingent solution. Imag-   6
ine the surprise of a Los Angeles woman, seriously injured in
an auto accident, when she recently asked a radiology technician at the hospital about a procedure. "Don't ask me," he
snapped. "I'm just a temp." In Appleton, Wisconsin, the Aid
Association for Lutherans is using temps to keep track of
$3.6 million in relief funds for victims of Hurricane Andrew.
The State of Maine uses temps as bailiffs and financial inves-
tigators. IBM, once the citadel of American job security, has
traded 10% of its staff for "peripherals" so far. Says IBM administrative manager Lillian Davis, in words that would have

been unimaginable from a Fortune 500 executive 20 years ago: "Now that we have stepped over that line, we have decided to use these people wherever we can."

The number of people employed full time by Fortune 500 companies has shrunk from 19% of the work force two decades ago to less than 10% today. Almost overnight, companies are shedding a system of mutual obligations and expectations built up since the Great Depression, a tradition of labor that said performance was rewarded, loyalty was valued and workers were a vital part of the enterprises they served. In this chilly new world of global competition, they are often viewed merely as expenses. Long-term commitments of all kinds are anathema to the modern corporation. For the growing ranks of contingent workers, that means no more pensions, health insurance or paid vacations. No more promises or promotions or costly training programs. No more lawsuits for wrongful termination or other such hassles for the boss. Says Secretary of Labor Robert Reich: "These workers are outside the traditional system of worker-management relationships. As the contingent work force grows—as many people find themselves working part time for many different employers—the social contract is beginning to fray."

As the underpinnings of mutual commitment crumble, time-honored notions of fairness are cast aside for millions of workers. Working temp or part time often means being treated as a second-class citizen by both employers and permanent staff. Says Michelle Lane, a former temp in Los Angeles: "You're just a fixture, a borrowed thing that doesn't belong there." Being a short-timer also can mean doing hazardous work without essential training, or putting up with sexual and racial harassment. Placement officers report client requests for "blond bombshells" or people without accents. Says an agency counselor: "One client called and asked us not to send any black people, and we didn't. We do whatever the clients want, whether it's right or not."

Workers have little choice but to cope with such treatment since most new job openings are the labor equivalent of uncommitted relationships. More than 90% of the 365,000 jobs created by U.S. companies last month were part-time positions taken by people who want to work full time. "The fill-ins are always desperate for full-time jobs," says one corporate personnel officer. "They always ask." Richard Belous, chief economist for the National Planning Association in Washington, has studied the proliferation of tenuous jobs. "If there was a national fear index," he says, "it would be directly related to the growth of contingent work."

Once contingent workers appear in a company, they mul-   10
tiply rapidly, taking the places of permanent staff. Says Manpower chairman Mitchell Fromstein: "The U.S. is going from
just-in-time manufacturing to just-in-time employment. The
employer tells us, 'I want them delivered exactly when I
want them, as many as I need, and when I don't need them I
don't want them here.' " Fromstein has built his business by
meeting these demands. "Can I get people to work under
these circumstances? Yeah. We're the ATMs of the job
market."

In order to succeed in this new type of work, says Carvel   11
Taylor, a Chicago industrial consultant, "you need to have
an entrepreneurial spirit, definable skills and an ability to articulate and market them, but that is exactly what the bulk
of the population holed up inside bureaucratic organizations
doesn't have, and why they are scared to death." Already
the temping phenomenon is producing two vastly different
classes of untethered workers: the mercenary work force at
the top of the skills ladder, who thrive; and the rest, many of
whom, unable to attract fat contract fees, must struggle to
survive.

The flexible life of a consultant or contract worker does   12
indeed work well for a relatively small class of people like
doctors, engineers, accountants and financial planners, who
can expect to do well by providing highly compensated services to a variety of employers. David Hill, 65, a former chief
information systems officer for General Motors, has joined
with 17 other onetime auto-industry executives (median
salary before leaving their jobs: $300,000) to form a top-of-
the-line international consulting group. "In the future," says
Hill, "loyalty and devotion are going to be not to a Hughes or
Boeing or even an industry, but to a particular profession or
skill. It takes a high level of education to succeed in such a
free-flowing environment. We are going to be moving from
job to job in the same way that migrant workers used to
move from crop to crop."

Many professionals like the freedom of such a life. John   13
Andrews, 42, a Los Angeles antitrust attorney, remembers
working seven weeks without a day off as a young lawyer. He
prefers temping at law firms. Says he: "There's no security
anymore. Partnerships fold up overnight. Besides, I never
had a rat-race mentality, and being a lawyer is the ultimate
rat-race job. I like to travel. My car is paid for. I don't own a
house. I'm not into mowing grass."

But most American workers do better with the comfort and   14
security of a stable job. Sheldon Joseph was a Chicago adver-

tising executive until he was laid off in 1989. Now he temps for $10 an hour in a community job-training program. Says the 56-year-old Joseph: "I was used to working in the corporate environment and giving my total loyalty to the company. I feel like Rip Van Winkle. You wake up and the world is all changed. The message from industry is, 'We don't want your loyalty. We want your work.' What happened to the dream?"

Employers defend their new labor practices as plain and simple survival tactics. American companies are evolving from huge, mass-production manufacturers that once dominated markets to a new species of hub-and-network enterprises built for flexibility in a brutally competitive world. The buzz phrase at many companies is "accordion management"—the ability to expand or contract one's work force virtually at will to suit business conditions.   15

Boardroom discussions now focus on what are called "core competencies"—those operations at the heart of a business—and on how to shed the rest of the functions to subcontractors or nonstaff workers. Managers divide their employees into a permanent cadre of "core workers," which keeps on shrinking, and the contingent workers, who can be brought in at a moment's notice. Most large employers are not even certain at any given time how many of these helpers are working for them—nor do they usually care. Says a manager: "We don't count them. They're not here long enough to matter." Some analysts wonder whether America's celebrated rise in productivity per worker (2.8% last year) is all it seems to be, since so many of those invisible hands are not being counted. So profound is the change that the word *core* has evolved a new meaning, as in "she's core," meaning that she is important and distinctive because she is not part of the contingent work force.   16

Indeed, managers these days can hire virtually any kind of temp they want. Need an extra lawyer or paralegal for a week or so? Try Lawsmiths in San Francisco or Project Professionals in Santa Monica, California. Need a loan officer? Bank Temps in Denver can help. Engineers? Sysdyne outside Minneapolis, Minnesota. CAD/CAM operators? You don't even need to buy the equipment: in Oakland, California, Western Temporary Services has its own CAD/CAM business, serving such clients as the U.S. Navy, the Air Force, Chevron, Exxon and United Technologies. Doctors and nurses? A firm called Interim in Fort Lauderdale, Florida, can provide them anywhere in the country. Need to rent a tough boss to clean up a bad situation? Call IMCOR, a Connecticut-based firm that boasts a roster of senior executives expert at   17 turnarounds. Says IMCOR chairman John Thompson: "Services like ours are going to continue to flourish when businesses change so rapidly that it's in no one's interest to make commitments. Moving on to the next place where you're needed is going to be the way it is. We will all be free-lancers."

For now, most citizens will have to scramble to adapt to   18
the new age of the disposable worker. Says Robert Schaen, a former comptroller of Chicago-based Ameritech who now runs his own children's publishing business: "The days of the mammoth corporations are coming to an end. People are going to have to create their own lives, their own careers and their own successes. Some people may go kicking and screaming into the new world, but there is only one message there: You're now in business for yourself."

READING FOR MEANING

Write to create meanings for Castro's explanation of contingent workers.

START MAKING MEANING

Begin by listing some of the advantages or disadvantages of being hired as a contingent worker. Continue by writing about anything else in the essay or in your experience that contributes to your understanding of the concept of contingent workers.

IF YOU ARE STUCK

If you cannot write at least a page, consider writing about

- the "system of mutual obligations and expectations" that guaranteed an earlier generation of long-term workers who performed well a number of benefits: employment, health care coverage, paid vacations, and pension plans (paragraph 7).

- the idea that being a contingent worker means you are "treated as a second-class citizen by both employers and permanent staff" (paragraph 8).

- the fact that contingent workers include chief executives, doctors, lawyers, and other highly paid professionals as well as sales clerks, word-processors, and assembly-line workers.

- how your own current or future career goals may be affected by this change in the American work force.

READING LIKE A WRITER
EXPLAINING THROUGH DEFINITION

Essays explaining concepts are essentially exercises in defining. By defining, we mean indicating what the concept—or, more precisely, what the words used to name the concept—mean. Writers usually define words by using synonyms, other words with similar meanings that might be more familiar to readers. Although the meanings may be very close, synonyms often have different connotations or associations. Writers sometimes use connotations to convey their attitude. Instead of stating what they think directly, they let readers infer it from their choice of words. This activity asks you to think about the implications of the synonyms Castro uses to define contingent workers.

ANALYZE

1. *Reread* the essay and *underline* each synonym you find for the term *contingent workers,* beginning with "temporary workers" in paragraph 2.

2. *Write* in the margin next to each synonym the connotations or associations it has for you.

WRITE

Write several sentences describing the synonyms Castro uses, their connotations, and the attitudes they reflect.

CONSIDERING IDEAS FOR YOUR OWN WRITING

Consider writing about other work- or business-related concepts, such as productivity, accordion management, glass ceiling, networking, collective bargaining, or sexual harassment. Some economic concepts you might consider explaining are junk bonds, portfolio, progressive tax, management style, and escrow. Another possibility would be to explain a concept related to a particular kind of work or craft with which you are familiar, such as computer programming.

BETH L. BAILEY

Dating

Beth L. Bailey (b. 1957) is a sociology professor in the Women's Studies Program at the University of New Mexico. She studies nineteenth- and twentieth-century American culture and has written several books, including From Front Porch to Back Seat: Courtship in Twentieth-Century America *(1988) and* The First Strange Place *(1992). "Dating" comes from Bailey's first book, a history of American courtship. Bailey tells us that she first became interested in studying courtship attitudes and behaviors when, as a college senior, she appeared on a television talk show to defend co-ed dorms, which were then new and controversial. Surprisingly, many people in the audience objected to co-ed dorms, not on moral grounds, but because they feared too much intimacy between young men and women would hasten "the dissolution of the dating system and the death of romance." Before reading Bailey's sociological explanation of dating, think about the attitudes and behaviors of people your own age in regard to courtship and romance.*

One day, the 1920s story goes, a young man asked a city girl if he might call on her (Black, 1924, p. 340). We know nothing else about the man or the girl—only that, when he arrived, she had her hat on. Not much of a story to us, but any American born before 1910 would have gotten the punch line. "She had her hat on": those five words were rich in meaning to early twentieth century Americans. The hat signaled that she expected to leave the house. He came on a "call," expecting to be received in her family's parlor, to talk, to meet her mother, perhaps to have some refreshments or to listen to her play the piano. She expected a "date," to be taken "out" somewhere and entertained. He ended up spending four weeks' savings fulfilling her expectations.

In the early twentieth century this new style of courtship, dating, had begun to supplant the old. Born primarily of the limits and opportunities of urban life, dating had almost completely replaced the old system of calling by the mid-1920s—and, in so doing, had transformed American courtship. Dating moved courtship into the public world, relocating it from family parlors and community events to restaurants, theaters, and dance halls. At the same time, it removed couples from the implied supervision of the private sphere—from the watchful eyes of family and local community—to the anonymity of the public sphere. Courtship among strangers offered couples new freedom. But access to the public world of the city required money. One had to buy entertainment, or even access to a place to sit and talk. Money—men's money—became the basis of the dating system and, thus, of courtship. This new dating system, as it shifted courtship from the private to the public sphere and increasingly centered around money, fundamentally altered the balance of power between men and women in courtship.

The transition from calling to dating was as complete as it was fundamental. By the 1950s and 1960s, social scientists who studied American courtship found it necessary to remind the American public that dating was a "recent American innovation and not a traditional or universal custom." (Cavin, as cited in "Some," 1961, p. 125). Some of the many commentators who wrote about courtship believed dating was the best thing that had ever happened to relations between the sexes; others blamed the dating system for all the problems of American youth and American marriage. But virtually everyone portrayed the system dating replaced as infinitely simpler, sweeter, more innocent, and more graceful. Hardheaded social scientists waxed sentimental about the "horse-and-buggy days," when a young man's offer of a ride home from church was tantamount to a proposal and when young men came calling in the evenings and courtship took place safely within the warm bosom of the family. "The courtship which grew out of the sturdy social roots [of the nineteenth century]" one author wrote, "comes through to us for what it was—a gracious ritual, with clearly defined roles for man and woman, in which everyone knew the measured music and the steps" (Moss, 1963, p. 151). 3

The call itself was a complicated event. A myriad of rules governed everything: the proper amount of time between invitation and visit (a fortnight or less); whether or not refreshments should be served (not if one belonged to a fashionable or semi-fashionable circle, but outside of "smart" groups in cities like New York and Boston, girls *might* serve iced drinks with little cakes or tiny cups of coffee or hot chocolate and sandwiches); chaperonage (the first call must be made on daughter and mother, but excessive chaperonage would indicate to the man that his attentions were unwelcome); appropriate topics of conversation (the man's interests, but never too personal); how leave should be taken (on no account should the woman "accompany [her caller] to the door nor stand talking while he struggles into his coat") ("Lady," 1904, p. 255). 4

Each of these "measured steps," as the mid-twentieth century author nostalgically called them, was a test of suitability, breeding, and background. Advice columns and etiquette 5 books emphasized that these were the manners of any "well-bred" person—and conversely implied that deviations revealed a lack of breeding. However, around the turn of the century, many people who did lack this narrow "breeding" aspired to politeness. Advice columns in women's magazines regularly printed questions from "Country Girl" and "Ignoramus" on the fine points of calling etiquette. Young men must have felt the pressure of girls' expectations, for they wrote to the same advisers with questions about calling. In 1907, *Harper's Bazaar* ran a major article titled "Etiquette for Men," explaining the ins and outs of the calling system (Hall, 1907, pp. 1095–97). In the first decade of the twentieth century, this rigid system of calling was the convention not only of the "respectable" but also of those who aspired to respectability.

At the same time, however, the new system of dating was 6 emerging. By the mid-1910s, the word *date* had entered the vocabulary of the middle-class public. In 1914, the *Ladies' Home Journal,* a bastion of middle-class respectability, used the term (safely enclosed in quotation marks but with no explanation of its meaning) several times. The word was always spoken by that exotica, the college sorority girl—a character marginal in her exoticness but nevertheless a solid product of the middle class. "One beautiful evening of the spring term," one such article begins, "when I was a college girl of eighteen, the boy whom, because of his popularity in every phase of college life, I had been proud gradually to allow the monopoly of my 'dates,' took me unexpectedly into his arms. As he kissed me impetuously I was glad, from the bottom of my heart, for the training of that mother who had taught me to hold myself aloof from all personal familiarities of boys and men" ("How," 1914, p. 9).

Sugarcoated with a tribute to motherhood and virtue, the 7 dates—and the kiss—were unmistakably presented for a middle-class audience. By 1924, ten years later, when the story of the unfortunate young man who went to call on the city girl was current, dating had essentially replaced calling in middle-class culture. The knowing smiles of the story's listeners had probably started with the word *call*—and not every hearer would have been sympathetic to the man's plight. By 1924, he really should have known better.

Dating, which to the privileged and protected would seem 8 a system of increased freedom and possibility, stemmed originally from the lack of opportunities. Calling, or even just visiting, was not a practicable system for young people whose families lived crowded into one or two rooms. For even the more established or independent working-class girls, the parlor and the piano often simply didn't exist. Some "factory girls" struggled to find a way to receive callers. The *Ladies' Home Journal* approvingly reported the case of six girls, workers in a box factory, who had formed a club and pooled part of their wages to pay the "janitress of a tenement house" to let them use her front room two evenings a week. It had a piano. One of the girls explained their system: "We ask the boys to come when they like and spend the evening. We haven't any place at home to see them, and I hate seeing them on the street" (Preston, 1907, p. 31).

Many other working girls, however, couldn't have done this even had they wanted to. They had no extra wages to pool, or they had no notions of middle-class respectability. Some, especially girls of ethnic families, were kept secluded— chaperoned according to the customs of the old country. But many others fled the squalor, drabness, and crowdedness of their homes to seek amusement and intimacy elsewhere. And a "good time" increasingly became identified with public places and commercial amusements, making young women whose wages would not even cover the necessities of life dependent on men's "treats" (Peiss, 1986, pp. 75, 51–52). Still, many poor and working-class couples did not so much escape from the home as they were pushed from it.   9

These couples courted on the streets, sometimes at cheap dance halls or eventually at the movies. These were not respectable places, and women could enter them only so far as they, themselves, were not considered respectable. Respectable young women did, of course, enter the public world, but their excursions into the public were cushioned. Public courtship of middle-class and upper-class youth was at least *supposed* to be chaperoned; those with money and social position went to private dances with carefully controlled guest lists, to theater parties where they were a private group within the public. As rebels would soon complain, the supervision of society made the private parlor seem almost free by contrast. Women who were not respectable did have relative freedom of action—but the trade-off was not necessarily a happy one for them.   10

The negative factors were important, but dating rose equally from the possibilities offered by urban life. Privileged youth, as Lewis Erenberg shows in his study of New York nightlife, came to see the possibility of privacy in the anonymous public, in the excitement and freedom the city offered (1981, pp. 60–87, 139–42). They looked to lower-class models of freedom—to those beyond the constraints of re-   11 spectability. As a society girl informed the readers of the *Ladies' Home Journal* in 1914: "Nowadays it is considered 'smart' to go to the low order of dance halls, and not only be a looker-on, but also to dance among all sorts and conditions of men and women.... Nowadays when we enter a restaurant and dance place it is hard to know who is who" ("A Girl," 1914, p. 7). In 1907, the same magazine had warned unmarried women never to go alone to a "public restaurant" with any man, even a relative. There was no impropriety in the act, the adviser had conceded, but it still "lays [women] open to misunderstanding and to being classed with women of undesirable reputation by the strangers present" (Kingsland, May 1907, p. 48). Rebellious and adventurous young people sought that confusion, and the gradual loosening of proprieties they engendered helped to change courtship. Young men and women went out into the world *together,* enjoying a new kind of companionship and the intimacy of a new kind of freedom from adult supervision.

The new freedom that led to dating came from other sources as well. Many more serious (and certainly respectable) young women were taking advantage of opportunities to enter the public world—going to college, taking jobs, entering and creating new urban professions. Women who belonged to the public world by day began to demand fuller access to the public world in general.   12

Between 1890 and 1925, dating—in practice and in name—had gradually, almost imperceptibly, become a universal custom in America. By the 1930s it had transcended its origins: Middle America associated dating with neither upper-class rebellion nor the urban lower classes. The rise of dating was usually explained, quite simply, by the invention of the automobile. Cars had given youth mobility and privacy, and so had brought about the system. This explanation—perhaps not consciously but definitely not coincidentally—revised history. The automobile certainly contributed to the rise of dating as a *national* practice, especially in rural and suburban areas, but it was simply accelerating and extending a process already well under way. Once its origins were located firmly in Middle America, however, and not in the extremes of urban upper- and lower-class life, dating had become an American institution.   13

Dating not only transformed the outward modes and conventions of American courtship, it also changed the distribution of control and power in courtship. One change was generational: the dating system lessened parental control and gave young men and women more freedom. The dating sys-   14 tem also shifted power from women to men. Calling, either as a simple visit or as the elaborate late nineteenth-century ritual, gave women a large portion of control. First of all, courtship took place within the girl's home—in women's "sphere," as it was called in the nineteenth century—or at entertainments largely devised and presided over by women. Dating moved courtship out of the home and into man's sphere—the world outside the home. Female controls and conventions lost much of their power outside women's sphere. And while many of the conventions of female propriety were restrictive and repressive, they had allowed women (young women and their mothers) a great deal of immediate control over courtship. The transfer of spheres thoroughly undercut that control.

Second, in the calling system, the woman took the initiative. Etiquette books and columns were adamant on that point: it was the "girl's privilege" to ask a young man to call. Furthermore, it was highly improper for the man to take the initiative. In 1909 a young man wrote to the *Ladies' Home Journal* adviser asking, "May I call upon a young woman whom I greatly admire, although she had not given me the permission? Would she be flattered at my eagerness, even to the setting aside of conventions, or would she think me impertinent?" Mrs. Kingsland replied: "I think that you would risk her just displeasure and frustrate your object of finding favor with her." Softening the prohibition, she then suggested an invitation might be secured through a mutual friend (Kingsland, 1909, p. 58).   15

Contrast these strictures with advice on dating etiquette from the 1940s and 1950s: An advice book for men and women warns that "girls who [try] to usurp the right of boys to choose their own dates" will "ruin a good dating career. . . . Fair or not, it is the way of life. From the Stone Age, when men chased and captured their women, comes the yen of a boy to do the pursuing. You will control your impatience, therefore, and respect the time-honored custom of boys to take the first step" (Richmond, 1958, p. 11).   16

This absolute reversal of roles almost necessarily accompanied courtship's move from woman's sphere to man's sphere. Although the convention-setters commended the custom of woman's initiative because it allowed greater exclusivity (it might be "difficult for a girl to refuse the permission to call, no matter how unwelcome or unsuitable an acquaintance of the man might be"), the custom was based on a broader principle of etiquette (Hart and Brown, 1944, p. 89). The host or hostess issued any invitation; the guest   17 did not invite himself or herself. An invitation to call was an invitation to visit in a woman's home.

An invitation to go out on a date, on the other hand, was an invitation into man's world—not simply because dating took place in the public sphere (commonly defined as belonging to men), though that was part of it, but because dating moved courtship into the world of the economy. Money—men's money—was at the center of the dating system. Thus, on two counts, men became the hosts and assumed the control that came with that position. 18

There was some confusion caused by this reversal of initiative, especially during the twenty years or so when going out and calling coexisted as systems. (The unfortunate young man in the apocryphal story, for example, had asked the city girl if he might call on her, so perhaps she was conventionally correct to assume he meant to play the host.) Confusions generally were sorted out around the issue of money. One young woman, "Henrietta L.," wrote to the *Ladies' Home Journal* to inquire whether a girl might "suggest to a friend going to any entertainment or place of amusement where there will be any expense to the young man." The reply: "Never, under any circumstances." The adviser explained that the invitation to go out must "always" come from the man, for he was the one "responsible for the expense" (Kingsland, Oct. 1907, p. 60). This same adviser insisted that the woman must "always" invite the man to call; clearly she realized that money was the central issue. 19

The centrality of money in dating had serious implications for courtship. Not only did money shift control and initiative to men by making them the "hosts," it led contemporaries to see dating as a system of exchange best understood through economic analogies or as an economic system pure and simple. Of course, people did recognize in marriage a similar economic dimension—the man undertakes to support his wife in exchange for her filling various roles important to him—but marriage was a permanent relationship. Dating was situational, with no long-term commitments implied, and when a man, in a highly visible ritual, spent money on a woman in public, it seemed much more clearly an economic act. 20

Dating, like prostitution, made access to women directly dependent on money. In dating, though, the exchange was less direct and less clear than in prostitution. One author, in 1924, made sense of it this way. In dating, he reasoned, a man is responsible for all expenses. The woman is responsible for nothing—she contributes only her company. Of 21 course, the man contributes his company, too, but since he must "add money to balance the bargain" his company must be worth less than hers. Thus, according to this economic understanding, she is selling her company to him. In his eyes, dating didn't even involve an exchange; it was a direct purchase. The moral "subtleties" of a woman's position in dating, the author concluded, were complicated even further by the fact that young men, "discovering that she must be bought, [like] to buy her when [they happen] to have the money" (Black, 1924, p. 342).

Yet another young man, the same year, publicly called a halt to such "promiscuous buying." Writing anonymously (for good reason) in *American Magazine,* the author declared a "one-man buyer's strike." This man estimated that, as a "buyer of feminine companionship" for the previous five years, he had "invested" about $20 a week—a grand total of over $5,000. Finally, he wrote, he had realized that "there is a point at which any commodity—even such a delightful commodity as feminine companionship—costs more than it is worth" ("Too-high," 1924, pp. 27, 145–50). The commodity he had bought with his $5,000 had been priced beyond its "real value" and he had had enough. This man said "enough" not out of principle, not because he rejected the implications of the economic model of courtship, but because he felt he wasn't receiving value for money.

In these economic analyses, the men are complaining about the new dating system, lamenting the passing of the mythic good old days when "a man without a quarter in his pocket could call on a girl and not be embarrassed," the days before a woman had to be "bought" ("Too-high," 1924, pp. 145–50). In recognizing so clearly the economic model on which dating operated, they also clearly saw that the model was a bad one—in purely economic terms. The exchange was not equitable; the commodity was overpriced. Men were operating at a loss.

Here, however, they didn't understand their model completely. True, the equation (male companionship plus money equals female companionship) was imbalanced. But what men were buying in the dating system was not just female companionship, not just entertainment—but power. Money purchased obligation; money purchased inequality; money purchased control.

The conventions that grew up to govern dating codified women's inequality and ratified men's power. Men asked women out; women were condemned as "aggressive" if they expressed interest in a man too directly. Men paid for everything, but often with the implication that women "owed" sexual favors in return. The dating system required men always to assume control, and women to act as men's dependents.

Yet women were not without power in the system, and they 26 were willing to contest men with their "feminine" power. Much of the public discourse on courtship in twentieth-century America was concerned with this contestation. Thousands of sources chronicled the struggles of, and between, men and women—struggles mediated by the "experts" and arbiters of convention—to create a balance of power, to gain or retain control of the dating system. These struggles, played out most clearly in the fields of sex, science, and etiquette, made ever more explicit the complicated relations between men and women in a changing society.

REFERENCES

A Girl. (1914, July). Believe me. *Ladies' Home Journal,* 7.

Black, A. (1924, August). Is the young person coming back? *Harper's,* 340, 342.

Erenberg, L. (1981). *Steppin' out.* Westport, Conn.: Greenwood Press.

Hall, F. H. (1907, November). Etiquette for men. *Harper's Bazaar,* 1095–97.

Hart, S., & Brown, L. (1944). *How to get your man and hold him.* New York: New Power Publications.

How may a girl know? (1914, January). *Ladies' Home Journal,* 9.

Kingsland. (1907, May). *Ladies' Home Journal,* 48.

———. (1907, October). *Ladies' Home Journal,* 60.

———. (1909, May). *Ladies' Home Journal,* 58.

Lady from Philadelphia. (1904, February). *Ladies' Home Journal,* 255.

Moss, A. (1963, April). Whatever happened to courtship? *Mademoiselle,* 151.

Peiss, K. (1986). *Cheap amusements: Working women and leisure in turn-of-the-century New York.* Philadelphia: Temple University Press.

Preston, A. (1907, February). After business hours—what? *Ladies' Home Journal,* 31.

Richmond, C. (1958). *Handbook of dating.* Philadelphia: Westminster Press.

Some expert opinions on dating. (1961, August). *McCall's,* 125.

Too-high cost of courting. (1924, September). *American Magazine,* 27, 145–50.

READING FOR MEANING

Write to create meanings for Bailey's explanation of dating.

START MAKING MEANING

Begin by listing the differences between calling and dating. Continue by writing about anything else in the essay or in your experience that contributes to your understanding of the concept of dating as Bailey defines it.

IF YOU ARE STUCK

If you cannot write at least a page, consider writing about

- how "lower-class" and "middle-class" values shaped the current conception and practice of dating (paragraphs 6–13).

- the identification of a "good time" with "public places and commercial amusements" (paragraphs 9 and 10).

- the connection between money and power in dating (paragraphs 24–26).

- the dating system described by Bailey in 1988 compared to the courtship system you know today.

A SPECIAL READING STRATEGY

Summarizing

Summarizing, a potent reading-for-meaning strategy, is also a kind of writing you will encounter in your college classes and on the job. By rereading Bailey's essay on dating with an eye toward finding its main ideas, you can do the groundwork for writing a summary of the selection. Taking the time to write a summary will help you remember what you have read and could help you convey to others the gist of Bailey's essay. For detailed guidelines on summarizing, see Appendix One (p. 462).

READING LIKE A WRITER
EXPLAINING THROUGH COMPARISON/CONTRAST

One of the best ways of explaining something new is to relate it, through comparison or contrast, to something that is familiar or well known. A *comparison* points out similarities between items; a *contrast* points out differences. Sometimes writers use both comparison and contrast; sometimes they use only one or the other. Bailey uses comparison and contrast a little differently. She is not explaining something new to readers by relating it to something already known to them. Instead, she is explaining something already known—dating—by relating it to something that is unknown to most readers—calling, an earlier type of courtship.

Since she is studying dating as a sociologist, this historical perspective enables her to consider the changing relationship between men and women and what it tells us about the larger social and cultural contexts.

ANALYZE

Put a line in the margin next to each sentence where Bailey compares or contrasts calling with dating, beginning with the last three sentences of the opening paragraph. Do not be concerned if you miss a few passages. The point is to see what Bailey's use of comparison and contrast adds to the explanation.

WRITE

Write several sentences, reporting what you have learned about Bailey's use of comparison and contrast. *Cite* examples from the reading. *Comment* on how informative you find her explanation given your own knowledge of dating.

COMPARE

Compare Bailey's use of comparison/contrast to help explain the concept of dating with either Quammen's use of it to explain parthenogenesis (paragraphs 11–14, pp. 166–67) *or* Elmer-DeWitt's use of it to explain cyberspace (paragraphs 12–15, pp. 182–83). What is being compared or contrasted in each essay? How does the comparison or contrast help explain the concept? *Write* a few more sentences, reporting what you have learned about how different writers use comparison/contrast in explanatory essays.

CONSIDERING IDEAS FOR YOUR OWN WRITING

Like Bailey, you might choose a concept that tells something about current or historical social values, behaviors, or attitudes. To look at changing attitudes toward immigration and assimilation, for example, you could write about the concept of the melting pot and the alternatives that have been suggested. Some related concepts you might consider are multiculturalism, race, ethnicity, masculinity or femininity, heterosexuality or homosexuality, and affirmative action.

MELISSA McCOOL

Reincarnation

Melissa McCool wrote this essay for her first-year com-position course. Her focus is reincarnation—a defining be-lief of several major Asian religions, notably Buddhism and Hinduism. Although reincarnation is not part of the Western Judeo-Christian tradition, interest in it has always been pres-ent in the United States. Several major writers have written about reincarnation or advocated it since the eighteenth century. Since late in the nineteenth century, the American Theosophical Society has nourished the concept; and, more recently, the New Age movement has embraced it.

Before you read, recall what you already know about reincarnation. With whom do you associate this belief? As you read, annotate details of the essay that contribute to your understanding of reincarnation and its twin concept of karma.

Recently, actor and New Age author Shirley MacLaine was   1
a guest on the David Letterman show. As she discussed some of her experiences, Letterman jokingly asked, "Now, was that in your fourth or fifth life?" The audience roared with laughter, as MacLaine stared at Letterman, visibly an-noyed. Readers of her books know that reincarnation is one of her most cherished beliefs, and it certainly must have upset her to have Letterman dismiss this ancient belief as a trivial joke in front of millions of viewers. Many Americans, unfortunately, have misconceptions about reincarnation be-cause it is not a familiar concept in Judeo-Christian society. It is often looked on as a passing New Age fad. In fact, how-ever, reincarnation has a rich history and hundreds of mil-lions of present-day believers worldwide, including, surpris-ingly, millions of Americans.

In simplest terms, reincarnation is the belief that the soul   2
passes from one body to another through a series of differ-ent lives. Some believe that the soul is reincarnated in a new body immediately after death, while others believe that it is reincarnated after some time has passed, perhaps while the soul rests somewhere else in the universe (Kelly 384). This immortal soul-self is neither body, nor mind, nor rationality, nor ego, but rather an invisible "subjective center of human personality" (Sharma 68). In effect, the soul is three dimen-sional: past, present, and future (Sharma 100). Ultimately, each soul has the same potential to attain spiritual perfec-tion, but some will reach this end sooner than others. The

freedom of will granted to individuals influences the choice of speed, hesitation, or even retreat on the path to spiritual perfection. Therefore, reincarnationists insist that at the very core of our nature we possess the right and responsibility to choose the path we will take.

Within the context of choice, reincarnation can be better understood. The entire blueprint of our development and rebirth is determined by the choices that we make. Every action has a reaction, and every decision has consequences— either positive, neutral, or negative. This is the moral law of cause and effect, or *karma*. This law of just retribution extends over a soul's various incarnations: the soul may reap in one lifetime what it has sown in another (Humphreys 15). For instance, someone who is generous with his or her money by giving it to needy people in one lifetime may in a following life win the lottery. Or, a person who performs acts of senseless violence in one lifetime may be the victim of similar crimes in the next life. In this way, karma can explain the inequalities in life that otherwise seem unfair.   3

It is difficult for many Westerners to take reincarnation seriously because it seems so foreign to the Judeo-Christian tradition. However, reincarnation is not in itself at odds with Christian, Jewish, or any other ideology. Rather, reincarnation is a philosophy that can be integrated into many different religious beliefs: one may be a reincarnationist and also a Christian, a Hindu, a Buddhist, a Jew.   4

In fact, belief in a concept related to reincarnation was widespread among early Christians. To attract converts after Christianity separated from Judaism in the first century A.D., Christians began preaching that when true believers died, their souls lived on in heaven. St. Paul, for example, preached "Brethren, be not deceived. God is not mocked, for whatever a man sows that shall he reap" (quoted in Humphreys 16). There is no evidence, however, that the early Christians ever believed in reincarnation as it had come to be defined by Eastern religions (Kelly 386). At the Council of Constantinople in A.D. 551, the Christian church leaders declared the concept of reincarnation a heresy. They reasoned that people had to be personally responsible for their sins. They believed that baptism, an important Christian practice, washed away all sins and relieved the person of any guilt or punishment. They decided that "each soul had to be created fresh for each person and only had one lifetime on earth" (Kelly 387). Regardless of the decision made in A.D. 551, it may be pointed out that in Christianity (and other religions that officially reject reincarnation) the   5 goal is spiritual perfection in a believer's lifetime. Reincarnation simply allows the individual more than one lifetime to achieve spiritual perfection.

In other religious traditions, such as Buddhism and Hinduism, the principle of reincarnation is an accepted reality. Some groups of people, such as the Tibetans and Indians, structure their entire social systems around belief in reincarnation. For example, Tibetans believe that the Dalai Lama, the spiritual and temporal leader of the six million Tibetan people, chose to be reborn for the purpose of serving other human beings. The current Dalai Lama, Tenzin Gyato, was recognized at the age of two as the reincarnation of his predecessor, the thirteenth Dalai Lama. As the leader of the Tibetan people, Gyato is recognized by most of the world as a great political and spiritual leader. In 1989, he was awarded the Nobel Peace Prize for leading Tibet's passive struggle against the Chinese. When the fourteenth Dalai Lama dies, the Tibetan government will not seek to appoint a successor, but rather to discover a child in whom the Dalai Lama has been reincarnated.

Many great Western thinkers throughout history have pondered the idea of the immortal soul, regardless of religious tradition. As early as the sixth century B.C., Greek and Roman philosophers and intellectuals pondered the idea of the immortal soul. In fact, the most influential philosophers of ancient Greece, Socrates and Plato, discussed reincarnation quite openly. As reported by Plato in the *Phaedo,* a dialogue from the last day of Socrates' life, Socrates commented, "I am confident that there truly is such a thing as living again, and that the living spring from the dead, and that the souls of the dead are in existence, and that the good souls have a better portion than the evil" (quoted in Head and Cranston 211). Plato explained his belief in the immortal soul in terms of motion: "Every soul is immortal—for whatever is in perpetual motion is immortal" (quoted in Head and Cranston 214). The teachings of Socrates and Plato have greatly influenced the modern fields of philosophy, sociology, and theology.

The Renaissance and Reformation produced a rebirth of progressive ideals and the abstract search for truth, a search that led to a revival of Western interest in reincarnation. The Italian painter and sculptor Leonardo da Vinci accepted the idea of the preexistence of the soul. During the Enlightenment, Voltaire, David Hume, and Immanuel Kant alluded to and wrote about reincarnation. Hence, history is saturated with references to reincarnation by many of the most enlightened people in Europe, and similar references can be found in the writings of American authors.

Most Americans are probably unaware of how many of their fellow citizens take reincarnation seriously and how influential the concept has been during the course of the history of our country. David Letterman would probably be surprised to know that several opinion polls in the 1980s "revealed that more than 20 percent of the American public believe in some form of reincarnation" (Kelly 384). In addition, several American religious leaders and other intellectuals have expressed their interest or belief in reincarnation. A group of psychologists has developed a counseling approach called post-life therapy that explores "traumatic events believed to have occurred in a patient's previous incarnations" (Kelly 384).   9

From a book that collects statements of belief in some form of reincarnation by Western thinkers over the centuries (Head and Cranston), I have selected several statements by famous American intellectuals and leaders. These statements show how seriously reincarnation has been taken by some Americans almost from the beginning of the United States. This selection may make the 20-percent figure less surprising and make Shirley MacLaine seem less of a New Age weirdo.   10

Benjamin Franklin (1706–1790), statesman, scientist, and philosopher: "Thus, finding myself to exist in the world, I believe I shall, in some shape or other, always exist; and, with all the inconveniences human life is liable to, I shall not object to a new edition of mine, hoping, however, that the *errata* of the last may be corrected."   11

Ralph Waldo Emerson (1803–1882), author: "As far back as I can remember I have unconsciously referred to the experiences of a previous state of existence."   12

Emily Dickinson (1830–1886), poet: "Afraid? Of whom am I afraid? Not death; for who is he? [...] / Twere odd I fear a thing / That comprehendeth me / In one or more existences / At Deity's decree."   13

Henry Ford (1863–1947), inventor and businessperson: "I adopted the theory of Reincarnation when I was twenty-six. [...] Religion offered nothing to the point. [...] Even work could not give me complete satisfaction. Work is futile if we cannot utilize the experience we collect in one life in the next. When I discovered Reincarnation it was as if I had found a universal plan. I realized that there was a chance to work out my ideas. Time was no longer limited. I was no longer a slave to the hands of the clock. [...] The discovery   14 of Reincarnation put my mind at ease. [...] If you preserve a record of this conversation, write it so that it puts men's minds at ease. I would like to communicate to others the calmness that the long view of life gives us."

Robert Frost (1874–1963), poet: "I'd like to get away from earth awhile / And then come back to it and begin over. / May no fate willfully misunderstand me / and half grant what I wish and snatch me away / Not to return." 15

Norman Mailer (b. 1923), author, has this to say in a biography of Marilyn Monroe: "Yet if we are to understand Monroe, and no one has [...] why not assume that [she] may have been born with a desperate imperative formed out of all those previous debts and failures of her whole family of souls. [...] To explain her at all, let us hold to that karmic notion as one more idea to support in our mind while trying to follow the involuted pathways of her life." 16

Reincarnation, it seems, is not so much a religion as it is a concept that has been fundamental in some religions and easily accommodated by others. It has had a surprisingly persistent appeal to American thinkers over the last three hundred years. The 1980s surveys and the popularity of Shirley MacLaine's books show that the appeal of reincarnation to Americans may be increasing. If so, the explanation could lie in Americans' growing interest in Asian religions since the 1950s (Long 269) and the increase in Asian immigrants to this country since the mid-1960s. The concept, with its twin concept of karma, is easy to understand and seems to provide some people the reassurance Henry Ford experienced. Perhaps that fact, more than anything else, explains its appeal to so many Americans. 17

WORKS CITED

Head, Joseph, and S. L. Cranston, eds. *Reincarnation.* New York: Julian-Crown, 1977.

Humphreys, Christmas. *Karma and Rebirth.* London: Curzon, 1983.

Kelly, Aidan A. "Reincarnation and Karma." *New Age Encyclopedia.* Ed. J. Gordon Melton. New York: Gale Research, 1990.

Long, J. Bruce. "Reincarnation." *The Encyclopedia of Religion.* Ed. Mircea Eliade. 16 vols. New York: Macmillan, 1987.

Sharma, Ishwar Chandra. *Cayce, Karma, and Reincarnation.* New York: Harper, 1975.

READING FOR MEANING

Write to create meanings for McCool's explanation of reincarnation.

START MAKING MEANING

Begin by briefly explaining reincarnation. Continue by writing about anything else in the essay or in your experience that contributes to your understanding of the concept of reincarnation.

IF YOU ARE STUCK

If you cannot write at least a page, consider writing about

- the concept of karma.

- your understanding of reincarnation before reading McCool's essay, pointing to particular places in the selection where your prior knowledge was confirmed or contested.

- the idea of an "immortal soul-self" being "neither body, nor mind, nor rationality, nor ego, but rather an invisible 'subjective center of human personality' " (paragraph 2).

- McCool's assertion that "reincarnation is a philosophy that can be integrated into many different religious beliefs" (paragraph 4), possibly exploring the connections between reincarnation and your own religious beliefs.

READING LIKE A WRITER
INTEGRATING SOURCES INTO YOUR WRITING

The two most common strategies for integrating quotations into your writing are using a signal phrase to introduce a long quotation and incorporating a shorter quote (words or phrases) into your sentence. *Signal phrases* may include the name of the person being quoted, the person's title, a verb such as *states, points out,* or *claims,* and a comma or colon. You can see an example in the first paragraph of McCool's essay ("... Letterman jokingly asked, 'Now, was that ...' "). Occasionally, a signal phrase follows the quote.

The second strategy—incorporating the quotation fit into your sentence—is especially useful when you want to quote individual words or brief phrases that are particularly apt or memorable. Here is an example from the second paragraph of McCool's essay:

This immortal soul-self is neither body, nor mind, nor rationality, nor ego, but rather an invisible *"subjective center of human personality"* (Sharma 68).

ANALYZE

1. *Reread* McCool's essay and put an "S" in the margin next to the passages where McCool quotes sources.

2. *Look closely* at the passages you marked and *underline* the signal phrase, if there is one.

3. In passages where the quotation is incorporated into McCool's sentence, *look closely* at the sentence to see how smoothly the quotation has been integrated into her writing.

WRITE

Write a few sentences, describing McCool's use of signal phrases and assessing how effectively she incorporates quotes into her writing. *Cite* examples of her different strategies for integrating sources into her writing.

COMPARE

Compare McCool's strategies for integrating quotations with those used by Quammen (pp. 166–67, paragraphs 11 and 16), Tannen (p. 176, paragraphs 26–27), *or* Elmer-DeWitt (p. 180, paragraphs 1–3). *Write* a few more sentences, indicating which strategies you found and how effectively they work in the essay.

CONSIDERING IDEAS FOR YOUR OWN WRITING

Religious studies and philosophy are subjects rich with abstract principles and themes. If reincarnation interests you, you might want to follow up on McCool's essay by writing about karma. Or you could skim the two encyclopedias in her list of works cited or a text you are using in one of your classes, looking for a concept that interests you. Some possibilities are animism, ancestor worship, pantheism, polytheism, mysticism, free will, Platonic forms, Jungian archetypes, halakah, Calvinism, and fundamentalism.

Reviewing What Makes Essays Explaining Concepts Effective

In this chapter, you have been learning how to read essays explaining concepts—reading for meaning and reading like a writer. Before going on to write an essay explaining a concept, pause here to review and contemplate what you have learned about the elements of effective concept explanations.

Analyze

Choose one reading from this chapter that seems to you especially effective. Before rereading the selection, *jot down* one or two reasons you remember it as an example of good concept explanation.

Continued

Reread your chosen essay, adding further annotations about what makes it so effective. *Consider* the essay's purpose and how well it achieves that purpose for its intended readers. Then focus on how well the essay

- devises a readable plan.

- uses appropriate explanatory strategies.

- integrates sources smoothly into the writing.

- engages readers' interest.

Your instructor may ask you to complete this activity on your own or to work with a small group of other students who have chosen the same essay. If you work with others, allow enough time initially for all group members to reread the selection thoughtfully and to add their annotations. Then discuss as a group what makes the essay effective. Take notes on your discussion. One student in your group should then report to the class what the group has learned about the effectiveness of essays explaining concepts. If you are working individually, write up what you have learned from your analysis.

Write

Write at least one page, justifying your choice of this essay as an example of effective concept explanation. Assume that your readers—your instructor and classmates—have read the selection but will not remember many details about it. They also might not remember it as an especially successful explanation. Therefore, you will need to *refer* to details and specific passages of the essay as you explain how it works and *justify* your evaluation of its effectiveness. You need not argue that it is the best essay in the chapter or that it is flawless, only that it is, in your view, a strong example of the genre.

A GUIDE TO WRITING ESSAYS EXPLAINING CONCEPTS

The readings in this chapter have helped you understand new concepts and learn more about concepts with which you are already familiar. Now that you have seen how writers use explanatory strategies that are appropriate for their readers, anticipating what their readers are likely to know, you can approach this type of writing confidently. This Guide to Writing will help you at every stage in the process of composing an essay explaining a concept—from choosing a concept and organizing your explanatory strategies to evaluating and revising your draft.

INVENTION

The following invention activities will help you choose a concept, explore what you already know, consider what your readers need to know, gather and sort through your information, and decide which explanatory strategies to use in presenting your information.

Choosing a Concept

List different concepts you could explain and then choose the one that interests you and would be likely to interest your readers. To make the best choice and have alternatives in case the first choice does not work out, you should have a full list of possibilities. You might already have a concept in mind, possibly one suggested to you for the Considering Ideas for Your Own Writing activities following the readings. Here are other concepts from various fields of study for you to consider:

- *Literature:* representation, figurative language, canon, postcolonialism, modernism, irony, epic

- *Philosophy:* Platonic forms, causality, syllogism, existentialism, nihilism, logical positivism, determinism, phenomenology

- *Business management:* autonomous work group, quality circle, management by objectives, zero-based budgeting, benchmarking, focus group

- *Psychology:* phobia, narcissism, fetish, emotional intelligence, divergent/convergent thinking, behaviorism, Jungian archetype

- *Government:* one person/one vote, minority rights, federalism, communism, theocracy, popular consent, exclusionary rule, political machine, political action committee

- *Biology:* photosynthesis, ecosystem, plasmolysis, phagocytosis, DNA, species, punctuated evolution, homozygosity, diffusion

- *Art:* composition, cubism, iconography, Pop Art, conceptual art, public sculpture, graffiti, forgery, auction, Dadaism, surrealism, expressionism

- *Math:* Mobius transformation, boundedness, null space, eigenvalue, complex numbers, integral, exponent, polynomial, factoring, Pythagorean theorem, continuity, derivative, infinity

- *Physical sciences:* gravity, mass, weight, energy, quantum theory, law of definite proportions, osmotic pressure, first law of thermodynamics, entrophy, free energy, fusion

- *Public health:* alcoholism, epidemic, vaccination, drug abuse, contraception, prenatal care, AIDS education

- *Environmental studies:* acid rain, recycling, ozone depletion, sewage treatment, toxic waste, endangered species

- *Sports psychology:* Ringelman effect, leadership, cohesiveness, competitiveness, anxiety management, aggression, visualization, runner's high

- *Law:* arbitration, strike, minimum wage, liability, reasonable doubt, sexual harassment, nondisclosure agreement, assumption of evidence

- *Meteorology:* jet stream, hydrologic cycle, El Niño, Coriolis effect, Chinook or Santa Ana wind, standard time system, tsunami

- *Nutrition and health:* vegetarianism, bulimia, diabetes, food allergy, aerobic exercise, obesity, Maillard reaction

Choose a promising concept to explore, one that interests you and that you think would interest your readers. You might not know very much about the concept now, but the guidelines that follow will help you learn more about it so that you can explain it to others.

Analyzing Your Readers

Write for five minutes, analyzing your potential readers. Begin by identifying your audience and what they would need to know. Even if you are writing only for your instructor, you should consider what he or she knows about your concept. Ask yourself the following questions to stimulate your thinking: Who would be interested in learning about the concept? What might these potential readers already know about the concept or about the field of study to which it applies? What new, useful, or interesting information about the concept could be provided for them? What questions might they ask?

Researching the Concept

Even if you know quite a bit about the concept, you may want to do additional library or Internet research or consult an expert. Before you begin, check with your instructor for special requirements, such as submitting photocopies of your written sources or using a particular documentation style.

EXPLORING WHAT YOU ALREADY KNOW ABOUT THE CONCEPT. *Write for five minutes about the concept to discover what you know about it.* Pose any questions you now have about the concept and try to answer questions you expect your readers would have.

FINDING INFORMATION AT THE LIBRARY OR ON THE INTERNET. *Learn more about your concept by finding sources, taking notes or making copies of relevant material, and keeping a working bibliography.* Before embarking on research, review any materials you already have at hand that explain your concept. If you are considering a concept from one of your courses, find explanatory material in your textbook and lecture notes. (See Appendix Two, Strategies for Research and Documentation, for detailed guidance on finding information at a library and on the Internet.)

CONSULTING EXPERTS. *Identify one or more people knowledgeable about the concept or the field of study in which it is used and request information.* If you are writing about a concept from a course, consult the professor, teaching assistant, or other students. If the concept relates to your job, consider asking your supervisor. If it relates to a subject you have encountered on television, in the newspaper, or on the Internet, you might email the author or post a query at a relevant Web site. Consulting experts can answer your questions as well as lead you to other sources— Web sites, chatrooms, articles, and books.

FOCUSING YOUR EXPLANATION. *With your own knowledge of the concept and that of your readers in mind, consider how you might focus your explanation.* Determine how the information you have gathered so far could be divided. For example, if you were writing about the concept of schizophrenia, you might focus on the history of its diagnosis and treatment, its symptoms, its effects on families, the current debate about its causes, or current preferred methods of treatment. If you were writing a book, you might want to cover all these aspects of the concept, but in a relatively brief essay you can focus on only one or two of these aspects.

CONFIRMING YOUR FOCUS. *Choose a focus for your explanation and write several sentences justifying the focus you have chosen.* Why do you think this focus will appeal to your readers? What interests you about it? Do you have enough information to plan and draft your explanation? Do you know where you can find any additional information you need? The following example shows how one writer began the research process and focused her work.

AN EXAMPLE

Melissa McCool's Research Process

Melissa McCool, whose essay you read earlier in the chapter (pp. 205–209), began her research by consulting a reference librarian. McCool followed the librarian's advice, looking for reincarnation in several encyclopedias and dictionaries of religion and philosophy and finding relatively brief entries that she photocopied for later reference. She then looked up reincarnation in the online book catalog and printed out the entries (author, title, and library call number) for twenty books. She found fourteen books on the shelves, skimmed them, and divided them into two groups: those concerned with either supporting or rejecting reincarnation and those either describing and evaluating it or collecting various statements about it from different historical periods. McCool did not take extended notes or photocopy any pages because she was not yet sure of her focus. In just over two hours, she had found much more information than she could possibly use in her essay, even if she only lightly sampled all of her sources.

After discussing these options with her instructor and other students, McCool decided to avoid the debate over the concept's validity and to focus instead on defining reincarnation and reviewing its history. She returned to the library to collect sources relevant to this more narrow focus. After she was well into her draft, she decided that the worldwide historical perspective was too sprawling and refocused her subject more specifically on the history of reincarnation in the United States, knowing that this topic would appeal to her American readers.

FORMULATING A WORKING THESIS.   Draft a thesis statement. A working thesis—as opposed to a final, revised thesis—will help you begin drafting your essay purposefully. The thesis in an essay explaining concepts simply announces the concept and focus of the explanation. Here are three examples from the readings.

- "What we are talking about here is celibate motherhood, procreation without copulation, a phenomenon that goes by the technical name *parthenogenesis*. Translated from the Greek roots: virgin birth" (Quammen, paragraph 1).

- "Each of the women at the conference had to make decisions about hair, clothing, makeup and accessories, and each decision carried meaning. Every style available to us was marked. The men in our group had made decisions, too, but the range from which they chose was incomparably narrower. Men can choose styles that are marked, but they don't have to, and in this group none did. Unlike the women, they had the option of being unmarked" (Tannen, paragraph 12).

- "Many Americans, unfortunately, have misconceptions about reincarnation because it is not a familiar concept in Judeo-Christian society. It is often looked on as a passing New Age fad. In fact, however, reincarnation has a rich history and hundreds of millions of present-day believers worldwide, including, surprisingly, millions of Americans" (McCool, paragraph 1).

Notice that McCool's thesis statement not only announces the concept, but also forecasts the main topics she takes up in her essay: the history of reincarnation and its American believers. Forecasts, though not required, can be helpful to readers, especially when the concept is unfamiliar or the explanation is complicated.

DRAFTING

The following guidelines will help you set goals for your draft and plan its organization.

Setting Goals

Establishing goals for your draft before you begin writing will enable you to move ahead more quickly and to make critical writing decisions more confidently. Consider the following questions now, and keep them in mind as you draft. They will help you maintain your focus while drafting as well as recall how the writers you have read in this chapter tried to achieve similar goals.

- *How can I begin engagingly so as to capture my readers' attention?* Should I try to be amusing, like Quammen and McCool? Should I begin with an anecdote, as Tannen, Elmer-DeWitt, and Bailey do? Should I present a surprising fact, as Castro does?

- *How can I orient readers so they do not get confused?* Should I provide an explicit forecasting statement, as McCool does? Should I add transitions to help readers see how the parts of my essay relate to one another, as Elmer-DeWitt and Bailey do? Should I use rhetorical questions and summary statements, as Quammen does?

- *How should I conclude my explanation?* Should I frame the essay by echoing the opening at the end, as Quammen and Tannen do? Should I end with a memorable line, as Elmer-DeWitt and Castro do? Should I end by stressing the importance of the concept, as McCool does?

Organizing Your Draft

With these goals in mind, make a tentative outline of the explanatory strategies you now think you will use. You might want to make two or three different outlines before choosing the one that looks most promising. Try to introduce new material in stages, so that readers' understanding of the concept builds slowly but steadily. You could base your essay on a series of implicit or explicit questions as Quammen does, interweave definition and explanation with a single extended example as Tannen does, or use a chronological and comparative organization as Bailey does.

READING A DRAFT CRITICALLY

Getting a critical reading of your draft will help you see how to improve it. Your instructor may schedule class time for reading drafts, or you may want to ask a classmate or a tutor in the writing center to read your draft. Ask your reader to use the following guidelines and to write out a response for you to consult during your revision.

Read for a First Impression

1. Read the draft without stopping to annotate or comment, and then write two or three sentences giving your general impression.

2. Identify one aspect of the draft that seems to you particularly effective.

Read Again to Suggest Improvements

1. Consider whether the concept is clearly explained and focused.

   • Restate briefly what you understand the concept to mean, indicating if you have any uncertainty or confusion about its meaning.

   • Identify the focus of the explanation and assess whether the focus seems appropriate, too broad, or too narrow for the intended readers.

   • If you can, suggest another, possibly more interesting, way to focus the explanation.

2. Recommend ways of making the organization clearer or more effective.

   • Indicate if a forecasting statement, topic sentences, or transitions could be added or improved.

   • Point to any place where you become confused or do not know how something relates to what went before.

   • Comment on whether the conclusion gives you a sense of closure or leaves you hanging.

3. Identify which explanatory strategies are being used (defining terms, classifying and dividing, comparing and contrasting, narrating a process, illustrating, reporting known causes or effects) and suggest ways of strengthening them.

- Point to any place where a strategy seems confusing or unhelpful—for example, if you do not get the point of a comparison or if the steps in a process seem vague.

- Circle any words that the writer could define or that you do not think need to be defined.

- Recommend adding a particular strategy that would help answer a question readers are likely to ask.

4. Assess whether quotations are integrated smoothly and acknowledged properly.

- Point to any place where a quotation is not smoothly integrated into the writer's sentence and offer a revision.

- Indicate any quotations that would have been just as effective if put in the writer's own words.

- If sources are not acknowledged correctly, remind the writer to consult Appendix Two.

- If you can, suggest other sources the writer might consult.

5. Suggest how the explanation could be more interesting to readers.

- If you feel overwhelmed with information, suggest where the explanation could be simplified or divided into smaller parts.

- Point to any passages where your attention wandered and suggest adding specific details, illustrations, anecdotes, or other material to enliven the writing.

- Tell the writer what questions still have not been answered.

REVISING

This section provides suggestions for revising your draft, suggestions that will remind you of the possibilities for developing a lively, engaging, and informative essay explaining a concept.

Keeping in mind any advice you have received, reread your draft carefully, noting which parts need revising and what specific changes you could make. These suggestions will help you solve problems and strengthen your explanation.

To Make the Concept Clearer and More Focused

- If readers are confused or uncertain about the concept's meaning, try defining it more precisely or giving concrete examples.

- If the focus seems too broad, explain one aspect of the concept in greater depth.

- If the concept seems too narrow, focus on a more significant aspect or try to make the significance clearer.

To Improve the Organization

- If readers have difficulty following the essay, improve the forecasting at the beginning of the essay by listing the topics in the order they will appear.

- If there are places in a paragraph where the topic gets blurred or is changed from one sentence to the next, make the connections between the sentences clearer.

- If the essay seems to lose steam before it comes to a conclusion, consider again what you want readers to learn from your essay.

To Strengthen the Explanatory Strategies

- If the content seems thin, consider whether you could add any other explanatory strategies or develop the ones you are using already.

- If some of the words you use are new to most readers, take the time to define them now, perhaps explaining how they relate to more familiar terms or adding analogy and example to make them less abstract.

- If the way you have divided or categorized the information is unusual or unclear, write a sentence or two making explicit what you are doing and why.

- If the concept seems vague to readers, try comparing it to something familiar or applying it to a real-world experience.

To Integrate Quotations Smoothly and Acknowledge Sources Properly

- Revise any sentences where quotations are not smoothly integrated by adding appropriate signal phrases or rewriting the sentences.

- If your critical reader has identified a quotation that could just as effectively be described in your own words, try paraphrasing or summarizing the quote.

- If your sources are not acknowledged properly, check Appendix Two for the correct citation form.

To Interest Readers More Effectively

- If readers feel overwhelmed with information, make your purpose for including that information clear, or if you cannot, consider cutting it.

- If readers' attention wanders in a particular section, enliven the writing or consider cutting the passage.

- If questions remain, either try to answer them or make clear to readers the focus of your explanation.

EDITING AND PROOFREADING

After you have revised your essay, be sure to spend some time checking for errors in usage, punctuation, and mechanics. If you have been keeping a list of errors you typically make, begin by checking your draft against this list. Ask someone else to proofread your essay before you print out a copy for your instructor.

From our research on student writing, we know that essays explaining concepts tend to have errors in essential or nonessential clauses beginning with *who, which,* or *that* as well as errors in the use of commas to set off these phrases that interrupt the flow of the sentence. Check a writer's handbook for guidance on these potential problems.

Reflecting on What You Have Learned

In this chapter, you have read critically several essays explaining concepts and have written one of your own. To better remember what you have learned, pause now to reflect on the reading and writing activities you completed in this chapter.

1. *Write* a page or so reflecting on what you learned. Begin by describing what you are most pleased with in your essay. Then *explain* what you think contributed to your achievement. Be specific about this contribution.

   - If it was something you learned from the readings, *indicate* which readings and specifically what you learned from them.

   - If it came from your invention writing, *indicate* the section or sections that helped you most.

   - If you got good advice from a critical reader, *explain* exactly how the person helped you—perhaps by helping you understand a particular problem in your draft or by adding a new dimension to your writing.

2. Now *reflect* more generally on explaining concepts, a genre of writing that plays an important role in education and in our society. *Consider* some of the following questions: As a reader of essays explaining concepts, how confident are you that the essay presents information that is well established and not actively disputed by other experts? Should writers of explanatory essays make explicit or defend their own assumptions and points of view?

Evaluation

We make evaluations every day, stating judgments about such things as food, clothes, books, classes, teachers, political candidates, television programs, performers, and films. Most of our everyday judgments simply express our personal preference—"I liked it" or "I didn't like it." But as soon as someone asks "Why?" we realize that evaluation goes beyond individual taste.

If you want others to take your judgment seriously, you have to give reasons for it. Instead of merely asserting that *"Titanic* was fantastic," for example, you must explain your reasons for thinking so: the spectacular special effects or the plausible re-creation of a particular period in history, for example.

For readers to respect your judgment, not only do you have to give them reasons, your reasons must also be recognized as appropriate for evaluating that particular kind of subject. An inappropriate reason for the judgment *"Titanic* is a great action movie" would be that the seats in the theater were comfortable. The comfort of the seats may contribute on one occasion to your enjoyment of the theater experience (and, indeed, would be an appropriate reason for judging the quality of a movie theater), but such a reason has nothing to do with the quality of a particular film.

For reasons to be considered appropriate, they must reflect the values or standards typically used in evaluating a certain kind of product, such as a film or a car. The standards you would use for evaluating a film obviously differ from those you would use for evaluating a car. Acting, musical score, and story are common standards for judging films. Handling, safety, and styling are some of the standards used for judging cars.

Readers expect writers of evaluations both to have relevant reasons and to support their reasons. If one of your reasons for liking the Dodge Stealth sports car is its quick acceleration, you could cite the *Consumer Reports* road-test results (0 to 60 mph in 6.3 seconds) as evidence. (Statistical support like this, of course, makes sense only when the rate is compared with the acceleration rates of other cars.) Similarly, if one of your reasons for liking *Titanic* is the special effects, you could give examples from the film to show as much. You might describe the opening underwater scenes where divers first discover the wreck of the ship on the ocean floor, or you might describe the final scenes of the movie where the ship sinks, water flooding the cabins and lower decks, as examples of powerful visual drama. Support is important because it deals in specifics, showing exactly what value terms like *quick* and *excellent* mean to you.

As you can see, evaluation of the kind you will read and write in this chapter is intellectually rigorous. In college, you will have many opportunities to write evaluations. You may be asked to critique a book or a journal article, judge a scientific hypothesis against the results of an experiment, assess the value of conflicting interpretations of a historical event or a short story, or evaluate a class you have taken. You will also undoubtedly read evaluative writing in your courses and be tested on what you have read.

Written evaluations will almost certainly play an important part in your work life, as well. On the job, you will probably be evaluated periodically and may have to evaluate people whom you supervise. It is also likely that you will be asked your opinion of various plans or proposals under consideration, and your ability to make fair and reasonable evaluations will affect your chances for promotion.

Evaluative arguments are basically about values, about what each of us thinks is important. Reading and writing evaluations will help you understand your own values, as well as those of others. You will learn that when your basic values meet with conflict, it may be impossible to convince others to accept a judgment different from their own. In such cases, you will know how to attempt to bridge the difference with mutual respect and shared concern.

As you read, discuss, and write about the essays in this chapter, you will learn a good deal about evaluative writing. You should also get ideas for an evaluative essay of your own, based perhaps on the ideas for writing that follow each reading. As you work through the selections in this chapter, keep in mind the following assignment and the situations for writing an evaluative essay.

Evaluation

Choose a subject that invites you to evaluate and to make a judgment. Write an essay, evaluating the subject, stating your judgment clearly, and backing it up with reasons and support. Describe the subject for readers unfamiliar with it, and give them a context for understanding the subject. Your principal aim is to convince readers that your judgment is informed and based on generally accepted standards for this kind of subject.

EVALUATIVE WRITING SITUATIONS

Following are a few examples to suggest the range of situations that may call for evaluative writing, including academic and work-related situations.

- For a conference on innovation in education, an elementary school teacher evaluates *Schoolhouse Rock,* an animated television series developed in the 1970s and recently reinvented in several new formats: books, CD-ROM learning games, and CDs. She praises the original series as an entertaining way of presenting information, giving two reasons the series remains an effective teaching tool: Witty lyrics and catchy tunes make the information memorable, and cartoonlike visuals make the lessons painless. She supports each reason by showing and discussing videotaped examples of popular *Schoolhouse Rock* segments, such as "Conjunction Junction," "We the People," and "Three Is a Magic Number." She ends by expressing her hope that teachers and developers of educational multimedia will learn from the example of *Schoolhouse Rock.*

- A supervisor reviews the work of a probationary employee. She judges the employee's performance as being adequate overall but still needing improvement in several key areas, particularly completing projects on time and communicating clearly with others. To back up her judgment, she cites several problems that the employee has had over the six-month probation period.

- An older brother, a college junior, writes a letter to his younger brother, a high-school senior who is trying to decide which college to attend. Because the older brother attends one of the colleges being considered and has friends at another, he feels competent to offer advice. He centers his letter on the question of what standards to use in evaluating colleges. He argues that if playing football is the primary goal, then college number one is the clear choice. But if having the opportunity to work in an award-winning scientist's genetics lab is more important, then the second college is the better choice.

A GUIDE TO READING EVALUATIONS

This guide is designed to introduce you to evaluative writing. We ask you to read, annotate, and write about your understanding of the essay that follows. Then, following guidelines we provide, you will reread the essay like a writer to analyze how it employs the features and strategies of strong evaluative writing.

AMITAI ETZIONI

Working at McDonald's

Sociology professor Amitai Etzioni (b. 1929) has written numerous articles and books, including The Spirit of Community: Rights, Responsibilities, and the Communitarian Agenda *(1993). He is also the founder of a journal,* The Responsive Community.

The following essay was originally published in 1986, in the Miami Herald, *a major newspaper that circulates in South Florida. The original headnote identifies Etzioni as the father of five sons, including three teenagers, and points out that his son Dari helped Etzioni write this essay— although it does not say what Dari contributed. As you read the essay, consider how this information—both about Etzioni's career and family and about his son's assistance— influences your willingness to accept his judgment.*

Annotate the essay as you read and as you complete the activities following the selection. For an illustration of the strategies and benefits of annotating, see Appendix One (p. 450).

McDonald's is bad for your kids. I do not mean the flat patties and the white-flour buns; I refer to the jobs teenagers undertake, mass-producing these choice items.   1

As many as two-thirds of America's high school juniors and seniors now hold down part-time paying jobs, according to studies. Many of these are in fast-food chains, of which McDonald's is the pioneer, trend-setter and symbol.   2

At first, such jobs may seem right out of the Founding Fathers' educational manual for how to bring up self-reliant, work-ethic-driven, productive youngsters. But in fact, these jobs undermine school attendance and involvement, impart few skills that will be useful in later life, and simultaneously skew the values of teen-agers—especially their ideas about the worth of a dollar.   3

It has been a longstanding American tradition that youngsters ought to get paying jobs. In folklore, few pursuits are more deeply revered than the newspaper route and the side-   4 walk lemonade stand. Here the youngsters are to learn how sweet are the fruits of labor and self-discipline (papers are delivered early in the morning, rain or shine), and the ways of trade (if you price your lemonade too high or too low . . .).

Roy Rogers, Baskin Robbins, Kentucky Fried Chicken, *et al.,* may at first seem nothing but a vast extension of the lemonade stand. They provide very large numbers of teen jobs, provide regular employment, pay quite well compared to many other teen jobs and, in the modern equivalent of toiling over a hot stove, test one's stamina.

5

Closer examination, however, finds the McDonald's kind of job highly uneducational in several ways. Far from providing opportunities for entrepreneurship (the lemonade stand) or self-discipline, self-supervision and self-scheduling (the paper route), most teen jobs these days are highly structured—what social scientists call "highly routinized."

6

True, you still have to have the gumption to get yourself over to the hamburger stand, but once you don the prescribed uniform, your task is spelled out in minute detail. The franchise prescribes the shape of the coffee cups; the weight, size, shape, and color of the patties; and the texture of the napkins (if any). Fresh coffee is to be made every eight minutes. And so on. There is no room for initiative, creativity, or even elementary rearrangements. These are breeding grounds for robots working for yesterday's assembly lines, not tomorrow's high-tech posts.

7

There are very few studies of the matter. One of the few is a 1984 study by Ivan Charper and Bryan Shore Fraser. The study relies mainly on what teen-agers write in response to questionnaires rather than actual observations of fast-food jobs. The authors argue that the employees develop many skills such as how to operate a food-preparation machine and a cash register. However, little attention is paid to how long it takes to acquire such a skill, or what its significance is.

8

What does it matter if you spend 20 minutes to learn to use a cash register, and then—"operate" it? What skill have you acquired? It is a long way from learning to work with a lathe or carpenter tools in the olden days or to program computers in the modern age.

9

A 1980 study by A. V. Harrell and P. W. Wirtz found that, among those students who worked at least 25 hours per week while in school, their unemployment rate four years later was half of that of seniors who did not work. This is an impressive statistic. It must be seen, though, together with the finding that many who begin as part-time employees in

10

fast-food chains drop out of high school and are gobbled up in the world of low-skill jobs.

Some say that while these jobs are rather unsuited for college-bound, white, middle-class youngsters, they are "ideal" for lower-class, "non-academic," minority youngsters. Indeed, minorities are "over-represented" in these jobs (21 percent of fast-food employees). While it is true that these places provide income, work and even some training to such youngsters, they also tend to perpetuate their disadvantaged status. They provide no career ladders, few marketable skills, and undermine school attendance and involvement.

The hours are often long. Among those 14 to 17, a third of fast-food employees (including some school dropouts) labor more than 30 hours per week, according to the Charper-Fraser study. Only 20 percent work 15 hours or less. The rest: between 15 to 30 hours.

Often the stores close late, and after closing one must clean up and tally up. In affluent Montgomery County, Md., where child labor would not seem to be a widespread economic necessity, 24 percent of the seniors at one high school in 1985 worked as much as five to seven days a week; 27 percent, three to five. There is just no way such amounts of work will not interfere with school work, especially homework. In an informal survey published in the most recent yearbook of the high school, 58 percent of the seniors acknowledged that their jobs interfere with their school work.

The Charper-Fraser study sees merit in learning teamwork and working under supervision. The authors have a point here. However, it must be noted that such learning is not automatically educational or wholesome. For example, much of the supervision in fast-food places leans toward teaching one the wrong kinds of compliance: blind obedience, or shared alienation with the "boss."

Supervision is often both tight and woefully inappropriate. Today, fast-food chains and other such places of work (record shops, bowling alleys) keep costs down by having teens supervise teens with often no adult on the premises.

There is no father or mother figure with which to identify, to emulate, to provide a role model and guidance. The work-culture varies from one place to another: Sometimes it is a tightly run shop (must keep the cash registers ringing); sometimes a rather loose pot party interrupted by customers. However, only rarely is there a master to learn from, or much worth learning. Indeed, far from being places where solid adult work values are being transmitted, these are places where all too often delinquent teen values dominate. Typically, when my son Oren was dishing out ice cream for Baskin Robbins in upper Manhattan, his fellow teen-workers considered him a sucker for not helping himself to the till. Most youngsters felt they were entitled to $50 severance "pay" on their last day on the job.

The pay, oddly, is the part of the teen work-world that is most difficult to evaluate. The lemonade stand or paper route money was for your allowance. In the old days, apprentices learning a trade from a master contributed most, if not all of their income to their parents' household. Today, the teen pay may be low by adult standards, but it is often, especially in the middle class, spent largely or wholly by the teens. That is, the youngsters live free at home, ("after all, they are high school kids") and are left with very substantial sums of money.   17

Where this money goes is not quite clear. Some use it to support themselves, especially among the poor. More middle-class kids set some money aside to help pay for college, or save it for a major purchase—often a car. But large amounts seem to flow to pay for an early introduction into the most trite aspects of American consumerism: Flimsy punk clothes, trinkets and whatever else is the last fast-moving teen craze.   18

One may say that this is only fair and square; they are being good American consumers and spend their money on what turns them on. At least, a cynic might add, these funds do not go into illicit drugs and booze. On the other hand, an educator might bemoan that these young, yet unformed individuals, so early in life are driven to buy objects of no intrinsic educational, cultural or social merit, learn so quickly the dubious merit of keeping up with the Joneses in ever-changing fads, promoted by mass merchandising.   19

Many teens find the instant reward of money, and the youth status symbols it buys, much more alluring than credits in calculus courses, European history or foreign languages. No wonder quite a few would rather skip school—and certainly homework—and instead work longer at a Burger King. Thus, most teen work these days is not providing early lessons in work ethic; it fosters escape from school and responsibilities, quick gratification and a short cut to the consumeristic aspects of adult life.   20

Thus, parents should look at teen employment not as automatically educational. It is an activity—like sports—that can be turned into an educational opportunity. But it can also easily be abused. Youngsters must learn to balance the   21 quest for income with the needs to keep growing and pursue other endeavors that do not pay off instantly—above all education.

Go back to school.   22

READING FOR MEANING

Write to create meanings for Etzioni's judgment that McDonald's is a problematic place for high-school students to work.

START MAKING MEANING

Begin by listing two or three of the main reasons Etzioni gives for his judgment. Continue by writing about anything else in the essay or in your experience that contributes to your understanding of Etzioni's evaluation. As you write, you will need to reread parts of the essay, adding to your annotations as you do so.

IF YOU ARE STUCK

If you cannot write at least a page, consider writing about

- the values Etzioni admires (self-reliance, the work ethic, and self-discipline, in paragraphs 3 and 4), considering how well your work (in or outside of school) supports these values.

- Etzioni's judgment that "these jobs ... skew the values of teenagers—especially their ideas about the worth of a dollar" (paragraph 3) and his support of this judgment (paragraphs 17–20).

- your experience of working in high school or college, reflecting on it in light of Etzioni's views about working while going to school.

- Etzioni's contrast between working at McDonald's and selling lemonade or delivering newspapers (paragraphs 4–7 and 17), commenting on the conclusions he draws from the contrast.

READING LIKE A WRITER

This section leads you through an analysis of Etzioni's evaluative writing strategies: *presenting the subject, asserting an overall judgment, giving reasons and support, counterarguing,* and *establishing credibility.* Each strategy is described briefly and followed by a critical reading and writing activity to help you see how Etzioni uses the strategy in his essay.

Consider this section a writer's introduction to evaluative writing. You will learn more about how different writers use these strategies later, from the Reading Like a Writer activities following the other selections in this chapter. Finally, at the end of the chapter a Guide to Writing Evaluations suggests how you can use these same strategies to write your own evaluative essay.

Presenting the Subject

Writers must present the subject so readers know what is being judged. Writers can simply name the subject, but usually they describe it in some detail. A film reviewer, for example, might identify the actors, describe the characters they play, and tell some of the plot. As a critical reader, you will note that the language used to present the subject also may serve to evaluate it. Therefore, you should look closely at how the subject is presented. Note where the writer's information about the subject comes from, whether the information is reliable, and whether anything important seems to have been left out.

ANALYZE

1. *Reread* paragraphs 5–7, 9, 12, 15, and 16, underlining and annotating the factual details that describe who works at fast-food restaurants and what they do. *Ask* yourself the following question as you analyze how Etzioni presents the subject: Where does the writer seem to get his information—from firsthand observation, conversation with others, reading published research?

2. Based on your own knowledge of fast-food jobs, *point* to those details you accept and those you think are inaccurate or only partially true. What seems to be missing from Etzioni's presentation of work at fast-food places?

WRITE

Write several sentences, discussing how Etzioni presents the subject to his intended readers—mainly adults, and particularly parents, concerned with education. *Give examples* from the reading. Then *write* a few more sentences, evaluating Etzioni's presentation of the subject in terms of accuracy and completeness.

Asserting an Overall Judgment

The writer's overall judgment is the main point of an evaluation—asserting that the subject is good or bad, or better or worse, than something comparable. Although readers expect a definitive judgment, they also appreciate a balanced one that acknowledges both good and bad qualities of the subject. Evaluations usually explicitly state the judgment up front in the form of a thesis and may restate it in different ways throughout the essay.

ANALYZE

1. *Reread* paragraphs 3 and 20–21, where Etzioni states his overall judgment. *Consider* whether his statements are clear.

2. *Decide* whether Etzioni qualifies his initial judgment when he restates it at the end of the essay.

WRITE

Write a few sentences, describing and evaluating Etzioni's presentation of his overall judgment.

Giving Reasons and Support

Any evaluative argument must explain and justify the writer's judgment. To be convincing, the reasons given as support must be recognized by readers as appropriate for evaluating the type of subject under consideration. That is, they must reflect the values or standards of judgment people typically use in similar situations. The reasons also must be supported by examples, quotations, facts, statistics, or personal anecdotes. The support may come from the writer's own knowledge and experience or from that of others, such as witnesses or authorities.

ANALYZE

1. Etzioni names three principal reasons for his judgment in the final sentence of paragraph 3. *Underline* these reasons and *consider* the appropriateness of each one, given Etzioni's intended reader—the largely middle-class adult subscribers to the *Miami Herald.* Why do you think they would or would not be likely to accept each reason as appropriate for evaluating part-time jobs for teenagers? What objections, if any, might a critical reader have to this kind of reasoning?

2. One reason Etzioni gives to clarify his view that working at McDonald's is "bad" for students is that the jobs "impart few skills that will be useful in later life" (paragraph 3). Etzioni then attempts to support or argue for this reason in paragraphs 4–9. *Reread* these paragraphs and *identify* in the margin where the writer uses the following strategies of argument: history, analogy, facts, benefits, comparisons, authorities, examples, assertions, research, and rhetorical questions.

3. *Evaluate* how well Etzioni supports his argument. Why do you think his readers will or will not find it appropriate, believable, and consistent? Which supporting details might they find most convincing? Least convincing?

WRITE

Write several sentences reporting what you have learned about how Etzioni gives reasons and support for his judgment. *Cite* a few examples of the support he gives for the "few skills" reason. How convincing do you think his readers will find this support?

Counterarguing

To gain credibility with their readers, writers often anticipate that some readers may resist the writer's judgments, reasons, or support. This strategy is called *counterarguing*, which involves responding to or countering readers' questions or objections. For example, some parents may question Etzioni's reasons for damning an easily available source of income for their high-school children. Other parents may object to his comparing fast-food jobs unfavorably to selling lemonade or delivering newspapers. A relatively poor parent may be firmly opposed to Etzioni's judgment that working part-time at McDonald's is bad for high-school students who must buy their own clothes and pay for their entertainment. Still other readers without any personal views about whether high-school students should or should not work part-time may wonder why Etzioni seems unaware that 21 percent of American children live in poverty and must work to help buy food and pay the rent, even if they would rather be doing homework.

Etzioni certainly is aware that some readers have questions and objections in mind. These objections do not cause him to waver in his own judgment, as you have seen, but they do persuade him to anticipate certain likely questions and objections and to respond. There are two basic ways to respond, or to counterargue, and Etzioni does both: A writer can *refute* readers' objections, arguing that they are simply wrong, or *accommodate* readers' objections, acknowledging that they are justified but do not irreparably damage the writer's reasoning.

ANALYZE

1. *Reread* paragraphs 8–11, 14, and 19, where Etzioni brings up either a reader's likely objection or an alternative judgment about the worth of part-time work. (Some alternative judgments are attributed to researchers, rather than readers, though it is likely some readers would have similar ideas.) *Underline* the alternative judgment or objection in these paragraphs.

2. *Choose* any two of these counterarguments and *look closely* at Etzioni's strategy. *Decide* first whether he refutes or accommodates the objection or alternative judgment. Then *note* how he goes about doing so.

3. *Evaluate* whether Etzioni's counterarguments are likely to convince skeptical readers.

WRITE

Write several sentences, identifying the objections and alternative judgments against which Etzioni counterargues. *Describe* his counterarguments, and *evaluate* how persuasive they are likely to be with his intended audience.

Establishing Credibility

The success of an evaluation depends to a large extent on readers' confidence in the writer's judgment. Evaluative writers usually try to establish their credibility by showing (1) they know a lot about the subject and (2) their judgment is based on valid values and standards. Biographical information can play a role in establishing a writer's authority by providing facts about his or her educational and professional accomplishments. It is the essay itself, however, that usually tells readers what the writer knows about the subject and from where that knowledge comes.

ANALYZE

1. Quickly *reread* the biographical headnote and the entire essay, putting a checkmark next to a few passages where you believe readers would find Etzioni especially credible or trustworthy. *Place a question mark* next to any passages where you think readers might question his credibility.

2. *Look* at the passages you marked and try to *determine* which words and bits of information contributed most to your evaluation of Etzioni's credibility in the eyes of his intended readers.

WRITE

Write a few sentences, summarizing your feelings about Etzioni's credibility. How credible is he? How could he be more credible? *Locate* the key words and sentences in the headnote and reading that influence how much trust, authority, and credibility readers will grant Etzioni. *Give examples* of what influenced you.

MICHAEL KINSLEY

Email Culture

> *Michael Kinsley is the editor-in-chief of the online maga-*
> *zine* Slate *(www.slate.com), an online magazine published*
> *by Microsoft Corporation, and which was founded in 1996.*
> *Previously, Kinsley served two stints as editor of the*
> New Republic. *For six and a half years he was co-host of*
> CNN's Crossfire. *He has also been editor of* Harper's *maga-*
> *zine, managing editor of the* Washington Monthly, *and*
> American Survey *editor of the* Economist. *For eleven years,*
> *he wrote the "TRB from Washington" column in the* New Re-
> public, *which appeared in the* Washington Post *and other*
> *newspapers. He also has written a regular column for the*
> Wall Street Journal. *His writing has appeared in the* New
> Yorker, Condé Nast Traveler, Vanity Fair, *and other publi-*
> *cations. He is the regular moderator of William F. Buckley's*
> Firing Line *debates on PBS.*
>
> *The following essay was originally published in 1996, in*
> Forbes, *a magazine for working professionals. Kinsley gives*
> *email an enthusiastically positive endorsement, and he of-*
> *fers several reasons for his positive evaluation. Although he*
> *focuses on email in the workplace, email is now widely used*
> *in many other settings. For some friends and families, email*
> *has almost replaced letters and phone calls. In some col-*
> *leges, email networks enable students to exchange their*
> *writing with other students or send it to an instructor for ad-*
> *vice. Whether or not you use email, you will want to know*
> *why Kinsley believes it to be "a marvelous medium of com-*
> *munication" for people in business.*

The way the new technology has affected my working life 1
most directly has nothing in particular to do with what I am
producing. My product happens to be an Internet-based
magazine, but this particular innovation would be just as
transforming if my business were manufacturing paper clips.
The innovation is email.

Until I came to Microsoft in January, I had never worked for 2
a big corporation. So I was having a hard time sorting out all
my new impressions. What was Microsoft (which prides itself,
of course, on being a different kind of corporation) and what
was (despite Microsoft's pretensions) corporate America in
general? Shortly after I arrived, I met someone who'd just
joined Microsoft from Nintendo North America—a similar

high tech, postindustrial, shorts-and-sandals sort of company, one would suppose. So I asked him, How is Microsoft different? He said, "At Microsoft, the phone never rings." And it's almost true. The ringing telephones that TV producers use as an all-purpose background noise to signify a business setting are virtually silent at Microsoft. At least in terms of intra-company communications, probably 99 percent take place through email. If you should happen to get an old-fashioned phone call, you may well be informed of that fact by email, even if the person who took the message is within eye-contact range.

Microsoft may still be a bit ahead of most of the rest of the country in developing an email culture, but I suspect it's only a tiny bit. Email is inevitable. Nineteen eighty-nine was the year you stopped asking people, "Do you have a fax machine?" and started asking, "What is your fax number?" Nineteen ninety was the year you started being annoyed (and, by around Christmastime), incredulous that anyone in the business or professional world would not have a fax number. Similarly, 1996 is the year you stopped asking people, "Do you have email?" and started asking, "What is your email address?" By the end of 1997 you will be indignant if anyone you're doing business with expects you to go to the trouble of communicating by less convenient methods.

This is an almost entirely positive development. Convenience aside, email is a marvelous medium of communication. It combines the immediacy of telephone or face-to-face talk with the thoughtfulness (or at least the opportunity for thoughtfulness) of the written word. At *Slate* we find it a wonderfully productive way to bounce around editorial ideas. And we use it in the online magazine as a medium of policy debate that we find intellectually superior to television chat.

Email has eased the burden of putting out a national magazine of politics and culture from Redmond, Washington (which is not the center of the universe, whatever some of its denizens may think). With a small budget and staff, we could not ordinarily afford to have a headquarters in Redmond plus bureaus in Washington and New York. But email enables us to spread the "headquarters" staff over all three places. Our East Coast representatives can pick up the local vibes in the traditional metropolitan manner (i.e., lunch) then plug back into Redmond in the modern manner (i.e., email). If you use email dozens of times a day—and save it—you end up with a pretty complete record of your activities and thoughts. As someone who (like many others) aspires to keep a diary but lacks the self-discipline, I find this comforting. Lawyers, of course, find it alarming, but you can't please everybody.

A social advantage of email is its egalitarianism. It's another blow to the old corporate culture in which Mr. Bigshot dictates letters and memos and the secretary types them, folds them, mails them, opens them at the receiving end, files them, and so on. Is there anyone in the business world who still thinks that he or she is too important to type? If so, that person had better wake up. Refusing to use a keyboard will soon be anachronistic as, say, refusing to speak on the telephone.   6

To be sure, egalitarianism has its limits. The ease and economy of sending email, especially to multiple recipients, makes us all vulnerable to any bore, loony, or commercial or political salesman who can set our email address. It's still a lot less intrusive than the telephone, since you can read and answer or ignore email at your own convenience. But as normal people's email starts mounting into the hundreds daily, which is bound to happen, filtering mechanisms and conventions of etiquette that are still in their primitive stage will be desperately needed.   7

Another supposed disadvantage of email is that it discourages face-to-face communication. At Microsoft, where people routinely send email back and forth all day to the person in the next office, this is certainly true. Some people believe this tendency has more to do with the underdeveloped social skills of computer geeks than with Microsoft's role in developing the technology email relies on. I wouldn't presume to comment on that. Whether you think email replacing live conversation is a good or bad thing depends, I guess, on how much of a misanthrope you are. I like it.   8

Historians looking back on our time, I suspect, will have no doubt that the arrival of email was a good thing. For decades now historians have been complaining about the invention of the telephone. By destroying the art of letter writing, telephones virtually wiped out the historians' principal raw material. Email, however, has reversed that development. Historians of the twenty-first century will be able to mine rich veins of written—and stored—material. People's daily lives will be documented better than ever before. Scholars specializing in the twentieth century will be at a unique disadvantage compared both with their colleagues writing about the nineteenth or earlier centuries and with those writing about the twenty-first or later.   9

So 1996 is not just the year business embraced email. In a way, it is the year history started again.   10

READING FOR MEANING

Write to create meanings for Kinsley's evaluation of email.

START MAKING MEANING

Begin by listing the main reasons Kinsley values email. (These reasons appear in paragraphs 4–6 and 9.) Continue by writing about anything else in the essay or in your experience that contributes to your understanding of Kinsley's evaluation.

IF YOU ARE STUCK

If you cannot write at least a page, consider writing about

- Kinsley's acknowledgment of two disadvantages of email (paragraphs 7 and 8), describing the disadvantages briefly and perhaps adding another one or more from your own experience.

- Kinsley's comparisons of fax machines and email (paragraph 3) and telephones and email (paragraph 8).

- your willingness or unwillingness to use email.

- a particular experience you have had with email, one that illustrates why you do or do not value email as Kinsley does.

READING LIKE A WRITER
GIVING REASONS AND SUPPORT

At the center of every evaluation are the writer's reasons for making a judgment and the line of support for those reasons. The reasons should be appropriate for evaluating the subject, and they should be convincing to readers. Furthermore, the reasons should be visible; you do not want readers to miss them. As a writer, you make reasons visible by cuing them strongly, for example, by putting them at the beginnings of paragraphs. Kinsley offers several reasons to support the high value he places on email, and he attempts to support each reason in various ways: examples, effects or benefits, questions, assertions, and comparisons or contrasts.

ANALYZE

1. *Underline* the reasons Kinsley gives for valuing email in paragraphs 4–6, and 9. *Look* for the one sentence in each paragraph that most concisely states the reason.

2. *Note* in the margin the kinds of supporting information you find in these paragraphs.

3. *Consider* whether Kinsley's reasons are likely to seem appropriate and believable to his readers. *Decide* whether the support he offers is convincing. What do you find most and least convincing about the reasons and support he offers?

WRITE

Write several sentences explaining what you have learned about how Kinsley attempts to justify his evaluation of email by giving reasons and support. *Give a few examples* from the reading. Then *write* a few more sentences, evaluating how successfully Kinsley supports his judgment.

CONSIDERING IDEAS FOR YOUR OWN WRITING

Kinsley's evaluation of email opens up the possibility of evaluating any device or technology you rely on for communication. Certainly, the telephone is important to you, but you may also have experience with a pager, car phone, or fax. You may have exchanged photographs, video-tapes, or audiotapes with someone. Maybe you still write letters or notes regularly. Choose one communication technology to evaluate—to praise or criticize.

How would you interest your readers in this technology and present it to them? For what reasons would you praise or criticize it? You could support these reasons convincingly only if you have considerable experience with the technology you are evaluating. What other technologies could you contrast it with?

J. C. HERZ

Game Boy's Toy Camera: Serious Business

A prominent and popular writer on computer games and the Internet, J. C. Herz (b. 1971) has authored two books, Joystick Nation *(1997), and* Surfing on the Internet: A Nethead's Adventures On-Line *(1995). Her writing has also appeared in many magazines, including* Esquire *and* Wired. *She now contributes reviews to the* New York Times' *weekly electronic section "Circuits," where the following essay appeared in 1998.*

Herz's evaluation focuses on a new digital electronic product, the Game Boy Camera. The device, when attached to the phenomenally popular Game Boy, functions as a digital camera. Herz does not describe the Game Boy product itself because she assumes that all or nearly all of her readers will know about it and that many own one. If you are not familiar with the product, Game Boy is the world's best-selling handheld computer game system, with over a thousand games available to users. As you read the selection, notice how Herz presents her evaluation of the Game Boy Camera and attempts to justify her positive judgment of it.

Nintendo's Game Boy camera is the Ginsu knife of digital imaging: an inexpensive mass-market device with seemingly endless repertory of functions. For $45, you get a cartridge that snaps into your handheld gaming device and takes black-and-white pictures. It stores up to 30 images at a time and displays them on screen.

Once you have taken these pictures, you can do all sorts of things to them. You can draw on them with a built-in paint program. You can decorate them with goofy facial features, captions and comments. You can use all sorts of trick lens effects to stretch the image, split the frame, superimpose frames or add borders. You can hot-link images together, so when you hit the fire button over a particular spot, you hear a sound effect and see a customized fade effect, and another picture pops onto the screen. You can convert your pictures into a Game Boy slide show. You can set the self-timer to snap at intervals, from a second to an hour, and string the resulting snapshots into a time-lapse animation.

It slices. It dices.

Once you have twisted and retouched an image, you can copy it and transfer it from one Game Boy to another via a separate cable. If you have a Super Game Boy adapter on a 16-bit Nintendo Super NES console, you can see the image on a television screen. You can also print out these images on the Game Boy Printer, a $55 calculator-size device that works like a tiny fax machine, burning stamp-size images onto a miniature roll of paper. The backing peels off. Voilà! Tradable stickers.

The resolution of these images is 128 by 112 pixels, a tiny   5
fraction of the resolution offered by high-end digital cameras that sell for 10 times the price. But the Game Boy camera is appealing in the way that all low-resolution, street-level things are appealing, the way that eight-millimeter film is appealing, the way that Fisher-Price Pixelvision cameras were appealing a decade ago. Pixelvision cameras can store only 5 minutes of grainy video on one side of a 90-minute audio tape. But there is something endearing about that graininess (the Pixelvision has become a kind of Holy Grail collector's item among independent filmmakers). And there is something appealing about the fact that it is a toy.

As a toy, the Game Boy camera is infinitely more cool   6
than its grown-up counterparts because it's not elite and fragile and expensive. It's cheap and rugged and unpretentious. It can be thrown into a backpack. It can be dropped. It's simple to control. It runs on two AAA batteries.

Plus it has the potential to become instantly ubiquitous.   7
There are 22 million Game Boys in North America, and this little cartridge snaps into all of them. Nintendo expects to sell 1.5 million of these cameras between June 1 and the end of the year. If those projections are met, a video game company will be manufacturing the No. 1 digital photography device in America within a very short period of time, despite the fact that its technology is hardly cutting edge—the same components have been running desktop teleconferences on Connectix Quickcams for years.

But in this case, leading-edge image technology is beside   8
the point. Because this device is not about taking beautiful pictures. It's about what you can do to pictures afterward. The visual information you capture is not an end in itself. It's a starting point. It's something to play with. It exists to be manipulated, the way a sound sample exists to be manipulated by a deejay.

And manipulation is increasingly what distinguishes vi-   9
sual media in the day-to-day world. When you look at an image in a magazine or on a movie screen or on television, the lingering question is what has been done to it. Egyptian pyramids have been digitally squeezed together on the cover of *National Geographic.* Fashion models and celebri-

ties are pared down and smoothed out after photo shoots, in what amounts to virtual cosmetic surgery. Feature films overlay real-life footage and computer-generated effects. Clever dialogue bubbles provide running commentary on VH1's "Pop-up Video." We have all become consumers of these digitally enhanced images.

It's only a matter of time before ordinary people start pro-   10
ducing them.

READING FOR MEANING

Write to create meanings for Herz's evaluation of the Game Boy Camera.

START MAKING MEANING

Begin by listing two or three of the main reasons Herz gives to clarify her favorable review of the Game Boy Camera. Then explain briefly why she considers it "serious business" (paragraphs 9 and 10). Continue by writing about anything else in the essay or in your experience that contributes to your understanding of Herz's evaluation.

IF YOU ARE STUCK

If you cannot write at least a page, consider writing about

- Herz's attempt to portray the Game Boy Camera's limitations—its low resolution and lack of new technology—as virtues (paragraphs 5, 7, and 8).

- other toys you know about that could be considered "serious business" culturally, connecting your ideas to Herz's ideas in paragraphs 9 and 10.

- Herz's statement that "manipulation is increasingly what distinguishes visual media" (paragraph 9).

- your experience using a regular or digital camera and how that influences your interest in the Game Boy Camera.

READING LIKE A WRITER
COUNTERARGUING OR REFUTING OBJECTIONS

Product evaluations like Herz's run the risk of sounding like advertising or hype if they offer only unqualified praise. They gain credibility when they acknowledge that the product may not be perfect or when they at least show an awareness that readers may have objections or questions. Herz anticipates at least two of her readers' possible objections: In paragraph 5, the objection seems to be, "But the resolution is so weak and the images so blurry, nothing like the quality you get with other digital cameras," and in paragraph 7, "But there's no new technology here." Herz attempts to refute both objections; that is, to argue that the objections are based on misunderstandings.

ANALYZE

1. *Underline* the two objections Herz anticipates, one at the beginning of paragraph 5, the other at the end of paragraph 7.

2. *Consider* how Herz attempts to refute the two objections (paragraphs 5, 6, and 8). *Note* in the margin the main points of her counterarguments.

3. *Evaluate* how successful Herz is in refuting the two objections. What seems most and least persuasive about her refutations?

WRITE

Write several sentences reporting on what you have learned about how Herz deals with readers' likely reservations. How does she bring up the potential objections to buying a Game Boy Camera and how does she counterargue? Then *add* a few more sentences, evaluating how persuasive these refutations are likely to be for Herz's intended readers.

COMPARE

Compare Herz's handling of readers' likely objections (paragraphs 5, 6, and 8) to Kinsley's handling of them in his evaluation of email (paragraphs 7 and 8, p. 236). *Identify* the objections Kinsley anticipates; then *decide* whether he attempts to refute them or to accommodate readers' concerns by acknowledging that their objections may be valid. Then *write* a few sentences, explaining what you have learned about how Herz and Kinsley raise and counter their readers' objections.

CONSIDERING IDEAS FOR YOUR OWN WRITING

Consider evaluating a game you own or one you remember from childhood. Examples include a computer game such as Mortal Kombat, Quake, or Myst, a board game such as Monopoly or Trivial Pursuit, a card game such as poker, or an athletic game such as handball or volleyball. The key is to choose a game that you have extensive experience playing and that you are willing to look at critically. Even if the game is easy to play, and even if your first thought is simply that it is fun, you still must follow the basic principles for evaluative writing and give substantial reasons explaining why the game works or does not work for you. You must judge the game according to recognized standards, such as its visual appeal, the simplicity or complexity of the rules, the degree of competitiveness or teamwork involved, the pace of the game, and the skills it requires. You also need to consider both the game's strengths and limitations.

JAMES WOLCOTT

Talking Trash

> *James Wolcott, a cultural critic for the* New Yorker, *often evaluates television programs.*
>
> *In the following essay, which originally appeared in that publication in 1996, Wolcott reviews* Night Stand, *a pseudo-talk show that makes fun of real talk shows. You may have seen the program, but Wolcott must assume that many of his readers will be unfamiliar with the show, which is not on a major network and is not especially popular. (*Night Stand *reruns could be seen in 1998 on late-night Comedy Central.) As you read his review, consider whether Wolcott tells readers enough about the program so that they can understand his evaluation and judgment of it.*

At first, the furor over "trash TV" (those daytime talk shows hosted by Ricki Lake, Geraldo Rivera, Richard Bey, Jerry Springer, Jenny Jones, Sally Jessy Raphael, Maury Povich, Montel Williams, and the others vying for Oprah's throne) divided along ideological lines, like a *Crossfire* panel.[1] On the right, wearing a gray suit and a grumpy expression, was William Bennett, the former Secretary of Education and "drug czar," the author of the best-seller *The Book of Virtues,* and the co-director (with Jack Kemp) of Empower America.[2] Having weighed in against gangsta rap, Bennett called a press conference in which he condemned daytime talk shows as degrading spectacles and specimens of "cultural rot," which fostered promiscuity and other forms of bad posture. His "J'accuse" was seconded by Republicans ranging from Colin Powell to Bruce Willis, with moderate Democrats such as Senators Sam Nunn and Joseph Lieberman making worried noises as well.[3] On the left, pundits beseeched us to look beyond the tawdry theatrics (e.g., black girls calling each other ho's) and pay heed to the Un-

[1] *Crossfire* is a political talk show. *(Ed.)*

[2] Jack Kemp was a vice-presidential candidate in 1996. He has served as a congressman and as secretary of housing and urban development. *(Ed.)*

[3] *J'accuse* is French for "I accuse." It was the title of a tract by Emile Zola that unmasked a conspiracy in the infamous Dreyfus case in late-nineteenth-century France. Colin Powell served as chairman of the Joint Chiefs of Staff under Presidents Bush and Clinton. Bruce Willis is an actor and supporter of Republican party causes. *(Ed.)*

derlying Social Issues. The *Times* columnist Frank Rich chastised Bennett for not being equally indignant about the tobacco giants, such as Philip Morris, that sponsor these programs (through their food divisions). In *Time,* Barbara Ehrenreich claimed that economic deprivation sometimes drove talk-show guests to shame themselves, and that the backlash against trash TV was an attempt to neuter the working class—a position also adopted by Ellen Willis in *The Nation.* She wrote, "On talk shows, whatever their drawbacks, the proles get to talk. . . ."

Meanwhile, TV has its own methods of policing itself. It chews its excesses and spits them out like bubble gum. The sharpest, funniest, and sanest critique of trash TV is a satire called *Night Stand* (syndicated nationally, and shown locally Saturday nights on WWOR–Channel 9), an imaginary talk show hosted by Dick Dietrick, played by Timothy Stack. Unlike E!'s popular series *Talk Soup,*[4] which serves tacky clips from talk shows in bite-size McNuggets, *Night Stand,* created by Stack, Paul Abeyta, and Peter Kaikko, doesn't peer through a porthole of smug irony. It presents sleaze and corruption as viable life-style alternatives. The program is taped in Los Angeles before a studio audience, with professional actors cast as the dysfunctional guests, and has become a cult favorite among standup comics and others with keen antennae. (Bill Maher, the host of *Politically Incorrect,* has called it "the funniest show on TV.") Each hour-long show consists of two segments, featuring such burning non-issues as "So You Think You're a Lesbian?" and "Addicted to Strip Clubs"; guests are I.D.'d onscreen with punchy tags ("BETH ANN MCCLEAR—Sexually Abused Christian Author/Centerfold"). The show also employs the guerilla tactics of trash TV—the ambush interview, the hidden camera, the inciting of catfights—and it captures the kangaroo-court, revival-tent ritualism of that realm, where bad guys are booted, sinners repent, and souls are healed.

Yet no one would mistake *Night Stand* for a real talk show. Its healthy sparkle is pure Hollywood. Unlike the human driftwood on daytime talk shows, the men and women on *Night Stand* are tan and buff, a master race of test-tube babies that didn't turn out so smart. These lap dancers, defrocked ministers, and shopaholics all speak as if they had attended self-help seminars, showing big rows of perfect teeth as they discuss the demons that possess them. The

2

3

[4]E! is the Entertainment channel. *Talk Soup* is a comedy program that makes fun of daytime talk shows. *(Ed.)*

show's put-on humor is somewhere between the old Steve Allen show and *Fernwood 2-Night,* with double-entendres that Benny Hill might have happily squirrelled away.[5]

What lends *Night Stand* its touch of the idiot sublime is   4
Stack's characterization of Dick Dietrick. He has a limber quality all his own, a guarded yet elastic self-deprecation reminiscent of George Plimpton's early writing or of Dick Martin rocking back on his heels on *Laugh-In.*[6] Lanky, boneless, pseudo-debonair, Stack's Dietrick is a one-man anthology of talk-show insincerity; the studio is his used-car lot, loaded with lemons. He can switch with seamless ease from badgering his guests to offering sympathy. He opens each segment with a brief topic intro, intoned with the news-bulletin urgency of Ted Koppel. On a recent *Night Stand,* the case of a white stripper losing a job to a black stripper raised the issue of affirmative action. "For those of you not familiar with affirmative action," Dick explained, "it's a government program originally set up to give minorities jobs that white people didn't want. Well, things are different now, white people have changed their minds, and they want those jobs back." As the show proceeds, Dick uses his body English to keep the dialogue in play: he fans his hand after he releases a tricky question, like a magician casting a spell, then does a Phil Donahue slouch as he awaits the answer; he snaps his fingers over his head, Sally Jessy Raphael style, to chastise his audience for hearing a dirty message in his innocent questions. ("Oh, *no,* no, people, no!")

Dietrick's professional aplomb is undercut by his verbal   5
haplessness. He is subject to malapropisms ("Let's cut to the heart of the meat of the matter") and has a spotty sense of history, referring to "the late Paul McCartney," to "the day Elvis was shot," and to events "indelibly paper-clipped" in the mind. With his female guests, he often drifts off into erotic reverie: "So anyway you're in bed, probably in pajamas or a nightgown, or a peekaboo teddy that rides high over your graceful yet powerful hips. Then what happened?"

[5]Steve Allen had several comedy programs on television in the 1950s and 1960s, including the original *Tonight Show. Fernwood 2-Night* was a comedy program starring Martin Mull that pretended to be a real talk show in the 1970s. Benny Hill was a British comic who had a comedy program on U.S. television in the 1970s. *(Ed.)*

[6]George Plimpton wrote several articles and books including *Paper Lion,,* which described his attempt to play football with a professional team. Dick Martin was co-host of *Laugh-In,* a popular, fast-paced comedy show of the 1960s. *(Ed.)*

Yet at the end of each segment he pulls himself together and addresses a sermonette to the camera (a takeoff on Jerry Springer): "So, what have we learned about fame? Well, we've learned that fame is usually limited to the well-known. . . . You see, people are always watching you when you're famous. And as a result things you take for granted are hardships for people like me. For example, I can't buy Preparation H without people gawking at me. I can't stiff a waiter. I can't hang around a Catholic girls' school waiting for that three-o'clock bell."

Snatches of autobiography sneak into each episode of *Night*   6
Stand: Dick's busted marriage and alimony payments. His bachelor life at Casa de Tuna, where he has been accused of nude bathing on the patio. His thing for white cotton panties ("the land of cotton"). His late nights alone with his remote-control clicker. In his sports jackets and loafers, Dietrick is the Sears-catalogue model of a classic underachiever. When one of his guests accuses him of being a third-rate talk-show host, he snaps, "I'll have you know I'm a *second*-rate talk-show host!" His proud, defensive second-rateness is what makes him a symptomatic American loser. He's the quintessential white guy who can't dance but snaps his fingers extra hard, a throwback to the "What kind of man reads *Playboy*?" ad, swirling a drink in a goblet beneath a black velvet bullfight painting. It's a persona that might be too dank and pathetic to enjoy if Stack didn't invest the role with such dry geniality.

Night Stand, like such recent pieces of pop sociology as *To*   7
Die For and *Natural Born Killers,*[7] portrays the TV audience as a nation of trained seals—fame junkies who clap on cue and crane their necks to see themselves on the studio monitors. There's no quality filter to celebrity today: serial killers and opera singers occupy the same glittery plane. On *Night Stand,* sitcom has-beens are hurrahed like Oscar winners, and even an attractive woman who appears only in the background of infomercials is treated like a star. ("Julianne, welcome to the show. I can see by the looks on the people in the audience that they almost recognize you.") In *To Die For* and *Natural Born Killers* the mass appetite for celebrity and notoriety is diagnosed as a national soul malady, but *Night Stand* doesn't trouble its empty little head over such matters. Like *Mad* magazine, it takes pop-culture garbage as a given—something beyond reform or redemption and full of absurd goodies. It assumes that all Americans crave the same thing:

[7]*To Die For* and *Natural Born Killers* are films that had been recently released at the time this essay was written in 1996. *(Ed.)*

cheap attention. After a religious groupie recounts to Dick how she decided to cash in on her notoriety, getting herself an agent and a new body, then posing naked everywhere she could ("It did wonders for my self-esteem"), he exclaims, "What a positive person!"

In the world according to Dick, the only categorical impera-   8
tive is to create good TV. Good TV means embarrassment ("Let's dredge up the heartache and trauma of that moment, if you don't mind") and conflict, no matter how contrived. When a gossip columnist announced that he was collaborating with a former maid to detail her exploitation at the hands of the former sitcom star Cindy Williams,[8] Dick said, "I think writing a book is good therapy, but facing your demons is good television." (Enter a scowling Cindy Williams.) And when a beauty-pageant consultant tried to play peacemaker between two beauty queens, Dick pointed a finger and issued a stern rebuke: "Don't *ever* stop a fight on my show." . . .

Right and left alike have exploited the trash-TV phenome-   9
non for their own ends. The right used trash TV to occupy a moral high ground that they vacated the moment they got bored. . . . The left used trash TV to pose as the defenders of the downtrodden by arguing that the domestic squabblers on daytime talk represent the authentic voice of the working class—even though it has been documented that these shows are plagued with impostors and deadbeats hired through classified ads. (The real working class is out working.) With both sides platitudinizing, Timothy Stack's Dick Dietrick emerges as the only honest phony around. And *Night Stand* is further evidence that in the nineties comedy is the only place where anyone can be both truthful and silly about race, sex, and class. Everything else is editorial.

READING FOR MEANING

Write to create meanings for Wolcott's evaluation of television talk shows.

START MAKING MEANING

Begin by describing briefly Wolcott's judgment of TV talk shows and listing the main reasons given for his judgment. (Look for the most concise statement of a reason in paragraphs 4–7.) Continue by writing about anything else in the essay or in your experience that contributes to your understanding of Wolcott's evaluation.

[8]Cindy Williams is a comic actress who became famous as Shirley in the popular 1970s sitcom *Laverne and Shirley*.

IF YOU ARE STUCK

If you cannot write at least a page, consider writing about

- the views of the political right and left toward trashy TV talk shows, listing typical views cited by Wolcott (paragraphs 1 and 9).

- your personal views of TV talk shows, connecting them, if possible, to the views of people on the political right or left.

- whether you accept *Night Stand*'s portrayal of the American TV audience (described in paragraph 7).

- a talk show you watch regularly, describing it briefly and noting which aspects of *Night Stand*'s satire apply to it and perhaps adding one or two other ways to satirize the show you watch.

READING LIKE A WRITER
PRESENTING THE SUBJECT

A published review of a movie or television program or series usually begins with a description of the subject, especially when the reviewer cannot assume that many readers have seen the program or series. Wolcott provides a relatively full description of *Night Stand* at the beginning of his evaluation, but he does even more: He gives readers a political context for the evaluation in terms of arguments in the 1990s between the political right and left about popular culture. By analyzing Wolcott's presentation of his subject, you can learn valuable strategies to use in your own evaluation.

ANALYZE

1. In paragraph 1, *underline* the views from the political left and right. *Consider* whether Wolcott presents a representative collection of views from each side. What other left or right views, or other views not so easily classified, might Wolcott have included in his essay?

2. In paragraphs 2 and 3, *identify* the different kinds of information Wolcott gives readers about *Night Stand,* beginning with the purpose of the program (satire), the time and channel in the New York area, the main character and actor, and so on. *Consider* whether you get enough information in these two paragraphs to enable you to understand what the program is about. What information seems most and least helpful to you?

WRITE

Write several sentences explaining how Wolcott establishes an ongoing political debate, fitting *Night Stand* into this context. *Give examples* from the review. Then *write* a few more sentences evaluating Wolcott's presentation.

A SPECIAL READING STRATEGY

Evaluating the Logic of an Argument

You can learn still more about Wolcott's evaluation by analyzing and evaluating its logic for appropriateness, believability, and consistency. For detailed guidelines on evaluating the logic of an argument, see Appendix One (p. 476).

CONSIDERING IDEAS FOR YOUR OWN WRITING

Consider evaluating a television series. You might evaluate your favorite weekday evening series that you watch regularly or a sports or hobby series that you watch occasionally. Because you would need to watch several programs closely and critically, you might need to videotape a few programs during the weeks before you begin working on this assignment. Or you could choose a series, like *Hard Copy* or *Inside Edition,* that appears nightly. Also, reruns of older programs are sometimes shown nightly. After watching several programs, you would need to settle on a judgment of the series, decide on reasons for your judgment, and take careful notes about features of the program to support your reasons. Your goal would be to become an expert on the series—a critical and evaluative expert, not just an enthusiastic viewer.

SCOTT HYDER

Poltergeist: It Knows What Scares You

Scott Hyder wrote this movie review for his first-year writing class. Like all reviewers, he cannot assume you have seen Poltergeist, *a movie released in 1982. But he probably assumes that you have seen other horror movies like it. As you read the review, think about how Hyder attempts to hold your interest in a movie you might not have seen in a theater or on video.*

You are an eight-year-old boy all tucked in for the night. 1
Your little sister is sleeping in the bed next to you. Suddenly, you hear a crash of thunder, and through the window, you can see the big, old, growling tree in the lightning. It seems to be, well, to be making faces at you! But, you are a big boy. Nothing scares *you*. Nothing at—BANG! WHOOSH! The tree comes to life as it tumbles through the window, grabbing you with its pulsating, hairy roots from your bed. As you scream for Mommy, the closet door slowly opens and an invisible, windlike presence kidnaps your sister. Your nice, cozy dreamhouse turns into a living hell. Watch out! "They're hee-re!"

In June 1982, producer-director-writer Steven Spielberg 2
defined "horror" with a new word: *Poltergeist*. At first and final glance, *Poltergeist* is simply a riveting demonstration of a movie's power to terrify. It creates honest thrills within the confines of a PG rating, reaching for shock effects and the forced suspension of disbelief throughout the movie. Spielberg wrote the story, coproduced it, and supervised the final editing. The directing credit goes to Tobe Hooper, best known for his cult shocker *The Texas Chainsaw Massacre,* which probably explains *Poltergeist's* violence and slight crudeness.

Nevertheless, *Poltergeist* cannot be classified in the same 3
horror category with such movies as *A Nightmare on Elm Street,* where a deformed psychotic slashes his victims with razor-edged fingernails. Unlike most horror flicks, *Poltergeist* works! Its success is due to excellent characters, music, and special effects—and to the fact that the story stays within the bounds of believability.

The movie takes place in a suburban housing tract. Steve 4
(Craig T. Nelson) and Diane (JoBeth Williams) Freeling have

just purchased a new home when their adorable five-year-old daughter, Carole Anne (Heather O'Rourke), awakes to odd voices coming from the snowy TV screen that Steve falls asleep in front of during the late movie. She calls them the "TV people," and with the help of special-effects producer George Lucas and his Industrial Light and Magic, these people abduct little Carol Anne, provoking turbulence and misery for this once-happy family.

A mere synopsis simply cannot give a real feeling for the story. As Steve Freeling says to the parapsychologists who have come to see the house, "You have to see it to believe it." Each character possesses a unique personality, which contributes to the overall feeling the audience has for the story. The characters are represented to be as normal and American as bologna sandwiches—Dad sells houses, Mom sings along to TV jingles. Spielberg likes these characters, illustrating their go-with-the-flow resilience. When things get suddenly hectic toward the climax, these people can display their fear and anger as well as summon their inner strengths. This is particularly evident when Tangina, the parapsychologist the Freelings hire, instructs Diane to lie to her daughter in order to lure Carol Anne into the light and save her. 5

"Tell her to go into the light," Tangina instructs. "Tell her that *you* are in the light!" 6

"No," Diane replies with betrayed emotions. 7

Tangina immediately puts everything into the proper perspective. "You can't choose between life and death when we're dealing with what's in between! Now tell her before it's too late!" 8

Such scenes clearly illustrate that Spielberg's characters are, in a sense, the ordinary heroes of the movies. 9

A horror movie, however, cannot rely on terror, anger, and disbelief to hold its audience for two hours. Something needs to accompany these emotions, equally expressing the full extent of the characters' fear and anger. Music composer Jerry Goldsmith contributes his share of eeriness with his Academy Award-winning sound track. The basic theme is a lullaby (entitled "Carol Anne's Theme") that soothes the watcher, providing a cheerful, childlike innocence to the picture. The inverse is the ghost music that accompanies the abduction of Carol Anne and forces our stomachs to writhe. The music brings a straining, vibrating tone that is responsible for 60 percent of the audience's terror. When the clown doll's hand wraps around Robbie's (Oliver Robbins) neck, the sudden blaring of Goldsmith's orchestra is what makes viewers swallow their stomachs. Without it, the scene would never slap 10 our face or give our necks a backward whiplash. Goldsmith matches the actions and emotions of the characters with the corresponding instrumental music, enabling the audience to parallel their feelings with those delivered on the screen.

If a horror movie has a well-developed plot with superior   11
actors and an excellent score to accompany their emotions, then it should be a sure winner at the box office, right? Looking back at such movies as *Rosemary's Baby, The Exorcist,* and the original *Psycho* one would obviously agree. *Poltergeist,* however, doesn't stop here. It goes even further by providing its audience with a special treat. With the help of *Star Wars* creator George Lucas, Spielberg and Hooper whip up a dazzling show of light and magic. There's an eerie parade of poltergeists in chiffons of light marching down the Freelings' staircase to the climactic scene as a huge, bright, nuclear-colored mouth strives to suck the Freeling children into their closet. Hooper's familiarity with film violence surfaces in a grotesque scene in which one of the parapsychologists hallucinates that he is tearing his face. Such shocking, hair-raising scenes as this make a huge contribution to horrifying the audience. Many horror films never achieve such reactions. *Poltergeist*'s precise timing with such effects makes it completely unpredictable as far as what is to come. From the first sign of a ghostlike hand jumping out of the TV to the staggering scene of dead bodies popping out of the half-dug swimming pool, the special-effects team draws every bit of energy out of the audience, dazzling them and forcing them to believe in the horror on the screen.

There have been many movies that possess superior rat-   12
ings in all of the above. Such movies as John Carpenter's *The Thing* and David Cronenberg's *Scanners* won raves for superior acting, background music, and special effects. Why was *Poltergeist* accepted at the box office more than other such movies? Every movie is forced to set up boundaries of believability through certain actions and concepts, and at one point these boundaries will be accepted by the viewer. In *Indiana Jones and the Temple of Doom,* Spielberg distinguished boundaries within which Indiana Jones defined his heroic stunts. Spielberg, however, unfortunately crossed his boundaries during a scene in which Indiana Jones jumps from one track to another with a moving train cart. From previous observations of Indiana Jones's capabilities, the audience is unable to accept this, nodding their heads with a "give me a break" expression.

In *Poltergeist,* Spielberg and Hooper remain within their es-   13
tablished boundaries. Unlike most horror movies that have

unfeasible killers who are incapable of dying or monsters that pop out of people's stomachs, *Poltergeist* focuses on the supernatural—a subject with *very wide* boundaries. Because of our lack of knowledge in the area, we are "at the mercy of the writers and directors," as Alfred Hitchcock has phrased it. The boundaries can be greater than most horror movies because of *Poltergeist*'s subject matter. The characters' disbelief of their surroundings encourages the audience to accept what is in front of them. Hence, *Poltergeist* successfully stays within its limits, taking them to their maximum, but luring the audience to believe the characters' situation.

Poltergeist reflects a lot of the fears that most of us grow   14
up with: seeing scary shadows from the light in your closet, making sure your feet are not dangling over the bed, forming scary images of the objects in your room. As Spielberg's *E.T.* reminisces about our childhood dreams, *Poltergeist* surfaces our childhood nightmares. With its characters, music, and special effects, and its clearly distinguished boundaries of belief, *Poltergeist* is able to capture its audience with its unique thrills, allowing viewers to link their most innerlocked fears to those on the screen. *Poltergeist:* It knows what scares you!

READING FOR MEANING

Write to create meanings for Hyder's evaluation of *Poltergeist.*

START MAKING MEANING

Begin by describing briefly Hyder's purpose in writing this movie review. Continue by writing about anything else in the essay or in your experience that contributes to your understanding of Hyder's evaluation.

IF YOU ARE STUCK

If you cannot write at least a page, consider writing about

• Hyder's claim that horror movies must "stay within the bounds of believability" to be considered excellent (paragraph 3).

• Hyder's view that the characters are the heroes of *Poltergeist,* recalling whether this is the case in most horror movies you have seen.

• why a movie director would choose an American suburb as the setting for *Poltergeist.*

• a horror movie you have seen recently, comparing it to what you have learned of *Poltergeist* from Hyder's review.

READING LIKE A WRITER
Supporting Reasons with Examples

For an arts review to be believable and convincing, it must offer readers many examples from the subject. These examples help readers imagine the subject. Perhaps better than anything in the review, examples help readers decide whether they find the reviewer's judgment plausible, worth taking seriously. Beginning writers of evaluations of all kinds usually err on the side of providing too few examples. Think of this fundamental requirement as one of piling up examples, of including a great many, perhaps more than you think readers can stand. If you discover that you have gone an inch or two too far, you can easily drop a few examples when you revise your draft. Hyder provides a good model, offering many examples to support his argument that *Poltergeist* is a fine horror movie.

ANALYZE

1. Hyder provides many examples to support his five reasons for his judgment (paragraphs 5–13). *Choose* any one of these paragraphs or paragraph sets and *underline* each separate example. (Some examples are references to other movies, which Hyder seems to assume readers will have seen.) *Skip* over the general statements and assertions to *look* for the specific or concrete examples.

2. *Place a checkmark* in the margin by the example that best helps you imagine the movie and *mark an X* in the margin by the example that you find least helpful.

WRITE

Write several sentences explaining how Hyder makes use of examples to substantiate his reasoning. *Quote* a few typical examples. Then *write* a few more sentences evaluating how plausible and convincing the examples are, in your view.

COMPARE

Compare Wolcott's presentation of the talk show *Night Stand* to Hyder's presentation of *Poltergeist. Look* back to paragraphs 1–4 of Hyder's review. How does he present his subject, and how well does he succeed in doing so? *Write* several sentences explaining how the two presentations are alike and different and evaluating each writer's success.

CONSIDERING IDEAS FOR YOUR OWN WRITING

Consider reviewing a current movie. Arrange to see it at least twice before you complete the first draft of your essay and a third time as you are revising. Only in this way can you collect relevant, concrete examples to support your evaluation. Or you might consider an earlier movie now available at video stores. That way you can view it in segments at home and scan forward or backward to review key scenes. Consider choosing a film in a genre—horror, noir, romance, Western, or others—that you are familiar with. By choosing a film in a recognized genre, your evaluation will be more astute and informed and you will be able to compare your movie to others in its genre, as does Hyder. In the same vein, consider evaluating a movie by a director whose other films you have seen, even one or two of them. These comparisons can strengthen your evaluation.

Which movie might you choose? What arrangements will you need to make in order to see it several times as you are working on your evaluation?

ILENE WOLF

Buzzworm: The Superior Magazine

*Ilene Wolf wrote the following essay in her first-year col-
lege composition course.*

The subject of the essay is a magazine, Buzzworm,
*which was new at the time the essay was written. If you
have seen* Buzzworm, *consider how accurately Wolf describes it and whether you agree with her judgment. If you
have not seen the magazine, ask yourself whether Wolf
gives you enough information to consider her judgment
sound.*

Many people today exist within their environment without really knowing anything about it. If this ignorance continues, we will undoubtedly destroy the world in which we
live. Only by gaining a better understanding of our planet
will we be able to preserve our fragile environment from pollution, hazardous waste, endangerment of species, and rav-
aging of the land. A new magazine is dedicated to enlighten-
ing the general public about these important issues. It is
called *Buzzworm.*

What makes *Buzzworm* superior to other magazines dealing with the same subject is that it not only fully explores all
of the aspects of the environment but does so in an objective manner. *Buzzworm* effectively tackles the controversial
question of how best to protect our planet and conveys the
information in a way that all audiences can understand. In
fact, the term *buzzworm,* borrowed from the Old West,
refers to a rattlesnake. The rattlesnake represents an effective form of communication, for when it rattles or buzzes it
causes an immediate reaction in those who are near. Thus
the purpose of *Buzzworm* is to create a reaction in its readers regarding the conservation and preservation of the environment.

One of *Buzzworm*'s most striking features is its visual appeal. Excellent photographs complement the articles. Contrasted with the photography in *Sierra,* another environmental magazine, the superb photographs in *Buzzworm* only
seem more striking. The Summer 1989 issue of *Buzzworm*
features a dramatic full-page color picture of the grey wolf,
which catches the reader's eye and draws attention to the
article concerning the endangerment of the grey wolf's habitat. The current issue of *Sierra* also has a picture of the grey
wolf, yet it is not only smaller but the colors are not as

1

2

3

clear—resulting in a less effective picture. Whereas both photographs of the animal pertain to their corresponding articles, it is the one in *Buzzworm* that makes the reader stop and discover the plight of the grey wolf.

Not only must a photograph be of excellent quality but it also must be placed correctly in the layout to enhance the article. The reader should be able to look at the picture and receive some information about the article it corresponds to. *Buzzworm*'s pictures of the East African Masai convey specific information about the tribe. Startling photographs depict the Masai in their traditional dress, focusing on the elaborate beadwork done by the women and the exquisite headdresses worn by the warriors. Looking at one picture of a young warrior wearing a lion's mane headdress, the reader gets a sense of the importance of the ritual and of the great respect that is earned by becoming a warrior. Another picture depicts a mother intently watching her daughter as she learns the art of beading. The look on the woman's face displays the care that goes into the beadwork, which has been an important part of their heritage for many generations. Thus, even before reading the article about the Masai, readers have some understanding of the Masai culture and traditions.

4

Another functional and informative aspect of *Buzzworm*'s layout is the use of subfeatures within an article. A subfeature functions in two ways, first by breaking up the monotony of a solid page of print, and second by giving the curious reader additional information. An article entitled "Double Jeopardy" in the current issue gives the reader an option of learning more about the subject through two subfeatures. The article itself describes the detrimental effects that excessive whale-watching and research are believed to have on the humpback whale. To find further information about what might be contributing to the already low numbers of the humpback whale, one can read the subfeature "Humpback Whale Survival." Furthermore, for the reader who is not familiar with the subject, there is a second subfeature, entitled "Natural History," which gives general information about the humpback whale. No such subfeatures can be found anywhere in *Sierra*.

5

In addition to being an effective way of adding pertinent information to the article, the subfeatures also add to the unity of the magazine. The subfeatures in *Buzzworm* all share a common gray background color, adding to the continuity in layout from one article to the next. This produces a cleaner, more polished, and visually appealing magazine.

6

Once again, *Buzzworm* shows superior layout design in keeping the articles from being overrun by advertisements. I realize that ads do generate necessary revenue for the magazine, but nothing is more annoying than an article constantly interrupted by ads. *Buzzworm*'s few ads are all in the back of the magazine. In fact, not once does an ad interrupt an article. On the other hand, *Sierra* is filled with advertisements that are allowed to interrupt articles, which only frustrates the reader and detracts from the article.

Buzzworm is unique in that it focuses on more than just one aspect of the environment. In contrast, *Sierra* devoted its entire September/October issue to one subject, the preservation of the public lands in the United States. Although it is a topic worthy of such discussion, readers prefer more variety to choose from. The content of *Buzzworm* ranges from the humpback whale to the culture of the Masai to a profile of three leading conservationists. The great variety of issues covered in *Buzzworm* makes it more likely to keep the reader's attention than *Sierra.*

Buzzworm's ability to inform the reader is not limited to the information in its articles. Captions also play a large part. Readers who are too lazy to read an entire article most often will look at the pictures and read the captions. Thus *Buzzworm*'s long and detailed captions are like miniature paragraphs, giving out more details than the terse captions in *Sierra,* which usually consist of only a few words. The difference in the amount of information in the two magazines is obvious from a look at a typical caption in *Buzzworm,* "Finding relaxation of a different kind, Earthwatch participants spend a vacation patrolling beaches and assisting female turtles in finding a secluded nesting area" compared to one in *Sierra,* "Joshua tree with Clark Mountain in background." Both captions give a description of their corresponding pictures, but only the caption found in *Buzzworm* gives any indication of what the article is about. The captions in *Buzzworm* supplement the articles, whereas the captions in *Sierra* only give brief descriptions of the pictures.

Finally, *Buzzworm* is objective, a rare quality in environmental magazines. An article on tourism versus environmental responsibility focuses on both the environmental and economic aspects of tourism, stating that while tourism generates income, it often destroys places of natural beauty that are so often visited. In contrast to this point of view, the article also cites examples where tourism has actually helped to preserve the environment. For every argument presented in *Buzzworm,* the counterargument is also presented. This balance is important, for readers must have all of the facts to be able to make well-informed judgments about controversial issues.

Despite all of its wonderful aspects, *Buzzworm* does have   11
its flaws. Some of its graphics pale next to the color photographs. Also, the photograph sizes should be varied more to create a visually more appealing layout. Except for these minor flaws, *Buzzworm* achieves its goal of appealing to its readers. In informing the general public about conservation and protection of our environment, *Buzzworm* is far more effective than *Sierra*.

READING FOR MEANING

Write to create meanings for Wolf's evaluation of the magazine *Buzzworm*.

START MAKING MEANING

Begin by listing three or four of the several reasons Wolf gives to justify her judgment. Continue by writing about anything else in the essay or in your experience that contributes to your understanding of Wolf's evaluation.

IF YOU ARE STUCK

If you cannot write at least a page, consider writing about

- Wolf's attention to the graphic design of the magazine—photographs in paragraph 3, layout in paragraphs 4–6, and captions in paragraph 9.

- Wolf's assumption that environmental magazines can persuade people to protect the environment.

- an environmental magazine you have read, comparing it to *Buzzworm*.

- your own views on the continuing struggle to strike a balance between encouraging industry/development and protecting the environment, comparing your views to those expressed by Wolf in paragraph 1.

READING LIKE A WRITER
ASSERTING A JUDGMENT

The purpose of an evaluative essay is to assert a judgment. Writers do not hide their opinion or merely imply it; instead, they assert it, nearly always toward the beginning of the essay, and usually they reassert it in various ways later in the essay. Since everything in the essay works toward supporting the judgment, writers do not want readers to lose sight of the judgment itself.

Wolf asserts her judgment in the second paragraph and reasserts it in the final paragraph. In between, as she presents the reasons for her judgment and the argument to support each reason, Wolf continually reminds readers of how much she values *Buzzworm*.

ANALYZE

1. *Underline* the judgment asserted in paragraphs 2 and 11.

2. *Skim* the essay, putting a checkmark next to any other statements that express a positive evaluation of *Buzzworm*.

3. *Evaluate* how successfully Wolf asserts and continually reminds readers of her judgment. How clear is her opinion or position? How frequently does she remind readers of her judgment? What role does comparison to *Sierra* play in these statements?

WRITE

Write several sentences explaining what you have learned about how Wolf asserts her overall judgment and keeps her readers aware of it. *Include* examples from the essay. Then *write* a few more sentences, evaluating how successfully Wolf manages this basic requirement of evaluation.

CONSIDERING IDEAS FOR YOUR OWN WRITING

Consider evaluating something published in series: a magazine or newspaper, for example. You would need to examine closely several issues, settle on a judgment of the series, decide on reasons for your judgment, and take careful notes of various kinds of support for your reasons. Clearly, you could not write an evaluation of the series from memory—instead, it is easy to immerse yourself in the series you choose to evaluate, becoming a knowledgable expert about it. Like Wolf, you could strengthen your evaluation by comparing your series to another of its type.

Reviewing What Makes Evaluations Effective

In this chapter you have been learning how to read evaluative writing for meaning and how to read it like a writer. Before going on to write an evaluation of your own, pause here to review and contemplate what you have learned about the elements of effective evaluations.

Analyze

Choose one essay from this chapter that you think works especially well. Before rereading the selection, *write* down one or two reasons you remember it as an example of good evaluative writing. *Reread* your chosen selection, adding further annotations as you proceed. *Consider* the selection's purpose and how well it achieves that purpose for its intended readers. Then *focus* on how well the essay

- presents the subject.

- asserts an overall judgment.

- gives reasons and supporting evidence.

- counterargues.

- establishes credibility.

You can review all of these basic features in the Guide to Reading Evaluations (pp. 225–33).

Your instructor may ask you to complete this activity on your own or to work with a small group of other students who have chosen the same essay. If you work with others, allow enough time initially for all group members to reread the selection thoughtfully and to add their annotations. Then discuss as a group what makes the essay effective. Although you all agree that the essay is good, do not be surprised if you disagree on the specifics. Take notes on your discussion, including what in the essay the group agrees works well and what the group is divided about. One student in your group should then report to the class what the group has learned about the effectiveness of evaluative writing. If you are working individually, write up what you have learned from your analysis.

Write

Write at least a page, explaining and justifying your choice of this reading as an example of effective evaluative writing. Assume that your readers—your instructor and classmates—have read the selection but will not remember many details about it. They also might not remember it as an especially successful evaluation. Therefore, you will need to *refer* to details and specific parts of the reading as you explain how it works and *justify* your evaluation of its effectiveness. You need not argue that it is the best essay in the chapter or that it is flawless, only that it is, in your view, a strong example of the genre.

A GUIDE TO WRITING EVALUATIONS

The readings in this chapter have helped you learn a great deal about evaluative writing. Now that you have seen how writers of evaluations argue to support their assertions, you are in a good position to approach this type of writing confidently. As you develop your essay, you can review the readings to see how other writers use various strategies to solve the problems you face in your own writing.

This guide is designed to assist you in writing an evaluation essay. Here you will find activities to help you choose a subject and discover what to say about it, organize your ideas and draft the essay, read the draft critically, revise the draft to strengthen your argument, and edit and proofread the essay to improve its readability.

INVENTION

Invention is a process of discovery and planning by which you generate something to say. The following invention activities will help you choose a subject and develop your evaluation of it. A few minutes spent developing each writing activity will improve your chances of producing a detailed and convincing first draft.

Choosing a Subject

The selections in this chapter suggest several different types of subjects you could write about. As you have seen, arts and entertainment products are popular subjects for review: fashion, sports, television programs, films, magazines, books, restaurants, and video games included. Technology, since it changes so quickly, also supplies many subjects: new hardware and software, new procedures and laws. There are countless other possibilities, such as public figures, businesses, educational programs, and types of equipment (cars, sporting gear).

To find a subject, list specific examples in several of the following categories. Although you may be inclined to pick the first idea that comes to mind, try to make your list as long as you can. This will ensure that you have a variety of subjects from which to choose and will encourage you to think of unique subjects.

- A film or group of films by a single director or actor
- A song or CD
- A live or videotaped concert or theatrical performance
- A magazine or newspaper
- A book (perhaps a work—either fiction or nonfiction—that you have recently read for one of your classes)

- A club or organized activity that people participate in—dance classes, camping or hiking trips, college sports programs, debate group. (You might, like Etzioni, consider a subject generally viewed positively that your experience leads you to evaluate more negatively or, alternatively, a subject generally viewed negatively that your experience leads you to evaluate more positively.)

- A contemporary political movement (perhaps evaluating the movement's methods as well as its goals and achievements)

- A proposed or existing law

- A noteworthy person—either someone in the news or a local professional, such as a teacher, doctor, social worker, auto mechanic, or minister (perhaps using your personal experience with such local figures to strengthen your evaluation)

- An artist or writer, or his or her works

- A local business

- Particular brands of machines or equipment with which you are familiar (perhaps comparing a "superior" to an "inferior" brand to make your evaluation more authoritative)

- One of the essays in this book (arguing that it is a strong or weak example of its type) or two essays (arguing that one is better than the other)

After you have a list of possibilities, consider the following questions as you make your final selection:

- *Do I already know enough about this subject, or can I get the information I need in time?* If, for instance, you decide to review a film, you should be able to see it soon. If you choose to evaluate a brand of machine or equipment, you should already be somewhat familiar with it or have time to learn enough about it to be able to write with some authority.

- *Do I already have strong feelings about this subject?* It is always easier to write about subjects on which you have formed opinions, although it is conceivable that you could change your mind as you write. If you choose a subject about which you feel indifferent, your readers will probably have the same reaction. The more sure you are of your judgment, the more persuasive you are likely to be.

Developing Your Argument

The writing and research activities that follow will enable you to explore your subject, analyze your readers, and begin developing your evaluation.

EXPLORING YOUR SUBJECT.   *To find out what you already know about the subject, list the main things you now know about it and then make notes about how you will go about becoming familiar enough with your subject to write about it like an expert or insider.* You may know little or much about your subject, and you may feel uncertain how to learn more about it. For now, discover what you do know.

ANALYZING YOUR READERS.   *Make notes about your readers.* Who exactly are your readers? They may be your classmates, or you may want to—or be asked by your instructor to—write for another audience. You could write for the general public, as all of the writers in this chapter seem to be doing. Or you could write for a more narrow audience: parents ready to purchase a new child's learning game, advanced users of email or some other technology, viewers who have seen several films by the director of the film you are reviewing, or viewers who have never seen one of the director's films. How much do your readers know about your subject and others of its type? How would you describe your readers' attitudes and opinions about the subject? What standards might they use to judge a subject like yours?

CONSIDERING YOUR JUDGMENT.   *Make a list of the good and bad qualities of your subject.* Then decide whether your judgment will be positive or negative. You can certainly acknowledge some of the good or bad qualities in your essay, but your judgment should not be ambivalent throughout. In a movie review, for example, you must ultimately decide whether you do or do not recommend that your readers try to see the film. If your list leaves you feeling genuinely ambivalent, you should see if you can *isolate* one part of your larger subject that you feel strongly about, and then write about that part. For instance, if John Travolta's acting as a whole leaves you feeling ambivalent, focus on a single movie or even a scene within a movie where you have sharp opinions one way or the other. Or you might want to trust the processes of learning and writing about your subject to help you decide whether you want to praise or criticize it. Another option, of course, is to choose a different subject to evaluate.

If you can judge your subject now, *write a sentence or two asserting your judgment.* At the end of these activities, you will have an opportunity to revise this assertion.

LISTING REASONS.   *List all the reasons you might give to persuade your readers of your judgment of the subject.* Reasons answer the question, "Everything considered, why do you evaluate this subject positively [or negatively]?" Write down all the reasons you can think of.

Then look over your list to consider which reasons you feel are the most important and which would be most convincing to your readers, given your understanding of the standards on which they ordinarily base their evaluations of subjects of this kind. *Put an asterisk by these convincing reasons.*

Consider this list only a starting point. Continue to revise it as you learn more about your subject. A preliminary list of reasons gives you a head start on planning your essay.

FINDING SUPPORT FOR YOUR REASONS. *Make notes about how to support your most promising reasons.* For support, most evaluations rely largely on details and examples from the subject itself. For that reason, you will have to reexamine the subject closely even if you know it quite well. Depending on the subject, an evaluation may make use of facts, quotations from experts, statistics, or personal experience.

Work back and forth between your list of reasons and notes for support. The reasons list will remind you of the support you need, and it will help you discover which reasons have substance. The credibility of your argument will depend to a large extent on the amount of specific, relevant support you can bring to your argument.

FORMULATING A WORKING THESIS. *Draft a thesis statement.* A working thesis—as opposed to a final, revised thesis—will help you begin drafting your essay purposefully. The thesis statement in an evaluation essay is simply a concise assertion of your overall judgment. Here are three examples from the readings.

- "This is an almost entirely positive development. Convenience aside, email is a marvelous medium of communication" (Kinsley, paragraph 4).

- "Meanwhile, TV has its own methods of policing itself. It chews its excesses and spits them out like bubble gum. The sharpest, funniest, and sanest critique of trash TV is a satire called *Night Stand* . . . an imaginary talk show hosted by Dick Dietrick, played by Timothy Stack" (Wolcott, paragraph 2).

- "Unlike most horror flicks, *Poltergeist* works! Its success is due to excellent characters, music, and special effects—and to the fact that the story stays within the bounds of believability" (Hyder, paragraph 3).

Notice that there is no ambivalence in these statements. They are clear, assertive, and unmistakably positive in their judgments. (An assertive judgment does not preclude a writer's later acknowledging problems or weaknesses in a subject judged positively or anticipating readers' likely reservations about the evaluation.) Hyder's thesis statement illustrates another interesting feature: It forecasts the major reasons for the judgment, the reasons that are at the heart of the evaluation. Forecasts are not required, but readers often find them helpful.

DRAFTING

The following guidelines will help you set goals for your draft and plan its organization.

Setting Goals

Establishing goals for your draft before you begin writing enable you to move ahead more quickly and to make critical writing decisions more confidently. Consider the following questions now, and keep them in mind as you draft. They will help you maintain your focus while drafting as well as recall how the writers you have read in this chapter tried to achieve similar goals.

- *What is my primary purpose in writing this evaluation?* What do I want to accomplish with my evaluation? Is my primary purpose to make a recommendation, as Herz and Wolf do? Do I want to celebrate my subject, like Kinsley, Wolcott, and Hyder do, or expose its flaws, like Etzioni?

- *How can I present the subject so that I can inform and interest my readers in my subject?* How much experience evaluating a subject of this kind can I expect my readers to have? Must I provide a full context for my subject, as Wolcott does, or describe it in a general way, as Hyder does? Can I assume familiarity with it, as does Etzioni? Will readers share my standards, as Hyder seems to assume his readers do, or will I need to explain or define some of my standards, as Wolf does?

- *How can I assert my judgment effectively?* How can I construct a clear, unambiguous thesis statement like those in all of the readings in this chapter? Should I assert my judgment in the first sentence and re-assert it at the end of my evaluation, as Etzioni does? Or should I first describe my subject or provide a context for evaluating it, as Wolcott, Kinsley, and Hyder do?

- *How can I give convincing reasons and adequate support for my reasons?* How can I ensure that the reasons I offer to justify my judgment will seem appropriate and convincing to my readers? Should I forecast my reasons, as Etzioni and Hyder do? For my subject, will I offer a wide range of types of support, as Etzioni does? How can I gather an adequate amount of support for my reasons, as do all of the writers in this chapter? Should I rely on comparisons to support my reasoning, as Kinsley and Hyder do?

- *How can I anticipate readers' reservations?* Should I pointedly anticipate my readers' likely reservations, objections, and questions, as Herz and Kinsley do?

- *How can I establish credibility with my readers?* Should I feature my personal experience with the subject, as Kinsley does? Or should I demonstrate my expertise with the subject by making comparisons with similar subjects, as Kinsley, Hyder, and Wolf do?

Organizing Your Draft

With goals in mind and invention notes at hand, you are ready to make a first outline of your draft. Review the list of reasons you have developed. Tentatively select from that list the reasons you think will most effectively convince your readers of the plausibility of your judgment. Then decide how you will sequence these reasons. Some writers prefer to save their most telling reason or reasons for the end, whereas others try to group the reasons logically (for example, the technical reasons in a movie review). Still other writers like to begin with reasons based on standards of judgment familiar to their readers. Whatever sequence you decide on for your reasons, make sure it will strike your readers as a logical or step-by-step sequence.

READING A DRAFT CRITICALLY

Getting a critical reading of your draft will help you see how to improve it. Your instructor may schedule class time for reading drafts, or you may want to ask a classmate or a tutor in the writing center to read your draft. Ask your reader to use the following guidelines and to write out a response for you to consult during your revision.

Read for a First Impression

1. Read the draft without stopping to annotate or comment, and then write two or three sentences giving your general impression.

2. Identify one aspect of the draft that seems to you particularly effective.

Read Again to Suggest Improvements

1. Recommend ways to strengthen the presentation of the subject.

   - Locate the places in the draft where the subject is described. The description might be spread out over several paragraphs, serving both to identify the subject and to provide support for the argument. Point to any areas where you do not understand what is being said or where you need more detail or explanation.

   - If you are surprised by the way the writer has presented the subject, briefly explain your expectations for reading about this particular subject or subjects of this kind.

   - Indicate whether any of the information given about the subject seems unnecessary.

- Finally and most importantly, raise questions wherever the information about the subject seems unconvincing, inaccurate, or only partially true.

2. Suggest ways to strengthen the thesis statement.

- Find and underline the single statement of the writer's overall judgment in the draft. If you cannot find a clear thesis, let the writer know.

- If you find several restatements of the thesis, examine them closely for consistency. Look specifically at the value terms the writer uses to see whether they are unclear or waffling.

3. Recommend ways to strengthen the supporting reasons.

- Highlight the reasons you find in the essay. The reasons in an evaluation may take the form of judgments of the subject's qualities, judgments that in turn need to be explained and supported. Look closely at any reasons that seem problematic and briefly explain what bothers you. Be as specific and constructive as you can, suggesting what the writer might do to solve the problem. For example, if a reason seems inappropriate, indicate what other kind of reason you would expect a writer to use when evaluating this subject.

- Look for instances of faulty logic. Note whether the writer's argument is based on personal tastes rather than on generally accepted standards of judgment. Point out any areas where you detect *either/or* reasoning (that is, seeing only the good *or* only the bad qualities) and weak or misleading comparisons.

4. Suggest ways to extend and improve the counterargument.

- Locate places where the writer anticipates readers' questions, objections, and reservations about the reasons and support. Consider whether these anticipations seem cursory or adequate, logical or questionable, considerate or dismissive. Point to specific problems you see and suggest possible revisions.

- Look for areas where the writer anticipates readers' alternative judgments of the subject (that is, where readers may value the subject, for different reasons or judge the subject in a different way). Note whether the writer addresses readers' alternative judgments responsibly and accurately and responds to them fairly.

- If the writer does not counterargue, consider where doing so might be appropriate. Help the writer anticipate any reservations and alternative judgments that have been overlooked, providing advice on how to respond to them. Keep in mind that the writer may choose to accommodate or refute readers' reservations or alternative judgments.

5. Suggest ways to strengthen the credibility of the writer and the writer's judgment.

   • Ignoring whether you agree or disagree with the writer's judgment on the subject, point to any places in the essay where you do not trust the writer's credibility. For instance, look for areas where the writer seems insufficiently knowledgeable, where the facts seem unconvincing or distorted, or where the writer is being unfair, perhaps criticizing a minor point unnecessarily or emphasizing something beyond the control of the subject's producers.

   • Let the writer know whether you think the judgment is sound or whether it is based on some idiosyncratic, trivial, or some other inappropriate standards of judgment.

6. Suggest how the organizational plan might be improved.

   • Consider the overall plan of the draft, perhaps by making a scratch outline. (Scratch outlining is illustrated in Appendix One.) Decide whether the sequence of reasons and counterarguments is logical or whether you can suggest rearrangements to improve it.

   • Indicate where new or better transitions might help identify different steps in the argument and keep readers on track.

REVISING

This section provides suggestions for revising your draft. Suggestions that will remind you of the possibilities for developing a well-argued evaluation. Revising means reenvisioning your draft, trying to see it in a new way, given your purpose and readers.

The biggest mistake you can make in revising is to focus initially on words or sentences. Instead, first try to see your draft as a whole in order to assess its likely impact on readers. Think imaginatively and boldly about cutting unconvincing material, adding new material, and moving material around to improve readability and strengthen your argument. Your computer makes even drastic revisions easy, but you still need to make the effort and decisions that will improve your draft.

You may have received a critical reading from classmates, a writing center tutor, or your instructor. If so, rely on this valuable help in deciding which parts of your draft need revising and what specific changes you could make.

To Present the Subject More Effectively

   • If more specific information about the subject is needed, review your invention writing to see if you have forgotten details you could now add to the draft. Or do some further invention work to generate and add new information.

- If critical readers have asked specific questions, consider whether you need to answer those questions in your revision.

- If you have included information that readers regard as unnecessary or redundant, consider cutting it.

- If any of the information strikes readers as inaccurate or only partially true, reconsider its accuracy and completeness and then make any necessary changes to reassure readers.

To Clarify the Overall Judgment

- If your overall judgment is not stated explicitly or clearly, make the thesis more obvious.

- If readers think your restatements of the judgment are contradictory, reread them with a critical eye and, if you agree, make them more consistent.

- If readers think your judgment is unemphatic or waffling, reconsider the value terms you use.

- If your essay discusses both the good and the bad qualities of the subject, be sure that your thesis statement is compatible with what you say about the subject in the essay.

To Strengthen the Reasons and Evidence

- If a reason seems inappropriate to readers, consider how you might better convince them that the reason is appropriate (for example, that it is used often by others or that it is based on widely shared and valid standards of judgment).

- If your readers do not fully understand how a particular reason applies to the subject, make your thinking more explicit.

- If the connection between a reason and its support seems vague or weak, explain why you think the support is relevant.

- Most important, if you have not fully supported your reasons with many examples from your subject, reread or reexamine your draft closely and collect further examples.

To Strengthen the Counterargument

- If you have not anticipated readers' likely questions, objections, or reservations, do so now.

- If you have not considered readers' alternative judgments, and it makes sense to do so for your particular audience, do so now.

- If any counterargument seems to attack your readers rather than their ideas, revise it to focus on the ideas.

To Enhance Credibility

- If readers question your knowledge of the subject or authority to evaluate it, reassure them by the way you discuss the subject and compare it to other subjects of the same kind.

- If the qualities you choose to emphasize seem minor, explain why you think they are important.

- If readers think your essay is too one-sided, consider whether there is any quality of the subject you could either praise or criticize.

EDITING AND PROOFREADING

After you have revised your essay, be sure to spend some time checking for errors in usage, punctuation, and mechanics. If you have been keeping a list of errors you typically make, begin by checking your draft against this list. Ask someone else to proofread your essay before you print out a copy for your instructor.

From our research on student writing, we know that evaluation essays have frequent problems in sentences that set up comparisons. The comparisons can be incomplete, illogical, or unclear. Edit carefully any sentences that set up comparisons between your subject and others. Refer to a writer's handbook for help with making all comparisons complete, logical, and clear.

Reflecting on What You Have Learned

In this chapter, you have read critically several evaluation essays and have written one of your own. To better remember what you have learned, pause now to reflect on the reading and writing activities you completed in this chapter.

1. *Write* a page or so reflecting on what you have learned. Begin by describing what you are most pleased with in your essay. Then *explain* what you think contributed to your achievement. Be specific about this contribution.

   - If it was something you learned from the readings, *indicate* which readings and specifically what you learned from them.

Continued

- If it came from your invention writing, *indicate* the section or sections that helped you most.

- If you received good advice from a critical reader, *explain* exactly how the person helped you—perhaps by helping you understand a particular problem in your draft or by adding a new dimension to your writing.

- Try to write about your achievement in terms of what you have learned about the genre of evaluation.

2. Now *reflect* more generally on evaluations, a genre of writing that plays an important role in our society. *Consider* some of the following questions: How confident did you feel about asserting a judgment and justifying it? How comfortable were you playing the role of judge and jury on the subject? How have your personal preferences and values influenced your judgment? How might your gender, ethnicity, age, or social class have influenced your ideas about the subject? What contribution might evaluation essays make to our society that other genres cannot make?

Speculation about Causes
or Effects

When something surprising occurs, we automatically look to the past and ask, "Why did that happen?" Whether we want to understand it, to make it happen again, or to find a way to prevent its recurrence, we need to speculate about what *caused* it.

Or our focus may shift from cause to *effect,* from "Why did that happen?" to "What is going to happen?" Anticipating possible effects can be useful in planning and decision making.

In many cases, questions about causes and effects are relatively easy to answer. Through personal experience or scientific experimentation, we know what causes some things to happen and what effects they will have. For example, scientists have discovered that the HIV virus causes AIDS, and we all know its potential deadly effects. We cannot be completely certain, however, what causes the virus to develop into AIDS in particular individuals or of the long-term effects of AIDS on society. In these situations, the best we can do is make educated guesses. In this chapter, you will read and write speculative essays about causes and effects that cannot be known for certain.

This kind of speculative cause or effect writing is published every day. A political analyst conjectures about the cause of a surprising election defeat. An economist suggests likely effects of the 1998 Asian economic crisis on the U.S. economy. A sportswriter speculates about why the Pacific Ten nearly always defeats the Big Ten in the Rose Bowl.

Speculation about causes or effects also plays an important role in government, business, and education. To give credit where it is due, a mayor asks the police commission to report on why complaints of police brutality against African Americans and Latinos have decreased recently. A salesperson writes a memo to the district sales manager explaining why a local advertising campaign may have failed to increase sales of Cadillac Cateras. Before proposing changes in the math curriculum, a school principal appoints a committee to investigate the causes for falling math test scores at the school.

Speculation about causes or effects is equally important in college study. For example, you might read a history essay in which a noted scholar evaluates other scholars' proposed causes of the Civil War in order to argue for a never-before-considered cause. (If the essay merely summarizes other scholars' proposed causes, the historian would be reporting established information, not speculating about new possibilities.) Or you might encounter a sociological report conjecturing about a recent increase in marriages among the elderly. The writer may not know for certain why this trend exists but could conjecture about its possible causes—and then argue with relevant facts, statistics, or anecdotes to support the conjectures.

Writing an essay in which you speculate about causes or effects involves some of the most challenging problem-solving and decision-making situations a writer can experience. You will test your powers of reasoning and creativity as you search out hidden, underlying causes or speculate about effects that are surprising yet plausible. You will continue to develop a sensitivity to your readers' knowledge and attitudes, anticipating their objections and discovering ways to convince them to take your speculations seriously.

Reading the essays in this chapter will help you see what makes arguments about causes or effects convincing. You will also get suggestions for writing your own essay about causes or effects, from the selections as well as from the ideas for writing that follow each essay. Keep the following assignment on speculating about causes or effects in mind as you evaluate the essays in this chapter and plan to write one of your own.

THE WRITING ASSIGNMENT

Speculating about Causes or Effects

Choose a subject that invites you to speculate about its causes or effects—why it may have happened or what its effects may be. Write an essay, arguing for your proposed causes or effects. Essays about causes look to the past to ponder why something happened, whereas essays about effects guess what is likely to happen in the future. Whether you choose to write about causes or effects, you need to do two things: (1) Establish the existence and significance of the subject (an event, a phenomenon, or a trend), and (2) convince readers that the causes or effects you propose are plausible.

CAUSE OR EFFECT WRITING SITUATIONS

The following examples suggest further the kinds of causal arguments writers typically make.

- A science writer notes that relatively few women get advanced degrees in science and speculates that social conditioning may be the major cause. To support her causal argument, she cites research on the way boys and girls are treated differently in early childhood. She also gives examples to attempt to show that the social pressure to conform to female role expectations may discourage junior-high-school girls from doing well in math and science. She acknowledges that other as-yet-unrecognized causes may contribute as well.

- A student writes in the school newspaper about the rising number of pregnancies among high-school students. Interviews with pregnant students lead her to speculate that the chief cause of the trend is a new requirement that parents must give written consent for minors to get birth-control devices at the local clinic. She explains that many of the students fail to get birth-control information, let alone devices, because of this regulation. She reports that her interviews do not support alternative explanations that young women have babies to give meaning to their lives, gain status among their peers, or live on their own supported by welfare.

- A psychology student writes about the effects—positive and negative—of extensive video-game playing among preteens. Based on his own experience and observation, he suggests that video games may improve children's hand-eye coordination, as well as their ability to concentrate on a single task. He speculates that, on the negative side, some children's grades may suffer as a result of spending too much time playing video games.

A GUIDE TO READING SPECULATIVE ESSAYS ABOUT CAUSES OR EFFECTS

This guide is designed to orient you to the possibilities and constraints associated with writings that speculate about causes or effects. As you read, you will gain insights into particular ways of making meaning; as you write, you will experiment with useful strategies for creating a plausible cause or effect argument. The guide begins with an essay by the well-known novelist and screenwriter, Stephen King. First read the essay for meaning, seeking to understand its causal argument and to make connections with your own knowledge and experience. Then read the essay like a writer, noting where and how King uses the special features of successful causal argument.

STEPHEN KING

Why We Crave Horror Movies

A preeminent writer of horror novels and films, Stephen King (b. 1947) may be best known for Misery *(1987),* Four Past Midnight *(1990),* Needful Things *(1991), and* Nightmares and Dreamscapes *(1993). The following essay originally appeared in* Playboy *magazine, in 1981. Most readers of* Playboy *are men in their twenties to forties. The most popular men's magazine for the last forty-seven years,* Playboy's *format, content, and readers have changed little since 1981. In addition to featuring scantily clad or unclad women,* Playboy *offers its readers information about health and fitness, social issues, and popular culture. Over the years, it has showcased many well-known writers in addition to Stephen King.*

As King's title indicates, "Why We Crave Horror Movies" attempts to explain the causes for a common phenomenon.

I think that we're all mentally ill; those of us outside the asylums only hide it a little better—and maybe not all that much better, after all. We've all known people who talk to themselves, people who sometimes squinch their faces into horrible grimaces when they believe no one is watching, people who have some hysterical fear—of snakes, the dark, the tight place, the long drop . . . and, of course, those final worms and grubs that are waiting so patiently underground. 1

When we pay our four or five bucks and seat ourselves at tenth-row center in a theater showing a horror movie, we are daring the nightmare. 2

Why? Some of the reasons are simple and obvious. To show that we can, that we are not afraid, that we can ride this roller coaster. Which is not to say that a really good horror movie may not surprise a scream out of us at some point, the way we may scream when the roller coaster twists through a complete 360 or plows through a lake at the bottom of the drop. And horror movies, like roller coasters, have always been the special province of the young; by the time one turns 40 or 50, one's appetite for double twists or 360-degree loops may be considerably depleted. 3

We also go to re-establish our feelings of essential normality; the horror movie is innately conservative, even reactionary. Freda Jackson as the horrible melting woman in *Die, Monster, Die!* confirms for us that no matter how far we may be removed from the beauty of a Robert Redford or a Diana Ross, we are still light-years from true ugliness. 4

And we go to have fun.   5

Ah, but this is where the ground starts to slope away,   6
isn't it? Because this is a very peculiar sort of fun, indeed.
The fun comes from seeing others menaced—sometimes
killed. One critic has suggested that if pro football has become the voyeur's version of combat, then the horror film
has become the modern version of the public lynching.

It is true that the mythic, "fairy-tale" horror film intends to   7
take away the shades of gray. . . . It urges us to put away our
more civilized and adult penchant for analysis and to become children again, seeing things in pure blacks and
whites. It may be that horror movies provide psychic relief
on this level because this invitation to lapse into simplicity,
irrationality and even outright madness is extended so
rarely. We are told we may allow our emotions a free rein . . .
or no rein at all.

If we are all insane, then sanity becomes a matter of de-   8
gree. If your insanity leads you to carve up women like Jack
the Ripper or the Cleveland Torso Murderer, we clap you
away in the funny farm (but neither of those two amateur-
night surgeons was ever caught, heh-heh-heh); if, on the
other hand, your insanity leads you only to talk to yourself
when you're under stress or to pick your nose on your
morning bus, then you are left alone to go about your business . . . though it is doubtful that you will ever be invited to
the best parties.

The potential lyncher is in almost all of us (excluding   9
saints, past and present; but then, most saints have been
crazy in their own ways), and every now and then, he has to
be let loose to scream and roll around in the grass. Our emotions and our fears form their own body, and we recognize
that it demands its own exercise to maintain proper muscle
tone. Certain of these emotional muscles are accepted—
even exalted—in civilized society; they are, of course, the
emotions that tend to maintain the status quo of civilization
itself. Love, friendship, loyalty, kindness—these are all the
emotions that we applaud, emotions that have been immor-
talized in the couplets of Hallmark cards and in the verses (I
don't dare call it poetry) of Leonard Nimoy.

When we exhibit these emotions, society showers us with   10
positive reinforcement; we learn this even before we get out
of diapers. When, as children, we hug our rotten little puke
of a sister and give her a kiss, all the aunts and uncles smile
and twit and cry, "Isn't he the sweetest little thing?" Such
coveted treats as chocolate-covered graham crackers often
follow. But if we deliberately slam the rotten little puke of a

sister's fingers in the door, sanctions follow—angry remon-
strance from parents, aunts and uncles; instead of a chocolate-covered graham cracker, a spanking.

But anticivilization emotions don't go away, and they de-   11
mand periodic exercise. We have such "sick" jokes as,
"What's the difference between a truckload of bowling balls
and a truckload of dead babies?" (You can't unload a truckload of bowling balls with a pitchfork . . . a joke, by the way,
that I heard originally from a ten-year-old.) Such a joke may
surprise a laugh or a grin out of us even as we recoil, a possibility that confirms the thesis: If we share a brotherhood of
man, then we also share an insanity of man. None of which is
intended as a defense of either the sick joke or insanity but
merely as an explanation of why the best horror films, like
the best fairy tales, manage to be reactionary, anarchistic,
and revolutionary all at the same time.

The mythic horror movie, like the sick joke, has a dirty   12
job to do. It deliberately appeals to all that is worst in us. It
is morbidity unchained, our most base instincts let free, our
nastiest fantasies realized . . . and it all happens, fittingly
enough, in the dark. For those reasons, good liberals often
shy away from horror films. For myself, I like to see the most
aggressive of them—*Dawn of the Dead,* for instance—as lifting a trap door in the civilized forebrain and throwing a basket of raw meat to the hungry alligators swimming around in
that subterranean river beneath.

Why bother? Because it keeps them from getting out,   13
man. It keeps them down there and me up here. It was
Lennon and McCartney who said that all you need is love,
and I would agree with that.

As long as you keep the gators fed.   14

READING FOR MEANING

Write to create meanings for King's speculations about why some
moviegoers crave horror movies.

START MAKING MEANING

Begin by restating two or three of the main causes King proposes to
explain why some moviegoers crave horror movies. Given his readers—
Playboy subscribers—and his reputation as a writer of horror novels and
films, write a sentence or two about what you think his purpose might be
in this essay. Continue by writing about anything else in the story or in
your experience that contributes to your understanding of the essay.

IF YOU ARE STUCK

If you cannot write at least a page, consider writing about

- the difference between pro- and anti-civilization emotions as King presents them in paragraphs 10–13, indicating what you think about his distinction.

- King's claim that "all you need is love" so "long as you keep the gators fed" (paragraphs 13 and 14).

- reasons, other than the ones King offers, some moviegoers crave horror films.

- your experience with horror novels or films, making connections to King's argument.

READING LIKE A WRITER

This section leads you through an analysis of King's causal-argument strategies: *presenting the subject, making a cause or effect argument, counterarguing,* and *establishing credibility.* Each strategy is described briefly and followed by a critical reading and writing task to help you see how King uses the strategy in his essay.

Consider this activity a writer's introduction to causal argument. In the activities following the readings by Natalie Angier, Andrew M. Greeley, and Sarah West later in this chapter, you will learn still more about how different writers create causal arguments. From the Jonathan Kozol and Steven Waldman readings and the accompanying activities, you will learn strategies for speculating about effects. Finally, at the end of the chapter, a Guide to Writing Speculative Essays about Causes or Effects suggests how you can use these same strategies to write your own essay.

Presenting the Subject

In trying to explain why something happened or what its effects may be, writers must be sure that readers will understand what happened. In some writing situations, a writer can safely assume that readers will already know a great deal about the subject; here the writer can simply identify the subject and immediately begin the speculations about causes or effects. In many cases, however, writers must present an unfamiliar subject in enough detail so readers will understand it fully. On occasion, writers may even need to convince readers that the subject is important and worth speculating about.

When writers decide they need to prove that the trend or phenomenon they are writing about exists, they may describe it in great detail, give examples, offer factual evidence, cite statistics, or quote statements by authorities. To establish the importance of the trend or phenomenon, writers may show that it involves a large number of people or has great importance to certain people.

ANALYZE

1. How does King present horror movies as a particular movie genre? *Skim* the essay to see which horror movies he mentions by title. Are the few examples of horror movies in the essay sufficient? Do you think readers need to have seen the movies mentioned to get the point? What does King seem to assume about his readers' experiences with horror films?

2. *Consider* how King establishes the importance of the subject. *Underline* one or two things King says that are likely to increase his readers' curiosity about why people crave horror movies.

WRITE

Write several sentences explaining how King presents his subject.

Making a Cause or Effect Argument

At the heart of an essay speculating about causes or effects is an argument. The argument is made up of at least two parts: the proposed causes or effects, and the reasoning and support for each cause or effect. In addition, the writer may anticipate readers' objections or questions, strategies we take up in the next section. In analyzing King's argument, we will look at some of the causes he proposes and how he supports them.

Writers speculating about causes or effects rarely consider only one possibility. They know that most puzzling phenomena (like people's attraction to horror movies) have multiple possible causes. However, they also know that it would be foolish to try to identify every possible cause. Writers must therefore be selective if they hope to make a convincing argument. The best arguments avoid the obvious. They offer imaginative, new ways of thinking—either proposing causes or effects that will surprise readers or arguing for familiar causes or effects in new ways.

Writers support their arguments with various kinds of evidence: facts, statistical correlations, personal anecdotes, testimony of authorities, examples, and analogies. In this activity, we focus on King's use of analogies.

ANALYZE

1. *Reread* paragraphs 3 and 12 and *identify* the analogy in each paragraph. An *analogy* is a special form of comparison in which one part of the comparison is used to explain the other. In arguing by analogy, the writer reasons that if two situations are alike, their causes will also be similar.

2. *Think about* how well the comparisons in paragraphs 3 and 12 hold up. For example, you may be able to use your personal experience to test whether watching a horror movie is much like riding a roller coaster. *Ask yourself* in what ways the two are alike—and different. Are they more alike than different? Also *consider* how you are or are not like a hungry alligator when you watch a horror movie.

WRITE

Describe and *evaluate* King's support-by-analogy in paragraphs 3 and 12. *Explain* the parts of each analogy—the two separate things being compared. *Evaluate* how well each analogy works logically. In what ways are the two things being compared actually alike? Also *evaluate* what the two analogies contribute to King's causal argument. How is the essay strengthened by them?

Counterarguing

When causes or effects cannot be known for certain, there is bound to be disagreement. Consequently, writers try to anticipate possible objections and alternative causes or effects readers might put forward. Writers bring these objections and alternatives directly into their essays and then either refute (argue against) them or find a way to accommodate them in the argument.

ANALYZE

1. King anticipates a possible objection from readers when he poses the question "Why bother?" in paragraph 13. *Reread* paragraphs 11 and 12 to understand the context in which King anticipates the need to pose that question. *Notice* his direct answer to the question in paragraph 13.

2. *Think about* the effectiveness of King's counterargument. *Consider* whether it satisfactorily answers the objection.

WRITE

Write a few sentences explaining why you think King asks the question at this point in his argument. *Consider* whether some of King's readers would ask themselves this question. *Evaluate* how satisfied they would be with King's response.

Establishing Credibility

Because cause or effect writing is highly speculative, its effectiveness depends in large part on whether readers trust the writer. Readers sometimes use information about the writer's professional and personal accomplishments in forming their judgments about the writer's credibility. The most important information, however, comes from the writing itself, specifically how writers argue for their own proposed causes or effects, as well as how they handle readers' objections.

Writers seek to establish their credibility with readers by making their reasoning clear and logical, their evidence relevant and trustworthy, and their handling of objections fair. They try to be authoritative (knowledgeable) without appearing authoritarian (opinionated and dogmatic).

ANALYZE

1. *Reread* the headnote that precedes King's essay, and *reflect* on what his readers might have known about King. King is more widely known now than he was when "Why We Crave Horror Movies" was published in 1981, but his *Playboy* readers would likely have heard of him.

2. With King's readers in mind, *skim* the essay in order to decide whether the reasoning is clear and logical and the examples and analogies relevant and trustworthy. *Notice* that King's reasoning is psychological: He argues that mental and emotional needs explain why some people crave horror films. Therefore, you, along with King's intended readers, can evaluate King's credibility in light of your own personal experience—your understanding of the role horror novels and films play in your own life. On the basis of your own experience and your evaluation of the logic and consistency of King's argument, *decide* whether King's readers would have found him a credible writer on the subject of horror films.

WRITE

Write several sentences, describing the impression readers might get of King from the headnote and from reading the essay. What might make them trust or distrust what he says about his subject?

READINGS

NATALIE ANGIER

Intolerance of Boyish Behavior

> *One of America's preeminent science writers, Natalie Angier (b. 1958) won a Pulitzer Prize in 1991 for her reports on various scientific topics published in the* New York Times, *where she has worked as a reporter since 1990. Her specialties are biology and medicine. Angier began her journalism career in 1980, after graduating magna cum laude from Barnard College with a degree in English and physics. As both a staff writer and freelancer she has published articles in several magazines, including* Discovery, Time, *and* The Atlantic. *Her 1988 book,* Natural Obsessions: The Search for the Oncogene, *won the Lewis Thomas Award for excellence in writing about the life sciences. She is also a 1990 recipient of the International Biomedical Journalism Prize for outstanding media coverage of cancer.*
>
> *The following selection appeared in the* New York Times *in 1994. The* Times *is a major newspaper in the New York City region; but because people living in dozens of mid- to large-sized American cities can have it delivered to their homes daily, the* Times *has wide national influence. Politicians, academics, and other journalists give it special attention. Journalists such as Angier who write about scientific topics for newspapers and magazines do not assume that readers have a high level of scientific training; they write for a broad audience, including college students interested in ideas and issues.*
>
> *In this reading Angier seeks to explain the increasing intolerance by teachers, parents, counselors, and therapists of certain kinds of behavior that have been labeled "boyish." Angier speculates not about the causes of a phenomenon but about the causes of a* trend—*an increase or decrease in something over time. Unexpected or alarming social trends—such as the increasing use of medication with boys for behavior that was previously tolerated or overlooked— especially invite causal speculation. You will notice that Angier is careful to demonstrate that there is in fact an increasing intolerance of boyish behavior.*
>
> *As you read, think about your own experience as a sibling, a friend of other young children, and a student in elementary school. Does Angier convince you that most boys are more rambunctious than most girls? Do you believe that many teachers and parents now see this as a big problem? Consider also how plausible you find Angier's proposed causes for the growing intolerance of boyish behavior.*

Until quite recently, the plain-spun tautology "boys will be boys" summed up everything parents needed to know about their Y-chromosome bundles. Boys will be very noisy and obnoxious. Boys will tear around the house and break heirlooms. They will transform any object longer than it is wide into a laser weapon with eight settings from stun to vaporize. They will swagger and brag and fib and not do their homework and leave their dirty underwear on the bathroom floor. 1

But they will also be ... boys. They will be adventurous and brave. When they fall down, they'll get up, give a cavalier spit to the side, and try again. Tom Sawyer may have been a slob, a truant and a hedonist; he may have picked fights with strangers for no apparent reason; but he was also resourceful, spirited and deliciously clever. Huckleberry Finn was an illiterate outcast, but as a long-term rafting companion he had no peer. 2

Today, the world is no longer safe for boys. A boy being a shade too boyish risks finding himself under the scrutiny of parents, teachers, guidance counselors, child therapists—all of them on watch for the early glimmerings of a medical syndrome, a bona fide behavioral disorder. Does the boy disregard authority, make snide comments in class, push other kids around and play hooky? Maybe he has a conduct disorder. Is he fidgety, impulsive, disruptive, easily bored? Perhaps he is suffering from attention-deficit hyperactivity disorder, or ADHD, the disease of the hour and the most frequently diagnosed behavioral disorder of childhood. Does he prefer computer games and goofing off to homework? He might have dyslexia or another learning disorder. 3

"There is now an attempt to pathologize what was once considered the normal range of behavior of boys," said Melvin Konner of the departments of anthropology and psychiatry at Emory University in Atlanta. "Today, Tom Sawyer and Huckleberry Finn surely would have been diagnosed with both conduct disorder and ADHD." And both, perhaps, would have been put on Ritalin, the drug of choice for treating attention-deficit disorder. 4

To be fair, many children do have genuine medical problems like ADHD, and they benefit enormously from the proper treatment. Psychiatrists insist that they work very carefully to distinguish between the merely rambunctious child, and the kid who has a serious, organic disorder that is disrupting his life and putting him at risk for all the demons of adulthood: drug addiction, shiftlessness, underemployment, criminality and the like. 5

At the same time, some doctors and social critics cannot help but notice that so many of the childhood syndromes now being diagnosed in record numbers affect far more boys than girls. Attention-deficit disorder, said to afflict 5 percent of all children, is thought to be about three to four times more common in boys than girls. Dyslexia is thought to be about four times more prevalent in boys than girls; and boys practically have the patent on conduct disorders. What is more, most of the traits that brand a child as a potential syndromeur just happen to be traits associated with young males: aggression, rowdiness, restlessness, loud-mouthedness, rebelliousness. None of these characteristics is exclusive to the male sex, of course—for the ultimate display of aggressive intensity, try watching a group of city girls engaged in a serious game of jump-rope—but boys more often will make a spectacle of themselves. And these days, the audience isn't smiling at the show.

"People are more sensitized to certain extremes of boyishness," said Dr. John Ratey, a psychiatrist at Harvard Medical School. "It's not as acceptable to be the class clown. You can't cut up. You won't be given slack anymore." Woe to the boy who combines misconduct with rotten grades; he is the likeliest of all to fall under professional observation. "If rowdiness and lack of performance go together, you see the button being pushed much quicker than ever before," he said, particularly in schools where high academic performance is demanded.

Lest males of all ages feel unfairly picked upon, researchers point out that boys may be diagnosed with behavioral syndromes and disorders more often than girls for a very good reason: their brains may be more vulnerable. As a boy is developing in the womb, the male hormones released by his tiny testes accelerate the maturation of his brain, locking a lot of the wiring in place early on; a girl's hormonal bath keeps her brain supple far longer. The result is that the infant male brain is a bit less flexible, less able to repair itself after slight injury that might come, for example, during the arduous trek down the birth canal. Hence, boys may well suffer disproportionately from behavioral disorders for reasons unrelated to cultural expectations.

However, biological insights can only go so far in explaining why American boyhood is coming to be seen as a state of protodisease. After all, the brains of boys in other countries also were exposed to testosterone in utero, yet non-American doctors are highly unlikely to diagnose a wild boy as having a conduct disorder or ADHD.

"British psychiatrists require a very severe form of hyper-   10
activity before they'll see it as a problem," said Dr. Paul R.
McHugh, chairman and director of psychiatry at the Johns
Hopkins School of Medicine in Baltimore. "Unless a child is
so clearly disturbed that he goes at it until he falls asleep in
an inappropriate place like a wastebasket or a drawer, and
then wakes up and starts it all over again, he won't be put on
medication." Partly as a result of this sharp difference in attitudes, the use of Ritalin-like medications has remained fairly
stable in Britain, while pharmaceutical companies here have
bumped up production by 250 percent since 1991.

Perhaps part of the reason why boyish behavior is sus-   11
pect these days is Americans' obsessive fear of crime.
"We're all really terrified of violence," said Dr. Edward
Hallowell, a child psychiatrist at Harvard. "Groups of people
who have trouble containing aggression come under suspicion." And what group has more trouble containing aggression than males under the age of 21? Such suspiciousness is
not helped by the fact that the rate of violent crime has
climbed most steeply among the young, and that everybody
seems to own a gun or know where to steal one. Sure, it's
perfectly natural for boys to roll around in the dirt fighting
and punching and kicking; but toss a firearm into the equation, and suddenly no level of aggression looks healthy.

Another cause for the intolerance of boyish behavior is   12
the current school system. It is more group-oriented than
ever before, leaving little room for the jokester, the tough,
the tortured individualist. American children are said to be
excessively coddled and undisciplined, yet in fact they
spend less time than their European or Japanese counterparts at recess, where kids can burn off the manic energy
they've stored up while trapped in the classroom. Because
boys have a somewhat higher average metabolism than do
girls, they are likely to become more fidgety when forced to
sit still and study.

The climate is not likely to improve for the world's   13
Sawyers or Finns or James Deans or any other excessively col-
orful and unruly specimens of boyhood. Charlotte Tomaino, a
clinical neuropsychologist in White Plains, notes that the
road to success in this life has gotten increasingly narrow in
recent years. "The person who used to have greater latitude
in doing one thing and moving onto another suddenly is the
person who can't hold a job," she said. "We define success
as what you produce, how well you compete, how well you
keep up with the tremendous cognitive and technical demands put upon you." The person who will thrive is not the
restless version of a human tectonic plate, but the one who

can sit still, concentrate and do his job for the 10, 12, 14 hours a day required.

A generation or two ago, a guy with a learning disability—   14
or an ornery temperament—could drop out of school, pick up a trade and become, say, the best bridge builder in town. Now, if a guy cannot at the very least manage to finish college, the surging, roaring, indifferent Mississippi of the world's economy is likely to take his little raft, and break it into bits.

READING FOR MEANING

Write to create meanings for Angier's speculations about why Americans are increasingly intolerant of boyish behavior.

START MAKING MEANING

Begin by listing a few of the basic facts about the trend Angier discusses in her essay. (She presents the trend mainly in paragraphs 1–6.) Then write a sentence or two explaining what you believe to be her purpose in this essay. Continue by writing about anything else in the essay or in your experience that contributes to your understanding of Angier's speculations.

IF YOU ARE STUCK

If you cannot write at least a page, consider writing about

- the causes Angier proposes in paragraphs 7, 8, 11, 12, and 13 to explain intolerance of boyish behavior, restating each cause briefly and writing about the one you find most plausible and the one you find least plausible.

- how Angier incorporates examples from Mark Twain's novels *Tom Sawyer* and *Huckleberry Finn* and how her use of them contributes to your understanding of the essay.

- Angier's assertion that it is "perfectly natural" (paragraph 11) for boys to fight, punch, and kick.

- a time when you experienced intolerance of boyish behavior, connecting your experience to ideas or examples in Angier's essay.

READING LIKE A WRITER

COUNTERARGUING

Writers speculating about causes must work imaginatively and persistently to support their proposed causes, using all the relevant resources available to them—quoting authorities, citing statistics and research findings, comparing and contrasting, posing rhetorical questions, offering literary allusions, and crafting metaphors, among others. (Angier uses all of the resources in this list.) In addition to supporting their proposed causes, writers usually do more. Because they aim to convince particular readers of the plausibility of their causal argument, writers try to be keenly aware that at every point in the argument their readers will have questions, objections, and other causes in mind. Anticipating and responding to these questions, objections, and alternative causes is known as *counterarguing.*

As readers work their way through a causal argument, nearly all of them will think of questions they would like to ask the writer; or they will resist or object to certain aspects of the support, such as the way the writer makes use of facts or statistics, relies on an authority, sets up an analogy, or presents an example or personal experience. Readers may doubt whether the support is appropriate, believable, or consistent with the other support provided by the writer. They may come to believe that the writer relies too much on emotional appeals and too little on reason. Readers may also resist or reject the writer's proposed causes, or they may believe that other causes better explain the trend. Experienced writers anticipate all of these predictable concerns. Just as imaginatively as they argue for their proposed causes, writers attempt to answer readers' questions, react to their objections, and evaluate their preferred causes. When you write your essay about causes or effects, anticipating and responding to your readers' concerns will be one of the most challenging and interesting parts of constructing your argument.

ANALYZE

1. Angier counterargues in at least three places in her causal argument: paragraphs 5, 6, and 8. *Reread* these paragraphs to *identify and underline* the objections to her argument that Angier anticipates from her readers. For example, in the first sentence of paragraph 5, she anticipates readers' likely objection that some boys do have medical problems requiring treatment.

2. *Examine* closely how Angier counterargues readers' objections and questions. For the three objections or questions you have identified in paragraphs 5, 6, and 8, *notice* the kinds of support she relies on to argue against each objection. *Decide* whether the support is similar or different among the three cases.

WRITE

Write several sentences reporting what you have learned about how Angier anticipates her readers' objections. Specifically, in each case, how does she support her counterargument? How appropriate do you, as one of her intended readers, find her support? How believable do you find it?

A SPECIAL READING STRATEGY

Evaluating the Logic of an Argument

To evaluate the logic of an argument speculating about causes, ask yourself three basic questions:

- How appropriate is the support for each cause being speculated about?

- How believable is the support?

- How consistent and complete is the overall argument?

Such an evaluation requires a comprehensive, thoughtful critical reading, but your efforts will help you to understand more fully what makes a causal argument successful. Follow the detailed guidelines for evaluating the logic of an argument in Appendix One (p. 476). There you will find definitions and explanations as well as an illustration based on an excerpt from a famous essay by Martin Luther King Jr. (The excerpt appears on pp. 451–56.)

CONSIDERING IDEAS FOR YOUR OWN WRITING

Think about other groups or categories of people you have the opportunity to observe, and try to identify changes in aspects of their behavior. For example, does it seem to you that girls or women are increasingly interested in math and science or in participating in team sports? If you have been working for a few years, have you noticed that employees have become more docile and more eager to please management? If you have young children, does it seem to you that day-care people have become increasingly professional?

Select one group whose behavior is changing and consider how you would convince readers that the behavior is in fact changing—increasing or decreasing over time. What kind of evidence would you need to gather in the library or on the Internet to corroborate your personal impressions? As a writer speculating about a behavioral change, consider how you would come up with some possible causes for the trend.

ANDREW M. GREELEY

Why Do Catholics Stay in the Church? Because of the Stories

An ordained Roman Catholic priest and a parish priest for ten years, Andrew M. Greeley (b. 1928) is also a leading American authority on the sociology of religion, with academic appointments at both the University of Arizona and the University of Chicago. He has published hundreds of articles and dozens of books. American universities have awarded him five honorary degrees in recognition of the importance of his scholarly work. As critical of the Catholic church as he is devoted to it, he has been a controversial figure within the church. Greeley's writings include the novels Fall from Grace *(1993) and* Wages of Sin *(1992), religious books such as* The Book of Irish American Prayers and Blessings *(1991) and* Love Affair: A Prayer Journal *(1992), and the highly regarded sociological studies* The Making of the Popes, 1978: The Politics of Intrigue in the Vatican *(1979) and* The Irish Americans: The Rise to Money and Power *(1980), among many other examples.*

The following essay was published in 1994, in the New York Times Magazine *supplement to the Sunday edition of the* Times. *Though most of the* Times' *readers live in and around New York City, the* Times *also circulates nationwide and has become an important national newspaper. These facts are essential to your understanding of Greeley's argumentative strategies. He knows that many of his readers are fellow Catholics eager to know why he thinks they remain Catholics, and that most of his other readers either belong to a different religious faith or never or only rarely attend church. He also knows that the high percentage of Americans who go to church may be interested in an argument about the appeal of religious faith, even one different from their own. (Twenty-three percent of Americans are Catholic, 52 percent Protestant, 19 percent not affiliated with any organized religious group.) In short, Greeley is writing for a diverse, national audience.*

In this selection, Greeley speculates about the causes of a phenomenon. He wants to try out some ideas about why Catholics remain Catholic. If you are not Catholic or not affiliated with any religious group, think about how Greeley attempts to engage your interest and hold it. Whatever your religious beliefs, notice as you read how carefully and fully Greeley supports the one cause he announces in his title for why Catholics remain faithful.

You can make a persuasive case against Catholicism if you want. The Church is resolutely authoritarian and often   1 seems to be proud of the fact that it "is not a democracy." It discriminates against women and homosexuals. It tries to regulate the bedroom behavior of married men and women. It tries to impose the Catholic position regarding abortion on everyone. It represses dissent and even disagreement. The Vatican seems obsessed with sex. The Pope preaches against birth control in countries with rapidly expanding populations. Catholics often cringe when the local bishop or cardinal pontificates on social policy issues. Bishops and priests are authoritarian and insensitive. Lay people have no control of how their contributions are spent. Priests are unhappy, and many of them leave the priesthood as soon as they can to marry. The Church has covered up sexual abuse by priests for decades. Now it is paying millions of dollars to do penance for the sexual amusements of supposedly celibate priests while it seeks to minimize, if not eliminate altogether, the sexual pleasures of married lay people.

One might contend with such arguments. Research indi-   2
cates that priests are among the happiest men in America. The Church was organized in a democratic structure for the first thousand years and could be so organized again. But let the charges stand for the sake of the argument. They represent the way many of those who are not Catholic see the Catholic Church, and with some nuances and qualifications the way many of those inside the church see the Catholic institution. Nonetheless this case against Catholicism simply does not compute for most Catholics when they decide whether to leave or stay.

Do they in fact remain? Are not Catholics leaving the   3
church in droves? Prof. Michael Hout of the Survey Research Center at the University of California at Berkeley has demonstrated that the Catholic defection rate has remained constant over 30 years. It was 15 percent in 1960 and it is 15 percent today. Half of those who leave the Church do so when they marry a non-Catholic with stronger religious commitment. The other half leave for reasons of anger, authority and sex—the reasons cited above.

How can this be, the outsider wonders. For one thing,   4
as the general population has increased, the number of Catholics has increased proportionately. Still, how can 85 percent of those who are born Catholic remain, one way or another, in the church? Has Catholicism so brainwashed them that they are unable to leave?

The answer is that Catholics like being Catholic. For the   5
last 30 years the hierarchy and the clergy have done just about everything they could to drive the laity out of the church and have not succeeded. It seems unlikely that they

will ever drive the stubborn lay folk out of the Church because the lay folk like being Catholic.

But why do they like being Catholic?   6

First, it must be noted that Americans show remarkable   7
loyalty to their religious heritages. As difficult as it is for members of the academic and media elites to comprehend the fact,
religion is important to most Americans. There is no sign that
this importance has declined in the last half century (as measured by survey data from the 1940's). Skepticism, agnosti-
cism, atheism are not increasing in America, as disturbing as
this truth might be to the denizens of midtown Manhattan.

Moreover, while institutional authority, doctrinal proposi-   8
tions and ethical norms[1] are components of a religious heritage—and important components—they do not exhaust the
heritage. Religion is experience, image and story before it is
anything else and after it is everything else. Catholics like
their heritage because it has great stories.

If one considers that for much of Christian history the   9
population was illiterate and the clergy semiliterate and that
authority was far away, one begins to understand that the
heritage for most people most of the time was almost entirely story, ritual, ceremony and eventually art. So it has
been for most of human history. So it is, I suggest (and my
data back me up), even today.

Roger C. Schank, a professor of psychology at Northwest-   10
ern University who specializes in the study of artificial intelligence, argues in his book *Tell Me a Story* that stories are
the way humans explain reality to themselves. The more and
better our stories, Schank says, the better our intelligence.

Catholicism has great stories because at the center of its   11
heritage is "sacramentalism," the conviction that God dis-
closes Himself in the objects and events and persons of ordinary life. Hence Catholicism is willing to risk stories about
angels and saints and souls in purgatory and Mary the
Mother of Jesus and stained-glass windows and statues and
stations of the cross and rosaries and medals and the whole
panoply of images and devotions that were so offensive to
the austere leaders of the Reformation.[2] Moreover, the

---

[1]*doctrinal propositions:* statements about the basic beliefs of a religion; *ethical norms:* widely shared beliefs about good and bad behavior. *(Ed.)*

[2]*Reformation:* a religious movement that swept Western Europe
during the sixteenth century, beginning as a reform movement
within the Roman Catholic church and eventuating in the establishment of Protestant churches dissenting from papal authority. *(Ed.)*

Catholic heritage also has the elaborate ceremonial rituals that mark the passing of the year—Midnight Mass, the Easter Vigil, First Communion, May Crowning, Lent, Advent, grammar-school graduation and the festivals of the saints.

Catholicism has also embraced the whole of the human life cycle in Sacraments (with a capital S), which provide rich ceremonial settings, even when indifferently administered for the critical landmarks of life. The Sacrament of Reconciliation (confession that was) and the Sacrament of the Anointing of the Sick (extreme unction that was) embed in ritual and mystery the deeply held Catholic story of second chances.   12

The "sacramentalism" of the Catholic heritage has also led it to absorb as much as it thinks it can from what it finds to be good, true and beautiful in pagan religions: Brigid is converted from the pagan goddess to the Christian patron of spring, poetry and new life in Ireland; Guadalupe is first a pagan and then a Christian shrine in Spain and then our Lady of Guadalupe becomes the patron of poor Mexicans. This "baptism" of pagan metaphors (sometimes done more wisely than at other times) adds yet another overlay of stories to the Catholic heritage.   13

The sometimes inaccurate dictum "once a Catholic, always a Catholic," is based on the fact that the religious images of Catholicism are acquired early in life and are tenacious. You may break with the institution, you may reject the propositions, but you cannot escape the images.   14

The Eucharist (as purists insist we must now call the Mass) is a particularly powerful and appealing Catholic ritual, even when it is done badly (as it often is) and especially when it is done well (which it sometimes is). In the Mass we join a community meal of celebration with our neighbors, our family, our friends, those we love. Such an awareness may not be explicitly on the minds of Catholics when they go to Church on Saturday afternoon or Sunday morning, but is the nature of metaphor that those who are influenced by it need not be consciously aware of the influence. In a *New York Times*–CBS News Poll last April, 69 percent of Catholics responding said they attend Mass for reasons of meaning rather than obligation.   15

Another important Catholic story is that of the neighborhood parish. Because of the tradition of village parishes with which Catholics came to America, the dense concentration of Catholics in many cities and the small geographical size of the parish, parishes can and often do become intense communities for many Catholics. They actuate what a University of   16

Chicago sociologist, James S. Coleman, calls "social capital," the extra resources of energy, commitment and intelligence that overlapping structures produce. This social capital, this story of a sacred place in the heart of urban America, becomes even stronger when the parish contains that brilliant American Catholic innovation—the parochial school.

Perhaps the Catholic religious sensibility all begins with the Christmas crib. A mother shows her child (perhaps age 3) the crib scene. The child loves it (of course) because it has everything she likes—a mommy, a daddy, a baby, animals, shepherds, shepherd children, angels and men in funny clothes—and with token integration! Who is the baby? the little girl asks. That's Jesus. Who's Jesus? The mother hesitates, not sure of exactly how you explain the communication of idioms to a 3-year-old. Jesus is God. That doesn't bother the little girl at all. Everyone was a baby once. Why not God? Who's the lady holding Jesus? That's Mary. Oh! Who's Mary? The mother throws theological caution to the winds. She's God's mommy. Again the kid has no problem. Everyone has a mommy, why not God?   17

It's a hard story to beat. Later in life the little girl may come to understand that God loves us so much that He takes on human form to be able to walk with us even into the valley of death and that God also loves us the way a mother loves a newborn babe—which is the function of the Mary metaphor in the Catholic tradition.   18

It may seem that I am reducing religion to childishness— to stories and images and rituals and communities. In fact, it is in the poetic, the metaphorical, the experiential dimension of personality that religion finds both its origins and raw power. Because we are reflective creatures we must also reflect on our religious experiences and stories; it is in the (lifelong) interlude of reflection that propositional religion and religious authority become important, indeed indispensable. But then the religiously mature person returns to the imagery, having criticized it, analyzed it, questioned it, to commit the self once more in sophisticated and reflective maturity to the story. . . .   19

When I was in grammar school in the mid-1930's, the nuns told a story that sums up why people stay Catholic. One day Jesus went on a tour of the heavenly city and noted that there were certain new residents who ought not to be there, not until they had put in a long time in purgatory and some of them only on a last-minute appeal. He stormed out to the gate where Peter was checking the day's intake on his Compaq 486DX Deskpro computer (I have edited the nuns'   20 story)—next to which, on his work station, was a fishing pole and a papal crown.

"You've failed again, Simon Peter," said the Lord.   21

"What have I done now?"   22

"You let a lot of people in that don't belong."   23

"I didn't do it."   24

"Well, who did?"   25

"You won't like it."   26

"Tell me anyway."   27

"I turn them away from the front gate and then they go   28
around to the back door and your mother lets them in!"

It is the religious sensibility behind that fanciful story that   29
explains why Catholics remain Catholic. It might not be your
religious sensibility. But if you want to understand Catholics—
and if Catholics want to understand themselves—the starting
point is to comprehend the enormous appeal of that sensibility. It's the stories.

READING FOR MEANING

Write to create meanings for Greeley's speculations about why so
many Catholics stay Catholic.

START MAKING MEANING

Begin by explaining what you think is Greeley's purpose in this essay,
given his diverse national audience, including yourself as one of his intended readers. Support your explanation with a few details from the
essay. Continue by writing about anything else in the essay or in your experience that contributes to your understanding of Greeley's argument.

IF YOU ARE STUCK

If you cannot write at least a page, consider writing about

- Greeley's criticism of the Catholic church (paragraphs 1–5), keeping
  in mind that the writer is a Catholic priest and that he is addressing
  an audience made up of non-Catholics as well as Catholics.

- your reaction to the religious story that Greeley claims (in paragraphs 17 and 18) is the most important one for Catholics.

- why you do or do not practice your own religion, comparing or contrasting your choice with why many Catholics stay in the church, according to Greeley.

- criticisms you have of your faith, comparing or contrasting them with
  Greeley's criticism of Catholicism.

READING LIKE A WRITER

MAKING A CAUSAL ARGUMENT THROUGH EXAMPLES

When writers argue for or support their causes, as Greeley does for his claim that stories keep Catholics faithful to the church, they have many resources available to them. For example, they may use statistics, quote authorities, evoke history, create dialogue, or tell a story. Greeley deploys all of these resources in paragraphs 8–29, where he attempts to convince readers that there is indeed one principal cause for Catholics' loyalty. However, he relies primarily on examples to support his argument. Because Greeley knows that many of his readers are unfamiliar with the Catholic stories he claims have such power, he names, describes, or tells many of these stories. These are his examples, and they give his argument whatever plausibility it may have with his readers.

ANALYZE

1. Greeley offers four religious stories from Catholicism as examples to support his speculations: the sacramentalism story (paragraphs 11–14), the Eucharist story (paragraph 15), the neighborhood parish story (paragraph 16), and the Christmas crib story (paragraphs 17 and 18). (Notice that Greeley uses the story concept broadly, to include narratives with a beginning and an end as well as institutions, events, and rituals.) *Choose* one of these stories to examine closely.

2. *Analyze* how Greeley presents the one story you have chosen. Where does he give examples, quote authorities, present statistics, or tell stories? *Consider* whether you find the story clear and convincing. Does it provide adequate detail, and is all of the detail relevant? Do you already have to know something of the story to understand what Greeley writes about it?

WRITE

Write several sentences reporting what you have learned about Greeley's use of the story to support his argument. Then *add* a few sentences evaluating how successful this example is in convincing readers that Catholics remain Catholic because of the stories.

CONSIDERING IDEAS FOR YOUR OWN WRITING

Greeley's selection may suggest to you several ideas for writing an essay that considers what causes a group of people to do something or to behave in some way. For example, what causes some people to stay in or drop out of college, devote themselves to strenuous exercise programs, abuse their spouses, join cults or gangs, become vegetarians, or listen to talk radio? You should be able to think of other examples.

Like Greeley, you might choose to speculate about why people stay in your religious faith or at your particular church. Or you might speculate about why people leave your faith or church. Because you would be writing for readers of other faiths and those who are nonbelievers, you would need to assume that they might initially consider your faith unusual, if not strange. For your speculations to be convincing, then, you would need to convey a certain detachment or distance from your own beliefs so readers could trust your judgment. You would need to avoid seeming to recruit others to your faith or attacking other faiths. Your purpose would be to speculate plausibly about why people stay in or leave your faith. Your readers, like Greeley's, would include members of your faith, members of other faiths, and nonbelievers.

JONATHAN KOZOL

The Human Cost of an Illiterate Society

A well-known critic of American schools, Jonathan Kozol (b. 1936) was in the forefront of educational reformers during the 1970s and 1980s. He has taught in the Boston and Newton, Massachusetts, public schools, as well as at Yale University and the University of Massachusetts at Amherst. In support of his writing and research, he has been awarded numerous prestigious fellowships from the Guggenheim, Ford, and Rockefeller Foundations. Kozol's books include Death at an Early Age *(1967), for which he won the National Book Award,* Free Schools *(1972),* Children of the Revolution *(1978),* On Being a Teacher *(1981),* Illiterate America *(1985),* Savage Inequalities: Children in America's Schools *(1991), and* Blueprint for a Democratic Education *(1992).*

The following selection is taken from Illiterate America, *a comprehensive study of the nature, causes, and effects of illiteracy. The book is intended for a broad readership. Certainly, you are among Kozol's intended readers. In this chapter from the book, Kozol speculates about the human consequences of illiteracy, outlining the limitations and dangers in the lives of adults who cannot read or write. Elsewhere in the book, Kozol conjectures about the causes of illiteracy, but here he concentrates on the effects of the phenomenon, speculating about what life is like for illiterates. He adopts this strategy to argue that the human costs of the problem pose a moral dilemma for our country.*

PRECAUTIONS. READ BEFORE USING.
Poison: Contains sodium hydroxide (caustic soda-lye).
Corrosive: Causes severe eye and skin damage, may cause blindness.
Harmful or fatal if swallowed.
If swallowed, give large quantities of milk or water.
Do not induce vomiting.
Important: Keep water out of can at all times to prevent contents from violently erupting. . . .

WARNING ON A CAN OF DRANO

Questions of literacy, in Socrates' belief, must at length be judged as matters of morality. Socrates could not have had in mind the moral compromise peculiar to a nation like our own. Some of our Founding Fathers did, however, have this question in their minds. One of the wisest of those Founding

1

Fathers [James Madison] recognized the special dangers that illiteracy would pose to basic equity in the political construction that he helped to shape:

> A people who mean to be their own governors must   2
> arm themselves with the power knowledge gives. A
> popular government without popular information or
> the means of acquiring it, is but a prologue to a farce or
> a tragedy, or perhaps both.

Tragedy looms larger than farce in the United States   3
today. Illiterate citizens seldom vote. Those who do are forced to cast a vote of questionable worth. They cannot make informed decisions based on serious print information. Sometimes they can be alerted to their interests by aggressive voter education. More frequently, they vote for a face, a smile, or a style, not for a mind or character or body of beliefs.

The number of illiterate adults exceeds by 16 million the   4
entire vote cast for the winner in the 1980 presidential contest. If even one third of all illiterates could vote, and read enough and do sufficient math to vote in their self-interest, Ronald Reagan would not likely have been chosen president. There is, of course, no way to know for sure. We do know this: Democracy is a mendacious term when used by those who are prepared to countenance the forced exclusion of one third of our electorate. So long as 60 million people are denied significant participation, the government is neither of, nor for, nor by, the people. It is a government, at best, of those two thirds whose wealth, skin color, or parental privilege allows them opportunity to profit from the provocation and instruction of the written word.

The undermining of democracy in the United States is one   5
"expense" that sensitive Americans can easily deplore because it represents a contradiction that endangers citizens of all political positions. The human price is not so obvious at first.

Illiterates cannot read the menu in a restaurant.   6

They cannot read the cost of items on the menu in the   7
window of the restaurant before they enter.

Illiterates cannot read the letters that their children bring   8
home from their teachers. They cannot study school department circulars that tell them of the courses that their children must be taking if they hope to pass the SAT exams. They cannot help with homework. They cannot write a letter to the teacher. They are afraid to visit in the classroom. They do not want to humiliate their child or themselves.

Illiterates cannot read instructions on a bottle of prescrip-   9
tion medicine. They cannot find out when a medicine is past
the year of safe consumption; nor can they read of allergenic
risks, warnings to diabetics, or the potential sedative effect
of certain kinds of nonprescription pills. They cannot observe preventive health care admonitions. They cannot read
about "the seven warning signs of cancer" or the indications
of blood-sugar fluctuations or the risks of eating certain
foods that aggravate the likelihood of cardiac arrest.

Illiterates live, in more than literal ways, an uninsured ex-   10
istence. They cannot understand the written details on a
health insurance form. They cannot read the waivers that
they sign preceding surgical procedures. Several women I
have known in Boston have entered a slum hospital with the
intention of obtaining a tubal ligation and have emerged a
few days later after having been subjected to a hysterec-
tomy. Unaware of their rights, incognizant of jargon, intimi-
dated by the unfamiliar air of fear and atmosphere of ether
that so many of us find oppressive in the confines even of
the most attractive and expensive medical facilities, they
have signed their names to documents they could not read
and which nobody, in the hectic situation that prevails so
often in those overcrowded hospitals that serve the urban
poor, had even bothered to explain.

Even the roof above one's head, the gas or other fuel for   11
heating that protects the residents of northern city slums
against the threat of illness in the winter months become uncertain guarantees. Illiterates cannot read the lease that
they must sign to live in an apartment which, too often, they
cannot afford. They cannot manage check accounts and
therefore seldom pay for anything by mail. Hours and entire
days of difficult travel (and the cost of bus or other public
transit) must be added to the real cost of whatever they consume. Loss of interest on the check accounts they do not
have, and could not manage if they did, must be regarded as
another of the excess costs paid by the citizen who is ex-
cluded from the common instruments of commerce in a nu-
merate society.

"I couldn't understand the bills," a woman in Washington,   12
D.C., reports, "and then I couldn't write the checks to pay
them. We signed things we didn't know what they were."

Illiterates cannot read the notices that they receive from   13
welfare offices or from the IRS. They must depend on word-
of-mouth instruction from the welfare worker—or from
other persons whom they have good reason to mistrust.
They do not know what rights they have, what deadlines and

requirements they face, what options they might choose to exercise. They are half-citizens. Their rights exist in print but not in fact.

Illiterates cannot look up numbers in a telephone direc-   14 tory. Even if they can find the names of friends, few possess the sorting skills to make use of the yellow pages; categories are bewildering and trade names are beyond decoding capabilities for millions of nonreaders. Even the emergency numbers listed on the first page of the phone book—"Ambulance," "Police," and "Fire"—are too frequently beyond the recognition of nonreaders.

Many illiterates cannot read the admonition on a pack of   15 cigarettes. Neither the Surgeon General's warning nor its reproduction on the package can alert them to the risks. Although most people learn by word of mouth that smoking is related to a number of grave physical disorders, they do not get the chance to read the detailed stories which can document this danger with the vividness that turns concern into determination to resist. They can see the handsome cowboy or the slim Virginia lady lighting up a filter cigarette; they cannot heed the words that tell them that this product is (not "may be") dangerous to their health. Sixty million men and women are condemned to be the unalerted, high-risk candidates for cancer.

Illiterates do not buy "no-name" products in the super-   16 markets. They must depend on photographs or the familiar logos that are printed on the packages of brand-name groceries. The poorest people, therefore, are denied the benefits of the least costly products.

Illiterates depend almost entirely upon label recognition.   17 Many labels, however, are not easy to distinguish. Dozens of different kinds of Campbell's soup appear identical to the nonreader. The purchaser who cannot read and does not dare to ask for help, out of the fear of being stigmatized (a fear which is unfortunately realistic), frequently comes home with something which she never wanted and her family never tasted.

Illiterates cannot read instructions on a pack of frozen   18 food. Packages sometimes provide an illustration to explain the cooking preparations; but illustrations are of little help to someone who must "boil water, drop the food—*within* its plastic wrapper—in the boiling water, wait for it to simmer, instantly remove."

Even when labels are seemingly clear, they may be easily   19 mistaken. A woman in Detroit brought home a gallon of Crisco for her children's dinner. She thought that she had bought the chicken that was pictured on the label. She had enough Crisco now to last a year—but no more money to go back and buy the food for dinner.

Illiterates cannot travel freely. When they attempt to do   20
so, they encounter risks that few of us can dream of. They cannot read traffic signs and, while they often learn to recognize and to decipher symbols, they cannot manage street names which they haven't seen before. The same is true for bus and subway stops. While ingenuity can sometimes help a man or woman to discern directions from familiar landmarks, buildings, cemeteries, churches, and the like, most illiterates are virtually immobilized. They seldom wander past the streets and neighborhoods they know. Geographical paralysis becomes a bitter metaphor for their entire existence. They are immobilized in almost every sense we can imagine. They can't move up. They can't move out. They cannot see beyond. Illiterates may take an oral test for drivers' permits in most sections of America. It is a questionable concession. Where will they go? How will they get there? How will they get home? Could it be that some of us might like it better if they stayed where they belong?

Travel is only one of many instances of circumscribed existence. Choice, in almost all its facets, is diminished in the   21
life of an illiterate adult. Even the printed TV schedule, which provides most people with the luxury of preselection, does not belong within the arsenal of options in illiterate existence. One consequence is that the viewer watches only what appears at moments when he happens to have time to turn the switch. Another consequence, a lot more common, is that the TV set remains in operation night and day. Whatever the program offered at the hour when he walks into the room will be the nutriment that he accepts and swallows. Thus, to passivity, is added frequency—indeed, almost uninterrupted continuity. Freedom to select is no more possible here than in the choice of home or surgery or food.

"You don't choose," said one illiterate woman. "You take   22
your wishes from somebody else." Whether in perusal of a menu, selection of highways, purchase of groceries, or determination of affordable enjoyment, illiterate Americans must trust somebody else: a friend, a relative, a stranger on the street, a grocery clerk, a TV copywriter.

Billing agencies harass poor people for the payment of   23
the bills for purchases that might have taken place six months before. Utility companies offer an agreement for a staggered payment schedule on a bill past due. "You have to trust them," one man said. Precisely for this reason, you end

up by trusting no one and suspecting everyone of possible deceit. A submerged sense of distrust becomes the corollary to a constant need to trust. "They are cheating me . . . I have been tricked . . . I do not know. . . ."

Not knowing: This is a familiar theme. Not knowing the right 24 word for the right thing at the right time is one form of subjugation. Not knowing the world that lies concealed behind those words is a more terrifying feeling. The longitude and latitude of one's existence are beyond all easy apprehension. Even the hard, cold stars within the firmament above one's head begin to mock the possibilities for self-location. Where am I? Where did I come from? Where will I go?

"I've lost a lot of jobs," one man explains. "Today, even if 25 you're a janitor, there's still reading and writing. . . . They leave a note saying, 'Go to room so-and-so. . . .,' You can't do it. You can't read it. You don't know."

"Reading directions, I suffer with. I work with chem- 26 icals. . . . That's scary to begin with. . . ."

"You sit down. They throw the menu in front of you. 27 Where do you go from there? Nine times out of ten you say, 'Go ahead. Pick out something for the both of us.' I've eaten some weird things, let me tell you!"

A landlord tells a woman that her lease allows him to 28 evict her if her baby cries and causes inconvenience to her neighbors. The consequence of challenging his words conveys a danger which appears, unlikely as it seems, even more alarming than the danger of eviction. Once she admits that she can't read, in the desire to maneuver for the time in which to call a friend, she will have defined herself in terms of an explicit importance that she cannot endure. Capitulation in this case is preferable to self-humiliation. Resisting the definition of oneself in terms of what one cannot do, what others take for granted, represents a need so great that other imperatives (even one so urgent as the need to keep one's home in winter's cold) evaporate and fall away in face of fear. Even the loss of home and shelter, in this case, is not so terrifying as the loss of self.

Another illiterate, looking back, believes she was not wor- 29 thy of her teacher's time. She believes that it was wrong of her to take up space within her school. She believes that it was right to leave in order that somebody more deserving could receive her place.

People eat what others order, know what others tell them, 30 struggle not to see themselves as they believe the world perceives them. A man in California spoke about his own loss of identity, self-location, definition:

"I stood at the bottom of the ramp. My car had broke 31
down on the freeway. There was a phone. I asked for the police. They was nice. They said to tell them where I was. I
looked up at the signs. There was one that I had seen before.
I read it to them: ONE WAY STREET. They thought it was a joke.
I told them I couldn't read. There was other signs above the
ramp. They told me to try. I looked around for somebody to
help. All the cars was going by real fast. I couldn't make
them understand that I was lost. The cop was nice. He told
me: 'Try once more.' I did my best. I couldn't read. I only
knew the sign above my head. The cop was trying to be nice.
He knew that I was trapped. 'I can't send out a car to you if
you can't tell me where you are.' I felt afraid. I nearly cried.
I'm forty-eight years old. I only said: 'I'm on a one-way
street. . . .'"

Perhaps we might slow down a moment here and look at 32
the realities described above. This is the nation that we live
in. This is a society that most of us did not create but which
our President and other leaders have been willing to sustain
by virtue of malign neglect. Do we possess the character and
courage to address a problem which so many nations,
poorer than our own, have found it natural to correct?

The answers to these questions represent a reasonable 33
test of our belief in the democracy to which we have been
asked in public school to swear allegiance.

READING FOR MEANING

Write to create meanings for Kozol's speculations about the effects of
illiteracy.

START MAKING MEANING

Begin by listing the four or five effects of illiteracy Kozol proposes
that seem to you most damaging. Then write a few sentences about
Kozol's purpose. What seems to be his motivation for writing? Does he
seem to be accepting a hopeless situation or hoping for reform? What response do you think he wants from readers? What in the text leads you to
your answers? Continue by writing about anything else in the reading or
in your experience that contributes to your understanding of Kozol's argument.

IF YOU ARE STUCK

If you cannot write at least a page, consider writing about

- how illiteracy may undermine democracy, summarizing Kozol's main ideas about this danger (from paragraphs 2–4) and, if possible, adding an idea or two of your own.

- Kozol's connection between morality and literacy (paragraph 1), explaining possible connections you see and speculating about whom Kozol seems to be accusing of immoral actions.

- other effects of illiteracy Kozol does not mention.

- "the power that knowledge gives," using examples from your own experience of the ways knowledge gained from reading has contributed to your achievements, sense of identity, or privileges.

READING LIKE A WRITER
SUPPORTING PROPOSED EFFECTS

Kozol proposes many effects of illiteracy. A mere list of possible effects would be interesting, but to convince readers to take all of these effects seriously, Kozol must argue for—or support—them in ways that enhance their plausibility. To do so, all writers speculating about effects have many resources available to them to support their proposed effects: examples, statistics, quotations from authorities, personal anecdotes, analogies, scenarios, quotes from interviews, and more. As a writer speculating about causes or effects, you will need to support your speculations in these ways in order to make them plausible. You can learn more about supporting speculations by analyzing how Kozol does it.

ANALYZE

1. *Choose* one of these effects of illiteracy proposed by Kozol: helplessness in financial affairs (paragraphs 11 and 12), confusion about supermarket purchases (paragraphs 16–19), limited travel (paragraph 20), or loss of self (paragraphs 28–31).

2. *Examine* the support carefully. What kind of support do you find? More than one kind? Does the support seem to come from many or few sources?

3. *Evaluate* the support. Does it seem appropriate for the proposed effect? Does it seem believable and trustworthy? Does it seem consistent with the other support for the effect? If so, how does it complement the other support?

WRITE

Write several sentences explaining how Kozol supports the effect you have chosen. Also *evaluate* the plausibility of the support he offers. *Give details* from the paragraphs you have analyzed. As one of Kozol's intended readers, how convincing do you find the support?

CONSIDERING IDEAS FOR YOUR OWN WRITING

Consider speculating, like Kozol does, about the effects of a significant social problem. List several major social problems (local or national) that concern you. Your list might include, for example, the high pregnancy rate among unmarried teenagers, high-school dropout rates, high costs of a college education, unsafe working conditions or high employee turnover at your job, poor academic advising or too many required courses at your college, traffic congestion or uncontrolled development in your community, lack of good bookstores in your area, or limited access to local news because your town has only one daily newspaper. Choose one problem, and consider how you can speculate about its effects. What effects can you argue for? As a writer, how could you convince readers that your proposed effects are plausible? Will you need to research the problem to write about it authoritatively? Remember, your purpose is not to propose a solution to the problem but to speculate about its possible effects.

Alternatively, you could recall a recent controversial decision by college or community leaders that concerns you, such as a decision about campus life (safety, recreation, tutoring, or other special services) or about the future of your community (growth, transportation, safety). List several such decisions, and then choose one you would like to write about. Consider how you would write a letter to your college or community newspaper speculating about the effects or consequences of the decision. What short-term and long-term consequences would you propose? How would you convince readers to take your ideas seriously?

STEVEN WALDMAN

The Tyranny of Choice

Steven Waldman is a Washington correspondent for Newsweek *and writes frequently for other newsmagazines such as the* New Republic, *from which this selection is taken. The* New Republic *is a weekly magazine whose current editor wants it to be compared to* Time *magazine, another weekly. It considers itself centrist, offering balanced coverage of issues. As a college student you are among its intended readers. Waldman's first book,* The Bill *(1995), is a study of national service legislation in Congress.*

In this half-serious, half-humorous essay published in 1992, Waldman conjectures about a fundamental change in our society: the proliferation of choice. He explains in the opening paragraphs that he first became aware of this disconcerting trend on a simple shopping expedition. His essay explores the effects of having to face so many choices in our daily lives.

Before reading the selection, stop to consider the wide range of choices you make every day, such as what clothes you wear and what food you eat. For you personally, what are the advantages and disadvantages of having so many choices to make? Do you find this range of choice frustrating or exhilarating?

Why did I nearly start crying the last time I went to buy socks? I'd stopped in a store called Sox Appeal, the perfect place, one might imagine, to spend a pleasant few minutes acquiring a pair of white athletic socks. After a brief visit to the men's dress sock department—dallying with more than 300 varieties, among them products embroidered with bikini-clad women, neckties, flowers, Rocky and Bullwinkle, and elegant logos such as "The Gold Bullion Collection: Imported" and "D'zin Pour Homme"—I finally made it into the athletics section. Here, the product-option high was even headier. Past the "Hypercolor" socks that change hue, combination "sport-and-dress" white socks, and "EarthCare" environmentally safe socks (which, unfortunately, boast of decomposing easily) were hosiery for every sport: raquetball, running, walking, cycling, hiking, basketball, and aerobics. I needed help.

"What if I play racquetball occasionally and run occasionally and walk sometimes, but don't want to get a different sock for each one?" I asked the saleswoman. She wrinkled her nose: "It's really a matter of personal preference." Did she have any standard-issue white tube socks? The nose-wrinkle again. "Well, yeah, you *could* get those, but. . . . " I started reading the backs of the boxes, elaborately illustrated with architects' renderings of the stress points in the "Cushion-Engineered (TM) Zone Defense." After briefly contemplating the implications of the Cross-Training Sock—"Shock-Woven elastic arch brace contours to arch, providing additional support and normal articulation of the bones in the foot, while keeping sock migration minimal"—I spent another five minutes studying shapes (anklet, crew, or quarter) and manufacturers, and grabbed a Cross Trainer, two walkers, and, in an environmental guilt-spasm, one pair of the EarthCare.

Since that day, the sock metaphor has crept constantly   3
into my mind—and not just when I'm buying consumer products. At work I pick through dozens of options on my cafeteria insurance benefits plan. At the doctor's I'm offered several possible treatments for a neck problem and no real way to decide. At the video rental store I end up renting four movies even though I'll watch only one. Choices proliferate everywhere. My mental "tilt" light flashes continuously. I keep thinking that the more choices there are, the more wrong choices there are—and the higher the odds I'll make a mistake.

Think it over. A typical supermarket in 1976 had 9,000   4
products; today it has more than 30,000. The average produce section in 1975 carried sixty-five items; this summer it carried 285. (Kiwi has hit the top 20 list.) A Cosmetic Center outside Washington carries about 1,500 types and sizes of hair care products. The median household got six TV stations in 1975. Thanks to deregulation of the cable TV industry, that family now has more than thirty channels. The number of FM radio stations has doubled since 1970. A new religious denomination forms every week. (The 1980s brought us major additions such as the Evangelical Presbyterian Church and smaller groups such as the Semjase Silver Star Center, which follows the Twelve Bids from Patule that were given by extraterrestrial Space Brothers to Edmund "Billy" Meier.) In 1955 only 4 percent of the adult population had left the faith of their childhood. By 1985 one-third had. In 1980, 564 mutual funds existed. This year there are 3,347.

There has been a sharp rise in the number of people   5
choosing new faces. More than twice as many cosmetic surgery operations were performed in the 1980s than in the 1970s, estimates the American Academy of Cosmetic Surgery. In the past decade a new periodical was born every day. Some have perished, but the survivors include: *Elvis*

International Forum, Smart Kids (recent cover headline: "Should Babies Learn to Read?"), *American Handgunner, Triathlete, Harley Women, Log Home Living, Musclecar Classics,* and (my favorite) *Contemporary Urology.*

The growth of variety predates this recession, will continue after it, and, to a large extent, has persisted during it. *New Product News* reports that despite the depressed economy 21 percent more new products were introduced in supermarkets and drug stores in 1991 than the year before. Obvious benefits abound, of course, and not just for people with money. Telephone deregulation has made it cheaper to stay in touch with faraway friends; periodical proliferation meant I had *Fantasy Baseball* magazine to help me prepare for Rotisserie draft day; increased social tolerance has allowed more people (including me) to marry outside their faith or ethnic group; low sodium orange juice means people with high blood pressure can drink it (and it has increased juice sales); more cosmetics mean black women have shades that match their complexions. And so on. And in the words of Morris Cohen, a professor at the Wharton Business School: "If you're overwhelmed by the sock store, don't go there anymore." The beauty of the free market, he explains, is that each individual can select which options to exploit and which to ignore.

But Cohen's rational approach fails to account for how the mind actually processes all this variety. In fact, choice can be profoundly debilitating. It forces us to squander our time, weakens our connections to people and places, and can even poison our sense of contentedness. What follows is a simple checklist—take your pick—of the drawbacks of our new way of choosing.

Choice Erodes Commitment. The same psychological dynamic that has led to a decline in brand loyalty can operate on more important decisions. The more options we have, the more tenuous our commitment becomes to each one. The compulsion to take inventory of one's wants and continually upgrade to a better deal can help explain everything from the rise of the pathological channel switcher who can never watch one TV show straight through to staggering divorce rates and employer-employee disloyalty. Baseball players have never had as many career options as they do now. As a result, sportswriter Thomas Boswell notes, the slightest sign of trouble leads the player or team to try someplace or someone better, producing many "insincere love affairs and very few committed marriages." Sound familiar? Yes, even the infamous male commitment problem results in part from the same thinking. I recently married a wonderful woman, but only after several years of embarrassingly tortured contemplation of what kind of "options" I might be foreclosing. There are, after all, 9,538,000 unmarried females aged 24–39, each with the potential to be more "perfect" than the one before.

Choice Leads to Inept Consumption. The more choice available, the more information a consumer must have to make a sensible selection. When overload occurs, many simply abandon the posture of rational Super-Consumer. Warning labels on products have become so common that many shoppers simply ignore them all, including the important ones. Several friends have confessed that the selection of car models—591 and rising—has become so dizzying that they tossed aside *Consumer Reports* and relied entirely on the recommendation of a friend. Some become so paralyzed by the quest for the better deal that they postpone decisions indefinitely, while others become so preoccupied with absorbing the new features touted by a manufacturer that they forget to consider the basics. After all the fretting over the migration patterns of the socks, I took them home and found them to be quite fluffy and supportive, but the wrong size.

9

Consumers may be better informed than they were two decades ago, but salespeople have more tools with which to fight back. I spent three days studying up for a trip to Circuit City to buy a CD player. Despite having read several magazine and newspaper articles, I was, within minutes, putty in the salesman's hands. When I asked for a particular model, he rolled his eyes and laughed, "You must have gotten that from *Consumer Reports.*" With a simple well-timed chuckle he made me doubt my entire research regimen. He then battered me with a flurry of technoterms and finally moved in for the kill by giving me an audio comparison test between two different systems that sounded exactly alike. My resistance was exhausted, so I bought the system he suggested, which, of course, cost more than I had intended to spend.

10

Choice Causes Political Alienation. Voters don't necessarily have more choices than they used to—an increase in primaries and referenda having been offset by the influence of incumbency and money—but the *way* voters choose has changed dramatically. As a result of the weakening of political parties, voting behavior now closely resembles the consumption of products. The biggest political group is not Democrats or Republicans, but "independents," shopper-equivalents who've dropped brand loyalty in favor of product-by-product analysis. Last century two-thirds of voters went

11

straight party line; in 1980 two-thirds split tickets. In theory, this means voters carefully weigh the candidate's policies, character, and history. In reality, it's nearly impossible to sort through a candidate's "stands" on the "issues" from a blizzard of untrustworthy ads, a newspaper editorial, or a blip on the TV news. Was he the one who wants a revolving loan fund for worker retraining or the one who gives flag burners early parole? No wonder voters, like shoppers, act impulsively or vote according to the wisdom of their favorite interest group. Many who vote for ballot initiatives or lower offices simply follow the recommendation of the local news-paper, which is like buying a car on the word of the local auto columnist. When I was voting absentee in New York I selected judicial candidates on the basis of gender and race since I knew little else about them. The ultimate political choice overload came in California in 1990, when voters re-ceived a 222-page ballot pamphlet to help them decide among twenty-eight initiatives.

Candidates have responded to the rise of the consumer-voter by turning to marketing professionals who've only made the voters' dilemma worse. In the 1950s political con-sultants were advertising men who selected a candidate at-tribute and then sold it, the way an automaker might remind consumers of a large car's natural advantages, like spacious-ness and safety. Political consulting has evolved, though. Candidates now rely heavily on market researchers—i.e., the pollsters—trying less to determine what part of their essence they should highlight than what they should be-come to match voters' desires. Sometimes that means candi-dates become more responsive to public thinking, but more often it means politicians forget to consult (or have) their own core beliefs. Witness the breathtaking spectacle of pro-life pols who once assailed the supreme immorality of baby-killing quickly becoming pro-choice because of the supreme importance of polls. This "politics as consumption" (in the phrase of University of Rochester professor Robert West-brook) seems to produce more gelatinous politicians—pre-cisely the sort that voters have the hardest time judging.   12

Choice Erodes the Self. In theory, choice enables an in-dividual to select the car, money market fund, or spouse that expresses herself most precisely. But if choice is self-definition, more choices mean more possible definitions. Kenneth Gergen, a professor of psychology at Swarthmore, argues in his new book, *The Saturated Self,* that the postmod-ern personality becomes "populated" with growing numbers of "selves" as it's bombarded by an ever increasing number   13 of potential relationships from TV, travel, telephones, faxes, computers, etc. From an insecure sense of self, you then spiral toward what Gergen calls "multiphrenia," in which the besieged, populated self frantically flails about trying to take advantage of the sea of choices. This condition may never merit its own telethon, but as choices increase so do the odds that multiphrenia will strike, leaving the scars of perpetual self-doubt. It's why the people who work hardest to improve their appearance never seem to feel much better than before they sampled the offerings of the Self-Perfection Industry (exercise videos, customized makeup, cosmetic surgery, health food). They become like politicians with their own private pollsters; the quest to recreate virtually supplants whatever person was once there.

Choice Reduces Social Bonding. The proliferation of choice   14
helps cause, and results from, another trend—social fragmentation. Together they ensure that Americans share fewer and fewer common experiences. A yuppie diet bears less and less resemblance to that of a lower-income family. I don't even know who's on the Wheaties box anymore because my cereal is located about ninety feet down the aisle. As marketers divide us into increasingly narrow segments, we inevitably see ourselves that way too. When there was one movie theater in a neighborhood, everyone sat under the same roof and watched the same film. Video rental stores enable you to be a movie junkie without ever having to sit next to another human being. Three decades ago, even when everyone was sitting in their own homes they were at least all watching "Gunsmoke." Today's viewing public scatters to its particular demographic niche on the cable dial.

Dealing with an abundance of choices mostly requires a   15
mental reorientation. Choice overload helped me finally understand what was so offensive about the stereotypical yuppie obsession with "quality," of which I have often been guilty. It's not that some coffee beans aren't, in fact, more flavorful than others, it's that people who spend so much of their lives thinking about small differences become small people.

Imagine instead a world in which we used our choice   16
brain lobes for the most important decisions and acted more arbitrarily on the rest. Perhaps you might select a brand name and buy all its products for the next four years, scheduling Choice Day during non-presidential election years. Or you might embrace the liberating powers of TV commercials. As everyone knows, ads brainwash us into

choosing products through insidious appeals to sex or other animal urges. But sometimes it feels good to let an ad take us by the hand. A few years ago I had an epiphany while deciding what to eat for dinner. I looked in the refrigerator, thought about nearby restaurants and markets, and grew puzzled. Just then an ad came on the TV for Burger King, featuring a luscious Whopper with fake charcoal stripes painted with perfect symmetry across the juicy meat. I put on my coat and immediately walked, zombielike, to the nearby Burger King and ordered a Whopper. I found it exhilarating, because I knew it wasn't the behavior of a rational economic player, and that it didn't matter.

READING FOR MEANING

Write to create meanings for Waldman's speculations about the effects of too many choices.

START MAKING MEANING

Begin by explaining briefly the experience that led Waldman to speculate about "the tyranny of choice" (paragraphs 1–3). Then survey the six effects Waldman proposes, select one you think is most compelling or surprising, and restate it briefly in two or three sentences. Continue by writing about anything else in the essay or in your experience that contributes to your understanding of Waldman's argument.

IF YOU ARE STUCK

If you cannot write at least a page, consider writing about

- the possibility that too many choices in consuming, voting, and relating to others leads to the inability to make a commitment to any one thing or person.

- Waldman's counterintuitive speculation that when we confront too many choices as consumers, we become more likely to make bad purchase decisions (paragraphs 9 and 10).

- why Waldman believes that having many choices turns voters off (paragraphs 11 and 12), perhaps testing his conviction against your own experience as a voter.

- Waldman's philosophical speculations that choice erodes the self and reduces social bonding (paragraphs 13 and 14), first explaining briefly what you think the writer means in these paragraphs and then telling what you find most and least convincing in his argument.

READING LIKE A WRITER
PRESENTING THE SUBJECT BY ESTABLISHING THE TREND

When speculating about the causes or effects of a trend, writers need to demonstrate that the trend exists by showing a significant increase or decrease in the trend over a period of time. It may also involve arguing that the subject is in fact a trend—a marked change that has lasted for some time. In establishing a trend, writers usually provide statistical information: When did it start? Is it still continuing, or has it ended? How rapidly has it increased or decreased? Has it changed steadily over time, or have there been noticeable stages of change? A thorough presentation of the trend may have to answer all of these questions.

Writers must also aim to convince readers of the social or cultural importance of the trend. They may attempt to demonstrate that the trend poses a danger or holds great promise. They may point out that it involves many people or groups and has led or may lead to changes in the way people live and work.

ANALYZE

1. *Reread* paragraphs 1–5, where Waldman presents the subject and establishes the trend by relying on two strategies: anecdote and statistics. *Focus* first on the anecdote (paragraphs 1–3), noting anything that contributes to your understanding of the trend and convinces you that it does indeed exist. Do you find the anecdote believable?

2. Then *look closely* at the statistics (paragraphs 4 and 5). How many sets of before-and-after statistics do you find? Are the products and services alike or different? How reliable do the statistics seem to be? Do they help you understand the trend and convince you that it is in fact a trend? How? Why do you think Waldman combines an anecdote and statistics in these paragraphs?

3. Finally, *consider* how Waldman demonstrates the importance or significance of the trend. Is he able to show that it has social or cultural significance?

WRITE

Write a page or so, explaining how the personal anecdote and the statistics help Waldman establish the existence of the trend. *Refer* to specific details to support your explanation. Then *evaluate* Waldman's success at establishing the trend he calls "the tryanny of choice" and at demonstrating its significance.

COMPARE

Compare the ways Waldman and Natalie Angier present their subjects. *Look back* at Angier's essay and *reread* paragraphs 1–6 about intolerance of boyish behavior (pp. 284–85). *Notice* the kinds of details and sources Angier uses to present her subject and, like Waldman, how she goes about demonstrating that the trend is increasing over time. *Notice* also how Angier attempts to demonstrate the importance or significance of her subject. Then *write* several sentences comparing the two writers' presentations of their subjects.

CONSIDERING IDEAS FOR YOUR OWN WRITING

Waldman's essay suggests a number of possible essay projects. For example, Waldman speculates on how choice contributes to the erosion of commitment. You could write about what causes people to develop a sense of commitment in the first place. Or you could focus on the possible effects of having or losing a sense of commitment. Similarly, whereas Waldman speculates about the role of choice in increasing political alienation, you could speculate about other possible causes of political alienation or its potential effects on democracy. Choose a subject you are interested in thinking more about, and propose one or more of its possible causes or effects.

On your own or with classmates, use the phrase *the tyranny of* from Waldman's title to think of more essay topics. Some examples include the tyranny of leisure time, working while in college, commuting, ambition, television, living at home, poverty, workplace rules, both parents working, or gun control. You should be able to think of many others. As you consider each tyranny, try to come up with two or three possible effects of it, as a way of testing quickly whether it has promise as an essay topic.

SARAH WEST

The Rise of Reported Incidents of Workplace Sexual Harassment

> *Sarah West wrote this essay for an assignment in her first-year college writing course.*
>
> *Like Natalie Angier and Steven Waldman, West speculates about a trend: a gradual increase in reported incidents of workplace sexual harassment over a thirty-year period. She begins by establishing that the trend exists. Notice that her concern is not whether workplace sexual harassment is increasing but whether reported incidents of it are increasing. She no doubt recognizes that it would be difficult to demonstrate that actual acts of harassment are increasing or decreasing; she may also recognize that such acts are very likely decreasing as reported incidents increase and receive wide publicity. West then launches her speculations about the causes for the increasing number of reports.*
>
> *As you read, keep in mind that the U.S. Supreme Court has defined illegal sexual harassment as "sufficiently severe or pervasive to alter the conditions of the victim's employment." In other words, it is not a casual or unthreatening one-time incident, but several incidents that create a hostile work environment and undermine victims' trust and ability to do their jobs.*

To those students who recently graduated from high   1
school, it may sound like the Dark Ages, but it wasn't: Until
1964, an employee who refused to give in to his or her employer's sexual advances could be fired—legally. An employee being constantly humiliated by a coworker could be
forced either to deal with the lewd comments, the stares,
and the touching or to just quit his or her job. It is truly
strange to think that sexual harassment was perfectly legal
in the United States until Congress passed the Civil Rights
Act of 1964.

But even after 1964, sexual harassment still persisted. It   2
was not widely known exactly what sexual harassment was or
that federal laws against it existed. Often when an employee
was sexually harassed on the job, he or she felt too alienated
and humiliated to speak out against it (Martell and Sullivan 6).
During the 1970s and 1980s, however, sexual-harassment victims began coming forward to challenge their harassers. Then
suddenly in the 1990s, the number of sexual-harassment complaints and lawsuits sharply rose. According to a 1994 survey
conducted by the Society for Human Resource Management,

the percentage of human-resource professionals who have reported that their departments handled at least one sexual-harassment complaint rose from 35 percent in 1991 to 65 percent in 1994. Why did this large increase occur in such a short amount of time? Possible answers to this question surely would include growing awareness of the nature of workplace sexual harassment, government action, efforts of companies to establish anti-harassment policies and encourage harassed employees to come forward, and prominence given by the media to many cases of workplace harassment.

One significant cause of the rise in reported incidents of   3
sexual harassment was most likely the increased awareness of what constitutes sexual harassment. There are two distinct types of sexual harassment, and although their formal names may be unfamiliar, the situations they describe will most certainly ring a bell. *Hostile environment* sexual harassment occurs when a supervisor, or coworker gives the victim "unwelcome sexual attention" that "interferes with (his or her) ability to work or creates an intimidating or offensive atmosphere" (Stanko and Werner 15). *Quid pro quo* sexual harassment occurs when "a workplace superior demands some degree of sexual favor" and either threatens to or does retaliate in a way that "has a tangible effect on the working conditions of the harassment victim" if he or she refuses to comply (Stanko and Werner 15).

A fundamental cause of the rise in reports of workplace   4
harassment was government action in 1964 and again in 1991. After the passage of the Civil Rights Act of 1991, which allowed, among other things, larger damage awards for sexually harassed employees, many more employees began coming forward with complaints. They realized that sexual harassment was not legal and they could do something about it. Suddenly, it became possible for a company to lose millions in a single sexual harassment case. For example, Rena Weeks, a legal secretary in San Francisco, sued the law firm of Baker & McKenzie for $3.5 million after an employee, Martin Greenstein, "dumped candy down the breast pocket of her blouse, groped her, pressed her from behind and pulled her arms back to 'see which one (breast) is bigger'" ("Workplace"). The jury awarded Weeks $7.1 million in punitive damages, twice what she sought in her lawsuit ("Workplace"). In addition, research revealed that the mere existence of sexual harassment in a company could lead to "hidden costs" such as absenteeism, lower productivity, and loss of valuable employees (Stanko and Werner 16). These "hidden costs" could add up to six or seven million dollars a

year for a typical large company, according to one survey of Fortune 500 companies (Stanko and Werner 16).

Concerned about these costs, most companies decided to   5
develop and publicize sexual-harassment policies, making every employee aware of the problem and more likely to come forward as early as possible so that employers have a chance to remedy the situation before it gets out of hand (Martell and Sullivan 8). Prior to 1991, sexual-harassment victims were often asked by their employers simply to remain silent (Martell and Sullivan 8). These new policies and procedures, along with training sessions, made it much more likely that employees would report incidents of sexual harassment. And we should not be surprised that the Internet has provided independent information to employees about dealing with workplace sexual harassment ("Handling"; "Sexual").

The media have also contributed to the rise of reports   6
of workplace sexual harassment by giving great attention to a few prominent cases. In 1991, Supreme Court Justice Clarence Thomas in Senate hearings on his nomination had to defend himself from sexual harassment charges by his former colleague Anita Hill. Later that same year, U.S. male navy officers were accused of sexually harassing female navy officers at the infamous Tailhook Convention, a yearly gathering of navy aviators (Nelton 24). During 1997 and 1998—and probably for many years beyond—Paula Jones's, sexual-harassment charges against President Clinton dominated the national news on many days. Jones was an Arkansas state employee at the time she said Clinton, who was then governor, harassed her. These three highly publicized cases made sexual harassment a much-discussed public issue that sparked debate and encouraged victims to come forward.

Not everyone believes that there has been an increase in   7
reports of the workplace sexual harassment. One journalist has argued that the rise in reported sexual-harassment complaints is actually a sort of illusion caused by insufficient research, since "research on this topic has only been undertaken since the 1970s" (Burke 23). Although this statement is largely true, it is only true because the Civil Rights Act did not exist until 1964. How could sexual harassment be measured and researched if it was not even acknowledged yet by society?

It has also been suggested that the trend is the result of a   8
greater percentage of women in the workplace (Martell and Sullivan 5). This may be a sufficient argument since women report sexual harassment in a significantly greater number of cases than men do (men report roughly one-tenth of what

women report). It has been noted, however, that there has been a rise in sexual-harassment complaints reported by male victims as well recently. According to the Equal Employment Opportunity Commission, the number of sexual-harassment complaints filed annually by men has more than doubled from 1989 to 1993 (Corey). Sexual harassment is by no means a new occurrence. It has most likely existed since workplace environments have existed. Yet, that there are more women in the workplace today has likely increased the percentage of women workers being sexually harassed, but it is also very plausible that the rise in reported incidents of sexual harassment is because of increased awareness of sexual harassment and the steps that one can legally take to stop it.

It has taken thirty years, but American society seems to be making significant progress in bringing a halt to a serious problem. *Sexual harassment,* a phrase that was unfamiliar to most of us only a few years ago, is now mentioned almost daily on television and in newspapers. We can only hope that the problem will end if we continue to hear about, to read about, and, most importantly to talk about sexual harassment and its negative consequences as we educate each other about sexual harassment. Then, perhaps someday, sexual harassment can be stopped altogether.

9

WORKS CITED

Burke, Ronald J. "Incidence and Consequences of Sexual Harassment in a Professional Services Firm." *Employee Counselling Today* Feb. 1995: 23–29.

Corey, Mary. "On-the-Job Sexism Isn't Just a Man's Sin Anymore." *Houston Chronicle* 30 Aug. 1993:D1.

"Handling Sexual Harassment Complaints." *Employer and Employee.* 8 Jan. 1998 http://www.employer-employee.com/sexhar1.html.

Martell, Kathryn, and George Sullivan. "Strategies for Managers to Recognize and Remedy Sexual Harassment." *Industrial Management* May/June 1994: 5–8.

Nelton, Sharon. "Sexual Harassment: Reducing the Risks." *Nation's Business* Mar. 1995: 24–26.

"Sexual Harassment: FAQ." *Employment: Workplace Rights and Responsibilities.* 8 Jan. 1998 http://www.nolo.com/ChunkEMP/emp7.html.

Sexual Harassment Remains a Workplace Problem, but Most Employers Have Policies in Place, SHRM Survey Finds. Alexandria: Society for Human Resource Management, 26 June 1994: 1.

Stanko, Brian B., and Charles A. Werner. "Sexual Harassment: What Is It? How to Prevent It." *National Public Accountant* June 1995: 14–16.

"Workplace Bias Lawsuits." *USA Today* 30 Nov. 1994: B2.

READING FOR MEANING

Write to create meanings for West's speculations about the rise in reported incidents of sexual harassment in the workplace.

START MAKING MEANING

Begin by restating briefly the causes West proposes to explain the increase in reports of sexual harassment at work. She identifies four causes, each in its own paragraph (paragraphs 3–6). Continue by writing about anything else in the essay or in your experience that contributes to your understanding of West's speculations.

IF YOU ARE STUCK

If you cannot write at least a page, consider writing about

- your understanding of the two types of workplace sexual harassment described by West (paragraph 3).

- a time when you or someone you know was sexually harassed at work, what happened, and what—if anything—was done about it.

- whether you think the federal government should have a role in protecting people at work.

- the possible implication of workplace sexual harassment laws for students' interactions on college campuses.

READING LIKE A WRITER
ESTABLISHING CREDIBILITY

To be credible is to be believable. When you write an essay speculating about the causes or effects of something, readers will find your argument believable when they sense that you are able to see the various complexities of your subject. Therefore, if you do not oversimplify, trivialize, or stereotype your subject, if you do not overlook possible alternative causes or effects that will occur to readers, and if you convey more than casual knowledge of your subject and show that you have thought about it deeply and seriously, you will establish your credibility with readers.

Before you attempt your own essay speculating about causes or effects, it will be helpful for you to consider carefully how West establishes her credibility to speculate about the rise in reported incidents of workplace sexual harassment.

ANALYZE

1. *Reread* this brief essay, and *annotate* it for evidence of credibility or lack of it. (Because you cannot know West personally, you must look

closely at the words, evidence, and arguments of her essay to decide whether she constructs a credible argument.) *Examine closely* how knowledgeable she seems about the subject. Where does her knowledge assure or even impress you as one of her intended readers? Where does her knowledge seem thin? *Consider* especially how she presents the subject and trend (paragraphs 1–3). *Assess* also the sources she relies on and how effectively she uses them.

2. *Look for* evidence that West has not trivialized a complex subject. Keeping in mind that she appropriately limits herself to speculating about possible causes, *note* how her argument reflects the complexity of her subject or fails to do so.

3. *Consider* how West's counterarguments (paragraphs 7 and 8) influence your judgment of her credibility.

4. *Examine* her approach to readers. What assumptions does she make about their knowledge and beliefs? What attitude does she have toward her readers? *Note* evidence of the writer's assumptions and attitude in the essay.

WRITE

Write a page or so presenting evidence of West's attempts to establish her credibility. Then *evaluate* how credible her essay is to you as one of her intended readers. To explain your judgment, *point to* parts of the essay and *comment on* the influence of your own attitudes about and knowledge of workplace sexual harassment.

CONSIDERING IDEAS FOR YOUR OWN WRITING

West speculates about a subject of great social significance—sexual harassment. She speculates about the causes of the rise in reported incidents, but she could have speculated about the phenomenon of sexual harassment itself, asking why it happens at all or why there seems to be so much of it in the workplace. Following her lead, you could speculate about the causes of other important social phenomena or trends that influence how people live and work and what their opportunities in life may be. Here are some examples: the increase in the number of students working part-time or full-time to get a college degree; the increase in hateful speech on some campuses; the increase in specific standards to be met before admission to college; the increase in the costs of a college education; the decline of neighborhood or community cohesion; the rise of the political influence of the religious right; the growing gap in wealth between the rich and the rest; the increasing reliance by technology companies on workers trained in other countries; and the stagnant wages over two decades for most workers.

Reviewing What Makes Speculative Essays about Causes or Effects Effective

In this chapter you have been learning how to read cause or effect argument for meaning and how to read it like a writer. Before going on to write a speculative essay about causes or effects, pause here to review and contemplate what you have learned about the elements of effective cause or effect essays.

Analyze

Choose one reading from this chapter that is for you an especially effective example of speculative writing. Before rereading the essay, *jot down* one or two things that led you to remember it as an example of effective cause or effect writing.

Then *reread* the essay, adding further annotations about what makes it effective. As a starting point, *consider* the writer's purpose, judging how well the essay achieves that purpose for its readers. Then *focus* on how well the writer of the essay

- presents the subject, trend, or phenomenon.

- makes a logical, step-by-step cause or effect argument.

- supports—or argues for—each cause or effect.

- handles likely objections to his or her own proposed causes or effects.

- evaluates readers' alternative or preferred causes or effects.

Your instructor may ask you to complete this activity on your own or to work with a small group of students who have chosen the same essay. If you work with others, allow enough time initially for all group members to read the essay and to add their annotations. Then discuss as a group what makes the essay effective. Take notes on your discussion. One student in your group should then report to the class what the group has learned about this effective essay. If you are working individually, write up what you have learned from your analysis.

Write

Write at least a page, justifying your choice of this essay as an example of effective cause or effect argument. Assume that your readers—your instructor and classmates—have read the selection but will not remember many details about it. Therefore, you will need to *refer* to details and specific parts of the essay as you explain how it works and *justify* your evaluation of its effectiveness. You need not argue that it is the best essay in the chapter or that it is flawless, only that it is, in your view, a strong example of the genre.

A GUIDE TO WRITING SPECULATIVE ESSAYS ABOUT CAUSES OR EFFECTS

The readings in this chapter have helped you learn a great deal about writing that analyzes causes or effects. Now that you have seen how writers present their subjects to particular readers, propose causes or effects readers may not think of, support those causes or effects so as to make them plausible to readers, and anticipate readers' questions and objections, you can approach this type of writing confidently. The readings remain an important resource for you as you develop your own essay. Use them to review how other writers have solved the problems you face and to rethink the strategies that help writers achieve their purposes.

This guide is designed to assist you in writing your essay. Here you will find activities to help you identify a subject and discover what to say about it, organize your ideas and draft the essay, read the draft critically, revise the draft to strengthen your argument, and edit and proofread the essay to improve readability.

INVENTION

The following invention activities will help you find a subject and begin developing your argument. A few minutes spent completing each writing activity will improve your chances of producing a detailed and convincing first draft. You can decide on a subject for your essay, explore what you presently know about it and gather additional information, think about possible causes or effects, and develop a plausible argument.

Choosing a Subject

The subject of an essay speculating about causes or effects may be a trend, an event, or a phenomenon, as the readings in this chapter illustrate. Before choosing a subject for your essay, look back at the Considering Ideas for Your Own Writing activities following the readings in this chapter. These varied possibilities for analyzing causes or effects may suggest a subject you would like to explore.

After reviewing these ideas for writing, you may still need to find an appropriate subject for your essay. Begin by listing as many possible topics as you can. Making such a list often generates ideas: As soon as you start listing subjects, you will think of new ideas you cannot imagine now.

Even if you feel confident about a subject you have selected, continue listing other possibilities to test your choice. Try to list specific subjects, and make separate lists for *trends, events,* and *phenomena.* Here are some other ideas to consider:

Trends

- Changes in men's or women's roles and opportunities in marriage, education, or work

- Changing patterns in leisure, entertainment, life-style, religious life, health, technology

- Completed artistic or historical trends (various art movements or historical changes)

- Long-term changes in economic conditions or political behavior or attitudes

- Increasing reliance on the Internet for research, entertainment, shopping, and conversation

Events

- A recent college, community, national, or international event that is surrounded by confusion or controversy

- A recent surprising event at your college such as the closing of a tutorial or health service, the cancellation of popular classes, a change in library hours or dormitory regulations, the loss of a game by a favored team, or some hateful or violent act by one student against another

- A recent puzzling or controversial event in your community, such as the abrupt resignation of a public official, a public protest by an activist group, a change in traffic laws, a zoning decision, or the banning of a book from school libraries

- A historical event about which there is still some dispute as to its causes or effects

Phenomena

- A social problem, such as discrimination, homelessness, child abuse, illiteracy, high-school dropout rates, youth suicides, or teenage pregnancy

- One or more aspects of college life, such as libraries too noisy to study in, large classes, lack of financial aid, difficulties in scheduling classes, shortcomings in student health services, or insufficient availability of housing (in this essay you would not need to solve the problems, only to speculate about their causes or effects)

- A human trait, such as anxiety, selfishness, fear of success or failure, leadership, jealousy, insecurity, envy, opportunism, curiosity, openness, or health and fitness

After you have completed your lists, reflect on the possible topics you have compiled. Because an authoritative essay analyzing causes or effects requires sustained thinking, drafting, revising, and possibly even research, you will want to choose a subject to which you can commit yourself enthusiastically for a week or two. Above all, choose a topic that interests you, even if you feel uncertain about how to approach it. Then consider carefully whether you are more interested in the causes or the effects of the event, trend, or phenomenon. Consider, as well, whether the subject in which you are interested invites speculation about its causes or effects or perhaps even precludes speculation about one or the other. For example, you could speculate about the causes for increasing membership in your church, whereas the effects (the results or consequences) of the increase might for now be so uncertain as to discourage plausible speculation. Some subjects invite speculation about both their causes and effects. For this assignment, however, you need not do both.

Developing Your Subject

The writing and research activities that follow will enable you to test your subject choice and to discover what you have to say about it. Each activity takes only a few minutes but will help you produce a fuller, more focused draft.

EXPLORING YOUR SUBJECT. *You may discover that you know more about your subject than you suspect if you write about it for a few minutes without stopping.* This brief sustained writing will stimulate your memory, help you probe your interest in the subject, and enable you to test your subject choice. As you write, consider the following questions:

- What interests me in this subject? What about it will interest my readers?

- What do I already know about the subject?

- Why does the trend, event, or phenomenon not already have an accepted explanation for its causes or effects? What causes or effects have others already suggested for this subject?

- How can I learn more about the subject?

CONSIDERING CAUSES OR EFFECTS. *Before you research your subject (should you need to), you want to discover which causes or effects you can already imagine. Make a list of possible causes or effects.* For *causes* consider underlying or background causes, immediate or instigating causes, and ongoing causes. For example, if you lost your job delivering pizzas, an underlying cause could be that years ago a plant-closing in your town devastated the local economy, which has never recovered; an immediate cause could be that the pizza-chain outlet you worked for has been hit hard by the recent arrival of a new pizza-chain outlet; an ongoing cause could be that for several years some health-conscious residents regularly eat salad, rather than pizza, for dinner. For *effects,* consider both short-term and long-term consequences, as well as how one effect may lead to another in a kind of chain reaction. Try to think not only of obvious causes or effects but also of ones that are likely to be overlooked in a superficial analysis of your subject.

Identify the most convincing causes or effects in your list. Do you have enough to make a strong argument? Imagine how you might convince readers of the plausibility of some of these causes or effects.

RESEARCHING YOUR SUBJECT.   *When developing an essay analyzing causes or effects, you can often gain great advantage by researching your subject.* (See Appendix Two, Strategies for Research and Documentation.) You can gain a greater understanding of the event, trend, or phenomenon; and you can review and evaluate others' proposed causes or effects in case you want to present any of these alternatives in your own essay. Reviewing others' causes or effects may suggest to you plausible causes or effects you have overlooked. You may also find support for your own counterarguments to readers' objections.

ANALYZING YOUR READERS.   *Write for a few minutes, identifying who your readers are, what they know about your subject, and how they can be convinced by your proposed causes or effects.* Describe your readers briefly. Mention anything you know about them as a group that might influence the way they would read your essay. Estimate how much they know about your subject, how extensively you will have to present it to them, and what is required to demonstrate to them the importance of the subject. Speculate about how they will respond to your argument.

REHEARSING PART OF YOUR ARGUMENT.   *Select one of your causes or effects and write several sentences about it, trying out an argument for your readers.* The heart of your essay will be the argument you make for the plausibility of your proposed causes or effects. Like a ballet dancer or baseball pitcher warming up for a performance, you can prepare for your first draft by rehearsing part of the argument you will make. How will you convince readers to take this cause or effect seriously? This writing activity will focus your thinking and encourage you to keep discovering new arguments until you start drafting. It may also lead you to search for additional support for your speculations.

FORMULATING A WORKING THESIS.   *Draft a thesis statement.* A *working*—as opposed to final—*thesis* enables you to bring your invention work into focus and begin your draft with a clearer purpose. At some point during the drafting of your essay, however, you will likely decide to revise your working thesis or even try out a new one. A thesis for an essay speculating about causes or effects nearly always announces the subject; it may also mention the proposed causes or effects and suggest the direction the argument will take. Here are three sample thesis statements from the readings in this chapter.

- Greeley: "If one considers that for much of Christian history the population was illiterate and the clergy semiliterate and that authority was far away, one begins to understand that the heritage for most people most of the time was almost entirely story, ritual, ceremony and eventually art. So it has been for most of human history. So it is, I suggest (and my data back me up), even today" (paragraph 9).

- Waldman: "In fact, choice can be profoundly debilitating. It forces us to squander our time, weakens our connections to people and places, and can even poison our sense of contentedness" (paragraph 7).

- West: "According to a 1994 survey conducted by the Society for Human Resource Management, the percentage of human-resource professionals who have reported that their departments handled at least one sexual-harassment complaint rose from 35 percent in 1991 to 65 percent in 1994. Why did this large increase occur in such a short amount of time? Possible answers to this question surely would include growing awareness of the nature of workplace sexual harassment, government action, efforts of companies to establish anti-harassment policies and encourage harassed employees to come forward, and prominence given by the media to many cases of workplace harassment" (paragraph 2).

Notice, for instance, that West's thesis clearly announces her subject—workplace sexual harassment—as well as how she will approach the subject: by focusing on the increase in reported incidents and speculating about the causes of the increase. Her thesis also forecasts her speculations, identifying the causes and the order in which she will argue for them in the essay.

DRAFTING

The following guidelines will help you set goals for your draft and plan its organization.

Setting Goals

Establishing goals for your draft before you begin writing will enable you to move ahead more quickly and to make critical writing decisions more confidently. Consider the following questions now, and keep them in mind as you draft. They will help you maintain your focus while drafting as well as recall how the writers you have read in this chapter tried to achieve similar goals.

- *How can I convince my readers that my proposed causes or effects are plausible?* Should I rely on statistical support like Waldman, give many examples like Greeley, quote authorities and published research like Angier and West, include personal anecdotes and cases like Kozol, or introduce analogies like King and Angier?

- *How should I anticipate readers' objections to my argument? What should I do about alternative causes or effects?* Should I anticipate readers' objections and questions like Angier or answer readers' likely questions like Greeley? Can I refute alternative causes as West does? How can I find common ground—shared attitudes, values, and beliefs—with my readers, even with those whose objections or alternative causes I must refute?

- *How much do my readers need to know about my subject?* Do I need to describe my subject in some detail, in the way that Waldman establishes the plethora of choices we face, that Greeley describes Catholicism for non-Catholics, or that West describes the legal context for the rise in reported incidents of workplace sexual harassment? Or can I assume that my readers have personal experience with my subject, as King seems to assume? If my subject is a trend, how can I demonstrate that the trend exists?

- *How can I begin engagingly and end conclusively?* Should I begin by emphasizing the importance or timeliness of my subject as Angier does? Might I begin with a personal anecdote like Waldman's, or with an unusual statement like King's? How can I conclude by returning to an idea in the opening paragraph like Kozol, restating the urgency of the problem like West, repeating the main cause like Greeley, or trying humor and irony like Waldman?

- *How can I establish my authority and credibility to argue the causes or effects of my subject?* Can I do this by citing personal experience and presenting a carefully researched consideration of the trend like Waldman, by showing a comprehensive understanding of the effects of the phenomenon like Kozol, by counterarguing responsibly like West, or by relying on what I have learned through research and interviews like Angier?

Organizing Your Draft

With goals in mind and invention notes at hand, you are ready to make a tentative outline of your draft. The sequence of proposed causes or effects will be at the center of your outline, but you may also want to plan where you will consider alternatives or counterargue objections. Notice that some writers who conjecture about causes consider alternative causes—evaluating, refuting, or accepting them—before they present their own. Much of an essay analyzing causes may be devoted to considering alternatives. Both writers who conjecture about causes and writers who speculate about effects usually consider readers' possible objections to their causes or effects along with the argument for each cause or effect. If you must provide readers with a great deal of information about your subject as context for your argument, you may want to outline this information carefully. For your essay, this part of the outline may be a major consideration. Your plan should make the information readily accessible to your readers. This outline is tentative; you may decide to change it when you start drafting.

READING A DRAFT CRITICALLY

Getting a critical reading of your draft will help you see how to improve it. Your instructor may schedule class time for reading drafts, or you may want to ask a classmate or a tutor in the writing center to read your draft. Ask your reader to use the following guidelines and write out a response for you to consult during your revision.

Read for a First Impression

1. Read quickly through the draft, without stopping to annotate or comment, and then write two or three sentences giving your general impression.

2. Identify one aspect of the draft that seems particularly effective.

Read Again to Suggest Improvements

1. Recommend ways to make the presentation of the subject more effective.

   - Read the opening paragraphs that present the subject to be speculated about and tell the writer what you found most interesting and useful.

   - Point out one or two places where a reader unfamiliar with the subject might need more information.

   - Suggest ways the writer could make the subject seem more interesting or significant.

   - If the subject is a trend, explain what you understand to be the increase or decrease and let the writer know whether you think further evidence is required to demonstrate conclusively that the subject is indeed a trend.

   - If the beginning seems unlikely to engage readers, suggest at least one other way of beginning.

2. Suggest ways to strengthen the cause or effect argument.

   - List the causes or effects. Tell the writer whether there seem to be too many, too few, or just about the right number. Point to one cause or effect that seems especially imaginative or surprising and to one that seems too obvious. Make suggestions for dropping or adding causes or effects.

- Evaluate the support for each cause or effect separately. To help the writer make every cause or effect plausible to the intended readers, point out where the support seems thin or inadequate. Point to any support that seems less than appropriate or believable or inconsistent with other support. Consider whether the writer has overlooked important resources of support: anecdotes, examples, statistics, analogies, or quotations from publications or interviews.

3. Suggest ways to strengthen the counterargument.

- Locate every instance of counterargument—places where the writer has anticipated readers' objections or questions or evaluated readers' preferred alternative causes. Mark these in the margin of the draft. Review these as a set, and then suggest objections, questions, and alternative causes or effects the writer seems to have overlooked.

- Identify counterarguments that seem weakly supported and suggest ways the writer might strengthen the support.

- Determine whether any of the refutations attack or ridicule readers and suggest ways the writer could refute without insulting or unduly irritating readers.

4. Suggest how credibility can be enhanced.

- Tell the writer whether the intended readers are likely to find the essay knowledgeable and authoritative. Point to places where it seems most and least authoritative.

- Identify places where the writer seeks common ground—shared values, beliefs, and attitudes—with readers. Try to identify places where the writer might attempt to do so.

5. Suggest how the organizational plan could be improved.

- Consider the overall plan, perhaps by making a scratch outline. Analyze closely the progression of the causes or effects. Decide whether the causes or effects follow a logical step-by-step sequence.

- Suggest ways the causes or effects might be more logically sequenced.

- Review the places where counterargument appears and consider whether it is smoothly woven into the argument. Give advice on the best places for the counterarguments.

- Indicate where new or better transitions might cue the steps in the argument and keep readers on track.

REVISING

This section provides suggestions for revising your draft, suggestions that will remind you of the possibilities for developing a plausible cause or effect argument. Revising means reenvisioning your draft, trying to see it in a new way, given your purpose and readers, in order to strengthen your cause or effect argument.

The biggest mistake you can make in revising is to focus initially on words or sentences. Instead, first try to see your draft as a whole in order to assess its likely impact on your readers. Think imaginatively and boldly about cutting unconvincing material, adding new material, and moving material around. Your computer makes even drastic revisions easy, but you still need to make the effort and decisions that will improve your draft.

You may have received help with this challenge from classmates who have given your draft a critical reading. If so, rely on their valuable help in deciding which parts of your draft need revising and what specific changes you should make.

To Present the Subject More Effectively

- If readers unfamiliar with the subject may not understand it readily, provide more information.

- If the importance or significance of the subject is not clear, dramatize it with an anecdote or highlight its social or cultural implications.

- If the subject is a trend, show evidence of a significant increase or decrease over an extended period of time.

To Strengthen the Cause or Effect Argument

- If you have proposed what seem like too many causes or effects, clarify the role of each one or drop one or more that seem too obvious, obscure, or relatively minor.

- If a cause or effect lacks adequate support, come up with further examples, anecdotes, statistics, or quotes from authorities.

To Strengthen the Counterargument

- If you have not anticipated readers' likely questions about your argument and objections to it, do so now. Remember that you can either accommodate these objections and questions in your argument, conceding their insightfulness by making them part of your own argument, or refute them, arguing that they are not worth taking seriously.

- If you have not anticipated readers' likely alternative causes or effects, do so now, conceding or refuting each one.

- If you have attacked or ridiculed readers in your refutations, seek ways to refute their ideas decisively while showing respect for them as people.

- If you have neglected to establish common ground with your readers, especially those who may think about your subject quite differently from you, attempt to show them that you share some common values, attitudes, and beliefs.

To Enhance Credibility

- If readers of your draft have questioned your credibility as a writer of cause or effect argument, learn more about your subject, support your argument more fully, anticipate a wider range of readers' likely objections, or talk with others who can help you think more imaginatively about your speculations.

- If your choice of words or approach to your readers has weakened your credibility, consider your word choices throughout the essay and look for ways to show readers respect and to establish common ground with them.

To Organize More Logically and Coherently

- If readers questioned the logical sequence of your causes or effects, consider strengthening your plan by adding or dropping causes or effects or resequencing them. Ensure that one cause or effect leads to the next in a logically linked chain of reasoning.

- If your logic seems sound but the links are not clear to your readers, provide meaningful transitions from one step in the argument to the next.

- If your various counterarguments are not smoothly integrated into your argument, move them around or smooth the connections.

EDITING AND PROOFREADING

When you have revised your essay, be sure to spend some time checking for errors in usage, punctuation, and mechanics. If you have been keeping a list of errors you frequently make, begin by checking your draft against this list. Ask someone else to proofread your essay before you print out a copy for your instructor.

From our research on student writing, we know that essays speculating about causes or effects have a high percentage of errors in the use of numbers and "reason is because" sentences. Because you must usually rely on numbers to present statistics when you support your argument or demonstrate a trend, you may find that you are unsure about the conventions for presenting different kinds of numbers. Because you are usually drawn into "reason is because" sentences when you make a causal argument, you will need to know options for revising such sentences. Refer to a writer's handbook for help with these two problems.

Reflecting on What You Have Learned

In this chapter, you have read critically several speculative essays about causes or effects and have written one of your own. To better remember what you have learned, pause now to reflect on the reading and writing activities you completed in this chapter.

1. *Write* a page or so reflecting on what you have learned. Begin by describing what you are most pleased with in your essay and what you think contributed to your achievement. Be specific about this contribution.

   - If it was something you learned from the readings, *indicate* which readings and specifically what you learned from them.

   - If it came from your invention writing, *point out* the section or sections that helped you most.

   - If you got good advice from a critical reader, *explain* exactly how the person helped you—perhaps by helping you to understand a particular problem in your draft or by adding a new dimension to your writing.

2. Now *reflect* more generally on speculation about causes or effects, a genre of writing that plays an important role in our society. *Consider* some of the following questions: How comfortable were you in dealing with possibilities (probable or likely causes or effects) rather than certainties (proven or scientifically verifiable facts)? How satisfying was it to speculate about the causes or effects of your subject without proposing a resolution or solution to it? How might your own values and beliefs influence the particular causes or effects you decided to support? Do you think it is possible that your speculations benefit you and others of your gender and social class but dis-
   Continued

serve people different from you? Could your essay or any of the readings be interpreted as exercises in assigning blame? What contribution might essays speculating about causes or effects make to our society that other genres of writing cannot make?

Proposal to Solve a Problem

P roposals are written every day in the workplace. A team of engineers and technical writers in a transportation firm, for example, might write a proposal to compete for a contract to build a new subway system. The manager of a fashion outlet might write a memo to a company executive proposing an upgrading of the computer system to include networking within the chain of stores. Seeking funding to support her research on the American poet Walt Whitman, a university professor might write a proposal to the National Endowment for the Humanities.

Other proposals address social problems and attempt to influence the direction of public policy. A special United Nations task force recommends ways to eliminate acid rain worldwide. The College Entrance Examination Board commissions a report proposing strategies for reversing the decline in Scholastic Assessment Test (SAT) scores. A specialist in children's television writes a book suggesting that the federal government fund the development of new educational programming for preschool and elementary school students.

Still other proposals are written by individuals who want to solve problems involving groups or communities to which they belong. A college student irritated by long waits to see a nurse at the campus health clinic writes the clinic director, proposing a more efficient way to schedule and accommodate students. After funding for dance classes has been cut by their school board, students and parents interested in dance write a proposal to the school principal, asking her help in arranging after-school classes taught by a popular high-school teacher who would be paid with community funds. The board of directors of a historical society in a small ranching community proposes to the county board of supervisors that it donate an unused county building to the society so it can display historical records, photographs, and artifacts.

Problem solving is not only the basis for a popular type of argumentative writing; it is also a way of thinking that is fundamental to much of the world's work. To solve a problem means to see it clearly, to look at it from new angles. The essay you write for this chapter will fully engage you in this special and important way of thinking.

Because a proposal tries to convince readers that its way of defining and solving the problem makes sense, proposal writers must be sensitive to readers' needs and expectations. As you plan and draft a proposal, you will want to determine whether your readers know about the problem and whether they are aware of its seriousness. In addition, you will want to consider how your readers might rate other possible solutions. Knowing what your readers know, what their assumptions and biases are, and what kinds of arguments will be appealing to them is crucial to proposal writing, as it is to all good argumentative writing.

Reading the proposal essays in this chapter will help you discover why the genre is so important and how it works. You will also get many ideas for writing a proposal to solve a problem that matters to you. The Guide to Writing Proposals following the readings will help you draft and revise your proposal. Keep the following assignment in mind as you evaluate the essays in this chapter and plan to write one of your own.

THE WRITING ASSIGNMENT

Proposals

Write an essay proposing a solution to a problem affecting a group or community to which you belong. Your task is to define the problem and establish that it exists, to offer a solution that can be reasonably implemented, to lay out the particulars by which your proposal would be put into effect, and to consider readers' objections and alternative solutions.

WRITING SITUATIONS FOR PROPOSING SOLUTIONS TO PROBLEMS

Writing that proposes solutions to problems plays a significant role in college and professional life, as the following examples show.

- The business manager of a large hospital writes a proposal to the board of directors requesting the purchase of a new word-processing and billing system that she recently saw demonstrated at a convention. She argues that the new system would both improve efficiency and save money. In support of her proposal, she reminds the board of the limitations of the present system and points out the advantages of the new one.

- For a political science class, a college student analyzes the question of presidential term limits. Citing examples from recent history, she argues that U.S. presidents spend the first year of each term getting organized and the fourth year either running for reelection or weakened by their status as a lame duck. Consequently, they are fully productive for only half of their four-year terms. She proposes limiting presidents to one six-year term, claiming that this change would remedy the problem by giving presidents four or five years to put their programs into effect. She acknowledges that it could make presidents less responsive to the public will, but insists that the system of legislative checks and balances would make that problem unlikely.

- For an economics class, a student looks into the many problems arising from *maquiladoras,* new industries in Mexico near the border with the United States that provide foreign exchange for the Mexican government, low-paying jobs for Mexican workers, and profits for American manufacturers. He discovers that in Mexico there are problems of inadequate housing, health care, injuries on the job, and environmental damage. His instructor encourages him to select one of the problems, research it more thoroughly, and propose a solution. Taking injuries on the job as the problem most immediately within the control of American manufacturers, he proposes that they observe standards established by the U.S. Occupational Safety and Health Administration.

A GUIDE TO READING PROPOSALS

This guide is designed to orient you to the special features and possibilities of writing that proposes solutions to problems. As you read, you will gain insights into the particular ways of making meaning. As you write, you will learn useful strategies for creating a convincing proposal of your own. The guide begins with a proposal by a well-known writer on social and economic issues, Robert J. Samuelson. You will first read this essay for meaning, seeking to understand its presentation of a problem and argument for a solution. Then you will read the essay like a writer, noting where and how Samuelson uses the special features of successful proposals to solve problems.

ROBERT J. SAMUELSON

Reforming Schools through a Federal Test for College Aid

Robert Samuelson (b. 1945) began his journalism career at the Washington Post. *For many years, he has been a free-lance writer, producing a biweekly column on socioeconomic issues that appears in* Newsweek, *the* Washington Post, *the* Los Angeles Times, *the* Boston Globe, *and other newspapers. He is the author of* The Good Life and Its Discontents: The American Dream and the Age of Entitlement 1945–1995 *(1996).*

In the following essay, published in Newsweek *in 1991, Samuelson proposes a solution to a problem facing American high schools.* Newsweek *is among the three or four most prominent national weekly newsmagazines. Offering reports on current events, politics, science, health, the arts and popular culture, along with editorials and essays, it is aimed at a broad national readership. As a college student interested in news and ideas, you are among its intended readers.*

As you read the essay, annotate anything that helps you understand Samuelson's view of the problem and his proposal for solving it. Write your comments and questions in the margin of the text. React to his argument on the basis of your experience in high school.

We are not yet serious about school reform. The latest plan from the Bush administration mixes lofty rhetoric (a pledge to "invent new schools") with vague proposals to rate our schools with national tests. It doesn't address the most dreary—and important—fact about American education: our students don't work very hard. The typical high-school senior does less than an hour of homework an evening. No school reform can succeed unless this changes. What's depressing is that we could change it, but probably won't.

We could require students receiving federal college aid to pass a qualifying test. This is a huge potential lever. Nearly two-thirds of high-school graduates go to college (including community colleges and vocational schools), and roughly two-fifths—6 million students—get federal aid. In fiscal 1991, government grants and guaranteed loans totaled $18.1 billion. As a practical matter any federal test would also affect many unaided students; most colleges couldn't easily maintain a lower entrance requirement for the rich. The message would be: anyone wanting to go to college can't glide through high school.

1

2

Just how well our schools perform depends heavily on student attitudes. This is one reason why the Bush plan, which proposes tests to evaluate schools, is so empty. The tests hold no practical consequences for students and, therefore, lack the power to motivate them. When students aren't motivated, they don't treat school seriously. Without serious students, it's hard to attract good people into teaching no matter how much we pay them. And bad teachers ensure educational failure. This is the vicious circle we must break.

Unfortunately, we don't now expect much of our students. For most high-school students, it doesn't pay to work hard. Their goal is college, and almost anyone can go to some college. There are perhaps 50 truly selective colleges and universities in the country, Chester Finn Jr., professor of education at Vanderbilt University, writes in his new book, *We Must Take Charge: Our Schools and Our Future*. To survive, the other 3,400 institutions of "higher learning" eagerly recruit students. Entrance requirements are meager and financial assistance from states and the federal government is abundant.

"Coast and get into college and have the same opportunities as someone who worked hard," says one senior quoted by Finn. "That is the system." It's this sort of silly rationalization that hurts American students, precisely because they can't always make up what they've missed in the past. Opportunities go only to those who have real skills—not paper credentials or many years spent on campus. The college dropout rate is staggering. After six years, less than half of students at four-year colleges have earned a degree. The graduation rate is even lower for community colleges.

Every other advanced society does it differently. "The United States is the only industrial country that doesn't have some (testing) system external to the schools to assess educational achievement," says Max Eckstein, an expert on international education. Their tests, unlike ours, typically determine whether students can continue in school. As the lone holdout, we can compare our system with everyone else's. Well, we rank near the bottom on most international comparisons.

In the media, the school "crisis" is often pictured as mainly a problem of providing a better education for the poor and minorities. Stories focus on immigrants and inner-city schools. Almost everyone else is (by omission) presumed to be getting an adequate education. Forget it. In fact, the test scores of our poorest students, though still

3

4

5

6

7

abysmally low, have improved. Likewise, high-school drop-out rates have declined. What we minimize is the slippage of our average schools.

COMMON SENSE

When mediocrity is the norm, even good students suffer. In international comparisons, our top students often fare poorly against other countries' top students, notes economist John Bishop of Cornell University. Grade inflation is widespread. In 1990 1.1 million high-school students took the college board exams. These are the best students: 28 percent had A averages, 53 percent B's and the rest C's. Yet, two-fifths of these students scored less than 390 on the verbal SAT.   8

The idea that college-bound students should be required (by test) to demonstrate the ability to do college-level work is common sense. It's hard to see how anyone could object, especially with so much public money at stake. But almost no educators or political leaders advocate it. The American belief in "equality" and "fairness" makes it hard for us to create barriers that block some students. Our approach is more indirect and dishonest: first, we give them meaningless high-school degrees; then we let them drop out of college.   9

The same spirit of self-deception pervades much of the school debate. We skirt the obvious—students will work if there's a good reason—and pursue painless and largely fictitious cures. There's a constant search for new teaching methods and technologies that will, somehow, miraculously mesmerize students and automatically educate them. Computers are a continuing fad. Liberals blame educational failure on inadequate spending; conservatives lambaste public schools as rigid bureaucracies. These familiar critiques are largely irrelevant.   10

Low spending isn't the main problem. Between 1970 and 1990, "real" (inflation adjusted) spending per student in public schools rose 63 percent. In 1989, U.S. educational spending totaled 6.9 percent of gross national product, which equals or exceeds most nations'. As for "vouchers" and "choice"—conservatives' current cure—the experiment has already been tried in higher education. It failed. Government loans and grants are vouchers that allow students choice. The perverse result is that colleges compete by reducing entrance requirements in order to increase enrollments and maximize revenues.   11

A test for college aid would stem this corrosive process. The number of college freshmen would decline, but not—   12 given the high dropout rates—the number of college graduates. Because high-school standards are so lax, the passing grade of any meaningful test would flunk many of today's seniors. Tests are available, because a few state college systems, such as New Jersey's and Tennessee's, give them to freshmen. Failing students must take remedial courses. In 1990, 37 percent of New Jersey freshmen flunked a verbal-skills test and 58 percent an algebra test.

AN UPROAR

Who would be hurt? Not students who can pass the test today: that's perhaps 40 to 60 percent of college freshmen. Not students who might pass the test with more study: that's another big fraction. (In New Jersey and Tennessee, most students pass remedial courses. If they can do it at 18 or 19, they can do it at 17.) Some students who now go to college wouldn't. Often, these students drop out after saddling themselves with a hefty student loan. Would they be worse off? On college loans, default rates range as high as 25 percent.   13

But let's be candid. None of this is about to happen soon. Requiring tests for college aid would cause an uproar. There would be charges of elitism, maybe racism. Colleges and universities would resist. They depend on the current open-ended flow of students and, without it, some would have to shut down. This wouldn't be bad for the country, because we now overinvest in higher education. With one-fifth the students, colleges and universities account for two-fifths of all educational spending. But today's waste has spawned a huge constituency.   14

Little wonder that President Bush—and all politicians— steer clear of this sort of reform. It's too direct. It wouldn't cure all our educational problems, but it would make a start. It would jolt students, parents and teachers. It would foster a climate that rewards effort. It would create pressures for real achievement, not just inflated grades. It would force schools to pay more attention to non-college-bound students, rather than assuming everyone can go somewhere. It would strip away our illusions, which, sadly, are precisely what we cherish most.   15

READING FOR MEANING

Write to create meanings for Samuelson's proposal that students take a test administered by the federal government in order to receive federal aid for college.

START MAKING MEANING

Begin by writing about Samuelson's definition of the problem as one of student motivation (paragraphs 3–6), restating briefly what he has to say and reacting to it. Continue by writing about anything else in the essay or in your experience that contributes to your understanding of Samuelson's proposal.

IF YOU ARE STUCK

If you cannot write at least a page, consider writing about

- the "vicious circle" (paragraph 3), explaining what Samuelson means to convey with that phrase and evaluating it from your perspective as a former high-school student.

- Samuelson's statement, "When mediocrity is the norm, even good students suffer" (paragraph 8).

- the alternative solutions Samuelson refutes in paragraphs 10 and 11, describing one or two of them and giving your opinion about their potential value in improving high-school students' preparation for college.

- who would benefit immediately from Samuelson's proposal and what might be its long-term social and economic benefits.

READING LIKE A WRITER

This section guides you through an analysis of Samuelson's argumentative strategies: *introducing the problem, presenting the solution, arguing directly for the proposed solution, counterarguing,* and *establishing credibility.* Each strategy is described briefly and followed by a critical reading and writing task to help you see how Samuelson uses the strategy in his essay.

Consider this section a writer's introduction to proposals. You will learn still more from the activities following the readings later in the chapter. Finally, at the end of the chapter, A Guide to Writing Proposals suggests how you can use these same strategies in writing your own proposal.

Introducing the Problem

Every proposal begins with a problem. Depending on what their readers know about the problem, writers may explain how it came to be or what attempts have been made to solve it. Sometimes, readers are already aware of a problem, especially if it affects them directly. In such cases, the writer can merely identify the problem and move directly to presenting a solution. At other times, readers may be unaware that the problem exists or may have difficulty imagining the problem. In these situations, the writer may have to describe the problem in detail, helping readers recognize its importance and the consequences of failing to solve it.

Writers may also believe that readers misunderstand the problem, failing to recognize it for what it really is. They may then decide that their first task is to redefine the problem in a way that helps readers see it in a different way. Samuelson does precisely that. Because he believes that efforts to reform American schools are doomed because they fail to recognize the real problem, his opening strategy must be to redefine the problem.

ANALYZE

1. *Reread* paragraphs 3 through 6, noting in the margin which kinds of support Samuelson uses to convince readers that the problem should be redefined as one of student motivation. Where does he point to causes of the problem and to its consequences, rely on comparisons, quote authorities, give examples, make use of statistics, or make judgments?

2. *Consider* how effectively Samuelson redefines the problem. As one of his intended readers, *explain* why you are or are not convinced of his redefinition. In what ways might he have made his argument more convincing?

WRITE

Write several sentences, explaining Samuelson's strategy for introducing the problem and evaluating how convincing you find his argument. *Give details* from the reading.

Presenting the Solution

The solution is the heart of a proposal essay: The writer's primary purposes are to convince readers of the wisdom of that solution and even to take action on it. In order to achieve these purposes, the writer must ensure that readers can imagine the solution and envision just how it would be implemented.

Some proposals have little chance of success unless every small step of implementing them is detailed for readers. For this reason, a proposed solution to a highly technical engineering problem might run many pages in length. In contrast, a more tentative proposal, such as Samuelson's idea for encouraging greater student preparedness for college, could be brief. This type of proposal might refer to implementation without fully explaining it, perhaps deferring to specialists who could step in later to work out the details. In this case, details of implementation may be premature; the real purpose may be to invite readers' reactions before committing the time required to work out all the details. Given his space limitations and readers' expectations of a weekly newsmagazine, Samuelson has limited opportunity to detail the implementation of a massive and complex national testing program involving some six million high-school graduates in America.

ANALYZE

1. *Reread* paragraph 12, underlining the few details Samuelson gives about his proposed solution.

2. Keeping in mind his space constraints, *list* two or three additional key details Samuelson might have included to help his readers more easily imagine how the solution would look.

WRITE

List the details Samuelson gives about his proposed test. Then *add* a few sentences, evaluating whether Samuelson gives enough details for you to imagine how the solution might be implemented, even though it is not spelled out.

Arguing Directly for the Proposed Solution

In arguing for solutions, writers rely on two interrelated strategies: arguing directly for the solution and counterarguing readers' likely objections and preferred solutions. We take up counterargument in the next section.

A proposal is not a proposal without some argument supporting the solution. It may describe a situation well or complain with great feeling about a problem; if it goes no further, however, it cannot be a proposal. Writers must try to convince readers that the solution presented will actually alleviate the problem. The solution should appear feasible, cost-effective, and more promising than alternative solutions.

Writers should ask themselves why the solution would work and support their argument. Such support may include personal experience, hypothetical cases and scenarios, statistics, facts, assertions, examples, speculations about causes or consequences, and quotations from authorities. The most convincing support surprises readers: They see it and think, "I never thought of it that way."

Whatever else proposal writers do, they must argue energetically, imaginatively, and sensitively for their proposed solutions. Although Samuelson describes his solution only briefly and says nothing about how it might be implemented, he does argue energetically for it, relying on a variety of strategies.

ANALYZE

1. *Reread* paragraphs 8, 9, 12, 13, and 15, where Samuelson argues directly for his solution. In each of these paragraphs, *underline* the one main reason Samuelson gives for advocating his solution.

2. *Review* these paragraphs, this time annotating each one for the kinds of support Samuelson offers. *Note* in the margin the kinds of support

you find. Then *consider* the range and variety of support. Where does Samuelson rely on one kind or on several kinds of support?

3. *Consider* the strengths of Samuelson's direct argument for his solution. What do you find most and least convincing in his reasons and support?

WRITE

Write several sentences, describing and evaluating Samuelson's argument in the paragraphs you analyzed. What kinds of reasons and support does he use? *Give key examples* from the reading. *Conclude* with a few sentences that evaluate the effectiveness of Samuelson's argument.

Counterarguing: Anticipating Readers' Objections, Questions, and Preferred Solutions

As they argue for their solutions, experienced writers are continually aware of readers' objections to the argument or questions about it. Writers may *accommodate* readers' likely objections and questions by modifying their own arguments. What better way to disarm a skeptical or antagonistic reader! Or writers may *refute* readers' objections and questions; that is, try to show them to be wrong. Experienced arguers bring their readers' questions and objections right into their arguments. They do not ignore their readers or conveniently assume that readers are on their side.

Experienced proposal writers may also acknowledge other solutions. If a writer knows or suspects readers may have alternative solutions in mind, it is better to discuss them directly in the argument. If Samuelson had failed to acknowledge obvious alternative solutions, readers would have regarded him as ill-informed about the problem. A writer can integrate all or part of an alternative solution into his or her own solution, or refute or dismiss the alternative as unworkable.

ANALYZE

1. *Reread* paragraphs 7 and 13, where Samuelson anticipates readers' likely objections and questions. *Underline* the specific objections or questions against which Samuelson seems to be counterarguing. Then *note* in the margin whether he accommodates or refutes the objections and the strategies he uses to do so.

2. *Reread* paragraphs 10 and 11, where Samuelson opposes some popular alternative solutions. *Identify* the alternative solutions. Then *consider* whether Samuelson accommodates or refutes the alternatives and how he goes about doing so.

WRITE

Write a few sentences, explaining how Samuelson counterargues. *Give at least one example* of an objection or question and one example of an alternative solution. Then *write* a few more sentences, evaluating Samuelson's counterarguments. How successfully do you think he handles readers' likely objections or questions? How do you think advocates of alternative solutions Samuelson evaluates would respond to his evaluation?

Establishing Credibility

For an argument to be considered credible by readers, they must find it authoritative, believable, or trustworthy. Readers have many ways of deciding whether an argument is credible. They may already know the writer by reputation. They may have confidence in the magazine or book where the argument is published. Or, they may learn current information about the writer—jobs held, degrees earned, books published, awards won, and so on—from a biographical note published with the reading. The most important basis for readers' judgments about credibility, however, is the argument itself—the attitudes toward readers revealed in the writer's choice of wording and use of sources, the ring of truth in interview quotes and personal experience stories, the step-by-step logic of the argument, the plausibility of reasons, the adequacy of support, and the sensitivity in handling readers' likely questions, objections, and preferred solutions.

ANALYZE

1. *Reread* the biographical note introducing Samuelson's essay. How do the facts given there contribute to the credibility of his argument? What do you know about the publications he has worked for and published in? What more might you want to know?

2. Keeping in mind that you are among the intended readers of Samuelson's argument, *skim* the essay with a focus on assessing the credibility of the writer and his argument. *Note* in the margin your impressions and judgments.

WRITE

Write several sentences, describing the impression you have of Samuelson from both the biographical headnote and his essay. What makes you trust or distrust his argument? *Choose* a few examples from his argument to support your answer.

READINGS

EDWARD J. LOUGHRAN

Prevention of Delinquency

Edward J. Loughran (b. 1939) served as commissioner of the Massachusetts Department of Youth Services from 1985 to 1993. From 1993 to 1996, he directed the National Juvenile Justice Project for the Robert F. Kennedy Memorial in Boston. He is presently executive director of the Council of Juvenile Correctional Administrators and president of Loughran and Associates, a juvenile justice consulting firm. His book Balancing Juvenile Justice, *coauthored with Susan Gorino-Ghezzi, was published in 1995.*

The following proposal was published in Education Week *in 1990, a newspaper read by public and private school administrators, school board members, and state and federal education policymakers. For Loughran, a specialist in youth services, the problem is the increasing number of young people who are jailed (or, as he says, incarcerated or institutionalized) each year. He has in mind a solution that requires early attention to troubled eight- to twelve-year-olds in their homes, schools, and neighborhoods. You will be interested to see the range of specific programs he recommends, one of them involving college students as paid tutors and mentors.*

Loughran begins by contrasting two responses to teenage delinquents: putting them in jail and assigning them to community-based programs. Before you read the essay, recall a sentenced delinquent you know about or remember reading about. What was the crime? What happened to this person? As you read, pay close attention in the early paragraphs to the way Loughran presents the problem and argues for its seriousness.

The National Council on Crime and Delinquency recently reported that the number of young people incarcerated in the United States reached 53,000 last year—the highest number in the nation's history, despite a decline over the last decade in the juvenile population. 1

Many of these youths are placed in large, overcrowded facilities, where physical and sexual abuse and substandard correctional practices are on the rise. Educational and clinical programs in these settings are often ineffective. 2

The study found that young people treated in such institutions had a significantly higher rate of recidivism[1] than 3

---

[1]*recidivism:* a return to delinquent behavior (*Ed.*)

those in community-based, rehabilitative programs. In a comparison between California's institutional system and Massachusetts' community-based program, the council determined that 62 percent of the former state's sample, as opposed to only 23 percent in Massachusetts, were re-incarcerated after leaving a facility.

Most states continue to operate large institutions as their   4
primary response to juvenile crime. But many are now examining the community-based approach as an alternative, for reasons of cost as well as rehabilitation. The shift in focus from correction to prevention that underlies such changes is essential if we are to help those children most likely to become delinquents.

Today's juvenile offenders, reflecting a growing under-   5
class, have a complex profile. They typically are poor and virtually illiterate. Chronic truants or dropouts, they possess no marketable job skills. Many are children of teenage parents, and nearly 50 percent of them have already repeated that cycle. Though years below the legal drinking age, most have serious drug and alcohol problems.

Like most states, Massachusetts has seen a dramatic in-   6
crease in the number of young people coming into its youth-services system. Since 1982, the number of juveniles detained with the youth-services department while awaiting trial has doubled, from 1,500 to 3,044 in 1989. In addition, there were 835 new commitments to the department in 1989—121 more than in the preceding year. Yet these increases come at a time when the juvenile population in the state and in the nation is shrinking. In 1990, there are fewer than 500,000 juveniles in Massachusetts; in 1970, there were 750,000. Even more perplexing, juvenile arraignments on delinquency charges have also dropped significantly in the state, from 25,943 in 1980 to 18,902 in 1989.

These numbers show that something is wrong with   7
the way that juvenile-justice systems, courts, schools, and social-service agencies are addressing the problem of delinquency.

Two primary factors explain the growing numbers of juve-   8
nile offenders. First, there is indeed a rise in serious crime among young people; fueled by the steady stream of drugs and weapons into their hands. These dangerous offenders are committed—legitimately—to juvenile-correction agencies for long-term custody or treatment.

But a second, larger group is also contributing to the in-   9
crease. It consists of 11-, 12-, and 13-year-old first-time offenders who have failed at home, failed in school, and fallen

through the cracks of state and community social-service agencies. These are not serious offenders, or even typical delinquents. But they are coming into the correctional system because we have ignored the warning signs among them.

Each year in Massachusetts, roughly 20,000 youths become involved with the justice system. Although many of them will not receive probation or commitment to the department, each is signaling a need for help. Studies indicate that youths at risk to offend will begin to show signs as early as 2nd or 3rd grade. School failure, child abuse and neglect, drug abuse, and teenage pregnancy may all be indicators of a future involving crime.

Waiting for "problem children" to outgrow negative behavior is a mistake—in most cases, they don't. Unless intensive community supports are developed to improve their school experiences and the quality of life in their families and neighborhoods, as many as one in four American young people—some 7 million youths—are in danger of destroying their opportunities in life.

If we want to interrupt criminal paths and reduce the number of juveniles launching criminal careers, a shift in our priorities is necessary. States must invest their money in delinquency-prevention programs—at the front end rather than the back end of problems. These efforts should be targeted at elementary-school students from poor, high-crime neighborhoods, where traditional avenues to success are blocked.

For youths appearing in court on petty larceny or trespassing charges, we should develop restitution programs or innovative alternatives to costly lockups. Young people will learn something positive from a work assignment in the community, but not from 15 days' incarceration spent rubbing shoulders with more sophisticated offenders. And—at a time when correction resources are scarce—states will spend less money, gaining a greater return on investment.

Our department spends an average of $60,000 a year on each of its most serious offenders; much needs to be done in a short period of time to change behavior reinforced over many years. Less serious offenders are placed in group homes, at half the cost of secure facilities. For the least serious offenders, we operate day-treatment and outreach and tracking programs, which annually cost between $9,000 and $15,000 per youth. All of these programs include intensive educational and clinical components tailored to the individual.

The cost of constructing a 30-bed secure facility for juvenile offenders in Massachusetts is approximately $6 million

dollars; annual operating expenses are $1.8 million. A delin-
quency-prevention program costs about $10,000 per year.

The efforts of youth-services departments must necessar-   16
ily remain accountable for public safety. But the juvenile-
justice system should join together with local schools and
social-service and religious organizations to implement prevention and intervention strategies such as the following:

- *Home-builders:* Dispatch workers to the homes of children   17
  who have been abused, neglected, or recently released
  from a juvenile-detention program. Keep workers in homes
  at times of high stress: early in the morning, when the children might resist leaving for school, and after school, to supervise homework and nightly curfews. The annual cost for
  1 worker to supervise 1 family is $4,000, with each worker
  responsible for 4 to 5 families.
- *Mentors:* Assign a teaching assistant or college student to   18
  work with youths who are beginning to fail in school.
  Mentors would serve as adult companions, helping children with homework and supervising them during after-
  school hours. The annual cost of 1 mentor working with 4
  youngsters is $8,500. Public schools should employ stu-
  dents from local colleges or citizens in the community as
  part-time mentors.
- *Restitution:* Establish a plan whereby youths are assigned a   19
  community service or job to reimburse their victims, as
  well as serve justice and instill a sense of accountability in
  the offenders. A restitution program would also introduce
  a young offender to the world of work.
- *Streetworkers:* More and more 8- to 12-year-olds are being   20
  swept up in the excitement and status that accompany
  gang membership and urban violence. To counter the influence of gang leaders and reduce incidents of violence
  among these youngsters, hire full-time "streetworkers"—
  residents of the target areas who are street savvy and
  who want change in their neighborhood. Estimated cost
  is $8,000 per youth.
- *After-school employment:* Arrange for local businesses to hire   21
  high-school students as paid interns to work with a designated professional and learn a particular aspect of business. This would not only expose youths to professional
  opportunities but also provide positive role models. These
  private-public ventures could be overseen by community
  and state agencies, and by the larger businesses.

There are many other possibilities. The important thing is   22
to begin reaching kids sooner. We must refocus our efforts

from correcting the problem after the crime to creating alternatives that prevent the crime—not only in the interest of dollars but also for the sake of lives.

READING FOR MEANING

Write to create meanings for Loughran's proposal for a community-based approach to reducing juvenile crime.

START MAKING MEANING

Begin by listing the advantages that Loughran attributes to his solution (paragraphs 12–15). Continue by writing about anything else in the essay or in your experience that contributes to your understanding of Loughran's proposal.

IF YOU ARE STUCK

If you cannot write at least a page, consider writing about

- Loughran's argument that young "problem children" need special help (paragraphs 9–11).

- the one activity among those outlined in paragraphs 17–21 that you would most like to participate in, describing its possibilities and explaining why it appeals to you.

- the unstated assumptions in Loughran's argument, one example being that the state should be responsible for preventing delinquency.

- a personal experience (or that of a friend or family member) with the juvenile justice system, describing what happened and evaluating it in light of Loughran's recommendations.

READING LIKE A WRITER
INTRODUCING THE PROBLEM

In introducing the problem, writers may define or describe it as well as argue for its seriousness. Depending on their purpose and readers, writers must decide whether they need to identify the problem briefly (as Samuelson does) or introduce it at some length. In the latter case, they may present its history and speculate about its causes. Loughran devotes a relatively large portion of his proposal to introducing the problem.

ANALYZE

1. *Reread* paragraphs 8–11, a key part of Loughran's introduction of the problem. *Annotate* each paragraph with a phrase or two identifying

its topic or purpose. *Notice* the contrast Loughran sets up in paragraphs 8 and 9.

2. *Analyze* how, in paragraphs 8–11, Loughran establishes the importance or significance of helping especially young offenders. *Note* the statements and evidence he gives that demonstrate the importance of helping young offenders.

WRITE

Write several sentences, describing how Loughran introduces the problem and emphasizes its importance in these paragraphs. What strategies and kinds of evidence does he use? *Give details* from the reading to support your answer. *Conclude* with a few sentences evaluating Loughran's presentation of the problem. Given his purpose and readers, how successful do you find his argument? Which parts do you find most convincing? Least convincing?

CONSIDERING IDEAS FOR YOUR OWN WRITING

What social problems in your community might you write about authoritatively? There may be large social issues about which you are aware—homelessness, for example—but until you talk with homeless people or interview local authorities working with them, you will not have a real knowledge base from which to write about this problem. Through interviews and observation you can learn about the *local* problem that homeless people encounter or pose for the community, thus bringing a general problem into tighter focus.

Another social issue of local implications would be the needs of a minority group within a community or college that are not being fully met. Yet another topic to consider is the lack of accessible, affordable child care for children of college students or working parents. Although this problem is national in scope, it too can only be solved locally—campus by campus, business by business, neighborhood by neighborhood. You would want to start by talking with people who experience the problem in order to enlarge your understanding of it. Then you might interview two or three people who have access to adequate child care. They can help you think about alternative solutions. You might address your proposal to the campus president, the chief executive officer of a business, or a neighborhood minister with an underutilized church building.

With these examples in mind, talk with your instructor and other students about other social problems that have unique local aspects or that can only be solved locally.

JOHN BEILENSON

Giving the Young a Voice in National Service Programs

John Beilenson (b. 1962) is a writer who produces public relations materials and develops communications strategies for various organizations. He is founder and director of the Youth Voice Project in Chapel Hill, North Carolina, which aims to give young people a greater role in decision making in organizations set up to serve them. His books include Sukarno: Indonesia's Revolutionary *(1989),* Educating the Whole Child *(1993), and* The Book of Coffee *(1995).*

The following proposal appeared in 1993 in the journal Social Policy, *read by academic social scientists and by federal and state policymakers. In 1994, with President Clinton's encouragement, Congress established the National Service Corporation, a volunteer service program for young people that is in many ways a domestic version of the popular international Peace Corps program launched by President Kennedy in the 1960s. Beilenson proposes to give the volunteers in Clinton's program a more important role in planning, administering, and evaluating local projects as well as in setting national policy.*

Before reading the essay, reflect for a moment on any volunteer work you have done. How big was the organization for which you worked, and what were its goals? Who was in charge? What role, if any, did you and other volunteers have in the operation of the program and in monitoring its success? As you read, note that Beilenson directly addresses the national and local adult administrators of the National Service Corporation as his readers.

Where are the young people?   1

This is the question I find myself asking as I make my way   2
around the offices of national and community service programs in Washington and across the country. I have worked in and for youth service and youth serving organizations since 1985, so I have few illusions. Offices are for adults. If you want to find the youth in youth service, you generally have to get out to project sites—schools and playgrounds and parks—where young people are actually doing service.

Some of the offices of the top programs around the country,   3
however, have a significantly more youthful ambiance. Young people are in the office for training sessions and meetings. They are helping with the administrative work or waiting to travel with staff to a funding or press meeting. It is

not your typical work environment. It is noisier, more dynamic. You can almost hear what many call "youth voice"— young people involved in planning the fundamentals of community service programs. . . .

WAYS TO INCLUDE YOUTH VOICE

In the rush to make application deadlines, it is easy to   4
consult only the people who are in the office. Programs and planners must resist this expediency and make deliberate and ongoing efforts to listen to young people—their ideas, their hopes and fears, and their expert knowledge of their peers. It's not always easy, but it is far from an insurmountable goal. Here are some basic ways to do it.

1. Put young people on the team. The easiest way to get   5
youth voice heard on the national level is to include young people in all upper-level planning meetings and groups for the burgeoning National Service Corporation.[1] The over-30 crowd, wary of letting inexperienced young people into the process, need not worry. Groups of young people— many with their own programs—are well-versed and well-prepared to present some of the best thinking in the field. One need only look as far as Young People for National Service, Youth Service America's Youth Action Council, the Points of Light Foundation's Youth Engaged in Service (YES) Ambassadors,[2] or the Participant Council developed during Summer of Service to find fistfuls of qualified young advisers.

2. Bring young people on the board. The National Service   6
Corporation should also appoint a significant number of young people (ages 16 to 25)—as many as four—to its planned 14-member board. This will ensure that young people have a meaningful role in the board decision-making that will take place in the coming months and years. Again, these need not be "token" appointments. Some recent college graduates involved in service have almost a decade of experience in the field. Young people's presence on this highly visible national board, as well as on state commissions on national and community service, sends an important message to young people

[1]*National Service Corporation:* an initiative of the Clinton administration begun in 1994, now called the Corporation for National and Community Service or AmeriCorps (*Ed.*)

[2]*Young People for National Service:* a lobbying group that pushed for passage of the National Service Act of 1993; *Youth Service America* was founded in 1985 by the Ford Foundation to advocate a variety of youth service programs; *Youth Engaged in Service* was one of the Points of Light volunteer organizations recognized by the Bush administration to promote community service (*Ed.*)

that their concerns are important and, through their representatives, their issues can be raised.

3. Get out of the office. National, state and local planners should also get out into the field to hear what community service program participants are saying and suggesting. PennSERVE, Pennsylvania's state office of volunteerism, has developed "speakouts," where administrators and board members travel to different communities to listen to what young people and adults in the field have to say. These "hearings" are informal and interactive and create a "safe" environment for young people to talk frankly with adults. Young people might well be hired to do this research themselves.

7

4. Create youth forums. Another way planners can get the feedback required to ensure their ideas meet the needs and inspire the hopes of young people is to fund and create national, state and local youth advisory councils. Many states—including Michigan, California, Maryland, and Ohio—have already formed these 15- to 25-member bodies that meet quarterly. Some point to the danger of marginalizing youth voice by locating it simply in these groups. Real decision-makers, the argument goes, can then more easily ignore youth input. From what I've seen, these councils are widely effective. They provide sound advice for service planners, but also train young people to participate in other local, state, and national forums around service—including state commissions and non-profit boards of directors.

8

The strength of youth advisory councils is that they create a sanctioned space for talented young people to think and act together, to gain a sense of their own power. Once involved on this kind of a state platform, they become savvy political players and articulate spokespeople.

9

5. Let young people decide. Finally, the Corporation, as well as state and local groups planning service initiatives, can ask young people to read and review grant and other proposals. The success of numerous mini-grant programs run entirely by young people (such as the scores now operating in Michigan under the aegis of the Michigan Council of Foundations) speaks to young people's proven seriousness and fiscal responsibility. Unused to throwing money at problems, young people gravitate to practical, low-cost alternatives that nevertheless meet their needs.

10

HOW YOUTH VOICE HELPS

Serious inclusion of youth voice in the national and community service initiatives will go a long way toward improving service programs. The stress and routine of young

11

people's lives are largely known only by young people themselves. Even team leaders, teachers, and community service staffers are a step removed. One junior high school program in Washington state, for example, foundered until *the students* pointed out that few could participate because after-school buses were not available. When City Year in Boston changed its year-round program to a nine-month one, adult planners intended to start the program in January and end in September, until a young corps member argued that it would be far better to coordinate with the school year, to start in September and end in June. Teach for America built in more training and support mechanisms for its teachers after listening to its first year of recruits, who found their teaching environments much tougher than expected. Aspects of day-to-day life that escape over-30 planners in a central office may seem obvious to young people, and can make all the difference in whether a program works. How can we succeed in providing meaningful service experiences for young people—and good services to the community—if we are not continually asking young people, "Does this make sense to you? Will this work?"

Making sure youth voice is heard at the policy level has a double benefit. On the one hand, it helps insure getting better programs. On the other, it gives young people an opportunity to take on leadership roles they otherwise have few opportunities to attain. At its best, national service can be a rite of passage in a society with few constructive routes into adulthood. Service, however, can only play this role if young people are challenged in work that builds skills and offers increasing amounts of responsibility. Though menial tasks may be part of the package when it is necessary to get a job done, national service should not be menial. Asking young people—working in a corps team, for example—to plan out their work each day, to take turns serving as a site leader, and to spend time investigating the impact their service is having on the community—distinguishes the service experience from entry-level jobs that demand little responsibility and allow no autonomy. 12

To reach its transformative potential, service must ultimately give young people an opportunity to act on their own ideas. Throughout our society and our educational system, young people are expected to follow along, to sit passively while a teacher or perhaps even Beavis and Butthead inform them about how the world works. Service gets young people off the couch, but may unwittingly reinstate societal codes that expect young people simply to follow orders. National service, of course, can do much better. 13

There are models of good, individual placement programs—like Southern Community Partners, for example—that allow young people to propose, start, and then run their own community initiative. Some may argue that this kind of fellowship is suitable only for an elite few, but even individual placements set in community agencies (like those proposed as a national service option) could well provide an analogous opportunity, where a young person might spend his or her second six months working on a self-designed project. When young people get this kind of a chance, they take responsibility for their successes and failures, and learn about the complexities decision-making involves. In short, they learn a little of what it's like to be an adult in our culture today. 14

Seeking out young people's ideas and involving them in the planning and decision-making of national service should be part of a larger process of seeking out and valuing important information and informants that mainstream culture and government planners often ignore. While adult society generally disregards young people, we must ask for their ideas on national service because young people know young people best. . . . 15

John Bell at YouthBuild USA[3] has described extensively the "adultism" in American society—adults' systematic mistreatment of young people simply because of their age. In YouthBuild's *Leadership Development* handbook, Bell argues that with the exception of prisoners, "young people's lives are more controlled than any other group in society." Adults tell young people when to eat, go to bed, go to school, and talk. They "reserve the right to punish, threaten, hit, take away 'privileges,' and ostracize young people," says Bell, all in the name of "discipline." Institutions, in particular school, reinforce this mistreatment, enabling young people to accept others evaluating their work, performance, thinking, and ultimately themselves. From "adultism," young people learn two important lessons—first, that it is all right to be disrespected, and second, that it is all right to disrespect others. 16

Of course, not all adults are "adultist." But all young people, Bell argues, are disrespected in some form or another. I highlight this analysis because it suggests an important role for the service initiatives. National and community service programs that encourage respectful youth-adult 17

---

[3]*YouthBuild USA:* a Boston organization that helps low-income youth learn carpentry and other skills to rehabilitate housing, noted for its strong leadership development program (*Ed.*)

partnerships, that encourage youth voice, can help to combat "adultism." Service programs can be safe places where young people are listened to, where their ideas are respected and acted upon, where decisions about them are made with them.

Creating these kinds of programs is not easy. It is not as simple as adults simply handing over all responsibility to young people. Nor is it simply using a young person on a board as "window dressing" to demonstrate a commitment to young people. Rather, it involves finding a middle ground. Adults must make the space for young people to take an active and engaged role in their service experience; in turn, young people must respect adults' skills and resources. Adults must provide enough support that young people have a chance to succeed, but not so much that their freedom to test out their ideas is too constrained or even too safe. Young people, in turn, must take their work seriously and commit to the ongoing effort success demands. Building youth voice into national and community service programs is a process that takes time and an unyielding belief in the potential of young people. It is worth the effort.

18

READING FOR MEANING

Write to create meanings for Beilenson's proposal to increase the participation of young people in the administration of youth programs.

START MAKING MEANING

Begin by listing the five aspects of the solution that Beilenson outlines in paragraphs 5–10. For each aspect, include at least one benefit Beilenson claims for it. Continue by writing about anything else in the essay or in your experience that contributes to your understanding of Beilenson's proposal.

IF YOU ARE STUCK

If you cannot write a least a page, consider writing about

- the main benefits Beilenson claims for his proposal (paragraphs 12–15), listing them and commenting on one or two of them.

- the concept of "adultism" (paragraphs 15 and 16), describing it and evaluating its usefulness for understanding adult behavior.

- why you think Beilenson, writing in his mid-thirties, seems in touch or out of touch with young volunteers in their late teens and early twenties.

- your personal experience as a volunteer in a school, community, religious group, or national program, describing what you did and connecting your experience to Beilenson's proposal.

A SPECIAL READING STRATEGY

Judging the Writer's Credibility

This special reading strategy consists of judging how writers establish credibility. A credible argument is one that seems to its readers authoritative, believable, and trustworthy. Readers rely on many sources of information in the text of the argument itself to determine whether the reading is credible. For detailed guidelines on how to judge the credibility of a writer's argument, see Appendix One (p. 481).

READING LIKE A WRITER
PRESENTING THE SOLUTION

Convincing managers of any organization—including youth programs—to make fundamental changes in their policies or practices is a daunting task for a proposal writer. Presenting the solution so that it speaks to managers in their own terms is one key to success. Being practical is another. Managers must understand how the solution would be implemented. They need to imagine how life would be different for themselves and all others in the organization after the solution is in place. Their basic concerns and anxieties must be allayed. Because Beilenson devotes considerable space to presenting the solution (and almost as much space arguing for it), it will be worthwhile analyzing how he presents the solution.

ANALYZE

1. *Reread* paragraphs 5, 7, and 10, annotating three different kinds of information about how the solution could be implemented: (a) specific actions that can be taken, including cost considerations, (b) examples of programs that have implemented a solution, and (c) gains to be made by adopting Beilenson's solution.

2. *Evaluate* Beilenson's success, in paragraphs 5, 7, and 10, in presenting the solution to National Service Corporation managers. Assuming you have observed several adult managers—teachers, coaches, school administrators, ministers or rabbis, bosses at work—you can fairly assess what would be convincing to them. (You may even have super-

vised younger people.) Where does Beilenson seem most successful? Least successful?

WRITE

Write several sentences, explaining how Beilenson presents the solution in paragraphs 5, 7, and 10. *Include* specific examples from these paragraphs. Also, briefly *evaluate* the success of Beilenson's presentation.

CONSIDERING IDEAS FOR YOUR OWN WRITING

Beilenson's example suggests a type of proposal you might want to consider for your essay—the proposal to improve the functioning of a goal-directed organization such as a sports team, business, or public institution (small-claims court, traffic offenders' school, welfare office, recreation center, or school). You could propose a solution to a problem in an institution in which you participated regularly or one in which you had a single disappointing experience. Your goal is not to ridicule or complain, but to attempt to bring about change that would make the organization more humane, efficient, productive, or successful in fulfilling its goals. Do not limit yourself to your own experience. Seek out former and current members who experienced problems like yours. They can help you understand the problem in a deeper way and refine your presentation of a solution and your argument for it.

Or you could follow Beilenson's example by choosing a problem that involves misunderstandings, a lack of communication, or wide gaps in experience between two groups. There is a wide range of groups to choose from: leaders and followers, workers and bosses, novices and professionals, full timers and part timers, educated and uneducated, powerful and powerless, insiders and outsiders, native speakers and second-language learners, experienced and inexperienced, instructors and learners, women and men, managers and managed. Your proposal could be aimed at either half of one of these pairs. Avoid simply complaining or expressing resentment. You want to make a reasoned argument for a solution that promises to bring about significant, lasting change.

ROB RYDER

10 Is a Crowd, So Change the Game

Rob Ryder writes screenplays and directs movies. Because of his experience playing and coaching basketball, he has served as an adviser on several recent hoop-related movies.

Ryder's proposal to turn basketball into an eight-player game was published in 1998, in the New York Times *sports section. His style is informal, like that of a sports announcer at work. The sentences and paragraphs tend to be short, and the words are familiar ones, except for a few technical terms from basketball. Ryder mentions several professional basketball players and coaches, but you need not recognize them or know much about the game to follow his proposal. Your experience with any sport will help you understand Ryder's attempt to make basketball a more challenging and entertaining game.*

Along with about a billion other people on this planet, I've had a lifelong love affair with basketball. I've known the game as a player (Princeton), as a coach (Hollywood Y.M.C.A. 5- to 8-year-olds), and as a basketball supervisor for the movies (*White Men Can't Jump, Blue Chips,* and *Eddie* among others). 1

So, it is with deep regret that I must finally go public with the truth: Basketball is a mess. A muddled, boring, chaotic, overcrowded, utterly predictable game of slapping, clawing, double and triple-teaming, endless stoppages, timeouts, whistles, whining, and countless trips to the free-throw line where players continue to stupefy us with their ineptitude. 2

Yet the game is still punctuated by enough moments of pure poetry, grace, power and creativity to keep us coming back for more. 3

So, now that we can admit the game is flawed, let's fix it. 4

I'm not tinkering here—this is no "raise the rim," "widen the lane" Band-Aid I'm proposing. Rather, I'm going straight to the heart of the problem. It's just too crowded out there. Basketball is meant to be played four on four. 5

Too radical? You're forgetting your American heritage. It's our game. We invented it; we can change it if we want to. (I'm sure there was a lot of groaning when the forward pass was introduced to football.) 6

When I ran the concept of four-on-four basketball, or 8-Ball, by Doc Rivers during the filming of *Eddie,* his eyes lighted up. 7

"Guards would rule," he said. Not necessarily, but we'll   8
get to that later. Working on another movie, *The Sixth Man,* I
proposed the change to Jerry Tarkanian, who replied: "I've
been saying that for years. I've been saying that for years."
When I asked Marty Blake, the crusty old N.B.A. war horse,
he responded, "What, are you nuts?"

Yeah. And so was James Naismith. The man almost got it   9
right. But how many realize that in the old days, there was a
jump ball after every basket scored? Or that teams were allowed to hold the ball indefinitely? Or that there wasn't always a 3-point shot?

The new game will be a lean, sleek, fluid game—domi-   10
nated by high-flying superbly coordinated athletes, with no
room for defensive ends. Charles Oakley, I love your work
ethic, but you're going to have trouble keeping up.

Kobe Bryant, Tim Duncan, Keith Van Horn, Ray Allen, the   11
future is yours.

Lisa Leslie, Teresa Edwards, Venus Lacey, you too will   12
love 8-Ball. As will all the little kids out there whose Saturday
morning games often resemble two swarms of bees fighting
over a Rollo.

Remember the pick-and-roll?—now it's more commonly   13
known as the pick-and-collide-into-two-defenders-coming-
from-the-weak-side. In 8-Ball, the pick-and-roll will rule. Help
from the weak side leaves the defense much more vulnerable without the fifth defender there to rotate over the
passing lane.

The old back-door play (which only Princeton seems to   14
pull off regularly these days) will be back. Only now, there
will be a cleaner path to the basket. Defenders, deny your
man the ball at your own peril.

But what about Doc Rivers's comment that guards would   15
rule playing four on four? Tell that to Hakeem Olajuwon, who
cannot only run the floor but will now also have enough
room for this dazzling array of post-up moves.

You see, everybody wins: The big men will finally have   16
some space, the shooters will get plenty of open looks from
the 3-point line, and the slashers, like Eddie Jones, should
have a field day with one fewer defender out there to clog
the lane.

So just what are we sacrificing by going to four on four?   17

Well, the lumbering big man will go the way of the dinosaur.   18
Sorry, George Mhuresan, but no one's going to cover for you
when your man releases and beats you downcourt. A four on
three is infinitely tougher to defend than a five on four.

And for you little guys, if you can't shoot, you're a liability.   19

There'll be a lot less room for the role player out there be-   20
cause 8-Ball will demand that every player on the floor polish his or her overall skills.

So where's the downside? Nolan Richardson knows—as   21
Arkansas' 94-feet-of-hell amoeba defense will be reduced to a
quick detour through purgatory. It'll be a lot tougher to
press full court with only four defenders. Any good ball-
handler will be able to break the press, and this will definitely hurt the college and high school game.

For the pros, it's a moot point—full-court pressure disap-   22
peared years ago. Even Rick Pitino's on his way to discovering how tough it is to ask pro athletes to press full court
over an 82-game season.

But will this mean a reduction of the 12-man roster, re-   23
duced playing time and howls from the N.B.A. Players'
Association?

Not at all, for two reasons. One, 8-Ball will be a running   24
game, and in some ways may adopt the more exciting characteristics of hockey (yes, hockey). Coaches may actually
find themselves injecting four new players into a game simultaneously (a line change)—a nifty way to ratchet up the
action while giving your starters a rest.

And secondly, in the world of 8-Ball, the time of game will   25
expand; in the pros, from 48 to 60 minutes. But how do you
keep these games from running over three hours?

In 8-Ball, the time wasted on stupor-inducing foul shoot-   26
ing will be reduced by two-thirds, allowing for extra minutes
of real action. Whenever a player is fouled but not in the act
of shooting, his team automatically gets the ball out of
bounds. When fouled in the act of shooting, a player gets
one free throw worth 2 points or 3 points, depending on the
shot he was taking. But in both cases, the offensive team
gets the option of skipping the foul line and taking the ball
out of bounds.

This will eliminate the ugly strategy of intentional fouling,   27
choke-induced shooting and subhuman fan behavior all in
one easy stroke.

A good basketball game is about rhythm, and 8-Ball will   28
flow.

The substitutions will make for marvelous matchups.   29
We'll see more fast breaks, cleaner inside moves, purer
shooting, more offensive rebounding, fewer turnovers, a lot
less standing around, more minutes of actual action, and
more scoring.

Plus, 8-Ball would bring forth the elimination of what must   30
be the stupidest addition to N.B.A. rules: the illegal defense

violation. Just try playing a four-man zone in 8-Ball. It'll turn
to a man-to-man real fast.

There it is, 8-Ball. Is there any realistic chance that the   31
N.C.A.A. or the N.B.A. will change over to four on four?
"Never happen," Dick Vitale answered.

That's why a group of former Princeton players is launch-   32
ing a professional basketball league—the "8BL." Look for it
in '99 following a televised exhibition this fall. In the meantime, all you rec league and intramural players out there—
with your smaller courts and running clocks and purists'
love for the game—8-Ball's for you, too. Show us the way.

READING FOR MEANING

Write to create meanings for Ryder's proposal to make basketball a
game with eight players.

START MAKING MEANING

Begin by explaining the problem Ryder has with current-day basketball, listing a few of the changes he envisions (paragraphs 10–16, 21, 24,
25, and 29). Continue by writing about anything else in the essay or
in your experience that contributes to your understanding of Ryder's
proposal.

IF YOU ARE STUCK

If you cannot write at least a page, consider writing about

- Ryder's point that the rules in professional sports do change and can
  be changed further (paragraph 6).

- the changes you imagine in eight-player basketball beyond those
  mentioned by Ryder.

- change you would like to see in some established sport, relating the
  change to the one Ryder proposes.

- how your personal experience of playing or watching basketball contributes to your understanding of Ryder's proposal.

READING LIKE A WRITER
COUNTERARGUING

Because proposal writers want their readers to accept their proposed
solutions and sometimes even take action to help implement them, they
must make an extraordinary effort to anticipate their readers' objections

and questions. This task is a major part of what is known as *counterarguing*. From trying out his proposal on several basketball experts (see paragraphs 7, 8, and 31), Ryder knows that some readers will resist it. In recognizing that he is "not tinkering" but proposing a substantial change, he assumes that most readers will at least be startled by his proposal, raising many questions if not also objections. In fact, the first question he anticipates—"Too radical?" (paragraph 6)—confirms that he knows his proposal will be a hard sell. Consequently, Ryder devotes a large part of his essay to counterargument. The following activity will guide you in analyzing his approach. It will also prepare you for counterarguing convincingly in your own proposal.

ANALYZE

1. *Reread* paragraphs 17, 21, 23, and 25, and *underline* the four readers' questions Ryder mentions in order to counterargue. *Choose* two of these questions and counterarguments to analyze closely.

2. *Notice* that Ryder answers the questions by countering them with the advantages of his proposal. For the two questions you have chosen, *underline* the specific advantages to the game he mentions in an attempt to allay readers' concerns.

3. *Evaluate* how successfully Ryder answers the two questions you have chosen. Does he offer enough advantages to the game to make his answer convincing? Which answer seems more convincing and why? What other questions do you have that Ryder overlooks?

WRITE

Write several sentences, explaining how Ryder anticipates and responds to readers' questions. *Cite* examples from the reading. Then *add* a few sentences, describing how successful you find Ryder's answers to the two questions you focused on in your analysis.

CONSIDERING IDEAS FOR YOUR OWN WRITING

Following Ryder's lead, consider proposing a way to improve a popular sport. Your idea need not revolutionize the sport, though it might. Or it could offer only a small refinement such as changing a rule or adding a feature to the game. (Recent developments such as the designated hitter in baseball and instant replays to resolve disputed official calls in football were originally subjects of proposals.) Your proposal could seek to improve the safety of the game for participants, the way records are kept, the way athletes are recruited into the sport, the way athletes are treated, or the entertainment value of the game to spectators. You could focus on either a professional or amateur sport, a team sport or individual competition, high school or college teams, or the National Hockey League. You could address your proposal to players, officials, fans, or the general public.

Another idea for writing is to identify a problem that needs to be solved in some activity or enterprise that everyone seems to think is working nearly perfectly, that no one seems to be questioning, or that people would initially strongly resist changing in any way. Capture readers' interest, as Ryder does, by announcing to readers that an activity as widely—and wildly—popular as playing basketball could be improved. Such a proposal would be in the respected American tradition of debunking authorities. Possible topics include the convention of taking honeymoons after a wedding, commuting to work or school by car, the institution of small-claims court, food or service at the most popular place to eat on or near campus, or the youth program at a local church.

BILL McKIBBEN

Curbing Nature's Paparazzi

Bill (William E.) McKibben (b. 1960) is a staff writer for
the New Yorker *magazine, where he served as an editor
from 1983 to 1987. His book* The End of Nature *(1989) argues that global warming will create an ecological disaster.
Known as an environmental writer, McKibben has also written a book about families,* Maybe One: A Personal and Environmental Argument for Single-Child Families *(1998).*

The following essay appeared in a 1997 issue of
Harper's Magazine, *a monthly magazine that has published
fiction and journalism since 1850. In the title McKibben al-
ludes to the paparazzi—free-lance photographers who aggressively pursue celebrities—who made headline news in
1997 because of the death of Britain's Princess Diana. Many
people blame the paparazzi for the car accident that caused
her death.*

*McKibben's particular concern is with the impact of na-
ture photographers on the ecosystem and on people's perceptions of nature. He believes the photographing of nature
and the system of publishing the photographs must be
changed, and he offers a specific proposal that he admits
will be hard to implement. His proposal requires "a new
ethic," he says, a new set of beliefs and reformed behavior.
As you read the essay, focus on understanding the problem
as McKibben sees it and on the solution he proposes.*

The art of wildlife photography employs quite a few   1
people scattered around the country. Filmmakers supply
hour upon hour of video for PBS, the major networks, and
cable channels. Still photographers take pictures for magazines, calendars, books, and advertisements, and they market countless trips for amateurs and aspiring professionals,
teaching them the tricks of the trade. Their images do a lot
of good: from Flipper and Jacques Cousteau to the mountain
lion nuzzling her kit on your latest mailing from an environmental group, they've helped change how we see the wild.
I've seen neighbors of mine, who had no use for wolves,
begin to melt during a slide show about the creatures. It is
no great exaggeration to say that dolphin-safe tuna flows directly from the barrel of a Canon, that without Kodak there'd
be no Endangered Species Act.

But it's not a completely benign enterprise. In the wild,   2
photographers often need to subtly harass wildlife to get
their shots: to camp near watering holes, say, where their
very presence may unnerve and scatter creatures. Worse,

and less recognized, is a sort of conceptual problem. After a lifetime of exposure to nature shows and magazine photos, we arrive at the woods conditioned to expect splendor and are surprised when the parking lot does not contain a snarl of animals mating and killing one another. Because the only images we see are close-ups, we've lost much of our sense of the calm and quotidian beauty of the natural world, of the fact that animals are usually preoccupied with hiding or wandering around looking for food.

There is something frankly pornographic about the animal horror videos (*Fangs!*) marketed on late-night TV, and even about some of the shots you see in something as staid as *Natural History* magazine. Here is an emerald boa eating a parrot—the odds, according to the photographers I talked to, were "jillions to one" that it was a wild shot. Indeed, the photographer who took it boasted to *People* magazine about how, in order to get other dramatic shots, he'd spray-painted ferrets to convert them to the endangered black-footed kind, and how he'd hoisted tame and declawed jaguars into tree branches for good shots, and starved piranhas so that they would attack with great ferocity. Another photographer took a game stab at defending the shot of the emerald boa munching the parrot: "It very graphically illustrates the relationship between higher and lower vertebrates," he said. So it does, but that's a little like saying that Miss September graphically illustrates the development of the mammary gland in *Homo sapiens.*

Even worse, perhaps, is the way the constant flow of images undercuts the sense that there's actually something wrong with the world. How can there really be a shortage of whooping cranes when you've seen a thousand images of them, seen ten times more images than there are actually whooping cranes left in the wild? We're rarely shown a photograph of the empty trees where there are no baboons anymore; whatever few baboons remain are dutifully pursued until they're captured on film, and even if all the captions are about their horrid plight, the essential message of the picture remains: baboons.

At this point we could—indeed we should—start talking about a new ethic. People have tried, from time to time, to promulgate ethics for most of the arts, and nature photography is no exception. Photographer Daniel Dancer, writing recently in *Wild Earth* magazine, suggested using photos for advocacy purposes—shooting the clear-cut next to the forest, for instance. One editor envisions sending a photographer out to document, say, the hour-by-hour life of a snake rather than a young grizzly striking poses at a game farm. Reading and talking to such thinkers, though, it's easy to find a note of resignation—the deep suspicion that such rhetoric is not going to affect very quickly or very profoundly the marketplace in which photographers operate.

"A big problem we see is an editor who says, 'I want this 6 kind of picture,' and then the word gets out," says Chuck Jonkel of the Wildlife Film Festival. "Editors will say, 'Give us a picture of a caribou running full tilt, and we'll give you $1,700.' Someone's going to hire a helicopter and run the shit out of the caribou to get that $1,700. I don't blame the photographer for that—I blame the editors." If one photographer or editor falters, chances are that there will be another to take his place. Dancer offers the wise advice of Wendell Berry that "one must begin in one's own life the private solutions that can only in turn become public solutions." That is so. But my work on environmental issues has made me wary of completely private solutions, for the momentum of our various tragedies makes the slow conversion of small parts of the society insufficient. Aren't we ethically impelled to also try to imagine ways that such private solutions might turn into public and widespread practice?

It's precisely for that reason that wildlife photography in- 7 terests me so much. It's a small enough world that, at least for purposes of argument, you could postulate real changes. Suppose the eight or nine magazines that run most of the nature photos and the three or four top TV nature shows formed among them a cooperative, or clearinghouse, for wildlife images and announced that, up to a certain date, anyone could mail them as many slides or reels of film as they wished. *And after that date they wouldn't take any new submissions.* Then, when the editors of *Natural History* decided they needed some elephant photos, the staff of the cooperative agency could send over a wide array to choose from. For the fact is, there are already plenty of elephant photos in the world (when *Wildlife Conservation Magazine* was planning a piece on elephants a few years ago, its editors reviewed ten thousand slides). And since most of the competing magazines and TV shows would belong to the cooperative, commercial pressure might diminish; no one else would have a two-inch-away close-up of the golden tamarind monkey either.

If some member of the consortium had a good reason for 8 needing a new picture—if there were a new species or a new behavior that needed illustrating, or someone was needed to accompany a scientific expedition—then the cooperative could assign a photographer, along with strict instructions about conduct: about, say, how far away to stay from the animals. These measures might solve some of the ethical problems surrounding the industry's treatment of animals. It's also possible that such a cooperative agency could eventually begin to deal with the larger questions—for instance, over time, it could cull from its stock extreme close-ups and other kinds of photos that miseducate viewers about the natural world. It's the kind of place where a new ethic might *adhere,* might grow into something powerful.

Imagining institutions allows you to test the strength of   9
the ethic on which they're based against very real and practical objections. In this case, the most obvious drawback is that the cooperative would put photographers out of work or force them to find new subjects, for if the agency worked as planned, it would need very few new wildlife photos annually. This potential clearinghouse for wildlife photos would announce, in effect: "We've got enough images now; we can recycle them more or less forever; please don't bother taking any more." And since negatives don't really degrade with use, that would be that. But this, we intuitively feel, is not fair. Who am I, or you, to tell someone else how he can or can't make a living?

It is an almost unknown thing in our society to say,   10
"That's enough." And it sounds especially heretical in any creative endeavor. The word "censorship" rises unbidden to one's lips. And even if you can convince yourself that it's not really censorship (it's not the government, after all; it's no more than some magazine telling you that it won't print your story for whatever damn reason; it's editing), even so, it seems repressive. It *is* repressive. It's the imposition of a new taboo. Consumers aren't supposed to have taboos; they're supposed to consume. And consume we do: not just goods and services but images, ideas, knowledge. Nothing is off-limits. So there's something a little creepy about saying, "We'll be buying no new photos of wildebeests. We don't think it's a good idea to be taking them." Do we really want any new taboos?

As I've become more interested in environmental matters,   11
I've thought a lot about these questions of restraint—about when one's curiosity or creative impulse can be bane as well as boon, about whether there are places where taboos once more make sense. The answers are easier to see when the questions concern things, not ideas. Clearly, for instance, we'd be better off environmentally if as a culture we frowned

on automobiles, if we said that the freedom they afforded was not worth the cost in terms of global warming, suburban sprawl, and so forth. And a taboo against the next, ever-larger version of the Ford Explorer, even if it somehow developed, wouldn't seem a real threat to the human spirit.

But the debate about limiting ideas is one we're incapable   12
of having, because we operate under the assumption that the limitation of creativity is repellent. We take as a given that we should find out everything we can, develop everything we can, photograph and write about everything we can, and then let the marketplace decide what to do with it. By definition, therefore, if it sells it is good. If we can clone animals, say, then we will; to suggest otherwise is to stand against not only free enterprise but also the free imagination. But in our blind defense of these things that seem "right," we may be short-circuiting the process of thinking things through as a culture, leaving ourselves no way to entertain the possibility of restraint.

And yet self-restraint is a uniquely human capacity, belong-   13
ing as exclusively to us as flight belongs to the birds. It's the one gift no other creature possesses—even as a possibility.

READING FOR MEANING

Write to create meanings for McKibben's proposal to reduce nature photography sharply.

START MAKING MEANING

Begin by listing a few details of the problem as presented by McKibben in paragraphs 1–4. Continue by writing about anything else in the essay or in your experience that contributes to your understanding of McKibben's proposal.

IF YOU ARE STUCK

If you cannot write at least a page, consider writing about

- McKibben's extended counterargument in paragraphs 9–12, restating the main objections he counterargues and responding to one or two of them.

- McKibben's ideas on the importance of personal and public restraint for protecting the environment (paragraphs 12 and 13).

- Wendell Berry's claim that "one must begin in one's own life the private solutions that can only in turn become public solutions" (paragraph 6).

- how you have been influenced by nature photography or television shows, relating your experience to McKibben's argument (paragraph 4).

READING LIKE A WRITER
IMPLEMENTING THE SOLUTION

Proposal writers must always offer solutions. Depending on the situation, however, writers are not obliged to detail how the solution should be implemented. Some writers might not know how to implement the solution; Robert J. Samuelson, for example, does not know the inner workings of student test development agencies, and Rob Ryder is not a member of the National Basketball Association owners' committee. This lack of knowledge need not preclude their making a proposal, though it may weaken their influence with those who would have to implement the solution. Moreover, some proposals are written primarily to influence public opinion, with the hope that some expert will step up to offer a detailed plan for implementation. Other writers, such as Edward J. Loughran, have worked for years implementing solutions like the ones they propose to others. In these situations readers are grateful for the expert advice.

McKibben devotes some attention to implementing his proposal. Perhaps knowing that readers will resist his proposal, especially professional nature photographers and publishers of nature magazines, McKibben realizes that he must attend to implementation. His plan is speculative, but it goes far enough to answer the predictable objection, "What you're proposing can't be done."

ANALYZE

1. *Reread* paragraphs 7 and 8, where McKibben describes how his proposal might be implemented. *Underline* any details of implementation—the actual physical arrangements.

2. Now *mark* the places in paragraphs 7 and 8 where McKibben supports his plan.

3. *Evaluate* how successfully McKibben presents his plan for implementation and argues to support it. McKibben understands that nature photographers (who make money from placing their work in magazines) will fiercely resist his plan. He seems to be writing not so much for them, however, as for general readers who might like to see wildlife protected. For these readers, including yourself, how convincing do you find McKibben's plan? Does he help readers see that it could be implemented? Does he succeed in making the plan seem timely and beneficial?

WRITE

Explain how McKibben presents a plan for implementing his proposed solution. Then *evaluate* how successful you find his plan. *Include* a few details from the reading to support your conclusions.

CONSIDERING IDEAS FOR YOUR OWN WRITING

Consider proposing curbs or limits on some activity in a group or organization to which you belong. You would be saying to members of the group, "We have to put a stop to this practice." Like McKibben, you might focus on the unintended consequences of an activity. Here are some examples: a sports team for which weekends without practice leave everyone too tired by the end of Monday practices or sore by Tuesday practices; a campus group that schedules meetings to accommodate the meal times of dorm residents rather than the commuting schedules of off-campus members; a workplace where certain rules or expectations create hardships for a certain group; a volunteer group in which training, supervision, or follow-up activities undermine the group's goals. You and your classmates will be able to think of other examples.

Choose a group and identify an activity that needs curbing. Begin thinking about how you could go about developing a proposal to curb the activity. Keep in mind that your proposal will fail to win support if it sounds like a complaint or if it blames individuals for creating the problem. You want to address all members of the organization and to convince many or most of them that the unintended consequences of the activity have created a serious problem. Then you need to propose a compelling solution and argue for it convincingly.

PATRICK O'MALLEY

More Testing, More Learning

Patrick O'Malley wrote the following proposal while he was a first-year college student. He proposes that college professors give students frequent brief examinations in addition to the usual midterm and final exams. After discussing his unusual rhetorical situation—a student advising professors—with his instructor, he decided to revise the essay into the form of an open letter to professors on his campus, a letter that might appear in the campus newspaper.

O'Malley's essay may strike you as unusually authoritative. This air of authority is due in large part to what O'Malley learned about the possibilities and problems of frequent exams as he interviewed two professors (his writing instructor and the writing program director) and talked with several students. As you read, notice particularly how he anticipates professors' likely objections to his proposals and their preferred solutions to the problem he identifies.

It's late at night. The final's tomorrow. You got a *C* on the   1
midterm, so this one will make or break you. Will it be like the midterm? Did you study enough? Did you study the right things? It's too late to drop the course. So what happens if you fail? No time to worry about that now—you've got a ton of notes to go over.

Although this last-minute anxiety about midterm and final   2
exams is only too familiar to most college students, many professors may not realize how such major, infrequent, high-stakes exams work against the best interests of students both psychologically and intellectually. They cause unnecessary amounts of stress, placing too much importance on one or two days in the students' entire term, judging ability on a single or dual performance. They don't encourage frequent study, and they fail to inspire students' best performance. If professors gave additional brief exams at frequent intervals, students would learn more, study more regularly, worry less, and perform better on midterms, finals, and other papers and projects.

Ideally, a professor would give an in-class test or quiz   3
after each unit, chapter, or focus of study, depending on the type of class and course material. A physics class might require a test on concepts after every chapter covered, while a history class could necessitate quizzes covering certain time periods or major events. These exams should be given weekly, or at least twice monthly. Whenever possible, they

should consist of two or three essay questions rather than many multiple-choice or short-answer questions. To preserve class time for lecture and discussion, exams should take no more than 15 or 20 minutes.

The main reason professors should give frequent exams is that when they do, and when they provide feedback to students on how well they are doing, students learn more in the course and perform better on major exams, projects, and papers. It makes sense that in a challenging course containing a great deal of material, students will learn more of it and put it to better use if they have to apply or "practice" it frequently on exams, which also helps them find out how much they are learning and what they need to go over again. A recent Harvard study notes students' "strong preference for frequent evaluation in a course." Harvard students feel they learn least in courses that have "only a midterm and a final exam, with no other personal evaluation." They believe they learn most in courses with "many opportunities to see how they are doing" (Light, 1990, p. 32). In a review of a number of studies of student learning, Frederiksen (1984) reports that students who take weekly quizzes achieve higher scores on final exams than students who take only a midterm exam and that testing increases retention of material tested.

Another, closely related argument in favor of multiple exams is that they encourage students to improve their study habits. Greater frequency in test taking means greater frequency in studying for tests. Students prone to cramming will be required—or at least strongly motivated—to open their textbooks and notebooks more often, making them less likely to resort to long, kamikaze nights of studying for major exams. Since there is so much to be learned in the typical course, it makes sense that frequent, careful study and review are highly beneficial. But students need motivation to study regularly, and nothing works like an exam. If students had frequent exams in all their courses, they would have to schedule study time each week and gradually would develop a habit of frequent study. It might be argued that students are adults who have to learn how to manage their own lives, but learning history or physics is more complicated than learning to drive a car or balance a checkbook. Students need coaching and practice in learning. The right way to learn new material needs to become a habit, and I believe that frequent exams are key to developing good habits of study and learning. The Harvard study concludes that "tying regular evaluation to good course organization enables stu-

4

5

dents to plan their work more than a few days in advance. If quizzes and homework are scheduled on specific days, students plan their work to capitalize on them" (Light, 1990, p. 33).

By encouraging regular study habits, frequent exams would also decrease anxiety by reducing the procrastination that produces anxiety. Students would benefit psychologically if they were not subjected to the emotional ups and downs caused by major exams, when after being virtually worry-free for weeks they are suddenly ready to check into the psychiatric ward. Researchers at the University of Vermont found a strong relationship between procrastination, anxiety, and achievement. Students who regularly put off studying for exams had continuing high anxiety and lower grades than students who procrastinated less. The researchers found that even "low" procrastinators did not study regularly and recommended that professors give frequent assignments and exams to reduce procrastination and increase achievement (Rothblum, Solomon, & Murakami, 1986, pp. 393, 394).

6

Research supports my proposed solution to the problems I have described. Common sense as well as my experience and that of many of my friends support it. Why, then, do so few professors give frequent brief exams? Some believe that such exams take up too much of the limited class time available to cover the material in the course. Most courses meet 150 minutes a week—three times a week for 50 minutes each time. A 20-minute weekly exam might take 30 minutes to administer, and that is one-fifth of each week's class time. From the student's perspective, however, this time is well spent. Better learning and greater confidence about the course seem a good trade-off for another 30 minutes of lecture. Moreover, time lost to lecturing or discussion could easily be made up in students' learning on their own through careful regular study for the weekly exams. If weekly exams still seem too time-consuming to some professors, their frequency could be reduced to every other week or their length to 5 or 10 minutes. In courses where multiple-choice exams are appropriate, several questions take only a few minutes to answer.

7

Another objection professors have to frequent exams is that they take too much time to read and grade. In a 20-minute essay exam a well-prepared student can easily write two pages. A relatively small class of 30 students might then produce 60 pages, no small amount of material to read each week. A large class of 100 or more students would produce

8

an insurmountable pile of material. There are a number of responses to this objection. Again, professors could give exams every other week or make them very short. Instead of reading them closely they could skim them quickly to see whether students understand an idea or can apply it to an unfamiliar problem; and instead of numerical or letter grades they could give a plus, check, or minus. Exams could be collected and responded to only every third or fourth week. Professors who have readers or teaching assistants could rely on them to grade or check exams. And the Scranton machine is always available for instant grading of multiple-choice exams. Finally, frequent exams could be given *in place of* a midterm exam or out-of-class essay assignment.

Since frequent exams seem to some professors to create   9 too many problems, however, it is reasonable to consider alternative ways to achieve the same goals. One alternative solution is to implement a program that would improve study skills. While such a program might teach students how to study for exams, it cannot prevent procrastination or reduce "large test anxiety" by a substantial amount. One research team studying anxiety and test performance found that study skills training was "not effective in reducing anxiety or improving performance" (Dendato & Diener, 1986, p. 134). This team, which also reviewed other research that reached the same conclusion, did find that a combination of "cognitive/relaxation therapy" and study skills training was effective. This possible solution seems complicated, however, not to mention time-consuming and expensive. It seems much easier and more effective to change the cause of the bad habit rather than treat the habit itself. That is, it would make more sense to solve the problem at its root: the method of learning and evaluation.

Still another solution might be to provide frequent study   10 questions for students to answer. These would no doubt be helpful in focusing students' time studying, but students would probably not actually write out the answers unless they were required to. To get students to complete the questions in a timely way, professors would have to collect and check the answers. In that case, however, they might as well devote the time to grading an exam. Even if it asks the same questions, a scheduled exam is preferable to a set of study questions because it takes far less time to write in class, compared to the time students would devote to responding to questions at home. In-class exams also ensure that each student produces his or her own work.

Another possible solution would be to help students pre-   11
pare for midterm and final exams by providing sets of questions from which the exam questions will be selected or
announcing possible exam topics at the beginning of the
course. This solution would have the advantage of reducing
students' anxiety about learning every fact in the textbook,
and it would clarify the course goals, but it would not motivate students to study carefully each new unit, concept, or
text chapter in the course. I see this as a way of comple-
menting frequent exams, not as substituting for them.

From the evidence and from my talks with professors and   12
students, I see frequent, brief in-class exams as the only way
to improve students' study habits and learning, reduce their
anxiety and procrastination, and increase their satisfaction
with college. These exams are not a panacea, but only more
parking spaces and a winning football team would do as
much to improve college life. Professors can't do much
about parking or football, but they can give more frequent
exams. Campus administrators should get behind this effort,
and professors should get together to consider giving exams
more frequently. It would make a difference.

REFERENCES

Dendato, K. M., & Diener, D. (1986). Effectiveness of cognitive/re-
laxation therapy and study-skills training in reducing self-
reported anxiety and improving the academic performance
of test-anxious students. *Journal of Counseling Psychology, 33,*
131–135.
Frederiksen, N. (1984). The real test bias: Influences of testing on
teaching and learning. *American Psychologist, 39,* 193–202.
Light, R. J. (1990). *Explorations with students and faculty about teaching, learning, and student life.* Cambridge, MA: Harvard University Graduate School of Education and Kennedy School of
Government.
Rothblum, E. D., Solomon, L., & Murakami, J. (1986). Affective, cognitive, and behavioral differences between high and low procrastinators. *Journal of Counseling Psychology, 33,* 387–394.

READING FOR MEANING

Write to create meanings for O'Malley's proposal for improving learning and study habits.

START MAKING MEANING

Begin by describing briefly the problem O'Malley sees and the solution he proposes (paragraphs 1–3). Then list the alternative solutions that

O'Malley counterargues (paragraphs 9–11). Continue by writing about anything else in the essay or in your experience that contributes to your understanding of O'Malley's proposal.

IF YOU ARE STUCK

If you cannot write at least a page, consider writing about

- the reasons so few professors give frequent exams, listing the main reasons O'Malley offers (paragraphs 7 and 8) and commenting on one or two of his responses (paragraphs 9–11).

- the relation O'Malley attempts to establish between high-pressure exams and poor performance (paragraph 2), testing it against your own experience.

- which classes, in your experience, are and are not suited to frequent brief exams.

- your own experience preparing for major exams such as midterms and finals, comparing it with the scenario O'Malley describes in paragraph 1.

READING LIKE A WRITER
ARGUING DIRECTLY FOR THE SOLUTION

Counterarguing readers' likely questions and preferred solutions is especially important in proposals. So is arguing directly for the solution. Writers argue directly for a proposed solution by explaining the reasons it should be implemented and then supporting those reasons with evidence or examples. Many types of support are available: personal experience, assertions, research, reviews of research, quotes from authorities, effects or consequences, benefits, contrasts, analogies, and causes. O'Malley makes use of all of these types of support.

ANALYZE

1. *Skim* paragraphs 4–6, underlining in each paragraph the sentence that announces the reason for the solution.

2. *Note* in the margin the kinds of support O'Malley relies on. Try to *categorize* all of his support.

3. *Evaluate* how effectively O'Malley argues to support his solution. Do the reasons seem plausible? Is one reason more convincing to you than the others? How believable do you find the support?

WRITE

Write several sentences, explaining what you have learned about O'Malley's attempt to convince readers to take his proposed solution seriously. *Give examples* from the reading. Then *add* a few sentences, evaluating how convincing you find his argument. Which parts do you find most convincing? Least convincing? *Explain* your choices.

COMPARE

Compare O'Malley's direct argument for his solution to the argument Beilenson makes in his essay (paragraphs 11 and 12, pp. 355–56). *Identify* Beilenson's reasons and *categorize* his support. Then *write* several sentences, explaining how the two writers attempt to convince readers to support their proposed solutions. *Cite* a few examples from each reading.

CONSIDERING IDEAS FOR YOUR OWN WRITING

Much of what happens in high school and college is predictable and conventional. Examples of conventional practices that have changed very little over the years are exams, classroom lectures, graduation ceremonies, required courses, and lower admission requirements for athletes. Think of additional examples of established practices in high school or college; then select one that you believe needs to be improved or refined in some way. What changes would you propose? What individual or group might be convinced to take action on your proposal for improvement? What questions or objections should you anticipate? How could you discover whether others have previously proposed improvements in the practice you are concerned with? Whom might you interview to learn more about the practice and the likelihood of changing it?

Reviewing What Makes Proposals Effective

In this chapter, you have been learning how to read proposals for meaning and how to read them like a writer. Before going on to write a proposal essay, pause here to review and consolidate what you have learned about the elements of effective proposals.

Analyze

Choose one reading from this chapter that seems to you to be especially effective. Before rereading the selection, *write* down one or two reasons you remember it as an example of good proposal writing.

Reread your chosen selection, adding further annotations about what makes it particularly successful as a proposal to solve a problem. *Consider* the selection's purpose and how well it achieves that purpose for its intended readers. (Look at the headnote preceding each reading in this chapter for information on the intended audience. You can also make an informed guess about readership by noting the publication source of the essay and inferring some of the writer's assumptions about what readers know and believe.) Then *focus* on how well the essay

- introduces the problem.

- presents the solution.

- argues directly for the proposed solution.

- anticipates readers' likely objections, questions, and preferred solutions.

- establishes credibility.

You can review all of these basic features in the Guide to Reading Proposals (pp. 337–46).

Your instructor may ask you to complete this activity on your own or to work with a small group of other students who have chosen the same essay. If you work with others, allow enough time initially for all group members to reread the selection thoughtfully and to add their annotations. Then discuss as a group what makes the essay effective. Take notes on your discussion. One student should then report to the class what the group has learned about the effectiveness of proposal essays. If you are working individually, write up what you have learned from your analysis.

Write

Write at least a page, explaining and justifying your choice of this essay as an example of an effective proposal. Assume that your readers—your instructor and classmates—have read the selection but will not remember many details about it. They also may not remember it as an especially successful proposal. Therefore, you will need to *refer* to details and specific parts of the essay as you explain how it works and *justify* your evaluation of its effectiveness. You need not argue that it is the best essay in the chapter or that it is flawless, only that it is, in your view, a strong example of the genre.

A GUIDE TO WRITING PROPOSALS

The readings in this chapter have helped you learn a great deal about writing that proposes solutions to problems. A proposal has two basic features: the problem and the solution. Now that you have seen how writers establish that the problem exists and is serious, offer a detailed analysis of the problem, attempt to convince readers to accept the solution offered, and demonstrate how the proposed solution can be implemented, you can approach this type of writing confidently. Using these strategies will help you develop a convincing proposal of your own.

This guide is designed to assist you in writing your essay. Here you will find activities to help you identify a subject and discover what to say about it, organize your ideas and draft the essay, read the draft critically, revise the draft to strengthen your argument, and edit and proofread the essay to improve readability.

INVENTION

Invention is a process of discovery and planning by which you generate something to say. The following invention activities will help you choose a problem for study, analyze the problem and identify a solution, consider your readers, develop an argument for your proposed solution, and research your proposal. A few minutes spent completing each writing activity will improve your chances of producing a detailed and convincing first draft.

Choosing a Problem

Begin the selection process by listing several groups or organizations to which you presently belong—for instance, a neighborhood or town, film society, dormitory, sports team, biology class. For each group, list as many problems facing it as you can. If you cannot think of any problems for a particular organization, consult with other members. Then reflect on your list of problems, and choose the one for which you would most like to find a solution. It can be a problem that everyone already knows about or one about which only you are aware.

Proposing to solve a problem in a group or community to which you belong gives you an important advantage: You can write as an expert, an insider. You know about the history of the problem, have felt the urgency to solve it, and perhaps have already thought of possible solutions. Equally important, you know precisely where to send the proposal and who would most benefit from it. You have the access needed to interview others in the group, people who can contribute different, even dissenting viewpoints about your problem and solution. You are in a position of knowledge and authority—from which comes confident, convincing writing.

The writers you have read in this chapter take on problems of national scope—poor achievement in high schools, the high rate of delinquency among teenagers, the need to give a younger generation a voice in the volunteer programs in which they work, the possibility of making basketball a more interesting game to watch, the unfortunate but unintended influence of nature photography, and the unintended consequences of infrequent exams in college courses. Each of these proposals requires a wide-ranging knowledge of the problem and its social context. Unless you have time to learn about the often-extensive history of current social problems, you will learn more about proposal writing and produce a stronger piece of writing that might bring about change if you choose a local problem affecting a group or community to which you presently belong. Doing so will put you in the same authoritative position as the writers represented in this chapter.

If you choose a problem that affects a wider group, concentrate on one with which you have direct experience and for which you can suggest a detailed plan of action.

Developing Your Proposal

The writing and research activities that follow will enable you to test your problem and proposal and develop an argument that your readers will take seriously.

ANALYZING THE PROBLEM. *Write a few sentences in response to each of these questions:*

- Does the problem really exist? How can you tell?

- What caused this problem? Consider immediate and deeper causes.

- What is the history of the problem?

- What are the negative consequences of the problem?

- Who in the community or group is affected by the problem?

- Does anyone benefit from the existence of the problem?

CONSIDERING YOUR READERS. *With your understanding of the problem in mind, write for a few minutes about your intended readers.* Will you be writing to all members of your group or to only some of them? To an outside committee that might supervise or evaluate the group or to an individual in a position of authority inside or outside the group? Briefly justify your choice of readers. Then gauge how much they already know about the problem and what solutions they might prefer. Consider the problem's direct or indirect impact on them. Comment on what values and attitudes you share with your readers and how they have responded to similar problems in the past.

FINDING A TENTATIVE SOLUTION.   *List at least three possible solutions to the problem.* Think about solutions that have already been tried as well as solutions that have been proposed for related problems. Find, if you can, solutions that eliminate causes of the problem. Also consider solutions that reduce the symptoms of the problem. If it seems too big to be solved all at once, list solutions for one or more parts of the problem. Maybe a series of solutions is required and a key solution should be proposed first. From your list, choose the solution that seems to you most timely and practicable and write two or three sentences describing it.

ANTICIPATING READERS' RESISTANCE.   *Write a few sentences defending your solution against each of the following predictable objections.* For your proposal to succeed, readers must be convinced to take the solution seriously. Try to imagine how your prospective readers will respond.

- It won't really solve the problem.
- I'm comfortable with things as they are.
- We can't afford it.
- It will take too long.
- People won't do it.
- Too few people will benefit.
- I don't see how to get started on your solution.
- It's already been tried, with unsatisfactory results.
- You're making this proposal because it will benefit you personally.

COUNTERARGUING ALTERNATIVE SOLUTIONS.   *Identify two or three likely solutions to the problem that your readers may prefer, solutions different from your own.* Choose the one that poses the most serious challenge to your solution. Then write a few sentences comparing your solution with the alternative solution, weighing the strengths and weaknesses of each. Explain how you might demonstrate to readers that your solution has more advantages and fewer disadvantages than the alternative solution.

SUPPORTING YOUR SOLUTION.   *Write down every plausible reason your solution should be heard or tried.* Then review your list and highlight the strongest reasons, the ones most likely to persuade your readers. *Write for a few minutes about the single most convincing reason for your solution.*

Support this reason in any way you can. You want to build an argument that readers will take seriously.

RESEARCHING YOUR PROPOSAL. *Try out your proposal on members of the group, or go to the library to research a larger social or political problem.* If you are writing about a problem affecting a group to which you belong, talk to other members of the group to learn more about their understanding of the problem. Try out your solution on one or two people; their objections and questions will help you to counterargue and to support your argument more successfully.

If you are writing about a larger social or political problem, you should do research to confirm what you remember and to learn more about the problem. You can probably locate all the information you need in a good research library or on the Internet; you could also interview an expert on the problem. Readers will not take you seriously unless you are well informed.

FORMULATING A WORKING THESIS. *Draft a thesis statement.* A working thesis helps you begin drafting your essay purposefully. The thesis statement in a proposal is simply a statement of the solution you propose. Keep in mind that you may need to revise your thesis as you develop a first draft and learn more about your proposal. Here are three examples from the readings.

- "If we want to interrupt criminal paths and reduce the number of juveniles launching criminal careers, a shift in our priorities is necessary. States must invest their money in delinquency-prevention programs—at the front end rather than the back end of problems. These efforts should be targeted at elementary-school students from poor, high-crime neighborhoods, where traditional avenues to success are blocked" (Loughran, paragraph 12).

- "I'm not tinkering here—this is no 'raise the rim,' 'widen the lane' Band-Aid I'm proposing. Rather, I'm going straight to the heart of the problem. It's just too crowded out there. Basketball is meant to be played four on four" (Ryder, paragraph 5).

- "If professors gave additional brief exams at frequent intervals, students would learn more, study more regularly, worry less, and perform better on midterms, finals, and other papers and projects" (O'Malley, paragraph 2).

Notice that each of these thesis statements makes clear what the writer is proposing. Each thesis also mentions or implies the problem to be solved, even though it has already been described in the essay. Note that O'Malley's thesis statement forecasts the benefits of solving the problem, a strategy that helps readers anticipate how the argument is sequenced.

DRAFTING

The following guidelines will help you set goals for your draft and plan its organization.

Setting Goals

Establishing goals for your draft before you begin writing will enable you to move ahead more quickly and to make critical decisions more confidently. Consider the following questions now, and keep them in mind as you draft. They will help you maintain your focus while drafting as well as recall how the writers you have read in this chapter tried to achieve similar goals.

- *How can I introduce the problem in a way that interests my readers and convinces them that it needs to be solved?* Like Ryder, do I have to convince my readers that there really is a problem? Like Beilenson, should I draw on my authority from having observed the group carefully for some time? Must I describe the problem at length, as Loughran does, or merely identify it, as O'Malley does?

- *How should I present the solution?* Should I list and describe the various parts of the solution, as Beilenson does? Should I describe in detail how the solution might be implemented, as do Loughran and McKibben? Or need I describe the solution only briefly, like Samuelson, Ryder, and O'Malley do, letting other interested parties work out the details and take action?

- *How can I argue convincingly for my proposed solution?* Should I give examples of similar solutions that have proven successful, like Beilenson does? Describe the benefits of my solution, as Beilenson and O'Malley do? Offer statistics like Loughran does? Provide visual scenarios for what the solution would look like, as Ryder does? Or refer to research like O'Malley does?

- *How should I anticipate readers' objections and their preferred alternative solutions?* Should I refute readers' likely objections to the argument for my solution, as O'Malley and Samuelson do? Should I concede the difficulty of implementing the solution, as McKibben does? Should I attempt to answer readers' questions, as Ryder does? Should I accommodate an objection from my readers, as Beilenson does? Should I consider and refute alternative solutions, as O'Malley and Samuelson do?

- *How will I establish my credibility so that members of my group will want to join me in taking action to solve the problem?* Should I feature my firsthand experience with the problem, as Loughran, Beilenson, and O'Malley do? Should I set up a logical step-by-step argument, as all the writers in this chapter do? Should I show my respect for and knowledge of my readers by counterarguing at length, as Ryder and O'Malley do? Should I reveal my efforts to learn about the problem by quoting some of the people I interviewed, as Ryder does? Should I show what I know from published sources, as O'Malley does?

Organizing Your Draft

With goals in mind and invention notes at hand, you are ready to make a first outline of your draft. The basic parts are quite simple: the problem, the solution, and the reasons in support of the solution. This simple plan is nearly always complicated by other factors, however. In outlining your material, you must take into consideration many other details, such as whether readers already recognize the problem, how much agreement exists on the need to solve the problem, how much attention should be given to alternative solutions, and how many objections and questions by readers should be expected.

Your outline should reflect your own writing situation. You should not hesitate to change this outline when you start writing. For example, you might discover a more convincing way to order the reasons for adopting your proposal, or you might realize that counterargument must play a larger role than you first imagined. The purpose of an outline is to identify the basic features of your proposal, not to lock you in to a particular structure.

READING A DRAFT CRITICALLY

Getting a critical reading of your draft will help you see how to improve it. Your instructor may schedule class time for reading drafts, or you may want to ask a classmate or a tutor in the writing center to read your draft. Ask your reader to use the following guidelines and to write out a response for you to consult during your revision.

Read for a First Impression

1. Read the draft without stopping to annotate or comment, and then write two or three sentences giving your general impression.

2. Identify one aspect of the draft that seems to you particularly effective.

Read Again to Suggest Improvements

1. Recommend ways to present the problem more effectively.

   • Locate places in the draft where the problem is defined and described. Point to places where you believe the intended readers will need more explanation or where the presentation seems un-clear or confusing.

- Consider whether readers might want to know more about the causes or effects of the problem. Suggest ways the writer might do more to establish the seriousness of the problem, creating a sense of urgency to gain readers' support and to excite their curiosity about solutions.

2. Suggest ways to present the solution more effectively.

- Find the solution, and notice whether it is immediately clear and readable. Point to places where it could be made clearer and more readable.

- Advise the writer whether it would help to lay out steps for imple-mentation.

- Tell the writer how to make the solution seem more practical, workable, and cost-effective.

3. Recommend ways to strengthen the argument for the solution.

- List the reasons the writer gives for adopting the solution or con-sidering it seriously. Point out the reasons most and least likely to be convincing. Let the writer know whether there are too many or too few reasons. If the reasons are not sequenced in a logical, step-by-step sequence, suggest a new order.

- Evaluate the support for each reason. Point out any passages where the support seems insufficient and recommend further kinds of support.

4. Suggest ways to extend and improve the counterargument.

- Locate places where the writer anticipates readers' objections to and questions about the proposal. Keeping in mind that the writer can accommodate or refute each objection or question, evaluate how successfully the writer does so. Recommend ways to make the response to each question or objection more convincing.

- Suggest any likely objections and questions the writer has overlooked.

- Identify any alternative solutions the writer mentions. Give advice on how the writer can present these alternative solutions more clearly and responsibly, and suggest ways to accommodate or re-fute them more convincingly.

5. Suggest ways to make the argument more credible.

- Tell the writer whether the intended readers are likely to find the proposal knowledgeable and authoritative. Point to places where it seems most and least authoritative.

- Identify places where the writer seems most insightful in anticipating what readers need to know, what questions and objections they may have, and what alternative solutions they may prefer. Note whether the writer responds to readers' concerns responsibly and respectfully.

6. Suggest how the organization might be improved.

   - Consider the overall plan, perhaps by making a scratch outline (see Appendix One, p. 461, for advice on scratch outlining). Decide whether the sequence of reasons and counterarguments follows a logical step-by-step sequence. Suggest a more logical sequence, if necessary.

   - Indicate where new or better transitions might help identify steps in the argument and keep readers on track.

REVISING

This section provides suggestions for revising your draft, suggestions that will remind you of the possibilities for developing a convincing proposal. Revising means reenvisioning your draft, trying to see it in a new way, given your purpose and readers, in order to develop your argument.

The biggest mistake you can make while revising is to focus initially on words or sentences. Instead, first try to see your draft as a whole in order to assess its likely impact on readers. Think imaginatively and boldly about cutting unconvincing material, adding new material, and moving material around to improve readability and strengthen your argument. Your computer makes even drastic revisions easy, but you still need to make the effort and decisions that will improve your draft.

You may have received a critical reading from classmates, a writing center tutor, or your instructor. If so, rely on this valuable help in deciding which parts of your draft need revising and what specific changes you could make.

To Present the Problem More Effectively

- If your readers are unfamiliar with the problem or doubt that it exists, briefly address its history or describe it in some detail to make its impact seem real.

- If your readers know about the problem but believe it is insignificant, argue for its seriousness, perhaps by dramatizing its current and long-term effects. Or speculate about the complications that might arise in the future if the problem is not solved.

To Present the Solution More Effectively

- If readers cannot see how to realize your proposed solution, outline the steps of its implementation. Lead them through it chronologically. Demonstrate that the first step is easy to take; or, if it is unavoidably challenging, propose ways to ease the difficulty.

- If a solution is beyond your expertise, explain where the experts can be found and how they can be put to use.

- If all readers can readily imagine how the solution would be implemented and how it would look once in place, reduce the amount of space you give to presenting the solution.

To Strengthen the Argument for the Solution

- If you have not given adequate reasons for proposing the solution, give more reasons.

- If your reasons are hidden among other material, foreground them. Consider announcing them explicitly at the beginnings of paragraphs (the first reason why, the second, the third; the main reason why; my chief reason for; and so on).

- If your argument seems unconvincing, support your reasoning with arguments, examples, anecdotes, statistics, quotes from authorities or members of the group, or any other appropriate support.

To Strengthen the Counterarguments

- If you have not anticipated all of your readers' weighty objections and questions, do so now. Consider carefully whether you can accommodate some objections by either granting their wisdom or adapting your solution in response to them. If you refute objections or dismiss questions, do so in a spirit of continuing collaboration with members of your group; there is no need to be adversarial. You want readers to support your solution and perhaps even to join with you in implementing it.

- If you have neglected to mention alternative solutions that are popular with readers, do so now. You may accommodate or reject these alternatives, or—a compromise—incorporate some of their better points. If you must reject all aspects of an alternative, do so through reasoned argument, without questioning the character or intelligence of those who prefer the alternative. You may be able to convince some of them that your solution is the better one.

To Enhance Credibility

- If readers of your draft have questioned your credibility, learn more about the problem, seek advice on presenting the solution in a more compelling way, make the feasibility of the solution clearer, and talk with more members of the group so that you can incorporate or address more viewpoints.

- If your attitude toward your readers weakens your credibility, look for ways to show readers more respect and to establish a common ground with them.

To Organize More Logically and Coherently

- If your argument lacks logical progression, reorganize the reasons supporting your proposed solution.

- If your various counterarguments are not smoothly integrated into your argument, try another sequence or add better transitions.

EDITING AND PROOFREADING

After you have revised your essay, be sure to spend time checking for errors in usage, punctuation, and mechanics. If you have been keeping a list of errors you typically make, begin by checking your draft against this list. Ask someone else to proofread your essay before you print out a copy for your instructor.

From our research on student writing, we know that proposal writers tend to refer to the problem or solution by using the pronoun *this* or *that* ambiguously. Edit carefully any sentences with *this* or *that* to ensure that a noun immediately follows the pronoun to make the reference clear. Refer to a writer's handbook for help with avoiding ambiguous pronoun reference.

Reflecting on What You Have Learned

In this chapter, you have read critically several proposals and have written one of your own. To better remember what you have learned, pause now to reflect on the reading and writing activities you completed in this chapter.

1. *Write* a page or so reflecting on what you have learned. Begin by describing what you are most pleased with in your essay. Then *explain* what you think contributed to your achievement. Be specific about this contribution.

Continued

- If it was something you learned from the readings, *indicate* which readings and specifically what you learned from them.

- If it came from your invention writing, *indicate* the section or sections that helped you most.

- If you got good advice from a critical reader, *explain* exactly how the person helped you—perhaps by helping you understand a particular problem in your draft or by adding a new dimension to your writing.

- Try to write about your achievement in terms of what you have learned about the genre.

2. Now *reflect* more generally on proposals, a genre of writing that plays an important role in our society. *Consider* some of the following questions: How confident did you feel in making a proposal that might lead to improvements in the functioning of an entire group or community? Does your proposal attempt fundamental or minor change in the group? How necessary is your proposed change in the scheme of things? Whose interest would be served by the solution you propose? Who else might be affected? In what ways does your proposal challenge the status quo in the group? What contribution might essays proposing solutions to problems make to our society that other genres of writing cannot make?

Position Paper

I f, as a college student, you have strong feelings about a recent event
(such as a student's dying as a result of fraternity hazing) or a new policy (such as the decision to end affirmative action admissions for un-
derrepresented minorities), you might write a position paper and try to
get it published in the school newspaper. Position papers enable writers
to express strong feelings, to think through difficult issues, and to influence others.

In college, you may also write position papers to fulfill assignments
asking you to construct arguments responding to the course reading. If
you were studying the Federalist Papers in an American history course,
for example, you might join in the debate, arguing with James Madison in
favor of the system of checks and balances. In a journalism course, you
might argue that there should be no holds barred when covering political
figures, but that the privacy of others, including celebrities, should be respected. In a management course, you might argue that taking care of the
environment is good business practice.

As these examples suggest, position papers take on controversial issues that are, by definition, issues about which people disagree, sometimes vehemently. Such issues have no obvious "right" answer, no truth
everyone accepts, no single authority everyone trusts. Consequently, simply gathering information—finding the facts or learning from experts—
will not settle these disputes because ultimately they are matters of opinion and judgment.

Although it is not possible to prove that a position on a controversial
issue is right or wrong, it is possible through argument to convince others to consider another position seriously or to accept or reject a position. To be convincing, a position paper must argue for its position by giv-

ing readers strong reasons and solid support. It also must anticipate opposing arguments.

As you read and discuss the selections in this chapter, you will discover why position papers play such an important role in college, the workplace, and civic life. You will also learn how position papers work. From the essays and from the ideas for writing that follow each selection, you will get many ideas for taking a position on an issue that you care about. As you analyze the selections and think about writing a position paper of your own, keep in mind the following assignment. The Guide to Writing Position Papers, which follows the readings, will support you as you write your own position paper.

THE WRITING ASSIGNMENT

Arguing a Position on an Issue

Choose an issue about which you feel strongly. Write an essay, arguing your position on the controversial issue. Your purpose is to try to convince readers to adopt your position or, at least, to take seriously the arguments you raise. Therefore, you will want to acknowledge readers' opposing views as well as any objections and questions they might have.

WRITING SITUATIONS FOR POSITION PAPERS

Writing that takes a position on a controversial issue plays a significant role in college work and professional life, as the following examples show.

- A committee made up of business and community leaders investigates the issue of regulating urban growth. After reviewing the arguments for and against government regulation, committee members argue against it on the grounds that supply and demand alone will regulate development, that landowners should be permitted to sell their property to the highest bidder, and that developers are guided by the needs of the market and thus serve the people.

- For a sociology class, a student writes a term paper on surrogate mothering. She first learned about the subject from television news but feels that she needs more information to write a paper on the topic. In the library, she finds several newspaper and magazine articles that help her understand better the debate over the issue. In her paper, she presents the strongest arguments on each side but concludes that, from a sociological perspective, surrogate mothering should not be allowed because it exploits poor women by creating a class of professional breeders.

- For a political science class, a student is assigned to write an essay on public employees' right to strike. Having no strong opinion herself, she discusses the issue with her mother, a nurse in a county hospital, and her uncle, a firefighter. Her mother believes that public employees like hospital workers and teachers should have the right to strike, but that police officers and firefighters should not because public safety would be endangered. The uncle disagrees, arguing that allowing hospital workers to strike would jeopardize public safety as much as allowing firefighters to strike. He insists that the central issue is not public safety, but individual rights. In her essay, the student supports the right of public employees to strike but argues that a system of arbitration should be used wherever a strike might jeopardize public safety.

A GUIDE TO READING POSITION PAPERS

This guide to reading is designed to introduce you to the special features and strategies of essays that argue for a position on a controversial issue. It focuses on a brief but forceful argument by Richard Estrada against the practice of naming sports teams and mascots after Native Americans. You will be asked to read this essay more than once. First, you will read for meaning, seeking to understand and respond to Estrada's argument. Then, you will read like a writer of position papers, analyzing Estrada's essay to see how he constructs his argument and evaluating his argument to see which parts work well and which do not work as effectively.

RICHARD ESTRADA

Sticks and Stones and Sports Team Names

> *Richard Estrada writes for a nationally syndicated newspaper column. This essay was first published on October 29, 1995 in the* Dallas Morning News *during the baseball World Series in which the Atlanta Braves played the Cleveland Indians. The Series, which was televised, drew attention to the practice of dressing team mascots like Native Americans on the warpath and encouraging fans to rally their teams with gestures like the "tomahawk chop" and pep yells like the "Indian chant." The controversy over these practices ignited a*

long-standing debate in the United States over sports teams using names associated with Native Americans. Various high schools and at least one university, Stanford, have changed the names of their sports teams in recent years because of this ongoing controversy.

The title of the essay, as you may know, refers to a children's chant: "Sticks and stones will break my bones, but words will never hurt me." As you read, consider why Estrada and his newspaper editor thought this title was appropriate.

When I was a kid living in Baltimore in the late 1950s, there   1
was only one professional sports team worth following. Anyone who ever saw the movie *Diner* knows which one it was. Back when we liked Ike, the Colts were the gods of the gridiron and Memorial Stadium was their Mount Olympus.

Ah, yes: The Colts. The Lions. Da Bears. Back when defen-   2
sive tackle Big Daddy Lipscomb was letting running backs know exactly what time it was, a young fan could easily forget that in a game where men were men, the teams they played on were not invariably named after animals. Among others, the Packers, the Steelers and the distant 49ers were cases in point. But in the roll call of pro teams, one name in particular always discomfited me: the Washington Redskins. Still, however willing I may have been to go along with the name as a kid, as an adult I have concluded that using an ethnic group essentially as a sports mascot is wrong.

The Redskins, along with baseball teams like the Atlanta   3
Braves, the Cleveland Indians and the Kansas City Chiefs, should find other names that avoid highlighting ethnicity.

By no means were such names originally meant to dispar-   4
age Native Americans. The noble symbols of the Redskins or college football's Florida Seminoles or the Illinois Illini are meant to be strong and proud. Yet, ultimately, the practice of using a people as mascots is dehumanizing. It sets them apart from the rest of society. It promotes the politics of racial aggrievement at a moment when our storehouse is running over with it.

The World Series between the Cleveland Indians and the   5
Atlanta Braves reignited the debate. In the chill night air of October, tomahawk chops and war chants suddenly became far more familiar to millions of fans, along with the ridiculous and offensive cartoon logo of Cleveland's "Chief Wahoo."

The defenders of team names that use variations on the   6
Indian theme argue that tradition should not be sacrificed at the altar of political correctness. In truth, the nation's No. 1 P.C. [politically correct] school, Stanford University, helped

matters some when it changed its team nickname from "the Indians" to "the Cardinals." To be sure, Stanford did the right thing, but the school's status as P.C. without peer tainted the decision for those who still need to do the right thing.

Another argument is that ethnic group leaders are too in-   7
clined to cry wolf in alleging racial insensitivity. Often, this is the case. But no one should overlook genuine cases of politi- cal insensitivity in an attempt to avoid accusations of hyper- sensitivity and political correctness.

The real world is different from the world of sports enter-   8
tainment. I recently heard a father who happened to be a Na- tive American complain on the radio that his child was being pressured into participating in celebrations of Braves base- ball. At his kid's school, certain days are set aside on which all children are told to dress in Indian garb and celebrate with tomahawk chops and the like.

That father should be forgiven for not wanting his family   9
to serve as somebody's mascot. The desire to avoid ridicule is legitimate and understandable. Nobody likes to be triv- ialized or deprived of their dignity. This has nothing to do with political correctness and the provocations of militant leaders.

Against this backdrop, the decision by newspapers in   10
Minneapolis, Seattle and Portland to ban references to Na- tive American nicknames is more reasonable than some might think.

What makes naming teams after ethnic groups, particu-   11
larly minorities, reprehensible is that politically impotent groups continue to be targeted, while politically powerful ones who bite back are left alone. How long does anyone think the name "Washington Blackskins" would last? Or how about "the New York Jews"?

With no fewer than 10 Latino ballplayers on the Cleveland   12
Indians' roster, the team could change its name to "the Ban- ditos." The trouble is, they would be missing the point: Lati- nos would correctly object to that stereotype, just as they rightly protested against Frito-Lay's use of the "Frito Ban- dito" character years ago.

It seems to me that what Native Americans are saying is   13
that what would be intolerable for Jews, blacks, Latinos and others is no less offensive to them. Theirs is a request not only for dignified treatment, but for fair treatment as well. For America to ignore the complaints of a numerically small segment of the population because it is small is neither dig- nified nor fair.

READING FOR MEANING

Write to create meanings for Estrada's argument to stop using Native American names for sports teams.

START MAKING MEANING

Begin by restating what you think is the *most* or *least* convincing part of Estrada's argument, and briefly explain why you think so. Continue by writing about anything else in the essay or in your experience that contributes to your understanding of Estrada's argument. As you write, you may want to reread parts of the essay and add further annotations.

IF YOU ARE STUCK

If you cannot write at least a page, consider writing about

- the apparent contradiction between Estrada's assumption that naming a sports team the *Redskins* was originally intended to be admiring and not disparaging, and his assertion in the next sentence that "ultimately, the practice of using a people as mascots is dehumanizing" (paragraph 4).

- the term "political correctness" (paragraph 6)—what you think it means and how Estrada's argument relates to it.

- the power of words to hurt, especially words that make people feel different or inferior—perhaps related to your own experience of being called demeaning names.

- a question you would like to ask Estrada, an addition you would make to his argument, or an alternative position you would argue for.

READING LIKE A WRITER

This section guides you through an analysis of Estrada's writing strategies: *defining the issue, asserting a clear, unequivocal position, arguing directly for the position, counterarguing objections and opposing arguments,* and *establishing credibility.* Each strategy is described briefly and followed by a critical reading and writing activity to help you see how Estrada uses the strategy in his essay.

Consider this section a writer's introduction to arguing a position. You will learn still more about how different writers use these strategies from the activities following readings later in the chapter. At the end of the chapter, A Guide to Writing Position Papers suggests how you can use these same strategies in writing your own position paper.

Defining the Issue

For position papers published in the midst of an ongoing public debate, writers may need only to mention the issue. In most cases, however, writers need to identify the issue as well as explain or define it for readers. To define the issue, writers may provide several kinds of information. They may, for example, place the issue in its historical or cultural context, cite specific instances to make the issue seem less abstract, or establish or redefine the terms of the debate.

Defining the issue, then, is hardly a matter of disinterestedly informing readers about the issue; it can be an important part of the argument. At the very least, how a writer defines the issue sets the stage for the argument. In "Sticks and Stones and Sports Team Names," Estrada tries to define the issue in a way that will make readers receptive to his argument, first by sharing a childhood memory and then by reminding readers of images many of them saw on television during the 1995 baseball World Series.

ANALYZE

1. *Reread* paragraphs 1 and 2, where Estrada introduces the issue, and underline any words that suggest why he begins his argument by telling his Dallas readers about his childhood in Baltimore.

2. Then, *reread* paragraph 5, where Estrada describes the events at the World Series that "reignited the debate." *Look closely* at his description of the television images and *underline* any words that might lead readers to take his argument seriously.

WRITE

Write several sentences, describing how Estrada defines the issue. Specifically, *consider* how he uses personal reminiscence and shared television images to raise concern about the issue. *Quote* any words he uses that seem likely to have an impact on readers. Then *add* a few sentences evaluating how successfully Estrada defines the issue and how well he prepares readers for his argument.

Asserting a Clear, Unequivocal Position

Writers of position papers always take sides. Their primary purpose is to assert a position of their own and to influence readers' thinking. This assertion is the main point of the essay, its thesis. Writers try to state the thesis simply and directly, although they may qualify the thesis by limiting its applicability. For example, a thesis in favor of the death penalty might limit capital punishment to certain kinds of crimes. The thesis statement often forecasts the stages of the argument as well, identifying the main reason or reasons that will be developed and supported in the essay.

Where the thesis is placed depends on various factors. Most likely, you will want to place the thesis early in the essay to let readers know right away where you stand. But when you need to spend more time establishing the issue or defining the terms of the debate, you might postpone introducing your own position. Restating the thesis at various points and at the end can also help keep readers oriented.

ANALYZE

1. *Find* the first place where Estrada explicitly asserts his position and *put brackets* ([]) around the sentence or sentences that state the thesis.

2. *Skim* paragraphs 3, 4, 9, and 13, and *put brackets* around the sentences in these paragraphs that restate the thesis.

3. *Examine* the context for each of these restatements to determine why Estrada thought it necessary to repeat his thesis. Also *look closely* at the language he uses to see whether he repeats key words, uses synonyms, or adds new words.

WRITE

Write a few sentences, explaining what you have learned about how Estrada states and restates his position. *Describe* the different contexts in which he restates the thesis and how the wording changes. *Cite* examples from the readings. Then *speculate about* the possible reasons for reasserting a thesis so often in a brief essay like this.

Arguing Directly for the Position

Not only do writers of position papers explicitly assert their positions, but they also give reasons for them. Moreover, they usually support each reason with facts, statistics, examples, anecdotes, quotes from authorities, and analogies.

Facts are statements that can be proven objectively to be true; but readers may need to be reassured that they indeed come from trustworthy sources. Although *statistics* may be mistaken for facts, they often are only interpretations or correlations of numerical data. Their reliability depends on how and by whom the information was collected and interpreted. *Examples* and *anecdotes,* in contrast, tend *not* to make truth claims or pretend to apply to everyone. Instead, they present particular stories and vivid images that work by appealing to readers' emotions. Somewhere in between these two extremes are expert opinions and analogies. Readers must decide whether to regard *quotes* from experts as credible and authoritative. They must also decide how much weight to e *analogies,* comparisons that encourage readers to assume that what ue about one thing is also true about something to which it is com-
1. As a critical reader, you should look skeptically at analogies to de-
e whether they are logical as well as persuasive.

ANALYZE

1. *Reread* paragraphs 11–13, where Estrada develops his final reason for opposing the use of Native American names for sports teams. *Find* the first place where Estrada explicitly asserts his reason and *put brackets* ([ ]) around the sentence or sentences that state the topic sentence of this part of his argument.

2. To see how Estrada argues by analogy, *underline* the three sports team names he facetiously proposes in paragraphs 11 and 12 and *compare* them to the teams in paragraphs 2–4 named after Native Americans.

3. *Consider* how persuasive his analogies are in paragraphs 11 and 12.

WRITE

Write several sentences, briefly describing Estrada's strategy of argument by analogy. *Cite* examples of his analogies. Then *add* a few sentences speculating about the persuasiveness of his strategy of arguing by analogy. Why do you think some readers would find the argument in this part of the essay compelling and other readers would not?

Counterarguing Objections and Opposing Arguments

Writers of position papers often try to anticipate likely objections and questions readers might raise as well as opposing arguments. Writers may concede points with which they agree and may even modify a thesis to accommodate valid objections. But when they think the criticism is groundless or opposing arguments are flawed, writers counterargue aggressively. They refute the challenges to their argument by poking holes in their opponents' reasoning and support.

ANALYZE

1. *Reread* paragraph 6 where Estrada presents the argument of those who disagree with his position. *Underline* the words he uses to characterize the opposing argument.

2. *Examine* paragraphs 7 and 8 to see how Estrada counterargues. For example, *notice* his use of the words "real" to describe the anecdote (paragraph 8) and "genuine" to describe the kinds of insensitivity that, in his opinion, should not be overlooked (paragraph 7).

3. *Consider* how well the anecdote supports his point, particularly why the anecdote might appeal to his *Dallas Morning News* readers.

WRITE

Write several sentences, briefly explaining Estrada's counterargument. Then *add* a few sentences evaluating the probable success of this strategy with newspaper readers.

Establishing Credibility

Readers judge the credibility of an essay that argues about a controversial issue by the way it defines the issue, argues, and counterargues. Critical readers expect writers to advocate forcefully for their position, but at the same time they expect writers to avoid misrepresenting other points of view, attacking opponents personally, or manipulating readers' emotions. To establish credibility, writers thus aim instead to support their argument responsibly with the help of authoritative sources and a well-reasoned, well-supported argument.

Another factor that may influence a reader's judgment of an argument's credibility is whether the writer seems to share at least some of the reader's values, beliefs, attitudes, and ideals. Readers often trust writers who express concerns they also have about an issue. Many readers respect arguments based on strong values even if they do not share those particular values or hold to them as strictly. Yet readers also tend to dislike moralizing and resent a condescending or belittling tone as much as a shrill or hectoring one. Instead, readers usually appreciate a tone that acknowledges legitimate differences of opinion, while seeking to establish common ground where possible.

ANALYZE

1. Quickly *reread* the entire essay, putting a question mark in the margin next to any passages where you doubt Estrada's credibility. *Put a checkmark* next to any passages where he seems especially trustworthy.

2. *Review* the passages you marked and, wherever you can, *put in the margin* a word or phrase to briefly describe the dominant tone of the passage.

3. Then *consider* what language, information, or other element in the marked passages contributed to your judgment of Estrada's credibility.

WRITE

Write several sentences, describing your impression of Estrada's credibility. *Cite* a few examples from the reading to support your view.

STEPHEN BATES

Religious Diversity
and the Schools

Stephen Bates (b. 1958) is a senior fellow at the Annen-
berg Washington Program, a conservative think tank. He has
written many articles and books, including Battleground:
One Mother's Crusade, the Religious Right, and the Struggle for Control of Our Classrooms *(1993) and, with Edwin*
Diamond, The Spot: The Rise of Political Advertising on
Television *(1992).*

The following essay was adapted from Battleground.
Bates writes in this position paper about religious tolerance,
an issue that many readers might assume was settled by the
constitutional guarantee of freedom of religion. But Bates re-
minds readers that the controversy continues, especially in
public schools. Although the separation of church and state
is inscribed in the Bill of Rights, every few years heated de-
bates flare over whether prayer should be permitted in the
schools or whether creationism should be taught as a scien-
tific theory comparable to evolution. In his essay, Bates fo-
cuses on whether fundamentalist Christian students should
be excused from "assignments that offend their beliefs."

Before reading, reflect on what you know about reli-
gious tolerance and its history. Then, as you read, annotate
the essay, noting anything that contributes to your under-
standing of the issue and Bates's position on it.

In countless ways, today's public schools tailor the edu-   1
cational experience to the individual student. Handicapped
students get assignments fashioned to their abilities. Pregnant students get prenatal care, and students with infants
get day care. Students who lack fluency in English spend the
day in bilingual classrooms. Several states excuse conscien-
tious objectors from dissecting animals. Some districts provide schools-within-schools for students fighting drug or
alcohol addiction, for the children of alcoholics, and for
chronic troublemakers or gang members. New York City and
Los Angeles have special high schools for gay students. Atlanta, Philadelphia, Newark, and other districts have implemented Afrocentric curricula, some of whose advocates
speak of tailoring education to black students' "special
learning patterns." The National Education Association
(NEA) has endorsed special programs for underachievers,

for "socially promoted" students (students who don't meet advancement standards but are advanced anyway), for "displaced students of desegregated districts," and for many others with special concerns.

When it comes to the special concerns of fundamentalist Christians, however, educators often turn a cold shoulder. Excusing fundamentalists from assignments that offend their beliefs, the NEA said in a 1986 *amicus* brief, "substitutes segregation and intolerance for the democratic values that public education is designed to foster." Tolerance may indeed be the dominant theme of the modern curriculum. The authors of a recent study of American high schools concluded that "tolerating diversity is the moral glue that holds schools together." One study of American history books found toleration presented as "the only 'religious' idea worth remembering." What was being tolerated, often as not, was omitted.

Tolerance, though, can be an expansive and even elusive concept. When a Jewish girl in Yonkers, New York, asked to be excused from singing Christmas hymns in 1949, her teacher scolded her. Refusing to sing, the teacher said, would be terribly intolerant of her. A decade later, a Baltimore administrator told atheist Madalyn Murray O'Hair that her son need not pray. To be tolerant of other students, however, he would have to "stand with the rest, maintain an attitude of reverence, and just move his lips as if he were saying prayers."

Teachers today often misconstrue toleration in a different fashion, by equating it with indifferentism—the belief that all religions have equal validity. In a 1987 case, Judge Danny Boggs of the U.S. Court of Appeals for the Sixth Circuit drew a vital distinction. *Civil toleration,* he pointed out, means that adherents of all faiths deserve equal rights as citizens, whereas *religious toleration* means that all faiths are equally valid as religions. Under civil toleration, all faiths are equal in the eyes of the state; under religious toleration, all faiths are equal in the eyes of God.

Unfortunately, educators don't always grasp the distinction. "I hear teachers telling kids, 'It doesn't matter how you pray, just pray,' or, 'It's wonderful to have faith, and does it really matter which one?' " says Charles C. Haynes of the First Liberty Institute at George Mason University. "But that kind of well-meaning relativism . . . undermines what parents are teaching, that it *does* matter to whom one prays and how one prays. It doesn't just matter, it matters ultimately."

From the school's perspective, another problem arises. The curriculum often seeks to foster respect for women, gays, minorities, and other groups. What happens when parents, for religious reasons, believe that the husband must head the household, that homosexuality is a sin, and that anyone who doesn't accept Jesus as Savior is bound for hell? Educators fear that if they excuse students with such beliefs from assignments, other students will infer that the school endorses the beliefs. "It is a mission of public schools," writes school administrator Frederick W. Hill, "*not* to tolerate intolerance."

Tolerating everything except intolerance, however, seems   7
self-contradictory. "If you are going to be tolerant," says Paul Vitz, a New York University psychology professor, "you are going to have to tolerate some things you don't like, including intolerance." As Tom Lehrer once quipped: "I know there are people in this world who do not love their fellow men. And I hate people like that."

The internal contradiction becomes more obvious in an   8
era of multicultural education. British educators Philip H. Walkling and Chris Brannigan observe: "What makes a particular culture identifiably that culture might include essentially sexist or racist practices and principles. . . . Sexism can be, in theory, rooted in beliefs . . . which are crucial to cultural identity. That is, they can be the very sort of belief which those of us who value a multicultural society think that minorities have the right to preserve."

In addition, a bedrock principle of civil liberties is that the   9
state must allow many things of which majorities disapprove: Jehovah's Witnesses distributing anti-Catholic literature in Catholic neighborhoods, Nazis marching through a predominantly Jewish suburb, and protestors setting fire to an American flag. The Constitution generally *does* tolerate intolerance. The schools ought to teach this principle and operate in accordance with it in order to prepare students for democratic citizenship.

Boundaries exist, of course. Parents can't expect the pub-   10
lic schools to teach religious dogma, and they can't expect the schools to insulate religious objectors from other children all day long (as New York City did by building a wall between Hasidic Jewish students and other students, until a court ruled the approach unconstitutional). But parents can reasonably request secular alternatives to religiously offensive assignments. Or they can ask to have their children sent to a study hall and take over responsibility for part of the curriculum themselves.

Parents can't expect the school to teach their children   11
creationism. But they can ask the school not to teach their

children evolution. Parents can't expect teachers to make religious judgments on their behalf. But they can expect teachers to respect the parents' judgments—unlike the teacher in the Midwest who told Jehovah's Witnesses that their parents were wrong, God wanted them to participate in the classroom Halloween party; and unlike the kindergarten teacher who told an atheist's daughter that her mother was wrong, God does exist.

Some materials, moreover, are indispensable; parents   12
can't expect to have their children excused from reading them. But as former Massachusetts education official Charles Glenn writes, "The number of specific texts that are truly essential to carrying out the mission of public education is surely very limited: the Declaration of Independence, the Bill of Rights, the Gettysburg Address, a handful of others."

We can differ over how far schools ought to go to accom-   13
modate religious objections to the curriculum—whether schools ought to release students only from supplementary books or from single or multiple textbooks and courses. But the presumption ought to be in favor of accommodation.

Without such a presumption, fundamentalists will in-   14
creasingly wind up in religious schools and home schooling. Unable to avoid part of the public school curriculum, they will avoid all of it—an option that has long dismayed supporters of public education. "The greater the proportion of our youth who fail to attend our public schools and who receive their education elsewhere, the greater the threat to our democratic unity," Harvard president James Bryant Conant wrote in 1952. "Letting subcultural groups split off and form their own private schools," writes educator James Moffett, "will seriously deepen community and national divisions." In Moffett's view, "America needs to accommodate plurality *within* unity, so that various parties can pursue, on the same sites, the ramifications of their goals and values and discover where these lead."

If we believe that pluralistic public education is an essen-   15
tial bulwark of a peaceful multicultural society, then we should do what we can to keep fundamentalists (and other religious dissidents) in the public schools. Even skipping the occasional book or class, they benefit from and contribute to the democratic mission of public education. They acquire socially beneficial information and attitudes that they might not otherwise get. By their presence, they also give other students an object lesson in diversity.

We shouldn't panic when the difference manifests itself,   16
as when some students leave the room or read a different

book. Embracing religious diversity but forbidding its public expression is a crabbed form of pluralism, one that our public schools should forsake.

READING FOR MEANING

Write to create meanings for Bates's argument that public schools should respond to students' religious objections by modifying the curriculum.

START MAKING MEANING

Begin by explaining briefly what you think is the main reason behind Bates's argument that public schools should tolerate intolerance. Continue by writing about anything else in the essay or in your experience that contributes to your understanding of Bates's argument.

IF YOU ARE STUCK

If you cannot write at least a page, consider writing about

- the examples Bates gives of tolerance in public schools (paragraph 1), choosing one example and explaining why you approve or disapprove of the practice.

- Bates's choice of words—such as "relativism" (paragraph 5), "sexism" (paragraph 8), and "pluralism" (paragraph 16)—and the connotations (attitudes and feelings) these words carry.

- how you learned the theory of evolution in school and whether the experience qualified as "tolerant."

- what Bates means by "indifferentism" (paragraph 4).

READING LIKE A WRITER
DEFINING THE ISSUE

For a well-known issue like the one Stephen Bates writes about in "Religious Diversity and the Schools," defining or redefining the issue can be an important part of the argument. In some debates, writers define the issue in the same terms their readers do. For example, many people see the death penalty in terms of "an eye-for-an-eye" justice, but still argue about whether justice is being applied equally. Often, however, writers define the terms differently than their readers. For example, instead of accepting the assumption that the death penalty is just (arguing only about whether it is applied equally), a writer might redefine the issue in legal or constitutional terms, presenting the death penalty as "cruel and unusual punishment." To redefine the terms of the argument, the writer needs to convince readers that this new way of defining the issue (in terms of what is appropriate punishment) is important and should be taken seriously.

As a critical reader, you will want to be attentive to the ways writers define and attempt to redefine the terms of an argument. Uncritical readers can become confused or even misled by arguments that surreptitiously shift the terms. To read critically, you need to identify and examine closely the key terms the writer uses. You may also need to do some additional reading to help you judge whether the writer fairly represents others' definitions of the issue and decide whether the writer's redefinition of the issue makes sense.

ANALYZE

1. *Reread* paragraphs 1–9, underlining the word *tolerance* in its various forms (such as *tolerating* and *tolerant*).

2. *Look closely* at the way Bates uses the concept of tolerance, noting how he defines it and shows that people differ in their understanding of it.

3. *Notice* the distinction Bates draws between civil and religious tolerance in paragraph 4, and the contradiction he identifies in paragraphs 7 and 8.

4. *Consider* how defining the issue serves as part of Bates's strategy to influence his politically conservative readers. *Think about* how readers with different points of view are likely to respond to his strategy.

WRITE

Write several sentences, describing what you have learned about how Bates defines the issue and about the role his definition plays in advancing his argument. *Cite* examples from the reading. *Tell* whether you think his strategy is effective and why.

CONSIDERING IDEAS FOR YOUR OWN WRITING

The first paragraph of Bates's essay presents several educational policy issues you could write about. Other school-related issues you might consider: Should college athletes whose teams help raise money for the school be paid for their labor? Should parent groups or school boards ban certain books from high-school reading lists? Should AIDS education be required in all schools? Should condoms be distributed free in high schools? Should community service be required for high-school graduation? Should federal loans be available to any high-school graduate who wants to go to college?

DONELLA MEADOWS

Rush and Larry, Coast to Coast: This Is Not Democracy in Action

Donella Meadows (b. 1941) is a professor of environmental studies at Dartmouth College. She has cowritten several books, including The Global Citizen *(1991) and* Beyond the Limits: Confronting Global Collapse, Envisioning a Sustainable Future *(1993). She is also the author of a nationally syndicated newspaper column, "The Global Citizen."*

Meadows wrote the following essay several months after the 1992 presidential election. It originally appeared in the Los Angeles Times, *a newspaper with a general readership. The issue—whether television and radio talk shows help foster democratic debate—came to the fore after Ross Perot declared his candidacy on the talk show* Larry King Live. *Perot promised to continue to hold the "electronic town meetings" he held during his campaign to debate solutions to the nation's problems. The town meeting, where all citizens meet to play a direct role in government (voting on issues instead of voting for the politicians who decide issues), is a New England institution dating from colonial times. It is often cited as a model of direct democracy.*

Before reading the essay, reflect on talk shows you have seen on television or heard on radio. In your experience, what do such shows contribute to the national debate on important issues? How democratic do you think they are? As you read and annotate Meadows's essay, notice how she defines democracy.

I'm a talk-show junkie. I'd rather listen to real folks stumbling to express their own thoughts than to polished puppets reading what others have written. I tune into Larry, Rush and the folks who call in, to keep myself awake, chuckling, thinking and every now and then yelling in outrage.

One item of talk I hear is about the power of talk shows. They are restoring democracy, it is said, to a nation that has concentrated too much power within one narrow East Coast Beltway. Just by venting our opinions into a national satellite feed, you and I can scuttle a congressional pay raise, elevate a wise-cracking Texan to a presidential candidacy or bring down a potential attorney general because she hired an illegal alien.[1]

[1]Washington, D.C., is the area within the "East Coast Beltway," Ross Perot is the "wise-cracking Texan," and Zoë Baird is the "potential attorney general" whose candidacy was withdrawn when it was discovered that she had hired an illegal alien to care for her children. *(Ed.)*

We don't need Ross Perot to create an electronic town   3
meeting, they say. It's already going on, coast-to-coast, on
multiple channels, 24 hours a day.

Now, much as I like the talk shows, I'm also from New En-   4
gland, and I can say that there's a big difference between the
Rush Limbaugh show and a town meeting. And much as I
like town meetings, they are not as effectively democratic as
they could be.

One problem with both call-in shows and town meetings   5
is that they're not representative. Only those who take
the trouble, and don't have to go to work, and aren't busy
with the kids can participate. Even within that set, the
loudest mouths and most made-up minds dominate the air
time. At town meetings, you can see the shy folks, the ones
who have trouble sounding off in public, leaning against
the back wall or bending over their knitting. On talk radio,
those people are invisible, but they're there. It's a mistake
to think that the blowhards who call in speak for the
nation.

A second problem is that, as we know well from town   6
meetings, the power isn't with the people, it's with the moderator. He or she establishes the rules, decides who to call
on, changes the subject, cuts people off. In talk radio, there
is only one rule: Break for the commercial on time.

Some call-in moderators are neutral and courteous. Then   7
there's Rush Limbaugh, who is funny and pompous and a
scapegoater and hatemonger. His popularity could cause
you to draw some terrible conclusions about the state of
mind of the American people. It helps to remember that Bill
Cosby is popular, too. I heard an interview the other day
with a psychologist who was hired by Cosby to go over each
script to be sure it contained no "put-down" humor—no joke
made at the expense of any person or group. Limbaugh's
show is pure put-down humor.

The purpose of the commercial media is not to foster   8
democracy, of course; it's to entertain in order to attract attention in order to sell. Therefore, talk shows have a fast
pace. They flip from topic to topic. There is time to spout
off, but no time for serious debate. Talk shows can only
transmit knee-jerk responses to hot-button items. They can
deal with Zoë Baird's child-care arrangements, but they
seem uninterested in Ron Brown's links to corporations and
foreign governments. They have plenty to say about gays in
the military, but they can't fathom Yugoslavia. They get ex-
ercised about Congress bouncing checks worth a few thou-

sand dollars, while billions of dollars slide away into the S&L disaster.[2]

The talk shows not only miss the biggest, most profound issues; they can be a breeding grounds for careening falsehoods. One man tells Larry King that a cellular phone gave his wife brain cancer, causing a national panic before there's a shred of evidence. Rush Limbaugh pronounces the greenhouse effect a fiction made up by commie-pinko environmentalists, and decades of good science are swept away.   9

Even if everyone could participate, even if the moderators were fair and responsible, even if the pace were deliberate enough to have a real conversation, there would be a final problem with democracy by talk radio. We are not very good at talking to one another. We are better at coming back with one-liners than at listening with open minds. We have few public role models showing us how to demand and judge evidence, how to weigh conflicting opinions, how to deal with uncertainty and complication.   10

What I hear every day on talk radio is America's lack of education—and I don't mean lack of college degrees. I mean lack of the basic art of democracy, the ability to seek the great truths that can come only by synthesizing the small truths possessed by each of us.   11

The world is richly varied and wildly complicated. Each person experiences only a piece of it. To make any sense of the world, to make the right decisions as a nation, we need many points of view—east and west, rich and poor, male and female, liberal and conservative, urban and rural, black and white, yes, even straight and gay. Democracy wins out over any government dominated by just one point of view, because only democracy has at least the potential of seeing the world complete and whole.   12

That's why talk shows and town meetings are good things. They will be even better when they let all voices be heard with respect, with inquiry, and with dedication to finding the truth, rather than ridiculing the opposition.   13

---

[2]Zoë Baird was a candidate for attorney general (referred to earlier), while Ron Brown was former head of the Democratic party and secretary of commerce. Gays in the military, the war in Yugoslavia, Congress bouncing checks, and the S&L (savings and loan) problem were all newsworthy events at the time the article was written. (*Ed.*)

READING FOR MEANING

Write to create meanings for Meadows's argument about the role of talk shows in fostering democratic debate.

START MAKING MEANING

Begin by restating the reasons Meadows gives for her position. Continue by writing about anything else in the essay or in your experience that contributes to your understanding of Meadows's argument.

IF YOU ARE STUCK

If you cannot write at least a page, consider writing about

- any show on television or radio that has influenced your thinking on a social or political issue, relating your experience to Meadows's argument.

- the idea that talk shows treat politics as a source of entertainment.

- another example of democratic discussion, such as an Internet chatroom, relating your example to Meadows's argument.

- which critical thinking skills, if any, are needed to participate meaningfully in democratic discussions.

READING LIKE A WRITER
ARGUING FOR A POSITION THROUGH DEFINITION

As we have seen, writers of essays arguing a position pay close attention to the words they use. The success of an argument often depends on how readers define certain key words. Sometimes writers try to win an argument by redefining the terms of the issue. We have seen this strategy in the essay by Stephen Bates, where he tries to shift the terms of the issue *from* a question of whether *diversity* should be a goal of public schools *to* whether diversity should include *toleration* of all things, including intolerance. If readers accept Bates's definition of the issue as "tolerating intolerance," then they are likely to accept his conclusion that schools should accommodate religious objections to the curriculum, permitting students to be excused from the study of evolution or any other subject to which they object.

In the essay by Donella Meadows we can see another way writers use definition to argue directly for their positions. As you will see from the following activity, Meadows bases her reasons on various meanings of the key term *democratic* in order to, as asserted in the thesis in paragraph 4, convince readers that talk shows are "not as effectively democratic as they could be."

ANALYZE

1. Here is a brief outline of Meadows's four reasons why talk shows are not sufficiently democratic: because they are "not representative" (paragraph 5), because they give all the power to the moderator instead of to the people (paragraphs 6–7), because they do not provide time for serious debate and breed falsehood (paragraphs 9–10), and because participants lack the "ability to seek the great truths by synthesizing the small truths possessed by each of us" (paragraphs 10–12).

2. *Choose* one of these reasons and *examine* the role of definition in the argument. *Look* specifically at how the idea of democracy relates to the reason you have chosen.

WRITE

Write several sentences, describing the role definition plays in the part of the argument you chose to analyze. Also, *speculate about* its effectiveness. What might make Meadows's readers, including yourself, accept or reject this particular definition?

CONSIDERING IDEAS FOR YOUR OWN WRITING

Consider any controversial issues involving the media—television, radio, film, performance art, music video, recording, or the Internet. For example, should sexually explicit material on the Internet be censored in some way? Should films or television programs that represent different nationalities or ethnic groups be monitored to prevent stereotyping? Should compact discs have an industry-designed rating system like the ones used for film and television?

CHARLES KRAUTHAMMER

Saving Nature, but Only for Man

Charles Krauthammer (b. 1950) has had a varied career as a research psychiatrist and political scientist. He has won many awards for his writing, including the Pulitzer Prize for Distinguished Commentary and the National Magazine Award for Essays and Criticism. He has published one book, Cutting Edges: Making Sense of the Eighties *(1985). Krauthammer writes a weekly syndicated column for the* Washington Post *as well as a monthly column for* Time *magazine, where the following essay appeared in 1991.*

In this position paper, Krauthammer attacks what he calls "sentimental environmentalism." Knowing from national polls that many adults who read general news-magazines like Time *support environmental causes, Krauthammer takes the risk of telling his readers they are wrong or they do not understand the issue very well. You might be one of these readers. As you read the essay, note your personal responses to Krauthammer's argument. How does it feel to be challenged? What do you think of the approach he takes and the tone or attitude he has toward readers?*

Environmental sensitivity is now as required an attitude in polite society as is, say, belief in democracy or aversion to polyester. But now that everyone from Ted Turner to George Bush, Dow to Exxon has professed love for Mother Earth, how are we to choose among the dozens of conflicting proposals, restrictions, projects, regulations and laws advanced in the name of the environment? Clearly not everything with an environmental claim is worth doing. How to choose?

There is a simple way. First, distinguish between environmental luxuries and environmental necessities. Luxuries are those things it would be nice to have if costless. Necessities are those things we must have regardless. Then apply a rule. Call it the fundamental axiom of sane environmentalism: Combatting ecological change that directly threatens the health and safety of people is an environmental necessity. All else is luxury.

For example: preserving the atmosphere—stopping ozone depletion and the greenhouse effect—is an environmental necessity. In April scientists reported that ozone damage is far worse than previously thought. Ozone depletion not only causes skin cancer and eye cataracts, it also destroys plankton, the beginning of the food chain atop which we humans sit.

The reality of the greenhouse effect is more speculative,   4
though its possible consequences are far deadlier: melting
ice caps, flooded coastlines, disrupted climate, parched
plains and, ultimately, empty breadbaskets. The American
Midwest feeds the world. Are we prepared to see Iowa acquire Albuquerque's climate? And Siberia acquire Iowa's?

Ozone depletion and the greenhouse effect are human   5
disasters. They happen to occur in the environment. But
they are urgent because they directly threaten man. A sane
environmentalism, the only kind of environmentalism that
will win universal public support, begins by unashamedly
declaring that nature is here to serve man. A sane environmentalism is entirely anthropocentric: it enjoins man to preserve nature, but on the grounds of self-preservation.

A sane environmentalism does not sentimentalize the   6
earth. It does not ask people to sacrifice in the name of other
creatures. After all, it is hard enough to ask people to sacrifice in the name of other humans. (Think of the chronic public resistance to foreign aid and welfare.) Ask hardworking
voters to sacrifice in the name of the snail darter, and, if
they are feeling polite, they will give you a shrug.

Of course, this anthropocentrism runs against the grain of   7
a contemporary environmentalism that indulges in earth
worship to the point of idolatry. One scientific theory—Gaia
theory—actually claims that Earth is a living organism. This
kind of environmentalism likes to consider itself spiritual. It
is nothing more than sentimental. It takes, for example, a
highly selective view of the benignity of nature. My nature
worship stops with the April twister that came through
Andover, Kans., or the May cyclone that killed more than
125,000 Bengalis and left 10 million (!) homeless.

A nonsentimental environmentalism is one founded on   8
Protagoras' maxim that "Man is the measure of all things."
Such a principle helps us through the thicket of environmental argument. Take the current debate raging over oil drilling
in a corner of the Alaska National Wildlife Refuge. Environmentalists, mobilizing against a bill working its way through
Congress to permit such exploration, argue that we should
be conserving energy instead of drilling for it. This is a false
either/or proposition. The country does need a sizable energy tax to reduce consumption. But it needs more production too. Government estimates indicate a nearly fifty-fifty
chance that under the ANWR lies one of the five largest oil
fields ever discovered in America.

We have just come through a war fought in part over oil: 9
Energy dependence costs Americans not just dollars but

lives. It is a bizarre sentimentalism that would deny ourselves oil that is peacefully attainable because it risks disrupting the calving grounds of Arctic caribou.

I like the caribou as much as the next man. And I would be   10
rather sorry if their mating patterns are disturbed. But you
can't have everything. And if the choice is between the welfare of caribou and reducing an oil dependency that gets
people killed in wars, I choose man over caribou every time.

Similarly the spotted owl. I am no enemy of the owl. If it   11
could be preserved at no or little cost, I would agree: the variety of nature is a good, a high aesthetic good. But it is no
more than that. And sometimes aesthetic goods have to be
sacrificed to the more fundamental ones. If the cost of preserving the spotted owl is the loss of livelihood for 30,000
logging families, I choose family over owl.

The important distinction is between those environmen-   12
tal goods that are fundamental and those that are merely
aesthetic. Nature is our ward. It is not our master. It is to be
respected and even cultivated. But it is man's world. And
when man has to choose between his well-being and that of
nature, nature will have to accommodate.

Man should accommodate only when his fate and that of   13
nature are inextricably bound up. The most urgent accommodation must be made when the very integrity of man's
habitat—e.g., atmospheric ozone—is threatened. When the
threat to man is of a lesser order (say, the pollutants from
coal- and oil-fired generators that cause death from disease
but not fatal damage to the ecosystem), a more modulated
accommodation that balances economic against health concerns is in order. But in either case the principle is the same:
protect the environment—because it is man's environment.

The sentimental environmentalists will call this saving na-   14
ture with a totally wrong frame of mind. Exactly. A sane—a
humanistic—environmentalism does it not for nature's sake
but for our own.

READING FOR MEANING

Write to create meanings for Krauthammer's essay about present-day
environmentalism.

START MAKING MEANING

Begin by briefly restating the reasons behind Krauthammer's argument against environmental sensitivity. Continue by writing about anything else in the essay or in your experience that contributes to your understanding of Krauthammer's argument.

IF YOU ARE STUCK

If you cannot write at least a page, consider writing about

- the distinction Krauthammer makes between "environmental sensitivity" (paragraph 1) and "sane environmentalism" (paragraphs 5 and 6).

- an environmental issue facing your hometown that fits Krauthammer's definition of an "environmental necessity" (paragraph 2).

- Krauthammer's notion of nature as "our ward . . . not our master" (paragraph 12).

- a question you would like to ask Krauthammer or an objection you have to his argument.

A SPECIAL READING STRATEGY

Looking for Patterns of Opposition

This special reading strategy involves looking for patterns of opposition in a position paper. In addition to presenting their own point of view on the issue, writers also represent opposing views. Looking for oppositions is a critical reading strategy that can help you analyze writers' assumptions about what's at stake for them in a debate. Note, for example, that Krauthammer introduces two pairs of oppositions: He names the first pair—"environmental luxuries and environmental necessities"—in paragraph 2, and he establishes the second pair—"sane environmentalism" and "sentimental environmentalism"—in the remaining paragraphs of the essay. For detailed guidelines on how to look for patterns of opposition, see Appendix One (p. 449).

READING LIKE A WRITER

COUNTERARGUING

Although counterarguing occasionally involves modifying your position to accommodate objections you consider valid, most often it simply means refuting opposing arguments. Refutation can be a small part of an argument or it can dominate the argument. Experienced writers know that a refutation's effectiveness depends largely on how staunch readers are in defending their opinions. If a reader's position is based on fundamental values and beliefs, then even the most compelling reasons and evidence are unlikely to shake his or her ideological foundations. But if a reader is at all uncertain, then supplying good counterarguments could influence his or her thinking on the issue.

Because refutation risks antagonizing readers, the tone of arguments is especially important. A tone perceived as hostile or sarcastic could be alienating, whereas a witty or easygoing tone could have the opposite effect of disarming readers, making them less defensive and more open to considering new ideas.

ANALYZE

1. *Reread* Krauthammer's essay, paying special attention to the tone of paragraphs 1 and 5–9. *Underline* the words and phrases that help convey the writer's tone.

2. *Note* in the margin where you find evidence of refutation, such as renaming or redefining the opposing position or countering an argument with examples.

3. *Check* to see whether Krauthammer acknowledges the validity of any opposing arguments or objections, or whether he modifies his own position to accommodate the views of others.

WRITE

Write a few sentences, reporting what you have learned about the strategies Krauthammer uses to counterargue.

COMPARE

Compare Krauthammer's method of counterargument with that of one other writer in this chapter, such as Jill Kuhn, whose essay on sex education in the schools begins on page 432.

CONSIDERING IDEAS FOR YOUR OWN WRITING

Krauthammer's essay opens up the possibility for you to write a position paper on an ecological issue. Consider the following examples: Should we continue to open up off-shore oil fields? Should we keep off-road vehicles out of the desert? Should we require a deposit on canned and bottled goods? Should all households be required to recycle glass, newspapers, plastic, and lawn or garden clippings?

You might instead consider writing a position paper on a local issue that affects residents' quality of life. Here are some possibilities: Should communities provide homeless people with free food and shelter? Should community growth be limited? Should height and design restrictions be placed on new commercial buildings? Should there be a police review board to handle complaints against the police? Should skateboarding be banned from all sidewalks? You and your classmates will think of other possibilities. One major advantage of writing a position paper on local quality-of-life issues is that you can gather information easily by reading community newspapers and talking with local leaders and residents.

SHELBY STEELE

Affirmative Action

Shelby Steele (b. 1946) is currently a research fellow at the Hoover Institution at Stanford University. He has written several award-winning books and essays, and he publishes regularly in popular newsmagazines and newspapers. Among his books are The Content of Our Character: A New Vision of Race in America *(1990), for which he won the National Book Critics Circle Award, and* A Dream Deferred: The Second Betrayal of Black Freedom in America *(1998).*

In the following essay from The Content of Our Character, *Steele argues for his position against affirmative action policies. Affirmative action became national policy in the 1960s as part of an effort to ensure equal opportunity for African Americans, Latinos, women, and other minority groups who in the past had been discriminated against in federally supported or regulated institutions such as colleges and television stations.*

As you read the essay, notice how Steele represents the spectrum of opinion on this complex, emotionally charged issue. Look for and annotate places where he acknowledges opposing points of view, and consider how he treats readers with whom he disagrees.

In a few short years, when my two children will be applying to college, the affirmative action policies by which most universities offer black students some form of preferential treatment will present me with a dilemma. I am a middle-class black, a college professor, far from wealthy, but also well-removed from the kind of deprivation that would qualify my children for the label "disadvantaged." Both of them have endured racial insensitivity from whites. They have been called names, have suffered slights, and have experienced firsthand the peculiar malevolence that racism brings out in people. Yet, they have never experienced racial discrimination, have never been stopped by their race on any path they have chosen to follow. Still, their society now tells them that if they will only designate themselves as black on their college applications, they will likely do better in the college lottery than if they conceal this fact. I think there is something of a Faustian bargain[1] in this.

Of course, many blacks and a considerable number of whites would say that I was sanctimoniously making affirma-

---

[1]*Faustian bargain:* from the medieval legend of Faust, a pact with the devil (*Ed.*)

tive action into a test of character. They would say that this small preference is the meagerest recompense for centuries of unrelieved oppression. And to these arguments other very obvious facts must be added. In America, many marginally competent or flatly incompetent whites are hired everyday—some because their white skin suits the conscious or unconscious racial preference of their employer. The white children of alumni are often grandfathered into elite universities in what can only be seen as a residual benefit of historic white privilege. Worse, white incompetence is always an individual matter, while for blacks it is often confirmation of ugly stereotypes. The Peter Principle[2] was not conceived with only blacks in mind. Given that unfairness cuts both ways, doesn't it only balance the scales of history that my children now receive a slight preference over whites? Doesn't this repay, in a small way, the systematic denial under which their grandfather lived out his days?

So, in theory, affirmative action certainly has all the moral symmetry that fairness requires—the injustice of historical and even contemporary white advantage is offset with black advantage; preference replaces prejudice, inclusion answers exclusion. It is reformist and corrective, even repentent and redemptive. And I would never sneer at these good intentions. Born in the late forties in Chicago, I started my education (a charitable term in this case) in a segregated school and suffered all the indignities that come to blacks in a segregated society. My father, born in the South, only made it to the third grade before the white man's fields took permanent priority over his formal education. And though he educated himself into an advanced reader with an almost professional authority, he could only drive a truck for a living and never earned more than ninety dollars a week in his entire life. So yes, it is crucial to my sense of citizenship, to my ability to identify with the spirit and the interests of America, to know that this country, however imperfectly, recognizes its past sins and wishes to correct them.

Yet good intentions, because of the opportunity for innocence they offer us, are very seductive and can blind us to the effects they generate when implemented. In our society, affirmative action is, among other things, a testament to white goodwill and to black power, and in the midst of these heavy investments, its effects can be hard to see. But after twenty years of implementation, I think affirmative action

3

4

---

[2]*The Peter Principle:* a popular business principle asserting that employees are promoted to the level of their incompetence (*Ed.*)

has shown itself to be more bad than good and that blacks—whom I will focus on in this essay—now stand to lose more from it than they gain.

In talking with affirmative action administrators and with blacks and whites in general, it is clear that supporters of affirmative action focus on its good intentions while detractors emphasize its negative effects. Proponents talk about "diversity" and "pluralism"; opponents speak of "reverse discrimination," the unfairness of quotas and set-asides. It was virtually impossible to find people outside either camp. The closest I came was a white male manager at a large computer company who said, "I think it amounts to reverse discrimination, but I'll put up with a little of that for a little more diversity." I'll live with a little of the effect to gain a little of the intention, he seemed to be saying. But this only makes him a halfhearted supporter of affirmative action. I think many people who don't really like affirmative action support it to one degree or another anyway.

I believe they do this because of what happened to white and black Americans in the crucible of the sixties when whites were confronted with their racial guilt and blacks tasted their first real power. In this stormy time white absolution and black power coalesced into virtual mandates for society. Affirmative action became a meeting ground for these mandates in the law, and in the late sixties and early seventies it underwent a remarkable escalation of its mission from simple anti-discrimination enforcement to social engineering by means of quotas, goals, timetables, set-asides and other forms of preferential treatment.

Legally, this was achieved through a series of executive orders and EEOC[3] guidelines that allowed racial imbalances in the workplace to stand as proof of racial discrimination. Once it could be assumed that discrimination explained racial imbalances, it became easy to justify group remedies to presumed discrimination, rather than the normal case-by-case redress for proven discrimination. Preferential treatment through quotas, goals, and so on is designed to correct imbalances based on the assumption that they always indicate discrimination. This expansion of what constitutes discrimination allowed affirmative action to escalate into the business of social engineering in the name of anti-discrimination, to push society toward statistically propor-

[3]*EEOC:* the Equal Employment Opportunity Commission, a federal agency charged with abolishing discrimination in hiring based on race, gender, and religion (*Ed.*)

tionate racial representation, without any obligation of proving actual discrimination.

What accounted for this shift, I believe, was the white mandate to achieve a new racial innocence and the black mandate to gain power. Even though blacks had made great advances during the sixties without quotas, these mandates, which came to a head in the very late sixties, could no longer be satisfied by anything less than racial preferences. I don't think these mandates in themselves were wrong, since whites clearly needed to do better by blacks and blacks needed more real power in society. But, as they came together in affirmative action, their effect was to distort our understanding of racial discrimination in a way that allowed us to offer the remediation of preference on the basis of mere color rather than actual injury. By making black the color of preference, these mandates have reburdened society with the very marriage of color and preference (in reverse) that we set out to eradicate. The old sin is reaffirmed in a new guise.

But the essential problem with this form of affirmative action is the way it leaps over the hard business of developing a formerly oppressed people to the point where they can achieve proportionate representation on their own (given equal opportunity) and goes straight for the proportionate representation. This may satisfy some whites of their innocence and some blacks of their power, but it does very little to truly uplift blacks.

A white female affirmative action officer at an Ivy League university told me what many supporters of affirmative action now say: "We're after diversity. We ideally want a student body where racial and ethnic groups are represented according to their proportion in society." When affirmative action escalated into social engineering, diversity became a golden word. It grants whites an egalitarian fairness (innocence) and blacks an entitlement to proportionate representation (power). *Diversity* is a term that applies democratic principles to races and cultures rather than to citizens, despite the fact that there is nothing to indicate that real diversity is the same thing as proportionate representation. Too often the result of this on campuses (for example) has been a democracy of colors rather than of people, an artificial diversity that gives the appearance of an educational parity between black and white students that has not yet been achieved in reality. Here again, racial preferences allow society to leapfrog over the difficult problem of developing blacks to parity with whites and into a cosmetic diversity that covers the blemish of disparity—a full six years after admission, only about 26 percent of black students graduate from college.

Racial representation is not the same thing as racial development, yet affirmative action fosters a confusion of these very different needs. Representation can be manufactured; development is always hard-earned. However, it is the music of innocence and power that we hear in affirmative action that causes us to cling to it and to its distracting emphasis on representation. The fact is that after twenty years of racial preferences, the gap between white and black median income is greater than it was in the seventies. None of this is to say that blacks don't need policies that ensure our right to equal opportunity, but what we need more is the development that will let us take advantage of society's efforts to include us. 11

I think that one of the most troubling effects of racial preferences for blacks is a kind of demoralization, or put another way, an enlargement of self-doubt. Under affirmative action the quality that earns us preferential treatment is an implied inferiority. However this inferiority is explained— and it is easily enough explained by the myriad deprivations that grew out of our oppression—it is still inferiority. There are explanations, and then there is the fact. And the fact must be borne by the individual as a condition apart from the explanation, apart even from the fact that others like himself also bear this condition. In integrated situations where blacks must compete with whites who may be better prepared, these explanations may quickly wear thin and expose the individual to racial as well as personal self-doubt. 12

All of this is compounded by the cultural myth of black inferiority that blacks have always lived with. What this means in practical terms is that when blacks deliver themselves into integrated situations, they encounter a nasty little reflex in whites, a mindless, atavistic reflex that responds to the color black with alarm. Attributions may follow this alarm if the white cares to indulge them, and, if they do, they will most likely be negative—one such attribution is intellectual ineptness. I think this reflex and the attributions that may follow it embarrass most whites today, therefore, it is usually quickly repressed. Nevertheless, on an equally atavistic level, the black will be aware of the reflex his color triggers and will feel a stab of horror at seeing himself reflected in this way. He, too, will do a quick repression, but a lifetime of such stabbings is what constitutes his inner realm of racial doubt. 13

The effects of this may be a subject for another essay. 14
The point here is that the implication of inferiority that
racial preferences engender in both the white and black
mind expands rather than contracts this doubt. Even when
the black sees no implication of inferiority in racial preferences, he knows that whites do, so that—consciously or unconsciously—the result is virtually the same. The effect of
preferential treatment—the lowering of normal standards to
increase black representation—puts blacks at war with an
expanded realm of debilitating doubt, so that the doubt itself becomes an unrecognized preoccupation that undermines their ability to perform, especially in integrated situations. On largely white campuses, blacks are five times more
likely to drop out than whites. Preferential treatment, no
matter how it is justified in the light of day, subjects blacks
to a midnight of self-doubt, and so often transforms their advantage into a revolving door.

Another liability of affirmative action comes from the fact 15
that it indirectly encourages blacks to exploit their own past
victimization as a source of power and privilege. Victimization, like implied inferiority, is what justifies preference, so
that to receive the benefits of preferential treatment one
must, to some extent, become invested in the view of one's
self as a victim. In this way, affirmative action nurtures a
victim-focused identity in blacks. The obvious irony here is
that we become inadvertently invested in the very condition
we are trying to overcome. Racial preferences send us the
message that there is more power in our past suffering than
our present achievements—none of which could bring us a
preference over others.

When power itself grows out of suffering, then blacks are 16
encouraged to expand the boundaries of what qualifies as
racial oppression, a situation that can lead us to paint our
victimization in vivid colors, even as we receive the benefits
of preference. The same corporations and institutions that
give us preference are also seen as our oppressors. At Stanford University minority students—some of whom enjoy as
much as $15,000 a year in financial aid—recently took over
the president's office demanding, among other things, more
financial aid. The power to be found in victimization, like any
power, is intoxicating and can lend itself to the creation of a
new class of super-victims who can feel the pea of victimization under twenty mattresses. Preferential treatment rewards us for being underdogs rather than for moving beyond that status—a misplacement of incentives that, along
with its deepening of our doubt, is more a yoke than a spur.

But, I think, one of the worst prices that blacks pay for   17
preference has to do with an illusion. I saw this illusion at
work recently in the mother of a middle-class black student
who was going off to his first semester of college. "They owe
us this, so don't think for a minute that you don't belong
there." This is the logic by which many blacks, and some
whites, justify affirmative action—it is something "owed," a
form of reparation. But this logic overlooks a much harder
and less digestible reality, that it is impossible to repay
blacks living today for the historic suffering of the race. If all
blacks were given a million dollars tomorrow morning it
would not amount to a dime on the dollar of three centuries
of oppression, nor would it obviate the residues of that oppression that we still carry today. The concept of historic
reparation grows out of man's need to impose a degree of
justice on the world that simply does not exist. Suffering can
be endured and overcome, it cannot be repaid. Blacks cannot be repaid for the injustice done to the race, but we can
be corrupted by society's guilty gestures of repayment.

Affirmative action is such a gesture. It tells us that racial   18
preferences can do for us what we cannot do for ourselves.
The corruption here is in the hidden incentive *not* to do
what we believe preferences will do. This is an incentive
to be reliant on others just as we are struggling for self-
reliance. And it keeps alive the illusion that we can find
some deliverance in repayment. The hardest thing for any
sufferer to accept is that his suffering excuses him from very
little and never has enough currency to restore him. To
think otherwise is to prolong the suffering.

Several blacks I spoke with said they were still in favor of af-   19
firmative action because of the "subtle" discrimination blacks
were subject to once on the job. One photojournalist said,
"They have ways of ignoring you." A black female television producer said, "You can't file a lawsuit when your boss
doesn't invite you to the insider meetings without ruining
your career. So we still need affirmative action." Others mentioned the infamous "glass ceiling" through which blacks can
see the top positions of authority but never reach them. But I
don't think racial preferences are a protection against this
subtle discrimination; I think they contribute to it.

In any workplace, racial preferences will always create   20
two-tiered populations composed of preferreds and unpreferreds. This division makes automatic a perception of enhanced competence for the unpreferreds and of questionable competence for the preferreds—the former earned his
way, even though others were given preference, while the

latter made it by color as much as by competence. Racial preferences implicitly mark whites with an exaggerated superiority just as they mark blacks with an exaggerated inferiority. They not only reinforce America's oldest racial myth but, for blacks, they have the effect of stigmatizing the already stigmatized.

I think that much of the "subtle" discrimination that   21
blacks talk about is often (not always) discrimination against the stigma of questionable competence that affirmative action delivers to blacks. In this sense, preferences scapegoat the very people they seek to help. And it may be that at a certain level employers impose a glass ceiling, but this may not be against the race so much as against the race's reputation for having advanced by color as much as by competence. Affirmative action makes a glass ceiling virtually necessary as a protection against the corruptions of preferential treatment. This ceiling is the point at which corporations shift the emphasis from color to competency and stop playing the affirmative action game. Here preference backfires for blacks and becomes a taint that holds them back. Of course, one could argue that this taint, which is, after all, in the minds of whites, becomes nothing more than an excuse to discriminate against blacks. And certainly the result is the same in either case—blacks don't get past the glass ceiling. But this argument does not get around the fact that racial preferences now taint this color with a new theme of suspicion that makes it even more vulnerable to the impulse in others to discriminate. In this crucial yet gray area of perceived competence, preferences make whites look better than they are and blacks worse, while doing nothing whatever to stop the very real discrimination that blacks may encounter. I don't wish to justify the glass ceiling here, but only to suggest the very subtle ways that affirmative action revives rather than extinguishes the old rationalizations for racial discrimination.

In education, a revolving door; in employment, a glass   22
ceiling.

I believe affirmative action is problematic in our society be-   23
cause it tries to function like a social program. Rather than ask it to ensure equal opportunity we have demanded that it create parity between the races. But preferential treatment does not teach skills, or educate, or instill motivation. It only passes out entitlement by color, a situation that in my profession has created an unrealistically high demand for black professors. The social engineer's assumption is that this high demand will inspire more blacks to earn Ph.D.'s and join the

profession. In fact, the number of blacks earning Ph.D.'s has declined in recent years. A Ph.D. must be developed from preschool on. He requires family and community support. He must acquire an entire system of values that enables him to work hard while delaying gratification. There are social programs, I believe, that can (and should) help blacks *develop* in all these areas, but entitlement by color is not a social program; it is a dubious reward for being black.

It now seems clear that the Supreme Court, in a series of recent decisions, is moving away from racial preferences. It has disallowed preferences except in instances of "identified discrimination," eroded the precedent that statistical racial imbalances are *prima facie* evidence of discrimination, and in effect granted white males the right to challenge consent degrees that use preference to achieve racial balances in the workplace. One civil rights leader said, "Night has fallen on civil rights." But I am not sure. The effect of these decisions is to protect the constitutional rights of everyone rather than take rights away from blacks. What they do take away from blacks is the special entitlement to more rights than others that preferences always grant. Night has fallen on racial preferences, not on the fundamental rights of black Americans. The reason for this shift, I believe, is that the white mandate for absolution from past racial sins has weakened considerably during the eighties. Whites are now less willing to endure unfairness to themselves in order to grant special entitlements to blacks, even when these entitlements are justified in the name of past suffering. Yet the black mandate for more power in society has remained unchanged. And I think part of the anxiety that many blacks feel over these decisions has to do with the loss of black power they may signal. We had won a certain specialness and now we are losing it.   24

But the power we've lost by these decisions is really only the power that grows out of our victimization—the power to claim special entitlements under the law because of past oppression. This is not a very substantial or reliable power, and it is important that we know this so we can focus more exclusively on the kind of development that will bring enduring power. There is talk now that Congress will pass new legislation to compensate for these new limits on affirmative action. If this happens, I hope that their focus will be on development and anti-discrimination rather than entitlement, on achieving racial parity rather than jerry-building racial diversity.   25

I would also like to see affirmative action go back to its original purpose of enforcing equal opportunity—a purpose   26 that in itself disallows racial preferences. We cannot be sure that the discriminatory impulse in America has yet been shamed into extinction, and I believe affirmative action can make its greatest contribution by providing a rigorous vigilance in this area. It can guard constitutional rather than racial rights, and help institutions evolve standards of merit and selection that are appropriate to the institution's needs yet as free of racial bias as possible (again, with the understanding that racial imbalances are not always an indication of racial bias). One of the most important things affirmative action can do is to define exactly what racial discrimination is and how it might manifest itself within a specific institution. The impulse to discriminate *is* subtle and cannot be ferreted out unless its many guises are made clear to people. Along with this there should be monitoring of institutions and heavy sanctions brought to bear when actual discrimination is found. This is the sort of affirmative action that America owes to blacks and to itself. It goes after the evil of discrimination itself, while preferences only sidestep the evil and grant entitlement to its *presumed* victims.

But if not preferences, then what? I think we need social 27 policies that are committed to two goals: the educational and economic development of disadvantaged people, regardless of race, and the eradication from our society—through close monitoring and severe sanctions—of racial, ethnic, or gender discrimination. Preferences will not deliver us to either of these goals, since they tend to benefit those who are not disadvantaged—middle-class white women and middle-class blacks—and attack one form of discrimination with another. Preferences are inexpensive and carry the glamour of good intentions—change the numbers and the good deed is done. To be against them is to be unkind. But I think the unkindest cut is to bestow on children like my own an undeserved advantage while neglecting the development of those disadvantaged children on the East Side of my city who will likely never be in a position to benefit from a preference. Give my children fairness; give disadvantaged children a better shot at development—better elementary and secondary schools, job training, safer neighborhoods, better financial assistance for college, and so on. Fewer blacks go to college today than ten years ago; more black males of college age are in prison or under the control of the criminal justice system than in college. This despite racial preferences.

The mandates of black power and white absolution out of 28 which preferences emerged were not wrong in themselves.

What was wrong was that both races focused more on the goals of these mandates than on the means to the goals. Blacks can have no real power without taking responsibility for their own educational and economic development. Whites can have no racial innocence without earning it by eradicating discrimination and helping the disadvantaged to develop. Because we ignored the means, the goals have not been reached, and the real work remains to be done.

READING FOR MEANING

Write to create meanings for Steele's argument against affirmative action.

START MAKING MEANING

Begin by listing the reasons you think readers must take seriously, whatever their position on the issue. Continue by writing about anything else in the essay or in your experience that contributes to your understanding of Steele's argument.

IF YOU ARE STUCK

If you cannot write at least a page, consider writing about

- the contrast between thinking of affirmative action as compensation for past discrimination versus thinking of it as preferential treatment, and how the contrast informs Steele's argument.

- what Steele means when he says affirmative action assumes an "implication of inferiority" (paragraph 14), and how this assumption influences Steele's argument as well as your own reception of it.

- the counterargument that affirmative action may no longer be needed to redress racial discrimination, but is still needed to level the playing field for poor people of any race or ethnicity.

- how being a member of a particular racial or ethnic group influences your reading of this essay.

READING LIKE A WRITER
ARGUING FOR A POSITION
THROUGH CAUSE-EFFECT REASONING

As suggested throughout this chapter, writers have much to do to create a successful position paper. Central to their efforts, however, must be developing an argument in support of their position. They may present opposing positions and counterargue, but that does not complete the argument. Readers also want to know in positive terms why the writer holds a particular position.

Steele's essay shows how writers can argue on the basis of cause and effect. If you have read Chapter Seven, Speculation about Causes or Effects, you already know a good deal about this type of argument.

ANALYZE

1. *Reread* paragraphs 12–18, where Steele argues directly against affirmative action by exploring its effects. *Underline* the phrase or sentence that identifies each effect he mentions, and then *make notes* in the margin describing each effect.

2. Also *note* in the margin how Steele supports his argument. Does he define, illustrate, compare or contrast, give examples, mention a personal experience, or offer statistics?

WRITE

Write several sentences, explaining Steele's argumentative strategies in paragraphs 12–18. Illustrate your explanation by referring to specific examples in the text. Then *add* a few sentences, evaluating Steele's argument. What do you find most and least convincing?

CONSIDERING IDEAS FOR YOUR OWN WRITING

If your view on affirmative action differs from Steele's, consider writing an essay arguing for your position. You could also take a position on other current political and social policy issues such as the following: Should HMOs be required to provide treatment recommended by physicians regardless of the cost? Should violence against people because of their sexual orientation be classified as hate crimes and subjected to extra penalties? Should fathers and mothers have equal opportunities of gaining custody of their children after a divorce? Should companies be free to replace workers who go on strike for better wages or working conditions, or should they be required to negotiate with workers or submit to binding arbitration? Should women eighteen years old and younger be required to obtain permission from their parents to get an abortion? Because these issues are currently being debated—and some have been in the news for years—you would probably want to begin your research not with books but with sources known for their currency published in print, on television, or on the Internet.

JILL KUHN

Sex Education in Our Schools

Jill Kuhn wrote this essay for a first-year composition course. Her intended readers are the parents of middle- and high-school students who are wrestling with the issue of whether they should permit their children to take sex education courses in public school. As you read the argument, consider how you would address these particular readers and how well Kuhn anticipates their concerns and possible opposing arguments.

According to a 1994 review of public schools, "forty-six states either strongly recommend or mandate the teaching of sexuality education, while all fifty states either recommend or mandate AIDS education programs" (Kirby). As of 1995, surveys show that courses on sexuality or HIV were taught in 90% of the nation's public high schools (CAPS). Even though sex education courses have been taught in many public schools since 1967, the debate still rages over whether it is appropriate to teach sex in the schools. Now that the AIDS epidemic is upon us, however, we have no choice but to teach young people about sex. As former Surgeon General C. Everett Koop said: "We have to be as explicit as necessary to get the message across. You can't talk of the dangers of snake poisoning and not mention snakes" (qtd. in Leo 138).

While few people object to sex education, most agree that ideally it should be taught at home by parents. Apparently, though, parents either are not teaching it at all or teach it ineffectively. The Sorenson report found, for example, that over 70% of the adolescents studied do not talk freely about sex with their parents (Gordon 5). The teenagers complain that while their parents tend to lecture them on morality and speak in abstractions, what they need is to learn specific facts about sex and contraception. A study of 1,873 youths found that 67% of the boys and 29% of the girls had never been given any advice on sex by their parents. Moreover, "of those who were 'advised' more than two-thirds of the boys and one-fourth of the girls felt that neither of their parents had helped them to deal effectively with the problem of sex" (Gordon 8).

Many people oppose delegating the responsibility of teaching sex education to the public schools because they assume that students are more likely to have sex after taking a sex education course. The anti-abortion activist Phyllis

1

2

3

Schlafly, for example, claims that "the way sex education is taught in the schools encourages experimentation" (qtd. in Leo 138). Research on the effects of sex education, however, should allay these fears. "Indeed," according to the British group AVERT, "several studies from different countries show that good quality sex education can actually decrease the likelihood that young people will have sex, and increase condom use among those who are already sexually active." According to Kirby's 1994 review of research on the effectiveness of sex education in the United States, "there is not sufficient evidence to determine if school-based programs that focus only upon abstinence delay the onset of intercourse or affect other sexual or contraceptive behaviors." In contrast, the "data strongly support the conclusion that sexuality and AIDS education curriculums that include discussions of contraception in combination with other topics—such as resistance skills—do not hasten the onset of intercourse" (Kirby).

Several studies even show that some students postpone their first sexual experience after taking sex education courses. Two sex-education programs designed to delay the onset of intercourse—Postponing Sexual Involvement and Reducing the Risk—"successfully reduce the proportion of sexually inexperienced students who initiated sex during the following twelve to eighteen months" (Howard and McCabe 1990, and Devlin and Sipe 1992, reported in Kirby). Studies by Laurie Schwab Zabin show that sex education combined with school-based reproductive health clinics where counseling and contraception were made available to students increased the likelihood that sexually inexperienced female high-school students would delay sex for an average of seven months (Zabin et al. 1986 and 1988, reported in Kirby).

4

Delaying by a few months or even years when adolescents begin sexual intercourse may not seem like a great accomplishment, but the fact is that many teenagers are sexually active, and nothing their parents or anyone else says is going to stop them. "Of the twenty-nine million teenagers between the ages of thirteen and nineteen," according to Madelon Lubin Finkel and Steven Finkel, "twelve million (41.1%) are estimated to have had sexual intercourse" (49). Moreover, they estimate that "more than one-fifth of first premarital pregnancies among teenagers occurred within the first month of initiating sex." According to 1986 statistics compiled by the Alan Guttmacher Institute, "a million American teenagers become pregnant each year, producing one of

5

the highest teenage pregnancy rates of any western industrialized country" (reported in Kirby).

Surely it is preferable for sexually active adolescents to have accurate information about sex and contraception than to live in ignorance. And they are amazingly ignorant. Takey Crist administered a questionnaire on sexual anatomy to six hundred female students at the University of North Carolina at Chapel Hill, and found that among sexually active women, over one-fourth could not answer any of the questions (Gordon 19). In a nationwide study, 41% of the pregnant unmarried teenagers polled said that they had thought they could not get pregnant because, as they put it, "it was the wrong time of the month" (Finkel and Finkel 49). A study of unwed pregnant teenagers in Baltimore found that less than half could name three kinds of birth control and that one-third of those who did not use contraceptives were unaware that they could have used them (Gordon 19). An astonishing 91% of those questioned felt that they lacked adequate knowledge about how to use birth control.

Sex education courses dispel myths and misconceptions about sexual behavior in general and birth control in particular. Kirby concludes that the most effective school-based programs cover the topics of contraception, pregnancy, sexually transmitted disease (STD), HIV-AIDS, as well as abstinence and resistance skills. Curricula that used "experiential activities," such as role-playing games that suggested how students could respond to common "lines" used to get someone to have sex, proved highly effective (Kirby). A course taught in twenty-three Atlanta public schools entitled "Postponing Sexual Involvement" was developed specifically in answer to students' requests for help in learning how to say no without hurting anyone's feelings (Leo 142). Studies of the "Postponing Sexual Involvement" program showed that when it was combined with instruction on human sexuality and contraception, it "increased use of contraception among those who initiated intercourse after the program, but not among those who were sexually experienced at pretest" (Howard and McCabe 1990, and Howard 1992, reported in Kirby). Another program designed to reduce unprotected intercourse, "Reducing the Risk," increased contraceptive use among sexually experienced females and lower risk students, but not among males or higher risk youth (Kirby 1991, reported in Kirby).

The advent of AIDS makes sex education a necessity rather than a luxury, particularly for young people because they are an especially high-risk population. Surgeon General Koop's report emphasizes the need to focus sex education on teenagers because even though they may consider themselves invulnerable, they are actually a great risk: "Adolescents and preadolescents are those whose behavior we wish especially to influence because of their vulnerability when they are exploring their own sexuality (heterosexual and homosexual) and perhaps experimenting with drugs." (qtd. in Lewis 348). At least 2.5 million teenagers, according to the American Social Health Association, contract a sexually transmitted disease every year, including AIDS (Lewis 348). "In 1994, 417 new AIDS cases were diagnosed among 13- to 19-year-olds, and 2,684 new cases among 20- to 24-year-olds" (CAPS).

Parents can no longer afford to be overprotective. If they   9
truly want to protect their children, they must give up the fantasy that what their sons and daughters don't know, won't hurt them. Sex kills, and we must teach our children how to defend themselves. It is not enough to preach, "Just say no!" Adolescents always have and will continue to explore their own sexuality. What they need from us is information and openness. Parents certainly have a key role to play, but they cannot do it alone. Sex education must be taught in the schools and, as the surgeon general urges, it should begin in the early grades.

WORKS CITED

AVERT. <http://www.avert.org/schsexed.html>. Apr. 1998.
CAPS (Center for AIDS Prevention Studies). University of California, San Francisco. <http://www.caps.ucsf.edu/capsweb/sexednews.html>. Sept. 28, 1995.
Finkel, Madelon Lubin, and Steven Finkel. "Sex Education in High School." *Society* (Nov.–Dec. 1985): 48–51.
Gordon, Sol. *The Sexual Adolescent.* North Scituate, MA: Duxbury, 1973.
Kirby, Douglas, et al. <http://www.epibiostat.ucsf.edu/capsweb/toolbox/SCIENCEschoolA.html>. "School-based Programs to Reduce Sexual Risk Behaviors: A Review of Effectiveness." *Public Health Reports* 109, 3 (May–June 1994): 339–61.
Leo, John. "Should Schools Offer Sex Education?" *Reader's Digest* (Mar. 1987): 138–42.
Lewis, Ann C. "A Dangerous Silence." *Phi Delta Kappan* (June 1987): 348–49.

READING FOR MEANING

Write to create meanings for Kuhn's essay about teaching sex education in the public schools.

START MAKING MEANING

Begin by restating the reasons Kuhn gives for her position and commenting on how well she supports them. Continue by writing about anything else in the essay or in your experience that contributes to your understanding of Kuhn's argument.

IF YOU ARE STUCK

If you cannot write at least a page, consider writing about

- sex education courses or lessons that you remember from your own school days, and how your experience leads you to support or challenge Kuhn's argument.

- how Kuhn tries to counter the opposing argument that sex education courses encourage experimentation, and how convincing you think her argument is likely to be with people who make this argument.

- whether you agree or disagree with Kuhn's argument "that while their parents tend to lecture them on morality and speak in abstractions, what [teenagers] need is to learn specific facts about sex and contraception" (paragraph 2).

- a question you would like to ask Kuhn or an objection you have to her argument.

READING LIKE A WRITER
MAKING AN ESSAY READABLE

Writers strive to present a clear, convincing argument. They know that all readers expect it and that readers who disagree with their argument may be eager for an excuse to reject it or to stop reading if, for example, the writing is unclear or the organization is hard to follow. Writers of position papers, therefore, usually go to some effort to make their writing clear and coherent, easy for readers to follow from point to point even when the argument is fairly complicated.

ANALYZE

1. *Reread* Kuhn's essay, noting phrases in the margin that identify both the topic of each paragraph and its apparent role or purpose in the argument. Although connections between paragraphs can remain implicit, usually they are made explicit. *Annotate* when and how Kuhn makes them explicit.

2. *Consider* how you could divide Kuhn's essay into two or three main parts. *Notice* particularly how she frames her argument by relating the end to the beginning.

WRITE

Write several sentences, explaining and evaluating how Kuhn sequences, connects, and frames her argument.

COMPARE

Choose any other position paper in this chapter to analyze. Use the same procedure you followed in analyzing the readability of Kuhn's essay. *Note* any similarities and differences in the strategies used to make the essay readable between Kuhn's essay and the essay you have chosen; for example, the explicitness of transitions connecting paragraphs, the forecasting and sequencing of main points, the use of framing (repeating material at the end from the opening). Then *write* a few more sentences, explaining what you have learned from your comparison.

A SPECIAL READING STRATEGY

Evaluating the Logic of an Argument

This special reading strategy involves evaluating the logic of an argument. Most writers try to make their argument convincing by presenting reasons and support for their position. This critical reading strategy can help you determine whether part or all of the argument meets what we call the *ABC test:* appropriateness, believability, and consistency.

For example, note that in the opening paragraph Kuhn asserts that the AIDS epidemic gives us "no choice but to teach young people about sex." This is one of her main reasons for arguing in favor of sex education in the public schools. She supports this reason by quoting a respected authority, the former Surgeon General C. Everett Koop. Readers who recognize Koop's name are likely to see him as an authoritative source, and therefore may be inclined to accept his judgment. Moreover, many readers will consider what he says—the analogy he makes between AIDS and snake poisoning—to be good common sense. Applying the ABC test, the Koop quotation seems *appropriate* because it directly supports the reason Kuhn has given. It seems *believable* because Koop is a trustworthy authority. And it seems *consistent* because it goes along with support Kuhn gives later to show that adolescents are an especially high-risk group for contracting AIDS and other sexually transmitted diseases.

For detailed guidelines on how to evaluate the logic of an argument, see Appendix One (p. 449). Your instructor may ask you to use this strategy on a particular section of the essay or to work with a group of students on the entire essay.

CONSIDERING IDEAS FOR YOUR OWN WRITING

What other controversial issues impact adolescents or young adults? List issues you think you might want to know more about. Here are a few possibilities to get you started: censorship of popular recordings, lowering the voting age, raising the driving age, increasing the minimum wage, requiring women eighteen years old and younger to obtain permission from their parents to get an abortion.

Reviewing What Makes Position Papers Effective

In this chapter, you have been learning how to read position papers for meaning and how to read them like a writer. Before going on to write a position paper, pause here to review and contemplate what you have learned about the elements of effective position papers.

Analyze

Choose one reading from this chapter that seems to you to be especially effective. Before rereading the selection, *write* down one or two reasons you remember it as an example of a good position paper.

Reread your chosen selection, adding further annotations about what makes it a particularly successful position paper. *Consider* the essay's purpose and how well it achieves that purpose for its intended readers. Then *focus* on how well the essay

- defines the issue.

- asserts the position.

- argues directly for the position.

- counterargues readers' objections and questions.

- establishes the writer's credibility.

You can review all of these basic features in the Guide to Reading Position Papers (pp. 395–402).

Your instructor may ask you to complete this activity on your own or to work with a small group of other students who have chosen the same essay. If you work with others, allow enough time initially for all group members to reread the selection thoughtfully and to add their annotations. Then discuss as a group what makes the essay effective. Take notes on your discussion. One student in your group should then report to the class what the group has learned about the effectiveness of position papers. If you are working individually, write up what you have learned from your analysis.

Write

Write at least a page, justifying your choice of this reading as an example of an effective position paper. Assume that your readers—your instructor and classmates—have read the essay but will not remember many details about it. They also may not remember it as an especially successful position paper. Therefore, you will need to *refer* to details and specific parts of the essay as you explain how it works and *justify* your evaluation of its effectiveness. You need not argue that it is the best essay in the chapter or that it is flawless, only that it is, in your view, a strong example of the genre.

A GUIDE TO WRITING POSITION PAPERS

The readings in this chapter have helped you learn a great deal about position papers. Now that you have seen how writers construct an argument supporting their position for particular readers, you can approach this type of writing confidently. The readings remain an important resource for you as you develop your essay. Use them to review how other writers have solved the types of problems you will encounter in your writing.

This guide is designed to assist you in writing your position paper. Here you will find activities to help you choose an issue and discover what to say about it, organize your ideas and draft the essay, read the draft critically, revise the draft to strengthen your argument, and edit and proofread the essay to improve readability.

INVENTION

The following invention activities will help you choose an issue to write about and develop an argument to support your position on the issue. A few minutes spent completing each writing activity will improve your chances of producing a detailed and convincing first draft.

Choosing an Issue

Rather than limiting yourself to the first issue that comes to mind, consider your options by making a list of the issues that interest you. Begin with those you wrote about for the Considering Ideas for Your Own Writing activities following the readings. List the issues in the form of questions, like these:

- Should local school boards have the power to ban books (like *The Adventures of Huckleberry Finn* and *Of Mice and Men*) from school libraries?

- Should teenagers be required to get their parents' permission to obtain birth-control information and contraceptives?

- Should businesses remain loyal to their communities or should they move to wherever labor costs, taxes, or other conditions are more favorable?

After you have completed your list, reflect on the possible topics you have compiled. Choose an arguable issue, one about which people disagree but that cannot be resolved simply with facts or authorities. Your choice also may be influenced by whether you have time for research and whether your instructor requires it. Some issues—such as whether weapon searches should be conducted on high-school campuses or whether affirmative action should be continued in college admissions—have been written about extensively and therefore would make excellent topics for extended research. Writing about still other issues—such as whether students should be required to perform community service or should be discouraged from taking part-time jobs that interfere with their studies—may be confidently based on personal experience.

Developing Your Argument

The writing and research activities that follow will enable you to test your choice of an issue and discover good ways to argue for it.

DEFINING THE ISSUE.   *To see how you can define the issue, write nonstop for about five minutes.* This brief but intensive writing will help stimulate your memory, letting you see what you know about the issue and whether you will need to do research to discover more about it.

CONSIDERING YOUR OWN POSITION AND REASONS FOR IT.   *Briefly state your current position and give a few reasons you take this position.* You may change your position as you develop your ideas and learn more about the issue, but for now say as directly as you can where you stand and why.

ANALYZING YOUR PROSPECTIVE READERS.   *Write for five minutes about your intended readers, describing what you expect them to know and think about the argument.* Begin by identifying your readers, considering who they are, where you think they stand on the issue, how they are likely to define the issue, and what kinds of reasons and support are likely to carry weight with them.

RESEARCHING THE ISSUE.   *If your instructor requires research or you decide your essay would benefit from research, see Appendix Two, Strategies for Research and Documentation, for guidelines on finding library and internet sources on an issue.* Research can help you look critically at your own thinking and help you anticipate your readers' arguments and their possible objections to your argument.

REHEARSING THE ARGUMENT FOR YOUR POSITION.   *Consider the reasons you could give for your position, and then write for ten minutes about the one or two reasons you think would be most convincing to your readers.* Which reasons do you think are the strongest? Which are most likely to appeal to your readers? Try to use these reasons to show your readers why they should adopt your position or at least take it seriously.

REHEARSING YOUR COUNTERARGUMENT.   *Consider what would be the one or two strongest opposing arguments or objections to your argument, and then write for ten minutes either refuting or accommodating them.* Try to think of arguments or objections your readers would expect you to know about and respond to, especially any criticism that could seriously undermine your argument.

FORMULATING A WORKING THESIS. *Draft a thesis statement.* A working thesis—as opposed to a final or revised thesis—will help you bring your invention writing into focus and begin your draft with a clear purpose. As you draft and revise your essay, you may decide to modify your position and reformulate your thesis. A thesis for a position paper asserts the position and nearly always forecasts the argument; it might also forecast the counterargument. The thesis and forecasting statement, therefore, may extend over several sentences. Here are three examples from the readings.

- "Still, however willing I may have been to go along with the name as a kid, as an adult I have concluded that using an ethnic group essentially as a sports mascot is wrong" (Estrada, paragraph 2).

- "If we believe that pluralistic public education is an essential bulwark of a peaceful multicultural society, then we should do what we can to keep fundamentalists (and other religious dissidents) in the public schools" (Bates, paragraph 15).

- "Sex kills, and we must teach our children how to defend themselves. . . . Parents certainly have a key role to play, but they cannot do it alone. Sex education must be taught in the schools and, as the surgeon general urges, it should begin in the early grades" (Kuhn, paragraph 9).

DRAFTING

The following guidelines will help you set goals for your draft and plan its organization.

Setting Goals

Establishing goals for your draft before you begin writing will enable you to move ahead more quickly and to make critical writing decisions more confidently. Consider the following questions now, and keep them in mind as you draft. They will help you maintain your focus while drafting as well as recall how the writers you have read in this chapter tried to achieve similar goals.

- *How can I define the issue in a way that will advance my argument?* Should I create an opposition between my position and that of others, as Krauthammer does when he distinguishes between two types of environmentalism? Should I base my argument on defining a key term, as Bates does when he argues for tolerating intolerance?

- *How can I provide reasons and support that will win the respect of my readers?* Should I quote authorities and cite statistics from research studies, as Kuhn does? Should I argue that my position is based on shared values and principles, as Bates and Estrada do? Should I provide examples, as Meadows and Krauthammer do? Should I support my argument with personal experience, as Steele does?

- *How can I counterargue effectively?* Should I acknowledge the legitimacy of opposing arguments but show that they are not realistic, as Kuhn does, or that they have become counterproductive, as Steele does? Should I try to refute the argument by arguing over key terms and their definitions, as Bates does?

- *How can I begin engagingly and end conclusively?* Should I begin on a personal note, as Estrada, Meadows, and Steele do? Or should I begin by giving readers examples that support my argument, as Bates does?

- *How can I establish my authority and credibility on the issue?* Should I support my argument by citing sources readers are likely to respect, as Kuhn does? Or should I try to base my argument on concerns and values I share with my readers as Steele, Kuhn, and others try to do?

Organizing Your Draft

With goals in mind and invention notes in hand, you are ready to make a tentative outline of your draft. List the reasons you think you will rely on as support for your argument. Decide how you will sequence these reasons. Once you have an outline, add any opposing arguments or objections that you plan to counterargue.

Writers often begin and end with the strongest reasons, putting weaker ones in the middle. This organization gives the best reasons the greatest emphasis. Meadows more or less follows this pattern. Another common plan is to begin with a definition like Bates does, letting the definition carry most of the argument's weight. Krauthammer organizes his essay around a refutation of opponents' arguments, whereas Estrada and Steele use both counterargument and direct argument.

READING A DRAFT CRITICALLY

Getting a critical reading of your draft will help you see how to improve it. Your instructor may schedule class time for reading drafts, or you may want to ask a classmate or a tutor in the writing center to read your draft. Ask your reader to use the following guidelines and to write out a response for you to consult during revision.

Read for a First Impression

1. Read the draft without stopping to annotate or comment, and then write two or three sentences giving your general impression.

2. Identify one aspect of the draft that seems to you particularly effective.

Read Again to Suggest Improvements

1. Suggest ways of defining the issue more effectively.

   • Read the paragraphs that define the issue, and tell the writer how they help you understand the issue or fail to help you.

   • Point to any key terms used to define the issue that seem surprising, confusing, antagonizing, or unnecessarily loaded.

2. Recommend ways of presenting the position more clearly and unequivocally.

   • Find the clearest statement of the position and underline it. If you cannot find a clear thesis, let the writer know.

   • If you find several restatements of the thesis, examine them closely for consistency.

   • If the position seems extreme or overstated, suggest how it might be qualified and made more reasonable.

3. Help the writer strengthen the argument.

   • Indicate any reasons that seem unconvincing and explain briefly why you think so.

   • If you find any supporting points ineffective, briefly explain why you think so and how they could be strengthened.

   • If you find any place where supporting evidence is needed, suggest what kind of support (facts, statistics, quotations, or examples) could be added.

4. Suggest ways of improving the counterargument.

   • If any part of the refutation could be strengthened, suggest what the writer could add or change.

   • If only the weakest objections or opposing arguments have been acknowledged, remind the writer of stronger objections or opposing arguments that should be taken into account.

5. Suggest how credibility can be enhanced.

- Tell the writer whether the intended readers are likely to find the essay authoritative and trustworthy. Point to places where the argument seems most and least trustworthy.

- Identify places where the writer seeks to establish a common ground—shared values, beliefs, and attitudes—with readers. Try to identify places where the writer might attempt to do so without undermining the position being argued.

6. Suggest ways of improving readability.

- Consider whether the beginning adequately sets the stage for the argument, perhaps by establishing the tone or forecasting the points of the argument.

- If the organization does not seem to follow a logical plan, suggest how it might be rearranged or where transitions could be inserted to strengthen the logical connections.

- Note whether the ending gives the argument a satisfactory sense of closure.

REVISING

This section provides suggestions for revising your draft, suggestions that will remind you of the possibilities for developing a well-argued position paper. Revising means reenvisioning your draft, trying to see it a new way, given your purpose and readers, in order to develop your argument.

The biggest mistake you can make while revising is to focus on words or sentences. Instead, first try to see your draft as a whole in order to assess its likely impact on readers. Think imaginatively and boldly about cutting unconvincing material, adding new material, and moving material around to enhance clarity and strengthen your argument. Your computer makes even drastic revisions easy, but you still need to make the effort and decisions that will improve your draft.

You may have received a critical reading from classmates, a writing center tutor, or your instructor. If so, rely on this valuable help in deciding which parts of your draft need revising and what specific changes you could make.

To Define the Issue More Effectively

- If readers do not fully understand what is at stake in the issue, consider adding anecdotes, examples, or graphic details to make the issue more specific and vivid, or explaining more systematically why you see the issue as you do.

- If the terms you use to define the issue are surprising, antagonizing, or unnecessarily loaded, consider redefining the issue in more familiar or neutral terms.

To Assert the Position More Clearly

- If the position seems unclear to readers, try reformulating it or spelling it out in more detail.

- If your thesis statement is not easy for readers to find, try to state it more directly to avoid misunderstanding.

- If your thesis is not appropriately qualified to account for valid arguments or objections, modify it by limiting its scope.

To Strengthen the Argument

- If a reason seems unconvincing, try to make it more explicit or to clarify its relevance to the argument.

- If you need better supporting evidence, review your invention notes or do more research to find facts, statistics, quotations, or examples to bolster your argument.

To Improve the Counterargument

- If your refutation seems unconvincing, provide more or better evidence, such as facts and statistics from reputable sources, to convince readers that your argument is not idiosyncratic or personal. Avoid attacking your opponents on a personal level; refute only their ideas.

- If you have ignored strong, opposing arguments or reasonable objections, revise your essay to address them directly. If you cannot refute them, acknowledge their validity—and, if necessary, modify your position to accommodate them.

- If you can make any concessions without doing injustice to your own views, consider doing so now.

To Enhance Credibility

- If readers find your sources questionable, establish your sources' credibility or choose more reliable sources to back up your argument.

- If readers think you have ignored opposing arguments, demonstrate to readers that you know and understand, even if you do not accept, different points of view on the issue.

- If your tone is harsh or off-putting, consider the implications and potential offensiveness of your word choices, looking for ways to show readers respect and to establish a common ground with them.

To Improve Readability

- If the beginning seems dull or unfocused, rewrite it, perhaps by adding a surprising or vivid anecdote.

- If readers have trouble following your argument, consider adding a brief forecast of your main points at the beginning of your essay.

- If the reasons and counterarguments are not logically arranged, reorder them. Consider announcing each reason more explicitly or adding transitions to make the connections clearer.

- If the ending seems weak, search your invention notes and draft for a memorable quotation or a vivid example that will strengthen your ending.

EDITING AND PROOFREADING

After you have revised your essay, be sure to spend some time checking for errors in usage, punctuation, and mechanics. If you have been keeping a list of errors you typically make, begin by checking your draft against this list. Ask someone else to proofread your essay before you print out a copy for your instructor.

From our research on student writing, we know that essays arguing positions have a high percentage of sentence fragments involving subordinating conjunctions and punctuation errors involving conjunctive adverbs. Because arguing a position often requires you to use subordinating conjunctions (such as *because, although,* and *since*) and conjunctive adverbs (such as *therefore, however,* and *thus*), you want to be sure you know the conventions for punctuating sentences that include these types of words. Refer to a writer's handbook for help with avoiding sentence fragments and using punctuation correctly in sentences with subordinating conjunctions and conjunctive adverbs.

Reflecting on What You Have Learned

In this chapter, you have read critically several position papers and have written one of your own. To better remember what you have learned, pause now to reflect on the reading and writing activities you completed in this chapter.

1. *Write* a page or so reflecting on what you have learned. Begin by describing what you are most pleased with in your essay.

Continued

Then *explain* what you think contributed to your achievement. Be specific about this contribution.

- If it was something you learned from the readings, *indicate* which readings and specifically what you learned from them.

- If it came from your invention writing, *indicate* the section or sections that helped you most.

- If you got good advice from a critical reader, *explain* exactly how the person helped you—perhaps by helping you understand a particular problem in your draft or by adding a new dimension to your writing.

- Try to write about your achievement in terms of what you have learned about the genre.

2. Now *reflect* more generally on position papers, a genre of writing that plays an important role in our society. *Consider* some of the following questions: As a reader and writer of position papers, how important are reasons and supporting evidence? When people argue their positions on television and radio talk shows, do they tend to emphasize reasons and support? If not, what do they emphasize? How do you think their purpose differs from the purpose of the writers you read in this chapter and from your own purpose in writing a position paper? What contribution might position papers make to our society that other genres of writing cannot make?

A Catalog of Critical Reading Strategies

Serious study of a text requires a pencil in hand—
how much pride that pencil carries.
IRVING HOWE

Here we present fourteen specific strategies for reading critically, strategies that you can learn readily and then apply not only to the selections in this book but also to your other college reading. Mastering these strategies may not make the critical reading process any easier, but it can make reading much more satisfying and productive and thus help you handle difficult material with confidence. These strategies are

- *Annotating:* recording your reactions to and questions about a text directly on the page

- *Previewing:* learning about a text before reading it closely

- *Outlining:* listing the main idea of each paragraph to see the organization of a text

- *Summarizing:* writing a passage that briefly presents the main ideas of a text

- *Paraphrasing:* relying on your own words to restate and clarify the meaning

- *Questioning to understand and remember:* inquiring about the content

- *Contextualizing:* placing a text within an appropriate historical and cultural framework

- *Reflecting on challenges to your beliefs and values:* examining your responses to reveal your own unexamined assumptions and attitudes

- *Exploring the significance of figurative language:* seeing how metaphors, similes, and symbols enhance meaning

- *Looking for patterns of opposition:* discovering what a text values by analyzing its system of binaries/contrasts

- *Evaluating the logic of an argument:* testing the argument of a text to see whether it makes sense

- *Recognizing emotional manipulation:* looking for false or exaggerated appeals

- *Judging the writer's credibility:* determining whether a text can be trusted

- *Comparing and contrasting related readings:* exploring likenesses and differences between texts to understand them better

ANNOTATING

For each of these strategies, annotating directly on the page is fundamental. *Annotating* means underlining key words, phrases, or sentences; writing comments or questions in the margins; bracketing important sections of the text; connecting ideas with lines or arrows; numbering related points in sequence; and making note of anything that strikes you as interesting, important, or questionable. (If writing on the text itself is impossible or undesirable, you can annotate a photocopy.)

Most readers annotate in layers, adding further annotations on second and third readings. Annotations can be light or heavy, depending on a reader's purpose and the difficulty of the material.

For several of the strategies in this appendix, you will need to build on and extend annotating by *taking inventory:* analyzing and classifying your annotations, searching systematically for patterns in the text, and interpreting their significance. An inventory is basically a list. When you take inventory, you make various kinds of lists in order to find meaning in a text. As you inventory your annotations on a particular reading, you may discover that the language and ideas cluster in various ways.

Inventorying annotations is a three-step process:

1. Examine your annotations for patterns or repetitions of any kind, such as recurring images or stylistic features, related words and phrases, similar examples, or reliance on authorities.

2. Try out different ways of grouping the items.

3. Consider what the patterns you have found suggest about the writer's meaning or rhetorical choices.

The patterns you discover will depend on the kind of reading you are analyzing and on the purpose of your analysis. (See Exploring the Significance of Figurative Language, p. 470, and Looking for Patterns of Opposition, p. 473, for examples of inventorying annotations.) These patterns can help you reach a deeper understanding of the text.

The following selection has been annotated to demonstrate the processes required by the critical reading strategies we describe in the remainder of Appendix One. As you read about each strategy, you will refer back to this annotated example.

MARTIN LUTHER KING JR.

An Annotated Sample from "Letter from Birmingham Jail"

Martin Luther King Jr. (1929–1968) first came to national notice in 1955, when he led a successful boycott against back-of-the-bus seating of African Americans in Montgomery, Alabama, where he was minister of a Baptist church. He subsequently formed a national organization, the Southern Christian Leadership Conference, that brought people of all races from across the country to the South to fight nonviolently for racial integration. In 1963, King led demonstrations in Birmingham that were met with violence: A black church was bombed, killing four little girls. King was arrested and, while in prison, he wrote the famous "Letter from Birmingham Jail" to answer local clergy's criticism. King begins by discussing his disappointment with the lack of support he received from white moderates, such as the group of clergy who published their criticism in the local newspaper. (The complete text of the clergymen's published criticism appears at the end of this appendix.)

The following brief reading selection is excerpted from the letter and annotated to illustrate some of the ways you can annotate as you read. Since annotating is the first step for all critical reading strategies in this catalog, these annotations are referred to throughout this appendix. As you read, add your own annotations in the right-hand margin.

¶1 White
moderates block
progress

... I must confess that over the past few years I have been gravely disappointed with the white moderate. I have almost reached the regrettable conclusion that the Negro's [great stumbling block in his stride toward freedom] is not the White Citizen's Counciler or the Ku Klux Klanner, but the white moderate, who is

1

order vs. justice

negative vs.
positive

ends vs. means
treating others
like children

¶2 Tension
necessary for
progress

Tension already
exists

Simile: hidden
tension like a
boil

True?

¶3 King
questions
clergymen's logic
of blaming the
victim

more devoted to "order" than to justice; who prefers a
negative peace which is the absence of tension to a
positive peace which is the presence of justice; who
constantly says: "I agree with you in the goal you seek,
but I cannot agree with your methods of direct action";
who paternalistically believes he can set the timetable
for another man's freedom; who lives by a mythical
concept of time and who constantly advises the Negro
to wait for a "more convenient season." Shallow understanding from people of good will is more frustrating
than absolute misunderstanding from people of ill will.
[Lukewarm acceptance is much more bewildering than
outright rejection.]

I had hoped that the white moderate would under-   2
stand that law and order exist for the purpose of establishing justice and that when they fail in this purpose
they become the [dangerously structured dams that
block the flow of social progress.] I had hoped that the
white moderate would understand that the present tension in the South is a necessary phase of the transition
from an [obnoxious negative peace,] in which the Negro
passively accepted his unjust plight, to a [substantive
and positive peace,] in which all men will respect the dignity and worth of human personality. Actually, we who
engage in nonviolent direct action are not the creators of
tension. We merely bring to the surface the hidden tension that is already alive. We bring it out in the open,
where it can be seen and dealt with. [Like a boil that can
never be cured so long as it is covered up but must be
opened with all its ugliness to the natural medicines of air
and light, injustice must be exposed, with all the tension
its exposure creates, to the light of human conscience
and the air of national opinion before it can be cured.]

In your statement you assert that our actions, even   3
though peaceful, must be condemned because they
precipitate violence. But is this a logical assertion?
Isn't this like condemning [a robbed man] because his
possession of money precipitated the evil act of rob-
bery? Isn't this like condemning [Socrates] because his
unswerving commitment to truth and his philosophical
inquiries precipitated the act by the misguided populace in which they made him drink hemlock? Isn't this
like condemning [Jesus] because his unique God-
consciousness and never-ceasing devotion to God's
will precipitated the evil act of crucifixion? We must
come to see that, as the federal courts have consistently affirmed, it is wrong to urge an individual to

cease his efforts to gain his basic constitutional rights because the question may precipitate violence. [Society must protect the robbed and punish the robber.]

4

Yes!

I had also hoped that the white moderate would reject the myth concerning time in relation to the struggle for freedom. I have just received a letter from a white brother in Texas. He writes: "All Christians know that the colored people will receive equal rights eventually, but it is possible that you are in too great a religious hurry. It has taken Christianity almost two thousand years to accomplish what it has. The teachings of Christ take time to come to earth." Such an attitude stems from a tragic misconception of time, from the strangely irrational notion that there is something in the very flow of time that will inevitably cure all ills. [Actually, time itself is neutral; it can be used either destructively or constructively.] More and more I feel that the people of ill will have used time much more effectively than have the people of good will. We will have to repent in this generation not merely for the [hateful words and actions of the bad people] but for the [appalling silence of the good people.] Human progress never rolls in on [wheels of inevitability;] it comes through the tireless efforts of men willing to be co-workers with God, and without this hard work, time itself becomes an ally of the forces of social stagnation. [We must use time creatively, in the knowledge that the time is always ripe to do right.] Now is the time to make real the promise of democracy and transform our pending [national elegy] into a creative [psalm of brotherhood.] Now is the time to lift our national policy from the [quicksand of racial injustice] to the [solid rock of human dignity.]

¶4 Justifies urgency

Quotes white moderate as example

Critiques assumptions

Silence as bad as hateful words and actions

not moving

elegy = death, psalm = celebration metaphors: quicksand, rock

You speak of our activity in Birmingham as extreme. At first I was rather disappointed that fellow clergymen would see my nonviolent efforts as those of an extremist. I began thinking about the fact that I stand in the middle of two opposing forces in the Negro community. One is a [force of complacency,] made up in part of Negroes who, as a result of long years of oppression, are so drained of self-respect and a sense of "somebodiness" that they have adjusted to segregation; and in part of a few middle-class Negroes, who because of a degree of academic and economic security and because in some ways they profit by segregation, have become insensitive to the problems of the masses. The other [force is one of bitterness and hatred,] and it comes perilously close to advocating

5

¶5 Refutes criticism, King not an extremist

Complacency vs. hatred

Malcolm X?

violence. It is expressed in the various black nationalist [groups that are springing up] across the nation, the largest and best-known being Elijah Muhammad's Muslim movement. Nourished by the Negro's frustration over the continued existence of racial discrimination, this movement is made up of people who have lost faith in America, who have absolutely repudiated Christianity, and who have concluded that the white man is an incorrigible "devil."

¶6 Claims to offer better choice

I have tried to stand between these two forces, saying that we need emulate neither the "do-nothingism" of the complacent nor the hatred and despair of the black nationalist. For there is the more excellent way of love and nonviolent protest. I am grateful to God that, through the influence of the Negro church, the way of nonviolence became an integral part of our struggle.   6

¶7 Claims his movement prevents racial violence.

If...Then... Veiled threat?

If this philosophy had not emerged, by now many streets of the South would, I am convinced, be flowing with blood. And I am further convinced that if our white brothers dismiss as "rabble-rousers" and "outside agitators" those of us who employ nonviolent direct action, and if they refuse to support our nonviolent efforts, millions of Negroes will, out of frustration and despair, seek solace and security in black-nationalist ideologies—a development that would inevitably lead to a frightening racial nightmare.   7

¶8 Change inevitable: evolution or revolution?

spirit of the times

Worldwide uprising against injustice

Why "he," not "I"?

Repeats "let him"

Not a threat?

[Oppressed people cannot remain oppressed forever.] The yearning for freedom eventually manifests itself, and that is what has happened to the American Negro. Something within has reminded him of his birthright of freedom, and something without has reminded him that it can be gained. Consciously or unconsciously, he has been caught up by the ⟨Zeitgeist,⟩ and with his black brothers of Africa and his brown and yellow brothers of Asia, South America and the Caribbean, the United States Negro is moving with a sense of great urgency toward the [promised land of racial justice.] If one recognizes this [vital urge that has engulfed the Negro community,] one should readily understand why public demonstrations are taking place. The Negro has many [pent-up resentments] and latent frustrations, and he must release them. So let him march; let him make prayer pilgrimages to the city hall; let him go on freedom rides—and try to understand why he must do so. If his repressed emotions are not released in nonviolent ways, they will seek expression through violence; this is not a threat but a fact of his-   8

"I" channel discontent

tory. So I have not said to my people: "Get rid of your discontent." Rather, I have tried to say that this normal and healthy discontent can be [channeled into the creative outlet of nonviolent direct action.] And now this approach is being termed extremist.

¶9 Justifies extremism for righteous ends

But though I was initially disappointed at being categorized as an extremist, as I continued to think about the matter I gradually gained a measure of satisfaction from the label. Was not Jesus an extremist for love: "Love your enemies, bless them that curse you, do good to them that hate you, and pray for them which despitefully use you, and persecute you." Was not (Amos) an extremist for justice: "Let justice roll down like waters and righteousness like an everflowing stream." Was not (Paul) an extremist for the Christian gospel: "I bear in my body the marks of the Lord Jesus." Was not (Martin Luther) an extremist: "Here I stand; I cannot do otherwise, so help me God." And (John Bunyan): "I will stay in jail to the end of my days before I make a butchery of my conscience." And (Abraham Lincoln:) "This nation cannot survive half slave and half free." And (Thomas Jefferson:) "We hold these truths to be self-evident, that all men are created equal. . . ." [So the question is not whether we will be extremists, but what kind of extremists we will be.] Will we be extremists for hate or for love? Will we be extremists for the preservation of injustice or for the extension of justice? In that dramatic scene on Calvary's hill three men were crucified. We must never forget that all three were crucified for the same crime—the crime of extremism. Two were extremists for immorality, and thus fell below their environment. The other, (Jesus Christ,) was an extremist for love, truth and goodness, and thereby rose above his environment. Perhaps the South, [the nation and the world are in dire need of creative extremists.]

Hebrew prophet

disciple

founded Protestantism

preacher

freed slaves

wrote Declaration of Independence

Redeemer—all extremists for good

9

¶10 Disappointed in white moderate critics; thanks supporters

I had hoped that the white moderate would see this need. Perhaps I was too optimistic; perhaps I expected too much. I suppose I should have realized that few members of the oppressor race can understand the deep groans and passionate yearnings of the oppressed race, and still fewer have the vision to see that [injustice must be rooted out] by strong, persistent and determined action. I am thankful, however, that some of our white brothers in the South have grasped the meaning of this social revolution and committed themselves to it. They are still all too few in quantity, but they are big in quality. Some—such as Ralph McGill,

10

Who are they?

Lillian Smith, Harry Golden, James McBride Dabbs, Ann Braden and Sarah Patton Boyle—have written about our struggle in eloquent and prophetic terms. Others have marched with us down nameless streets of the

left unaided

South. They have (anguished) in filthy, roach-infested jails, suffering the abuse and brutality of policemen who view them as "dirty nigger-lovers." Unlike so many of their moderate brothers and sisters, they have recognized the urgency of the movement and sensed the

framing—recalls
boil simile

need for powerful ["action" antidotes] to combat the [disease of segregation.]

CHECKLIST

Annotating

To annotate a reading:

1. Mark the text using notations such as these:

   • circle words to be defined in the margin

   • underline key words and phrases

   • bracket important sentences and passages

   • use lines or arrows to connect ideas or words

   • use question marks to note any confusion or disagreement

2. Write marginal comments such as these:

   • number each paragraph for future reference

   • summarize each paragraph

   • define unfamiliar words

   • note responses and questions

   • identify interesting writing strategies

   • point out patterns

3. Layer additional markings on the text and comments in the margins as you reread for different purposes.

PREVIEWING

Previewing enables you to get a sense of what the text is about and how it is organized before reading it closely. This simple critical reading strategy includes seeing what you can learn from headnotes, biographical notes about the author, or other introductory material; skimming to get an overview of the content and organization; and identifying the genre and rhetorical situation.

Learning from Headnotes

Many texts provide some introductory material to orient readers. Books often have brief blurbs on the cover describing the content and author, as well as a preface, an introduction, and a table of contents. Articles in professional and academic journals usually provide some background information. Scientific articles, for example, typically begin with an abstract summarizing the main points. In this book, as in many textbooks, headnotes introducing the author and identifying the circumstances under which the selection was originally published precede the reading selections.

Because Martin Luther King Jr. is a well-known figure, the headnote might not tell you anything you do not already know. If you know something else about the author that could help you better understand the selection, you might want to make a note of it. As a critical reader, you should think about whether the writer has authority and credibility on the subject. Information about the writer's education, professional experience, and other publications can help. If you need to know more about a particular author, you could consult a biographical dictionary or encyclopedia in the library, such as *Who's Who, Biographical Index, Current Biography, Dictionary of American Biography,* or *Contemporary Authors.*

Skimming for an Overview

When you *skim* a text, you give it a quick, selective, superficial reading. For most explanations and arguments, a good strategy is to read the opening and closing paragraphs; the first usually introduces the subject and may forecast the main points, while the last typically summarizes what is most important in the essay. You should also glance at the first sentence of every internal paragraph because it may serve as a topic sentence, introducing the point discussed in the paragraph. Because narrative writing is usually organized chronologically rather than logically, often you can get a sense of the progression by skimming for time markers such as *then, after,* and *later.* Heads and subheads, figures and charts, also provide clues for skimming.

To illustrate, turn back to the King excerpt and skim it. Notice that the opening paragraph establishes the subject: the white moderate's criticism of Dr. King's efforts. It also forecasts many of the main points that are taken up in subsequent paragraphs; for example, the moderate's greater devotion to order than to justice (paragraph 2), the moderate's criticism that King's methods, though nonviolent, precipitate violence (paragraph 3), and the moderate's "paternalistic" timetable (paragraph 4).

Identifying the Genre and Rhetorical Situation

Reading an unfamiliar text is like traveling in unknown territory: You can use a map to check what you see against what you expect to find. In much the same way, previewing for genre equips you with a set of expectations to guide your reading. *Genre* means "kind" or "type," and is generally used to classify pieces of writing according to their particular social function. Nonfiction prose genres include autobiography, reflection, observation, explanations of concepts, and various forms of argument, such as evaluation, analysis of cause or effect, proposal to solve a problem, and position on a controversial issue. These genres are illustrated in Chapters Two through Nine with guidelines to help you analyze and evaluate their effectiveness. After working through these chapters, you will be able to identify the genre of most unfamiliar pieces of writing you encounter.

You can make a tentative decision about the genre of a text by first looking at why the piece was written and to whom it was addressed. These two elements—purpose and audience—constitute the rhetorical or writing situation. Consider the writing of "Letter from Birmingham Jail." The title explicitly identifies this particular selection as a letter. We know that letters are usually written with a particular reader in mind, but can also be written for the reading public (as in a letter to the editor of a magazine); that they may be part of an ongoing correspondence; and that they may be informal or formal.

Read the clergymen's statement at the end of this appendix (pp. 487–89) to gain some insight into the situation in which King wrote his letter and some understanding of his specific purpose for writing. As a public letter written in response to a public statement, "Letter from Birmingham Jail" may be classified as a position paper, one that argues for a particular point of view on a controversial issue.

Even without reading the clergymen's statement, you can get a sense of the rhetorical situation from the opening paragraph of the King excerpt. You would not be able to identify the "white moderate" with the clergymen who criticized King, but you would see clearly that he is referring to people he had hoped would support his cause but who, instead, have become an obstacle. King's feelings about the white moderate's lack of support are evident in the first paragraph, where he uses such words as *gravely disappointed, regrettable conclusion, frustrating,* and *bewildering.* The opening paragraph, as noted earlier, also identifies the white moderate's specific objections to King's methods. Therefore, you not only learn very quickly that this is a position paper, but you also learn the points of disagreement between the two sides and the writer's attitude toward those with whom he disagrees.

Knowing that this is an excerpt from a position paper allows you to appreciate the controversiality of the subject King is writing about and the sensitivity of the rhetorical situation. You can see how he asserts his own position at the same time that he tries to bridge the gap separating him from his critics. You can then evaluate the kinds of points King makes and the persuasiveness of his argument.

Previewing

To orient yourself before reading closely:

1. See what you can learn from headnotes or other introductory material.

2. Skim the text to get an overview of the content and organization.

3. Identify the genre and rhetorical situation.

OUTLINING

Outlining is an especially helpful critical reading strategy for understanding the content and structure of a reading. Outlining, which identifies and organizes the text's main ideas, may be part of the annotating process, or it may be done separately. Writing an outline in the margins of the text as you read and annotate makes it easier to find information later. Writing an outline on a separate piece of paper gives you more space to work with and thus usually includes more detail.

The key to outlining is distinguishing between the main ideas and the supporting material such as examples, factual evidence, and explanations. The main ideas form the backbone, which holds the various parts and pieces of the text together. Outlining the main ideas helps you uncover this structure.

Making an outline, however, is not simple. The reader must exercise judgment in deciding which are the most important ideas. Reading is never a passive or neutral act; the process of outlining shows how active reading can be.

You may make either a *formal, multileveled outline* with roman (I, II) and arabic (1, 2) numerals together with capital and lowercase letters, or you can make an *informal, scratch outline* that lists the main idea of each paragraph. A formal outline is harder to make and much more time consuming than a scratch outline. You might choose to make a formal outline of a reading about which you are writing an in-depth analysis or evaluation. For example, here is a formal outline a student wrote for a paper evaluating the logic of the King excerpt. Notice that the student uses roman numerals for the main ideas or claims, capital letters for the reasons, and arabic numerals for supporting evidence and explanation.

 I. The Negro's great stumbling block in his stride toward freedom is . . .
    the white moderate
    A. *Because* the white moderate is more devoted to "order" than to
       justice (paragraph 2)
       1. Law and order should exist to establish justice
       2. Law and order compare to dangerously structured dams that
          block the flow of social progress
    B. *Because* the white moderate prefers a negative peace (absence of
       tension) to a positive peace (justice) (paragraph 2)
       1. The tension already exists
       2. It is not created by nonviolent direct action
       3. Society that does not eliminate injustice compares to a boil that
          hides its infections. Both can be cured only by exposure (boil
          simile)
    C. *Because* even though the white moderate agrees with the goals, he
       does not support the means to achieve them (paragraph 3)
       1. The argument that the means—nonviolent direct action—are
          wrong because they precipitate violence is flawed
       2. Analogy of the robbed man condemned because he had money
       3. Comparison with Socrates and Jesus
    D. *Because* the white moderate paternalistically believes he can set a
       timetable for another man's freedom (paragraph 4)
       1. Rebuts the white moderate's argument that Christianity
          will cure man's ills and man must wait patiently for that to
          happen
       2. Argues that time is neutral and that man must use time cre-
          atively for constructive rather than destructive ends
 II. Creative extremism is preferable to moderation
    A. Classifies himself as a moderate (paragraphs 5–8)
       1. I stand between two forces: the white moderate's complacency
          and the Black Muslim's rage
       2. If nonviolent direct action were stopped, more violence, not
          less, would result
       3. "Millions of Negroes will, out of frustration and despair, seek so-
          lace and security in black-nationalist ideologies" (paragraph 7)
       4. Repressed emotions will be expressed—if not in nonviolent
          ways, then through violence (paragraph 8)
    B. Redefines himself as a "creative extremist" (paragraph 9)
       1. Extremism for love, truth, and goodness is creative extremism
       2. Identifies himself with the creative extremists Jesus, Amos,
          Paul, Martin Luther, John Bunyan, Abraham Lincoln, and
          Thomas Jefferson
    C. Not all white people are moderates, many are creative extremists
       (paragraph 10)
       1. Lists names of white writers
       2. Refers to white activists

Making a scratch outline, in contrast to a formal outline, takes less time but still requires careful reading. A scratch outline will not record as much information as a formal outline, but it is sufficient for most critical reading purposes. To make a scratch outline, you need to locate the topic of each paragraph. The topic is usually stated in a word or phrase, and it may be repeated or referred to throughout the paragraph. For example, the opening paragraph of the King excerpt (p. 451) makes clear that its topic is the white moderate.

After you have found the topic of the paragraph, figure out what is being said about it. To return to our example: If the white moderate is the topic of the opening paragraph, then what King says about the topic can be found in the second sentence, where he announces the conclusion he has come to—namely, that the white moderate is "the Negro's great stumbling block in his stride toward freedom." The rest of the paragraph specifies the ways the white moderate blocks progress.

When you make an outline, you can use the writer's words, your own words, or a combination of the two. An outline appears in the margins of the selection, with numbers for each paragraph (see pp. 451–55). Here is the same outline on a separate piece of paper, slightly expanded and reworded:

¶1 White moderates block progress in the struggle for racial justice
¶2 Tension is necessary for progress
¶3 The clergymen's criticism is not logical
¶4 King justifies urgent use of time
¶5 Clergymen accuse King of being extreme, but he claims to stand between two extreme forces in the black community
¶6 King offers a better choice
¶7 King's movement has prevented racial violence by blacks
¶8 Discontent is normal and healthy but must be channeled creatively rather than destructively
¶9 Creative extremists are needed
¶10 Some whites have supported King

CHECKLIST

Outlining

To make a scratch outline of a text:

1. Reread each paragraph systematically, identifying the topic and what is being said about it. Do not include examples, specific details, quotations, or other explanatory and supporting material.

2. List the main ideas in the margin of the text or on a separate piece of paper.

SUMMARIZING

Summarizing is one of the most widely used strategies for critical reading because it helps you understand and remember what is most important in a text. Another advantage of summarizing is that it creates a condensed version of the reading's ideas and information, which you can refer to later or insert into your own written text. Along with quoting and paraphrasing, summarizing enables you to refer to and integrate other writers' ideas into your own writing.

Relatively brief restatements of the reading's main ideas, summaries have many functions, depending on context. When you search for sources through your college library's online catalog, summaries help you decide whether you want to read the complete source. You may also notice summaries at key points in your textbooks, points where the author wants you to review information covered in previous pages. When you begin using journal articles in your field of study, brief summaries called abstracts can help you tell right away whether the report is relevant to your research.

Summaries also vary in length. Some summaries are very brief—a sentence or even a subordinate clause. For example, if you were referring to the excerpt from "Letter from Birmingham Jail" and simply needed to indicate how it relates to your other sources, your summary might focus on only one aspect of the reading. It might look something like this:

> There have always been advocates of extremism in politics. Martin Luther King Jr., in "Letter from Birmingham Jail," for instance, defends nonviolent civil disobedience as an extreme but necessary means of bringing about racial justice.

If, however, you were surveying the important texts of the civil rights movement, you might write a longer, more detailed summary, one that not only identifies the reading's main ideas but also shows how the ideas relate to one another.

Many writers find it useful to outline the reading as a preliminary to writing a summary. A paragraph-by-paragraph scratch outline (like the one illustrated on the preceding page) lists the reading's main ideas following the sequence in which they appear in the original. But writing a summary requires more than merely stringing together the entries in an outline. A summary has to make explicit the logical connections between the ideas. Writing a summary shows how reading critically is a truly constructive process of interpretation involving both close analysis and creative synthesis.

To summarize, you need to segregate the main ideas from the supporting material, usually by making an outline of the reading. You will want to use your own words for the most part because it confirms that you understand the material you have read, but you may use key words and phrases. You may also want to cite the title and refer to the author by name, using verbs like *expresses, acknowledges,* and *explains* to indicate the writer's purpose and strategy at each point in the argument.

Following is a sample summary of the King excerpt. It is based on the outline on page 460, but is much more detailed. Most important, it fills in connections between the ideas that King left for readers to make.

> King expresses his disappointment with white moderates who, by opposing his program of nonviolent direct action, have blocked progress toward racial justice. He acknowledges that his program has raised tension in the South, but he explains that tension is necessary to bring about change. Furthermore, he argues that tension already exists. But because it has been unexpressed, it is unhealthy and potentially dangerous.
>
> He defends his actions against the clergymen's criticisms, particularly their argument that he is in too much of a hurry. Responding to charges of extremism, King claims that he has actually prevented racial violence by channeling the natural frustrations of oppressed blacks into nonviolent protest. He asserts that extremism is precisely what is needed now—but it must be creative, rather than destructive, extremism. He concludes by again expressing disappointment with white moderates for not joining his effort as many other whites have.

CHECKLIST

Summarizing

To restate briefly the main ideas in a text:

1. Make an outline.

2. Write a paragraph or more that presents the main ideas largely in your own words. Use the outline as a guide, but reread parts of the original text as necessary.

3. To make the summary coherent, fill in connections between ideas.

PARAPHRASING

Unlike a summary, which is much briefer than the original text, a *paraphrase* is generally as long as the original and often longer. Whereas summarizing seeks to present the gist or essence of the reading and leave out everything else, paraphrasing tries to be comprehensive and leave out nothing that contributes to the meaning. (For more on summarizing, see pp. 462–63).

Paraphrasing works as a critical reading strategy for especially complex and obscure passages. Because it requires a word-for-word or phrase-by-phrase rewording of the original text, paraphrasing is too time consuming and labor intensive to use with long texts. But it is perfect for making sure you understand the important passages of a difficult reading. To paraphrase, you need to work systematically through the text, looking up in a good college dictionary many of the key words, even those you are somewhat familiar with. You can quote the author's words, but if you do, put quotation marks around them and be sure to define them.

Following are two passages. The first is excerpted from paragraph 2 of the excerpt from "Letter from Birmingham Jail." The second passage paraphrases the first.

Original

I had hoped that the white moderate would understand that law and order exist for the purpose of establishing justice and that when they fail in this purpose they become the dangerously structured dams that block the flow of social progress. I had hoped that the white moderate would understand that the present tension in the South is a necessary phase of the transition from an obnoxious negative peace, in which the Negro passively accepted his unjust plight, to a substantive and positive peace, in which all men will respect the dignity and worth of human personality.

Paraphrase

King writes that he had hoped for more understanding from the white moderate—specifically that they would recognize that law and order are not ends in themselves but means to the greater end of establishing justice. When law and order do not serve this greater end, they stand in the way of progress. King expected the white moderate to recognize that the current tense situation in the South is part of a transition process that is necessary for progress. The current situation is bad because although there is peace, it is an "obnoxious" and "negative" kind of peace based on blacks passively accepting the injustice of the status quo. A better kind of peace, one that is "substantive," real and not imaginary, as well as "positive," requires that all people, regardless of race, be valued.

When you compare the paraphrase to the original, you can see that the paraphrase tries to remain true to the original by including *all* the important information and ideas. It also tries to be neutral, to avoid inserting the reader's opinions or distorting the original writer's ideas. But because paraphrasing requires the use of different words and putting those words together into different sentences, the resulting paraphrase will be different from the original. The paraphrase always, intentional or not, expresses the reader's interpretation of the original text's meaning.

CHECKLIST

Paraphrasing

To paraphrase information in a text:

1. Reread the passage to be paraphrased, looking up unknown words in a college dictionary.

2. Relying on key words in the passage, translate the information into your own sentences.

3. Revise to ensure coherence.

QUESTIONING TO UNDERSTAND AND REMEMBER

As a student, you are accustomed to teachers asking you questions about your reading. These questions are designed to help you understand a reading and respond to it more fully, and often they work. When you need to understand and use new information, however, it may be more beneficial for *you* to write the questions. Using this strategy, you can write questions while you read a text the first time. In difficult academic reading, you will understand the material better and remember it longer if you write a question for every paragraph or brief section.

We can demonstrate how this strategy works by returning to the excerpt from "Letter from Birmingham Jail" and examining, paragraph by paragraph, some questions that might be written about it. Reread the King selection (pp. 451–56). When you finish each paragraph, look at the question numbered to match that paragraph in the following list. Assume for this rereading that your goal is to comprehend the information and ideas. Notice that each question in the list asks about the content of a paragraph and that you can answer the question with information from that paragraph.

Paragraph	Question
1	How can white moderates be more of a barrier to racial equality than the Ku Klux Klan?
2	How can community tension resulting from nonviolent direct action benefit the civil rights movement?
3	How can peaceful actions be justified even if they cause violence?
4	Why should civil rights activists take action now instead of waiting for white moderates to support them?
5	How are complacent members of the community different from black nationalist groups?
6	What is King's position in relation to these two forces of complacency and anger?
7	What would have happened if King's nonviolent direct action movement had not started?
8	What is the focus of the protest, and what do King and others who are protesting hope to achieve?
9	What other creative extremists does King associate himself with?
10	Who are the whites who have supported King, and what has happened to some of them?

Each question focuses on the main idea in the paragraph, not on illustrations or details. Note, too, that each question is expressed partly in the reader's own words, not just copied from parts of the paragraph.

How can writing questions during reading help you understand and remember the content—the ideas and information—of the reading? Researchers studying the ways people learn from their reading have found that writing questions during reading enables readers to remember more than they would by reading the selection twice. Researchers who have compared the results of readers who write brief summary sentences for a paragraph with readers who write questions have found that readers who write questions learn more and remember the information longer. These researchers conjecture that writing a question involves reviewing or rehearsing information in a way that allows it to enter long-term memory, where it is more easily recalled. The result is that you clarify and "file" the information as you go along. You can then read more confidently because you have more of a base on which to build your understanding, a base that allows meaning to develop and that enables you to predict what is coming next and add it readily to what you have already learned.

This way of reading informational material is very slow, and at first it may seem inefficient. In those reading situations where you must use the information in an exam or a class discussion, it can be very efficient, however. Because this reading strategy is relatively time consuming, you would, of course, want to use it selectively.

CHECKLIST

Questioning to Understand and Remember

To use questioning to understand and remember a reading, especially one that is unfamiliar or difficult:

1. Pause at the end of each paragraph to review the information.

2. Try to identify the most important information—the main ideas or gist of the discussion.

3. Write a question that can be answered by the main idea or ideas in the paragraph.

4. Move on to the next paragraph, repeating the process.

CONTEXTUALIZING

The texts you read were all written sometime in the past and often embody historical and cultural assumptions, values, and attitudes different from your own. To read critically, you need to become aware of these differences. *Contextualizing* is a critical reading strategy that involves making inferences about a reading's historical and cultural contexts and examining the differences between those contexts and your own.

We can divide the process of contextualizing into two steps:

1. Reread the text to see how it represents the historical and cultural situation. Compare the way the text presents the situation with what you know about the situation from other sources—such as what you have read in other books and articles, seen on television or in the movies, and learned in school or from talking with people who were directly involved.

   Write a few sentences, describing your understanding of what it was like at that particular time and place. Note how the representation of the time and place in the text differs in significant ways from the other representations with which you are familiar.

2. Consider how much and in what ways the situation has changed. Write another sentence or two, exploring the historical and cultural differences.

The excerpt from "Letter from Birmingham Jail" is a good example of a text that benefits from being read contextually. If you knew little about the history of slavery and segregation in the United States, Martin Luther King Jr., or the civil rights movement, it would be very difficult to understand the passion for justice and the impatience with delay expressed in the King selection. Most Americans, however, have read about Martin

Luther King Jr., and the civil rights movement or have seen television histories such as *Eyes on the Prize* or films such as Spike Lee's *Malcolm X*.

Here is how one reader contextualized the excerpt from "Letter from Birmingham Jail":

> 1. I am not old enough to remember what it was like in the early 1960s when Dr. King was leading marches and sit-ins, but I have seen television documentaries of newsclips showing demonstrators being attacked by dogs, doused by fire hoses, beaten and dragged by helmeted police. Such images give me a sense of the violence, fear, and hatred that King was responding to.
>
> The tension King writes about comes across in his writing. He uses his anger and frustration creatively to inspire his critics. He also threatens them, although he denies it. I saw a film on Malcolm X, so I could see that King was giving white people a choice between his nonviolent way and Malcolm's more confrontational way.
>
> 2. Things have certainly changed since the sixties. Legal segregation has ended. The term *Negro* is no longer used, but there still are racists like the detective in the O. J. Simpson case. African Americans like General Colin Powell are highly respected and powerful. The civil rights movement is over. So when I'm reading King, I'm reading history.
>
> But then again, police officers still beat black men like Rodney King, and extremists like Ice T still threaten violence. I don't know who's playing Dr. King's role today (Jesse Jackson?).

CHECKLIST

Contextualizing

To contextualize:

1. Describe the historical and cultural situation as it is represented in the reading and in other sources with which you are familiar.

2. Compare the text's historical and cultural contexts to your own historical and cultural situations.

REFLECTING ON CHALLENGES TO YOUR BELIEFS AND VALUES

Reading often challenges our attitudes, our unconsciously held beliefs, or our positions on current issues. We may feel anxious, irritable, or disturbed; threatened or vulnerable; ashamed or combative. We may feel suddenly wary or alert. When we experience these feelings as we read, we are reacting in terms of our personal or family values, religious beliefs, racial or ethnic group, gender, sexual orientation, social class, or regional experience.

You can grow intellectually, emotionally, and in social understanding if you are willing (at least occasionally) to *reflect* on these challenges instead of simply resisting them. Learning to question your unexamined assumptions and attitudes is an important part of becoming a critical thinker.

This reading strategy involves marking the text where you feel challenged, and then reflecting on why you feel challenged. As you read a text for the first time, simply mark an X in the margin at each point where you sense a challenge to your attitudes, beliefs, or values. Make a brief note in the margin about what you feel at that point or about what in the text seems to create the challenge. The challenge you feel may be mild or strong. It may come frequently or only occasionally.

Review the places you have marked in the text where you felt challenged in some way. Consider what connections you can make among these places or among the feelings you experienced at each place. For example, you might notice that you object to only a limited part of a writer's argument, resist nearly all of an authority's quoted statements, or dispute implied judgments about your gender or social class.

Write about what you have learned. Begin by describing briefly the part or parts of the text that make you feel challenged. Then write several sentences, reflecting on your responses. Keep the focus on your feelings. You need not defend or justify your feelings. Instead, try to give them a voice. Where do they come from? Why are they important to you? Although the purpose is to explore why you feel as you do, you may find that thinking about your values, attitudes, and beliefs sends you back to the text for help with defining your own position.

Here, for example, is how one writer responded to the excerpt from "Letter from Birmingham Jail":

> I'm troubled and confused by the way King uses the labels *moderate* and *extremist*. He says he doesn't like being labeled an extremist but he labels the clergymen moderate. How could it be OK for King to be moderate and not OK for the clergymen? What does *moderate* mean anyway? My dictionary defines *moderate* as "keeping within reasonable or proper limits; not extreme, excessive, or intense." Being a moderate sounds a lot better than being an extremist. I was taught not to act rashly or to go off the deep end. I'm also troubled that King makes a threat (although he says he does not).

CHECKLIST

Reflecting on Challenges to Your Beliefs and Values

To reflect on challenges to your beliefs and values:

1. Identify the challenges by marking where in the text you feel your beliefs and values are being opposed, criticized, or unfairly characterized.

2. Select one or two of the most troubling challenges you have identified and write a few sentences describing why you feel as you do. Do not attempt to defend your feelings; instead, analyze them to see where they come from.

EXPLORING THE SIGNIFICANCE OF FIGURATIVE LANGUAGE

Figurative language (metaphors, similes, and symbols) takes words literally associated with one object or idea and applies them to another object or idea. Because it embodies abstract ideas in vivid images, figurative language can often communicate more dramatically than direct statement. Figurative language also enriches meaning by drawing on a complex of feeling and association, indicating relations of resemblance and likeness. Here are definitions and examples of the most common figures of speech.

Metaphor implicitly compares two things by identifying them with each other. For instance, when King calls the white moderate "the Negro's great stumbling block in his stride toward freedom" (paragraph 1, p. 451), he does not mean that the white moderate literally trips the Negro who is attempting to walk toward freedom. The sentence makes sense only when it is understood figuratively: the white moderate trips up the Negro by frustrating every effort to eliminate injustice. Similarly, King uses the image of a dam to express the abstract idea of the blockage of justice (paragraph 2).

Simile, a more explicit form of comparison, uses *like* or *as* to signal the relation of two seemingly unrelated things. King uses simile when he says that injustice is "like a boil that can never be cured so long as it is covered up" (paragraph 2). This simile makes several points of comparison between injustice and a boil. It suggests that injustice is a disease of society, as a boil is a disease of the body, and that injustice, like a boil, must be exposed or it will fester and worsen. A simile with many points of comparison is called an *extended simile* or *conceit.*

A *symbol* is something that stands for or represents something else. Critics do not agree about the differences between a metaphor and a symbol, but one popular line of thought is that a symbol relates two or more items that already have a strong recognized alliance or affinity; metaphor, more general, would be the association of two related or unrelated items. By this definition, King uses the white moderate as a symbol for supposed liberals and would-be supporters of civil rights who are actually frustrating the cause.

How these figures of speech are used in a text reveals something of the writer's feelings about the subject and attitude toward prospective readers, and may even suggest the writer's feelings about the act of writing. Annotating and taking inventory of patterns of figurative language can thus provide insight into the tone and intended emotional effect of the writing.

Exploring the patterns of figurative language involves (1) annotating and then listing all the metaphors, similes, and symbols you find in the reading; (2) grouping the figures of speech that appear to express similar feelings and attitudes, and labeling each group; and (3) writing to explore the meaning of the patterns you have found.

The following sample inventory and analysis of the King excerpt demonstrate the process of exploring the significance of figurative language.

Listing Figures of Speech

Step 1 produced the following inventory:

order is a dangerously structured dam that blocks the flow

social progress should flow

stumbling block in the stride toward freedom

injustice is like a boil that can never be cured

the light of human conscience and air of national opinion

time is something to be used, neutral, an ally, ripe quicksand of racial injustice

the solid rock of human dignity

human progress never rolls in on wheels of inevitability

men are co-workers with God

groups springing up

promised land of racial justice

vital urge engulfed

pent-up resentments

normal and healthy discontent can be channeled into the creative outlet of nonviolent direct action

root out injustice

powerful action is an antidote

disease of segregation

Grouping Figures of Speech

Step 2 yielded three common themes:

Sickness: segregation is a disease; action is healthy, the only antidote; injustice is like a boil

Underground: tension is hidden; injustice must be rooted out; extremist groups are springing up; discontent can be channeled into a creative outlet

Blockage: forward movement is impeded by obstacles—the dam, stumbling block; human progress never rolls in on wheels of inevitability; social progress should flow

Exploring Patterns

Step 3 entailed about ten minutes of writing to explore the themes listed in step 2:

The patterns of blockage and underground suggest a feeling of frustration. Inertia is a problem; movement forward toward progress or upward toward the promised land is stalled. There seems to be a strong need to break through the resistance, the passivity, the discontent and to be creative, active, vital. These are probably King's feelings both about his attempt to lead purposeful, effective demonstrations and his effort to write a convincing letter.

The simile of injustice being like a boil links the two patterns of underground and sickness, suggesting something bad, a disease, is inside the people or the society. The cure is to expose, to root out, the blocked hatred and injustice and to release the tension or emotion that has so long been repressed. This implies that repression itself is the evil, not simply what is repressed.

CHECKLIST

Exploring the Significance of Figurative Language

To understand how figurative language—metaphor, simile, and symbol—contributes to a reading's meaning:

1. Annotate and then list all the figures of speech you find.

2. Group them and label each group.

3. Write to explore the meaning of the patterns you have found.

LOOKING FOR PATTERNS OF OPPOSITION

All texts contain patterns or voices of *opposition*. These voices may echo the views and values of critical readers the writer anticipates or predecessors to which the writer is responding; they may even reflect the writer's own conflicting values. You may need to look closely for such a dialogue of opposing voices within the text.

When we think of oppositions, we ordinarily think of polarities such as *yes* and *no, up* and *down, black* and *white, new* and *old.* Some oppositions, however, may be more subtle. The excerpt from "Letter from Birmingham Jail" is rich in such oppositions: *moderate* versus *extremist, order* versus *justice, direct action* versus *passive acceptance, expression* versus *repression.* These oppositions are not accidental; they form a significant pattern that gives a critical reader important information about King's letter.

A careful reading shows that one of the two terms in an opposition is nearly always valued over the other. In the King excerpt, for example, *extremist* is valued over *moderate* (paragraph 9, p. 455). This preference for extremism is surprising. The critical reader should ask why, when white extremists like the Ku Klux Klan have committed so many outrages against black southerners, King would prefer extremism. If King is trying to convince his readers to accept his point of view, why would he represent himself as an extremist? Moreover, why would a clergyman advocate extremism instead of moderation?

By studying the patterns of opposition, you can answer these questions more fully. You can see that King sets up this opposition to force his readers to examine their own values and realize that they are in fact misplaced. Instead of working toward justice, he says, those who support law and order maintain the unjust status quo. Getting his readers to think of the white moderate as blocking rather than facilitating peaceful change brings them to align themselves with King and perhaps even embrace his strategy of nonviolent resistance.

Looking for patterns of opposition is a four-step method of analysis:

1. Divide a piece of paper in half lengthwise by drawing a line down the middle. In the left-hand column, list those words and phrases from the text that you have annotated as indicating oppositions. Enter in the right-hand column the word or phrase that seems, according to this writer, the opposite of each word or phrase in the left-hand column. You may have to paraphrase or even supply this opposite word or phrase if it is not stated directly in the text.

2. For each pair of words or phrases, put an asterisk next to the one that seems to be preferred by the writer.

3. Study the list of preferred words or phrases, and identify what you think is the predominant system of values put forth by the text. Do the same for the other list, identifying the alternative system or sys-

tems of values implied in the text. Take about ten minutes to describe the oppositions in writing.

4. To explore these conflicting points of view, write a few sentences presenting one side, and then write a few more sentences presenting the other side. Use as many of the words or phrases from the list as you can—explaining, extending, and justifying the values they imply. You may also, if you wish, quarrel with the choice of words or phrases on the grounds that they are loaded or oversimplify the issue.

The following sample inventory and analysis of the King excerpt demonstrate the method for exploring patterns of opposition in a text.

Listing Oppositions

Steps 1 and 2: This list of oppositions uses asterisks to identify King's preferred word or phrase in each pair:

white moderate	*extremist
order	*justice
negative peace	*positive peace
absence of justice	*presence of justice
goals	*methods
*direct action	passive acceptance
*exposed tension	hidden tension
*robbed	robber
*individual	society
*words	silence
*expression	repression
*extension of justice	preservation of injustice
*extremist for love, truth, and justice	extremist for immorality

Analyzing Oppositions

Step 3 produced the following description of the conflicting points of view:

> In this reading, King addresses as "white moderates" the clergymen who criticized him. He sees the moderate position in essentially negative terms, whereas extremism can be either negative or positive. Moderation is equated with passivity, acceptance of the status quo, fear of disorder, perhaps even fear of any change. The moderates believe justice can wait, whereas law and order cannot. Yet, as King points out, there is no law and order for blacks who are victimized and denied their constitutional rights.
>
> The argument King has with the white moderates is basically over means and ends. Both agree on the ends but disagree on the

means that should be taken to secure those ends. What means are justified to achieve one's goals? How does one decide? King is willing to risk a certain amount of tension and disorder to bring about justice; he suggests that if progress is not made, more disorder, not less, is bound to result. In a sense, King represents himself as a moderate caught between the two extremes—the white moderates' "do-nothingism" and the black extremists' radicalism.

At the same time, King substitutes the opposition between moderation and extremism with an opposition between two kinds of extremism, one for love and the other for hate. In fact, he represents himself as an extremist willing to make whatever sacrifices—and perhaps even to take whatever means—are necessary to reach his goal of justice.

Considering Alternative Points of View

Step 4 entailed a few minutes of exploratory writing about the opposing point of view, and then several more minutes of writing about King's possible response to the opposition's argument:

The moderates' side: I can sympathize with the moderates' fear of further disorder and violence. Even though King advocates nonviolence, violence does result. He may not cause it, but it does occur because of him. Moderates do not really advocate passive acceptance of injustice, but want to pursue justice through legal means. These methods may be slow, but since ours is a system of law, the only way to make change is through that system. King wants to shake up the system, to force it to move quickly for fear of violence. That strikes me as blackmail, as bad as if he were committing violence himself. Couldn't public opinion be brought to bear on the legal system to move more quickly? Can't we elect officials who will change unjust laws and see that the just ones are obeyed? The *vote* should be the weapon in a democracy, shouldn't it?

King's possible response: He would probably have argued that the opposing viewpoint was naive. One of the major injustices at that time was that blacks were prevented from voting, and no elected official would risk going against those who voted for him or her. King would probably have agreed that public opinion needed to be changed, that people needed to be educated, but he would also have argued that education was not enough when people were being systematically deprived of their legal rights. The very system of law that should have protected people was being used as a weapon against blacks in the South. The only way to get something done was to shake people up, make them aware of the injustice they were allowing to continue. Seeing their own police officers committing violence should have made people question their own values and begin to take action to right the wrongs.

Looking for Patterns of Opposition

To explore and analyze the patterns of opposition in a reading:

1. Annotate the selection to identify the oppositions, and list the pairs on a separate page.

2. Put an asterisk next to the writer's preferred word or phrase in each pair of opposing terms.

3. Examine the pattern of preferred terms to discover the system of values the pattern implies; then do the same for the unpreferred terms.

4. Write to analyze and evaluate these alternative systems of value.

EVALUATING THE LOGIC OF AN ARGUMENT

An *argument* has two essential parts: the claim and support. The *claim* asserts a conclusion—an idea, an opinion, a judgment, or a point of view—that the writer wants readers to accept. The *support* includes *reasons* (shared beliefs, assumptions, and values) and *evidence* (facts, examples, statistics, and authorities) that give readers the basis for accepting the writer's conclusion.

When you assess the logic of an argument, you are concerned about the process of reasoning as well as the argument's truthfulness. Three conditions must be met for an argument to be considered logically acceptable—what we call the ABC test:

A. The support must be *appropriate* to the claim.

B. All of the statements must be *believable*.

C. The argument must be *consistent* and *complete*.

A. Testing for Appropriateness

To assess whether a writer's reasoning is appropriate, you look to see if all of the evidence is relevant to the claim it supports. For example, if a writer claims that children must be allowed certain legal rights, readers could readily accept as appropriate support quotations from Supreme Court justices' decisions but might question quotations from a writer of popular children's books. Readers could probably accept the reasoning that if women have certain legal rights then so should children, but few readers would agree that all human rights under the law should be extended to animals.

As these examples illustrate, appropriateness of support comes most often into question when the writer is invoking authority or arguing by analogy. For example, in the excerpt from "Letter from Birmingham Jail," King argues by analogy and, at the same time, invokes authority: "Isn't this like condemning Socrates because his unswerving commitment to truth and his philosophical inquiries precipitated the act by the misguided populace in which they made him drink hemlock?" (paragraph 3, p. 452). Readers not only must judge the appropriateness of comparing the Greek populace's condemnation of Socrates to the white moderates' condemnation of King's action, but also must judge whether it is appropriate to accept Socrates as an authority on this subject. Because Socrates is generally respected for his teaching on justice, his words and actions are likely to be considered appropriate to King's situation in Birmingham.

In paragraph 2, King argues that if law and order fail to establish justice, "they become the dangerously structured dams that block the flow of social progress." The analogy asserts a logical relationship: that law and order are to social justice what a dam is to water. If readers do not accept this analogy, then the argument fails the test of appropriateness. Arguing by analogy is usually considered a weak kind of argument because most analogies are parallel only up to a point, beyond which they may fail.

B. Testing for Believability

Believability is a measure of the degree to which readers are willing to accept the assertions supporting the claim. Whereas some assertions are obviously true, most depend on the readers' sharing certain values, beliefs, and assumptions with the writer. Readers who agree with the white moderate that maintaining law and order is more important than establishing justice are not going to accept King's claim that the white moderate is blocking progress.

Other statements such as those asserting facts, statistics, examples, and authorities present evidence to support a claim. Readers must put all of these kinds of evidence to the test of believability.

Facts are statements that can be proven objectively to be true. The believability of facts depends on their *accuracy* (they should not distort or misrepresent reality), their *completeness* (they should not omit important details), and the *trustworthiness* of their sources (sources should be qualified and unbiased). In the excerpt from "Letter from Birmingham

Jail," for instance, King asserts as fact that the African American will not wait much longer for racial justice (paragraph 8). His critics might question the factuality of this assertion by asking: Is it true of all African Americans? How much longer will they wait? How does King know what the African American will and will not do?

Statistics are often assumed to be factual, but they are really only interpretations of numerical data. The believability of statistics depends on the *accuracy* of the methods of gathering and analyzing data (representative samples should be used and variables accounted for), the *trustworthiness* of the sources (sources should be qualified and unbiased), and often on the *comparability* of the data (are apples being compared to oranges?).

Examples and *anecdotes* are particular instances that if accepted as believable lead readers to accept the general claim. The power of examples depends on their *representativeness* (whether they are truly typical and thus generalizable) and their *specificity* (whether particular details make them seem true to life). Even if a vivid example or gripping anecdote does not convince readers, it strengthens argumentative writing by bringing home the point dramatically. In paragraph 5, for example, King supports his generalization that there are black nationalist extremists motivated by bitterness and hatred by citing the specific example of Elijah Muhammad's Muslim movement. Conversely, in paragraph 9, he refers to Jesus, Paul, Luther, and others as examples of extremists motivated by love. These examples support his assertion that extremism is not in itself wrong, that any judgment must depend on the cause for which one is an extremist.

Authorities are people whom the writer consults for expertise on a given subject. Such authorities not only must be appropriate, as mentioned earlier, but must be believable as well. The believability of authorities, their *credibility,* depends on whether the reader accepts them as experts on the topic. King cites authorities repeatedly throughout the essay, referring not only to religious leaders such as Jesus and Luther but also to American political leaders such as Lincoln and Jefferson. These figures are certain to have a high degree of credibility among King's readers.

C. Testing for Consistency and Completeness

Be sure that all the support works together, that no supporting statement contradicts any of the others, and that no important objection or opposing argument is unacknowledged. To test for consistency and completeness, ask yourself: Are any of the supporting statements contradictory? Are there any objections or opposing arguments that are not refuted?

In his essay, a potential contradiction is King's characterizing himself first as a moderate between the forces of complacency and violence, and later as an extremist opposed to the forces of violence. King attempts to reconcile this apparent contradiction by explicitly redefining extremism in paragraph 9. Similarly, the fact that King fails to examine and refute every legal recourse available to his cause might allow a critical reader to question the sufficiency of his supporting arguments.

Following is one student's written evaluation of the logic of King's argument. The student wrote these paragraphs after applying the ABC test, evaluating the appropriateness, believability, consistency, and completeness of King's supporting reasons and evidence.

King writes both to the ministers who published the letter in the Birmingham newspaper and to the people of Birmingham. He seems to want to justify his group's actions. He challenges white moderates, but he also tries to avoid antagonizing them. Given this purpose and his readers, his supporting statements are generally appropriate. He relies mainly on assertions of shared belief with his readers and on memorable analogies. For example, he knows his readers will accept assertions like "law and order exist for the purpose of establishing justice"; it is good to be an extremist for "love, truth, and goodness"; and progress is not inevitable, but results from tireless work and creativity. His analogies also seem acceptable and are based on appropriate comparisons. For example, he compares injustice to a boil that nonviolent action must expose to the air if it is to be healed. Throughout his argument, King avoids fallacies of inappropriateness.

Likewise, his support is believable in terms of the well-known authorities he cites (Socrates, Jesus, Amos, Paul, Luther, Bunyan, Lincoln, Jefferson); the facts he asserts (for example, that racial tension results from injustice, not from nonviolent action); and the examples he offers (such as his assertion that extremism is not in itself wrong—as exemplified by Jesus, Paul, and Luther). If there is an inconsistency in the argument, it is the contradiction between King's portraits of himself both as a moderating force and as an "extremist for love"; but his redefinition of extremism as a positive value for any social change is central to the overall persuasiveness of his logical appeal to white moderates.

CHECKLIST

Evaluating the Logic of an Argument

To determine whether an argument makes sense, apply the ABC test:

1. *Test for appropriateness* by checking to be sure that each piece of evidence is clearly and directly related to the claim it is supposed to support.

Continued

2. *Test for believability* by deciding whether you can accept as true facts, statistics, and the testimony of experts, and whether you can accept generalizations based on the examples given.

3. *Test for consistency and completeness* by ascertaining whether there are any contradictions in the argument and whether any important objections or opposing arguments have been ignored.

Then write a few sentences, exploring the appropriateness, believability, and consistency and completeness of the argument.

RECOGNIZING EMOTIONAL MANIPULATION

Writers often try to arouse emotions in readers—to excite their interest, make them care, move them to action. Although nothing is wrong with appealing to readers' emotions, it is wrong to manipulate readers with false or exaggerated emotional appeals.

Many words have connotations, associations that enrich their meaning and give words much of their emotional power. For example, we used the word *manipulation* in naming this particular critical reading strategy to arouse an emotional response in readers like you. No one wants to be manipulated. Everyone wants to feel in control of his or her attitudes and opinions. This is especially true in reading arguments: We want to be convinced, not tricked.

Emotional manipulation often works by distracting readers from relevant reasons and evidence. To keep from being distracted, you will want to pay close attention as you read and try to distinguish between emotional appeals that are acceptable and those that you consider manipulative or excessive.

Here is an example of one student's reaction to the emotional appeal of the excerpt from "Letter from Birmingham Jail":

As someone King would probably identify as a white moderate, I can't help reacting negatively to some of the language he uses in this reading. For example, in the first paragraph, he equates white moderates with members of the Ku Klux Klan even though he admits that white moderates were in favor of racial equality and justice. He also puts down white moderates for being paternalistic. Finally, he uses scare tactics when he threatens "a frightening racial nightmare."

CHECKLIST

Recognizing Emotional Manipulation

To assess whether emotional appeals are unfairly manipulative:

1. Annotate places in the text where you sense emotional appeals being used.

2. Write a few sentences exploring your responses and identifying the kinds of appeals you found.

JUDGING THE WRITER'S CREDIBILITY

Writers often try to persuade readers to respect and believe them. Because readers may not know them personally or even by reputation, writers must present an image of themselves in their writing that will gain their readers' confidence. This image cannot be made directly but must be made indirectly, through the arguments, language, and the system of values and beliefs implied in the writing. Writers establish *credibility* in several ways:

- By showing their understanding of the subject
- By building common ground with readers
- By showing their ability to reason logically
- By responding fairly to objections and opposing arguments
- By choosing words precisely to show that they care

Testing for Knowledge

Writers demonstrate their knowledge through the facts and statistics they marshal, the sources they rely on for information, and the scope and depth of their understanding. As a critical reader, you may not be sufficiently expert on the subject yourself to know whether the facts are accurate, the sources reliable, and the understanding sufficient. You may need to do some research to see what others are saying about the subject. You can also check credentials—the writer's educational and professional qualifications, the respectability of the publication in which the selection first appeared, any reviews of the writer's work—to determine whether the writer is a respected authority in the field. King brings with him the authority that comes from being a member of the clergy and a respected leader of the Southern Christian Leadership Conference.

Testing for Common Ground

One way writers can establish common ground with their readers is by basing their reasoning on shared values, beliefs, and attitudes. They use language that includes their readers (*we*) rather than excludes them (*they*). They qualify their assertions to keep them from being too extreme. Above all, they acknowledge differences of opinion and try to make room in their argument to accommodate reasonable differences. As a reader, you will be affected by such appeals.

King creates common ground with readers by using the inclusive pronoun *we,* suggesting shared concerns between himself and his audience. Notice, however, his use of masculine pronouns and other references ("the Negro . . . he," "our brothers"). Although King intended this letter to be published in the local newspaper, where it would be read by an audience of both men and women, he addressed it to male clergy. By using language that excludes women, King missed the opportunity to build common ground with half his readers.

Testing for Fairness

Writers display their character by how they handle objections to their arguments. As a critical reader, you want to pay particular attention to how writers treat possible differences of opinion. Be suspicious of those who ignore differences and pretend everyone agrees with their viewpoints. When objections or opposing views are represented, you should consider whether they have been distorted in any way; if they are refuted, you want to be sure they are challenged fairly—with sound reasoning and solid evidence.

One way to gauge an author's credibility is to identify the tone of the argument. *Tone,* the writer's attitude toward the subject and toward the reader, is concerned not so much with what is said as with how it is said. By reading sensitively, you should be able to detect the writer's tone. To identify the tone, list whatever descriptive adjectives come to mind in response to either of these questions: How would you characterize the attitude of this selection? What sort of emotion does the writer bring to his or her writing? Judging from this piece of writing, what kind of person does the author seem to be?

Here is an answer to the second question, based on the excerpt from "Letter from Birmingham Jail":

> I know something about King from television programs on the civil rights movement. But if I were to talk about my impression of him from this passage, I'd use words like *patient, thoughtful, well*

educated, moral, confident. He doesn't lose his temper but tries to convince his readers by making a case that is reasoned carefully and painstakingly. He's trying to change people's attitudes; no matter how annoyed he might be with them, he treats them with respect. It's as if he believes that their hearts are right, but they're just confused. If he can just set them straight, everything will be fine. Of course, he also sounds a little pompous when he compares himself to Jesus and Socrates, and the threat he appears to make in paragraph 8 seems out of character. Maybe he's losing control of his self-image at those moments.

CHECKLIST

Judging the Writer's Credibility

To decide whether you can trust the writer:

1. As you read and annotate, consider the writer's knowledge of the subject, how well the writer establishes common ground with readers, and whether the writer deals fairly with objections and opposing arguments.

2. Write a few sentences exploring what you discover.

COMPARING AND CONTRASTING RELATED READINGS

When you *compare* two reading selections, you look for similarities. When you *contrast* them, you look for differences. As critical reading strategies, comparing and contrasting enable you to see both texts more clearly.

Both strategies depend on how imaginative you are in preparing the grounds or basis for comparison. We often hear that it is fruitless, so to speak, to compare apples and oranges. It is true that you cannot add or multiply them, but you can put one against the other and come up with some interesting similarities and differences. For example, comparing apples and oranges in terms of their roles as symbols in Western culture (say, the apple of Adam and Eve compared to the symbol for Apple computers) could be quite productive. The grounds or basis for comparison, like a camera lens, brings some things into focus while blurring others.

To demonstrate how this strategy works, we compare and contrast the excerpt from "Letter from Birmingham Jail" (pp. 451–56) with the following selection by Lewis H. Van Dusen Jr.

LEWIS H. VAN DUSEN JR.

Legitimate Pressures and Illegitimate Results

A respected attorney and legal scholar, Lewis H. Van Dusen Jr. served as chair of the American Bar Association Committee on Ethics and Professional Responsibility. This selection comes from an essay, "Civil Disobedience: Destroyer of Democracy," that first appeared in the American Bar Association Journal. *As you read it, notice the annotations we made comparing this essay to the one by King.*

There are many civil rights leaders who show impatience with the process of democracy. They rely on the sit-in, boycott, or mass picketing to gain speedier solutions to the problems that face every citizen. But we must realize that the legitimate pressures that [won concessions in the past] can easily escalate into the illegitimate power plays that might [extort] demands in the future.] The victories of these civil rights leaders must not shake our confidence in the democratic procedures, as the pressures of demonstration are desirable only if they take place within the limits allowed by law. Civil rights gains should continue to be won by the persuasion of Congress and other legislative bodies and by the decision of courts. Any illegal entreaty for the [rights of some] can be an injury to the [rights of others,] for mass demonstrations often trigger violence.

1

to get something by force or intimidation

Those who advocate [taking the law into their own hands] should reflect that when they are disobeying what they consider to be an immoral law, they are deciding on a possibly immoral course. Their answer is that the process for democratic relief is too slow, that only mass confrontation can bring immediate action, and that any injuries are the inevitable cost of the pursuit of justice. Their answer is, simply put, that the end justifies the means. It is this justification of any form of demonstration as a form of dissent that threatens to destroy a society built on the rule of law.

2

King's concern with time

ends/means debate

any form?

Our Bill of Rights guarantees wide opportunities to use mass meetings, public parades and organized demonstrations to stimulate sentiment, to dramatize issues and to cause change. The Washington freedom march of 1963 was such a call for action. But the rights

3

these are legal

of free expression cannot be mere force cloaked in the garb of free speech. As the courts have decreed in labor cases, free assembly does not mean mass picketing or sit-down strikes. These rights are subject to limitations of time and place so as to secure the rights of others. When militant students storm a college president's office to achieve demands, when certain groups plan rush-hour car stalling to protest discrimination in employment, these are not dissent, but a denial of rights to others. Neither is it the lawful use of mass protest, but rather the unlawful use of mob power.

right to demonstrate is limited

can't deny others' rights

Justice Black, one of the foremost advocates and defenders of the right of protest and dissent, has said:

. . . Experience demonstrates that it is not a far step from what to many seems to be the earnest, honest, patriotic, kind-spirited multitude of today, to the fanatical, threatening, lawless mob of tomorrow. And the crowds that press in the streets for noble goals today can be supplanted tomorrow by street mobs pressuring the courts for precisely opposite ends.

Society must censure those demonstrators who would trespass on the public peace, as it must condemn those rioters whose pillage would destroy the public peace. But more ambivalent is society's posture toward the civil disobedient. Unlike the rioter, the true civil disobedient commits no violence. Unlike the mob demonstrator, he commits no trespass on others' rights. The civil disobedient, while deliberately violating a law, shows an oblique respect for the law by voluntarily submitting to its sanctions. He neither resists arrest nor evades punishment. Thus, he breaches the law but not the peace.

Isn't he contradicting himself?

But civil disobedience, whatever the ethical rationalization, is still an assault on our democratic society, an affront to our legal order and an attack on our constitutional government. To indulge civil disobedience is to invite anarchy, and the permissive arbitrariness of anarchy is hardly less tolerable than the repressive arbitrariness of tyranny. Too often the license of liberty is followed by the loss of liberty, because into the desert of anarchy comes the man on horseback, a Mussolini or a Hitler.

Threatens repression as retaliation

4

5

6

We had already read and annotated the King excerpt, so we read the Van Dusen selection looking for a basis for comparison. We decided to base our contrast on the writers' different views of nonviolent direct action. We carefully reread the Van Dusen selection, annotating aspects of his argument against the use of nonviolent direct action. These annotations led directly to the first paragraph of our contrast, which summarizes Van Dusen's argument. Then we reread the King excerpt, looking for how he justifies nonviolent direct action. The second paragraph presents King's defense, plus some of our own ideas on how he could have responded to Van Dusen.

King and Van Dusen present radically different views of legal, nonviolent direct action, such as parades, demonstrations, boycotts, sit-ins, or pickets. Although Van Dusen acknowledges that direct action is legal, he nevertheless fears it; and he challenges it energetically in these paragraphs. He seems most concerned about the ways direct action disturbs the peace, infringes on others' rights, and threatens violence. He worries that even though some groups make gains through direct action, the end result is that everyone else begins to doubt the validity of the usual democratic procedures of relying on legislation and the courts. He condemns advocates of direct action like King for believing that the end (in this case, racial justice) justifies the means (direct action). Van Dusen argues that demonstrations often end violently and that an organized movement like King's can in the beginning win concessions through direct action but then end up extorting demands through threats and illegal uses of power.

In contrast, King argues that nonviolent direct action preserves the peace by bringing hidden tensions and prejudices to the surface where they can be acknowledged and addressed. Direct action enhances democracy by changing its unjust laws and thereby strengthening it. Since direct action is entirely legal, to forgo it as a strategy for change would be to turn one's back on a basic democratic principle. Although it may inconvenience people, its end (a more just social order) is entirely justified by its means (direct action). King would no doubt insist that the occasional violence that follows direct action results always from aggressive, unlawful interference with demonstrations, interference sometimes led by police officers. He might also argue that neither anarchy nor extortion followed from his group's actions.

Notice that these paragraphs address each writer's argument separately. An alternative plan would have been to compare and contrast the two writers' arguments point by point.

CHECKLIST

Comparing and Contrasting Related Readings

To compare and contrast two reading selections:

1. Read them both to decide on a basis or grounds for comparison or contrast.

2. Reread and annotate one selection to identify points of comparison or contrast.

3. Reread the second selection, annotating for the points you have already identified.

4. Write up your analyses of the two selections, revising your analysis of the first selection to correspond to any new insights you have gained. Or write a point-by-point comparison or contrast of the two selections.

Martin Luther King Jr. wrote "Letter from Birmingham Jail" in response to the following public statement by eight Alabama clergymen.

Public Statement by Eight Alabama Clergymen

April 12, 1963

We the undersigned clergymen are among those who, in January, issued "An Appeal for Law and Order and Common Sense," in dealing with racial problems in Alabama. We expressed understanding that honest convictions in racial matters could properly be pursued in the courts, but urged that decisions of those courts should in the meantime be peacefully obeyed.   1

Since that time there has been some evidence of increased forebearance and a willingness to face facts. Responsible citizens have undertaken to work on various problems which cause racial friction and unrest. In Birmingham, recent public events have given indication that we all have opportunity for a new constructive and realistic approach to racial problems.   2

However, we are now confronted by a series of demonstrations by some of our Negro citizens, directed and led in   3 part by outsiders. We recognize the natural impatience of people who feel that their hopes are slow in being realized. But we are convinced that these demonstrations are unwise and untimely.

We agree rather with certain local Negro leadership   4
which has called for honest and open negotiation of racial issues in our area. And we believe this kind of facing of issues can best be accomplished by citizens of our own metropolitan area, white and Negro, meeting with their knowledge and experience of the local situation. All of us need to face that responsibility and find proper channels for its accomplishment.

Just as we formerly pointed out that "hatred and violence   5
have no sanction in our religious and political traditions," we also point out that such actions as incite to hatred and violence, however technically peaceful those actions may be, have not contributed to the resolution of our local problems. We do not believe that these days of new hope are days when extreme measures are justified in Birmingham.

We commend the community as a whole, and the local   6
news media and law enforcement officials in particular, on the calm manner in which these demonstrations have been handled. We urge the public to continue to show restraint should the demonstrations continue, and the law enforcement officials to remain calm and continue to protect our city from violence.

We further strongly urge our own Negro community to   7
withdraw support from these demonstrations, and to unite locally in working peacefully for a better Birmingham. When rights are consistently denied, a cause should be pressed in the courts and in negotiations among local leaders, and not in the streets. We appeal to both our white and Negro citizenry to observe the principles of law and order and common sense.

Signed by:

C. C. J. CARPENTER, D.D., LL.D., *Bishop of Alabama*

JOSEPH A. DURICK, D.D., *Auxiliary Bishop, Diocese of Mobile-Birmingham*

Rabbi MILTON L. GRAFMAN, *Temple Emanu-El, Birmingham, Alabama*

Bishop PAUL HARDIN, *Bishop of the Alabama-West Florida Conference of the Methodist Church*

Bishop NOLAN B. HARMON, *Bishop of the North Alabama Conference of the Methodist Church*

GEORGE M. MURRAY, D.D., LL.D., *Bishop Coadjutor, Episcopal Diocese of Alabama*

EDWARD V. RAMAGE, *Moderator, Synod of the Alabama Presbyterian Church in the United States*

EARL STALLINGS, *Pastor, First Baptist Church, Birmingham, Alabama*

Strategies for Research and Documentation

A s many of the essays in *Reading Critically, Writing Well* show, writers often rely on research to expand and test their own ideas about a topic. This appendix offers advice on conducting research, guidelines for evaluating sources, and instructions for documenting the sources in your writing.

CONDUCTING RESEARCH

In your college career, you may have opportunities to do many different kinds of research, including laboratory experiments and statistical surveys. Here we introduce the three basic types of research you are most likely to use to satisfy the assignments in *Reading Critically, Writing Well* and to fulfill requirements of other lower-division courses: field research using observation and interview, library research, and Internet research.

Field Research

Observation and *interview* are the two major kinds of *field* or *ethnographic research*. The observational essays in Chapter Three illustrate some of the ways you might use field research. You might also use these research techniques when proposing a solution to a problem (Chapter Eight) or when arguing a position on a controversial issue (Chapter Nine). You may be asked to read and write essays based on field research in other courses as well, such as in sociology, political science, anthropology, psychology, communication, or business.

OBSERVATION

Following are guidelines for planning an observational visit, taking notes on your observations, and reflecting on what you observed.

Planning the Visit

To ensure that you use your time productively during observational visits, you must plan them carefully.

Getting Access. If the place you propose to visit is public, you probably will have easy access to it. Ask yourself whether everything you need to see is within casual view. If not, you have encountered a potential problem of access. If you require special access or permission, you will need to call ahead or make a get-acquainted visit to introduce yourself and explain your purpose.

Announcing Your Intentions. Explain politely who you are, where you are from, and why you would like access. You may be surprised at how receptive people can be to a student on assignment from a college course. Not every place you wish to visit will welcome you, however. A variety of constraints on outside visitors exist in private businesses as well as public institutions. But generally, if people know your intentions, they may be able to tell you about aspects of a place or an activity you would not have thought to observe.

Bringing Tools. Take a notebook with a firm back so that you will have a steady writing surface, perhaps a small stenographer's pad with a spiral binding across the top. Take a few pens or pencils. If you prefer to use a tape recorder to note your observations, bring along extra tapes and batteries. Also take a notebook in case something goes wrong with the tape recorder.

Observing and Taking Notes

Here are some practical suggestions for making observations and taking notes.

Observing. Some activities invite multiple vantage points, whereas others seem to limit the observer to a single perspective. Explore the space as much as possible, taking advantage of every vantage point available to you. Consider it from different angles, both literally and figuratively. Since your purposes are to analyze as well as to describe your subject, look for its typical and atypical features, how it is like and unlike similar subjects. Think also about what would make the subject interesting to your readers.

Notetaking. You undoubtedly will find your own style of notetaking, but here are a few pointers:

- Write only on one side of the page. Later, when you organize your notes, you may want to cut up the pages and file notes under different headings.

- Along with writing words, phrases, or sentences, draw diagrams and sketches that will help you see and recall the place later on.

- Use abbreviations as much as you like, but use them consistently and clearly.

- Note any ideas or questions that occur to you.

- Use quotation marks around any overheard conversation you take down.

Because you can later reorganize your notes easily, you do not need to take observational notes in any planned or systematic way. Your notes should include information about the place, the people, and your personal reactions to both:

The Place. Begin by listing objects you see. Then add details of some of these objects—color, shape, size, texture, function, relation to similar or dissimilar objects. Although visual details will probably dominate your notes, you might also want to note sounds and smells. Be sure to include some notes about the shape, dimensions, and layout of the place. How big is it? How is it organized?

The People. Note the number of people, their activities, their movements, and behavior. Describe their appearance or dress. Record parts of overheard conversations. Note whether you see more men than women, more of one racial group than of another, more older than younger people. Most important, note anything surprising or unusual about people in the scene and how they interact with one another.

Your Impressions. Include in your notes any feelings, ideas, or insights you have about what you observe.

Reflecting on Your Observations

Immediately after your visit (within a few minutes, if possible), find a quiet place to reflect on what you saw, review your notes, and add any images, details, insights, or questions you now recall. Give yourself at least a half hour for quiet thought. Finally, review all your notes, and write a few sentences about your main impressions of the place. What did you learn? How did this visit change or confirm your preconceptions? What impression of the place and people would you like to convey to readers?

INTERVIEW

Here are guidelines for setting up an interview, conducting an interview, and reflecting on what you learned.

Planning the Interview

Choosing an Interview Subject. If you will be interviewing a person who is the focus of your research, consider beginning with one or two background interviews with other people. If several people play important roles, be sure to interview as many of them as possible. Try to be flexible, however, because you may be unable to speak with the people you targeted initially and may wind up interviewing someone else—an assistant, perhaps. You might even learn more from an assistant than you would from the person in charge.

Arranging an Interview. You may be nervous about calling a busy person and asking for some of his or her time. Indeed, you may get turned down. If so, do ask if someone else might talk with you: Many people are genuinely flattered to be asked about themselves and their work. Moreover, because you are a college student on assignment, some people may feel that they are doing a public service by allowing you to interview them. When arranging the interview, introduce yourself with a short, simple, and enthusiastic description.

Keep in mind that the person you interview is donating time to you. When you call ahead to arrange a specific time for the interview, be sure to ask what time is most convenient. Arrive at the appointed time and bring all the materials you will need to conduct the interview. Remember, too, to express your thanks when the interview has ended.

Preparing for the Interview. Make any necessary observational visits and do any essential background reading before the interview. Consider your objectives: for example, do you want the "big picture," answers to specific questions, or clarification of something you heard in another interview, observed, or read?

The key to good interviewing is flexibility. You may be looking for facts, but your interview subject may not have any to offer. In that case, you should be able to shift gears and go after whatever insight your subject has to offer.

Composing Interview Questions. You probably will want to mix specific questions requesting factual information with open-ended questions likely to generate anecdotes and reveal attitudes that could lead to other, more penetrating questions. If you were interviewing a small-business owner, for example, you might begin with a specific question about when the business was established and then follow up with an open-ended question such as, "I wonder if you would take a few minutes to tell me something about your early days in the business. I'd be interested to hear about how it got started, what your hopes were, and what problems you had to face." Also consider asking directly for an anecdote ("What happened when your employees threatened to strike?"), encouraging reflection ("What do you think has helped you most? What has hampered you?"), or soliciting advice ("What advice would you give someone trying to start a new business today?").

The best questions encourage the interview subject to talk freely but to the point. If the answer strays too far from the point, a follow-up question may be necessary to refocus the talk. Another way to direct the conversation is to rephrase the subject's answer, saying: "Let me see if I have this right . . ." or "Am I correct in saying that you feel . . . ?" Often, the interview subject will take the opportunity to amplify the original response by adding just the anecdote or quotation for which you have been looking.

One type of question to avoid during interviewing is the *leading question*. Such questions assume too much. Consider, for example, this question: "Do you think the increase in the occurrence of rape is due to the fact that women are perceived as competitors in a severely depressed economy?" The question makes several assumptions, including that there is an increase in the occurrence of rape, that women are perceived (apparently by rapists) as competitors, and that the economy is severely depressed. A better way of asking the question might be to make the assumptions more explicit by dividing the question into its parts: "Do you think there is an increase in the occurrence of rape? What could have caused it? I've heard some people argue that the economy has something to do with it. Do you think so? Do you think rapists perceive women as competitors? Could the current economic situation have made this competition more severe?" This form of questioning allows you to voice what others have said without bullying your subject into echoing your terms.

Bringing Tools. You will need several pencils or pens and a notebook with a firm back so you can write without a table. We recommend dividing the page into two columns. Use the left-hand column (one-third of the page) to note your impressions and descriptions of the scene, the person, and the mood of the interview. Title this column *Impressions*. Title the wider right-hand column *Information*. Before the interview, write down a few basic questions to jog your memory. During the interview, however, listen and ask questions based on what your interview subject says. Do not mechanically go through your list of questions.

Taking Notes during the Interview

Your interview notes might include a few full quotations, key words, and phrases to jog your memory, as well as descriptive jottings about the scene, the person, and the mood of the interview. Remember that how something is said may be as important as what is said. Do not try to record everything your subject says during the interview. Except for the occasional quotation that you will cite directly, you do not want to make a verbatim transcript of the interview. You may not have much confidence in your memory, but if you pay close attention to your subject you are likely to recall a good deal of the conversation immediately after the interview, when you should take the time to add to your notes.

Reflecting on the Interview

Soon after the interview has concluded, find a quiet place to review your notes. Spend at least half an hour adding to your notes and thinking about what you learned. At the end of this time, write a few sentences about your main impressions from the interview:

- What were the highlights of the interview for you?

- Which questions did not get as much of a response as you anticipated or seem less important to you now?

- How did the interview change your attitude toward or understanding of the subject?

- How has this experience influenced your plans to interview others or to reinterview this person?

Library Research

Library research involves a variety of activities: checking the card or online catalog, browsing in the stacks, consulting bibliographical indexes, and evaluating sources. Although librarians are there to help, all college students should learn basic library research skills. You should familiarize yourself with your college library's resources and keep careful notes as you research so that you will not have to go back over the same ground.

Library research can be useful at various stages of the writing process, depending on the kind of essay you are writing and the special needs of your subject. You may, for example, need to do research immediately to choose a subject. Or you may choose a topic without the benefit of research, then use the library to find specific information to develop and support your thesis. But no matter when you enter the stacks, you need to follow a systematic strategy: Keep a working bibliography; prepare to search for sources by determining the appropriate subject headings or other criteria; consult standard reference works, such as bibliographical indexes and computer databases; and search for books, articles, and other sources on your topic. Later in this appendix, in Evaluating Sources Critically (pp. 509–12), you will find guidelines to help you evaluate the relevancy and credibility of these and other sources.

KEEP A WORKING BIBLIOGRAPHY

A *working bibliography* is a preliminary, ongoing record of all the references you consult as you research, even including those that you do not plan to cite in your essay. Encyclopedias, bibliographies, and indexes, for example, should go into the working bibliography, though you will not list these resources in your final bibliography. The working bibliography thus is a record of the *research process* as a whole; the final bibliography is a record of the *research paper* that you ultimately write.

Since the working bibliography is a first draft of your final list of sources, it is a good idea to use the same documentation style from the start. In Documenting Sources (pp. 512–35), later in this appendix, two styles of documentation are discussed and illustrated: the style adopted by the Modern Language Association (MLA) and widely used in the humanities, and the style advocated by the American Psychological Association (APA) for use in the social sciences. Individual disciplines often have their own preferred styles of documentation, which your instructor may wish you to use.

You can keep your working bibliography on index cards, in a notebook, or in a computer file. Whatever method you choose, make your entries accurate and complete. If the call number for a book is missing a single digit, for example, you might not be able to find the book in the stacks.

PREPARE TO SEARCH FOR SOURCES

To find sources in the library you need to determine subject headings and possibly use other search criteria.

How to Search by Subject Headings

Most information in libraries is referenced by *subject headings.* Book catalogs as well as periodical and newspaper indexes are arranged by subject. Therefore, when you begin library research, you need to identify possible subject headings, the specific words and phrases under which information on your topic is categorized. You might start with *The Library of Congress Subject Headings (LCSH),* a reference book that lists the standard subject headings used in catalogs and indexes and in many encyclopedias and bibliographies. Here is what the *LCSH* entry for "Home schooling" looks like:

Home schooling *(May Subd Geog)*   Place names may follow heading

Here are entered works on the provision of compulsory education in the home by parents as an alternative to traditional public or private schooling. General works on the provision of education in the home by educational personnel are entered under Domestic Education.

Used for ———▶ **UF** Education, Home
Home-based education
Home education **NT** ◀——— Narrower term
Home instruction **SA** ◀——— See also
Home teaching by parents
Homeschooling

Continued

Instruction, Home
Schooling, Home

Broader term   ━━▶ **BT** Education

Related term   ━━▶ **RT** Education—United States

Education—Parent participation

To find relevant sources, you also may need to break your topic into subtopics (also known as *subdivisions* or *subheadings*) and browse in related subject areas. You would find the following subdivisions for "Home schooling" in the *Academic Index,* an index of magazine and journal articles, for example:

Home schooling

- Athletics

- Demographic aspects

- Equipment and supplies

- Finance

- History

- Laws, regulations, etc.

- Moral and ethical aspects

- Services

Most subject listings in catalogs and indexes include cross-references: related terms or "see also" lines that point you to more information. Note in the preceding example from *The Library of Congress Subject Headings* that "Education—Parent participation" is listed as a related term for "Home schooling."

Selecting Other Search Criteria

In addition to subject searches, you may be able to use other search criteria, such as author's name, title, call number, location, type of media (audiotape, videotape, CD-ROM), and publication date. You could search by author name for a particular author mentioned frequently in your sources, search by library call number to determine what other sources are available in a specific subject area, or search by date in a newspaper index to research a particular event—for example, May 1980 would yield references to the eruption of Mount Saint Helens.

CONSULT STANDARD REFERENCE WORKS

To get an overview of your topic, look up your subject headings in *standard reference works.* Usually, these resources are found in the reference section of the library and cannot be checked out, so budget your library time for consulting reference works accordingly.

The most useful standard reference works include *specialized encyclopedias, disciplinary guides, government publications,* and *bibliographies.* In addition, a general encyclopedia such as the *Encyclopedia Americana* might help provide a very general overview of your topic, while almanacs, atlases, and dictionaries are sometimes useful as well.

Specialized Encyclopedias

A specialized encyclopedia such as the *Encyclopedia of Crime and Justice* or a disciplinary guide such as *Social Sciences: A Cross-Disciplinary Guide to Selected Sources* offers background on a subject and starting points for further research. Specialized encyclopedias often include an explanation of issues related to the topic, definitions of specialized terminology, and selective bibliographies naming additional sources. Specialized encyclopedias can be found in the catalog under the subject heading for the discipline, such as "psychology," and the subheading "dictionaries and encyclopedias." Three particular reference sources can help you identify specialized encyclopedias covering your topic:

- *ARBA Guide to Subject Encyclopedias and Dictionaries* (1997). Lists specialized encyclopedias by broad subject category, with descriptions of coverage, focus, and any special features.

- *First Stop: The Master Index to Subject Encyclopedias* (1989). Lists specialized encyclopedias by broad subject category and provides access to individual articles within them. By looking under the key terms that describe a topic, you can find references to specific articles in any of over four hundred specialized encyclopedias.

- *Kister's Best Encyclopedias: A Comparative Guide to General and Specialized Encyclopedias* (1994). Describes over 1,000 encyclopedias, both print and electronic. Includes major foreign-language encyclopedias.

Disciplinary Guides

Disciplinary guides can help you locate the major handbooks, encyclopedias, bibliographies, journals, periodical indexes, and computer databases in various academic fields. These types of works are published rarely and are not known for their currency. However, they can be valuable references, if you take the time to check dates and supplement your sources as needed. Here is a sample of disciplinary guides:

- *The Humanities: A Selective Guide to Information Sources*, 4th ed. (1994). By Ron Blazek and Elizabeth S. Aversa.

- *Introduction to Library Research in Anthropology,* 2nd ed. (1997). By John M. Weeks.

- *The American Historical Association's Guide to Historical Literature*, 3rd ed. (1995). Edited by Mary Beth Norton and Pamela Gerardi.

- *Political Science: A Guide to Reference and Information Sources* (1990). By Henry E. York.

- *Literary Research Guide: A Guide to Reference Sources for the Study of Literatures in English and Related Topics*, 3rd ed. (1998). By James L. Harner.

Government Resources

Some government publications and statistical reports may be found in the reference section or in a special government documents section of a library. If you are researching current issues, for example, you might want to consult *Congressional Quarterly Almanac* or *Congressional Quarterly Weekly Report.* On the Internet, try the home page of the U.S. Congress for the Congressional Record (<http://thomas.loc.gov/home/thomas2.html>). For compilations of statistics, try *Statistical Abstract of the United States, Statistical Reference Index,* or *The Gallup Poll: Public Opinion.* The Gallup Organizational Web site (<http://www.gallup.com>) provides descriptions of some of its most recent polls.

Bibliographies

A bibliography is simply a list of books on a given topic, which can be more or less exhaustive depending on its purpose. (To discover how selections were made, check the bibliography's preface or introduction.) A good way to locate a comprehensive, up-to-date bibliography on your subject is to look in the *Bibliographic Index.* A master list of bibliographies that contain fifty or more titles, the *Bibliographic Index* draws from articles, books, and government publications. The index, published yearly, is not cumulative, so check the most recent volume for current information.

SEARCH FOR BOOKS

The primary source of information on books is the library catalog. Just a decade ago a library's catalog consisted of small file cards organized alphabetically into rows of drawers, by subject, title, and author's name. Today the same type of information is organized electronically in an online catalog. The *online catalog* provides more flexibility in searching and often tells you whether the book is available or checked out. Another distinct advantage is that you can print out source information, making it unnecessary for you to copy it by hand. You should, however, check to make sure that the online catalog goes far enough back in time for your purposes. If the computerized records do not date far enough back, see whether your library has maintained its hard-copy card catalog for the period in question.

Each catalog card or computer entry gives the same basic information: the name of the author, the title of the book, the subject heading(s) related to the book, and the call number you will need to find the book on the library shelves. Most libraries provide a map showing where the various call numbers are shelved. Following is one college library's online catalog display of the author entry for a book on home schooling. Notice the call number in the middle of the bottom line. (On cards, look for the call number in the upper left-hand corner.)

```
AUTHOR:         Guterson, David, 1951–
TITLE:          Family matters: Why homeschooling makes
                sense
EDITION:        1st Harvest ed.
PUBLISHER:      San Diego: Harcourt Brace & Co., c1992
PHYSICAL DESC:  x, 254 p.; 18 cm.
NOTES:          Includes bibliographical references and
                index.
SUBJECTS:       Education—United States
                Education—parent participation
                Teaching methods
LOCATION / CALL NUMBER          STATUS
UCSD Undergrad / 649.68 g 1993  Available
```

Even if you attend a large research university, your library is unlikely to hold every book or journal article you might need. Remember that your library's catalog and serial record (a list of the periodicals the library holds) is only that particular institution's record of the books and magazines it holds. As you will learn in the following section on Internet research, you can access the online catalogs of other libraries to find sources not within your library's holdings. At that point, you can request an interlibrary loan from another college library, a procedure handled by email or in person at the reference desk. Keep in mind, however, that it may take a couple of weeks to obtain a source by way of interlibrary loan.

SEARCH FOR ARTICLES

Articles published in periodicals (magazines or journals that publish periodically) and in newspapers usually are not listed in the library catalog. To find them, you will want to use *periodical indexes*, which originally appeared in book form but today are just as likely to take the form of a CD-ROM, an online database, or a hybrid of the two. As computer technology becomes more sophisticated, some database services have begun to offer full-text articles along with the listings of articles. *Indexes* list citations of articles; *abstracts* summarize the articles as well. *Full-text retrieval* means you can view an entire article online and potentially download it (often excluding graphics) for reading offline.

Following are some of the computer database services that your library might subscribe to:

- *Readers' Guide to Periodical Literature* (1900–; CD-ROM, 1983–). The classic index for periodicals, updated quarterly, offering about two hundred popular periodicals.

- *ERIC (Educational Resources Information Center)* (1969–; online). Houses indexes, abstracts, and the full text of selected articles from 750 education journals. (<http://www.ericir.syr.edu>)

- *Business Periodicals Ondisc* (1988–), and *ABI/INFORM* (1988–). Provides the full text of articles from business periodicals. If your library has a laser printer attached to a terminal, you can print out articles, including illustrations.

- *Carl/Uncover* (1988–). An online document delivery service that lists over three million articles from twelve thousand journals. For a fee, you can receive the full text of the article by fax, usually within a few hours. (<http://www.carl.org>)

- *Lexis-Nexis* (1973–; online and CD-ROM). An information service for journalists, lawyers, and financial analysts. (<http://www.lexis-nexis.com>)

- *InfoTrac* (CD-ROM). An information supplier that provides access to the following three indexes: (1) *General Periodicals Index*, which lists information on over twelve hundred general-interest publications; (2) *Academic Index*, which provides the full text of articles from five hundred popular and academic periodicals; and (3) *National Newspaper Index*, which covers the *Christian Science Monitor, Los Angeles Times, New York Times, Wall Street Journal,* and *Washington Post.*

Using the *Academic Index* to do a search for "home schooling" would yield several listings, including the two examples shown here. Notice that the results specify whether an abstract is available and where the periodical can be found in the library.

```
Home Schooling
    Mommy, what's a classroom? (the merits of home
schooling are still being debated) Bill Roorback.
The New York Times Magazine, Feb 2, 1997 p30 col1 (112
col in).
    —Abstract Available—
    Holdings: 10/92—present  Periodicals—1st Floor Paper
01/66—present  Microfilm (Room #162)

Microfilm
    The natural curriculum. (educating children at home)
Rosie Benson-Bunch. Times Education Supplement, Dec 27,
1996 n4200 pA25(1).
    —Abstract Available—
```

While InfoTrac was created for popular and academic reference purposes, *Business Periodicals Ondisc* and ERIC were evidently designed for use within specific disciplines. Other discipline-specific databases include *Accountant's Index, Art Index, Education Index, Historical Abstracts, MLA International Bibliography* (literature), *Psychological Abstracts*, and *Sociological Abstracts*. Most of these resources use the Library of Congress subject headings, but some have their own systems of classification. *Sociological Abstracts,* for example, has a separate volume for subject headings. Check the opening pages of the index or abstract you are using or, to see how subjects are classified, refer to the system documentation.

When you look for the periodicals in your library, you will typically find that they are arranged alphabetically by title in a particular section of the building. For previous years' collections of popular magazines and many scholarly journals, look for bound annual volumes rather than individual issues. Some older periodicals and newspapers may be stored on microfilm (reels) or microfiche (cards) that must be read in viewing machines.

Internet Research

The *Internet* is a global computer network that enables users to store and share information and resources from the comfort of their own computers. The World Wide Web is a network of Web sites, each with its own address, or *uniform resource locator (URL)*. You may be able to gain access to the Internet through your library, or through a commercial Internet service provider. To search the Web, you also need a Web browser such as Netscape Navigator or Internet Explorer.

Research on the Internet is very different from library research. As you use the Internet for conducting research, be sure to keep the following concerns and guidelines in mind.

- *The Internet has no central system of organization.* On the Internet, a vast amount of information is stored on many different networks, on different servers, and in different formats, each with its own system of organization. There is no central catalog, reference librarian, or standard classification system for the vast resources available on the Internet.

- *Internet sources are generally less reliable than print sources.* Because it is relatively easy for anyone with a Web page to "publish" on the Internet, judging the reliability of online information is a special concern. Depending on your topic, purpose, and audience, the sources you find on the Internet may not be as credible or authoritative as library sources, and for some topics most of what you find may be written by amateurs. In most cases, you will probably want to balance or supplement Internet sources with print sources. When in doubt about the reliability of online sources for a particular assignment, check with your instructor. (See Evaluating Sources Critically, page 509, for more specific suggestions.)

- *Internet sources must be documented.* The requirements for documenting source material found on the Internet and source material found in more traditional sources are the same, though the formats are slightly different. As with print sources you locate in the library, you will need to follow appropriate conventions for quoting, paraphrasing, and documenting the online sources you cite. (See Documenting Sources, page 512, for guidelines.)

As with library research, you will need to follow a systematic research strategy: Keep a working bibliography; learn how to navigate the Web; prepare to search the Web by determining appropriate keywords and using online search engines; access online library catalogs; and use email to contact other researchers and experts. Later in this appendix, in Evaluating Sources Critically (pp. 509–12), you will find guidelines to help you evaluate the relevancy and credibility of your Internet sources.

KEEP A WORKING BIBLIOGRAPHY

A working bibliography for Internet research serves the same purpose as one for library research: supplying an ongoing record of all the sources you discover as you research your subject. This working bibliography becomes the draft for the list of works cited at the end of your essay, even though you may not list these resources in your final bibliography. In this case, it also helps you keep track of the URLs for Web sites you visit. You can store URLs in your Web browser as bookmarks or favorites or copy them to a text file.

You will notice that some documents you find on the Web are untitled and that some do not make the name of their author obvious. You may be able to create a title from the first words or heading of the text. Or you can give it a descriptive title. For an apparently unnamed document, look for an email address or open the document's source information window to find the document's "owner." In addition, you should be sure to note each document's publication date (or date of last revision or modification) as well as the date you accessed it.

LEARN HOW TO NAVIGATE THE WEB

For many academic users, an especially useful feature of the World Wide Web is that it allows *hypertext links* to other documents or files, so that with a simple click of the mouse a reader might find more detailed information on a subject or access a related document. Most material on the Web is available twenty-four hours a day, as long as your server is up and running.

A *Web browser* is a software program that allows you to display and navigate Web pages on your computer. Web browsers have evolved from basic text-driven browsers such as Lynx (still used today) into graphical, point-and-click interfaces such as Netscape Navigator and Microsoft Internet Explorer, which support not only text and hypertext links but also images, sound, animation, and even video.

A browser lets you move around a *Web site,* a set of connected pages (programming files) made available to the public. The central or starting point for a Web site is often called its *home page.* Web sites may be sponsored by companies, institutions, government agencies, organizations, clubs, or individuals.

As noted earlier, each Web site has its own address or uniform resource locator (URL). The URL for the Ecology Action Centre is typical:

http://www.cfn.cs.dal.ca/Environment/EAC/EAC-Home.html

The first part of a URL usually consists of the abbreviation *http://* that tells the sending and receiving computers the type of information being sent and how to transfer it. The second part usually includes the standard *www.* to establish that the location being accessed is on the World Wide Web, and the country, if outside of the United States, where the document is located. After a slash, the rest of the URL gives the address of the directory and file where the page is found as well as the name of the page itself, separated by slashes. URLs can be rather long, so you may need to insert a line break when citing one in an essay. *Wired Style* (1996) recommends breaking a line after the *http://* or before a punctuation mark such as a period or slash.

Many organizational and resource sites list the URLs of their home pages in print publications so that readers can access the Web sites for further information. Keep an eye out for such resources related to your research projects.

PREPARE TO SEARCH THE WEB

To find sources on the Web you need to use search engines, which are typically based on keyword searches.

Determining How to Search the Web by Keyword

Search engines on the World Wide Web and other specialized software allow you to enter keywords to retrieve related information. Before you can use a search engine, however, you need to identify possible *keywords*—words you think are likely to appear in a title, summary, full-text document, or Web page related to your subject. In a *keyword search,* you direct the software to search a database and list any resources that match your terms. On the Internet, keyword searches are more useful than focused subject searches of the kind you would do in the library because information on the Web is not organized systematically by subject.

Some keyword search software looks for the specified terms in the whole document, whereas others search only headings, summaries, or titles. Read the instructions on the screen or ask your reference librarian or instructor for help. To launch a keyword search, type in the search terms. In most cases, a logical connector such as *and, or,* or *not* can be used to focus the search. For example, the keywords *home schooling and socialization* will retrieve references to documents that contain both of those terms. If you are researching the topic of euthanasia and want to find instances of assisted suicide other than those involving Dr. Jack Kevorkian (a doctor famous for helping terminally ill patients commit suicide), entering the phrase *euthanasia not Kevorkian* will yield references to sources containing the term *euthanasia,* but excluding sources that also contain the term *Kevorkian.* Some search software allows you to search by phrases, asking you to enclose a phrase in quotation marks. For example, if the phrase *"working mothers"* is entered, only references containing that phrase will be returned. Use capital letters for proper nouns and titles, and remember that correct spelling is essential.

Using Search Engines to Locate Sources

Once you have some keywords about your topic in mind, you can choose any number of search engines to locate sources. In most cases, you will want to use several search engines because the results can vary considerably. You might begin by clicking *Search* on the home page for either Netscape Navigator or Microsoft Internet Explorer, where you can access a list of links to such popular search engines as Infoseek, Lycos, and Yahoo! Or you can access these and other common search engines directly at their URL addresses:

Alta Vista	http://www.altavista.digital.com
Excite	http://www.excite.com
Infoseek	http://www.infoseek.com
Lycos	http://www.lycos.com
WebCrawler	http://www.webcrawler.com
Yahoo!	http://www.yahoo.com

The functions of a search engine are to scan its directory of the Web for your keyword and to produce a list of direct links to Web pages containing the keyword. Most programs search both the titles of Web pages and the actual text of those pages for the keyword. Usually, the list of search results includes a brief description of each page. By clicking on the links in the list, you can directly access the Web pages. When you find a page you think might be useful, you should create a bookmark for it in your Web browser. Bookmarks (or Favorites) record the locations of Web pages within your browser so that you can return to a page later just by clicking on its bookmark. By bookmarking potentially useful Web pages you can keep track of your Internet research and maintain a working bibliography of your Internet sources.

Keep in mind that each search engine works a bit differently and will yield different results from the same keyword. Therefore, before you enter your keyword, read the on-screen instructions or help information for each search engine to see how it works. Also, try more than one search engine.

The success of a Web search and the number of hits or responses it yields depends on the keywords you choose and the comprehensiveness of the search engine. If a search yields too few sources or too many irrelevant ones, try rephrasing your keywords or choosing more specific ones to locate the most useful information. If your topic is ecology, for example, you might find information by searching with the keywords *ecosystem, environment, pollution,* and *endangered species,* among others. As with library searches, however, you should narrow your topic if the number of sources becomes unmanageable. Most search engines invite you to refine your search and help by offering related keywords. For instance, when an Alta Vista search using the keyword *ecology* resulted in 374,576 matches, a series of keyword groups with percentages was provided. If you choose the *ecology, biology, biological research, and genetics* group, you cut down to 88% of the matches, but if you choose *habitats, freshwater, extinction* group, you cut down to 15% of the original 374,576 possibilities. You could refine your search this way in several stages and wind up with a manageable number of sources.

For current events and other topics in the news, you can narrow your results by starting with a local or national newspaper or one whose coverage you respect. The following newspapers have high-powered search engines on their own sites:

New York Times	http://www.nytimes.com
San Jose Mercury News	http://www.mercurycenter.com
Los Angeles Times	http://www.latimes.com

Be warned, though, that some online news publishers now charge a fee for the full-text retrieval of articles. Finding the article is usually free of charge, but downloading the full text of an article to your computer will cost a small fee. Whichever search engines you choose, allow yourself enough time to sort through the results.

ACCESS ONLINE LIBRARY CATALOGS

Many library catalogs throughout the world can be accessed online, whether by a Web browser, a *telnet* connection, or direct modem-to-modem dialing. Contact your college library to see whether it offers Web-based, telnet, or modem access to the online catalogs of other libraries. Searches of the book catalogs of local and remote libraries may yield lists of valuable resources or, in some cases, complete articles. For more information, as well as a comprehensive list of links to searchable library catalogs, visit the Library of Congress site at <http://lcweb.loc.gov>. The Library of Congress Web site, as well as such other sites as the WWW Virtual Library at <http://vlib.org/Overview.html> and the Internet Public Library (IPL) at <http://www.ipl.org/ref/index.text.html>, provide an extensive list of subjects arranged according to the Library of Congress Subject Headings. An added advantage to the IPL site is that librarians are available to answer your questions by email.

USE EMAIL TO CONTACT OTHER RESEARCHERS AND EXPERTS

You can contact others directly through *email* (electronic mail). Some authors include their email addresses along with their articles, so you may be able to write to them for further information. Web pages often include email links to individuals who have further information on specific topics. In addition, you might consider logging on to a chatroom, where real-time communication can take place between two or more participants.

Another important email resource for some projects, *newsgroups,* are interest groups in which people post email messages in a public forum for discussion. The messages are usually posted on the Internet for anyone to read and respond to, much like a public bulletin board. A *listserv* is like a newsgroup except that listserv messages are not posted in a public forum but are sent automatically to all subscribers of the group by private email. In addition, the discussion that takes place on a listserv tends to be more serious and focused than that of newsgroups. One student researching language acquisition, for instance, subscribed to a listserv made up primarily of teachers of English as a second language. She read the group's email discussions for a while to determine whether her questions would be appropriate to the list, rather than posting her message immediately. She decided to post a message to the listserv with questions related to her research. In return, she received a great deal of useful information from professionals in the field.

Finally, note that most newsgroups and some listservs maintain searchable archives of previous postings. Contact a reference librarian for help in identifying useful email research tools, or start with a search engine that specializes in newsgroups, such as Deja News: <http://www.dejanews.com>. If all else fails, you can try a keyword search online combining the keyword *listserv* or *newsgroup* with your topic to see what you can find.

EVALUATING SOURCES CRITICALLY

From the very beginning of your search for sources, you should evaluate each potential source to determine whether it will be useful and relevant to your essay. Obviously, you must decide which sources provide information relevant to the topic, but you also must read sources with a critical eye to decide how credible or trustworthy they are. Just because a book or essay appears in print does not necessarily mean the information or opinions within it are reliable.

Criteria for Evaluating Sources

To help you evaluate the sources you have found, try using the following criteria. Your goal is to determine the relevance, currency, range of viewpoints, and authoritativeness of each potential source. In addition, you want to take special care when evaluating sources gathered from the Internet.

DETERMINE THE RELEVANCE OF POTENTIAL SOURCES

Begin your evaluation of sources by narrowing your working bibliography to the most relevant works. To decide how relevant a particular source is to your topic, you need to examine the source in depth. Do not depend on title alone, for it may be misleading. If the source is a book, check its table of contents and index to see how many pages are devoted to the precise subject you are exploring. In most cases you will want an in-depth, not a superficial, treatment of the subject. Read the preface or introduction to a book, the abstract or opening paragraphs of an article, and any biographical information given about the author to determine the author's basic or distinctive approach to the subject. As you look at all these elements, consider the following questions:

- Does the source provide a general overview or a specialized point of view? General sources are helpful early in your research, but ultimately you will need the authoritative and up-to-date coverage of specialized sources (excluding those that are overly technical).

- Is the source long enough to provide adequate detail?

- Is the source written for general readers or specialists? Advocates or critics?

- Is the author an expert on the topic? Does the author's way of looking at the topic support or challenge other views?

DETERMINE THE CURRENCY OF POTENTIAL SOURCES

Currency—or the timeliness of a source—is more important for some topics than for others. In an essay about changes in tax laws, for instance, you would need to use the most current information available to describe changes in the law. Although you should always consult the most up-to-date sources available on your subject, older sources often establish the principles, theories, and data on which later work is based and may provide a useful perspective for evaluating more current sources. For an Internet source, check the publication date and any revision or modification dates. Also make a note of the date you accessed the site.

DETERMINE THE VIEWPOINT OF POTENTIAL SOURCES

Your sources should represent a variety of viewpoints on the topic. Just as you would not depend on a single author for all of your information, you would not want to use authors who all belong to the same school of thought. Authors come to their subjects with particular viewpoints derived from their philosophies, experiences, educational backgrounds, and affiliations. In evaluating your sources, then, consider carefully how these viewpoints are reflected in the writing and how they affect the way authors present their arguments.

Although the text of a source gives you the most precise indication of the author's viewpoint, you can often get a good idea by also looking at the preface or introduction or at the sources the author cites. You will want to determine whether the document fairly represents other views on the topic with which you are familiar. When you examine a reference, you can often determine the point of view it represents by considering the following elements:

- *Title:* Look closely at the title and subtitle to see if they use words that indicate a particular viewpoint. Watch for "loaded" words or confrontational phrasing.

- *Author:* Consider how the author's professional affiliation might affect his or her perspective on the topic. Look also at the tone of the writing and any biographical information provided about the author.

- *Editorial slant:* Notice where the selection was published. To determine the editorial slant of a newspaper or periodical, all you have to do is read some of its editorials, opinion columns, or letters to the editor. You can also check such sources as the *Gale Directory of Publications and Broadcast Media* (1990) and *Magazines for Libraries,* 9th ed. (1997). For books, read the preface or introduction as well as the acknowledgments and sources cited to get an idea of how the authors position themselves in relation to other specialists in the field. For Internet sources, notice what organization, if any, stands behind the author's work.

DETERMINE WHETHER THE SOURCES ARE AUTHORITATIVE

Just because a book or essay appears in print or online does not guarantee that it is a reliable source of information. Check the author's professional credentials, background, and publication history to verify that he or she is an established voice in the field. To help determine which authors are established, note whether they are cited in encyclopedia articles, bibliographies, and recent works on the subject. For books, you can also look up reviews in newspapers or academic journals.

Experts will (and should) disagree on topics, and each author will naturally see the topic in his or her own way. Yet authoritative authors will explain and support, not just assert, their opinions. They will also cite their sources. Because articles published in most academic journals and books published by university presses are judged by other experts in the field, you can assume that these authors' views are respected even if they are controversial. Allowing for differences of viewpoint, information about the topic provided in the source should be consistent with information you have found on the topic in other sources.

USE SPECIAL CARE IN EVALUATING INTERNET SOURCES

Unlike most published print resources, which have been reviewed and selected by editors in a "filtering" process to ensure their accuracy and credibility, most publications on the Internet have been through no comparable filtering process. Anyone who can upload material to a server can publish on the Internet. Web sites may be sponsored by academic institutions, government agencies, companies, organizations, clubs, or individuals—for recreational or professional use. This variety makes it essential that you take extra care in evaluating the credentials of the author and the credibility of the information before you use an Internet publication as a source.

Often, the information needed to evaluate Internet sources is more difficult to locate than it is for print sources. Books, for example, display the name of their publisher on the spine and the title page, include information about the author in the beginning or at the end of the book, and often make the purpose of the work clear in a preface or introduction. Determining the publisher, the purpose, and sometimes even the author of a Web page, however, can often be more difficult because of the technical differences between print and online media. For example, Web pages that are part of a larger Web site might—when they are accessed by a search engine—give few pointers to the rest of the site. These Web pages may carry little or no indication of who published or sponsored the site or of its overall purpose or author. In this situation, the researcher should not use the source unless more information about the Web site can be tracked down. The following specialized techniques for reading and evaluating Web pages will help:

- *Look for a Web site that provides information on its history.* Look for the following information on any online articles you retrieve: the author's professional title, affiliation, and other credentials; the sponsor of the page and the Web site; a link to the site's home page; and the date the site was created or last revised. Check the title, headers, and footers of the Web page for this information. If it is provided, it may indicate a willingness to publish in a professional manner, and it will help you evaluate the source according to the criteria discussed earlier. Checking the home page of the Web site will help you discover, for example, if its purpose is commercial (a site published to sell radar detectors) or one of public safety (a site established by the Highway Patrol to give information on speed limits).

- *Alter the URL in the browser's "location" box, and try to contact the sponsoring institution.* By deleting all but the initial directory from a lengthy URL, you may be able to determine the sponsoring institution for the Web page. For example, in <http://lcweb.loc.gov/z3950/gateway.html>, taking away the subdirectory (z3950) and filename (gateway.html) will reveal the sponsoring computer's address: <http://lcweb.loc.gov> (which in this case is the Library of Congress home page). Enter the abbreviated URL address in your browser to access the site and to determine where the information comes from.

- *Follow links out from the site to others.* Internet sources sometimes provide direct links to other sources so you can see the context from which a fact, statistic, or quotation has been taken. Many also link to Web site "consumer reports" that have rated the site favorably, but you need to consider whether the site doing the ratings is trustworthy.

- *Use any other evaluation techniques available.* Even if you cannot discover the author's credentials, you can check his or her facts, details, and presentation: Does the information make sense to you? Can you verify the facts? You may find that, even though the author is not a recognized expert in the field, he or she offers information valuable to your project. One advantage of the Web is that anyone, not just recognized experts, can express views and relate firsthand experiences that may be useful in developing your topic.

DOCUMENTING SOURCES

Much of the writing you will do in college requires you to use outside sources in combination with your own firsthand observation and reflection. When you get information and ideas from reading, lectures, and interviews, you are using sources. In college, using sources is not only acceptable, it is expected. Writers should acknowledge sources for two reasons—to give credit to those sources and to enable readers to consult the sources for further information.

Although there is no universally agreed-on system for documenting sources, there is agreement on the need for documentation, on the type of information that should be included, and on the placement of citations.

The following guidelines cover two popular styles of documentation: the *Modern Language Association (MLA)* system, which is used in English and the humanities, and the *American Psychological Association (APA)* system, which is used in the social sciences.

Document Sources Using MLA Style

The following guidelines are sufficient for most college research assignments in English and other humanities courses that call for MLA-style documentation. For additional information, see the *MLA Handbook for Writers of Research Papers,* Fifth Edition (1999), or check the MLA Web site <http://www.mla.org>.

USE IN-TEXT CITATIONS TO SHOW WHERE YOU HAVE USED MATERIAL FROM SOURCES

In-text citations mark places in the text of an essay where information, ideas, or quotations from sources are included. Each in-text citation has a corresponding entry in the list of sources at the end of the essay that tells readers how to find the source. In MLA style this list is titled *Works Cited.*

Place an in-text citation in parentheses as near as possible to the borrowed material without disrupting your sentence. Include a citation each time you refer to a source, except when all of the sentences in a single paragraph refer to the same source—and no reference to another page in the source or to another source intervenes. In this case, you may use a single parenthetical citation, positioned after the last reference in the paragraph. Do not cite common knowledge or personal knowledge.

Use the Following Models for In-Text Citations

1. When the author is indicated in a signal phrase

"Despite his immense working vocabulary, Shakespeare did not mention chocolate at all," Sokolov points out, even though by 1569 chocolate was available in England (134).

2. When the author and page are indicated in a parenthetical citation

Dr. James is described as a "not-too-skeletal Ichabod Crane" (Simon 68).

While automotive design improvements have made American cars safer than ever at high speeds (Kaye 73), speed limits in many places still remain low.

3. When the source has more than one author

Dyal, Corning, and Willows identify several types of students, including the "Authority-Rebel" (4).

Authority-rebels see themselves as "superior to other students in the class" (Dyal, Corning, and Willows 4).

The drug AZT has been shown to reduce the risk of transmission from HIV-positive mothers to their infants by as much as two-thirds (Van de Perre et al. 4-5).

For three or more authors, you may list everyone or only the first author followed by *et al.*, as in the example above.

4. When the author is not named

In 1992, five years after the Symms legislation, the number of deaths from automobile accidents reached a thirty-year low ("Highways" 51).

5. When the source has a corporate or government author

A tuition increase has been proposed for community and technical colleges to offset budget deficits from Initiative 601 (Washington State Board for Community and Technical Colleges 4).

6. When two or more works by the same author are cited

When old paint becomes transparent, it sometimes shows the artist's original plans: "A tree will show through a woman's dress" (Hellman, Pentimento 1).

Because more than one of Hellman's works is listed in the list of works cited, the title follows the author's name in the parentheses.

7. When two or more authors have the same last name

According to Edgar V. Roberts, Chaplin's Modern Times provides a good example of montage used to make an editorial statement (246).

Chaplin's Modern Times provides a good example of montage used to make an editorial statement (E. V. Roberts 246).

Note that Roberts's first and middle initials are included in the parentheses because another author with the same last name is included in the list of works cited.

8. When a work without page numbers is cited

The average speed on Montana's interstate highways, for example, has risen by only 2 miles per hour since the repeal of the federal speed limit, with most drivers topping out at 75 (Schmid).

There is no page number for this source because it comes from the Internet.

9. When a quotation is taken from a secondary source

```
Chancellor Helmut Kohl summed up the German attitude: "For
millions of people, a car is part of their personal freedom"
(qtd. in Cote 12).
```

Create a works-cited entry for the secondary source in which you found the quote, rather than for the original source.

10. When a citation comes from a multivolume work

```
"Double meaning," according to Freud, "is one of the most
fertile sources for [. . .] jokes" (8: 56).
```

In the parentheses, number 8 indicates the volume and 56 indicates the page. For the works cited reference to a single volume in a multivolume work, see page 518, entry 8. The brackets placed around the ellipsis points are recommended by the MLA to distinguish them from ellipses the author may have used.

11. When the source is a literary or religious work

For a novel or other prose work available in various editions, provide the page numbers from the edition used. To help readers locate the quota-tion in another edition, add the part and/or chapter number as in the following:

```
In Hard Times, Tom reveals his utter narcissism by blaming
Louisa for his own failure: "'You have regularly given me up.
You never cared for me'" (Dickens 262; bk. 3, ch. 9).
```

For a play in verse, such as a Shakespearean play, indicate the act, scene, and line numbers instead of the page numbers.

```
At the beginning, Regan's fawning rhetoric hides her true
attitude toward Lear: "I profess / myself an enemy to all other
joys [. . .] / And find that I am alone felicitate / In your
dear highness' love" (King Lear I.i.74-75, 77-78).
```

For a poem, indicate the line numbers and stanzas (if they are num-bered), instead of the page numbers.

```
In "Song of Myself," Whitman finds poetic details in busy
urban settings, as when he describes "the blab of the pave,
tires of carts [. . .] the driver with his interrogating
thumb" (8.153-54).
```

If the source gives only line numbers, use the term *lines* in the first cita-tion; in subsequent citations, give only the numbers. For the Bible, indi-cate the book, chapter, and verse instead of the page numbers. Abbrevi-ate books with names of five or more letters in parenthetical citation, but spell out full names of books in your text.

```
She ignored the admonition "Pride goes before destruction, and
a haughty spirit before a fall." (New Oxford Annotated Bible,
Prov. 16.18).
```

12. When the citation comes from a work in an anthology

In "Six Days: Some Rememberings," Grace Paley recalls that
when she was in jail for protesting the Vietnam War, her pen
and paper were taken away and she felt "a terrible pain in the
area of my heart—a nausea" (191).

If you are discussing the editor's *preface* or *introduction,* name the editor.

13. When two or more works are cited in the same parentheses

When two or more different sources are used in the same passage, it may
be necessary to cite them in the same parentheses. Separate the citations
with a semicolon:

A few studies have considered differences between oral and
written discourse production (e.g., Scardamalia, Bereiter, and
Goelman, 1982; Gould, 1980).

14. When an entire work is cited

In The Structure of Scientific Revolutions, Thomas Kuhn
discusses how scientists change their thinking.

15. When material from the Internet is cited

In handling livestock, "many people attempt to restrain
animals with sheer force instead of using behavioral
principles" (Grandin).

If the author is not named, give the document title. Include page, section,
paragraph, or screen numbers, if available.

INCLUDE ALL OF YOUR SOURCES IN A WORKS-CITED LIST
AT THE END OF YOUR ESSAY

The works-cited list provides information that enables readers to find
the sources cited in the essay. Every source referred to in the text of your
essay must have a corresponding entry in the list of works cited at the
end of your essay. Conversely, every entry in the works-cited list must
correspond to at least one in-text citation in the essay.

Although there are many varieties of works-cited entries, the information generally follows this order:

Entry for a Book

Author's last name, First name, Middle initial. Book Title.
    City of publication: Publisher's name, year published.

Entry for a Journal

```
Author's last name, First name, Middle initial. "Title of the
     Article." Journal Name Volume number. issue number (year
     published): page range.
```

Copy the author's name and the title from the book's title page or the first page of the article. Do not worry about including information that is unavailable within the source, such as the author's middle initial or the issue number for a periodical. If your instructor permits, you may italicize rather than underline book titles and periodical names. *Note:* The MLA recommends that the list of works cited be placed at the end of the paper, beginning on a new page with pages numbered consecutively; that the first line of each entry begins flush with the left margin; that subsequent lines of the same entry indent five character spaces; and that the entire list be double-spaced, between and within entries.

Use the Following Models for Books

1. A book by a single author

```
Arnold, Marion I. Women and Art in South Africa. New York: St.
     Martin's, 1996.
```

2. Multiple works by the same author (or same group of authors)

```
Vidal, Gore. Empire. New York: Random, 1987.

---. Lincoln. New York: Random, 1984.
```

3. A book by an agency, organization, or corporation

```
Association for Research in Nervous and Mental Disease. The
     Circulation of the Brain and Spinal Cord: A Symposium on
     Blood Supply. New York: Hafner, 1966.
```

4. A book by two or more authors

For two or three authors:

```
Gottfredson, Stephen G., and Sean McConville. America's
     Correctional Crisis. Westport: Greenwood, 1987.
```

For three or more authors, name all the authors or only the first author plus *et al.* (and others):

```
Belenky, Mary F., Blythe M. Clinchy, Nancy R. Goldberger, and
     Jill M. Tarule. Women's Ways of Knowing: The Development
     of Self, Voice, and Mind. New York: Basic Books, 1986.

Belenky, Mary F., et al. Women's Ways of Knowing: The
     Development of Self, Voice, and Mind. New York: Basic
     Books, 1986.
```

5. A book with an unlisted author

Rand McNally Commercial Atlas. Skokie: Rand, 1993.

6. A book with one or more editors

Axelrod, Steven Gould, and Helen Deese, eds. Robert Lowell:
      Essays on the Poetry. Cambridge: Cambridge UP, 1986.

7. A book with an author and an editor

If you refer to the work itself:

Arnold, Matthew. Culture and Anarchy. Ed. J. Dover Wilson.
      Cambridge: Cambridge UP, 1966.

If you discuss the editor's work in your essay:

Wilson, J. Dover, ed. Culture and Anarchy. By Matthew Arnold.
      Cambridge: Cambridge UP, 1966.

8. One volume of a multivolume work

If only one volume from a multivolume set is used, indicate the volume number after the title:

Freud, Sigmund. The Complete Psychological Works of Sigmund
      Freud. Vol. 8. Trans. James Strachey. London: Hogarth, 1962.

9. Two or more volumes of a multivolume work

Sandburg, Carl. Abraham Lincoln. 6 vols. New York: Scribner's,
      1939.

10. A book that is part of a series

Include the series name, without underlining or quotation marks, followed by the series number. If the word *Series* is part of the name, include Ser. before the number.

Kirsch, Gesa and Duane H. Roen. A Sense of Audience in Written
      Communication. Written Communication Annual: An
      International Survey of Research and Theory. 5. Newbury
      Park: Sage Publications, 1990.

11. A republished book

Provide the original publication date after the title of the book, followed by normal publication information for the current edition:

Takaki, Ronald. Strangers from a Different Shore: A History of
      Asian Americans. 1989. New York: Penguin, 1990.

12. A later edition of a book

Rottenberg, Annette T. The Structure of Argument. 2nd ed.
      Boston: Bedford, 1997.

13. A book with a title in its title

Do not underline a title normally underlined when it appears within the title of a book or other work that is underlined:

Kinney, Arthur F. Go Down Moses: <u>The Miscegenation of Time</u>.
    New York: Twayne, 1996.

Brooker, Jewel Spears, and Joseph Bentley. <u>Reading</u> The Waste
    Land: <u>Modernism and the Limits of Interpretation</u>.
    Amherst: U of Mass P, 1990.

Use quotation marks around a work normally enclosed in quotation marks when it appears in the title of a book or other work that is underlined:

Miller, Edwin Haviland. <u>Walt Whitman's "Song of Myself": A</u>
    <u>Mosaic of Interpretation</u>. Iowa City: U of Iowa P, 1989.

14. A work in an anthology or a collection

Fairbairn-Dunlop, Peggy. "Women and Agriculture in Western
    Samoa." <u>Different Places, Different Voices</u>. Ed. Janet H.
    Momsen and Vivian Kinnaird. London: Routledge, 1993. 211-26.

15. Two or more works from the same anthology

To avoid repetition, you may create an entry for the collection and cite the collection's editors to cross-reference individual works to the entry:

Atwan, Robert, and Jamaica Kincaid, eds. <u>The Best American</u>
    <u>Essays, 1995</u>. New York: Houghton, 1995.

Paley, Grace. "Six Days: Some Rememberings." Atwan and Kincaid
    187-92.

16. A translation

If you refer to the work itself:

Tolstoy, Leo. <u>War and Peace</u>. Trans. Constance Garnett. London:
    Pan, 1972.

If you discuss the translation in your essay:

Garnett, Constance, trans. <u>War and Peace</u>. By Leo Tolstoy.
    London: Pan, 1972.

17. An article in a reference book

Suber, Howard. "Motion Picture." <u>The Encyclopedia Americana</u>.
    1991 ed.

18. An introduction, preface, foreword, or afterword

Holt, John. Introduction. <u>Better than School</u>. By Nancy
    Wallace. Burnett: Larson, 1983. 9-14.

Use the Following Models for Articles

19. An article from a newspaper

```
Wilford, John Noble. "Corn in the New World: A Relative
     Latecomer." New York Times 7 Mar. 1995, late ed.: C1+.
```

20. An article from a weekly or biweekly magazine

```
Kaye, Steven D. "Hello 75, So Long 55." U.S. News and World
     Report 18 Dec. 1995: 71-75.
```

21. An article from a monthly or bimonthly magazine

```
Spencer, Paula. "No More Whining." Parenting Apr. 1997:
     151-56.
```

22. An article in a scholarly journal with continuous annual pagination

```
Jackson, Jeremy S. H., and Roger Blackman. "A Driving
     Simulator Test of Wilde's Risk Homeostasis Theory."
     Journal of Applied Psychology 79 (1994): 950-58.
```

23. An article in a scholarly journal that paginates each issue separately

```
Epstein, Alexandra. "Teen Parents: What They Need to Know."
     High/Scope Resource 1.2 (1982): 6.
```

24. An article by an unidentified author

```
"Highways Become Safer." Futurist Jan.-Feb. 1994: 51-52.
```

25. An editorial or letter to the editor

```
"Meth Lab Charades." Editorial. Press-Enterprise [Riverside] 2
     Oct. 1997: A8.

Rissman, Edward M. Letter. Los Angeles Times 29 June 1989: B5.
```

26. A review

If the review is titled:

```
Anders, Jaroslaw. "Dogma and Democracy." Rev. of The Church
     and the Left, by Adam Minchik. New Republic 17 May 1993:
     42-48.
```

If the review is untitled:

```
Lane, Anthony. Rev. of The English Patient, dir. Anthony
     Minghella. New Yorker 25 Nov. 1996: 118-21.
```

If the review has no title and no named author, start with the words *Rev. of* and the title of the work being reviewed.

Use the Following Models for Internet Sources

Some of the following guidelines for citing Internet sources, authorized by the MLA, can be found at *<http://www.mla.org>*. Models for citing other kinds of Internet sources not covered by the MLA guidelines are based on Andrew Harnack and Eugene Kleppinger, *Online! A Reference Guide to Using Internet Sources* (New York: St. Martin's, 1998).

Although there are many varieties of Internet works-cited entries, the information generally follows this order:

```
Author's last name, First name, Middle initial. "Title of
    Short Work." Title of Book, Periodical, or Site.
    Publication date or date of last revision. Page numbers
    or number of paragraphs. Name of sponsoring institution
    or organization. Date of access. <URL>.
```

Entry for an Internet Source

27. A professional or personal World Wide Web site

Professional site:

```
Center for Immigration Studies. Washington, D.C. 8 Sept. 1998.
    <http://www.cis.org>.
```

Personal site:

```
Johnson, Suzanne H. Home page. 5 Oct. 1997
    <http://members.aol.com/suzannehi/hello.htm>.
```

28. A book or poem

Book:

```
Blind, Mathilde. Dramas in Miniature. London: Chatto & Windus,
    1891. Victorian Women Writer's Project. Ed. Perry
    Willett. 3 Oct. 1997. Indiana U. 13 Oct. 1997
    <http://www.indiana.edu/-letrs/vwwp/blind/dramas.html>.
```

Poem:

```
Mosko, Marc. "Muir Woods." Home page. 1996. 13 Oct. 1997
    <http://www.tear.com/poems/mosko/muirwoods.html>.
```

29. An article in a reference database

```
Linsk. "Thrills Spills." IRE Resource Center. 12338. Aug.
    27-29, 1995. Asbury Free Press. 15 pages.
    <http://www.ire.org/resources/center/search.html>.
```

30. An article from an online journal

```
Killiam, Rosemary. "Cognitive Dissonance: Should Twentieth-
    Century Women Composers Be Grouped with Foucault's Mad
```

Criminals?" Music Theory Online 3.2 (1997): 30 pars. 10
   May 1997 <http://smt.ucsb.edu/mto/mtohome.html>.

31. An article from an online magazine

Keillor, Garrison. "Why Did They Ever Ban a Book This Bad?"
   Salon 13 Oct. 1997. 14 Oct. 1997 <http://www.salon 1999.
   com/feature/>.

32. A posting to a discussion list

A newsgroup:

Sherman, Matthew. "Writing Process and Self-Discipline."
   Online posting. 15 Feb. 1995. 16 Feb. 1995 <eng13764@
   ebbs.english.vt.edu>.

33. Material from an online subscription service

Private subscription:

Weeks, W. William. "Beyond the Ark." Nature Conservancy
   Mar.-Apr. 1999. America Online. 2 Apr. 1999. Keyword:
   Ecology.

Library subscription:

"Breaking the Dieting Habit: Drug Therapy for Eating
   Disorders." Psychology Today Mar. 1995: 12+. Electric
   Lib. Main Lib., Columbus, OH. 31 Mar. 1999
   <http://www.elibrary.com/>.

34. A scholarly project

The Ovid Project. Ed. Hope Greenberg. 13 Mar. 1996. U of
   Vermont. 13 Oct. 1997 <http://www.uvm.edu/hag/ovid/
   index.html>.

Use the Following Models for Other Electronic Sources

35. Material from a CD-ROM database

Braus, Patricia. "Sex and the Single Spender." American
   Demographics 15.11 (1993): 28-34. ABI/INFORM. CD-ROM.
   UMI-ProQuest. 1993.

If no print version is available, include the author, title, and date (if provided) along with information about the electronic source.

36. Material published on a CD-ROM, magnetic tape, or diskette

Picasso: The Man, His Works, the Legend. CD-ROM. Danbury:
   Grolier Interactive, 1996.

Use the Following Models for Other Sources

37. An interview

Published interview:

Lowell, Robert. "Robert Lowell." Interview with Frederick
    Seidel. Paris Review 25 (1975): 56-95.

Personal interview:

Harkness, Edward. Personal interview. 7 May 1996.

Broadcast interview:

Calloway, Cab. Interview with Rich Conaty. The Big Broadcast.
    WFUV, New York. 10 Dec. 1990.

38. A lecture or public address

Timothy, Kristen. "The Changing Roles of Women's Community
    Organizations in Sustainable Development and in the
    United Nations." UN Association of the United States.
    Seattle. 7 May 1997.

39. A government document

United States Dept. of Health and Human Services. Clinical
    Classifications for Health Policy Research, Version 2:
    Hospital Inpatient Statistics. Rockville: AHCPR
    Publications Clearinghouse, 1996.

If the author is known, the author's name may either come first or be
placed after the title and introduced with the word *By.*

40. A pamphlet

Harborview Injury Prevention and Research Center. A Decade
    of Injury Control. Seattle: Harborview Medical Center,
    1995.

41. A published doctoral dissertation

Hilfinger, Paul N. Abstraction Mechanisms and Language
    Design. Diss. Carnegie-Mellon U, 1981. Cambridge: MIT P,
    1983.

42. An unpublished doctoral dissertation

Bullock, Barbara. "Basic Needs Fulfillment among Less
    Developed Countries: Social Progress over Two Decades of
    Growth." Diss. Vanderbilt U, 1986.

43. A dissertation abstract

Bernstein, Stephen David. "Fugitive Genre: Gothicism,
     Ideology, and Intertextuality." Diss. Yale U, 1991. DAI
     51 (1991): 3078-79A.

44. Published proceedings of a conference

Duffett, John, ed. Against the Crime of Silence. Proc. of the
     International War Crimes Tribunal, Nov. 1967, Stockholm.
     New York: Clarion-Simon, 1970.

If the name of the conference is part of the title of the publication, it
should not be repeated. Use the format for a work in an anthology (see
14) to cite an individual presentation.

45. A letter or email message

Hamilton, Alexander. "To William Seton." 3 Dec. 1790. The
     Papers of Alexander Hamilton. Ed. Harold C. Syrett.
     Vol. 7. New York: Columbia UP, 1969. 190.

Hannah, Barry. Letter to the author. 10 May 1990.

To cite an email message, substitute *Email to the author.*

46. A map or chart

Mineral King, California. Map. Berkeley: Wilderness P, 1979.

47. A cartoon

Wilson, Gahan. Cartoon. New Yorker 14 July 1997: 74.

Provide the cartoon's title (if given) in quotes.

48. An advertisement

Reliance National Employment Practices Liability.
     Advertisement. Wired May 1997: 196.

49. A work of art or a musical composition

De Goya, Francisco. The Sleep of Reason Produces Monsters.
     Norton Simon Museum, Pasadena.

Beethoven, Ludwig van. Violin Concerto in D Major, op. 61.

Gershwin, George. Porgy and Bess.

50. A performance

Hamlet. By William Shakespeare. Dir. Jonathan Kent. Perf.
     Ralph Fiennes. Belasco Theatre, New York. 20 June 1995.

Include the names of any performers or other contributors who are relevant to or cited in your essay.

51. A television or radio program

"The Universe Within." <u>Nova</u>. Narr. Stacy Keach. Writ. Beth
      Hoppe and Bill Lattanzi. Dir. Goro Koide. PBS. WNET, New
      York. 7 Mar. 1995.

Include the names of any contributors who are relevant to or cited in
your essay. If you are discussing the work of a particular person (for example, the director or writer), begin the entry with that person's name.

52. A film or videotape

<u>Othello</u>. Perf. Laurence Fishburne, Irene Jacob, and Kenneth
      Branagh. Castle Rock Entertainment, 1995.

<u>Casablanca</u>. Dir. Michael Curtiz. Perf. Humphrey Bogart. 1942.
      Videocassette. MGM-UA Home Video, 1992.

Include the names of any performers or other contributors who are relevant to or cited in your essay. If you are discussing the work of a particular person (for example, an actor), begin the entry with that person's
name:

Bogart, Humphrey, perf. <u>Casablanca</u>. Dir. Michael Curtiz. 1942.
      Videocassette. MGM-UA Home Video, 1992.

53. A sound recording

Bach, Johann Sebastian. Italian Concerto in F, Partita No. 1,
      and Tocata in D. Dubravka Tomsic, piano. Polyband, 1987.

Jane's Addiction. "Been Caught Stealing." <u>Ritual de lo</u>
      <u>Habitual</u>. Audiocassette. Warner Brothers, 1990.

If the year of issue is not known, add *n.d.*

Document Sources Using APA Style

The following guidelines are sufficient for most college research reports that call for APA-style documentation. For additional information,
see the *Publication Manual of the American Psychological Association,*
Fourth Edition (1994) or check the APA Web site <http://www.apa.org>.

USE IN-TEXT CITATIONS TO SHOW WHERE YOU HAVE USED MATERIAL FROM SOURCES

In-text citations mark places in the text of an essay where information,
ideas, or quotations from sources are included. Each in-text citation has a
corresponding entry in the list of sources at the end of the essay that tells
readers how to find the source. In APA style title this list *References.*
    Place an in-text citation as near as possible to the borrowed material
without disrupting your sentence. Include a citation each time you refer

to a source, except when all of the sentences in a single paragraph refer to the same source—and no mention of another source intervenes. In this case, you may use a single parenthetical citation for the entire paragraph. Do not cite common knowledge or personal knowledge.

Use the Following Models for In-Text Citations

1. When the author is indicated in a signal phrase

As Allis (1990) noted about home-schooling environments, "There are no drugs in the bathroom or switchblades in the hallways" (p. 85).

2. When the author and year are indicated in a parenthetical citation

"The children in my class made fun of my braids, so Sister Victoire, the principal, sent a note home to my mother asking her to comb my hair in a more 'becoming' fashion" (Lorde, 1982, pp. 59-60).

While home schoolers are a diverse group--libertarians, conservatives, Christian fundamentalists, and a growing number of ethnic minorities (Wahisi, 1995)--most cite one of two reasons as their primary motive for home schooling.

Always give the page numbers for quotations, but not for more general references.

3. When the source has two authors

Gallup and Elam (1988) show that lack of proper financial support ranked third on the list of the problems in public schools, while poor curriculum and poor standards ranked fifth on the list.

In a 1988 Gallup poll, lack of proper financial support ranked third on the list of the problems in public schools; poor curriculum and poor standards ranked fifth on the list (Gallup & Elam).

With two or more authors, use an ampersand (&) instead of the word *and* before the last author.

4. When the source has three or more authors

First citation for a source with three to five authors:

Dyal, Corning, and Willows (1975) identify several types of students, including the "Authority-Rebel" (p. 4).

One type of student that can be identified is the "Authority-Rebel" (Dyal, Corning, Willows, 1975, p. 4).

Subsequent citations for a source with three to five authors:

According to Dyal et al. (1975), Authority-Rebels "see
themselves as superior to other students in the class" (p. 4).

Authority-Rebels "see themselves as superior to other students
in the class" (Dyal et al., 1975, p. 4).

For a source with six or more authors, use the last name of the first author and et al. in all in-text citations. But in the list of references, give all the authors' names, regardless of the number.

5. When the author is not named

As reported in the 1994 Economist article "Classless Society,"
estimates as late as 1993 placed the number of home-schooled
children in the 350,000 to 500,000 range.

An international pollution treaty still to be ratified would
prohibit all plastic garbage from being dumped at sea
("Awash," 1987).

6. When the source has a corporate author

First in-text citation, with signal phrase:

According to the Washington State Board for Community and
Technical Colleges, a tuition increase has been proposed to
offset budget deficits from Initiative 601 (1995).

First parenthetical citation:

Tuition increases proposed for Washington community and
technical colleges would help offset budget deficits brought
about by Initiative 601 (Washington State Board of Community
and Technical Colleges [WSBCTC], 1995).

Subsequent parenthetical citation:

The tuition increases would amount to about 3 percent and
would still not cover the loss of revenue (WSBCTC, 1995).

7. When two or more authors have the same last name

"Women are more in the public world, the heretofore male
world, than at any previous moment in history," transforming
"the lives of women and men to an extent probably unparalleled
by any other social or political movement" (W. Brown, 1988,
pp. 1, 3).

If two or more primary authors are listed in the references, include the author's first initial in all text citations, even if the year of publication of the authors' works differs.

8. When two or more works are cited in the same parentheses

Through support organizations and programs offered by public
schools, home-schooled children are also able to take part in
social activities outside the home, such as field trips and
sports (Guterson, 1992; Hahn & Hasson, 1996).

When citing two or more works by different authors, arrange them alphabetically by the authors' last names, as in the preceding example. However, when citing multiple works by the same author in the same parentheses, order the citations by date, with the oldest reference first:
(Postman, 1979, 1986).

9. When two or more works by the same author are cited

When old paint becomes transparent, it sometimes shows the
artist's original plans: "A tree will show through a woman's
dress" (Hellman, 1973b, p. 1).

When two or more works by the same author or authors are cited, the
years of publication are usually enough to distinguish them. An exception
occurs when they share the same publication date. In this case, arrange
the works alphabetically by title, and then add *a*, *b*, *c*, and so on after
the years to distinguish works published in the same year by the same
author(s).

10. When a quotation is taken from a secondary source

Forster says "the collapse of all civilization, so realistic
for us, sounded in Matthew Arnold's ears like a distant and
harmonious cataract" (as cited in Trilling, 1955, p. 11).

Create an entry in the list of references for the secondary source in which
you found the quote, not for the original source.

11. When material from the Internet is cited

Each type of welfare recipient "requires specific services or
assistance to make the transition from welfare to work"
(Armato & Halpern, 1996, par. 7).

12. When a personal communication is cited

According to Linda Jones (personal communication, May 2,
1997), some parents believe they must maximize their day-care
value and leave their children at day-care centers for up to
ten hours a day, even on their days off.

Do not list personal correspondence, including email, in your reference
list.

INCLUDE ALL OF YOUR SOURCES IN A REFERENCE LIST
AT THE END OF YOUR ESSAY

The reference list provides information that enables readers to find the sources cited in the essay. Every source referred to in the text of your essay (except personal communication) must have a corresponding entry in the list of references at the end of your essay. Likewise, every entry in the reference list must correspond to at least one in-text citation in the essay. If you want to show the sources you consulted but did not cite in the essay, list them on a separate page titled *Bibliography.*

Although there are many varieties of references, the information generally follows this order:

Entry for a Book

```
Author's last name, First initial. Middle initial. (year
     published). Book title. City of publication: Publisher's
     name.
```

Entry for a Journal

```
Author's last name, First initial. Middle initial.
     (publication date). Title of the article. Journal Name,
     volume number (issue number), page range.
```

Copy the author's name and the title from the first or title page of the source but do not use first names, only initials. Do not worry about including information that is unavailable, such as the author's middle initial and the issue number for a journal article. *Note:* The APA recommends that all references be double-spaced and that only the first line of each entry be indented five to seven spaces for manuscripts intended for publication. However, instructors may require students to use a *hanging indent:* The first line of the entry is not indented, but subsequent lines are indented five to seven spaces. Ask your instructor which format is preferred. The examples in this section demonstrate a hanging-indent style. The APA discourages the use of italics, but your instructor may approve of or even prefer italics. The underlined titles and other elements in the models that follow can be italicized instead of underlined.

Use the Following Models for Books

1. A book by a single author

```
Guterson, D. (1992). Family matters: Why homeschooling makes
     sense. San Diego: Harcourt.
```

2. A book by more than one author

Gottfredson, S. G., & McConville, S. (1987). America's correctional crisis. Westport, CT: Greenwood.

Dyal, J. A., Corning, W. C., & Willows, D. M. (1975). Readings in psychology: The search for alternatives (3rd ed.). New York: McGraw-Hill.

3. A book by an agency, organization, or corporation

Association for Research in Nervous and Mental Disease. (1966). The circulation of the brain and spinal cord: A symposium on blood supply. New York: Hafner.

4. A book with an unlisted author

Rand McNally commercial atlas. (1993). Skokie, IL: Rand McNally.

When the word *Anonymous* appears on the title page, cite the author as *Anonymous.*

5. A later edition of a book

Lewis, I. M. (1996). Religion in context: Cults and charisma (2nd ed.). New York: Cambridge University Press.

6. Multiple works by the same author (or same group of authors)

Ritzer, G. (1993). The McDonaldization of society. Newbury Park, CA: Pine Forge Press.

Ritzer, G. (1994). Sociological beginnings: On the origins of key ideas in sociology. New York: McGraw-Hill.

Two or more works published by the same author or authors are listed in chronological order, as shown above. However, when the works also have the same publication date, arrange them alphabetically by title and add a lowercase letter after the date: *1996a, 1996b.*

7. A multivolume work

Sandburg, C. (1939). Abraham Lincoln: Vol. 2. The war years. New York: Scribner's.

Sandburg, C. (1939). Abraham Lincoln (Vols. 1–6). New York: Scribner's.

8. A book with an author and an editor

Baum, L. F. (1996). Our landlady (N. T. Koupal, Ed.). Lincoln: University of Nebraska Press.

9. An edited collection

Carter, K., & Spitzack, C. (Eds.). (1989). Doing research on women's communication. Norwood, NJ: Ablex.

10. A work in an anthology or a collection

Fairbairn-Dunlop, P. (1993). Women and agriculture in western
    Samoa. In J. H. Momsen & V. Kinnaird (Eds.), Different
    places, different voices (pp. 211-226). London:
    Routledge.

11. A republished book

Arnold, M. (1966). Culture and anarchy (J. D. Wilson, Ed.).
    Cambridge: Cambridge University Press. (Original work
    published 1869)

Note: Both the original and the republished dates are included in the in-text citation, separated by a slash: *(Arnold, 1869/1966)*.

12. A translation

Tolstoy, L. (1972). War and peace (C. Garnett, Trans.).
    London: Pan Books. (Original work published 1869)

Note: Both the original publication date and the publication date for the translation are included in the in-text citation, separated by a slash: *(Tolstoy, 1869/1972)*.

13. An article in a reference book

Suber, H. (1991). Motion picture. In Encyclopedia Americana
    (Vol. 19, pp. 505-539). Danbury, CT: Grolier.

14. An introduction, preface, foreword, or afterword

Holt, J. (1983). Introduction. In N. Wallace, Better than
    school (pp. 9-14). Burnett, NY: Larson.

Use the Following Models for Articles

15. An article in a scholarly journal with continuous annual pagination

Natale, J. A. (1993). Understanding home schooling. Education
    Digest, 9, 58-61.

16. An article in a scholarly journal that paginates each issue separately

Mayberry, M., & Knowles, J. G. (1989). Family unit objectives
    of parents who teach their children: Ideological and
    pedagogical orientations to home schooling. Urban Review,
    21(4), 209-225.

17. An article from a newspaper

Wilford, J. N. (1995, March 7). Corn in the New World: A
    relative latecomer. The New York Times, pp. C1, C5.

18. An article from a magazine

Rohn, A. (1988, April). Home schooling. Atlantic Monthly, 261,
    20-25.

19. An unsigned article

Awash in garbage. (1987, August 15). The New York Times,
    p. A26.

20. A review

Anders, J. (1993, May 17). Dogma and democracy [Review of the
    book The church and the left] The New Republic, 42-48.

If the review is untitled, use the bracketed information as the title, retaining the brackets.

21. An editorial or a letter to the editor

Meader, R. (1997, May 11). Hard to see how consumers will
    benefit from deregulation [Letter to the editor]. Seattle
    Post-Intelligencer, p. E3.

22. Two or more articles by the same author in the same year

Selimuddin, A. K. (1989a, March 25). The selling of America.
    USA Today, pp. 12-14.

Selimuddin, A. K. (1989b, September). Will America become #2?
    USA Today Magazine, 14-16.

Use the Following Models for Internet Sources

APA citation guidelines for online resources are currently being discussed and evaluated. If your source is available both in print and online, the APA prefers that you cite the print version. The following models, taken from Andrew Harnack and Eugene Kleppinger, *Online! A Reference Guide to Using Internet Sources* (New York: St. Martin's, 1998), offer more specific guidelines for citing Internet sources than the APA provides at present.

Entry for an Internet Source

Author's last name, First initial. Middle initial.
    (Publication date). Title of document. Title of Complete
    Work. <URL> (Date of access).

23. A World Wide Web site

Gibson, B. E. (1995). Still going on exhibit. Still Going On:
    An Exhibit Celebrating the Life and Times of William

Grant Still. <http://scriptorium.lib.duke.edu
/sgo/home.html> (1997, July 14).

24. Linkage data

To help readers access a file through a link to a source document:

Gwitch'in Steering Committee. (n.d.). The Arctic wildlife
refuge: America's last great wilderness. Lkd. Alaska Web
Servers, at "Virtual Tourist." <http://www.tourist.com>
(1996, July 11).

25. A telnet site

Earthquake report for 6/27/96. (1996, July 6). Weather
Underground. telnet.madlab.sprl.umich.edu:3000/Latest
Earthquake Reports (1996, July 11).

26. An FTP (file transfer protocol) site

If accessed directly:

Altar, T. W. (1993, January 14). Vitamin B12 and vegans. ftp
wiretap.spies.com Library/Article/Food/b12.txt (1996,
May 28).

If accessed through a URL:

Greig, A. (1995, November 21). Home magazines and modernist
dreams: Designing the 1950s house. <ftp://coombs
.anu.edu.au/coombs papers/coombs archives/urban-
research-program/working-papers/wp-047-1995.txt> (1996,
July 11).

27. A gopher site

If accessed directly:

Africa on the brink of a brighter future. (1997). gopher
hafaus01.unicef.org Public Information/1997 Publications
and Information Items/1997 Press Releases/Africa on the
Brink of a Brighter Future (1997, July 11).

If accessed through a URL:

Gipe, P. (n.d.). Tilting at windmills: Public opinion toward
wind energy. <gopher://gopher.igc.apc.org:70/0
/orgs/awea/faq/surv/gipe> (1997, September 11).

28. A posting to a discussion list

Conrad, E. (1996, July 8). Proof of life after death.
<sci.archeology> (1996, July 9).

Use the Following Models for Other Electronic Sources

The following guidelines are from the *Publication Manual of the American Pyschological Association,* Fourth Edition.

29. A newspaper article

Chass, M. (1998, September 8). Big Bang: McGwire Breaks
    Maris's Home Run Record. New York Times on the Web.
    [Newspaper]. Retrieved September 9, 1998 from the World
    Wide Web: http://www.nyt.com/library/sports
    /baseball/090998bbo-mcgwire.html

30. An article from an online journal

Banker, B. S., & Gaertner, S. L. (1998). Achieving stepfamily
    harmony: An intergroup relations approach. Journal of
    Family Psychology, 12, 3, 310-325. Retrieved September 9,
    1998 from the World Wide Web: http://www.apa.org
    /journals/fam/998ab.html.

31. An abstract

Ryan, A. M., Gheen, M. H., & Midgley, C. (1998). Why do some
    students avoid asking for help? [Abstract]. Journal of
    Educational Psychology, 90, 3, 528-535. Retrieved
    September 9, 1998 from the World Wide Web: http://
    www.apa.org/journals/edu/998ab.html.

32. Material from an online computer service

Reece, J. S. (1978). Measuring investment center performance.
    Harvard Business Review [On-line], 56(3), 28-40.
    Available: Dialog file 107, item 673280 047658

33. Material from a CD-ROM database or other electronic media

For information retrieved from electronic media, follow general citation models. (For date of publication, cite the year copies of the data were first made generally available.) Insert, in brackets, the type of medium from which you are citing (*CD-ROM, Data file, Database*) after the title of the work. Give the location and name of both the producer and the distributor.

Legal wear and tear of school uniforms. (1996, July 31). The
    Oakland Post, 33(15). Ethnic NewsWatch [CD-ROM]. Stam-
    ford, CT: SoftLine Information [Producer and Distributor].

34. Computer software

Bergman, L. R., & El-Khouri, B. M. (1995). SLEIPNER. A
    statistical package for pattern-oriented analysis
    (Version 1.0) [Computer software]. Stockholm, Sweden:
    Stockholm University Department of Psychology.

Use the Following Models for Other Sources

35. An interview

Do not list personal interviews in your references list. Cite the person's name in your text, and give the notation *personal communication.* Cite a published interview like an article from a magazine (see 18).

36. A government document

U.S. Department of Health, Education and Welfare. (1979). Healthy people: The surgeon general's report on health promotion (DHEW Publication No. 79-55071). Washington, DC: U.S. Government Printing Office.

37. A dissertation abstract

Fairhall, J. L. (1989). James Joyce, history, and the political unconscious. (Doctoral dissertation, State University of New York at Stony Brook, 1989). Dissertation Abstracts International, 51, 3582A.

38. An unpublished doctoral dissertation

Bullock, B. (1986). Basic needs fulfillment among less developed countries: Social progress over two decades of growth. Unpublished doctoral dissertation, Vanderbilt University, Nashville.

39. Published proceedings of a conference

Bingman, C. F. (1985). The president as manager of the federal government. In C. L. Harriss (Ed.), Control of federal spending (pp. 146-161). New York: Proceedings of the Academy of Political Science.

40. A technical or research report

Brown, B. B., Kohrs, D., & Lazarro, C. (1991, April). The academic costs and consequences of extracurricular participation in high school. Chicago: American Education Research Association.

41. A television program

Hoppe, B., & Lattanzi, B. (Writers). (1995). The universe within (G. Koide, Director). In P. Apsell (Producer), Nova. Boston: WGBH.

42. A film or videotape

Parker, O. (Director). (1995). Othello [Film]. New York: Castle Rock Entertainment.

Acknowledgments

Deborah Tannen. "Marked Women." Taken from "Marked Women, Unmarked Men" in *The New York Times Magazine*, June 20, 1993. Copyright © Deborah Tannen. Originally titled in NYT as "Wears Jump Suit. Sensible Shoes. Uses Husband's Last Name." This article is based in part on material in the author's book *You Just Don't Understand* (Ballantine, 1990). Reprinted by permission of the author.

Nicollette Toussaint. "Hearing the Sweetest Songs." From *Newsweek*, May 23, 1994. Originally titled "On Being Deaf." Copyright © 1994, Newsweek, Inc. All rights reserved. Reprinted by permission.

Steven Waldman. "The Tyranny of Choice." From *The New Republic*, January 22, 1992. Copyright © 1992, The New Republic, Inc. Reprinted by permission.

James Wolcott. "Talking Trash." Copyright © 1996 by James Wolcott. Originally in *The New Yorker*, April 1, 1996. Reprinted by permission.

This index lists the readings in the text according to the methods of writing the authors used to develop their ideas. For readings relying predominately on one method or strategy, we indicate the first page of the reading. If a method plays a minor role in a reading, we provide both the first page of the reading as well as the paragraph number(s) where the method is put to use.

Comparison and Contrast

Definition

Index of Authors, Titles, and Terms